WALKS&TOURS
in Britain

Published by
The Automobile Association, Fanum House, Basingstoke, Hampshire RG21 2EA
and
The Ordnance Survey, Romsey Road, Maybush, Southampton SO9 4DH

Cover picture: footpath near Cwmyoy in the Vale of Ewyas

Introductory features by Paul Sterry

Typeset by Avonset, Midsomer Norton, Bath. Repro by LC Repro Ltd., Aldermaston. Printed and ring binder made by Fabrieken Brepols N.V., Turnhout, Belgium.

Maps extracted from The Ordnance Survey's 1:250,000 Routemaster Series, 1:25,000 Pathfinder and Outdoor Leisure Map Series and 1:50,000 Channel Islands Map, with permission of Her Majesty's Stationery Office, Crown Copyright.

Additions to the maps by the Cartographic Depts of The Automobile Association and The Ordnance Survey.

Produced by the Publishing Division of The Automobile Association.

Published and distributed in the United Kingdom by The Ordnance Survey, Romsey Road, Maybush, Southampton S09 4DH, and the Publishing Division of The Automobile Association, Fanum House, Basingstoke, Hampshire RG21 2EA.

AA ISBN 0 7495 0031 X

OS ISBN 0 31900 209 8

CONTENTS & INTRODUCTION

*D*iscover the best that Britain has to offer with this unique walking and touring guide featuring loose-leaf pages.

Covering some of the most beautiful country in England, Scotland and Wales, these routes lead you through rolling scenery and dramatic landscapes, through elegant towns and tranquil villages — picking out features of interest which include wildlife, history and architecture, and describing places to visit along the way.

Each walk and drive is plotted on a superb, appropriately-scaled Ordnance Survey map, accompanied by detailed route directions and illustrated with beautiful colour photographs.

Ideal for anyone who enjoys exploring Britain's countryside either on foot or by car, this book brings together a host of information to form an attractive and practical guide that can be enjoyed both inside and outside the home.

ABOUT THIS BOOK

All the routes in this book have been carefully researched and every effort has been made to ensure accuracy. However, the landscape can change and features mentioned as landmarks may alter or disappear in time. The changing seasons also greatly affect the appearance of the landscape and paths may become overgrown in mid summer. Please note that some of the walks need particular care if children are in the party and wherever possible hazards are highlighted in the text. See also page 5.

How the Book Works
The tours, numbered 1 to 50, can be located by referring to the maps on pages 17 and 18.

Each tour in the book is followed by a selection of walks that begin within striking distance of the motor route. These walks, labelled 1A, 1B etc, can be easily located as they are clearly marked on the relevant tour map.

To locate the walks even more precisely, the National Grid reference number of the start point is given at the beginning of the route directions. This will enable you to find the start point from an Ordnance Survey Pathfinder, Landranger or Outdoor Leisure map of that area. See page 313 for an explanation of the National Grid system.

Parking
The walks in this book should have adequate parking space available at their start point, but sometimes this space is limited and thoughtless parking can cause considerable inconvenience to nearby residents, or cause a traffic hazard. It is an offence to park in such a way that your car obstructs the highway, and a landowner can sue for damages if a car is parked on his land without permission. Remember, too, that whatever the time of day or year, farm vehicles must always have clear access to field entrances and tracks.

Opening Times
Opening times of places of interest are not given in this book. It is always advisable to check the current details in advance when planning a visit to avoid disappointment.

Useful Addresses
Several organisations concerned with the countryside and places to visit are referred to throughout the book and anyone wishing to learn more about them can do so by writing to the following addresses.

Council for the Protection of Rural England (CPRE)
4 Hobart Place, London SW1W 0HY

Council for the Protection of Rural Wales (CPRW)
Tŷ Gwyn, 31 High Street, Welshpool, Powys SY21 7JP

Countryside Commission
John Dower House, Crescent Place, Cheltenham, Gloucestershire GL50 3RA

Countryside Commission for Scotland
Battleby House, Redgorton, Perth PH1 3EW

County Naturalists' Trusts (CNT)
See Royal Society for Nature Conservation

English Heritage (EH) formerly known as Ancient Monuments (AM)
Fortress House, 23 Savile Row, London W1X 1AB

Ancient Monuments in Wales are the responsibility of CADW, Brunel House, 2 Fitzalan Road, Cardiff CF2 1UY

Ancient Monuments in Scotland are the responsibility of the Scottish Development Office, 20 Brandon Street, Edinburgh EH5 5DX

Forestry Commission
231 Corstorphine Road, Edinburgh EH12 7AT

National Trust (NT)
36 Queen Anne's Gate, London SW1H 9AS

National Trust for Scotland (NTS)
5 Charlotte Square, Edinburgh EH2 4DU

Nature Conservancy Council (NCC)
Northminster House, Peterborough PE1 1UA

Ramblers' Association
1/5 Wandsworth Road, London SW8 2XX

Royal Society for Nature Conservation (RSNC)
The Green, Nettleham, Lincoln LN2 2NR

Royal Society for the Protection of Birds (RSPB)
The Lodge, Sandy, Bedfordshire SG19 2DL

COMFORT AND SAFETY

Before setting off on a walk of any distance it is always advisable to make sure you are well prepared, and mountain walking in particular needs careful planning.

A pair of robust, stout-soled shoes is essential for walking and even on a hot day you will not regret wearing them when traversing rough or boggy terrain.

A lightweight, waterproof anorak and overtrousers are also a good idea, especially when they can be folded away and carried in a rucksack. When climbing mountains these items, together with a hat and gloves, are essential, and it is best to dress in several layers of thin clothing which can easily be taken off and put on again as required. Climbing over rocky slopes soon warms you up, but once you stop you will begin to feel chilled again. The weather in our hills and mountains is often fickle: as you reach the summit of a mountain you may be greeted by brilliantly clear, sunny skies but within minutes this can change to pouring rain and limited visibility.

If you choose one of the more demanding walks on mountains or moorland an Ordnance Survey map of the area and a compass to help you get your bearings are advisable. Food and drink to last a whole day should be carried, together with glucose tablets as an energy supplement and a simple first aid kit. Plan the length of your journey carefully to take into account your own stamina and the number of hours of daylight but take a torch in case your return is delayed. A whistle may be useful to attract attention in an emergency. The recognised emergency signal is six blasts repeated every minute.

Unless extremely experienced, always use recognised routes: these are usually far easier than venturing across country. Besides which, you are far less likely to get lost and will be easier to trace in an emergency. It is always best to walk with a friend, not only for the company but also because there will be someone to raise the alarm should there be an accident. Never set off without telling someone of your planned route and your estimated return time.

On the Coast

Many of the most exhilarating walks take the rambler along dramatic coastal paths. Cliffs often seem to inspire

people to take risks but at all costs this should be avoided. Stay away from the edge because the soil is generally loose and often overhanging. Even comparatively gently sloping cliffs should be treated with caution because the vegetation, which often includes thrift and sea campion, is very slippery and soil may give way underfoot.

Before venturing on to the seashore itself it is advisable to consult a tide timetable. On gently shelving beaches the waves often rush in at an alarming speed and can easily catch you unawares. During bad weather, it is best to stay well above the waves, especially on the west coast of Britain. Once in a while, freak waves sweep high up the shoreline and in a rough sea this could have unfortunate consequences.

MAPS

The 1:50,000 series of Ordnance Survey maps are invaluable to the walker and rambler with 1¼ inches on the map representing approximately 1 mile. They can help you pinpoint your position, especially when used in conjunction with a compass, and by using their clear, colour-marked symbols (see pages 313 and 314), the courses of public footpaths, bridlepaths and almost every feature of the landscape can be identified with certainty.

Walkers enjoying a rest – and getting their bearings – on Hadrian's Wall

PHOTOGRAPHY

With recent advances in SLR cameras, more and more people are recording their trips to the countryside on film, and for more serious photographers a few of the following tips are worth bearing in mind.

Lenses

As a rule, 35mm cameras are supplied with a 50mm focal length standard lens which records more or less the same field of view as the human eye. Smaller focal length lenses (wide-angle) include a greater field of view and longer focal length lenses magnify a small area of view. Wide-angle lenses are often useful for taking landscape photographs but may cause some distortion, for example curved horizons. Longer focal length lenses (telephoto) are often used for bird and mammal photography since they allow the photographer to increase his or her distance from the subject. Above a focal length of 300mm they become almost impossible to hand-hold without resulting in camera shake on the image and so a tripod support is necessary.

Specially designed macro lenses can be bought to facilitate close-up photography of plants and insects. A

5

good lens will allow a magnification of 1:2 (image size on film : image size in real life). Not all so-called macro lenses do this so check before you buy one.

Extension rings can be fitted between an ordinary lens and the camera body affording similar results in terms of magnification. Although much cheaper to buy, they restrict the subject distance over which you can focus.

Films
Unless you want to experiment, stick to well-known makes of film and remember that, in general, the slower the film speed the better its definition. A film speed of 64 ASA for slide film and 100 ASA for print film is usually adequate.

Tripods
Although an extra weight to carry, many walkers with a serious interest in photography use a tripod for extra stability: lightweight, carbon-fibre models are not much of an extra burden. Tripods are essential for macro photography of insects and flowers and when using a slow shutter speed in poor light.

Direction of the Sun
Although there is seldom anything you can do about it, the direction of the sun has a marked effect upon the resulting photograph. In general, it is best to shoot with the sun behind you: photographing into the sun may give the image too much contrast or make it look hazy without the use of extra filters. Strong light conditions may also play tricks on your camera's light meter so if uncertain about the camera settings, take additional shots 'bracketing' half an 'f' stop either side of the indicated correct setting.

Composition
The composition of a picture is an extremely personal and subjective thing but there are a few golden rules which may help. Try to ensure that your horizon is straight (sometimes not as easy as it sounds). When composing a shot of a landscape, try to have an interesting feature in the foreground, such as a tree or a gate. If you do manage to find a suitable foreground subject try to remember to focus nearer to it than to infinity. With 'f' numbers greater than 8, the depth of field should ensure that the rest of the picture is in focus. Remember that

more depth of field lies beyond the plane of focus than in front of it so focussing on infinity may result in an out of focus foreground.

BIRDWATCHING
Another very enjoyable pastime when out walking is birdwatching, and with a little preparation can be taken up by anyone.

Binoculars
In order to get really good views of birds, binoculars are an essential part of the birdwatcher's kit. They help in identifying the species as well as revealing plumage details invisible at a distance. A wide range of makes, models and prices is available and it is sometimes difficult to choose. All models of binoculars are accompanied by two numbers such as 8×30 or 10×40. The first number refers to the magnification and the second to the field of view (and hence brightness) of the lenses.

From the point of view of the active birdwatcher, it does not always follow that the bigger the magnification the better the binoculars: beyond a magnification of 10 times, they tend to be too cumbersome to lift without causing arm strain and too heavy to carry for any great distance. For most people's purposes, 8×30 or 8×40 binoculars are more than adequate and useful for looking not only at birds but also at many other features of the landscape. Choose a pair that is comfortable to hold and easy to use, and avoid buying second-hand binoculars as they could be out of alignment which will result in eye-strain.

Books
Visit any good bookshop and you will be bewildered by the choice of bird books. Pocket identification guides are especially varied so choose one carefully to suit your needs as a beginner or as a proficient birdwatcher. Some cover birds from the whole of Europe, many of which stray to Britain, whilst others concentrate on the more regular breeding and migrant species. Look for a book with thorough descriptions and pictures large enough to see the features described.

Identification
Having bought your binoculars and your bird book, you can now set forth into the countryside and identify some birds. Initially you may be baffled by

many things you see, but you will soon learn that there are several key features to look and listen for. The size of the bird, the shape of the bill, the bird's overall colour and markings on the tail and wing are all important, but look also for the way it flies and listen for any unusual calls it may make.

Tips
Getting good views is often the birdwatcher's most frustrating task. Birds are alert and generally rather wary of people, not without good reason since many species have been persecuted over the centuries. However, in many places in Britain conservation bodies have built hides to which birds are often indifferent. Cars often serve a similar purpose – many birds being used to the sight of vehicles on roads.

Sitting quietly beside a favoured feeding spot, such as a muddy lake margin, may also yield good views since the birds will be preoccupied. Nesting birds are also often more tolerant of man than would otherwise be the case, but should under no circumstances be disturbed. If put off the nest, the bird may desert the eggs or young which may then be robbed by ever-alert predators.

Birdwatching on the Coast
Our sea cliffs provide a rich spectacle for the birdwatcher. Between Cornwall and Scotland many are occupied by vast seabird colonies from April until July – the sight, sound and smell of which are unforgettable. In some areas, special viewing areas with powerful, mounted binoculars have been provided. Elsewhere around the coast, it is best, from the point of view of safety and optimum viewing, to look along the coastline at the birds rather than down the cliff. Although many seabirds are tolerant of human presence some, for instance guillemots which nest on narrow ledges, are extremely vulnerable to disturbance.

From autumn until spring estuaries around our coast are alive with waders, gulls and wildfowl. At low tide they are often distant specks, feeding on the mudflats, but as the tide rises they move further up the shore. Consult a tide timetable and seat yourself inconspicuously as the tide is rising and watch the birds move towards you. Never sit where you could be trapped by the rising tide.

RIGHTS OF WAY

All routes covered in this book follow public rights of way or cross areas with open access to the public. When walking you should be aware not only of your rights of access but also the rights of landowners.

Although it is the responsibility of the landowner to maintain a right of way across his land, it is still private property, and whereas the public has a perfect right to use the footpath they should not stray from it – to do so is to trespass. If requested to return to a footpath by a landowner or his representative you should do so immediately. If you do not comply, you could be prosecuted. In Scotland, the laws of trespass are more relaxed than in England and Wales and with the exception of certain areas, at particular times of year, you are more or less free to roam at will so long as you use your common sense and respect people's property.

Study any Ordnance Survey map and you will find a network of paths and tracks radiating from the heart of most villages and towns in Britain. Although their importance to the communities they served has declined, the routes of these paths are laid down in law and cannot easily be altered and the Ordnance Survey maps provide an accurate and definitive record of all public footpaths, bridleways and roads used as public paths. You should have little trouble finding these routes when out walking since local authorities are obliged by law to mark the point where they depart from metalled roads. Conspicuous signposts are generally used and, in some areas, the course of a footpath away from roads may be waymarked.

OTHER AREAS OF PUBLIC ACCESS

In addition to rights of way, the public has access to many other areas of countryside in Britain and there are several categories of land where the public are free to walk.

Commonlands

These date back to medieval times when villagers had the right to graze their livestock on certain pieces of land. The tradition of access has remained to this day and although all commons are privately owned, and in theory public access is not automatic, access is seldom denied.

Access Land

This has been made accessible to walkers through an agreement between the landowner and the local authority. The most extensive of these areas are in the Peak District National Park, Yorkshire Dales National Park and Lake District National Park.

Unofficial Access Land

Legislation in certain areas has not been necessary because landowners such as the Forestry Commission, the National Trust, the National Trust for Scotland and the County Naturalists' Trusts allow free public access. The Scottish Highlands, the North York Moors, Dartmoor, Exmoor and the Cheviots are other similar areas. However, sensitive areas of vegetation are often fenced off and whole areas are sometimes closed during the breeding season to protect nesting birds.

Access to grouse moors is also restricted during the grouse shooting season (August 12 – December 10) as is access to some areas of Scottish moorland during the deer 'stalking' season (July 1 to October 20).

Country Parks

These are run by local authorities or private landowners for recreational pursuits as well as for their wildlife interest and public access is normally less restricted than in many other areas.

PROTECTED AREAS

Many areas of countryside are given special protection of various kinds which aims to preserve the landscape and wildlife for the enjoyment of future generations.

National Parks

Created by Act of Parliament, and soon to be joined by the Norfolk Broads, the ten National Parks of England and Wales preserve for the nation some of the wildest and most beautiful regions of our countryside. However, the land is always privately owned and unless a local arrangement has been made the public has no more rights of way than elsewhere. The interests of wildlife and

Green lanes, such as this one in Hampshire, are old country roads which have not been given a metalled surface

scenery in the Parks often have to compete with those of forestry, mineral extraction, farming and the military.

Areas of Outstanding Natural Beauty
These, and their Scottish equivalents, National Scenic Areas, are regions of attractive countryside whose status or size is not considered sufficient to warrant National Park status. The designation does not normally confer any additional rights of access to the public.

Heritage Coasts
These were established to help protect the natural beauty of many of our coastal regions. As with many other areas, unlimited public access would inevitably lead to erosion of the very beauty that people come to enjoy and the status of these areas mediates between the interests of conservation and access.

Sites of Special Scientific Interest
The Nature Conservancy Council (NCC) designates certain areas particularly rich in wildlife or geological interest as Sites of Special Scientific interest. They are usually privately owned, and the landowner then has to notify the NCC of any changes in land use which might affect the site. Although this affords the wildlife a degree of protection, its survival is not guaranteed because the Secretary of State for the Environment has the power to overrule the authority of the NCC.

National Nature Reserves
Owned or leased by the NCC, these areas are managed by full-time wardens and, because wildlife interests have priority, access other than to

Right of access varies greatly between reserves. This is the NNR at Benacre, Suffolk

public rights of way is sometimes restricted to permit holders.

Local Nature Reserves
Run by local authorities, these sites have legal status and are managed for their wildlife interest. Access varies from site to site, so comply with the regulations.

Other Nature Reserves
Many County Naturalists' Trusts and conservation bodies such as the RSPB own or lease areas which are managed as nature reserves. Access other than to public rights of way is sometimes restricted to members only, so check the regulations for each site.

WILDLIFE AND THE LAW

In our increasingly overcrowded island, development, change in land-use and public pressure are ever present threats to our wildlife. Whilst most people who use the countryside are responsible and share in the delights of our natural heritage, a small minority are less enlightened. In order to protect our wildlife and to help ensure its survival for future generations, the Wildlife and Countryside Act of 1981 protects by law some of our most endangered species. In general, the views of most responsible walkers and ramblers would be in accord with the legislation but a brief summary may be of interest.

Wild Flowers
It is illegal to uproot any wild plant without the permission of the landowner and more than 60 species are further protected from picking, sale or collection of seed. These most vulnerable species include many of our orchids as well as other less showy flowers. The best policy for ramblers is not to pick any wild flowers and leave them for others to enjoy.

Birds
It is illegal to kill, injure or take any wild bird as well as to take or destroy the nest or eggs of any species. There are certain exceptions to the Act which enable, for example, landowners to control certain 'pest' species, or permit bird ringers, under licence, to trap and ring birds for study. It is also illegal to disturb certain particularly vulnerable (Schedule 1) species whilst nest building, brooding or caring for young.

This applies even to photography of these species at the nest without a licence. For further details and a current list of Schedule 1 birds consult a copy of the Act or contact the Nature Conservancy Council (see page 4).

Other Wildlife
Many of our threatened mammals are protected from disturbance or injury and these include all species of bats and shrews as well as badgers and dormice. Invertebrates too are covered by the Act and several species of butterfly, moth, beetle, dragonfly and cricket have protection.

THE COUNTRY CODE

Ultimately, the continuing survival of our beautiful landscape and its varied wildlife depends on our attitude towards it. This applies both to landowners and landusers and to minimise conflict between the two the voluntary Country Code should be adhered to:
– Avoid damage to fences, gates and walls. These are there for a purpose and to repair damage is often expensive.
– Always close fences and gates to prevent livestock escaping.
– Keep to footpaths and other rights of way and avoid causing damage to crops.
–Respect other people's property. Farm machinery is often left unattended, close to where it will be needed, and should, therefore, be left untouched.
– Keep dogs under control and if necessary keep them on a lead. If you cannot control your pet you should not take it out into the countryside. This applies not only where farm livestock is concerned but to many other areas. Rampaging dogs pose a serious threat to deer, especially when they have young, and desertion and even premature abortion sometimes result. Other wild mammals are disturbed as well as ground-nesting and ground-feeding birds.
– Do not leave litter and especially do not discard lighted cigarettes, matches or anything else that could cause a fire.
– Drive slowly and safely in the country. Always assume that there might be a herd of cows or a stationary tractor round the next bend.
– When walking on country roads always remember to keep to the right, in single file.

Shag: both parents incubate the eggs on nests built of sticks and seaweed

THE COAST

For the birdwatcher, Britain's coastline is its crowning glory. So varied is its nature that whether you visit dramatic cliffs and rocky shores on the west coast or sheltered estuaries, mudflats and harbours elsewhere, there will be something to see throughout the year.

Cliffs

With a few notable exceptions, such as Beachy Head in Sussex and the Needles on the Isle of Wight, our more dramatic cliffs and rocky coasts are generally a feature of the north and west. Such places provide memorable and exhilarating walks – always accompanied by the sight and sound of coastal birds.

Jackdaws are one of the birds often seen on clifftops, nesting in inaccessible crevices in the rocks below. Occasionally, they are joined by the largest member of the crow family found in Britain, the raven. Recognised by its wedge-shaped tail in flight and loud 'cronking' call, this majestic bird scavenges carrion around the coast.

Ancestor of the feral pigeon, so familiar to visitors to London, the rock dove is now restricted to the west coast of Scotland. Many of its town relatives have, however, returned to the wild and flocks of pigeons are becoming increasingly common wherever there are cliffs. This spread has benefited one of our most elegant and threatened birds, the peregrine. Once severely reduced in numbers by egg-collectors and pesticides, their numbers are again increasing and there can be few more memorable sights than a peregrine 'stooping' at over 70mph towards its quarry.

Our cliffs are, of course, perhaps best known for their seabird breeding colonies, and for some species provide the most important sites in the world.

Although nesting on offshore islands, gannets often pass close to shore whilst the cliffs themselves support herring gulls, lesser black-backed gulls and the larger great black-backed gulls which build untidy nests of seaweed and flotsam amongst the rocks and clumps of thrift.

On sheer rock faces nearer to sea-level, kittiwakes nest on precipitous ledges. This species, named after its loud call, is the only British gull that can truly be called a 'sea' gull, only returning to land for a few weeks each year to nest. Fulmars, although superficially similar to kittiwakes and other gulls, are more closely related to albatrosses. Unlike many seabirds, their numbers are increasing.

Members of the auk family are also true seabirds, spending most of their lives out of sight of land. Guillemots prefer to lay their single, conical egg on ledges crowded with fellow

Grass-covered cliffs are puffins' chief breeding sites

guillemots, relying on the principle of safety in numbers. Razorbills, on the other hand, are more solitary and find security under boulders and in rock crevices. It is the puffin, however, that captures the imagination of most visitors to our sea cliffs. Their brightly coloured and outsize beaks, together with their rather awkward gait, give them a most comical appearance as they shuffle toward their burrow entrance, beaks laden with small fish.

Estuaries and Mudflats

Coastal birdwatching interest is not restricted to cliffs and rocky shores. Our estuaries, mudflats and sandy beaches also provide wonderful opportunities for the birdwatcher and are important staging posts for vast numbers of migrant birds. At low tide, estuaries such as the Exe in Devon, the Wash in Norfolk, the Severn Estuary and the Ythan in Scotland empty out

to reveal vast areas of mud and silt, rich in invertebrate life. Waders, ducks and gulls, each with beaks specially adapted to search for different food sources, feast on this rich supply.

Redshank, so-called sentinels of the marsh because of their alert nature and loud alarm call, are numerous around the coast throughout the year. In autumn and winter they are joined by dunlin, black-tailed and bar-tailed godwits, knot and grey plover – the identification of which can sometimes prove difficult. Less of an identification problem are the shelduck which dabble in the surface mud for small molluscs and whose black, white and chestnut plumage make them visible at a considerable distance. Autumn sees the return of brent geese, which despite their name are no bigger than the resident shelduck. Brent geese fly to Britain from their high Arctic breeding grounds and concentrate on certain estuaries in north Norfolk and along the Exe in Devon.

Beaches

Although most of the low-lying coastline of southern England is rich in marine life and consequently supports large numbers of feeding birds, most of the shingle and sandy beaches are too disturbed for birds to nest on. However, a few beaches, particularly around the Norfolk and Suffolk coasts, are protected for a few weeks in the year to safeguard birds such as the oystercatcher, ringed plover and common, Sandwich and little terns who nest on the ground. The further north and west you travel in Britain, the more likely you are to find birds nesting on the beach, so keep your eyes open for the signs of an alarmed bird in May and June and leave it in peace.

Oystercatchers, the most distinctive of our shorebirds, nest on scapes lined with shells

Birds around Britain

FRESHWATER

Many of the tours and walks in this book pass close to freshwater and whether it be tumbling mountain streams or lowland lakes, birds will be much in evidence.

Streams and Rivers

Lowland streams and rivers in southern England are the haunt of kingfishers which thrive on the rich supply of minnows and sticklebacks they contain. This most colourful of British birds is sometimes seen perched on an overhanging branch but more frequently darts past in a flash of blue and orange. Little grebes, which often share the river with the kingfishers, make floating nests of vegetation and are more secretive in their behaviour.

Larger rivers often attract wildfowl such as mute swan, Canada goose and mallard which normally feed on submerged water plants but readily learn to respond to food from visitors. More wary are grey herons which lurk in the shallow river margins, patiently waiting for a passing fish.

Marshes and Reedbeds

By June, the waterside vegetation has burgeoned and the lush foliage supports a wealth of smaller birds. Sedge warblers sing their scratchy song from cover while reed buntings often watch visitors from the vantage point of a bush. In a few places, this marshy habitat extends over a large area and sometimes forms extensive reedbeds. Places such as Minsmere in Suffolk and Slapton Ley in Devon are the haunt of reed warblers, marsh harriers and the occasional bittern.

Great crested grebe nesting, typically, on open, inland freshwater

Open Water

Open stretches of water often attract great crested grebes which nest among the emergent vegetation. In autumn and winter they are usually joined by large numbers of gulls and wildfowl such as teal, wigeon, pintail and shoveler, while water rails skulk around the margins. Although present throughout the year, numbers of water rails increase dramatically in the winter due to influxes of continental birds. It is more common to hear the bird's pig-like squeal than to see it, but harsh winter weather sometimes forces them into the open.

Upland Lakes and Rivers

Upland lakes are often rather disappointing for the birdwatcher, sometimes harbouring only coot and tufted duck. However, upland streams and rivers in the west and north of Britain are the haunt of the dipper, a fascinating bird so-named because of its habit of walking underwater in search of food. Grey wagtails – also found on some lowland rivers – often share the dipper's river, and goosanders try to breed on surprisingly small watercourses in Wales and Scotland.

GRASSLAND

Grasslands throughout lowland Britain are the haunt of the skylark. A rather nondescript brown bird on the ground, the skylark is immediately recognised by its song – a ceaseless warble delivered in flight and often from a great height. Meadow pipits share the same habitat as the skylark and also deliver their song in flight. Whereas the song of the skylark may be heard almost throughout the year, that of the meadow pipit is only sung in the spring. In wetter meadows they may be joined in spring by colourful yellow wagtails, as well as by breeding waders such as snipe and redshank.

Wherever hedgerows or areas of scrub persist, yellowhammers and linnets may be found, using the cover provided to build their nest. They generally feed on the ground and hence are often inconspicuous whereas goldfinches, which also prefer this habitat, feed prominently on the seeds of thistles, teasels and other grassland flowers.

Small birds have to keep a wary eye open for kestrels, which hover effortlessly overhead scanning the ground below. In the winter a number

Kestrel, Britain's commonest bird of prey

of other predators, such as short-eared owl, hen harrier and merlin, join their numbers – especially in coastal areas.

FARMLAND AND VERGES

From the rolling wheat fields of the Sussex Downs to the patchwork of small fields so typical of the West Country, farming has shaped the British countryside. These changes have favoured a few species of bird and coveys of common and red-legged partridges and pheasants, and flocks of woodpigeons are a familiar sight.

Open Fields

Most species which feed in open fields prefer to nest in the field margins or hedgerows, but not so the lapwing. This elegant wader makes a small scrape in a furrow and lays its camouflaged eggs on the bare soil. Lapwings are rather solitary in the breeding season but for the rest of the year form large flocks which take to the air at the first sign of danger.

Hedgerows

Hedgerows and roadside verges, in many respects, fulfil the same habitat requirements as woodland edge and so often have a high density of nesting songbirds. Blackbird, chaffinch, robin, dunnock, blackcap and yellowhammer all find the mixture of hawthorn, blackthorn and hazel much to their liking. Corn buntings prefer a more open field system where there is a good view across their territory. Their song, which is supposed to resemble jangling keys, is generally sung from a fence post or strand of barbed wire.

Barn owls, once a familiar sight at dusk throughout Britain, are now much reduced in numbers but can still be seen in parts of southern England and the west of Scotland.

HEATHLAND AND MOORLAND

Heathland

Sandy and acidic soils in lowland Britain provide ideal conditions for one of our most interesting types of habitat – heathland. Characterised by plants such as gorse and heather, heaths are home to many unique animals and plants and, although becoming increasingly fragmented due to the pressures of development, many fine areas still exist in Suffolk, Dorset, Hampshire, Devon and Cornwall.

The stonechat is perhaps the most characteristic bird of the southern heaths. Resplendent in its black, white and buff plumage, it perches conspicuously on gorse sprays, ever alert for danger. Yellowhammers and tree pipits nest on many of our heathlands where clumps of gorse and birch are allowed to flourish, but Dartford warblers, on the other hand, are seldom found outside Surrey, Hampshire and Dorset. Small birds have good reason to be wary because, from April until September, our heaths are the breeding ground for the hobby – a small but acrobatic falcon which catches small birds and insects alike while on the wing.

Although most heathland birdlife is best seen by day, one summer resident is strictly nocturnal. The nightjar, whose superbly camouflaged plumage renders it almost invisible by day, takes to the wing after dusk in search of moths and other night-flying insects. Its capacious mouth acts like a net as it flies swiftly through the air and the heaths echo with the sound of its strange call, somewhat reminiscent of a sewing-machine in action.

Preferring uncultivated land, the stonechat's decline may be due to loss of habitat

Moorland

Areas of moorland are found in upland parts of Britain from Dartmoor to the Scottish highlands. As on the lowland heaths, ling and heather often predominate but patches of rushes and purple moor grass offer alternative nesting sites for many species of bird.

Many regions of moorland, particularly in the North York Moors and Yorkshire Dales, are carefully managed for one particular species of bird – the red grouse. Systematic burning of small patchwork areas of moor ensure fresh growth of heather, the staple diet of the grouse, whilst areas of lusher vegetation are used for nesting. A stroll across one of these areas will soon afford the visitor good views of these birds as they take to the air in alarm with a loud call of 'go-back, go-back, go-back'.

A variety of wading birds, which spend a brief month or two on the moors during the breeding season, also benefit from this land management. Curlew, dunlin, golden plover and lapwing all seek out wet flushes and recently burned areas on which to nest. Predatory birds such as merlin and hen harrier prefer to nest in areas of overgrown heather while wheatears often choose crevices in the stone walls so characteristic of many moorlands.

MOUNTAINS

Our mountainous regions provide the walker with some of the finest scenery and most challenging routes to be found in Britain. They also offer the birdwatcher the chance of seeing some of our rarest and most rewarding species, and although the initial reaction to mountain birdwatching may be disappointment at the lack of birds, this only serves to make the excitement of spotting a golden eagle or peregrine falcon all the more intense.

The birdwatcher may be surprised at the number and variety of lowland birds which can be found at comparatively high elevations. Chaffinches call from bushes of mountain ash while dunnocks and wrens forage for insects among boulders and alongside mountain streams. Wheatears, too, often breed among boulders and rocks on steep mountain slopes, their presence being given away by the conspicuous white rump seen in flight and their loud alarm call which sounds like two stones being knocked together. They

Red grouse, about the size of a chicken, are almost invisible on heather moorland

share similar breeding requirements with another species, the ring ouzel, a bird which, unlike the wheatear, is only seen at lower elevations during migration. With the size, shape and overall colouring of a blackbird, the ring ouzel is distinguished from its relative by the white, crescent-shaped marking on its chest.

It is not until you climb some of the Scottish peaks that you start to see birds found exclusively in the mountains. Snow bunting and dotterel are scarce but regular visitors to the Cairngorms, but one of the most characteristic and regularly seen species is the ptarmigan, a medium-sized gamebird related to the grouse. Its mottled plumage renders it almost invisible as it crouches among the lichen-covered boulders and it will sometimes allow an approach to within 10ft before quietly creeping away.

Even during the summer, weather conditions on the mountain tops can be harsh, as many walkers know to their cost, and during the winter months many peaks are covered in a blanket of snow. For ground-dwelling birds such as the ptarmigan this could render their camouflage useless and so they moult their grey and brown feathers in favour of pure white plumage.

Rocky crags and mountain slopes are the haunt of peregrine falcons – always exciting birds to see – but pride of place must go to the majestic golden eagle. With its immense wingspan, it soars for hours on end in search of carrion as well as live quarry. The Scottish mountains are its stronghold although it is beginning to grace the skies over the Lake District once more.

Birds around Britain

BROADLEAVED WOODLAND

A woodland walk, taken early on a fine spring morning when the air is full of the chorus of breeding birds, is a memorable experience. The warblers are perhaps the best known of our songsters, with most wooded areas holding willow warblers, chiffchaffs, blackcaps and garden warblers. It is sometimes difficult to get good views among the dappled foliage so a knowledge of the different songs of each species can be useful.

In areas of mature beech woodland wood warblers sing their trilling song while in denser patches of scrub, especially around woodland edge or patches of coppice, nightingales may be heard. These incredible songsters sing at almost any time of night or day and their rich, fluty song carries a considerable distance on a still evening.

Many of our garden birds are also quite at home in broadleaved woodlands. Chaffinch, greenfinch, robin, dunnock, song thrush and mistle thrush are all common in woods throughout most of Britain although they are generally more wary of people here than in the urban environment. Among the most characteristic birds of our woodlands, however, are the tits: blue, great, coal, marsh and willow can all be found, each with slightly different habitat preferences, but most endearing of all is the long-tailed tit which looks just like an animated feather duster.

Many of the smaller woodland birds forage for insects among the leaf canopy or on the woodland floor but the nuthatch and treecreeper both search among crevices in the bark. Powerful toes and well-developed

Female great spotted woodpecker. The male has a red patch on the back of its neck

claws in both species enable them to keep a firm grip as they climb up tree trunks. Three species of woodpecker are also found in our woodlands. The smallest, the lesser spotted woodpecker, is hardly bigger than a sparrow and is rather inconspicuous, while the great spotted woodpecker is considerably bigger and often calls or 'drums' loudly, announcing its presence. The green woodpecker is larger still and drills large holes in tree trunks in which to nest. Unlike its relatives, it is sometimes seen on the ground, foraging for ants.

Early spring sees the return of rooks to colonial nests high in the tree tops, while woodpigeons are more retiring, constructing a neat arrangement of twigs among the lower branches. Stock doves, on the other hand, nest in holes in trees – a site also favoured by tawny owls whose familiar call can sometimes be heard at dusk. A dusk walk may also reveal the strange squeak of woodcock as they fly over their territory. During the daytime their mottled plumage renders them almost impossible to see among the fallen twigs and leaves.

The small songbirds have to be ever-alert for sparrowhawks which dash through woodland glades, taking their prey by surprise. After killing, the bird is taken to a stump or log to be plucked. Sparrowhawks, widespread in Britain, often occupy an abandoned nest of a jay.

CONIFEROUS WOODLANDS AND PLANTATIONS

Scottish Pine Forests
The highlands of Scotland hold the last remnants of natural pine forest left in Britain. This so-called Caledonian forest is sadly still being fragmented, but forests such as Abernethy and Rothiemurchus give a wonderful insight into the past and harbour a surprising variety of birds ranging from tiny songbirds to the immense capercaillie.

The isolation of the Scottish forests is also reflected in their birdlife. Scots pines, mainly in the Cairngorm region, are home to a bird unique to the British Isles, the Scottish crossbill. Distinguished from its more widespread relative, the common crossbill, by a larger bill and salmon-pink plumage in the male, this species is often extremely trusting as it prises seeds out of pine cones with its strangely shaped bill.

Crested tit – mainly confined to the old pine woods of Highland Scotland

Mature Pine Plantations
Elsewhere in Britain, pine forests have almost invariably been planted in recent years by man. The use of non-native species and the uniform age-structure of the woods means that they are of less interest to the birdwatcher than most deciduous woodlands, but most general woodland species can still be found – albeit in small numbers.

Chaffinch, greenfinch, robin, wren, dunnock and many of the tits all occur although the dense leaf canopy can often make observation rather difficult. When mature and cone-bearing, pine plantations may harbour small flocks of common crossbills which feed noisily among the branches: this species has certainly benefited from the spread of conifers.

Siskins and redpolls can also be seen. Small, mixed flocks – including birds which have migrated from the continent to our milder climate – often form in the winter. These flocks are sometimes joined briefly by blue, coal and long-tailed tits, as well as by one of our smallest birds, the goldcrest, which often hovers alongside a branch in order to pick off a hidden insect.

Young Plantations
For a few years after planting, upland conifer plantations are highly beneficial to ground-nesting species of birds. Black grouse, meadow pipits, grasshopper warblers and whinchats all thrive, as do predatory birds such as merlin, hen harrier and short-eared owl.

Flowering thrift, or sea pink, is a common sight around the coast of Britain in summer

THE COAST

Cliffs

Our rocky sea cliffs are a rich habitat for plants. Throughout the year a wealth of seaweeds can be seen at low tide while above the high tide mark lichens cover the rocks. Bright orange patches grow alongside encrusting species with nodules like crab eyes and are fascinating to study through a hand lens.

The first flowering plants begin to appear just above the spray zone and, not surprisingly, are much more tolerant to salt spray than inland species. Scurvy grass and the nodding white flowers of sea campion grow from crevices in the rocks and grab a tenuous hold between boulders; they often seem to thrive where the droppings from seabirds enrich the soil. Tussocks of thrift are next to colonise and soon consolidate the loose soil. During May and June they produce a dazzling display of brightly coloured flowers which rightfully earn the plant its other name of sea pink.

Here and there around our coasts immense plants of tree mallow can be found and, like the scurvy grass, they often seem to thrive around seabird colonies. Where rocky outcrops defy colonisation by most plants, English stonecrop is sometimes found. Its white flowers lie close to the ground, and its fleshy, red-green leaves help prevent water loss – such a threat to most plants in the drying sea breezes

and salt-laden air. Patches of thyme and devil's bit scabious often grow alongside the stonecrop and help complete the impression of a formally planted rock garden.

Sandy and Shingle Beaches

A surprising number of flowers have become adapted to this inhospitable habitat which is both well-drained and unstable. Yellow-horned poppy, sea sandwort and sea rocket are able to colonise the shifting terrain just above the high tide line, often accompanied by attractive plants of the aptly named sea holly. Where conditions are more stable, sea spurreys, sea kale and sea beet (the latter two forerunners of our garden vegetables) and a variety of clovers, such as haresfoot and strawberry clover, complete the array of plants.

Sand Dunes

Extensive areas of sand soon become stabilised by marram grass, which in turn allows many other plants to colonise. In the shelter of the dune slacks viper's bugloss, sea spurge, marsh orchids, marsh helleborines and a long list of other herbaceous plants provide a dazzling array of colour throughout the summer.

Estuaries

The higher reaches of estuaries mark the transition zone between sea and land where colonisation by plants

helps establish saltmarshes and subsequently dry land. Glasswort, sea arrow grass and cord grass grow on bare mud while higher up the shore clumps of sea purslane, sea aster and sea lavender can be found.

FRESHWATER

Streams and Rivers

Streams and rivers throughout Britain support a wide variety of colourful plants, the exact species varying according to the nature of the stream and its geographical position. Different species of water-crowfoot occur widely, their white, buttercup-like flowers appearing throughout the summer. Muddy shallows, exposed boulders and streamside banks are soon colonised by plants, and water speedwell, great willowherb and brooklime are widely found, while yellow mountain saxifrage is only seen beside upland streams in the north.

Water margins beside slow-flowing, lowland rivers and streams often harbour colourful plants such as lesser spearwort, yellow flag iris, monkeyflower and water forget-me-not. More local in their distribution, often being found beside canals, are flowering rush, frogbit, water violet and arrowhead. Marsh plants often grow right up to the riverside and several species of water dropwort, meadowsweet and meadow rue are sometimes found.

Yellow flag iris, the most common of Britain's two native species of wild iris. Stinking iris is the other

The Plant Life of Britain

Lakes and Ponds

Larger lakes and ponds are often carpeted with the leaves and flowers of white water lilies, while on smaller ponds duckweed blankets the surface. There is usually a similar profusion of plants lying beneath the surface of the water and the growth of Canadian pondweed, water milfoil and hornwort often clogs the water by the end of the summer. More acidic ponds sometimes hold bladderwort, which supplements its nutrient intake by catching and digesting small, aquatic insects. Often the only sign of its presence is the small yellow flower, produced on a long stalk.

Marshes

Throughout the summer months the wet meadows which adjoin many of our lowland rivers are a riot of colour. Southern marsh and early marsh orchids flower in May and June while later in the summer a more local orchid, the marsh helleborine, appears. May is also the month to see marsh marigolds, whose large, yellow flowers often seem to glow in the sunshine, and meadow vetchling and ragged robin, although less showy, are nonetheless extremely attractive when viewed closely. Tussock sedge and reedmace often appear to predominate but a careful search may reveal flowers of bistort, marsh cinquefoil and water avens.

GRASSLAND

A haven for insects and small mammals, natural grasslands throughout Britain burgeon with wild flowers throughout the summer. As with other habitats, many grassland

Musk orchid: over 40 species of orchid grow wild in Britain; 7,500 are to be found worldwide

Meadow cranesbill is widespread in the west and north of Britain

plants are strongly linked to the nature of the underlying soils, some being found only on neutral soils with others preferring chalky conditions.

Although generally considered to be botanically inferior to chalk grassland, meadows on neutral soils still harbour red and white clovers, meadow buttercup, marsh thistle and ox-eye daisy. *En masse*, this latter species is a wonderful sight as the flower heads sway in the breeze, interspersed with the occasional poppy or cornflower.

Considered one of the botanical gems of Britain, stretches of chalk downland can be found across southern England. Created by man's clearance of forests for sheep grazing, the short turf greatly favours herbaceous plants which cannot compete where more vigorous species are allowed to thrive. Consequently, the diversity of both species and colour can be truly amazing, many flowers needing to be studied at close range for best effect.

It is perhaps for the orchids that chalk grassland is best known. Pyramidal, fragrant, common spotted and bee orchids are all widespread and in places abundant, while burnt, musk, man and frog orchids occur more locally. Although their names often sound rather strange, a close study of the appearance or smell of their flowers soon reveals how appropriate these are.

Chalk grassland is a wonderful place for insects, in particular butterflies, and with the wealth of colourful flowers it is easy to see why. Cowslips appear early in the year, soon to be followed by thyme, basil thyme, marjoram, carline thistle, harebell, hay rattle, yellow-wort, autumn gentian and many more. Many of our chalk-loving plants have limited growing areas,

with field fleawort and round-headed rampion being extremely rare outside the Sussex Downs. Fortunately however, many, such as knapweeds and field scabious, occur more widely.

Although lacking the variety of southern chalk grasslands, meadows further north in Britain are often equally colourful. In the Yorkshire Dales, for example, you may find hay rattle, meadow cranesbill and buttercups, and on sheep-grazed turf covering limestone, particularly in the Teesdale area, a careful search may yield more unusual species such as globeflower, alpine bistort and sometimes even spring gentian or alpine bartsia.

FARMLAND AND HEDGEROWS

Open Fields

With the advent of modern farming practices agricultural fields full of flowers are a thing of the past. Although a few species, such as common chickweed and poppies, often flourish despite the application of modern herbicides, many of our 'arable weeds' have become decidedly scarce.

Fortunately, weed species often produce copious quantities of seed which can germinate after considerable periods of dormancy. Consequently, if spraying ceases, field margins and footpaths across arable fields may support unusual species such as corn buttercup, pheasant eye, ground pine and Venus's looking-glass, as well as more widespread plants such as pineapple mayweed, field bindweed and field pansy.

Snakeshead fritillary, a lover of damp meadowland, is becoming increasingly scarce

Roadside Verges and Hedgerows

With the disappearance of much of our woodland and increasingly rigorous modern farming practices, roadside verges and hedgerows are fast becoming major refuges for wildlife. So much so that in some counties stretches of roadside have been declared nature reserves and it is not uncommon, for example on the Sussex Downs, to find several species of orchid growing side by side on the verge.

In early spring patches of lesser celandine put on a fine display, being particularly fond of sunny banks. Roadside verges in the West Country are often especially lush and sometimes the beautiful yellow flowers of the celandine are accompanied by early purple orchids and primroses. Here and there patches of greater stitchwort add a splash of white to the fresh green of emerging leaves, and later in the season foxgloves and red campion grow clear of the grass and brambles.

Many of our remaining hedgerows date back several centuries to a time when they were essential for marking boundaries and containing livestock. With increasing age, hedgerows acquire more and more species of tree and shrub and a mature example can hold field maple, elm, elder, hazel, spindle and many others. In spring, these hedges are a delightful sight with sprays of the white flowers of hawthorn and blackthorn.

Although at the height of summer our roadside verges and hedgerows are colourful enough to be the envy of many cottage gardens, many people consider them to be at their best

Early purple orchid – traditionally associated with love and reproduction. It thrives on lime-rich soil

Foxgloves flower in open woodland from May to September. Local names include fairy fingers and goblin's thimble

during the autumn when the berries, fruits and seeds, which ensure the survival of future generations of hedgerow plants, can be found.

In the shade provided by shrubs and trees tall spikes of red berries appear – the fruiting stage of cuckoo pint which flowered earlier in the year. Dense patches of bramble produce a feast of blackberries so beloved of ramblers and wild animals alike, while the berries of white and black bryony, although no less appealing to look at, are not for human consumption. By September the dog rose which looked so attractive in June will have produced hips, and traveller's joy the hairy seeds which gave it its other name of old man's beard.

HEATHLAND AND MOORLAND

Although heathland plants are generally low-growing, their lack of stature is generally made up for in colour. From June until September the pinks and purples of the heathers contrast with the yellow flowers of gorse and the resulting mosaic can be striking.

Ling and bell heather are the two dominant plants of our heathlands and are at their best in July and August. Where not burnt or overgrazed, they often grow to sizeable clumps and dotted among them will be shrubs of gorse and broom. The three species of gorse found in this country all have extended and slightly differing flowering periods, so, whatever the time of year, gorse flowers can generally be found on our heathlands.

Where the heathland soil becomes waterlogged, cross-leaved heath begins to flourish, thriving in conditions

where its roots are permanently wet. Raised tussocks of soil provide slightly drier conditions, however, and here heath spotted orchids and tormentil appear.

In heathland valleys, where pools of standing water occur, only the most specialised plants can survive. Fragrant-smelling bog myrtle grows around the pool margins while, often completely submerged in peaty water, *Sphagnum* moss is characteristic. Here and there yellow spikes of bog asphodel can be seen, together with marsh St John's wort and tassels of aptly named cotton grass and pink spikes of lousewort.

These acidic soils are poor in nutrients which has encouraged one family of bog plants, the sundews, to adopt the following extraordinary feeding strategy: their sticky leaves trap any small insect which touches their glistening surface then secrete enzymes which digest the unfortunate creature. The nutrients released are then absorbed by the plant.

Ling and bell heather also dominate our upland moorlands. Management of moorland by mosaic burning for grouse generally impoverishes the flora, but in unmanaged areas low-growing shrubs of bilberry, cowberry and crowberry can be found. The white, flower-like bracts of dwarf cornel are a local but widespread sight in northern Britain and in wet areas sundews, insectivorous butterworts, grass of Parnassus and bog rosemary can all be found. Needless to say, drainage of moorland, which is becoming increasingly frequent, does not favour these species and they soon disappear.

Bell heather (shown here) prefers the drier areas of moorland, cross-leaved heath the wetter

The Plant Life of Britain

Mountain avens flowers from June to August and has feathery, plumed fruits

MOUNTAINS

A mountain's bedrock has a profound influence upon the distribution of flowers to be found on it. Bands of alkaline limestone support a far wider variety of plants than the more widespread areas of acidic rocks like granite, and as a result most of Britain's mountains support a comparatively small variety of plants. In addition to this, British mountain flowers have been drastically influenced by man. Trees and shrubs have long-since been cleared from most areas and many of our peaks are so popular with the public that soil erosion is becoming a problem. Countless generations of sheep have also nibbled the vegetation to the point where they have seriously affected the flora and the plants that survive tend to be those not favoured by them.

Nevertheless, there are isolated pockets of alkaline soils – rich in mountain flora – which are protected either by their inaccessibility or by their status, and National Nature Reserves at Cwm Idwal in Snowdonia and Glen Clova in the Cairngorms are well worth exploring.

The sight and scent of a thick carpet of bluebells in spring is unforgettable

Saxifrages are one of the most characteristic families of mountain plants with purple, starry and mossy saxifrages being widespread. A variety of other species, such as drooping, tufted and highland saxifrages, occur on isolated mountain peaks, sometimes in the company of plants such as alpine forget-me-not and rock speedwell.

Acid rocks do support some plants of interest, and alpine lady's mantle, mountain everlasting and clubmosses are common. Ferns grow among crevices in the rocks with lemon scented or mountain fern and holly fern being characteristic, while on scree slopes in the Snowdonia range beautiful clumps of parsley fern can be found. The boulders themselves also support lichens, the most common being the map or mountain lichen, named because of its resemblance to a coloured map.

Paradoxically, it is not always necessary to climb mountains to find mountain flora in Britain. Along the north coast of Scotland, especially between Strathy Point and Bettyhill, conditions are right for alpine and arctic species such as mountain avens, purple mountain milk-vetch, northern bedstraw and yellow mountain saxifrage to grow near to sea level.

BROADLEAVED WOODLAND

During the summer months the leaf canopy of broadleaved woodland casts dense shade on the woodland floor. However, in early spring, before the leaves are formed, plenty of light is available and this is the time when many woodland flowers are at their best.

Dog's mercury persists for most of the summer, but for many plants the growing and flowering period is short. Some of these spring flowers grow in carpets given the right conditions and, particularly under ash, you are likely to find large patches of ramsons, wood sorrel or wood anemone. Here and there a careful search may reveal early purple orchid, herb paris, yellow archangel, goldilocks buttercup or even yellow star of Bethlehem.

Later in the season, in more ancient woodlands, flower spikes of greater butterfly orchids stand well above the surrounding vegetation. Honeysuckle begins to flower in June and its strong smell pervades woods where it is allowed to flourish.

In many parts of southern England the woodland practice of coppicing still persists. Practised mainly on hazel, but also occasionally on ash and hornbeam, it involves periodic cutting back to the stump with the result that thin, straight shoots appear which are eventually ideal for hurdles and fenceposts. The amount of light reaching the woodland floor is greatly increased and one plant in particular does extremely well – the bluebell. Thanks to this forestry practice woods full of bluebells, which are almost unknown on mainland Europe, are widespread in England.

Beechwoods, which often grow on lime-rich soils, produce an extremely dense leaf canopy so that the woodland floor is often rather bare. Before the leaves have appeared on the trees, hellebores, spurge laurel and mezereon sometimes grow, while later in the year shade-loving plants such as broadleaved and white helleborine, birdsnest orchid or yellow birdsnest can be found by careful searching.

Oak woodlands, particularly in the west and north of Britain, are often festooned with lichens and the woodland floor carpeted with ferns and mosses. Spring flowers generally include common dog violet and wood spurge, together with more widespread species like bluebell, early purple orchid and yellow archangel, to be followed later in the year by foxgloves and bracken.

CONIFEROUS WOODLANDS

Most coniferous woodlands in England and Wales are the result of forestry plantation policies and many are now quite mature. However, the tree species used are often not native to Britain and consequently the floral interest is somewhat limited compared to the range which is found in more natural woodlands.

In their initial stages, the ground flora of conifer plantations generally reflects the vegetation that would have been there prior to planting: bilberry, ling and bell heather on acid soils and chalk flora on lime-rich soils. However, once mature enough to form an unbroken canopy, very little can survive underneath and botanical interest is confined to the woodland rides. Fortunately, because these are kept wide enough to allow future extraction of timber, the rides are often a haven for wildlife.

HOW TO FIND THE TOURS AND WALKS

The maps on either side of this page show where the tours in the book are located, and the key gives the start points of both the tours and their accompanying walks.

Wherever possible the walks are keyed to the nearest village, but sometimes a well-known landmark is given instead.

To find the precise location of a walk, refer to the relevant tour map. See also page 4.

Tour 1 St Helier *27½ miles*
Walk 1A La Corbière
Walk 1B St Ouen
Walk 1C St Lawrence
Walk 1D Vallée des Vaux

Tour 2 St Helier *25 miles*
Walk 2A Trinity Church, Bouley Bay
Walk 2B Gorey

Tour 3 St Peter Port *29½ miles*
Walk 3A Jerbourg Point
Walk 3B Pleinmont
Walk 3C L'Erée
Walk 3D L'Ancresse

Tour 4 Penzance *46 miles*
Walk 4A Lamorna Cove
Walk 4B St Levan
Walk 4C Bosullow
Walk 4D Zennor
Walk 4E Godrevy Point
Walk 4F Hendra

Tour 5 Wadebridge *79 miles*
Walk 5A New Polzeath
Walk 5B Boscastle

Tour 6 Looe *79 miles*
Walk 6A Cawsand
Walk 6B Polkerris

Tour 7 Plymouth *57 miles*
Walk 7A Merrivale
Walk 7B Noss Mayo

Tour 8 Ashburton *44 miles*
Walk 8A Two Bridges
Walk 8B Drewsteignton

Tour 9 Exeter *64 miles*
Walk 9A Silverton
Walk 9B Weston

Tour 10 Lynton *59 miles*
Walk 10A Hillsford Bridge
Walk 10B Tarr Steps

Tour 11 Bristol *63 miles*
Walk 11A Monkton Combe
Walk 11B Chilcompton
Walk 11C Westonzoyland
Walk 11D Burrington

Tour 12 Weymouth *67 miles*
Walk 12A Child Okeford
Walk 12B Worth Matravers

Tour 13 Salisbury *76 miles*
Walk 13A Tollard Royal
Walk 13B Lower Woodford

Tour 14 Newport *72 miles*
Walk 14A Arreton
Walk 14B Wootton
Walk 14C Alverstone
Walk 14D St Helens
Walk 14E Bembridge Point
Walk 14F Luccombe
Walk 14G Wroxall
Walk 14H St Lawrence
Walk 14I Godshill
Walk 14J Blackgang
Walk 14K Brighstone
Walk 14L Brook
Walk 14M Shalfleet
Walk 14N Carisbrooke

Tour 15 Chichester *53 miles*
Walk 15A East Marden
Walk 15B Singleton
Walk 15C Sutton
Walk 15D Amberley
Walk 15E Fontwell
Walk 15F Pagham Harbour

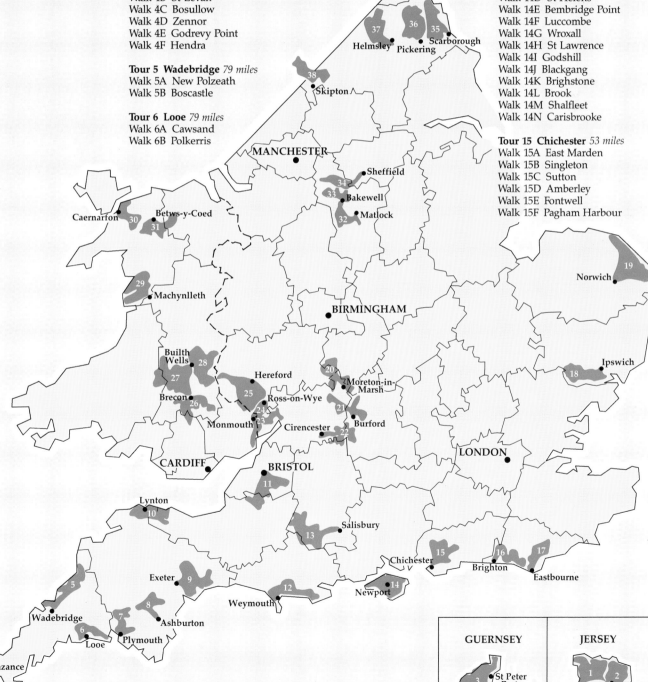

HOW TO FIND THE TOURS AND WALKS

Tour 16 Brighton *48 miles*
Walk 16A Worthing
Walk 16B Washington
Walk 16C Coombes
Walk 16D Devil's Dyke
Walk 16E Clayton
Walk 16F Firle

Tour 17 Eastbourne *53 miles*
Walk 17A Westdean
Walk 17B Alfriston

Tour 18 Ipswich *64 miles*
Walk 18A Shotley
Walk 18B Stutton
Walk 18C Lavenham
Walk 18D Hadleigh

Tour 19 Norwich *79 miles*
Walk 19A Reepham
Walk 19B Weybourne
Walk 19C Horsey
Walk 19D Framingham Earl

Tour 20 Moreton-in-Marsh *65 miles*
Walk 20A Broadway
Walk 20B Chipping Camden
Walk 20C Elmley Castle
Walk 20D Chastleton

Tour 21 Burford *71 miles*
Walk 21A Fifield
Walk 21B Windrush
Walk 21C Bourton-on-the-Water
Walk 21D Hailes Abbey
Walk 21E Kilkenny
Walk 21F Astall

Tour 22 Cirencester *67 miles*
Walk 22A Ampney St Peter
Walk 22B Bibury
Walk 22C Radcot
Walk 22D Sapperton

Tour 23 Monmouth *40 miles*
Walk 23A Vallets Wood
Walk 23B Mallards Pike Lake

Tour 24 Ross-on-Wye *50 miles*
Walk 24A Ross-on-Wye
Walk 24B Howle Hill
Walk 24C Christchurch
Walk 24D Tidenham
Walk 24E Upper Wyndcliff
Walk 24F Abbey Bridge

Tour 25 Hereford *77 miles*
Walk 25A Lower Bullingham
Walk 25B King's Thorn
Walk 25C Mordiford
Walk 25D Brockhampton
Walk 25E Llanfihangel Crucorney
Walk 25F Llanveynoe

Tour 26 Brecon *65 miles*
Walk 26A Pont Cadwgan
Walk 26B Llangattock
Walk 26C Talybont-on-Usk
Walk 26D Pont ar Daf
Walk 26E Porth yr Ogof
Walk 26F Blaen Llia

Tour 27 Brecon *73 miles*
Walk 27A Brecon
Walk 27B Carreg Cennen Castle

Tour 28 Builth Wells *65 miles*
Walk 28A New Radnor
Walk 28B Kington
Walk 28C Little Black Hill
Walk 28D Cwm Sorgwm

Tour 29 Machynlleth *59 miles*
Walk 29A Machynlleth
Walk 29B Cors y Gedol Hall
Walk 29C Penmaenpool
Walk 29D Coed Groe

Tour 30 Caernarfon *80 miles*
Walk 30A Newborough Forest
Walk 30B Nantmor
Walk 30C Beddgelert Forest
Walk 30D Llanaelhaearn

Tour 31 Betws-y-coed *62 miles*
Walk 31A Llyn Tecwyn Isaf
Walk 31B Pont-y-pant

Tour 32 Matlock *51 miles*
Walk 32A Blore
Walk 32B Alstonefield
Walk 32C Wetton
Walk 32D Pikehall
Walk 32E Hartington
Walk 32F Birchover

Tour 33 Bakewell *40 miles*
Walk 33A Monyash
Walk 33B Parsley Hay
Walk 33C Hollinsclough
Walk 33D Topley Pike

Tour 34 Sheffield *51 miles*
Walk 34A Birchen Edge
Walk 34B Castleton
Walk 34C Ladybower Dam
Walk 34D Hathersage

Tour 35 Scarborough *73 miles*
Walk 35A West Ayton
Walk 35B Saltergate
Walk 35C Littlebeck
Walk 35D Whitby
Walk 35E Robin Hood's Bay
Walk 35F Cloughton

Tour 36 Pickering *55 miles*
Walk 36A Sinnington
Walk 36B Rosedale Abbey
Walk 36C Danby
Walk 36D Goathland

Tour 37 Helmsley *68 miles*
Walk 37A Sutton Bank
Walk 37B Osmotherley
Walk 37C Gribdale Gate
Walk 37D Chop Gate

Tour 38 Skipton *67 miles*
Walk 38A Malham Tarn
Walk 38B Settle
Walk 38C Clapham
Walk 38D Kettlewell
Walk 38E Hebden
Walk 38F Bolton Abbey

Tour 39 Hawes *57 miles*
Walk 39A Hawes
Walk 39B Muker
Walk 39C Reeth
Walk 39D Askrigg
Walk 39E Countersett
Walk 39F West Burton
Walk 39G Hubberholme
Walk 39H Dent

Tour 40 Broughton-in-Furness *57 miles*
Walk 40A Nether Wasdale
Walk 40B Dunnerdale Forest

Tour 41 Coniston *35 miles*
Walk 41A Monk Coniston
Walk 41B Bowness-on-Windermere

Tour 42 Ambleside *46 miles*
Walk 42A Grasmere
Walk 42B Keswick
Walk 42C Keswick boat landings
Walk 42D Hartsop

Tour 43 Keswick *60 miles*
Walk 43A Ashness Bridge
Walk 43B Rosthwaite
Walk 43C Buttermere
Walk 43D Mire House

Tour 44 Barnard Castle *60 miles*
Walk 44A Barnard Castle
Walk 44B Bowlees

Tour 45 Hexham *80 miles*
Walk 45A Blanchland
Walk 45B Westgate
Walk 45C Keenleywell House
Walk 45D Steel Rigg

Tour 46 Alnwick *86 miles*
Walk 46A Old Bewick
Walk 46B Carey Burn Bridge
Walk 46C Holy Island
Walk 46D Craster

Tour 47 Wooler *90 miles*
Walk 47A Alwinton
Walk 47B Holystone

Tour 48 Oban *102 miles*
Walk 48A Head of Glen Nevis
Walk 48B Dalmally

Tour 49 Inverness *119 miles*
Walk 49A Inverfarigaig
Walk 49B Dog Fall, Glen Affric

Tour 50 Lairg *126 miles*
Walk 50A Balnakeil
Walk 50B Handa Island

50

Lairg

49 Inverness

48

Oban

EDINBURGH

GLASGOW

Wooler

47

46
Alnwick

Hexham

45

44

43

Keswick

42

40

41

Broughton
-in-
Furness

Ambleside

Coniston

Barnard
Castle

39

Hawes

38

ROUTE DIRECTIONS

The drive starts from St Helier ①.

From the Weighbridge, follow signs to the West, St Aubin A1, to leave by the Esplanade. In ½ mile, at the traffic signals, go forward into Victoria Avenue A2. Just under two miles further, bear left on to the A1 to reach Beaumont. At the mini-roundabout go forward, signed St Aubin. About ¾ mile further, reach St Aubin ②.

Turn right on to the A13, signed St Brelade, Corbière, and ascend St Aubin's Hill. In just over one mile, branch left on to the B66, signed St Brelade's Church and Bay, and descend to St Brelade's Bay ③.

At the far end of the Bay by St Brelade's Church (on the left) turn left on to an unclassified road, then at the T-junction turn right, signed Beau Port Bay, and ascend. The road has hairpin bends. After a short distance pass the road to Beau Port Bay Car Park (on the left), then in ½ mile, at the T-junction, turn left into the B83 Route du Sud to reach La Corbière Lighthouse ④.

Continue with the B44, passing Petit Port Bay, then in ¾ mile turn left on to the B35, signed La Pulente, St Ouen's Bay, and descend to La Pulente. Proceed along St Ouen's Bay ⑤.

In 1½ miles, an AA telephone is passed on the right. In 1¼ miles, pass La Mielle de Morville Country Park and Nature Reserve on the right. In ¼ mile bear right, signed L'Étacq, St Ouen. After ½ mile, pass a quarry and turn sharp left, signed L'Étacq, to reach L'Étacq ⑥.

After a mile, L'Étacq Point is reached. Ascend the hill and at the top turn sharp left on to the B55, signed Gros Nez, Plémont. In ¾ mile turn left on to an unclassified road, signed Grosnez, to reach Grosnez Point (with car park) ⑦.

Return to the T-junction and turn left into the B55 Route de Grosnez. In ¾ mile go straight over the crossroads, signed Léoville, passing the road to Plemont Candlecraft (on the left). After 1⅓ miles turn sharp left on to the B65, signed La Grève de Lecq, and descend into La Grève de Lecq ⑧.

Continue with the B40, passing Grève de Lecq Army Barracks on the left. In just over one mile, go over the crossroads, then ⅓ mile further go forward on the B33, signed St John. An AA telephone is passed on the right. Go straight on for 1¾ miles to St John's Church. Go straight over the crossroads and turn immediately right on to the A10, signed St Lawrence, St Helier, to reach Le Carrefour Selous, and go straight over the crossroads. In one mile pass St Lawrence's Church (on the right) ⑨.

The route follows a level coastal road from St Helier then winds uphill, allowing a magnificent view of La Corbière Lighthouse. More fine views follow along St Ouen's Bay – the longest in the Channel Islands.

In 1⅓ miles, at the T-junction, turn left on to the A1, signed St Helier. In 1¼ miles, at the roundabout, take the second exit then go forward at the traffic signals. Proceed along the Esplanade to re-enter St Helier.

POINTS OF INTEREST

① St Helier, Jersey's capital town, is a pleasant mixture of spacious parks, historic buildings and pedestrianised shopping precincts – including an attractive enclosed market. The Fort Regent Entertainment and Sports Centre above the town has entertainments to suit the whole family.

② Acknowledged as Jersey's second town, St Aubin is a charming place to explore on foot with its harbour and quaint streets. The Royal Channel Islands Yacht Club is located here.

③ One of the island's most popular beaches, St Brelade's Bay is ideal for both bathing and windsurfing.

St Brelade's Church nestles close to the sea with the Fishermen's Chapel – which has some fine 14th- and 15th-century wall paintings inside – standing alongside.

④ La Corbière is a reef of jagged rocks on which stands the 62ft-high lighthouse. It is not open to the public but the lower gallery can be reached by a causeway at low tide. This is dangerous when the tide rises and a bell is rung to warn visitors that it is time to leave.

⑤ The sandy bay of St Ouen – stretching for almost the entire length of the west coast – is used for surfing and sand racing. Families will find the waves at the southern end gentler. There are two Martello towers on the beach, one of which – Kempt Tower – now houses an Interpretation Centre for the whole bay.

⑥ L'Étacq marks the northern extremity of St Ouen's Bay. From here to the ruins of Gros Nez

Castle, a distance of 1½ miles, cliffs rise vertically to nearly 250ft. The workshops of L'Étacq Woodcraft are open to the public, as is the Potter's Wheel nearby where pottery and leatherwork may be seen.

⑦ This north-westerly tip of the island has magnificent views of the other main Channel Islands, spectacular scenery of its own, a holy rock, a rifle range and a racecourse. Gros Nez Castle was already a ruin by 1540.

⑧ Coarse, yellow sand – once used to purify the island's water – distinguishes the beach of La Grève de Lecq. To the east is a 270ft mound known as Le Castel de Lecq. This is thought to have been used as a hillfort during the Iron Age, and a refuge from invaders in medieval times.

⑨ Known to have existed in the early 12th century, St Lawrence's Church has a Norman saddle-back tower and some Norman windows. The Hamptonne Chapel, built in 1524, is reckoned to be one of the finest examples of ecclesiastical architecture on the island.

Probably built during the 14th century, Gros Nez Castle may well have been dismantled during the French Occupation

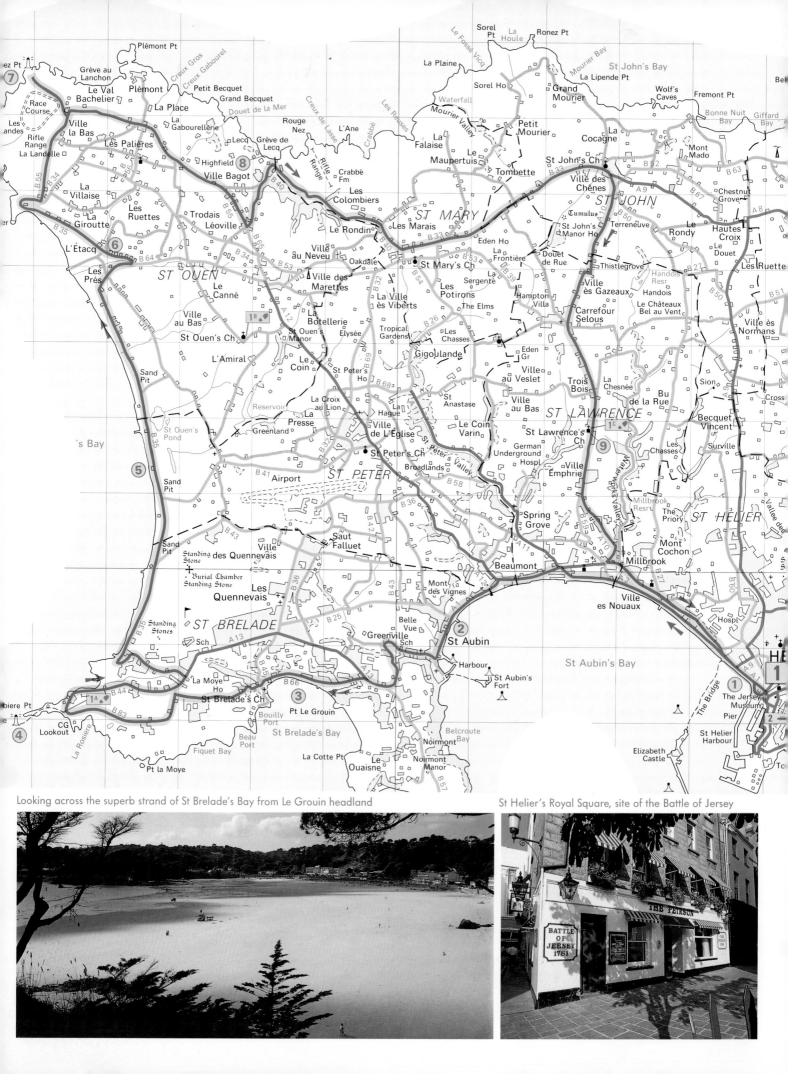

Looking across the superb strand of St Brelade's Bay from Le Grouin headland

St Helier's Royal Square, site of the Battle of Jersey

ROUTE DIRECTIONS

Allow 3 hours
Start from the car park to the right of the old railway station above La Corbière (grid ref. WV554481). (There is a convenient No 12 bus stop and a phone box.)

Walk on to the old railway line which runs parallel to the road and turn right①.

The track crosses two roads, then continues past La Moye Golf Club on the left. Take the next turn left, off the main track, opposite Les Quennevais Secondary School. On the right are playing fields and on the left the golf course and then a pumping station. After an avenue of trees there is access on to the dunes to your left. Go through these and you are now on Les Blanches Banques②.

Keeping the magnificent view of St Ouen's Bay in front of you, make your way down any of the many paths to the foot of the dunes. As you reach the lower sandhills look out to sea. If La Rocco Tower, the round tower situated on rocks to the south of the bay, is on your left, you should be able to see a standing stone beneath you on the sandy plain. Head for that③.

Now keep walking south, towards La Corbière. The route goes past a car park and up some steps, with a German bunker on the right. After the next car park, cross La Grande Route des Mielles (Five Mile Road) on to the footpath, still heading towards the lighthouse④.

Stay on this side of the road, past a drinking trough (abreuvoir) dated 1871, until the bend in the road. There is now a footpath leading round the cliff. Take the path up the cliff, which is private but a permitted footpath, to the top⑤.

Return to the top of the steps and take the path through zig-zag gates opposite. At the bottom turn left along a bridlepath, left again and then right on to the road. This leads round to La Corbière, past a German bunker, and so back to the starting point.

Standing 500yds from the shore, La Corbière Lighthouse can be reached on foot at low tide. However, this should not be attempted when the tide is coming in

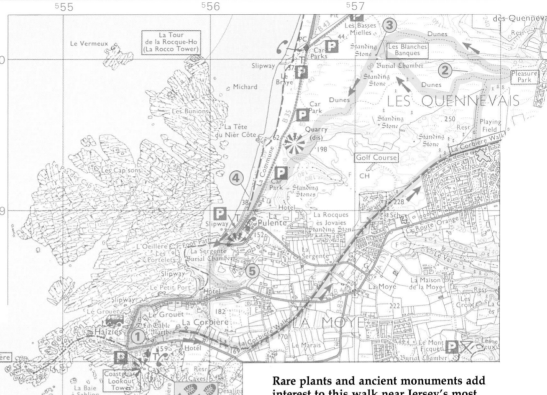

Rare plants and ancient monuments add interest to this walk near Jersey's most south-westerly point. Apart from two short climbs towards the end, the walk is not strenuous, but walkers with young children will need to take care where the route is on or near roads.

POINTS OF INTEREST

①The large slab of red granite just here is La Table des Marthes. Probably the capstone from some megalithic structure, it was once of considerable local importance because contracts signed on the stone before 1850 were held to be binding. The tower away to the right of the track has a more modern significance: it belongs to a desalination plant, used in serious water shortages.

②This is one of the most important dune systems in Europe, and is particularly rich in plant life. Creamy-white burnet roses fill the air with their scent in June, and Jersey thrift, dwarf pansies and rare orchids are among more than 400 species here.

③Standing stones, or menhirs, often mark burial sites. Here, the burial chamber can still be seen, and there is a sister stone just to the south.

④Seashore plants thrive beside this stretch of the path by the sea. Among the more unusual species likely to be seen are wild fennel and sea stock.

⑤Just off the route here (turn left, then right) is a prehistoric burial chamber called La Sergenté. Dating from about 3700BC, it is believed to be the oldest tomb in Jersey.

Le Val de la Mare Reservoir, now a well-established wildlife haven. Inset: Dolmen des Monts at Grantez

Wonderfully varied scenery is the main attraction of this energetic but beautiful walk around Le Val de la Mare Reservoir and Les Mielles Country Park. The path can be wet in places.

POINTS OF INTEREST

① Dedicated to a 7th-century archbishop of Rouen, the church was probably founded by an early member of the de Carteret family – landowners here since before 1066.

② On both sides of the road are strips of land separated by grass banks. These are fields still farmed in the medieval strip manner.

③ Constructed in the early 1960s, the dam measures 535ft along its crest, which rises 75ft above the valley floor.

④ Between the dam and the road, the walk follows the track of a railway which ran from the granite quarries at St John to La Pulente. Built by the Germans during the Occupation in World War II, it was never opened.

⑤ Plants to be found in this damp terrain include galingale, a species of sedge which can be used for basket-weaving and to make paper.

⑥ The Dolmen des Monts, Grantez, is a bottle-shaped grave, about 5ft below the present ground level. It was originally covered by a circular mound, and was virtually undisturbed when investigated in 1912. Eight skeletons were found inside, dating back some 5,000 years.

⑦ Ahead is St Ouen's Mill. This is now a shipping marker and the headquarters of a Scout group. There has been a mill here since the 14th century and medieval strip fields can be seen around it.

ROUTE DIRECTIONS

Allow 3 hours
Start from the car park behind St Ouen's Parish Church (grid ref. WV579530) ①.

In front of the church turn right and then first left (La Rue de la Campagne) ②.

At the T-junction turn right and then left on to a track marked La Val de la Mare Reservoir. Take the left-hand fork and, by a small parking area, go through the gate to the left.

Follow the path down to the water, then north up the Y-shaped reservoir's western arm, across a gravel causeway, up the hill between the two arms (with fantastic views – and seats – at the summit) and so down to the tip of the eastern arm, around and south down its length to the dam ③.

Take the path down to the foot of the dam, and out to the road, then turn right ④.

After the junction with Mont Matthieu and an area of sand-removal, turn right up a track, and when it forks bear left. The area soon becomes wooded and the path narrow, overgrown and sometimes wet ⑤.

Continue past La Ville au Bas farm and turn left along a ridge giving more panoramic views of the bay below. Take the second track to the left, marked as a footpath only (not the first steep path as this leads straight down!). This leads into another valley, Les Vaux Cuissin, with a brook and a recently planted copse. Finally, climb out on to Les Chemins des Monts.

Turn left into the road, and in about 400yds on the left go past a Neolithic passage grave ⑥.

After leaving the dolmen, cross the road on to a track. Keep bearing right into La Rue de Grantez ⑦.

Turn left at the next junction to get back to the church.

ROUTE DIRECTIONS

Allow 2 hours or 1½ hours Start from Rue de l'Eglise, where you can park alongside the church (grid ref. WV626518) ①.

Turn left on to the main road and then right opposite the parish hall down a metalled track marked 'no road'. This soon becomes rough and steep and leads down into La Vallée de St Laurens②.

Those who are taking the shorter walk will turn left on to the road at the bottom and should skip the next section until the more energetic return to this point. The others will turn right, following a winding road to Millbrook Reservoir③.

Turn left, up Ruelle de St Clair. At the top of the road, turn left down a grass track between two private drives. Continue down into the valley again④.

Turn right up the road picking up those who chose the shorter walk and continue past Dannemarche Reservoir, turning left up Mont de la Chenaie. At the top, turn left, then right on to the main road and immediately left again into Rue Milbrae. Keep straight on at the next crossroads, down a road marked 'no entry'⑤.

Beyond Morel Farm, turn left into Les Charrières de Malorey and when the road curves to the right, keep straight on into Le Chemin des Montagnes. Then turn left past Badier Farm. This is marked private but there is a public right of way leading straight past the house and on to a track. This leads down into a valley and then curves to the right. It eventually comes out on to the road behind the church.

The 17th-century double roadside arch of Morel Farm, a property of the National Trust for Jersey

This is a pretty walk, showing the best of this lush parish with its brooks, reservoirs and National Trust properties. Much of the route is on metalled roads, but some of the tracks can be overgrown.

POINTS OF INTEREST

①The St Lawrence Pillar, standing inside the church, was found below the floor during restoration work in 1890 and proves that there was already a church here at the beginning of the 7th century. St Lawrence's has the oldest bell in Jersey, dating from 1592. The 16th-century Hamptonne Chapel is a fine example of the French Flamboyant Gothic style. The church has an unusual Norman saddle-back tower, a distinctive landscape feature. Note the contained setting of this little community with the church, school, arsenal and parish hall all in a straight line, and the public house and shop just across the road.

②La Vallée de St Laurens is often referred to as Waterworks Valley. Six or seven mills were at one time powered by the stream that runs through it, but over the last 100 years three reservoirs have been built in the valley bottom.

③The abreuvoir on the right of the road provided water for the horses carrying granite to build the St Aubin's sea wall at the turn of the century. Millbrook Reservoir was the first to be built in the valley, in 1898, to provide water for St Helier (the Jersey Fresh Water Angling Association have fishing rights here, but the public can stroll around it).

④In the valley bottom is the site of the mill pond of Moulin à Sucre, a mill which once crushed sugar. On the right various paths lead past the site of Vicart Mill and back to the original junction.

⑤At the bottom of the hill are several National Trust for Jersey properties. On the left are two wooded côtils (steep fields) while on the right is Le Rât Cottage, a delightful 17th-century dwelling. Just past the junction to this cottage is La Fontaine de St Martin, an ancient sacred spring said to have healing powers. Just beyond, on the right, is an unusual abreuvoir, with the stream running on to the road and back. This was built as a lavoir (washing place) in the 17th century. Keep straight up the road to reach Morel Farm, a National Trust for Jersey property, which has interesting outbuildings. This is a working farm and the tenant cannot always show people round.

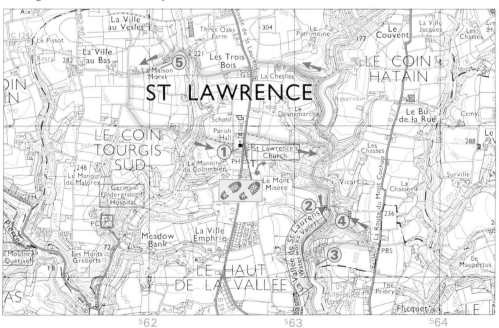

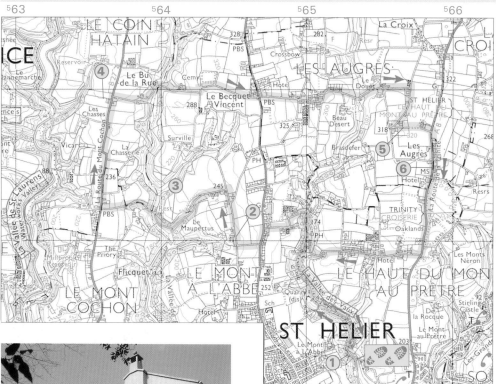

Peaceful farmland between La Vallée de St Laurens and La Vallée des Vaux

ROUTE DIRECTIONS

Allow 2 hours
Start near the water garden about ¼ mile along Vallée des Vaux, where there is roadside parking (grid ref. WV654503).

Walk up the valley with the stream on your right①.

The route follows the road past the Harvest Barn Inn and yet more National Trust land. Take the first left up Rue des Côtils (very steep), which leads to the main road. Turn left on to Queen's Road, and then first right down a narrow lane. Turn right at the bottom past Fernhill②.

Turn left and into Fern Valley③.

When the junction with La Route du Mont Cochon is reached, turn right and walk along the road, turning right down the next public road, Ruette Pinel④.

La Ruette Pinel leads back into the valley, past another farm and eventually up to Surville cemetery.

Cross the main road and follow the strawberry signs (during the picking season) along Rue du Becquet Vincent. This eventually descends to the top of Vallée des Vaux. Past Le Douet Farm turn left past Lyndale, right at the T-junction, and then left again⑤.

Turn right on to Trinity main road (La Route de la Trinité)⑥.

Turn right into La Route du Petit Clos, which wends its way past another farm and so to the western slope of La Commune des Melèches. Some may wish to brave the gorse bushes of the common to reach the foot of the valley, but the road leads gently down to the entrance of the Harvest Barn. Turn left along the valley to your parking spot.

The Sir Francis Cook Gallery hosts a varied programme of art exhibitions

This is an easy, rural walk, close to St Helier yet with some surprisingly unspoilt views. The route follows country lanes that wind up and down between the valleys leading into the town, each with its cluster of working farms.

POINTS OF INTEREST

①The roadside stream, which meanders through the water garden, once drove a watermill that served St Helier. Two National Trust properties are to be found in this valley: Le Don Le Gallais – the first property given to the National Trust for Jersey – and, higher up, Les Déserts, whose arboretum contains many unusual trees.

②Originally called L'Ancienne Maison Le Geyt, this 17th-century house was the home of a distinguished lawyer, Philippe Le Geyt, born in 1635.

③Totally unspoilt views are a feature of this part of the walk, and it is hard to believe that aptly named Fern Valley is less than a mile from St Helier.

④West of the main road, the view extends across La Vallée de St Laurens (known as Waterworks Valley on account of its three reservoirs) to the unusual tower of St Lawrence's Church beyond.

⑤Vegetables and fruit, including strawberries in season, may be picked at La Grange fruit farm.

⑥On the right can soon be seen the Sir Francis Cook Gallery, a converted chapel used by local artist Sir Francis Cook and given by his widow to the Jersey Heritage Trust in 1982. Different exhibitions are held here throughout the year. Past the Gallery and the Oaklands Lodge Hotel is Le Don Sparkes-Davies, a property of the National Trust for Jersey. This curious, windowless building was probably erected to give its owner or occupier an influence or vote in the town parish.

ROUTE DIRECTIONS

The drive starts from St Helier ①.

From the Weighbridge in St Helier follow signs The West, St Aubin A1, leaving the town by The Esplanade. In ½ mile, at the traffic signals, drive forward into Victoria Avenue, A2. In nearly ¾ mile turn right, signed Waterworks Valley A1. Continue to a crossroads, at which go forward on the B27, signed Mont Cochon. In nearly 3 miles, at the T-junction, turn left on to an unclassified road, then turn right. After a further ½ mile, at a crossroads, turn right, then at a fork bear left. In ½ mile at the T-junction turn right to follow the A9 to Les Hautes Croix.

At the next T-junction turn left on to the A8, signed Trinity Church, Bouley Bay, then immediately turn right. In almost a mile take the second turning left, C96, signed Bouley Bay, and in nearly ½ mile at another T-junction bear left and descend through sharp bends to Bouley Bay ②.

Return from the bay and ascend through sharp bends, with views of the French coast and Ecrehous Reefs. After nearly a mile take the first left turn on to the C95. Some ¾ mile further continue forward, then at the T-junction turn left on to the C93, signed Rozel Bay. For the beach keep left at the foot of the hill ③.

Continuing, bear right on to the B38 and climb. In a mile turn left on to the B91, signed Flicquet, St Catherine's, and in ½ mile at a crossroads go forward on to an unclassified road (not for large cars, which should turn right at the crossroads for St Catherine's) signed Flicquet Bay. Descend a narrow, winding hill road to Flicquet Bay.

Ascend, and just after ½ mile at a T-junction turn left on to the B91. After another ½ mile, at a crossroads, turn left on to the B29, signed St Catherine's. Continue round a one-way system for St Catherine's Breakwater and a return to the crossroads ④.

On rejoining the crossroads after the one-way system turn left, signed Anne Port, Gorey. In just over a mile reach L'Archirondel. In just over ½ mile pass Anne Port and then Mont Orgueil Castle ⑤.

At a T-junction turn sharp left, signed Gorey Harbour, St Helier A3. At the harbour keep right on the A3, signed St Helier, and in ½ mile pass on the right a road for Gorey Village and on the left the Royal Jersey Golf Course.

After passing the golf course, pass an AA telephone box on the right. Pass Grouville Post Office and keep left on the A4, signed La Rocque, St Helier, to La Rocque Harbour ⑥.

In just over a mile, reach Le Hocq

When France was the enemy the picturesque northern beaches and bays of Jersey were part asset, part liability. Their quiet secretiveness, which enchants so many visitors today, made them vulnerable as hidden routes for stealthy invasion from the sea.

Wooded Rozel Valley

Rozel's attractive fishing harbour was built during 1829 when the oyster trade was at its peak on the island

(Le Hocq Inn), then in just over 2 miles, at a mini-roundabout, turn left, signed Mount Bingham. Pass a bathing pool to Mount Bingham. Turn left, then turn sharp right, passing the harbour to re-enter St Helier.

POINTS OF INTEREST

① Among St Helier's attractions (see also Tour 1) is the Jersey Museum in Pier Road. Here some of the island's finest art treasures can be seen, as well as exhibitions depicting Jersey life through the ages.

② The shingle beach of Bouley Bay shelves steeply, so whereas it is excellent for skin-divers, it is dangerous for children and inexperienced swimmers. In fact the water is so deep that in the 19th

century there were plans to build a large harbour here. The winding road leading from the top of the 500ft cliff to the beach is famous for hill motor climbs.

③ Rozel has everything to recommend it – gift shops, restaurants, a pretty harbour and a sheltered beach. There is a pleasant walk along Rozel Valley where 19th-century botanist Samuel William Curtis lived and planted many plants and trees; the giant Himalaya pink tulip tree is a particular attraction when in bloom during the early spring.

④ The breakwater at St Catherine's Bay was built by the British Government in the mid-19th century as a response to French coastal fortification, but work was abandoned because of design faults

and the advent of steamships. The arm extending from L'Archirondel is some 2,300ft long.

⑤ Mont Orgueil Castle is a formidable 13th-century and later fortress that towers over the port of Gorey and its tiny harbour from a rocky summit some 310ft above sea level. Open to the public in summer, it affords magnificent views. The Jersey Pottery, in the village, can also be visited.

⑥ Situated at the southern end of the Royal Bay of Grouville, La Rocque, with its natural harbour, is one of the oldest fishing villages on Jersey. The bay is a birdwatchers' paradise where curlews and oystercatchers number among the waders, and brent geese are a common sight between November and April.

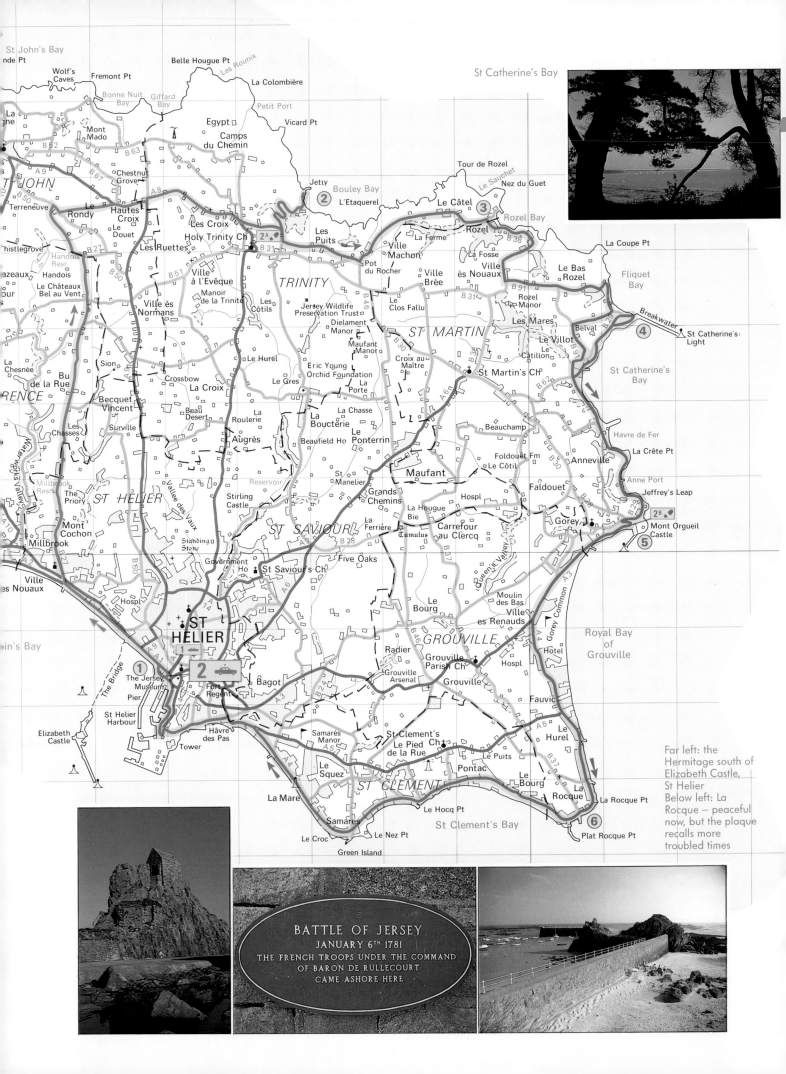

St John's Bay
nde Pt
Wolf's Caves
Fremont Pt
Belle Hougue Pt
Les Rounix
La Colombière
St Catherine's Bay

Bonne Nuit Bay
Giffard Bay
Petit Port
Egypt
Vicard Pt

B 52
Mont Mado
B 63
Camps du Chemin

ST JOHN
Chestnut Grove
A 9
Tour de Rozel
Nez du Guet
Le Sauchet

Terrenêuve
Le Rondy
Hautes Croix
A 8
Jetty
Bouley Bay
L'Etaquerel
Le Câtel
Rozel Bay
Rozel

Le Douet
Les Croix
Holy Trinity Ch
2A
Les Puits
La Ferme
Ville Machon
La Fosse
La Coupe Pt

histlegrove
Les Ruettes
B 31
Pot du Rocher
Ville Brée
Ville ès Nouaux
Le Bas Rozel
Fliquet Bay

Handois Resr
B 27
Ville à l'Evêque
B 51
Le Clos Fallu
B 31
Rozel Manor
B 91
Breakwater

azeaux
Handois
Manoir de la Trinité
Les Côtils
TRINITY
Les Mares
Le Villot
Belval
B 29
St Catherine's Light

Le Châteaux Bel au Vent
Ville ès Normans
Jersey Wildlife Preservation Trust
ST MARTIN
Le Catillon
B 30

La Chesnée
Sion
Dielament Manor
Maufant Manor
Croix au Maître
St Martin's Ch
B 62
St Catherine's Bay

Bu de la Rue
Crossbow
Le Hurel
Eric Young Orchid Foundation
La Porte
Havre de Fer
La Crête Pt

RENCE
Becquet Vincent
La Croix
Le Gres
La Chasse
Beauchamp
Anneville

Les Chasses
Beau Desert
La Roulerie
La Bouctérie
Le Ponterrin
Foldouët Fm
Le Côtil
Anne Port
Jeffrey's Leap

Surville
L'Augrès
Beaufield Ho
St Manelier
Maufant
Hospl
La Hougue Bie
Faldouet
2B
Mont Orgueil Castle

Millbrook Resr
The Priory
ST HELIER
Stirling Castle
Reservoir
Grands Chemins
Carrefour au Clercq
Gorey
5

Mont Cochon
Standing Stone
Government Ho
St Saviour's Ch
ST SAVIOUR
La Ferrière
Tumulus
B 28
Moulin des Bas
Royal Bay of Grouville

Millbrook
A 2
Five Oaks
Le Bourg
Ville es Renauds

Ville es Nouaux
Hospl
A 6
GROUVILLE
Hotel

in's Bay
Radier
Grouville Parish Ch
Hospl

ST HELIER
1
The Jersey Museum
2
Bagot
Grouville Arsenal
Grouville

The Bridge
Pier
Fort Regent
B 24
Fauvic

St Helier Harbour
Hâvre des Pas
Samarès Manor
St Clement's Le Pied de la Rue
Le Puits
Le Hurel
A 5

Elizabeth Castle
Tower
Le Squez
La Mare
ST CLEMENT
Pontac
Le Bourg
La Rocque
La Rocque Pt

Samarès
Le Croc
Le Nez Pt
Le Hocq Pt
St Clement's Bay
Le Bourg
6
Plat Rocque Pt

Green Island

Far left: the Hermitage south of Elizabeth Castle, St Helier
Below left: La Rocque – peaceful now, but the plaque recalls more troubled times

BATTLE OF JERSEY
JANUARY 6TH 1781
THE FRENCH TROOPS UNDER THE COMMAND
OF BARON DE RULLECOURT
CAME ASHORE HERE

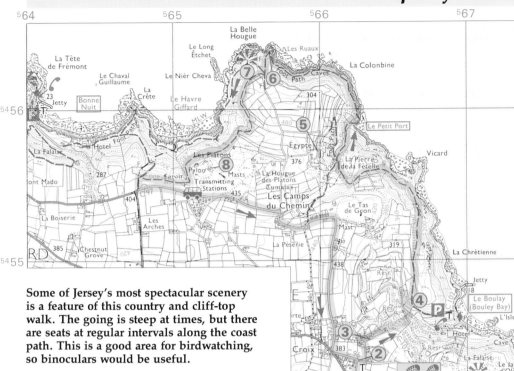

ROUTE DIRECTIONS

Allow 2½ hours
Start from Rue du Presbytère, where there is parking, east of Trinity Church (grid ref. WV662540) ①.

Head north, past the parish hall on your right, and turn right at a T-junction (signposted to Bouley Bay) ②.

Take the first turning left down a lane which bears left. Turn right down a narrow path to the left of a private drive to 'Fresh Springs' ③.

Follow the path through zig-zag gates down through woods and past iris beds on the left to the main road. Turn left on to the road, then left again up a one-way road. Turn right up the next track opposite a 'no entry' junction and follow the track round to the left ④.

Continue along the westward path until faced with a wooded valley, a small cove and a fishing hut ⑤.

At the junction in the woods turn right and go down a steep incline. At the next junction take the right turn, marked Bonne Nuit (a 100yd detour over the stream leads to another ruined cottage). The path now goes past the beach of Petit Port and Wolfs Lair, the fishing hut, and along an area rich in wild flowers ⑥.

Next there is the headland of La Belle Hougue. To make a detour to the summit, take the path to the right, another few yards up the slope, ignoring the sign to the main road ⑦.

Take the upper path, then at the white sign forbidding motor-cycles, take the minor path left, towards a bungalow. Turn right on to a track, and then left on to the metalled road ⑧.

Keep to the road until the junction at Le Vescont Monument (a granite obelisk commemorating a Trinity constable or mayor) and then take the first turning left. This road returns to the starting point.

Some of Jersey's most spectacular scenery is a feature of this country and cliff-top walk. The going is steep at times, but there are seats at regular intervals along the coast path. This is a good area for birdwatching, so binoculars would be useful.

POINTS OF INTEREST

① The interior of 11th-century Trinity Church is plain, but note a fine 17th-century mural memorial against the north wall of the Lady Chapel to Sir Edouard de Carteret, Black Rod under Charles II.

② The strip of land on the right of the path belongs to the National Trust for Jersey, and is planted with hydrangeas, fuchsias and other flowering shrubs.

③ This spot is called Le Puchot (a watercourse in the form of a pond). The streams run through an enclosure containing a lavoir (to do the washing) and a well-head fronted by a wrought-iron gate.

④ There are superb views from this point, and it is also possible to see remnants of a military guardhouse, on the right towards the top of the climb. At the summit are views of the French coastline and, to the right, the north coast of the island is a glorious tapestry of colour.

⑤ The ruined houses to the left of the modern house on the facing hillside are the remains of Égypte (Egypt), a farm used by the Germans during the Occupation to practise street-to-street fighting.

⑥ As the path approaches the headland of La Belle Hougue, a short detour can be made down a little path to the right, to La Fontaine ès Mittes, a mineral spring said to give speech to the dumb and to cure eye complaints. Nonetheless it is a little murky these days.

⑦ From the summit of La Belle Hougue, Bonne Nuit Bay can be seen to the west.

Between it and the headland lies Le Havre Giffard (Giffard Bay), sometimes known as Dead Man's Bay as the protruding rock resembles a human body.

⑧ To the left is Les Platons, the highest point on the island, with its radio transmission masts.

Spectacular scenery can be enjoyed from the cliff path at the headland of La Belle Hougue, including views of Bonne Nuit Bay to the west

Mont Orgueil Castle towers over the harbour of Gouray

ROUTE DIRECTIONS

Allow 2½ hours or 1 hour
Start from a parking spot on the coast road near Gorey (Gouray) Pier or by Castle Green (grid ref. WV714504).

If below the castle, walk up the footpath just round the corner from the pier to Castle Green. Turn left and, crossing the road, go up Mont de la Garenne, marked 'no entry'. At the top, turn right (Rue des Marettes) and follow the sign to a dolmen, which is found through an avenue of trees on the left①.

After making this detour, continue down Rue des Marettes in the same direction, turning left into La Grande Route de Faldouet, and then first right after the Garden Centre, passing an old house called Grassfort on the right②.

About 300yds down the road, turn left. Bear left at the next fork and then take the second turning right at a 'no entry' sign, passing the prize-winning Gorey Village development and the back entrance to the Jersey Pottery③.

After the initial climb, this is an easy walk through country lanes. As well as marvellous views, there is plenty of historical interest.

POINTS OF INTEREST

① The Dolmen de Faldouët, like other Neolithic passage-graves, was probably once covered by a mound. Though altered since it was discovered in the 17th century, its original form was probably a horseshoe-shaped chamber with a 24-ton capstone.

② Grassfort has a fine double archway, though the original arch over the pedestrian entrance has been replaced by a straight lintel engraved 17 CCL 25. Further down the road is another double arch incorporating an 18th-century marriage stone.

③ A popular tourist attraction, the Jersey Pottery is the largest in the Channel Islands. More than 200 kinds of pot are made and sold here.

④ Popular with birdwatchers and bird-ringers, Grouville Marsh is host to wintering wildfowl, including teal and snipe. This important stretch of wetland is also a stop-over point for migrating birds.

⑤ A memorial outside the historic Church of St Martin of Grouville commemorates soldiers killed at La Rocque on the day of the Battle of Jersey in 1781.

⑥ The last lap is along the track of the old eastern railway, past colourful flower-beds and the memorial to Gorey shipbuilders. The public gardens opposite the monument are a pleasant and scented finale.

Snipe, a Grouville Marsh resident whose numbers increase in winter when flocks also arrive from Scandinavia and Iceland

Those taking the short walk can now cut through Gorey Village on to the coast road and back to the pier. For the full walk, keep on the same road past Grouville Marsh④.

Turn left into La Rigondaine, and left again to go past the parish church⑤.

Take the second turn right past a tiny chapel and, crossing the Coast Road, take the road towards the Grouville Bay Hotel and the sea, passing the Royal Jersey Golf Course. Either head back towards the castle along the sea-wall or go along the beach⑥.

ROUTE DIRECTIONS
The drive starts from St Peter Port ①.

From the Weighbridge in St Peter Port follow the coast north for just over 2½ miles to St Sampson ②.

At a mini-roundabout turn right and continue for a mile to Bordeaux Harbour ③.

At the T-junction at the end of the harbour turn right. Follow the main road, passing on the right the road to Déhus Dolmen ④.

Continue past the L'Ancresse Golf Course and an AA telephone box on the left. Almost immediately, at a crossroads, turn right, signed Bay, car park. Follow the coast road in a circular route and in almost a mile, at a T-junction, turn left. In about ¾ mile arrive back at the crossroads and turn right to rejoin the main road to reach Vale church and turn right, signed West Coast. In ¼ mile bear left, then shortly right. In about ½ mile, at L'Islet crossroads, turn right and follow the coast road about 2½ miles to Grandes Rocques, then, after ½ mile, Cobo ⑤.

In just over another mile reach Vazon Bay ⑥.

Leave Vazon Bay and in nearly 2 miles pass Perelle Garage, with the road to Les Rouvets Tropical Vinery and Gardens on the left ⑦.

Keep right, for the main route, and continue to Fort Saumarez and bear left to follow the coast road. After just over 1¼ miles reach Rocquaine Bay and Fort Grey ⑧.

After running north along Les Banques, this round-the-island tour follows a coast road alongside pleasant bays and over picturesque cliffs, affording fine sea views, then switches between coastal and inland ways until it finally cuts across country and returns to St Peter Port.

After ½ mile, at the Imperial Hotel, turn left, signed St Peter Port, and ascend. At the top of the climb (where a path leads off right to the cliffs), turn left with the major road. In 1¼ miles pass Torteval church on the left, and in another ½ mile bear right then keep to the main road. At Forest Road crossroads turn right to pass the Airport, then bear left – passing a road to the German Occupation Museum on the right ⑨.

After passing the road to the museum on the right, immediately turn sharp right, signed Petit Bôt Bay, and descend to Petit Bôt Bay ⑩.

Ascend from the bay and take the first turning sharp right. After ½ mile, at a T-junction, turn right, then immediately bear right. At the next T-junction turn right, and in nearly ½ mile at another T-junction turn right again, signed Icart. Continue to Icart car park ⑪.

Return from the car park to the main road and keep forward. In ¼ mile, at a T-junction, turn right and immediately left. In ¾ mile, at the crossroads, turn left, then at the T-junction turn right. After another ¼ mile, at the traffic signals, go forward, signed Jerbourg, to reach Jerbourg car park, then return to the traffic signals and turn sharp right, signed St Peter Port. In just over a mile bear right and descend. Re-enter St Peter Port by Le Val des Terres.

POINTS OF INTEREST

① St Peter Port, Guernsey's capital town, boasts one of the most attractive shopping centres in Britain. Its waterfront, dating back to medieval times, is delightful too – as is the harbour from which trips can be made to the other islands.

② St Sampson was developed as a shopping centre in the early 19th century when the channel that originally separated this northern corner of Guernsey from the rest of the island was reclaimed.

③ Crammed with small fishing boats, Bordeaux Harbour is particularly charming and two jetties on the south side make good swimming platforms at high tide. Medieval Vale Castle surveys the scene from its vantage point midway between Bordeaux and St Sampson.

④ Déhus Dolmen is a particularly fine prehistoric burial chamber with good carvings and a passageway with side chambers – all lit.

⑤ Windsurfers, sunbathers and observers of marine life are all well catered for at Cobo Bay. It is also popular with the young and the glamorous.

⑥ Vazon Bay is another good spot for beach sports and a variety of races are held here in the summer months.

⑦ Five former tomato greenhouses house the subtropical and tropical plants of Les Rouvets Gardens. The greenhouse names – citrus, Mediterranean, Madeira, tropical and desert – indicate the range of species on show.

⑧ Fort Grey, at the southern end of Rocquaine Bay, was originally built to fend off French invaders. It has since been restored to house a maritime museum with particular emphasis on shipwrecks around the Guernsey coast.

⑨ The German Occupation Museum tells the story of the Occupation of Guernsey and contains an extensive collection of German military artefacts.

⑩ Sheltered Petit Bôt Bay is best loved as a sun trap. Its two hotels were demolished by the Germans and the only buildings now are a cottage, a café and an 18th-century tower.

⑪ Icart Point, a promontory joined to the headland by a narrow ledge, is known as Château d'Icart and separates Petit Bôt from Saint's Bay – so called from two rocks known as The Saints.

A view of St Peter Port from the citadel on top of Castle Cornet. The other islands and parts of the French coast can also be seen from here

Above left: Grandes Rocques, haunt of sunbathers

Above: Beaucette Marina, an inspired use of an old quarry

Left: working boats at Bordeaux – a natural harbour

Fermain Bay (above) and Moulin Huet Bay (right) provide good swimming on either side of the Jerbourg peninsula

ROUTE DIRECTIONS

Allow 2½ hours
Start from Jerbourg Point, where there is parking available (grid ref. WV340749)① .

Take the steps of the cliff path, going down from the left seaward corner②.

At the seat, take the steps leading off to the left. A little way down, turn left again, on a path which is marked with sign stones and goes towards Fermain Bay, one mile away. At a T-junction above the bay, turn right to pass some seats overlooking the sea③.

At the next junction, turn left up a narrower path (if going down to the bay, turn right). The path climbs steeply to a road on a bend. Keep right, passing through an S-bend to take the left turning opposite Varclin Cottage.

Turn left again at the next junction. Coming to the main Jerbourg Road (Route de Jerbourg), turn left and, after 140yds, right at a crossroads.

This road descends ever more steeply towards Moulin Huet passing a right and a left turning. Bear left uphill on a narrow road and watch for railings on the right which mark the head of a few steps descending to the cliff path④.

The cliff path goes back to the starting point, with an occasional sign stone marked 'Jerbourg' or 'Cliff Path' for guidance.

Much of this rather strenuous walk is on Guernsey's coast path, but spectacular views make the steep stretches well worth the effort. The walk encircles the peninsula at the island's south-eastern tip – the last rock-bound refuge of the islanders from French raiders in the Middle Ages.

POINTS OF INTEREST

① Jerbourg Point car park is the first of several fine viewpoints on the walk. Jersey, Sark and the French coast can be seen from here, and as the walk continues views open up eastwards to take in the smaller islands of Herm and Jethou.

② During World War II the squat Bréhon Tower in the channel mounted a German anti-aircraft battery which shot down two aircraft, one from each side. The white, box-like lighthouse marks St Martin's Point, where the pirate Richard Higgins was hanged in 1565 and left to rot.

③ Like many of Guernsey's beaches, Fermain Bay has its share of fortifications. Its Martello tower and stout sea wall, once topped by guns, are overlooked by a conical sentry box on the hillside above known as the Pepper Pot.

④ Views from the coast path above Moulin Huet take in the Pea Stacks, a group of rocks at the end of Jerbourg Point. Various legends are attached to the third peak from the end, which looks something like a cowled monk. He was known as Le Petit Bonhomme Andriou and fishermen would salute him as they passed. Also visible ahead is the Doyle Column, a memorial to General Sir John Doyle.

ROUTE DIRECTIONS

Allow 2¼ hours
Start from Pleinmont, where there is parking available (grid ref. WV242753).

Walk along the cliff path, with the sea on the left①.

Cross the car park bearing left, and turn left where a sign stone indicates Cliff Path and Portelet, descending to another car park②.

Continue past Fort Pezeries, going past little Portelet Harbour to Rocquaine Bay③.

Rejoin the coast road at Fort Grey and walk back south for about 80yds. Turn left by the cottage called Le Crocq du Sud. The road climbs gently up a sheltered valley. Take the fourth right turning, up a road towards the spire of Torteval church. Turn left at the top into the pathway and go over a car park and through the churchyard to the road. Turn left④.

After 100yds turn right into a lane. Bear right at the first junction and continue to the main road. Turn left and, after 100yds, turn right where a sign stone indicates Les Tielles⑤.

Turn right on the cliff path (sign stone 'Pleinmont Pt'). After about a mile, near the watch house on a hill, the path joins a partly tarmac-surfaced track which eventually bends right round a field⑥.

At this point take the path again to the left, to go back to the starting point.

Known as 'Cup and Saucer', Fort Grey, built on a castle, overlooks some dangerous reefs

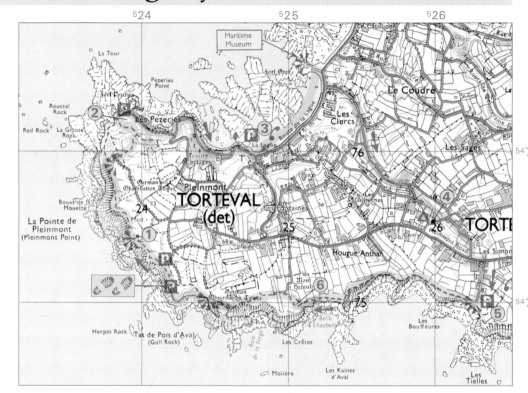

The cliff path around Pleinmont Point follows one of the most dramatic stretches of Guernsey's coast. Below, fishing boats pick their way among rocks that other sailors go miles to avoid. There is nothing between here and America.

POINTS OF INTEREST

① About a mile offshore can be seen the Hanois Lighthouse, built in 1859 on a notorious granite reef which had long taken a steady toll of ships.

Overlooking the sea is a German watchtower, one of a chain which fixed targets by triangulation – a method made obsolete by radar.

② The circular mound near Fort Pezeries is the Table des Pions, a traditional resting place for the 'Chevauchée de S. Michel', an historic procession of the Court which inspected the roads and sea defences.

③ Rocquaine Bay can be crossed on foot at most states of the tide. The broad expanse of sand and rocks is backed by the highest sea wall in Guernsey, reaching 40ft in places. Built almost 100 years ago to prevent coastal erosion, it was reinforced by the Germans during World War II.

Each August, numerous visitors come to Rocquaine Bay for the one-day Rocquaine Regatta, one of Guernsey's most fun-packed summer events.

④ The spire of Torteval church is a prominent local landmark. Built in 1818, the church replaces an older one, and still has one of the original bells, cast in 1432.

⑤ The cliffs of the south-facing promontory known as Les Tielles give fine views out to sea. On a clear day, the lighthouse 23 miles away on the Plateau des Roches Douvres can be seen.

⑥ The 1804 watch house was one of a chain which stood guard against Napoleon. Just before it note Belle Elizabeth and Petite Elizabeth – a conical rock at the foot of the cliff, with a smaller rock nearby. The story goes that Elizabeth, a beautiful local girl, had an illegitimate child and was banished from home by her indignant father. In despair she threw herself from the cliff, her baby in her arms, and both were turned into the rocks you see.

WALK 3C · Witches and Fairies GUERNSEY

Tales of witches and fairies surround two of the prehistoric sites on this walk in western Guernsey. Most of the walking is on roads, with an alternative of going along the beach on the coastal sections.

POINTS OF INTEREST

①A short detour can be made by following the sign to Le Creux ès Faies, a prehistoric tomb which, according to local folklore, is the entrance to fairyland. Some older Guernsey residents still avoid the place, especially at night.

②Monks from the now ruined Priory of St Mary Lihou built the first causeway to Lihou Island. The island can still be reached at low tide. A disastrous shipwreck here is recalled by the 'Prosperity' memorial in the car park.

③Near the road's most northerly point, a detour can be made by following the sign pointing to an ancient monument and climbing to Le Trépied dolmen. This Neolithic tomb is mentioned in the transcripts of local witchcraft trials in the 17th century, and there are eye-witness accounts of the Friday-night sabbaths.

④A 10ft-high standing stone known as La Longue Rocque can be seen through a gateway on the right. Within living memory this has been the site of Guy Fawkes' night bonfires. Traditionally the guy was called the Bout'lot (now Budloe), a corruption of Bout de L'an – end of the year. The custom derives from pagan winter solstice ceremonies.

⑤In a wall on the left, a little way down, there is a stone inscribed 'James de Garis 1895'. He was a renowned carpenter and boat builder who made very fine fishing boats here.

ROUTE DIRECTIONS

Allow 1¾ hours
Start at L'Erée (grid ref. WV254781).

With the sea on the left, walk a short distance up the main road and take the left turning just past an old bunker, on to the headland of L'Erée①.

The walk continues to the car park overlooking the strait to Lihou Island②.

Return up the approach road and bear left at the fork below the German tower. Turn left on to the coast road or walk over the beach to the next slipway③.

The walk follows the path over an old gun position and through a pine wood, and becomes a macadamed lane. Cross over the main crossroads and turn right past the Tropical Gardens.

At the top of the hill, double back on the right turning and, in 80yds, turn left on to a footpath. Coming to the main road, cross over to the footway, turn left and in a few yards turn right down a lane. At the next junction, turn left and, ignoring a left turning, keep going to the main Les Paysans Road, bearing right up the hill④.

Take the next right turn at a staggered crossroads, then take the first left and, at the end of this road, turn right⑤.

Bear right at the first fork and left at the second. Keep going towards the sea. Reaching the coast, turn right to return to the starting point.

Finds from Le Trépied, a Neolithic tomb, included bones, arrowheads and beaker fragments

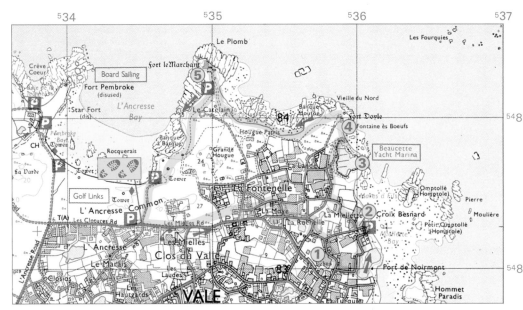

Guernsey supplied the granite used in some of England's finest buildings, including the steps of St Paul's Cathedral. Many of the old quarries have now found other uses, such as the wildfowl sanctuary, the marina and the fish farm seen on this walk, in the north-east corner of the island. The route also takes in a 5,000-year-old chambered tomb, made of massive granite slabs.

POINTS OF INTEREST

① Guernsey's most impressive passage grave, the Déhus Dolmen, is known for the unusual carvings on one of its capstones. Visitors can explore the four side-chambers inside the 30ft-long tomb, which has electric lighting.

② This was the site of the Chapel of St Magloire, the 6th-century missionary saint who, with St Sampson, brought Christianity to Guernsey.

③ Beaucette Marina was formed from a vast granite quarry, by blasting away the neck of land which separated it from the sea. In 1967 the owner of the quarry arranged for the Royal Marines to do the blasting as a training exercise in exchange for food and accommodation. But the exercise planned to take a few days, took nine months.

④ Just beyond the white watch house is Fort Doyle, built as part of the British response to the fortification of Cherbourg in the mid 19th century. From the gun platform there are fine views over the northern approaches to Guernsey, including Alderney and Cap de la Hague.

⑤ Built around 1800 on Guernsey's most northerly headland, Fort Le Marchant has been reinforced several times. Until recent years it had a Victorian façade, now demolished, though the 19th-century gun tracks can still be seen. Today there is a rifle range here, used by the local shooting club.

ROUTE DIRECTIONS

Allow 1½ hours
Start from the car park by L'Ancresse Lodge Hotel (grid ref. WV345834).

Walk on the grass beside the main road with the common on the left and the road on the right.

Opposite the bus-turning loop on the far side of the road bear left over the common making for the white gable-end of an isolated cottage whose top is seen in a dip between banks of gorse. A path runs that way and crosses a narrow roadway. Go forward past two semi-detached houses, and carry on over another road and into a winding lane on the other side.

Where the lane meets a wider road on a bend, go straight on into the smaller lane, and turn left at the next crossroads. At the next junction keep right through a sharp bend and enjoy the good view of Paradis Quarry, now an emergency reservoir and a sanctuary for wildfowl. Take the next left turning. After the houses a right bend is reached with a mound on the right①.

Take the next left turning, the Rue des Hougues de Noirmont. As it twists down to the sea you get glimpses of another huge quarry, now used as a fish farm. Yet another quarry further south is the island's rubbish tip and is nearly full. After the lane has taken a final twist away from the sea, turn right on to another winding lane (not the track on the corner)②.

At the staggered crossroads turn right and then right at the end into Beaucette Marina③.

Leave the marina with the sea on the right and walk over the Common to the white watch house④.

The walk now follows the coast path round Fontenelle Bay, past a Martello tower to Fort le Marchant⑤.

Return from Fort le Marchant to carry on around the shore. Coming to the next Martello tower, follow the roadway from the car park there back to the starting point. (This walk includes Beaucette Marina by kind permission of the proprietors.)

An anti-tank wall, built by the Germans in 1940, now provides shelter for the sands of L'Ancresse Bay – a popular beach for windsurfers with its own surfing school

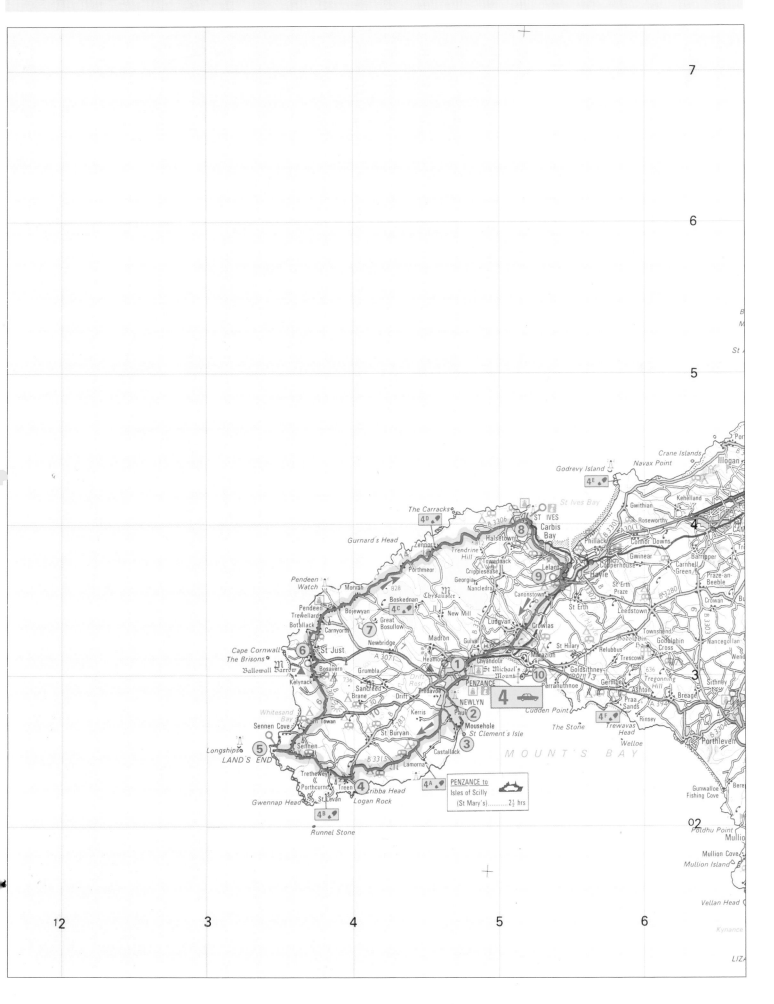

PENZANCE to
Isles of Scilly
(St Mary's)..........2½ hrs

ROUTE DIRECTIONS
The drive starts from Penzance ①.

Follow signs to Newlyn and Mousehole along an unclassified road beside the harbour②.

At Newlyn cross a bridge and turn left on to an unclassified road to Mousehole③.

Turn left for the harbour, then turn right and right again, signed Paul. Go past the church, signed Land's End. In just over ½ mile, turn left on to the B3315. Continue through Sheffield and in 1¾ miles pass the turning to Lamorna Cove.

Remain on the B3315 for 3¼ miles. At the T-junction, turn left. The road descends steeply, with a hairpin bend, then goes up to Treen④.

Continue on the B3315 for ¾ mile, then turn left, unclassified, to Porthcurno. Rejoin the B3315 and continue westwards. In ½ mile turn right. After 2 miles, turn left on to the A30 and drive for about ½ mile to Land's End⑤.

Return along the A30, to reach Sennen. Leave Sennen on the A30. After 1¾ miles, turn left on to the B3306, signed St Just. After 3 miles turn left at the T-junction on to the A3071 and enter St Just⑥.

Continue on the St Ives road, B3306, to Pendeen and Morvah⑦.

Continue on the B3306 to Zennor and St Ives⑧.

Starting at Penzance, the drive visits the fishing villages of Newlyn and Mousehole, then veers inland and continues to Land's End. The coastal road to St Ives passes through rugged moorland interspersed with farms. Beyond St Ives Bay a detour is made to view St Michael's Mount.

Leave St Ives on the A3074, signed Hayle. Pass Carbis Bay on the left and continue into Lelant on the River Hayle⑨.

At Lelant turn right and in ½ mile bear right at the mini-roundabout, signed Penzance. At the next roundabout, take the third exit on to the A30, passing Canonstown and Crowlas. After a mile, at the next roundabout, take the second exit on to an unclassified road, signed Marazion⑩.

Return along the unclassified road, signed Penzance. Cross the railway bridge and keep left. Pass through Longrock then in ¾ mile at the roundabout rejoin the A30.

POINTS OF INTEREST

①The mild climate has drawn visitors to Penzance since Regency times – as several handsome buildings in the town testify. The attractive Museum of Nautical Art and the Penlee Memorial Gardens are just a few of the reasons for spending time here.

②Newlyn, a busy fishing port, became famous for its artist colony in the 19th century. Painters still live and work among the quaint old cottages and fish-cellars.

③Pronounced locally as 'Mouzell', Mousehole is a typical Cornish fishing village – narrow alleyways, flower-filled courtyards, a busy harbour and squat stone cottages jumbled together.

④The tiny village of Treen stands near the end of a fortified headland known as Treen Castle – owned by the National Trust. A relative of Oliver Goldsmith overturned the 66-ton Logan Rock, a rocking stone reached by a footpath from Treen, and was made to replace it at his own expense.

⑤On a fine day the Isles of Scilly are visible 28 miles away to the west of Land's End – England's most westerly mainland point. The Longships Lighthouse can be seen offshore, and, on the horizon, Wolf Rock Lighthouse.

⑥St Just was an important centre last century when the nearby tin and copper mines were in full production. Now all closed, the mines and their ruined buildings are an interesting element of the surrounding landscape.

⑦About a mile south of the village of Morvah, which lies on the edge of Penwith moorland, are Chûn Castle and Chûn Quoit – an Iron Age stone fort and a Neolithic chamber tomb.

⑧Old houses and winding alleys cluster beneath the 120ft spire of the 15th-century church in St Ives. The village became the haunt of artists in the 1880s and today there are numerous galleries selling works of art. St Ives remains popular for its beaches – Porthmeor for surfers, Porthminster for families.

⑨Lelant, originally a port on the Hayle Estuary, declined when the river silted up. Now the marshland – the Saltings – is a sanctuary for wading birds. Near the village is Cornucopia and Lelant Model Village where there are smuggling, mining and shipwreck displays.

⑩St Michael's Mount, with its splendid castle and priory, can be reached by boat from Marazion, or on foot along a cobbled causeway at low tide. Marazion itself is an attractive place with Georgian and Victorian houses and ancient inns built to serve pilgrims who had journeyed to the priory.

The headland of Cape Cornwall, crowned by a mine chimney, lies to the east of St Just. This is the only cape in England

ROUTE DIRECTIONS

Allow 3½ hours
Start from the café and shop in Lamorna Cove car park (grid ref. SW450240).

Walk from the car park past a row of cottages and over the stream, then continue along the coast footpath, passing large heaps of granite on the left ①.

Keep to the coast path until reaching the Kemyel Woods ②.

Keep to the path through the woods then go down right to the coast before a steep uphill climb leads to the coastguard look-out at Penzer Point. Look for a stile on the left several hundred yards ahead by a wooden signpost. Cross the stile and reach another stile in the left-hand corner of the small field. After crossing this, go diagonally right across a field to a stile, in the middle of the opposite wall. Cross the next field diagonally right to a stile in the top corner, then follow a line of stiles to the farm at Kemyel Drea ③.

At Kemyel Drea cross the system of stiles and gates to the road. Turn left and follow the road round to the right, then go sharp right at a signpost. This leads through a marshy wood to the road at Kemyel Crease. Turn left here and go through the buildings to a stile in the right-hand wall. Cross this and go diagonally right across the field to a stile, then follow the line of stiles to the farm at Kemyel

Lamorna's inn sign

Wartha. At the road turn left and go through the farm, then take the left-hand path at the signpost in front of the last house. Follow the path down into the valley ④.

Follow the path to a rocky open space. Go left here until reaching a large quarry on the left, then follow the path past a ruined building. A little further on, bear to the left and return downhill to Lamorna Cove.

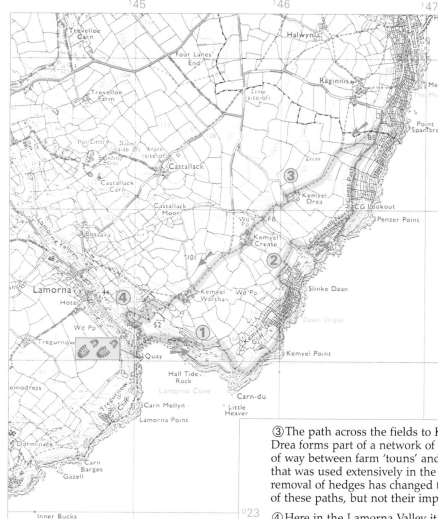

Around Lamorna Cove the coast is less rugged than the rest of the Land's End sea-cliffs. Here the shoreline faces east across Mount's Bay and catches a great deal of sunlight. From Lamorna the walk follows the coast then turns inland across a well-trodden field path that leads back to the cove. The path may be muddy.

POINTS OF INTEREST

① Last century, the Lamorna Quarries were worked extensively for their high-quality stone, some of which was used for building the Thames Embankment. In 1851 a solid block of Lamorna granite was carved into a 22ft obelisk weighing 21 tons, and sent to the Great Exhibition in Hyde Park.

② Kemyel Woods contain fine examples of Monterey pines and cypresses, horse chestnut, privet and wild cherry. They were planted in the 1940s by a local farmer as a windbreak for small meadows, which were used for growing violets and early potatoes. This type of farming was once essential to the local economy.

③ The path across the fields to Kemyel Drea forms part of a network of old rights of way between farm 'touns' and hamlets that was used extensively in the past. The removal of hedges has changed the nature of these paths, but not their importance.

④ Here in the Lamorna Valley it is interesting to note the way nature reclaims the land and that now the abandoned quarry workings are nature reserves in their own right.

The peaceful and lovely Lamorna Cove lies between towering peaks of weathered granite. It has a small crescent of sand and a stone pier

The sea forms a dramatic backdrop for the Minack Theatre, hewn out of the headland rock

POINTS OF INTEREST

① St Levan, a genial eccentric, was one of a number of Celtic saints who settled in Cornwall in the 6th century.

The present church has a remarkable font in the Norman style and in the churchyard there is a large granite rock, split in two, known as St Levan's Stone.

② The cliffs around Gwennap Head rise magnificently above the sparkling Atlantic. A mile offshore lies the Runnel Stone Buoy, marking the outer end of a notorious reef.

③ There is a beautiful little beach at Porthgwarra flanked by granite bluffs, with caves and tunnels carved from the rock. They were once used by fishermen for storing gear and beaching their small boats.

④ St Levan's holy well was said to cure eye troubles. It stands next to a roofless baptistry and just below is the site, now empty, of St Levan's original cell and chapel.

⑤ On the far edge of Pedn-mên-an-mere headland is the open-air Minack Theatre which has been carved out of the cliff to resemble a classical amphitheatre.

From the little granite church of St Levan, the walk follows an ancient field track before joining the coast path above the spectacular cliffs at Gwennap Head, the 'Fisherman's Land's End'.

ROUTE DIRECTIONS

Allow 2 hours
Start from the field above St Levan's Church, where you can park (grid ref. SW381222).

Walk to the road end, ignoring the beach path on the left①.

Turn left at the road end and walk uphill past a cottage. A narrow path leads to a granite stile into a field, whose left edge is followed for 50yds to another stile. As you cross, on the right is another stile by a Celtic cross. Follow the left side of two fields to stiles, then cross three fields to stiles, all the time aiming north west for a single house and farm buildings. Follow the left side of

St Levan's Well, near the beach where the saint caught fish

another field to a stile and a road that leads south past Lower Roskestal Farm.

After about ¾ mile, where the road bends sharply left, take the second obvious track on the right. This leads downhill across a stream, and up to the coastguard road. Turn right for a few yards then take the track on the right up to the coastguard look-out at Gwennap Head②.

Turn left in front of the look-out and follow the coast path to Porthgwarra Cove③.

Go past the café/shop at Porthgwarra and turn right at the signpost. Then go left, uphill, and pass a house before turning right along the cliff top. Keep right at the next junction until reaching St Levan's holy well above Porth Chapel beach④.

Go down the rocky path towards the beach then continue along the top of the cliff to the next headland of Pedn-mên-an-mere⑤.

Follow the path to the theatre car park. (The theatre can be viewed if no play is in progress.) Follow the track from the car park to the road, then turn left and return to St Levan's Church.

ROUTE DIRECTIONS

Allow 1¾ hours
Start outside the Mên-An-Tol Print Studio (grid ref. SW418344).

Take the broad track leading inland①.

Some distance along the track, pass the sign to the Mên-An-Tol, which we visit later on, and continue to the Mên Scryfa, an inscribed stone in the middle of a field on the left. Rejoin the track and continue to a junction of several paths. Nearby is a large 'whaleback' rock, with a cross-hole carved in it②.

Return to the junction and take the right hand of the two paths leading east uphill to the stone circle of Boskednan, known as 'Nine Maidens'③.

Continue along the path that leads on from Nine Maidens.

On reaching a pot-holed track, turn right towards Greenburrow mine shaft④.

From the mine shaft, and facing the distant rocky tor of Carn Galver, walk a few yards down the slope then take the left-hand path. Keep left at the next junction. About 100yds before a gate in a low wall, take the right-hand junction. Continue along the path, passing a square, granite boundary stone. A few yards further on, ignoring the gate on the left, bear left along a track, then cross a low wall and go right following an obvious path that crosses a stream before leading to the Mên-An-Tol⑤.

Continue to the rough lane and turn left to the car park.

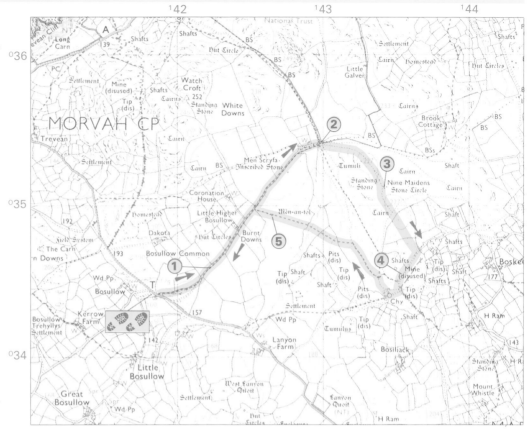

The wild granite hills and heath-covered moors that lie north of Penzance are rich in archaeological remains and this exhilarating walk takes in several ancient monuments including a stone circle – one of four in Cornwall known as the Nine Maidens.

The curious Mên-An-Tol – one of the most perfect examples of a 'port-hole' entrance in existence. The upright stones on either side were placed there quite recently

POINTS OF INTEREST

①The track across the moors is said to be part of the ancient 'Tinners Way' from Sennen to St Ives, along which the early traders collected copper and tin from moorland smelting works.

②Called 'Four Parishes', this rock was the original meeting place of the ancient parishes of Madron, Morvah, Zennor and Gulval, names that excite interest in their own right.

③A Neolithic or Bronze Age monument of the period 2,000 – 1,500BC, the Nine Maidens circle probably originally had 20 upright stones. Its present name is a traditional one that perhaps reflects early Christian superstition related to young ladies dancing on the Sabbath and being turned to stone for their sins.

④Greenburrow was the pumping house for the old Ding Dong mine, which extends beneath the surrounding moorland.

⑤The 'holed stone', Mên-An-Tol, has an almost perfectly round hole through its centre. Little is known for certain about its history, but it was probably once part of a prehistoric tomb. Mên-An-Tol was traditionally held to have magical properties: local people believed that crawling through it would cure their ailments.

WALK 4D · From Zennor   CORNWALL

Zennor, a village with a handsome Norman church, lies between high rocky moorland and a magnificent coast. It is the ideal starting point for a coast and inland walk through this most ancient and impressive of Cornish landscapes.

POINTS OF INTEREST

① D H Lawrence drank in the Tinner's Arms when he lived nearby during World War I, but, suspected of being a German spy because his wife was German, he was driven out of the village.

The Wayside Museum contains a traditional Cornish kitchen and an outdoor exhibition of domestic and mining implements.

② It was to Pendour Cove that the legendary Mermaid of Zennor is supposed to have lured the squire's son after hearing him sing in the church choir. He was never seen again, but it is said his voice could be heard beneath the waves. There is a mermaid bench-end in Zennor church.

③ The cliffs here in the Carnelloe area are a mixture of greenstone (a much older rock than granite) and killas, which is the Cornish name for the ancient sedimentary rocks that once lay beneath the sea. It is along the junctions of these older rocks with the inland granite that mineral seams occur. The surrounding land through which the path leads was once heavily mined.

The 12th-century Church of St Senara at Zennor

④ From the edge of Trewey the traditional field path that once linked all the small farms and hamlets to the coast road leads back to Zennor through characteristic small Cornish fields, bordered by 'hedges' of stone and witch-like blackthorn.

Farming country near Zennor

ROUTE DIRECTIONS

Allow 2 hours
Start from the car park between the Wayside Museum and the Tinner's Arms (grid ref. SW454384) ①.

Take the lane between the pub and the church (both worth a visit) and continue sharply left. The lane leads to the coast path at a National Trust sign and a waymarking stone. (Go straight ahead for a detour to Zennor Head, only a few hundred yards away.) The main walk goes left and down some steep steps and slippery rocks, and across a small stream. To the right is Pendour Cove ②.

Follow the path across the slope then turn left and go uphill to a wayside seat. The path now skirts the steep slopes that run down to Veor Cove, and reaches the edge of the next headland with superb views of Zennor Head across the bay ③.

Continue round the base of the headland. Where a path branches by some rocky pillars, take the left-hand branch that leads uphill and along the back wall of an isolated cottage. (This section is sometimes overgrown.) Join a track that leads inland past some old mine workings with fine views of Gurnard's Head. At the coast road, turn left in front of some houses close to Trewey, and where the track swings sharply left, go straight ahead over a granite stile ④.

Cross a second stile and go past an open gateway, keeping the hedge on your left. Then cross a stile and go straight across the next field to another stile. Continue with Zennor church tower directly ahead to yet another stile, then across the next two fields at a slight angle to the right to a final stile. From here, make for the farm buildings ahead, and into a muddy lane. At the main road turn left and take the steep hill past the museum and head back to the car park.

WALK 4E · To the Lighthouse CORNWALL

Views to dramatic cliffs and coves below are a feature of the cliff path leading round the headlands of Godrevy and Navax Points. Much of the walk is on National Trust land, and the area is rich in wild flowers. The path goes close to the cliff edge, so care must be taken with children.

POINTS OF INTEREST

① From the west-facing cliff tops of Godrevy Point there are fine views to Godrevy lighthouse. It was built in 1859 in the hope of reducing the number of wrecks that occurred on the notorious reef known as The Stones, running for a mile directly offshore. Moves to close the lighthouse in the 1930s were thwarted after protests by local fishermen and it is now automatic and unmanned. Its walled gardens, cultivated by the early keepers, can still be seen. The writer Virginia Woolf is said to have based her novel *To the Lighthouse* on Godrevy's romantic island.

② The cliffs here are of sedimentary rocks that once lay beneath the ocean. They have been greatly altered by heat and by vast earth movements that have folded them into fantastic shapes. In the coves below the cliffs, the grey (or Atlantic) seal can sometimes be glimpsed playing.

③ In summer the predominant colours along these paths and lanes are the purple of foxglove and the brilliant yellow of ragwort.

④ The sand to the west covers much of the medieval town of Conerton, which was steadily overwhelmed by the shifting dunes from the 13th century onwards. The modern village of Gwithian a few hundred yards away has a handsome church with a fine 15th-century tower.

Navax Point (top) and Godrevy Point (above) are the most dramatic features of the six-mile stretch of coast — largely owned by the National Trust — between Gwithian and Portreath

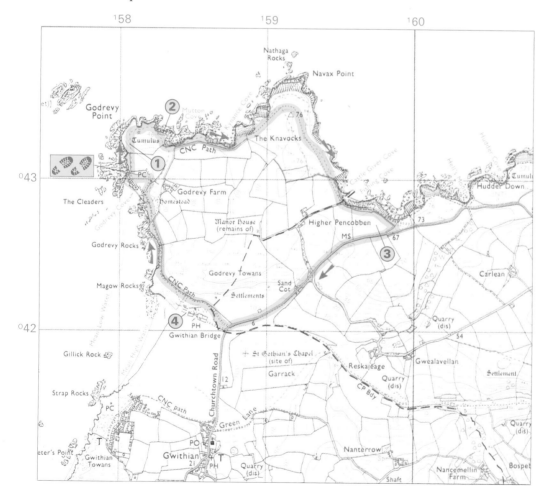

ROUTE DIRECTIONS

Allow 2½ hours
Start from the National Trust car park (grid ref. SW582431).

Walk in the direction of the lighthouse, crossing a stone stile in the boundary wall. Follow the broad track directly uphill①.

Continue across the headland, following the track with care where it occasionally skirts the abrupt edge of the cliff②.

Continue along the path until you reach a stile into a field. Keep left and go down the side of the hedge to another stile. Cross this and continue as far as the road③.

Turn right at the road and go downhill to the track (second on the right) that leads right on to Godrevy headland④.

Continue along the road across Godrevy Towans, with fine views to St Ives, and back to the car park.

Wheal Prosper Mine at Rinsey

ROUTE DIRECTIONS

Allow 2½ hours
Start from the car park above the beach at the end of Hendra Lane (grid ref. SW585276).

Turn right at the car park entrance and walk a few yards uphill, then take the footpath on the left. Go left at the next junction until you reach a metalled road by some houses. This leads towards the charming little hamlet of Higher Trevurvas.

Continue along the road and where it swings sharply left, cross the stile into a field on the right. Keep the hedge on your right and continue over two more stiles before reaching a lane that leads to the road at Hendra①.

Turn right at Hendra then left by a cottage. Go right across a stile then left to another stile. Cross the centre of the next field and follow the hedges, crossing stiles, until you reach the road at Rinsey, by a large barn.

Turn right and go through Rinsey, leaving the National Trust car park sign to the right. Between the buildings on the right ahead there is a footpath sign pointing the way to Rinsey Cove. Follow the path to Rinsey mine stack②.

Go left from the mine stack and follow the track across two stiles by a connecting wall until you reach an open field. Go along the left edge of the field then join a grass track that leads down to a granite stile in a wire fence. Turn right on to the coast path which crosses Trewavas Head③.

Continue along the coast path on to National Trust land. Go along the coast path below the Wheal Prosper mine stack and continue uphill to the National Trust car park. Go through the car park, then turn left and then right④.

Follow the coast path, avoiding all paths right and left, to the car park above the beach.

Beginning and ending near a sandy beach – tempting in favourable weather – this is a pleasant walk through fields and along the coast on the eastern shores of Mount's Bay. The walk passes the remains of some 19th-century mine stacks and skirts the granite headlands of Rinsey and Trewavas.

It is easy to see why Camel Rock was so named

POINTS OF INTEREST

① From the fields around Hendra, out of sight and sound of the sea, the twin hills of Godolphin and Tregonning can be seen inland. On the right is Tregonning. It was in this neighbourhood that the 18th-century chemist William Cookworthy found the first Cornish deposits of china-clay (decomposed and altered granite). The site was not extensive and the main clay extraction now takes place near St Austell's 'Cornish Alps'.

② Rinsey's restored mine engine-house served the Wheal Prosper Mine which was first worked for copper in 1836 and runs for some distance beneath the sea. Both Rinsey and Trewavas are granite headlands on this coast of sedimentary rocks.

③ From Trewavas Head look back along the coast to the remarkable formation known as Camel Rock. Millions of years ago, as the molten granite cooled, vertical and horizontal shrinkage cracks appeared and subsequent weathering along these joints has produced such characteristic shapes as the Camel.

④ At the foot of Rinsey West Cliff below the path is a small cove intriguingly named on older maps as 'Basher's Harbour'.

ROUTE DIRECTIONS

The drive starts from Wadebridge ①.

Leave Wadebridge on the A39, following signs to Bude. Cross the river bridge, then at the mini-roundabout turn left. In ½ mile, at the traffic signals, turn left on to the B3314, signed Port Isaac. In 1½ miles Trewornan Bridge is crossed over the River Amble. In 2 miles turn left on to the unclassified road, signed Rock. 1¼ miles further, keep left for Pityme ②.

From Pityme the main tour turns right on to the Polzeath road. Continue through Trebetherick and descend steeply (1 in 5) to Polzeath ③.

Leave Polzeath and ascend sharply (1 in 7). After 2 miles branch left on to a road signed Port Isaac. In ½ mile turn left on to the B3314 for St Endellion ④.

Leave St Endellion and continue along the B3314 for 1 mile, then turn left on to the B3267 for Port Isaac ⑤.

At Port Isaac turn right, unclassified, and descend to Portgaverne. Pass through the village and ascend (1 in 10). After 2¼ miles turn left on to the B3314 and continue to Delabole ⑥.

Leave Delabole and continue on the B3314 for 1¾ miles, then turn left on to an unclassified road, signed Tintagel, B3263. Join the B3263, and pass through Trewarmett to Tintagel ⑦.

From the Wharncliffe Arms Hotel in Tintagel turn right, signed Boscastle. In about ¾ mile descend (1 in 9) then ascend steeply (1 in 6). Two miles further on turn left, signed Bude. The road descends with a hairpin bend to Boscastle ⑧.

Leave Boscastle on the Bude road, B3263, cross a river bridge, and ascend steeply (1 in 6). After 3½ miles turn left and immediately left again on to an unclassified road signed Crackington Haven. In 2½ miles descend steeply (1 in 5) into the village of Crackington Haven ⑨.

Continue through Crackington Haven and ascend steeply (1 in 6). After 3 miles reach Wainhouse Corner and turn left on to the A39, signed Bude. Continue past Treskinnick Cross and Poundstock, then ½ mile further turn left on to an unclassified road, signed Widemouth. After ¾ mile follow the wide sweep of Widemouth Bay to Bude ⑩.

Leave Bude following signs for Bideford (A39). Shortly turn right, signed Camelford, A39. After 1 mile turn right on to the A39 then turn left on the unclassified road, signed Marhamchurch. At Marhamchurch turn left, signed Week St Mary, then

This is a drive of contrasts, including Tintagel – rich in romance and legends, Boscastle – with its stern cliffs and picturesque harbour, the sweeping sands of Bude and, inland, villages steeped in the past.

bear right. At Week St Mary turn right, signed Canworthy Water, and at the end of the village branch right. In 3½ miles, at the T-junction, turn left. Just over a mile further, turn right and cross the river bridge to Canworthy Water. Continue with the Hallworthy road, and pass through Warbstow to Hallworthy. At Hallworthy turn right on to the A395, not signed. In 2¾ miles turn left on to the A39, signed Wadebridge, to reach Camelford ⑪.

Leave Camelford on the A39 and keep straight on, passing the edge of St Kew Highway to re-enter Wadebridge.

POINTS OF INTEREST

① Wadebridge claims the longest bridge in Cornwall, built by wealthy wool merchants in the 15th century. Today the town serves a wide agricultural area and is a busy shopping centre.

② From Pityme a detour can be made to Porthilly, via Rock, where the small church of St Michael was dug from drifting sand. It has a simple Norman font.

③ The main attractions at Polzeath are safe bathing and excellent sands that offer some of the best surfing in Cornwall. The tiny church of St Enodoc, on the golf links, was excavated from the sand in 1863. Sir John Betjeman, who spent many childhood holidays in the area, is buried there.

④ Standing by the road at St Endellion is the lovely little church of St Endellienta. Inside are several quaint bell-ringers' rhymes, and a number of amusing Georgian epitaphs can be seen in the churchyard.

⑤ Narrow alleyways known as 'drangs' wind between Port Isaac's slate cottages. Protected by high headlands, the harbour has seen fishing boats come and go since the Middle Ages.

⑥ The Delabole region has been famous for its slate for nearly 600 years and at Delabole Slate Quarry there is a museum and viewing area.

⑦ Linked by many writers with King Arthur, 12th-century Tintagel Castle on its wave-lashed promontory has traces of a Celtic

settlement, identified as the trading port of a chieftain's stronghold. The Old Post Office – now in the care of the National Trust – in the village High Street is a 14th-century manor house. King Arthur's Hall nearby was built in 1933 and contains an exhibition of Arthurian legends.

Sheltered by cliffs, the beach at Crackington Haven used to serve as a small port dealing with Welsh limestone and coal, and local slate

⑧ The village of Boscastle is ranged round a long, broad street that climbs steeply through woodland from the tiny 16th-century pier. Close to the harbour is an intriguing Museum of Witchcraft.

⑨ At Crackington Haven a long, peaceful, gorse-clad valley owned by the National Trust opens out on to a sandy beach. Surf is good here, but it can be dangerous.

⑩ Strong winds that have caused hundreds of wrecks over the centuries provide a constant supply of rollers, ideal for surfing, at Bude. The town was developed as a family resort in Victorian and Edwardian times.

⑪ One tradition places King Arthur's Camelot at Camelford. Slaughterbridge, which crosses the Camel River a mile north of the town, is one of the contenders for his last battleground.

TOUR 5 · King Arthur's Country   CORNWALL

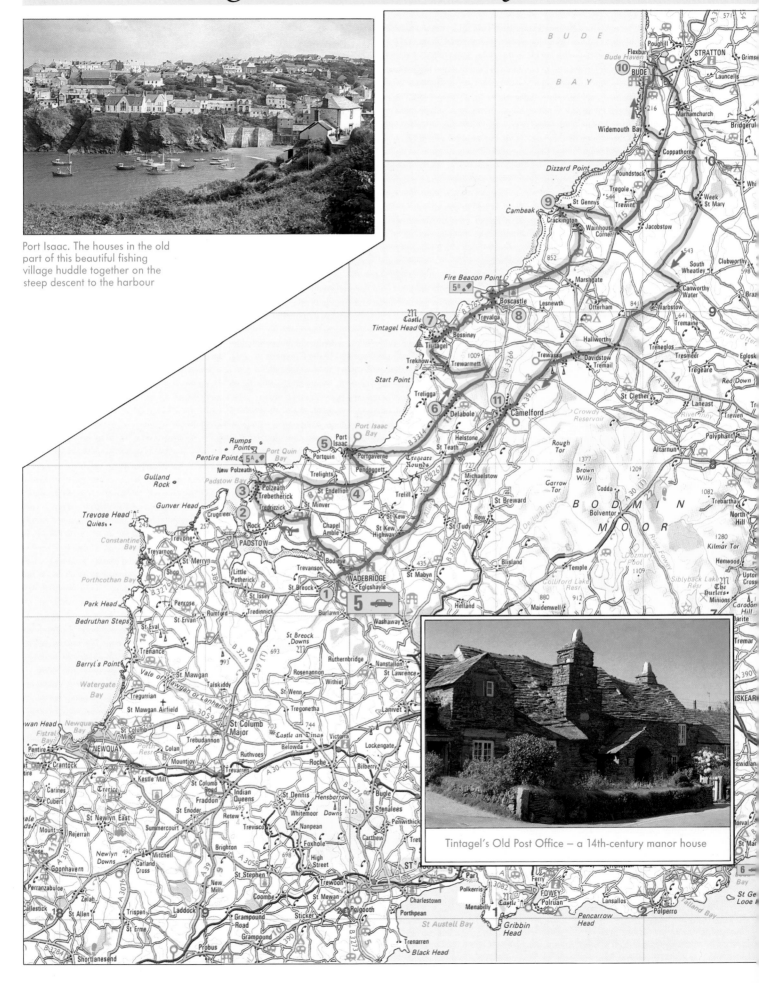

Port Isaac. The houses in the old part of this beautiful fishing village huddle together on the steep descent to the harbour

Tintagel's Old Post Office – a 14th-century manor house

WALK 5A · *Above Doom Bar* CORNWALL

Pentire Point – viewed from Polzeath

ROUTE DIRECTIONS

Allow 2½ hours
Start from the the main entrance of the car park at New Polzeath (grid ref. SW936795).

Turn right and then right again into Gulland Road. At the end of this road, where it joins Baby Beach Lane, take the coast path opposite. Go round the small cove of Pentireglaze Haven on to National Trust property and continue to Pentire Point, ignoring any paths on the right①.

From Pentire Point, with its off-lying Newland Rock, continue along the coast path until reaching the path that leads on to the Rumps headland. Follow this path on to the head②.

Return to the main path and continue with the wall on your right③.

Where the coast path turns sharply left at the junction of two walls, go right over a stile and head for a line of tamarisk shrubs④.

At the National Trust sign turn left. On reaching Pentire Farm, go straight through the yard. Opposite the farmhouse, go through a gateway on the right into a lane (muddy in wet weather). This becomes a path leading downhill to the coast path above Padstow Bay, where a left turn up some wooden steps leads back to New Polzeath.

Pentire Point and Rumps Point lie on the eastern side of Padstow Bay. Both headlands dominate this dramatic stretch of coastline, with the great cliff faces of Pentire best viewed from Rumps Point.

POINTS OF INTEREST

①The views across Padstow Bay from Pentire Point are magnificent. In fine conditions, the Camel Estuary appears to be a calm, secure waterway but it is marred by the suitably named Doom Bar – a dangerous ridge of sand and silt that has built up between the headlands. Yet Padstow, which lies on the west bank of the River Camel, was a busy port in years past and is still a flourishing fishing harbour.

②The Rumps, with their remarkable pinnacles, are composed of greenstone (a hard igneous rock), whereas the rest of Pentire is pillow lava that erupted from ancient volcanoes. From the Rumps the vast main wall of Pentire is visible.

③Looking back to the Rumps, it is obvious why the promontory made an ideal cliff castle. Three Iron Age earth ramparts with ditches were constructed across the saddle.

④Tamarisk grows well in these coastal areas. It is particularly attractive in July and August when its graceful, slender branches are covered in rosy-pink, scented flowers.

ROUTE DIRECTIONS

Allow 3½ hours
Start from the car park at Boscastle Harbour (grid ref. SX100913).

Walk to the bridge over the River Valency. Cross the bridge and turn right along by the harbour, then go up some steps and bear left along the cliff path①.

At this point it is worth making a detour to Willapark headland with its disused coastguard look-out, where there are magnificent views along the coast②.

On returning to the main path, turn right. Walk carefully along the cliff top, ignoring inland paths, before going down some wooden steps and over a stile. From here the path is obvious.

Where the path drops into a shallow valley just before the 'Manor House', turn left through a gate and go straight up the lane past the farm to St Petroc's Church at Trevalga③.

From the church, walk to the main road. Cross over and continue up the steep lane past a chapel on the right before reaching the Old Rectory. By the rectory gate there is a path leading off to the left. It is sometimes overgrown but does not run far before it reaches a field.

From here a right of way lies ahead but is not always obvious. On reaching Trehane Farm go on past the farmhouse to a field gate. You must now cross four fields before reaching the next lane. Follow the right-hand hedge of the first field to a gap then cross the next field at a leftward diagonal angle until reaching a gate. Stay in this field, but from the gate follow the hedge round to the right until reaching a stile. Climb this, then go diagonally left across the next field to the middle of the opposite wall. Cross the wall and go across the next field to a stile near the bottom corner. This leads into a lane. Go left down the lane and at its end turn right (not on to the main road) then left at a crossroads and on past the Napoleon Inn④.

Go straight on at the next crossroads and then downhill through the delightful older part of Boscastle to the car park.

Boscastle Harbour lies at the mouth of the Valency Valley, from where this walk follows the coastline to the south west before striking inland.

POINTS OF INTEREST

①Boscastle Harbour, impressively situated in a break in the dramatic cliffs, dates from the mid 16th century. For many years it served the inland town of Launceston as a port, the two being linked by pack horse and wagon transport. Slate and corn were shipped from the 16th-century pier.

②This stretch of the coast can be hostile in bad weather. Its reputation in the days of sail is recalled by a local saying:

'From Padstow Bar to Lundy Light
Is a sailor's grave by day or night.'

③St Petroc's Church, said to have been founded in the 13th century, was extensively restored in 1875. It has some charming features, including a 'squint'.

④During the Napoleonic Wars soldiers were recruited in two old coaching inns in Boscastle – one was the Napoleon, the other was the Wellington.

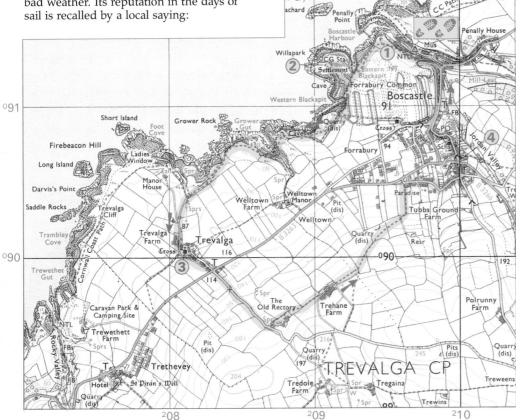

ROUTE DIRECTIONS
The drive starts from Looe①.

Follow signs to Plymouth, via Torpoint, along the A387. In ½ mile branch right on to the B3253. In 3¾ miles rejoin the A387 and at Hessenford turn right on to the B3247, signed Seaton. From Seaton an unclassified road on the right may be taken to the Woolly Monkey Sanctuary at Murrayton②.

From Seaton take the steep ascent (1 in 7) to Downderry. An ascent with a hairpin bend follows. After ¾ mile, bear right, signed Crafthole. At Crafthole go straight on, signed Millbrook, then in 2 miles turn right, unclassified, signed Whitsand Bay. On the outskirts of Cawsand keep left, and in ½ mile turn left. (To visit Kingsand, turn right.) Ascend and turn left on to the B3247, signed Millbrook. Alternatively, turn right to visit Mount Edgcumbe House and Country Park③.

Continue with the B3247, signed Millbrook. At Millbrook, turn left, signed Torpoint, then bear right. The road ascends steeply (1 in 6). In 2¾ miles turn right, signed Torpoint A374. The road descends steeply (1 in 7) to Antony. From here a 1¾-mile detour to the right can be made, to Antony House④.

From Antony, follow the A374 Liskeard road and continue through Sheviock to Polbathic. Here turn right on to the B3249, signed St Germans. In 1 mile keep left under the railway bridge, signed Saltash, and enter St Germans⑤.

At the far end of the village branch left on to an unclassified road, signed Liskeard. In 1 mile go over the crossroads and in another ¾ mile turn right on to the A374. At Trerulefoot roundabout take the second exit to join the A38. In 5½ miles branch left on to the A390 to reach Liskeard⑥.

From Liskeard follow signs for Bodmin and later rejoin the A38 to reach Dobwalls. From Dobwalls, remain on the Bodmin road and descend into the Fowey Valley.
After crossing the River Fowey a road on the right, signed St Neot, leads to Carnglaze Slate Caverns⑦.

Continue on the A38 for another 2 miles, then turn left on to the unclassified road, signed Looe scenic route. In 1 mile turn left on to the A390. After another mile turn right on to the B3359, signed Looe. In 4½ miles pass the turning, on the right, to Lanreath⑧.

Continue along the B3359 to Pelynt. In 1½ miles turn right, signed Polperro, then right again on to the A387. The road descends steeply (1 in 10) to Polperro⑨.

Return along the A387 to Looe.

Running through a region of deep wooded valleys stretching to the sea, the route takes in one of Cornwall's finest houses, a miniature cathedral city and a sanctuary for monkeys.

POINTS OF INTEREST

①East and West Looe, facing each other across an estuary, attract numerous holidaymakers to the busy quayside where boat trips and shark-fishing expeditions set off. The guildhall houses a museum of the town's history, and a former fish cellar nearby houses a museum of Cornish folk items.

②Part of the wooded valley at Murrayton has been turned into a sanctuary where visitors can observe a breeding colony of Amazonian woolly monkeys at close quarters.

③First built in the 16th century, Mount Edgcumbe House was a victim of the 1941 Plymouth Blitz. Since restored, it has fine Hepplewhite furniture and most of the large estate has been turned into a country park with scenic walks.

④Antony House, a dignified Queen Anne mansion, is one of the most impressive houses in Cornwall. It has panelled rooms and is surrounded by 250 acres of wooded parkland sloping down to the riverside.

⑤Until 1043 the little village of St Germans was Cornwall's cathedral city. The existing church, consecrated in 1261, is one of Cornwall's best examples of Norman architecture. In the village itself are six gabled almshouses and a fine 19th-century gatehouse.

⑥A pleasant market town with steep, narrow streets, Liskeard was one of Cornwall's four stannary towns. Charles I slept at Stuart House during 1644, and the water of Pipe Well in Well Lane is said to have healing properties.

⑦The quarry at Carnglaze Slate Caverns (open to the public) has been producing slate since the 14th century. One of the most remarkable features in the caverns is a blue-green underground lake.

⑧Lanreath Farm and Folk Museum has vintage tractors, engines and old farm implements such as a turnip and cattle-cake cutter and grappling irons. The earthwork running through the village, believed to be an ancient rampart, is known as the 'Giant's Hedge'.

⑨Parking is restricted in Polperro's narrow streets so it is best to park at the top of the approach road through the valley. The colour-washed cottages and inns piled up behind the harbour crowded with fishing boats have attracted artists over the years and studios and gift shops abound here.

Looe, formerly a pilchard fishing community, is now mainly devoted to holidaymakers during the summer

The magnificent Norman doorway of the church at St Germans

PLYMOUTH to
Roscoff .... 7-9 hrs
Santander .... 24 hrs

View from the clifftop down to Polperro, an artist's haven. Its narrow streets run down to one of Cornwall's quaintest harbours

A circular walk on the Rame Peninsula, starting and finishing at Cawsand village, with views across Plymouth Sound to the Devon shore. After a pleasant stretch of woodland the second part of the route takes in Rame Head and the eastern shore of Whitsand Bay.

POINTS OF INTEREST

① The linked villages of Cawsand and Kingsand were once divided by the ancient Cornwall-Devon boundary. Both very Cornish now, they are worth exploring. The Cawsand Bay fishermen were noted smugglers and it is said that in 1804 17,000 casks passed through the two villages.

② Rame Head and the 14th-century Chapel of St Michael are worth a visit. The headland was once an Iron Age fort and has been much used ever since – as a chapel, a hermitage and a light beacon for shipping.

③ Whitsand Bay has over three miles of sand and is reached by paths which zig-zag down cliffs more than 250ft high in places.

④ The road above Whitsand Bay was originally a military road, part of the mid-18th-century system of batteries and forts created to protect Plymouth Sound.

Rame Head, on the Rame Peninsula, is part of the Cornwall Coast Path which runs from Marsland Mouth on the north coast, round Land's End, and on to the shores of Plymouth Sound. It forms the central section of the South West Way

ROUTE DIRECTIONS
Allow 2½ hours
Start from the large car park at Cawsand village (grid ref. SX432503).

Take the road towards the village square (signposted) and turn right at Pier Lane by a small coast path sign①.

Continue to Penlee Point along the 'Earl's Drive', built in the 19th century by the Earl of Edgcumbe. Keep to the lower track before climbing towards Penlee Point. From the Point follow the metalled track until it turns inland. Keep straight ahead over a stile and go on to Rame Head②.

Rejoin the path and turn left below the coastguard look-out to a wooden stile. Continue along the side of the headland with the great sweep of Whitsand Bay on your left③.

Cross two more stiles then go left down some stone steps and straight across a track by the gate of a house. Go down more steps and through a gate until you reach another track. Turn right here and follow the track uphill④.

On reaching the road go straight across and down the opposite lane for about 50yds. Just before a farm go left into a field at the signpost and follow the path, keeping the hedge on your right. At a gap turn right and go down to a stile into a lane. Turn right then left on to the road and return to Cawsand car park.

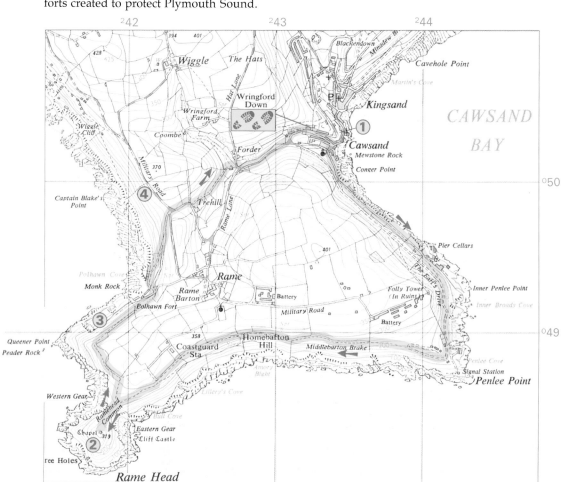

Cormorants lay their eggs on cliff tops in the early spring

ROUTE DIRECTIONS

Allow 3 hours
Start from the large car park a few hundred yards before Polkerris (grid ref. SX094523).

At the beach turn left and go up the path, ignoring a flight of steps on the right. Continue uphill until reaching a quiet road. Turn right here①.

Follow the road, keeping straight ahead at Tregaminion Chapel until reaching Menabilly Barton. Follow the track, keeping left at the junction as you pass through the farm, that leads down to Polridmouth Cove②.

At the wooden stile above the cove, turn right and follow the coast path. On reaching an open field, make directly for the tall beacon tower above Gribbin Head③.

From the beacon, follow the coast path along the western side of the headland, keeping left at all junctions④.

Where the path reaches the trees above Polkerris, walk along the brow of the wood, ignoring the stiles, until reaching a coast footpath sign. This path leads down a series of inclines to the cove and back to the car park.

Gribbin Head seems a gentle and unspectacular headland but it is ringed by rocks against which the sea crashes dramatically during storms.

From the small, secluded cove of Polkerris, the walk skirts the Menabilly Estate, long associated with the novelist Daphne du Maurier – best known for her book *Rebecca*.

POINTS OF INTEREST

①Polkerris was one of the busiest fishing harbours of the last century and beside the beach are the ruins of one of the largest 'pilchard palaces' in Cornwall. Here the pilchards were 'baulked' in salted piles and pressed for their oil.

②Inland from Polridmouth Cove lies the old Rashleigh family estate of Menabilly, associated in recent times with Daphne du Maurier who lived there for a while.

③ Gribbin Head provides a magnificent view towards Fowey and the fine eastern headlands. The remarkable 84ft-high beacon was erected by Trinity House in 1832 to help vessels navigate the headland.

④On leaving Gribbin Head the views across St Austell Bay form a broad mix of coast and landscape, from cliffs to sandy beaches and from the industrial complex round Par to the china-clay 'alps' above St Austell.

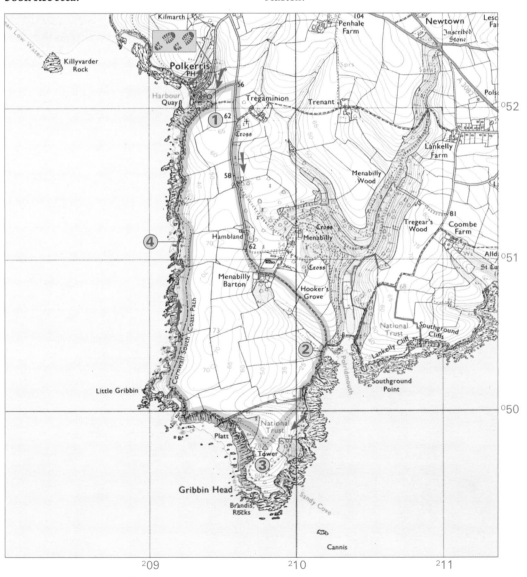

ROUTE DIRECTIONS
The drive starts from Plymouth ①.

From the city centre or the Tamar Bridge road A38, follow signs to Exeter to reach Marsh Mills roundabout. Here take the exit signed Plympton on to the B3416. In ½ mile, on the right, is a road

Open moorland dotted with sheep and ponies is the predominant feature of the first part of this tour. Later, it follows lovely Devon lanes to reach the reconstructed quay at Morwellham, and Buckland Abbey, once the home of Sir Francis Drake.

Buckland Abbey ⑨.

In 1¼ miles the drive starts to cross Roborough Down and at a crossroads bear left to reach a T-junction with the A386. Here turn right (no sign) on to the main road and later pass the edge of Roborough. Plymouth Airport is then skirted before the long gradual descent to Plymouth city centre.

Built in the 13th century as a monastery, Buckland Abbey was turned into a handsome house by Sir Richard Grenville in 1586

leading past the entrance to Saltram House ②.

Nearly ¾ mile farther, at the mini-roundabout, turn left, signed Exeter. Alternatively, turn right to visit Plympton ③.

In ½ mile turn left, signed Sparkwell, Cornwood, and in ¼ mile, at a mini-roundabout, turn right. Proceed through pleasant countryside to Sparkwell, beyond which is the entrance (on the left) to the Dartmoor Wildlife Park ④.

Continue to Lutton before reaching Cornwood. At the crossroads in Cornwood turn left, signposted Tavistock, and start a long, gradual ascent on to Lee Moor, situated beneath Penn Beacon (1,402ft) and Shell Top (1,546ft). Continue with wide views over the whole of the Plymouth area and after 2½ miles, at a crossroads, turn right on to the Cadover Bridge road. Alternatively, keep forward and pass through the village of Shaugh Prior to Shaugh Bridge – the meeting point of the rivers

Meavy and Plym at the entrance to the National Trust's Goodameavy Estate.

The main route continues northwards to reach Cadover Bridge, spanning the infant River Plym. Bear left across the bridge and ascend, and at the top turn right, signed Sheepstor, Meavy. In 1 mile descend (1 in 6) into the Meavy Valley and in ½ mile cross the river to reach the edge of Meavy. Here keep forward, signed Princetown, and in ½ mile turn sharp right, signposted Burrator. In ¾ mile turn right, signed Sheepstor, across the dam wall of the Burrator Reservoir ⑤.

In almost ¾ mile turn left (no sign) along a narrow road, and continue the drive round the reservoir's wooded bank. After 3 miles turn sharp right, signed Princetown, and ascend, and in ¾ mile at crossroads turn right on to the B3212, signed Princetown. The drive then climbs on to open moorland with extensive views on the left into east and north Cornwall. The BBC television transmitter on North Hessary Tor (1,695ft) is seen to the left on the approach to Princetown ⑥.

Turn left on to the Tavistock road, B3357, and shortly pass the prison,

then in 1 mile, at a T-junction, turn left again. With Great Mis Tor (1,768ft) on the right and extensive views ahead stretching from the Tamar Estuary to Bodmin Moor, the drive gradually descends from Dartmoor, past Merrivale Quarry in the Walkham Valley, to reach Tavistock ⑦.

Leave by the Liskeard road, A390, and in 2½ miles, at the Harvest Home public house, branch left on to an unclassified road, signed Morwellham. In 1 mile, at a crossroads, go forward and start a long descent to reach Morwellham ⑧.

Return to the crossroads and turn sharp right, signed Bere Alston, to proceed along a high ridge between the Tamar and Tavy valleys. After 2¾ miles turn sharp left, signed Denham Bridge, Plymouth, and start a long descent (1 in 4 at the end) along a narrow road to cross the River Tavy at the secluded Denham Bridge. Immediately turn right, signposted Plymouth, to ascend out of the valley, and in ¾ mile at a T-junction turn right, signed Buckland Abbey. In ½ mile, at a crossroads, turn right then left, signed Roborough, Plymouth, passing the entrance immediately on the right to

POINTS OF INTEREST

① Plymouth has been an important port for centuries and there is much of interest to see in the city that reflects its maritime history. The Sound, one of the finest deepwater anchorages in Europe, is a magnificent sight.

② Saltram House, owned by the National Trust, is a handsome 18th-century mansion set in attractive grounds. Robert Adam designed two of the rooms, and there are paintings by Joshua Reynolds – who was born at nearby Plympton.

③ The village of Plympton has two interesting old churches – Plympton St Mary and Plympton St Maurice – and there is also a 16th-century guildhall, a 17th-century grammar school and the keep of a Norman castle.

④ More than 100 species of animals – including the big cats, bears, wolves and seals – are kept in 25 acres of countryside at the Dartmoor Wildlife Park.

⑤ Burrator Reservoir, attractively situated between Sharpitor (1,312ft) and Sheepstor (1,150ft), supplies Plymouth with water.

⑥ Named after George IV when he was Prince of Wales, Princetown is a bleak, grey place – famous for its prison which was completed in 1809.

⑦ Important as a market town, Tavistock, beside the River Tavy, owes much of its present appearance to the Dukes of Bedford who dominated it from the 16th to the 20th centuries. Remains of the town's once great 10th-century abbey can be seen, and the market, which dates from that time, is still held outside the gate every Friday.

⑧ A former copper loading port on the River Tamar, Morwellham has been turned into a major 'living' industrial museum of the port, the local copper mines and the lives of the people who dwelt there in the last century.

⑨ Once owned by Sir Francis Drake, Buckland Abbey was converted into a mansion at the Dissolution. The medieval tithe barn is used by Plymouth City Museum to house a collection of carts and carriages.

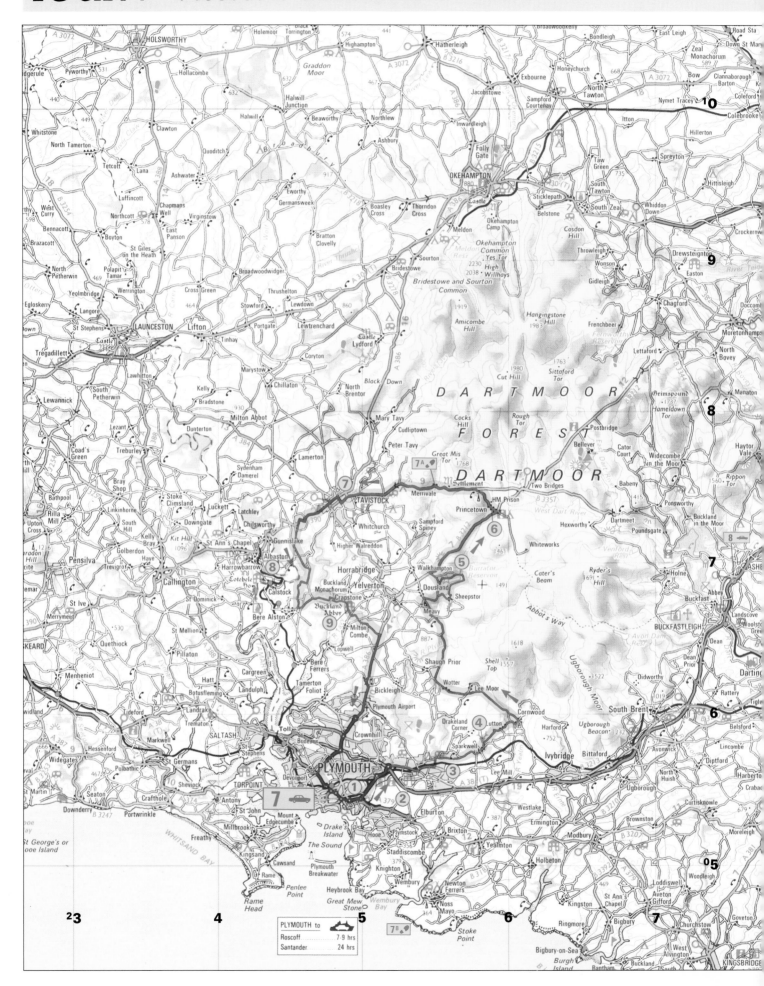

PLYMOUTH to
Roscoff .... 7-9 hrs
Santander .... 24 hrs

A dense collection of Bronze Age hut circles at Merrivale, near ceremonial stone rows

Here is a varied walk through the beautiful scenery of the Walkham Valley. It returns along the line of the defunct Princetown railway, past once-busy quarries, and ends by visiting an impressive group of Bronze Age antiquities.

POINTS OF INTEREST

① Across the valley from Longash Farm – which is no longer actively farmed – is Vixen Tor, one of Dartmoor's finest granite outcrops. The Longash Brook (or the Pila Brook: some Dartmoor streams have alternative names) is crossed, and then the track passes through Hucken Tor, a charming little tor where a gate is hung between the rocks. A fine view now opens up, the track becomes a road and several farms are passed.

② The old Princetown line began as a horse-drawn tramway in the 1820s, was converted to a railway, and finally closed in 1956. There was a halt here from 1936 which displayed a sign warning of the danger to dogs from snakes. As you continue to walk, you will see the track of the old tramway taking a longer route round Yes Tor Bottom, the name of this shallow valley. Soon the waste tips of Swelltor Quarry will be seen, with the grass-covered Royal Oak siding beyond.

③ The stone on the skyline, known as a guidestone, is one of a number erected in about 1700 to help travellers find their way between Ashburton and Tavistock. An A and a T are cut into the sides of the stone facing these towns.

④ Ancient relics at this point date from 750BC to 2500BC and consist of groups of hut circles (the stone foundations of circular dwellings), burials in the form of stone cairns or stone chests, menhirs (standing stones) and a stone circle (a temple, perhaps). Most enigmatic of all are the lines of upright stones, usually called stone rows.

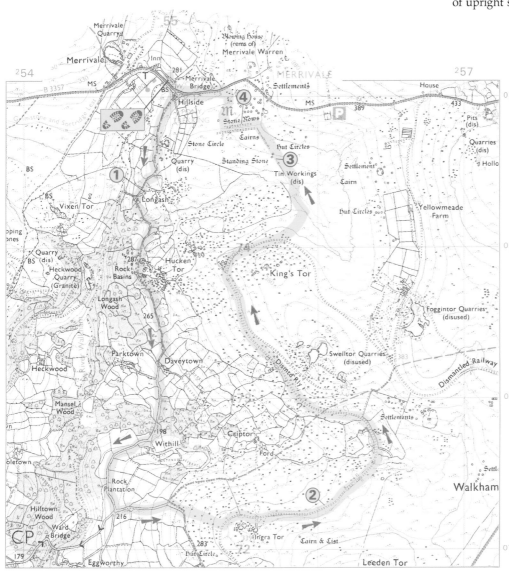

ROUTE DIRECTIONS

Allow 3 hours
Start from the car parking area at Merrivale near the old bridge over the River Walkham (grid ref. SX550751).

Cross the 'new' road and take the signposted farm track next to Hillside Cottages. This will be your route for the next 2½ miles. On your left you will pass a disused quarry, then Longash Farm①.

At the first crossroads turn up left, signposted Criptor. After crossing a cattle grid, bear off right towards the prominent pile of Ingra Tor where you will meet the track of the old Princetown railway. Follow this left②.

As the line curves tightly to the right (east), keep a look out for the bold face of Yellowmeade Farm. When it comes into sight, bear down left off the track and make for the wall corner, following it round left and crossing the upper reaches of the Longash Brook which you crossed earlier. Head for a prominent stone on the skyline immediately ahead③.

By aiming north west from the stone towards Merrivale Quarry you will pass through the most interesting, comprehensive and convenient group of prehistoric antiquities on Dartmoor④.

Return to Merrivale Bridge in the dip beneath Merrivale Quarry.

ROUTE DIRECTIONS

Allow 2½ hours
Start from the National Trust's Warren Cliffs car park (grid ref. SX541466).

Leave the car park by the way you came in. Turn left and then right after 35yds down a gravel track that eventually leads to Noss Mayo①.

Turn left opposite Noss Mayo car park and then right along a narrow road with a 7ft width restriction. After the last cottage on the left, climb a few steps on the left into Fordhill Plantation. This National Trust path leads off Revelstoke Drive②.

Where the path rejoins the drive, back-track for about 25yds, turn sharp left and take the track leading to the (summer only) ferry slip. The path continues to rejoin Revelstoke Drive. Pass by Battery Cottage – a sprawling country house on the site of a one-time defensive position. After passing through Brakehill Plantation the path reaches open cliff land, with the Great Mew Stone visible ahead③.

At Gara Point the path bears left above the coastguard look-out④.

Having rounded the corner beyond Warren Cottage, the path turns inland through a gate and then returns to the car park.

A view of the boats down-river from the charming village of Newton Ferrers, whose old-fashioned gabled houses and white cottages sprawl across a hillside a few miles from Plymouth

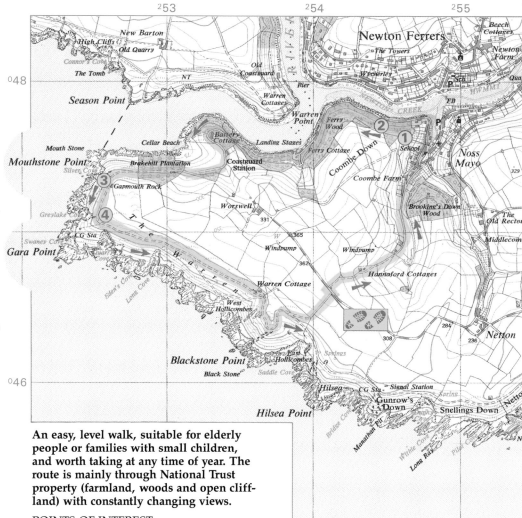

An easy, level walk, suitable for elderly people or families with small children, and worth taking at any time of year. The route is mainly through National Trust property (farmland, woods and open cliff-land) with constantly changing views.

POINTS OF INTEREST

①Noss Mayo is a delightful village clustered around Noss Creek and flanked by National Trust woodland. Across this creek of the River Yealm (pronounced 'yam') is the prosperous yachting resort of Newton Ferrers.

②Revelstoke Drive, also known as the Ten Mile Drive, was built as a carriage road in the last century by Lord Revelstoke. The family seat was at Membland, to the east of Noss Mayo, and his Lordship laid out the drive so that he could tour his property from the comfort of his carriage. The undulating path leads through beech, sycamore and sweet chestnut trees. Soon the mouth of the River Yealm can be seen coming in from the north.

③The Great Mew Stone is a steep-sided islet which forms part of the HMS *Cambridge* gunnery school on Wembury Point. On a clear day Eddystone Lighthouse can be seen to the south west.

④Gara Point is a convenient place from which to see cormorants or shags resting on a waterline rock. These gently sloping cliffs, Warren Cliffs, are so called because rabbits were encouraged to breed here for their meat and skins. Warren Cottage is where the warrener lived. Sheep graze the sidelands, so dogs should be kept on leads.

ROUTE DIRECTIONS

The drive starts from Ashburton ①.

From the town centre follow the Buckland signs along an unclassified road, shortly turning left across the River Ashburn before starting a long ascent through well-wooded country. The drive later keeps forward to pass beneath the slopes of Buckland Beacon, 1,282ft②.

Continue along a narrow, winding road through Buckland in the Moor. One mile farther, at a T-junction, turn left, signed Widecombe, and descend into the attractive East Webburn Valley. Cross the river and ascend to another T-junction and turn right. In 1 mile enter Widecombe in the Moor③.

Leave by the Bovey Tracey road, B3387, bearing right past the green, and ascend steeply on to open moorland④.

Start the long descent to the Bovey Valley and, after 3 miles, at the crossroads by the Edgemoor Hotel, turn left, unclassified. From this point a short detour can be made to visit the Parke Rare Breeds Farm and Dartmoor National Park Centre near Bovey Tracey by keeping forward at the crossroads and in ½ mile turning right. The entrance is ¼ mile farther on the left⑤.

On leaving, turn right and rejoin the main route near Yarner Wood. The main tour turns left again after ½ mile, signed Manaton, Becky Falls. In a further ¾ mile pass on the left an entrance to the Yarner Wood National Nature Reserve (guided walks available). Continue the winding climb across the slopes of Trendlebere Down, with excellent views of the thickly wooded Bovey

Valley to the right, before entering dense woodland surrounding the picturesque Becky Falls (entrance on right). Continue past the hamlet of Manaton⑥.

At the T-junction, ¾ mile beyond Manaton's church, turn right on to the North Bovey road. Descend steeply along a narrow, winding road and after 1½ miles cross the River Bovey and ascend into North Bovey⑦.

Leave by following signs for Postbridge and in ½ mile, at a crossroads, turn left. Three-quarters of a mile farther, at a T-junction, turn left on to the B3212, signed Princetown. Ascend, with good views to the right, on to open moorland; to the left rises high ground leading to Hameldown Tor, 1,737ft. Near the Warren House Inn, where a peat fire is always burning, the road reaches its highest point, at 1,426ft. Continue to Postbridge⑧.

After leaving Postbridge a detour along the next turning on the left, unclassified, can be taken past Bellever Wood to Bellever picnic site and nature trail⑨.

At the edge of Two Bridges turn left on to the Dartmeet, Ashburton road, B3357, following the line of the West Dart. After 4¼ miles the drive descends steeply to reach the picturesque Dartmeet Bridge, where the East and West Dart rivers converge, before starting a long winding ascent (1 in 5) up the

Ashburton road, unclassified, to the vicinity of Sharp Tor, 1,250ft, from where there are fine views down the valley.

From Poundsgate, a steep, winding descent (maximum 1 in 4) leads to a crossing of the River Dart at New Bridge, adjacent to which is a picnic site. After entering the woods of Holne Chase, an unclassified road on the right leads to Holne⑩.

The River Dart is crossed for the second time, at Holne Bridge. One mile farther the drive passes the entrance, on the right, to the River Dart Country Park⑪.

In a further ¾ mile turn left to re-enter Ashburton.

POINTS OF INTEREST

① One of Devon's four stannary towns, Ashburton's origins go back to a Saxon settlement. Today, it is a real country town with many old and attractive buildings, including a 15th-century church with a magnificent Devonshire tower.

② On the summit of Buckland Beacon stands the Ten Commandments Stone, carved by a local stonemason. To the left are occasional views over the deep and thickly wooded Dart Valley.

③ The village of Widecombe is dominated by the 120ft-high tower of its fine 14th-century church. Adjacent are the 13th-century

Church House (National Trust) and the village green, whose connection with the well-known song *Widecombe Fair* is celebrated by the carved sign.

④ The B3387 passes Rippon Tor, 1,560ft, on the right and then reveals a magnificent view from 1,250ft over south Devon to Torbay. On the left are Saddle Tor, 1,350ft, and the famous Haytor Rocks, which rise to 1,490ft and make a fine viewpoint.

⑤ The Parke Rare Breeds Farm is set in the beautiful grounds of the Dartmoor National Park Authority which offer delightful woodland and riverside walks.

⑥ Manaton was once the home of the novelist John Galsworthy, who wrote much of the *Forsyte Saga* here. The hamlet has a 15th-century church.

⑦ Set around a pleasant green, North Bovey is one of Dartmoor's most attractive villages.

⑧ Standing at the very heart of Dartmoor, Postbridge comprises a scattering of farms, an inn and a chapel. To the left from the road bridge, a medieval stone clapper bridge can be seen crossing the East Dart River.

⑨ A reasonable cross-section of birds can be found in Bellever Woods, a relatively new coniferous woodland. Its setting beside the East Dart River is extremely attractive.

⑩ Holne Bridge was built in the 15th century and the Church of St Mary dates from 1300. It has a fine screen and much detailed work. Charles Kingsley was born at the vicarage here in 1819.

⑪ The Park has children's adventure playgrounds, a bathing lake, pony rides and nature trails.

Haytor Rocks – the most accessible and probably the most well known of Dartmoor's rugged granite outcrops known as tors

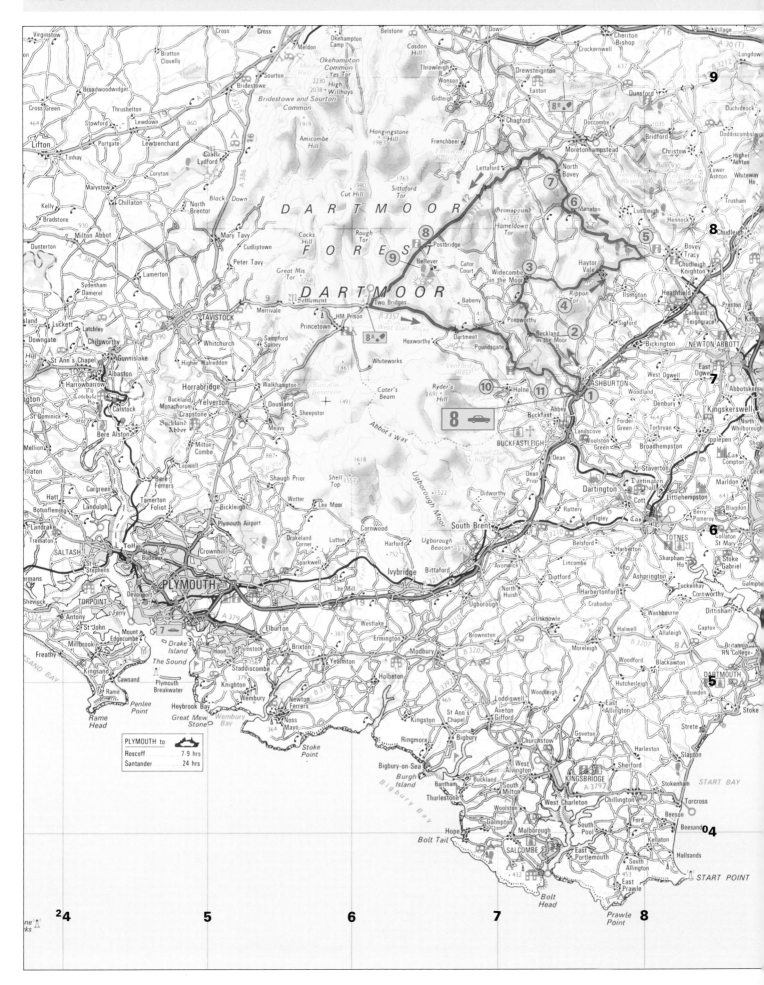

Lichen, ferns and moss add interest to Wistman's Wood. Artificial warrens around the edge, where rabbits were bred for their flesh and fur, date from medieval times

ROUTE DIRECTIONS

Allow 2½ hours
Start from the quarry car park at Two Bridges (grid ref. SX609751).

Walk north along the track past Crockern. Bear up right following the signpost directions and yellow waymarks to a ladder stile. Once you are over the stile Wistman's Wood and Beardown Tors come into view①.

Climb the stile and continue on to reach Wistman's Wood②.

At the northern limit of the wood, head uphill to Longaford Tor, from which a splendid view unfolds③.

Now walk south along the ridge over Littaford Tors④.

Continue to walk on until you reach a gap in the wall ahead, where three walls meet. Pass through the gap, still heading south. The summit of Crockern Tor soon comes into view⑤.

With Crockern Tor in view ahead, go west and downhill to the first stile climbed on the outward walk, and return to the car park.

An easy walk over open moorland to the curious grove of ancient gnarled oaks known as Wistman's Wood, visiting several typical tors on the return route.

POINTS OF INTEREST

①Crowning the hill to the west of Wistman's Wood are the Beardown Tors, one of which carries a flagpole. A red flag flies when firing is taking place on the Merrivale field firing range.

② Wistman's Wood grows at between 1,300ft and 1,400ft – which is high and very exposed for an oak wood. Visitors are asked not to venture into the wood as it is a National Nature Reserve.

③Cut Hill, which can be seen to the north on a clear day from Longaford Tor, is the most remote summit on Dartmoor. In the nearby valley to the south east are the ruined buildings of the 19th-century Powder Mills, where gunpowder was made.

④Some of the blocks that make up Littaford Tors look like masonry, but they are entirely natural. Dartmoor's tors have not been satisfactorily explained and even geologists disagree as to their origin.

⑤Crockern Tor was the assembly point for the Stannary Parliament (the Great Court of the Dartmoor tinners) from 1494 to 1703. It was chosen because it was almost equidistant from the Stannary towns of Ashburton, Chagford, Tavistock and Plympton, all of which sent representatives.

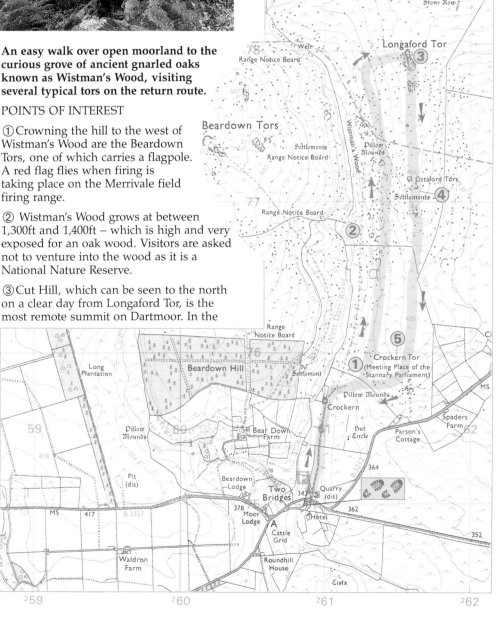

ROUTE DIRECTIONS

Allow 3 hours
Start from the car park on the south side of Fingle Bridge (grid ref. SX743898).

Walk back over the bridge for 170yds, then take the signposted path through the woods of the Teign Gorge①.

At a rocky promontory — Sharp Tor — a path leads off right to Castle Drogo. It is well worth a detour if the castle is open②.

If you make a detour to the castle, the Hunters' Path can be rejoined further on③.

Follow the path as it turns away from the valley, then doubles back on itself at a lower level to reach the River Teign at an anglers' metal bridge. Turn left, downstream, and follow this Fisherman's Path past a weir④.

Continue beside the river back to the car park⑤.

Castle Drogo (below), built of granite above the Teign Valley; and the River Teign — famed for its salmon — flowing under Fingle Bridge (below right)

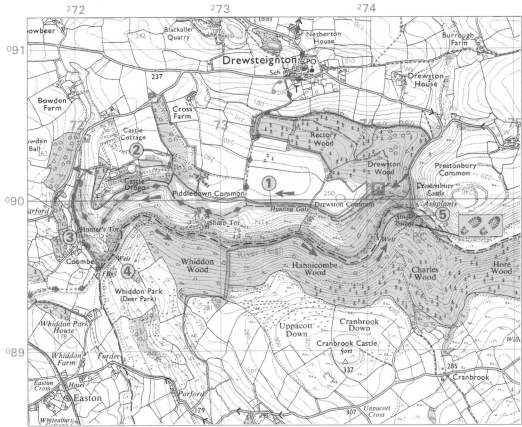

A long but gentle climb at the beginning of the walk leads to a panoramic high-level track. The return route follows a riverside path with one short, stepped climb over a rocky buttress. From April to October it is possible to visit Castle Drogo, owned by the National Trust.

POINTS OF INTEREST

①This is the Hunters' Path, and high Dartmoor forms the western skyline. The trees in the woods are initially oaks, but silver birch become dominant further up. Large domed wood-ants' nests punctuate the path verges and fallow deer can sometimes be seen.

②The striking neo-medieval mock fortress of Castle Drogo was built for Julius Drewe between 1910 and 1930 by Sir Edwin Lutyens. The house has much to fascinate all the family, including its own telephone and hydro-electric systems.

③The Hunters' Path reaches the western end of the Teign Gorge at Hunts Tor (not Hunters Tor as shown on some maps). Across the valley is Whiddon (deer) Park, surrounded by a high stone wall.

④The weir in the Teign, which forms a deep pool, diverts some of the flow to a turbine house on the south bank which provides electricity to Castle Drogo. As you walk downriver a scree of frost-shattered shale is crossed, and where Sharp Tor's lower buttresses meet the river a steep climb up and then down has to be made.

⑤A short distance before Fingle Bridge there is another weir which took water to the waterwheel of Fingle Mill, destroyed by fire in 1894. Its ruins are visible at the far end of the car park.

ROUTE DIRECTIONS
The drive starts from Exeter ①.

From the city centre follow the signs Exmouth (A376) to leave by the B3182 Topsham Road. In 2 miles, at a roundabout, take the second exit, unclassified, signed Topsham. Later pass under the M5 viaduct and enter Topsham②.

Pass the Lord Nelson public house then turn left, signed Exmouth (for town centre keep forward). Go over the level crossing then bear right. On the descent, pass the 16th-century Bridge Inn before crossing the River Clyst. In ¾ mile, at the roundabout, turn right on to the A376. This road runs parallel, but inland, to the estuary of the River Exe, skirting Exton and Lympstone before continuing to Exmouth③.

Leave by the Budleigh Salterton road, A376, and enter Budleigh④.

Keep forward through the town, and at the end of the seafront ascend and turn sharp left, then leave by following the main A376 northwards through the Otter Valley. Later skirt East Budleigh village and after another ¾ mile you pass the Brick Cross, a curious obelisk at a crossroads with directions in biblical phrases. At this point a short detour across the valley to the right can be made to visit Otterton. The main drive then skirts Bicton Park⑤.

Continue through Colaton Raleigh and in 1½ miles, turn right on to the A3052, signed Sidmouth, entering Newton Poppleford. At the end, cross the River Otter and ascend (1 in 8). Shortly beyond the summit turn right on to the B3176 and later descend to the edge of Sidmouth town centre⑥.

At the mini-roundabout turn left, signed Honiton, Lyme Regis, into All Saints Road. (For the seafront and car parks go forward.) At the end turn left and leave by the B3175 to reach Sidford. Here, turn right on to the Lyme Regis road, A3052. Shortly, pass an old packhorse bridge over the River Sid, on the left, then ascend (1 in 7) on to higher ground. Three miles farther, turn left on to the B3174, signed Ottery and Honiton. After 2½ miles a detour to the right leads to Farway Countryside Park⑦.

Continue with the B3174 and in ¾ mile branch right, unclassified, signed Farway. Keep forward along the top of the forested Farway Hill and in 2¾ miles, at the T-junction, turn left, signed Honiton. A 1-in-5 descent is then made to reach Honiton⑧.

Turn left into the main street and in ¾ mile turn left again on to the Sidmouth road, A375. An ascent is then made of Gittisham Hill to cross Gittisham Common. After a further

As well as seaside resorts, such as Exmouth and Sidmouth, this tour explores the countryside of east Devon, passing many pretty villages and several notable churches.

The Exe Estuary: yachtsmen are well catered for along Devon's south coast

1½ miles, at the Hare and Hounds public house, turn right on to the B3174, signed Ottery. One mile farther, a diversion to the left, signed Sidbury, may be taken to the White Cross Picnic Site, 2¾ miles, from where there are magnificent views.

The main drive descends Chineway Hill (1 in 5) to reach Ottery St Mary⑨.

Turn right, signed Exeter, then bear left, one-way, through the square. At the end turn right on to the B3176, signed Fairmile and Talaton. Later cross the River Otter and pass the entrance to Cadhay House⑩.

At Fairmile cross the A30, signed Talaton and Clyst Hydon. Continue along this secondary road through Talaton to Clyst Hydon. At the end of the village turn right, signed Cullompton, then in ¾ mile turn left on to the unclassified Hele road. Follow this byroad round to the broad Culm Valley.

At the junction with the B3181 turn left on to the Exeter road and 2 miles farther pass the junction with the B3185. From here a detour to the right leads to the National Trust property of Killerton House⑪.

The main tour remains on the B3181 past Broad Clyst and later enters the suburbs of Exeter at

Pinhoe. Go forward at the mini-roundabouts, signed Ring Road, then in 1 mile, at the traffic signals, turn right, B3212, for the return to Exeter city centre.

POINTS OF INTEREST

①The cathedral city of Exeter is the county town of Devon and has many fine buildings of architectural and historical interest, a rat-run of underground passages and a number of museums, including the splendid Maritime Museum.

②The ancient port of Topsham has a number of old houses, including several attractive 17th- and 18th-century examples in the Strand built by Dutch merchants.

③Exmouth is a traditional seaside resort, with 2 miles of golden sands, which offer fine views across the estuary to Dawlish Warren and Torbay.

④A small resort at the mouth of the River Otter, Budleigh's shingle beach is strictly for swimmers rather than paddlers. The thatched Fairlynch Museum and Arts Centre stands opposite Mackerel Square.

⑤Within the extensive grounds at Bicton Park are some magnificent gardens, including an Italian garden laid out in 1735. There are also theme halls, a woodland railway and a countryside museum.

⑥Retaining an air of genteel tranquillity, Sidmouth is a Regency and Victorian resort whose mainly shingle beach is bounded by fine red cliff scenery to both the east and west.

⑦Farway Countryside Park offers the opportunity to see rare breeds and present-day farm animals in a picturesque farm setting.

⑧One of the first of the great serge manufacturing towns in Devon, Honiton is best known for its lace-making. The Honiton Lace Shop in the main street sells all you need to make your own, as well as ready-made samples.

⑨Charming and unspoilt, Ottery St Mary has literary associations with Thackeray and Coleridge and was the birthplace of the latter. The 14th-century church, with its twin towers, is one of the finest in Devon.

⑩Cadhay is an Elizabethan manor house built around a central courtyard. Its Great Hall has a fine timber roof.

⑪Killerton House was rebuilt in 1778 to the design of John Johnson. It houses the Paulise de Bush collection of costumes and has 15 acres of hillside gardens containing rare trees and shrubs.

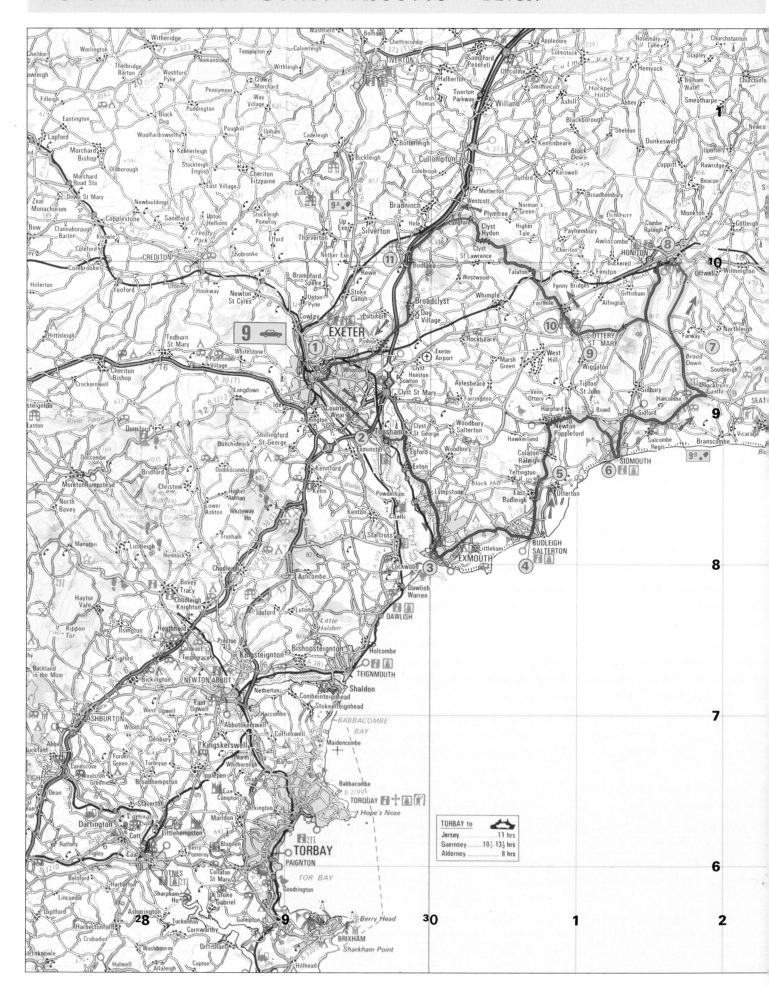

The nocturnal badger, with its handsome coat of silver and black, lives in hedgerows or woodland and is an inhabitant of the farmland near Silverton

ROUTE DIRECTIONS

Allow 2½ hours
Start from the car park near the Health Centre in Silverton (grid ref. SS957030).

Walk to Fore Street and turn right①.

Turn right up Parsonage Lane beside the Methodist Chapel②.

Carry on up, passing the school on your right. Where the track deteriorates, go through a hunting gate on the left and continue up the field with the hedge on your right. At the end of the third field, join the road, turn right and climb steeply to Christ Cross③.

Turn right along a gently falling road, and right again down a steep rough track just as the ridge road begins to climb, and follow it helter-skelter down and through Greenslinch Farm④.

At Greenslinch, take the gently climbing track behind the cottages, and turn left over a stile where the track turns sharp right. Aim for the stile at the top of the field — Silverton is now spread out in the foreground. After crossing the stile, walk down the field with the hedge on your right⑤.

Pass through the gate, turn half right and follow the track to the road. Silverton is now ½ mile to the west. The church is worth a visit on the way back to your car⑥.

A wonderful viewpoint rewards the walker on this steep climb in rolling farmland not far from Exeter. It is a walk best done in summer on a clear day, and sturdy shoes or boots are essential. Allow time to have a look at Silverton.

POINTS OF INTEREST

①Silverton is a large, attractive village with a lot of thatched houses in the older part.

②The cob (dried mud) walls of the cottages on the right of Parsonage Lane are built on stone plinths to give them solid footings.

③Known locally as Criss Cross, Christ Cross stands at about 850ft, and the view from here extends to Somerset, with the Wellington Monument prominent on the northern shoulder of the Blackdown Hills.

④The rough lane descending to Greenslinch Farm recalls how all Devon's roads used to be. Badger runs through the hedges are very noticeable here.

⑤Dolbury Hill, on the National Trust's Killerton estate, is the wooded hill which can be seen 2½ miles away to the south east. The park is open to the public, as is the house, between April and October.

⑥Silverton church – about 500 years old – stands between the Culm and the Exe. The west gallery is one of its best features.

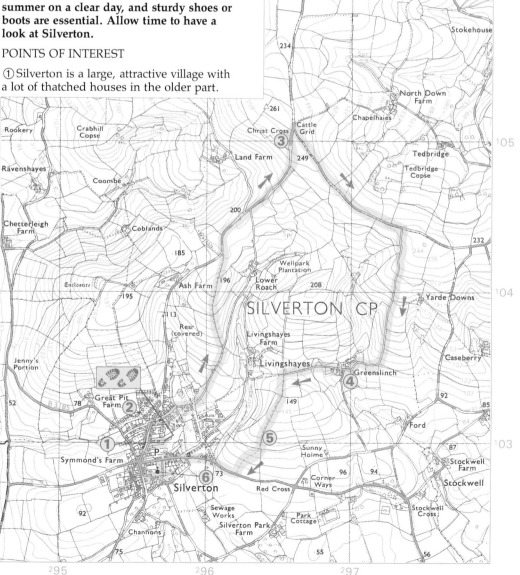

A walk along the east Devon coast between Weston Combe and the village of Branscombe. There is likely to be mud where the path passes through cattle pasture. One steep climb follows a visit to Branscombe church, one of Devon's most interesting parish churches.

POINTS OF INTEREST

① Weston Combe, with its steep, uncultivated sides but fertile valley bottom providing pasture, is typical of the deep combes which dissect the plateau of east Devon. Weston Cliff is reached at the end of the combe where there is a 500ft drop, and **walkers are warned not to go near the cliff edge as the subsoil is unstable.** The view here extends from Portland in Dorset to Scabbacombe Head beyond Torbay. A few chalets mark Weston Mouth, but the beach cannot be reached by car, so it is always quiet.

② This part of the walk follows the South West Way, which starts at Minehead in Somerset and follows the coast for over 600 miles, via Land's End, to Poole Harbour in Dorset.

③ Branscombe church, Norman in origin but somewhat altered in medieval times, remains unspoilt. Much of the furniture is Jacobean, but the splendid pulpit is 18th century. About 200yds down from the church is a thatched forge and a traditional country bakery whose oven is still heated by ashen faggots.

Branscombe, a scattered village of attractive stone and thatched cottages, in the combes of the tributaries which eventually join and flow out to sea at Branscombe Mouth

④ This area is very much the preserve of badgers, who find the steep, scrub-covered hillsides to their liking.

ROUTE DIRECTIONS

Allow 3 hours
Start from Weston car park by the bottom track (grid ref. SY166889).

Bear round left, leaving the flint-surfaced track for a narrow footpath where a signpost reads Weston Cliff①.

Take the coast path heading east, following the signposts, waymarks and stiles. One field after the National Trust sign, the path bears left away from the cliff and meets a hedged track at the point where another track comes in from the left②.

Carry on eastwards, looking out for Branscombe church through the trees to the left. When you are nearly level with the church, turn left down a steep path through the woods at a waymark post. This leads to the churchyard③.

Leave the churchyard by the main gate, walk left up the road and turn down and immediately up across a steep field just before the old chapel. Climb a stile into the woods and follow the path to rejoin the outward route. Turn right here, and right again where the track comes in from the right④.

At Berry Barton Farm turn left and return along a relatively quiet road to Weston, about 1¼ miles away.

TOUR 10 · Exmoor – Combes and Cliffs   DEVON

ROUTE DIRECTIONS

The drive starts from the large hill-top village of Lynton ①.

Leave by the Lynmouth road and on the descent turn sharp left with the B3234. Continue the steep descent of Lynmouth Hill to the small resort of Lynmouth ②.

Follow the signs Minehead A39 and ascend Countisbury Hill (1 in 4) ③.

After the long climb to the hamlet of Countisbury, the road emerges on to the northern extremity of Exmoor. Three miles farther the drive enters Somerset and shortly passes the turning to Oare, on the right ④.

The main tour continues along the A39 for almost 6 miles and then makes the notorious twisting descent of Porlock Hill (1 in 4) to reach the village of Porlock ⑤.

A diversion to the left along the B3223 leads to the coast at Porlock Weir, 1½ miles away, with its small harbour ⑥.

At Porlock go forward through the village with the Minehead road and at the end keep left then turn right with the one-way system. Half a mile farther turn right on to an unclassified road, signed Horner and Luccombe, and proceed through the attractive Horner Valley.

In 1½ miles, at the crossroads, turn right, signed Dunkery Beacon. (Alternatively keep forward to visit the delightful village of Luccombe, ½ mile away.) The main tour immediately ascends (1 in 5) and after ¾ mile it bears left in order to continue the long climb over the shoulder of Dunkery Hill ⑦.

There is an easy descent for 2¾ miles after which turn right on to the Simonsbath road, B3224. Continue through undulating countryside for 3¾ miles before turning left on to an unclassified road, signed Winsford. This pleasant byroad later enters the valley of the River Exe to reach Winsford. At the telephone kiosk turn right, signed Molton, then bear left. After another 1½ miles meet the crossroads junction with the B3223. The road ahead leads to Tarr Steps ⑧.

The main route turns right on to the Lynton, Simonsbath road, B3223, and crosses Winsford Hill (1,405ft). Proceed through more open countryside and in 4 miles, at the crossroads, turn left and enter Simonsbath ⑨.

At Simonsbath branch left with the B3358, signed Blackmoor Gate and Ilfracombe. Follow this moorland road to Challacombe and after a further 2¼ miles, at the T-junction, turn right on to the B3226. At Blackmoor Gate turn left then immediately right, A399, signed Combe Martin. Two miles farther

turn right on to an unclassified road, signed Trentishoe and Hunter's Inn.

In another 1¼ miles turn right again and later pass the car park for Holdstone Down, on the left, from where there are fine views. Almost a mile farther bear right, still signed Hunter's Inn, and descend into the wooded valley of the River Heddon to the beautifully situated Hunter's Inn ⑩.

Here turn left, signed Martinhoe, and ascend along a narrow byroad. At the top turn left again and continue to the hamlet of Martinhoe. Pass the church and in almost ½ mile branch left, signed Woody Bay Hotel, then take the next turning left. After the descent continue with signs Lynton via Toll Road, passing the Woody Bay Hotel, with impressive views across the Bristol Channel.

Follow the narrow coast road and in 1¼ miles pass through a tollgate. Later go forward at the roundabout, entering the spectacular Valley of the Rocks with its many jagged tors and rocky outcrops, before the return to Lynton.

POINTS OF INTEREST

① Standing 600ft above its sister town of Lynmouth, Lynton is mainly Victorian. The Exmoor Museum, in a restored 16th-century house, displays tools and products of former local craftsmen.

② Picturesquely situated at the mouth of the East and West Lyn rivers, Lynmouth has been described as the 'English Switzerland'. It has suffered terribly from torrential floods, most recently in August 1952, when more than 30 people were killed and many houses washed away.

③ One of the most famous hills in the West Country, Countisbury affords good seascape views over the Bristol Channel to the Welsh coast.

④ Oare is the remote hamlet popularised by R D Blackmore in *Lorna Doone*, and the diminutive square-towered church is where, in the novel, Lorna was shot by Carver Doone. The nearby village of Malmsmead provides access to the legendary 'Doone Country'.

⑤ Porlock has an old-world charm with its narrow, winding streets and thatched roofs. Its sheltered position and mild climate create a paradise of flowers.

⑥ Porlock Weir is a picturesque place, with pebbles on the beach and bracken-covered hillsides. A cliff path leads to Culbone, less than 2 miles from Porlock Weir, where there is the Church of St Beuno, the smallest complete parish church in England (35ft by 12ft).

⑦ Dunkery is Exmoor's highest point, and at the summit of the hill (1,453ft), a footpath on the right leads to the AA Viewpoint on Dunkery Beacon. Red deer can often be seen on the moors from here in the early morning and at twilight.

⑧ The medieval clapper bridge of Tarr Steps is a well-known Exmoor beauty spot on the River Barle.

⑨ Simonsbath is a walkers' paradise with wild moorland and heather-clad hills on all sides. The village contains a handful of cottages, a hotel dating back to 1654, a pottery and a National Park Information Centre.

⑩ Heddon's Mouth, where the River Heddon reaches the sea, is a particularly attractive spot which can only be reached by delightful footpaths.

The pretty harbour at Porlock Weir, formed from a natural creek

The rolling uplands of Exmoor are a dominant feature of this tour, which also makes its way along the magnificent coastline with its steep hills and dramatic sea views.

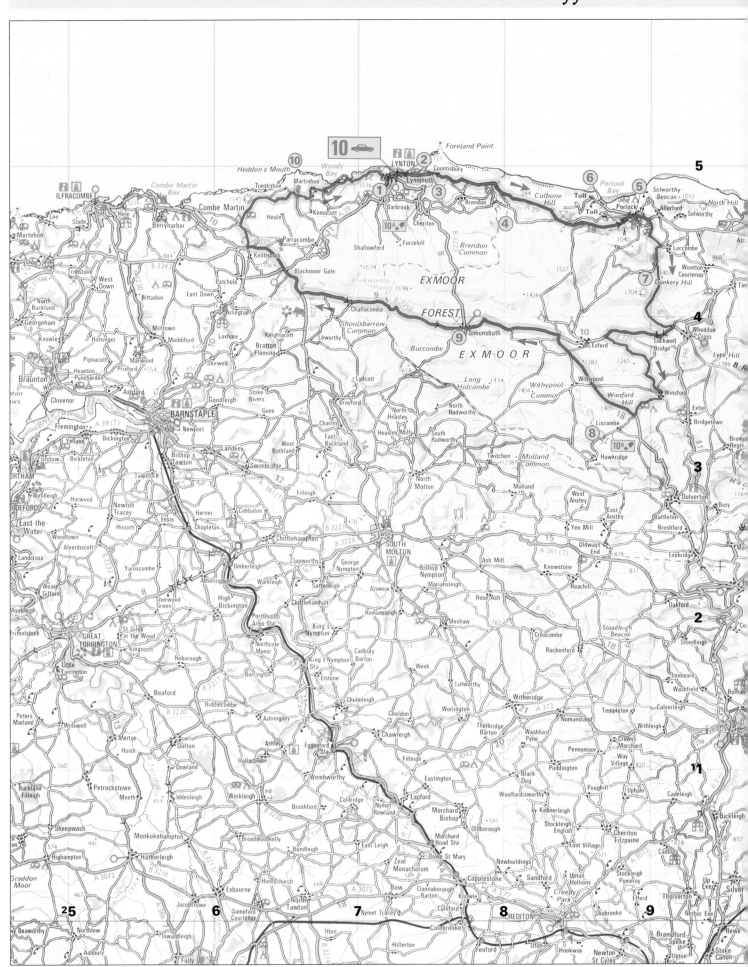

A beautiful, easy walk through oak woodlands in the steep valleys of the East Lyn and the Hoar Oak Water, with fine views of hills and valleys.

POINTS OF INTEREST

① At this point Lynton is visible on its hillside platform towards the sea. This bright, airy town – mainly Victorian – with terraces of small hotels and boarding houses crowns the brow of the great cliff, 600ft high, above its sister town of Lynmouth on the far shore. The two are linked by a zig-zag road and a cliff railway.

② Watersmeet is so named because here the East Lyn river and Hoar Oak Water come together. Watersmeet House is an 1832 fishing lodge now owned by the National Trust and open from April to October as a café, shop and information centre.

③ This valley still carries the scars caused by the great flood disaster of August 1952. About 9in of rain fell on Exmoor in 24 hours, and 90 million tons of water surged down the valleys converging on Lynmouth,

carrying debris, boulders and tree trunks which pounded the town throughout the night. The community was shattered by the terrible event in which 34 people tragically lost their lives.

Two rivers meet: the East Lyn and Hoar Oak Water flow together at the appropriately named Watersmeet, with its pretty 19th-century fishing lodge

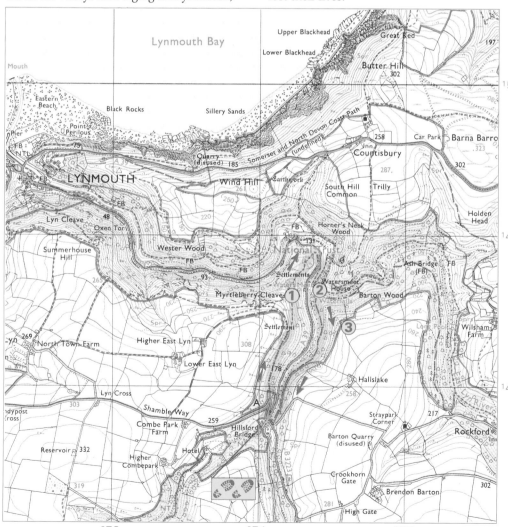

ROUTE DIRECTIONS
Allow 2 hours
Start from Hillsford Bridge car park and picnic site past Combe Park Lodge (grid ref. SS740477).

Walk up the grass verge of the A39 behind the AA box. Where it tapers, head for the National Trust sign ahead. Pass through the gateway and walk up the track.

At a signpost by a seat, take the path marked Watersmeet. It re-enters the woods and goes downhill, reaching open ground again and meeting a path from the left. Turn right here ①.

The path reaches the road, which should be crossed with care to a small lay-by. Steps from here are signposted Watersmeet. Go down and cross two footbridges to Watersmeet House ②.

Return from the house over the first (the East Lyn) footbridge, and opposite the National Trust money box turn steeply up left, signposted Hillsford Bridge, bearing right at the top. (These steep steps do not last long.) After ¼ mile, opposite a seat on the left, it is worth taking a detour along a short path that goes down right to an attractive waterfall ③.

By continuing along up the river-bank path, Hillsford Bridge car park is easily reached.

WALK 10B · *River Bank and Hilltop* DEVON

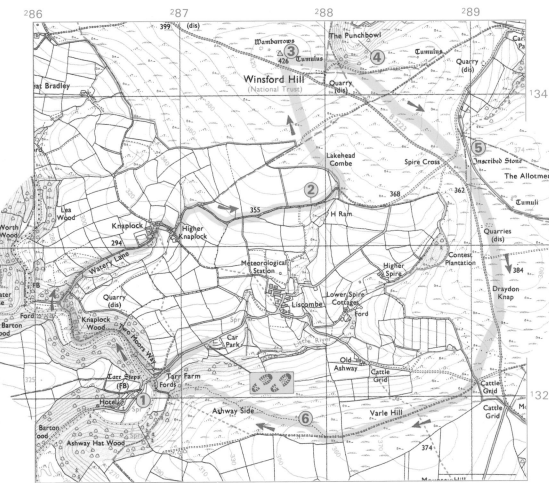

ROUTE DIRECTIONS

Allow 4 hours

Start from the car park to Tarr Steps (grid ref. SS872323) ①.

Walk downhill following the permitted path upstream. It is soon joined by a bridleway, and this should be traced to the point where the first side valley comes in from the right.

Turn up Watery Lane, a rocky track that becomes a muddy lane near Knaplock Farm. Pass both the Knaplock farms and stay on the approach track until reaching the open moor at a cattle grid ②.

At the cattle grid turn left, cross a small stream and make for the top of Winsford Hill, which is out of sight until you are nearly there ③.

Head due east to the rim of the Punchbowl ④.

Keeping a short distance east of the B3223, make for the small building which protects the Caractacus Stone ⑤.

Continue walking south a short distance east of the road, cross it and pass over the cattle grid on the Tarr Steps side road. Now follow the footpath to Tarr Steps ⑥.

At Tarr Steps, walk back up the road to the car park.

A varied walk along the River Barle and over the open moorland of Winsford Hill, best made on a fine, dry and clear day.

POINTS OF INTEREST

① Tarr Steps is a 17-span clapper bridge, 55yds long, dating from medieval times. Over the years it has been damaged several times by floods, so a debris-arrester-cable is now positioned upstream to intercept floating logs.

② The beech hedges on the farm track are noted features of the Exmoor landscape. They were planted as windbreaks by the Knight family who, having acquired 10,000 acres of the moor in the 19th century, set about taming it.

③ There are Bronze Age barrows on the summit of Winsford Hill (1,399ft) and views in every direction. In spring and summer the area is alive with the song of skylarks and meadow pipits, as well as the buzz of insects when the heather is in flower.

④ The Punchbowl is a deep, steep combe in the northern flank of Winsford Hill, where trees have managed to gain a hold.

⑤ So named because of the inscription *Caractaci Nepus*, the Caractacus Stone probably dates from between AD450 and 650 and is thought to be a memorial.

⑥ Ashway Farm, the birthplace of Sir George Williams, the founder of the YMCA, is just out of sight to the south as the path descends to the river.

Visitors make their way over Tarr Steps, Exmoor's famous ancient clapper bridge

ROUTE DIRECTIONS

The drive starts from Bristol①.

From the city centre follow the signs Taunton, The South West, A38②.

After 1¼ miles, follow the signs The South West to cross the impressive Cumberland Basin Swing Bridge then continue with Taunton signs. In 1 mile turn left, one-way, then right and right again, then turn left to the A38. After ¼ mile, at the Cross Hands Public House, branch left, signed Bishopsworth, on to an unclassified road.

Proceed through suburbs and after 1 mile keep forward at a mini-roundabout then shortly branch left. Proceed through Withywood and shortly begin the winding ascent of Dundry Hill. The drive reaches a height of 669ft but the actual summit of 764ft lies away to the right③.

In 1½ miles cross a main road, signed Chew Stoke, and ¾ mile further on turn right on to the B3114, signed West Harptree, and go through Chew Stoke. Beyond the Blue Bowl Inn, at the edge of West Harptree, keep forward on to an unclassified road signed Cheddar. In ½ mile cross the main road and ascend on to the main Mendip ridge. At the crossroads immediately beyond the Wells Way Inn, turn right and in ¼ mile at the next crossroads turn left signed Cheddar to cross high open agricultural land.

In 1¼ miles, at a crossroads, go forward on to the B3371. Continue through open scenery for some distance before descending into a shallow valley and turning right at a T-junction on to the B3135. From here the drive starts the long, winding and at first thickly wooded descent of Cheddar Gorge④.

Enter Cheddar village⑤.

Continue with the Wells road and in ¼ mile at the market cross turn left on to the A371. The drive then proceeds along the foot of the escarpment, with the broad flat Axe Valley to the right. After about 5 miles, at Easton, on the near side of the church, turn left, no sign, on to a narrow unclassified road. Climbing over a low hill the drive reaches the car park and entrance to the spectacular Wookey Hole Caves and Paper Mill⑥.

Continue on the Wells road passing the Wookey Hole Inn and in 1½ miles turn left on to the A371 for the centre of Wells⑦.

Leave the city following signs for Bath A39 and begin a long gradual climb to an 850ft summit on the Mendip scarp. Prominent to the left is the television transmitter on the summit of Pen Hill (1,002ft). Continue across undulating country through Chewton Mendip⑧.

Continue north with the A37 and ¾ mile beyond Farrington Gurney

village turn right to rejoin the A39, signposted Bath. Proceed through Hallatrow then High Littleton and then, 1 mile further, turn right on to the B3114, signposted Timsbury.

Continue through agricultural countryside to pass through the villages of Timsbury and Tunley, then, 1¾ miles beyond Tunley, turn left on to the A367. After a further 1½ miles, at a roundabout, keep forward, signed City Centre, to enter the city of Bath by the Wells Road. At the next roundabout, 1¾ miles further on, take the second exit under a railway bridge and cross the River Avon before turning left to enter the city centre⑨.

Leave Bath following signs Bristol A4 along either the Lower or Upper Bristol roads. In 4¾ miles the drive passes through Saltford. After a further 1¼ miles at a roundabout take the second exit. In 2 miles, at the next roundabout, take the second exit again to pass through the suburbs of Bristol, returning to the city centre along the Bath Road.

POINTS OF INTEREST

①The university and cathedral city of Bristol has a rich maritime and industrial heritage with many fine buildings, museums and galleries. Most notable of its many churches is St Mary Redcliffe, which was described by Elizabeth I as 'the fairest, goodliest and most famous parish church in England'.

②As you skirt the northern side of the Floating Harbour along Hotwell Road there are brief views of Brunel's fully restored SS *Great Britain* to the left. The famous ship was built here and launched by Prince Albert in 1843.

③From the start of the descent of Dundry Hill, there are views ahead to the attractive Chew Valley Lake, a reservoir opened in 1956.

④Cheddar Gorge is a huge natural chasm nearly 500ft in depth at its greatest point. At the mouth of the gorge the drive passes the entrance to the Cheddar Caves with their magnificent stalagmite and stalactite formations. Guided tours of the caves are available.

⑤Apart from the Caves, Cheddar offers all manner of other amusements, souvenir shops and cafés.

⑥Madame Tussaud's own the unusual tourist complex at Wookey

Hole, comprising the prehistoric caves with their weird formations, a 19th-century paper mill, where paper is made by hand, and a fairground collection.

⑦Wells is a charming city (England's smallest) that has retained its medieval atmosphere. The west front of the Cathedral has been described as the finest sculpture gallery in Europe. St Cuthbert's Church, at the west end of the High Street, is the largest

parish church in Somerset and has a magnificent tower.

⑧The church at Chewton Mendip has a 15th-century tower which stands at 126ft, making it one of the highest parish churches in England. You can see Cheddar cheese being made by hand at the Chewton Cheese Dairy.

⑨Bath is a splendid city with its magnificent Georgian buildings, Roman baths and Abbey. The city centre offers a wealth of museums and places to visit, including the Pump Room, Pulteney Bridge and the Assembly Rooms with the Museum of Costume in the basement.

The West Front of Wells Cathedral, adorned with 356 statues set in their own niches

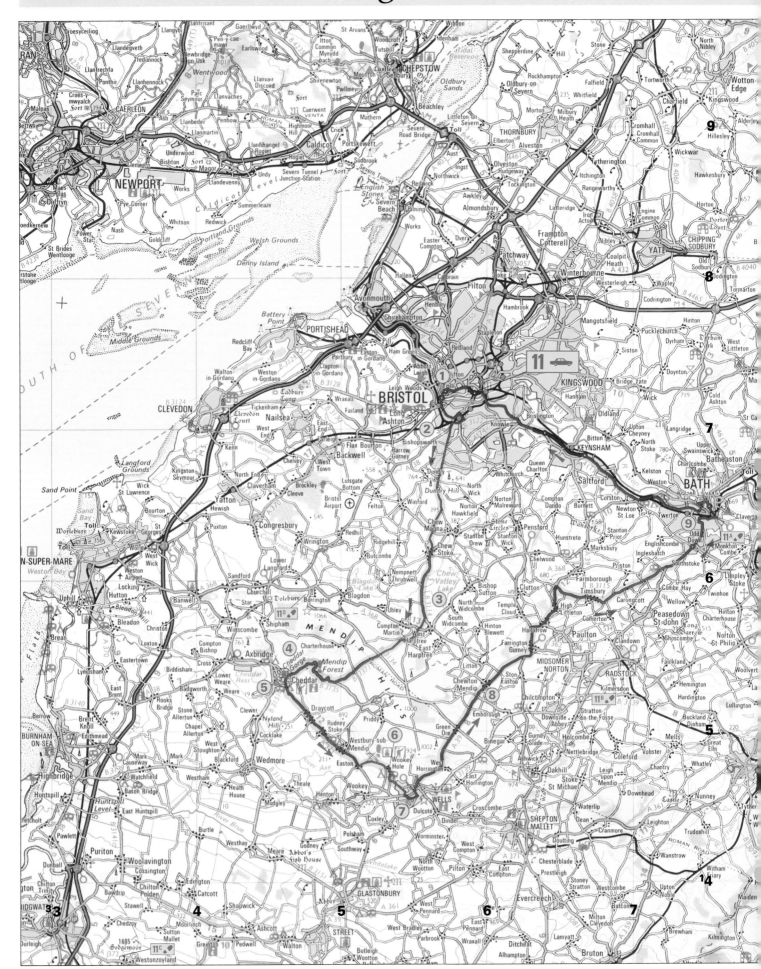

ROUTE DIRECTIONS

Allow 2 hours
Start from the long lay-by a mile south of Claverton on the A36 (grid ref. ST783625).

At the lower end of the lay-by turn left. Walk down the track to the wharf by the canal.

Continue past the wharf to go up and across the higher bridge, then double back on the other side to cross the Dundas Aqueduct①.

Turn left down some earth steps into the field just before the canal sweeps around to the right. Walk along the line of the trees and then down to the river.

Carry on walking across the fields. Ahead, up on the right, is Sheephouse Farm. Continue by the river until you meet the broad track leading to the farm. Follow the track. At the fork near the farmhouse bear left towards a step stile. Go into the farmyard and left out on to the road. Go left at the road and walk down②.

At a house called Hanover Square, follow the public footpath to the right, going steeply up over a field to Warleigh Wood. Cross the stile by a telegraph pole and continue the hard climb up through the wood③.

Cross a stile and turn right down a well-marked footpath. In 10yds go left and up between two trees on another footpath. Climb for 20yds. The path goes right above the top of the wood, then levels out and follows the contour round the side of the hill④.

When the track forks, go right, down and into the wood on the well-defined path. Eventually you come to the edge of the woods. Go over a step stile and on to the road. Go left along the road and up through the wood until you come to a T-junction. Turn right, following the sign to Conkwell.

On reaching Conkwell go right, down the very steep hill. Where the road divides go left by Cromwell's Rest Cottage. The path enters a wood of bluebells and mossy boulders, past a little public footpath notice. When it joins another path at a right angle, you will see a fence directly in front of you. Turn right, and walk downhill keeping the wire fence on your left.

Go over a step stile at the bottom of the wood and out into a field. The metal fence is still on your left. Eventually you pass through some beech trees and then over a step stile to get back to the Dundas Aqueduct. Cross the aqueduct and the bridge over the canal to retrace your steps to the car.

The sweeping curve of the Avon Valley east of Bath carries river and canal side by side between steep, tree-clad slopes. This walk follows the river before climbing to return through Warleigh Wood.

POINTS OF INTEREST

①Built, appropriately, of Bath stone, the splendid Dundas Aqueduct carries the Kennet and Avon Canal across the River Avon. It is one of two aqueducts on the canal, both designed by the architect and engineer John Rennie, who masterminded the construction of the canal, in the late 18th century, to link Bristol with London.

②On this stretch of the walk the weir can be heard and seen on the Avon below. Beyond it is Claverton Pumping Station, where an early 19th-century pump, powered by a waterwheel, still lifts water from the river to the canal, 47ft above. Above Claverton village on the opposite bank can be seen the handsome building of Claverton Manor, which now houses the American Museum.

John Rennie's classical Dundas Aqueduct

③These deciduous woodlands above the Avon are a delight in spring, when primroses, bluebells, ramsons (wild garlic) and wild strawberries carpet the ground.

④The stone wall that runs parallel with the path here marks the county boundary between Avon and Wiltshire. After reaching the road, the walk crosses into Wiltshire before re-crossing into Avon.

WALK 11B · Downside Abbey   SOMERSET

Downside Abbey is the target of this rural ramble. Short sections may be overgrown and muddy and *please take care with children – this walk crosses a main road*.

POINTS OF INTEREST

① To the left of the farmhouse there is a bell tower folly, and behind the house is an outhouse with Corinthian columns.

② Holcombe has two churches, but the one standing alone on the edge of Holcombe Wood is the oldest – as might be expected – and the prettiest. Evidence of its Norman origins is still visible.

③ The village of Stratton-on-the-Fosse has the distinction of having part of the Fosse Way as its main street. Here the A367, the road was built by the Romans to link Lincolnshire with the south coast.

④ Originally from Flanders, the Benedictine monks of Downside (both monastery and school) came here early in the 19th century. The magnificent Abbey Church was designed by Sir Giles Gilbert Scott.

⑤ Chilcompton, with the River Somer flowing through the main part in waterfalls, is a pleasant, sprawly village with a number of old houses dating back two to three hundred years.

Downside Abbey – monastery and school – set in lovely Avon countryside at Stratton-on-the-Fosse

ROUTE DIRECTIONS

Allow 2½ hours
Start from the long lay-by on the B3139 by the 'Chilcompton' sign, approaching from the north (grid ref. ST655519).

From the lay-by, walk up the track towards Tyning House. Near the house go through a metal gate leading into the field and follow the wall round to the right. Go over the stile and straight across the next field to another stile. Walk along the edge of the next field with the hedge to your left. Go carefully out on to the A367, cross over and turn right. After 20yds go left down Manor Farm drive. Walk round to the right of the green and swing right to go behind the farmhouse①.

Climb the stile into the field, and walk down with the hedge on your left. At the end of the garden go left through a kissing gate, through the trees and over another stile. Turn immediately left over another stile and walk along the top of the field, then go down, over the stile at the bottom of the field, and across the footbridge.

Walk up the field edge, keeping the woods to your left. Shortly, go over the stile on your left, into the wood. There is no obvious path through the wood, but bear right round the hill for a few yards into a clearing. Go down to the footbridge at the bottom of the clearing, then take the path up out of the hollow.

Follow the path out of the wood and cross diagonally right to the top of the field. Climb the stile and walk with the wood on your right. Where the wood ends, go across the fence and straight across the field to a gate. Here a detour can be made left to Holcombe church②.

Continue along the track to the road. Go left for 30yds to an iron gate on your right. Cross the first field (or go round it, if sown) to the overgrown gate in the far right corner. Climb the gate and walk straight on to a farmyard. Continue on to the right of the barns to the road. Turn right at the King's Arms on to the main road at Stratton-on-the-Fosse③.

Walk past the entrance to Downside Abbey school on your left and the war memorial on your right. Turn left up Abbey Road to visit Downside Abbey Church④.

Walk back towards Abbey Road but hairpin left on to the right of way. Walk up the field and on to the metalled path which goes back to Chilcompton through three kissing gates. Turn right on to the main road through the village. From here it is about ¾ mile to the car⑤.

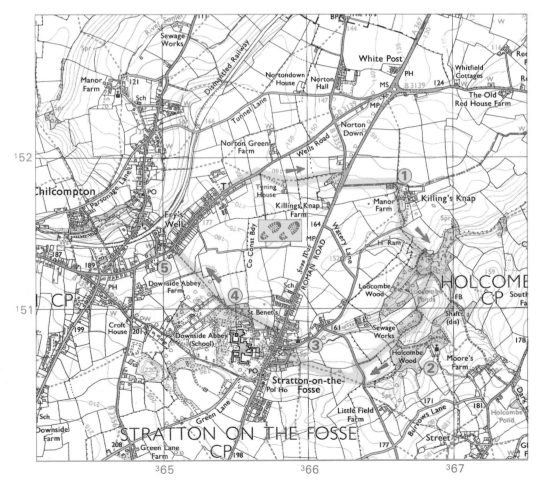

WALK 11C · On Sedgemoor   SOMERSET

ROUTE DIRECTIONS

Allow 2½ hours
Start from the track leading north from the A372 just west of Westonzoyland (grid ref. ST346351). There is space to park about 50yds along the track.

Walk back to the road, turn left and go into the village①.

Turn left down Standards Road and left again into Broadstone. Turn right into Monmouth Road and follow this to Bussex Farm. Follow signs to the battlefield②.

Walk back to the road, cross it and go down Liney Road. At a T-junction turn left down the private road (a right of way for pedestrians). After a short distance go left across the ditch and through a metal gate. Turn immediately right and walk parallel with the road, through a wooden gate and on beside the ditch. Go right at the next metal gate and out on to the road. At a small brick shelter where the road bends right, turn left down the track, keeping the drainage ditch on your left③.

Go through the removable barbed wire fence. Almost immediately go left across the ditch and continue alongside it. At the next hedge go through a metal gate, then left beside a row of trees and another ditch. Go through another metal gate and on until you meet another ditch. Go through yet another metal gate and right on to a well-used track with a largish drainage channel on your left. Cross the fourth bridge and continue to King's Sedgemoor Drain④.

Just before the footbridge turn left and walk with King's Sedgemoor Drain on your right, for about 1½ miles. Continue over Chedzoy New Cut⑤.

After the footbridge the track eventually veers left. It soon branches to the right but you continue straight on alongside Moor Drove Rhyne. Pass under the power cables, then count the drainage ditches coming in on the left. After the fifth drain go left through a metal gate; soon there will be a hedge on your left. Cross the footbridge, go left and then right along the hedge. At the next fence, turn left through a metal gate. At the main track, go right and walk back to your car.

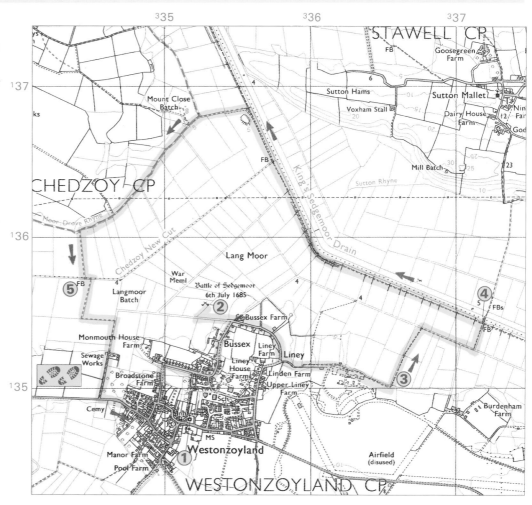

An extraordinary landscape, rich in wildlife, can be seen on this flat walk over the Somerset Levels. Sedgemoor Battlefield is included in the walk.

POINTS OF INTEREST

① Westonzoyland church has a fine Somerset tower that serves as a landmark for miles around. A register inside records the nearby battle.

② Here at Sedgemoor hundreds of Monmouth's followers were killed in the rebellion of 1685 – the last great battle on English soil.

③ A widespread drainage system was first dug in the 13th century and farmers still work together to adjust the water level so that rivers feed the land with rich silt.

④ In late spring and summer, spectacular dragonflies may be seen around the ditches, as well as butterflies and aquatic plants. Birdlife is rich too. In spring and summer there are lapwings, redshanks, kestrels and skylarks.

⑤ At the cut, it can be seen how the sluice has been built into the bridge to contain the flow of water.

Sedgemoor, where the Duke of Monmouth, illegitimate son of Charles II, was executed after his army was cut to pieces by James II's men

WALK 11D · *Mendip Ramble*   SOMERSET

ROUTE DIRECTIONS

Allow 2½ hours
Start from the car park near the public conveniences just south of the Burrington pub off the B3134 (grid ref. ST477588).

Turn right on to the B3134, go past the Burrington pub and the garden centre, then cross with care and turn left up the lane by the postbox. The lane becomes a track. Keep going up, past a house on the right, until you reach a fire-risk notice. Turn left on to the track in front of the notice and follow the broad track you see stretching across heathland①.

After 200yds on the bridle-path you come to a crossroads of tracks. Turn left. Follow this well-trodden path, ignoring a right turn after 20yds and a wider fork to the left. At the next fork, go straight on where one branch of the path swings right uphill and a small path goes left. Follow the well-trodden path, used by horses, down to West Twin Brook. Cross the brook just below a small waterfall, and take the well-trodden path to the left. This takes you up and away from the brook②.

The path levels out and then goes down the steep-sided valley to East Twin Brook③.

Cross the stream-bed and take the well-trodden path, sharp left, out of the valley. Continue with fields to your left and heathland to your right for about ¾ mile④.

Eventually your path bends left as other tracks join from the right, and goes down between fields. Pass Ellick House on your left and reach the B3134. Turn left and walk down the B3134. After 40yds cross with care to the car park on the right. Take the right-most broad track up and away from the road.
Go straight on through a gap in trees and on to a track used by cattle. The track veers left in front of a metal gate. Walk along the track with the hedge and then the wood on your right. At the junction of tracks keep going straight, heading downhill and ignoring two right turns. When you come to a distinct fork where both paths wind downhill and into trees, take the right fork and enter a wood.
Follow this track, which eventually bends sharp right round fir trees. Go down past

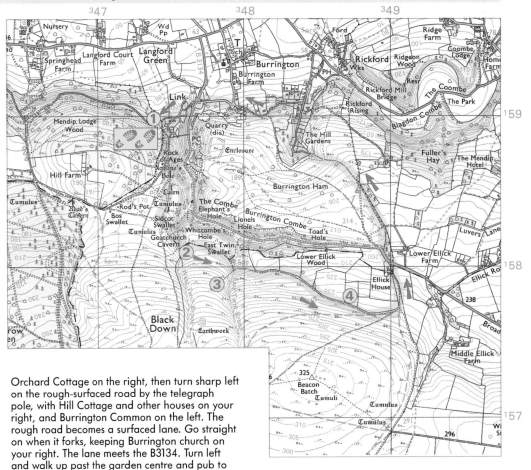

Orchard Cottage on the right, then turn sharp left on the rough-surfaced road by the telegraph pole, with Hill Cottage and other houses on your right, and Burrington Common on the left. The rough road becomes a surfaced lane. Go straight on when it forks, keeping Burrington church on your right. The lane meets the B3134. Turn left and walk up past the garden centre and pub to your car.

An exhilarating, undulating ramble on the Mendip Hills which includes streams and waterfalls. Take care to follow the directions, as the heathland paths can be confusing. This walk should be taken only in fine weather and in strong shoes.

POINTS OF INTEREST

①It was in this part of Burrington Combe that a curate from Blagdon, Augustus Toplady, sheltered during a storm and while waiting composed the well-known hymn *Rock of Ages*.

②On emerging from the valley, the rock face of the cliff above Burrington Combe, running parallel on your left, is visible. Artefacts of Early Stone Age people have been found in the cave called Aveline's Hole, in the combe.

③At East Twin Brook the stream disappears underground into a hole known as a swallet. These are a typical feature of limestone country – as are the area's gullies, potholes and caves – all caused by water percolating through the cracks and fissures of the rock.

④Lowland heaths, with a unique mix of plants, animals and insects, are superb areas for wildlife. Butterflies, damselflies and dragonflies are all much in evidence on a warm summer's day, and the nightjar can often be heard during the evening.

The rock face of the cliff above Burrington Combe, seen running parallel with the walk

ROUTE DIRECTIONS
The drive starts from Weymouth ①.

Follow the Wareham signs to leave by the A353. After skirting the bay, the route turns inland through Overcombe and Preston before ascending on to downland ②.

Shortly, pass the village of Osmington and, after 2¾ miles, at the roundabout, take the third exit on to the A352. In another 3¾ miles, at the Red Lion Hotel, turn right, unclassified, signed Lulworth Cove. In Winfrith Newburgh, at the church, turn left and continue through chalk downland.

If you wish, after 2½ miles you can take the toll road on the right to a car park and the footpath to the arch in the rocks known as Durdle Door.

A descent is made into West Lulworth. Turn right, B3070, to visit Lulworth Cove. Return along the B3070 through West Lulworth. Follow signs to Wool, and ascend towards Lulworth Camp.

From this point a scenic drive is made across the Purbeck Hills to Corfe Castle. This road may be closed by the army if they are using the nearby tank ranges. A large notice-board indicates the situation. Alternative routes are available via the B3070 or B3071, thence A352 and Wareham.

Assuming the road is open, turn right with the B3070, signed Wareham, and in 1½ miles at the edge of East Lulworth turn right, unclassified, signed Whiteway Hill. In ¼ mile branch right, no sign, pass through an army barrier, then climb Whiteway Hill.

This tour takes you over chalk downs to Lulworth Cove and along the Purbeck Hills to Corfe Castle, through some delightful villages and on to Dorchester. A diversion may be made to the Swannery and Sub-tropical gardens at Abbotsbury.

Almost a mile further turn right on to the Church Knowle/Corfe Castle road. In ¾ mile pass the hamlet of Steeple and then the turning, on the right, to Kimmeridge ③.

Continue to Church Knowle, then in 1½ miles turn right on to the A351 and enter Corfe Castle ④.

Return along the A351, signed Wareham. In 2¾ miles, at the roundabout, take the third exit, B3075, for Wareham ⑤.

Follow the signs to Dorchester to leave by the B3070 and A352. In 5 miles turn right, unclassified, signed Bovington Camp. After ½ mile turn left and enter Bovington Camp, home of the Royal Armoured Corps and the Tank Museum.

After 1¾ miles pass the entrance to Clouds Hill ⑥.

At the next T-junction turn left, signed Dorchester, then in ¼ mile turn right, signed Bere Regis. Continue through dense woodland and after ½ mile turn left on to the Briantspuddle road. Pass through Briantspuddle, following the Bere Regis signs. Cross the River Piddle or Trent and in a mile turn left on to the A35, signed Dorchester, to reach Tolpuddle ⑦.

Another 1¼ miles along the A35 is Athelhampton House ⑧.

Continue through Puddletown ⑨.

Later descend Yellowham Hill, passing, on the left, the turning to Higher Bockhampton ⑩.

Continue on the A35 and in 1½ miles at the roundabout turn right, B3150, and enter Dorchester ⑪.

Follow the Bridport signs out of Dorchester. In 1½ miles at a roundabout take the second exit, unclassified, signed Martinstown. In another 1½ miles turn right, B3159, and enter Martinstown. Beyond the village turn left, unclassified, signed Portesham, and climb up on to the downland. There are good views from the monument to Nelson's flag-captain, Admiral Hardy.

In ¾ mile, at the crossroads, turn left, then descend and later bear left to enter Portesham. From here a short detour can be made westwards along the B3157 to the village of Abbotsbury ⑫.

At Portesham the main tour turns left on to the B3157, signed Weymouth. After Chickerell follow town centre signs to return to Weymouth.

POINTS OF INTEREST

① A pleasant seaside town, popular in Georgian times, Weymouth's greatest feature is the Bay with its gently sloping sandy beach.

② To the left is White Horse Hill, 519ft. The mounted figure cut into the chalk commemorates King George III.

③ Near to Kimmeridge village is the Jacobean, Queen Anne and Georgian Smedmore House. It has pretty walled gardens filled with unusual plants and shrubs.

④ Corfe, dominated by the ruins of its Norman castle, is a delightful village with its grey stone slab roofs, mullion windows and picturesque square.

⑤ A charming town, Wareham remains confined within the earth embankments of the 10th-century town walls. St Martin's Church is the only Saxon church in Dorset in anything like its original shape.

⑥ Clouds Hill, now owned by the National Trust, was the home of Lawrence of Arabia before his premature death, and contains his furniture and other relics.

⑦ Tolpuddle is celebrated for its Martyrs and the old sycamore under which they used to meet is still on the village green. There is also a small museum devoted to them.

⑧ Athelhampton is a fine example of 15th-century architecture. Its baronial Great Hall has a spectacular timber roof and its attractive gardens include fountains and waterfalls.

⑨ The 'Wetherby' of Thomas Hardy's novel *Far From The Madding Crowd*, Puddletown's church has a perfect 17th-century interior and some exceptional tombs and effigies.

⑩ The small thatched cottage where Thomas Hardy was born in 1840 can be visited at Higher Bockhampton. It belongs to the National Trust now.

⑪ The county town of Dorset and Hardy's 'Casterbridge', Dorchester is rich in history and fascinating buildings. The County Museum is a must.

⑫ Abbotsbury is a beautiful stone-built village whose Swannery was established by monks in the 14th century. Between 400 and 800 mute swans make their home here in the mating season. West of the village, the Sub-tropical Gardens, started in 1760, have a walled garden which is a mass of azaleas, camellias and rhododendrons.

The River Piddle, manor house and church at Tolpuddle

ROUTE DIRECTIONS

Allow 3 hours
Start from the village hall at Child Okeford (parking nearby), which is on the main road at the north end of the village, going towards Manston (grid ref. ST834130).

Walk back towards the village up the road, and turn left at the war memorial to the church①.

Continue out through the back gate of the church on to a gravel road. Cross a stile over a fence to the right, into a field. Go straight across the field, over another stile, and slightly left across the next meadow to a gate and stile. Keep the hedge near to your right.

At the road, go over the stone stile and immediately left up a deep, rutted track signed 'Bridleway'. Continue up the hill and, at the wood, take a path right into it. At the end of the wood, climb out over the metal bar fence and continue up the hill. The way becomes a track②.

Return to the path. Cross the field to the right and go through a metal gate. Continue by the fence for about 50yds to a low stile (on the right), then go straight down the field with the hedge on your right, through a gate and down between the hedge and fence on to the road. Go left along the road, taking care, for about 200yds③.

Turn right along the road marked No Through Road and Hanford Farm④.

At the crossroads of tracks, turn right. Go across to a signed footpath between houses and gardens. At the end, go over a stile and right on to a gravel track through the gate and wood beyond. Half-way up the track, Little Hanford House is ahead on your left. Turn left through the gate and cross the field below the house, turning right around its grounds and keeping to the top of the field, until you come to a footpath sign by the red brick farmhouse. Turn left, going down and across to a metal gate in the corner of the field. Go left through the gate and immediately right into the lower field, keeping the fence to your right, past two water troughs.

Through the next gateway, walk left around the field to the River Stour and then right along the river to a metal footbridge⑤.

Do not cross the bridge but cut across the field to a metal gate

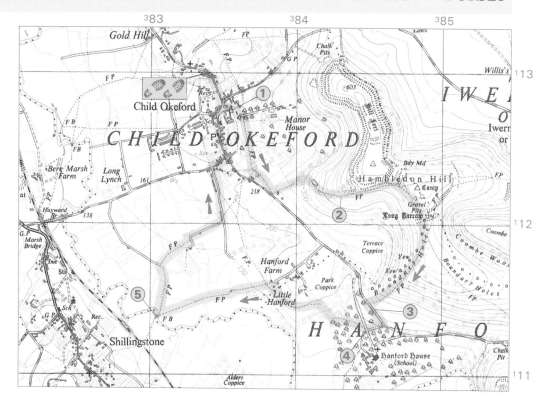

and then go diagonally left, over a stile and into a green lane. Turn left and then right into a field. Go straight across from the gateway to another stile on the far side of the field. Turn left into the green lane. At a T-junction by farm buildings, turn left and go along the lane, past bungalows, to the road. Turn right at the T-junction then left, to walk through the village and back to your car.

A magnificent Iron Age hillfort is the literal high point of this walk, and the climb up to it is steep and strenuous in places. After returning to the Stour Valley, the walk meanders back to Child Okeford across the gentler farmland that borders the river. Some parts of the walk may be muddy.

POINTS OF INTEREST

① The Church of St Nicholas, mostly dating back to the mid 1800s, stands at the upper end of the village beneath the slopes of Hambledon Hill. It has some lovely stained glass, and an old Bible.

② As the path begins to level out, you can clearly see the ramparts of Iron Age Hambledon Hill hillfort to the left. It may be reached by climbing up to the left, and the effort will be rewarded with superb views. Enclosing over 30 acres, the fort has double ramparts most of the way round, with extra defences to the south-east, and is thought to have been built in three phases over a number of centuries.

③ On the skyline ahead a fine yew copse

and the ramparts of Hod Hill can be glimpsed. After conquering the Iron Age fort here, the Romans built their own fort in the north-west corner of the site – and remains of both are clearly visible.

④ Off to the left of this path is the impressive Hanford House, now a school. Dating from the end of the 16th century, the exterior is practically unaltered.

⑤ The River Stour is wide and meandering here, and the bridge makes a pleasant place to pause. Across the river and the railway line is the ancient village of Shillingstone. Its church was begun in Norman times and retains windows and a doorway from these days.

The steeply shelving ramparts of Hambledon Hill

Stone houses cluster round a duck pond in the pretty village of Worth Matravers near Swanage

This walk includes a section of the Dorset coast protected by the Heritage Coast Scheme. There is a steep climb up some steps, with superb views at the top that make the effort worthwhile. *Please take care: the path goes very close to the cliff edge in places.*

POINTS OF INTEREST

①The cottages in the village of Worth Matravers are built of local Purbeck limestone. Much of the church dates from about 1100; it is one of Dorset's oldest.

②On the hills over to the left is a good example of strip lynchets. These are the long terraced banks on the contours of a hill, caused by ploughing.

③Limestone from the South Purbeck Downs, quarried since the 17th century, has been used for kerbs, headstones, flagstones, walls and buildings – notably Salisbury Cathedral which was begun in 1220.

④On reaching the coast there is a magnificent view to the west of the cliffs of the Kimmeridge Ledges. Kimmeridge Bay is overlooked by a folly, Clavell's Tower.

⑤Next to the coastguard station is St Aldhelm's Chapel, about 350ft above sea level. It is a small Norman building, possibly built as a chapel dedicated to St Aldhelm.

⑥At this point the coastal cliffs as far ahead as Durlston Head can be seen. On the right lie the ruins of an old RAF telecommunications station.

ROUTE DIRECTIONS

Allow 2½ hours
Start from the Worth Matravers car park near the Square and Compass pub (grid ref. SY974776).

Turn right out of the car park and walk through Worth Matravers, keeping the duck pond on your left①.

Pass the church and then the children's play area on your right and go out along the road towards a farm silo. The sea can now be seen on your left. Beyond Weston Farm fork left, following the signpost indicating a footpath to St Aldhelm's Head 1½ miles. Soon climb a stile at a signpost indicating Chapman's Pool. Shortly you cross another stile at a signpost to Renscombe ¼ mile. As you walk straight ahead across the field, Renscombe Farm appears on the right. At the track, turn left where the milestone indicates St Aldhelm's Head 1½ miles. You are now walking due south along a wide track towards the sea②.

Turn right on to a track at a sign indicating Pier Bottom and the coast path ½ mile. Shortly after another track joins from the right, turn right, over a stile and into a field. Turn left and walk down into the valley past St Aldhelm's Head Quarry③.

Eventually you arrive at a step stile near the sea④.

Turn left to tackle the steps of the coast path. Pause for a rest and look back at the breathtaking scenery of the Dorset coast. At the top, you will see the mast of the coastguard station. **Care must be taken here: you are very close to the cliff edge⑤.**

Continue along the coast path, heading east⑥.

Follow the coast path sign to Winspit. Eventually the path turns left and inland to skirt an old quarry. Go around the northern edge of the quarry and turn left to walk up into Winspit Bottom. Where the path divides into two, bear right and follow the path through a field, over two stiles and into Worth Matravers. Bear right to return to the car park.

ROUTE DIRECTIONS

The drive starts from Salisbury ①.

Leave on the A354 following signs to Blandford. After 4 miles turn right in Coombe Bissett on to an unclassified road alongside the River Ebble, signed Bishopstone. Then keep left, signed Broad Chalke, to go through Bishopstone and into Broad Chalke ②.

At the Queen's Head Inn turn left, signed Bowerchalke, then in nearly ¼ mile, at the church, turn right and follow the road for 2 miles to Bowerchalke. Continue to follow signs to Sixpenny Handley and in 4½ miles, at the crossroads, turn right on to the B3081, signed Shaftesbury, and enter Sixpenny Handley. Ahead of you is Cranborne Chase. After 4 miles reach Tollard Royal, lying in a hollow on Cranborne Chase ③.

Follow the B3081 across Cranborne Chase and after 4 miles descend the aptly named Zig Zag Hill. After 1 mile, at a T-junction, turn right and in another mile turn left on to the A30, then at the roundabout take the second exit, B3081, signed Town Centre, into Shaftesbury ④.

From the centre follow the signs All Through Traffic and then Gillingham. Shortly, at the T-junction, go left under a road bridge, then right, unclassified, signed Motcombe. At Motcombe bear right, signposted Mere, and later, at a T-junction, turn left. After ¾ mile turn left again at crossroads. After 5 miles enter Mere. In Mere turn left on to the B3095, no sign, and then go straight ahead on the B3092, signed Frome. After 2½ miles turn left, unclassified, to Stourton ⑤.

Return to the B3092 and turn left, then continue to Maiden Bradley. After 2 miles turn right, unclassified, signed Horningsham, Longleat. At Horningsham a detour may be made to Longleat House and Safari Park ⑥.

One mile after Horningsham follow the sign to Shear Water/Longbridge Deverill and after another mile, at the T-junction, turn left, and then take the next left again. The road passes close to Shear Water before you reach Crockerton. At the T-junction turn right, signed Blandford, and at the next T-junction, right again, A350. After 1 mile enter Longbridge Deverill. Five and a half miles after Longbridge Deverill turn left on to the B3089, signed Salisbury. After another 1½ miles reach Hindon. Follow the B3089 to Fonthill Bishop. Continue for 2¼ miles to Chilmark ⑦.

Follow the B3089 for another 1½ miles to Teffont Magna. At the Black Horse Inn, turn right on to an unclassified road, signed Tisbury, and enter Teffont Evias.

Shortly after the church, turn left and left again, signposted Salisbury. After ½ mile, at a T-junction, turn right and rejoin the B3089. After ¾ mile, at a crossroads, turn right, unclassified, signed Fovant ⑧.

In Fovant turn left on to the A30, signed Salisbury, and reach Wilton ⑨.

At the roundabout at the end of Wilton, take the third exit, A36, to return to Salisbury.

POINTS OF INTEREST

① One of England's most attractive cities, Salisbury's cathedral has the tallest spire in the land, and the Cathedral Close, with its rich variety of architectural styles, is the largest in England. The city has a network of medieval streets and a 15th-century Poultry Cross, and is also a fine shopping centre.

② Broad Chalke is an attractive village with thatched cottages, barns and a big 13th-century church.

③ Cranborne Chase, a hunting preserve since Saxon times, is an area of great beauty and rich in flora and fauna. General Pitt-Rivers, the archaeologist, lived near Tollard Royal and is commemorated by a carved urn in the 14th-century church.

④ A hilltop town of Saxon origins, many royal names are linked with Shaftesbury's Abbey, including that of King Canute. Steeply cobbled Gold Hill will be familiar to many as the location of the Hovis advertisement on television.

⑤ At Stourton you may visit Stourhead House, with fine furniture by Thomas Chippendale, and its magnificent gardens, with the famous temples and grottoes (National Trust).

⑥ Longleat is a grand Elizabethan house in a glorious wooded, lakeside setting. The landscaped park was created by Capability Brown in 1757. The Safari Park, famous for its lions, also contains elephants, rhinos, giraffes, zebras and many other animals.

⑦ The village of Chilmark is the home of Chilmark stone, used through the ages in many handsome buildings, notably Salisbury Cathedral.

⑧ On the downs above the village of Fovant are the regimental badges cut into the chalk hillside by World War I soldiers.

⑨ Once an ancient capital of Wessex, Wilton is famous for the beautiful stately home, Wilton House, rebuilt after a fire in 1647 to the designs of Inigo Jones and John Webb, and for the Royal Wilton Carpet Factory in King Street, which is open to visitors.

This tour starts by going through the Ebble Valley villages and across Cranborne Chase to Shaftesbury, and continues via Mere to Stourhead and Longleat. It then crosses Salisbury Plain and returns via Wilton.

This attractive weather-boarded barn stands on the banks of the Ebble beside the road at Coombe Bissett

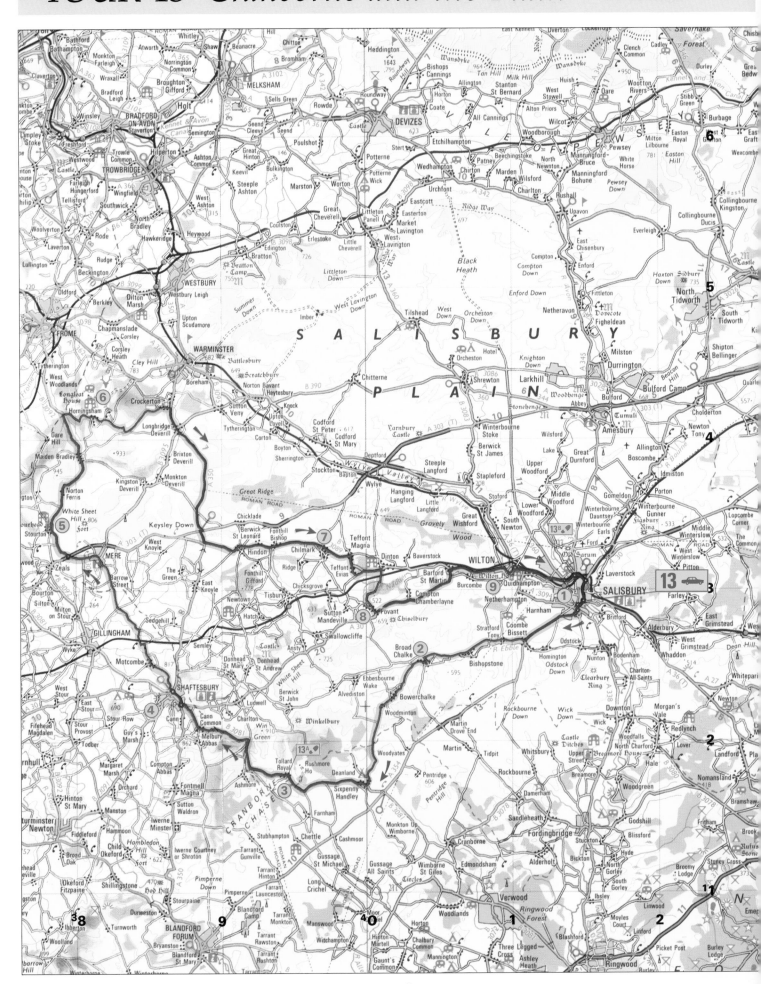

ROUTE DIRECTIONS

Allow 2½ hours
Start from Tollard Royal, where you can park (grid ref. ST944178)①.

Walk south through Tollard Royal past the Grundfos Well. About 50yds past the well go left through a gate and up the track which forks off the road. At the brow, veer left over the hill, keeping the fence on your left.

Go on through a metal gate and down to Tinkley Bottom. Turn right to walk along the bottom of the valley, with Tollard Farm at the top of the hill on your right. Just before the main road, at a junction of tracks, turn left across the adjacent track and go diagonally left up the field following the route marked by a yellow arrow on the gate. Go over a stile at the top left of the field, again arrow marked, and go towards the woods. South Lodge appears to your left. At the edge of the woods, go over the stile across the road and into the wood. Shortly, at a junction of tracks, go right. Keep straight on the footpath②.

Follow the fence as it eventually takes a sharp right turn. When you come to an open field on your left go through the gate with the yellow arrow and follow the path as it veers left. The woods on your left eventually give way to estate buildings. Go on along the edge of the field, through a metal gate and straight ahead on a track, keeping the parkland and then woods to your left – your way leads into a field. Cross the stile, keeping to the left of the field. Through the gate by a cottage, turn immediately left into the woods along the left fork track③.

Continue along the well-defined track and pass Bridmore Lodge on your left. Walk on up to the road at the handsome lodge gate house. Turn right on the road and, within 30yds, left over a stile. Go through the trees to the field edge and turn left.

Walk around the field keeping the trees on your left. Continue on the track down the hill. When the track goes left through the fence, carry straight on, down to the corner of the field, over a stile and on steeply down into the valley.

At the bottom turn left through a gate and continue straight on down. Go through the gate next to Munday's Pond④.

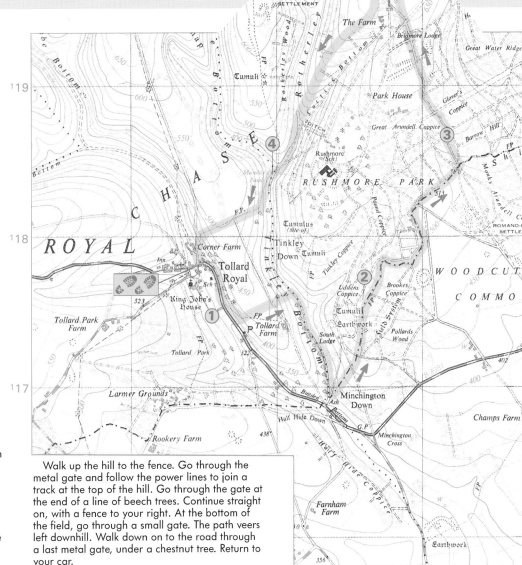

Walk up the hill to the fence. Go through the metal gate and follow the power lines to join a track at the top of the hill. Go through the gate at the end of a line of beech trees. Continue straight on, with a fence to your right. At the bottom of the field, go through a small gate. The path veers left downhill. Walk down on to the road through a last metal gate, under a chestnut tree. Return to your car.

Cranborne Chase, a hunting preserve from Saxon times until the 19th century, is fine walking country. Although much of it is now arable land, there are still lovely tracts of open woodland.

POINTS OF INTEREST

①The handsome medieval King John's House, near the 14th-century church, was a hunting lodge used by King John.

②The fence on your left is the perimeter of Rushmore Park. From 1880 this was the home of General Pitt-Rivers, the archaeological pioneer.

③The names on the map either side of this path show that coppicing (cutting back tree growth to the ground) has been a regular practice here for centuries. Ash, oak and hazel are most usually coppiced, and the wood's uses range from thatching spars to pea sticks.

④Dew ponds (commonly named as such since the early 19th century) such as Munday's Pond were once a familiar feature of chalkland. Invaluable as watering holes for sheep – whether natural depressions or man made – they occurred where moisture collected naturally.

The Grundfos Well in Tollard Royal

ROUTE DIRECTIONS

Allow 1¾ hours
Start from the road at the north end of Lower Woodford (grid ref. SU126353).

Walk south through Lower Woodford keeping to the road and up the hill to the road junction. Little Durnford Manor and Farm are on the left. Go left down the private road and through the well-maintained estate①.

Your route finally emerges through a doorway in the wall on to the road. Go straight over the road and up the lane by the wood (marked as The Avenue on the map). Turn left at the crossroads at the top by an attractive thatched cottage. The road becomes a track②.

The village of Lower Woodford, one of three Woodfords in the beautiful Avon Valley

Go straight up over the ridge to the end of the track③.

The footpath continues through a copse (the path is indicated on a post by a disc). Go through the gate at the opposite edge of the copse and walk across the edge of the field, keeping the fence close to your left. At the end of the field there is a barbed wire gate which can be opened, and closed again, by a wire loop around the post.

Turn left and walk down the track through the farmyard and on to the road. Turn left and almost immediately right down a lane marked with a dead-end sign. The lane develops into a footpath which goes over two footbridges④.

The path comes back on to the road in Lower Woodford, where you left your car.

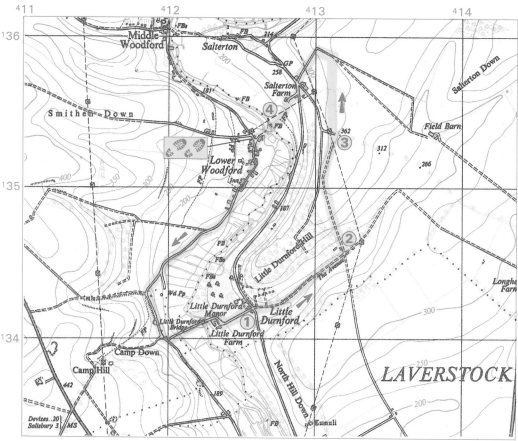

An easy walk past the water meadows and trout-rich waters of the River Avon, with a gentle climb up Little Durnford Hill. Military aircraft will probably be seen, and a variety of other planes from Old Sarum Airfield, home of the Optica spotter plane.

POINTS OF INTEREST

①The walk passes through some beautiful water meadows, once important to Wessex chalkland sheep farming. They were made because, until recent times, March and April were difficult months to ensure that sheep had enough feed. The solution was the creation of a system of trenches and drains, leading off and eventually back into a main river. Controlled flooding protected grass from frost early in the year, without the meadows becoming swamps. The person who harnessed the water was called a 'drowner' and this was a skilled occupation.

Hatches or sluices were used to control the flow of water, and examples can be seen at Lower Woodford and many other places around Salisbury, where the five rivers of South Wiltshire were extensively used to irrigate water meadows.

②Large flints are plentiful on the ground here, and flintwork is characteristic of local houses.

③There are fine views north to Salisbury Plain. The plain, roughly 20 miles from west to east and 12 miles from north to south, stretches from the Vale of Pewsey southwards towards Salisbury, and is fringed by the attractive river valleys of the Avon, the Bourne and the Wylye. To the south can be seen Old Sarum and Salisbury Cathedral spire.

④Here anglers fly-fishing for trout may be seen, as well as swans, water voles and coots.

Water, water everywhere – the bridge at Little Durnford Manor in the water meadows area

High chalk cliffs, sandy bays, bird-haunted mudflats and a windswept coastline all feature on this tour around the Island, which visits pretty villages, seaside resorts, manor houses, Victorian churches and lighthouses.

POINTS OF INTEREST

① Newport, the Island's 'capital', is an old market town with narrow streets, wide squares and hidden riverside quays.

② Situated at the mouth of the River Medina, Cowes is best known as Britain's yachting capital. Of interest is the Maritime Museum at the public library.

③ With its stone quays and old harbour, Yarmouth is a picturesque town as well as being a busy ferry terminal and popular boating centre.

④ The Needles Pleasure Park is at Alum Bay, where facilities include a chair lift to view the fascinating multicoloured sand cliffs and famous detached chalk stacks – The Needles – and their lighthouse. The Needles Old Battery, a 19th-century fort, is also of interest.

⑤ Tennyson Down is so called because the poet walked the cliff-top path – one of the most attractive on the Island. Tennyson's former home, Farringford House (now a hotel), stands to the right of the road just to the west of Freshwater Bay.

⑥ Compton Bay has an excellent sandy beach, and the beautiful cliff-top road offers fine views out to sea, with the rolling slopes of Compton Down to the left.

⑦ Blackgang Chine is a spectacular cleft in the cliff face, once used by the 'Black Gang' smugglers. A Fantasy Theme Park has been established here and adjacent to it is the Blackgang Sawmill and St Catherine's Quay.

⑧ Ventnor is given a somewhat Continental appearance by the terraces on which it is built. They zig-zag down to the sea on the slope of St Boniface Down (National Trust). At 785ft, this is the Island's highest point.

⑨ The 'old village' of Shanklin has thatched cottages and one of the prettiest inns on the Island, The Crab. Shanklin Chine is a natural gorge of great scenic beauty.

⑩ Sandown has an extensive sandy beach and its many attractions include the Isle of Wight Zoo and a local geology museum in the public library.

⑪ For hundreds of years a rough fishing hamlet, Bembridge was turned by the Victorians into a fashionable resort. A large village still remains though, with a street of shops, a spacious church and a fine maritime museum. Bembridge Windmill, built around 1700, is the only windmill to survive on the Island.

⑫ Flamingo Park slopes down to the old salterns and visitors can wander among many kinds of waterfowl and visit the flamingos and tropical house.

⑬ The largest resort on the Island, Ryde is also one of the busiest points of entry. There is a fine beach and excellent views of the Solent.

⑭ The church at Whippingham, with its fairytale tower, was designed by Prince Albert in 1861 for the use of Queen Victoria and her family when they stayed at Osborne House.

⑮ Built in the 19th century in the style of an Italian Renaissance villa, Osborne was for some time the home of Queen Victoria and was where she died.

ROUTE DIRECTIONS

The drive starts from Newport, but it is not difficult to join the tour at any location en route ①.

From Newport follow signs to Cowes to leave by the A3020. In ¾ mile, at the roundabout, go forward.
    Two miles further, at Northwood,

Freshwater Bay. The cliffs offer splendid walks in both directions and from the bay there are walks through the marshes to Freshwater town

branch left on to the B3325 then in ½ mile bear right. After another ¾ mile there is a mini-roundabout. A detour to the right may be taken to visit the town centre of Cowes②.

The main tour turns left on to an unclassified road, no sign. In ¼ mile go over the crossroads and descend Church Road, then shortly turn right into Lower Church Road. At the next T-junction turn left, signed Yarmouth, and pass Gurnard Bay. In 1¼ miles, turn right at the T-junction, then bear right. In another 1½ miles bear right again and proceed to Porchfield. Continue through wooded countryside and after ½ mile bear right. In just over another ½ mile turn right, signed Newtown. One mile further is the 18th-century Old Town Hall (National Trust).

Continue past an inlet of the Newtown River and, at the T-junction, turn right, signed Yarmouth. In ¾ mile, at the next T-junction, turn right again on to the A3054 and enter Shalfleet. Later there are good coastal views before reaching Yarmouth③.

Follow signs to Freshwater and cross the Yar Bridge. Half a mile further a turning on the right leads to the Fort Victoria Country Park.

Remain on the A3054 and in almost ½ mile bear right, signed Totland. After another ½ mile, on the left, is the road to Golden Hill Fort.

Continue through Colwell Bay and shortly go forward to the Alum Bay road, B3322, to enter the small resort of Totland. At a roundabout keep forward and proceed to Alum Bay④.

From the Royal Needles Hotel return along the same road. In nearly ½ mile pass the Museum of Clocks then branch right, unclassified, signed Freshwater Bay, with 6ft width restriction. In another ½ mile, at the High Down Inn, bear right then turn left. To the right is Tennyson Down (National Trust)⑤.

Continue to Freshwater Bay. Bear right to join the A3055, no sign, and climb to skirt Compton Bay⑥.

The drive passes the car parks for Compton, Hanover and Brook Chines before skirting Brook Bay and the village of Brook. Continue along the coast road for 7 miles, signed Ventnor, to reach Chale. Half a mile beyond the village, at the roundabout, take the second exit for Blackgang⑦.

Return to the roundabout and turn right with the A3055, signed Ventnor, then pass beneath St Catherine's Hill, 773ft.

At Niton keep left (one-way) then turn right. Half a mile further a turning to the right leads to St

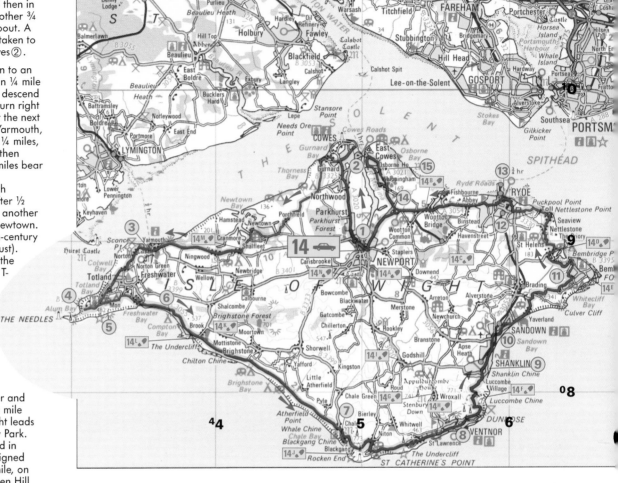

Catherine's Lighthouse, situated 136ft above the sea.

Continue along the picturesque, thickly wooded Undercliff, with steep cliffs rising to the left, and pass through St Lawrence. In Old Park, near by, there is a tropical bird park.

Continue for 1 mile. Here you pass the entrance to the Ventnor Botanic Gardens, with the Museum of Smuggling History.

Proceed into the town centre of Ventnor⑧.

Leave by following the Shanklin signs to remain on the A3055. A winding ascent (1 in 8) is then made. This passes beneath St Boniface Down.

Later descend (1 in 10). Here you reach the resort of Shanklin⑨.

Follow the main road through the town to the residential district of Lake. Here pass the Stag Inn and in ¼ mile bear right at the war memorial. Pass beneath the railway and in just over ½ mile turn right into Station Avenue, signed Town Centre, to enter Sandown⑩.

Follow the Bembridge signs to leave by the seafront, B3395. In 1¼ miles pass 12th-century Yaverland church, and at the T-junction turn right. After another ¼ mile a detour to the right is available via Bembridge Down (Napoleonic Fort

and AA Viewpoint) to reach Culver Down.

The main drive continues along the B3395 and in 1¼ miles passes Bembridge Airport. Bear left and almost a mile further, at the mini-roundabout, turn left on to an unclassified road. Shortly on the left is the footpath to Bembridge Windmill. Enter the village of Bembridge⑪.

From the one-way system, follow the Ryde signs, B3395, and skirt Bembridge Harbour. At St Helens turn right at the T-junction, B3330, signed Nettlestone. In just over ¼ mile turn left, signed Ryde, and continue to Nettlestone. Here branch right on to the B3340, signed Seaview, and almost ¼ mile further branch right again with an unclassified road, signed Sea Front. The coast is reached again at Seaview. Descend the High Street and follow the Esplanade, then keep forward into Bluett Avenue. At the T-junction turn right then keep left along the shoreline. From here there are fine views over Spithead to Portsmouth.

Shortly, pass through a tollgate, passing on the left Oakhill Road. This road leads to Flamingo Park waterfowl and water gardens⑫.

Continue along the coast road, then veer inland and ½ mile further

turn right on to the B3330. Shortly, turn right again with the A3055. Later join the Esplanade to enter Ryde⑬.

Follow signs to Newport to leave by the A3054. After 1½ miles pass through Binstead then in 1¼ miles pass, on the right, the turning to the Fishbourne car ferry. Shortly, enter Wootton Bridge, which stands at the head of a creek, and in 1½ miles, at the roundabout, turn right on to the A3021, signed East Cowes. One mile further turn left on to an unclassified road, signed Whippingham church. In ½ mile the road passes the church⑭.

Continue for almost a mile and at a T-junction turn left into Victoria Grove. Join Adelaide Grove and at the end turn left again, A3021, into East Cowes, the busy car ferry terminal which connects with Southampton.

Follow signs to Newport, A3054, to leave by the A3021. On the southern outskirts of the town is the entrance to Osborne House, on the left⑮.

Remain on the A3021 and ½ mile further pass the turning to Barton Manor Vineyard and Gardens, on the left. In 1½ miles, at the roundabout, take the second exit, A3054, and return to Newport.

Watch out for the Arreton Manor ghost!

There is something for everyone on this walk: two manor houses and a craft village to visit, an ancient church, a bracing stretch of downland, and a tucked-away valley to discover near the end of the walk. Most of the route is on tracks and footpaths, parts of which may be muddy in wet weather.

POINTS OF INTEREST

① The stout 14th-century tower of St George's Church hides what is probably the Isle of Wight's oldest church doorway, dating from Saxon times. Treasures inside the surprisingly light and airy building include a brass commemorating a soldier who fought at Agincourt in 1415.

② Originally a farmhouse built by the Cistercian monks of Quarr Abbey, Arreton Manor was largely rebuilt in the early 17th century. Now open to the public in summer, it houses a folk museum which includes a collection of old wirelesses. Nearby is the Arreton Country Craft Village, where craftsmen can be watched making items ranging from jewellery to dolls' houses.

③ Arreton Down commands stunning views southwards over the fertile farmland of the Vale of Arreton. All kinds of vegetables are available in season here on 'pick-your-own' farms.

④ Shepherd's Lane is the old drive leading to Haseley Manor. This historic house – dating partly from Norman times – has been rescued from dereliction and restored by its present owners. Once the home of Lord Fleming, the judge who tried Guy Fawkes, it is now open to the public. There is a pottery studio, offering regular demonstrations, and a restaurant.

⑤ In early summer the damp valley bottom here glows with the blooms of the marsh-loving yellow iris.

ROUTE DIRECTIONS

Allow 2 hours (excluding visits to the manors) Start at the White Lion pub (grid ref. SZ534867; parking is available on the verge opposite).

Cross the road and proceed to the church behind the pub①.

Follow footpath A12, signposted to the Downs. After the farm buildings, keep the fence on your right, passing the rear entrance to Arreton Manor②.

Continue uphill and near the top of the field branch right up some steps and over a stile. Continue diagonally across the hillside, passing the electricity pole on your right. Pass close to the south-east corner of the quarry fence then continue on the same diagonal route, aiming for a tall electricity pole behind the roadside hedge on the skyline③.

Strike the road by signpost A11, turn right, and follow the roadside fence for 270yds. Branch right down bridleway A17, signposted to Haseley Manor (do not continue along the roadside path).

Follow the sunken lane diagonally downhill, bend round to the left, and descend to the metal gate on your right (if this part of the route is muddy, follow the left-hand bank). Turn right through the gateway marked by the blue arrow, and follow the dead straight Shepherd's Lane to Haseley Manor④.

Turn right at the Manor gates and follow the access road until you reach the main road. Cross over and follow the footpath diagonally opposite by Arbutus Cottage.

Enter the field behind the houses and go straight across to the stile on the far side, then continue along the edge of the next field as waymarked, with the fence on your right. After 80yds, where another path joins from the right, fork left and follow the trodden path gently downhill through the marshy field.

Cross the second ditch on the concrete bridge, then bear right uphill to a gate. Pass through and follow the blue arrow along the broad grassy track with a bank on your left and a valley on your right⑤.

Pass through the next gate and continue along the bridleway with the copse on your right.

Turn right 190yds past the end of the copse, where there is a gap in the bank, and walk down across the field to the stream on the far side. Cross the stream on the culvert and go straight up the steep hill to the stile at the top. Cross the wide open field by following the right of way (straight ahead, and usually well trodden) indicated by the HT waymark. Strike the road by the community centre, cross over, and turn left back to the White Lion.

ROUTE DIRECTIONS

Allow 2¾ hours
Start from the car park in Brannon Way (grid ref. SZ544919).

Walk down High Street, turning right at the bottom into Lakeside Holiday Centre①.

Inside the entrance, fork right on a good gravel track through woodlands and fields to the railway crossing. Cross over and go through the yard of Woodhouse Farm, continuing to the T-junction.

Turn left to Great Briddlesford, passing round the pond and through the gate on to the enclosed track, which you follow to the road. Turn left and follow the road, passing under the railway arch and, shortly after, the bridge over Blackbridge Brook②.

Shortly after crossing the brook take the track to the right just before the garage (footpath R8), and follow it to the end. Continue over the stile, along the edge of the field to the twin stiles, and after a short distance turn left over another stile to the road ahead. Continue, turning right at the next two T-junctions.

Shortly after Havenstreet Post Office, at the right-hand bend, continue straight ahead to the stile and hill, keeping to the right of the war memorial on the summit③.

Maintain this direction over the stile and down a long field to a further stile, crossing the narrow meadow and going through the gate to Newnham Farm ahead. Follow the concrete track to the road, and at the bend take the stile on the left.

On footpath R4 cross the field as indicated, keeping left of the largest and nearest oak, and enter the wood by the bridge, bearing right through the wood to the stile and field. Pass along the left side of the field to the road and cross to the track opposite. (Beware of fast-moving traffic.) Follow to the T-junction and turn left④.

Pass over the crossing and maintain this direction to the road where you turn left into Fishbourne⑤.

At the telephone box on the right take the footpath R1 to the T-junction and turn left along the private road to the bend.

Continue ahead, descending to the concrete bridge over the brook, and climb to the main road. Turn right to Wootton Bridge and on to the car park.

The upper reaches of Wootton Creek on the Solent shore are fed by a brook running from the central downland ridge. This walk runs parallel with the west side of the creek and returns via a monastery. Stout footwear is advisable.

POINTS OF INTEREST

① The part of Wootton Creek above the bridge is known as the Old Mill Pond. Here fields and copses slope down to the water's edge – a peaceful contrast with the tidal part of the creek, busy with boatyards and small craft.

② On the left above the railway arch is the Isle of Wight Railway Centre at Havenstreet station, now a mecca for steam enthusiasts. A section of the Newport-to-Ryde railway has been reopened, and volunteers have restored the station, rolling-stock and locomotives, including the *Calbourne*, the last engine to go out of service. The privately owned railway now offers trips to Wootton and back at weekends in summer.

③ Enclosed by a low stone wall, Havenstreet's unusual war memorial houses an altar and inscribed slate tablets. The hill on which it stands, though only 200ft high, commands fine views.

Once the centre of life in Binstead, the old Quarr Abbey was dissolved by Henry VIII

④ The old and new Cistercian abbeys of Quarr can be seen at this point. A little to the west are the striking 20th-century buildings that house the community today.

⑤ Fishbourne is perhaps best known as the terminal for the Portsmouth car ferry. Boats have sailed between here and the mainland for centuries: at one time fares were doubled in bad weather.

Maize – a main crop locally

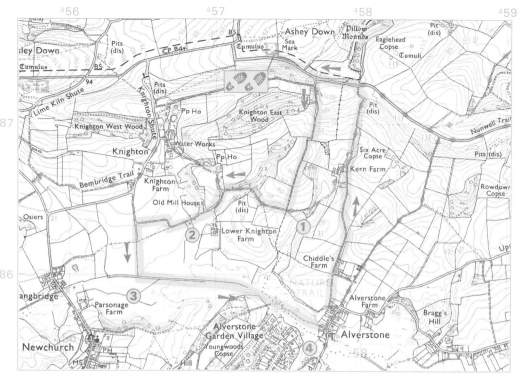

ROUTE DIRECTIONS

Allow 2 hours
Start from the car park below Ashey Down (grid ref. SZ574874).

Cross the road from the car park and turn left along the roadside path to the bridleway sign. Turn right through the metal gate and continue straight ahead down the bridleway, ignoring NC4 on your right. In just over ½ mile you reach a T-junction with another track①.

Turn right along the track and keep to the right, passing the entrance to the sandpit on your right. Follow the sandy path past the plantation and at the next junction fork left towards Newchurch. When the track joins the road turn slightly right and follow it over a little bridge②.

Continue along the road and, 160yds past the dog-leg, turn left down the bridleway signposted to Alverstone. When it joins the old railway track turn left again towards Alverstone③.

Pass the black iron bridge, and in 220yds branch left over the stile and follow the riverside path to the old Alverstone Mill④.

Turn left up the road and after 160yds turn left along the footpath by the old school. Turn right after the last house, up the path with a garden on your right. Go through a metal gate and, keeping the fence on your left, follow the edge of the field to join the road by a stone barn.

Continue ahead up the road towards the Downs. Near the bungalow go straight ahead by the bridleway signposted to Ashey Down. Pass Kern Farm on your left, go through the metal gate, and continue ahead towards the Downs along the farm track.

At the top of the Downs go through the gate and turn immediately left along the Downland Way path, parallel to the road, and follow this back to the car park.

Though quite close to the busy resort of Sandown, this walk offers a complete contrast. The peaceful valley of the River Yar (one of two rivers on the Island to share the name) is rich in wild flowers and birdlife. The walking is gentle, but stout shoes are needed as parts of the route may be muddy after rain.

POINTS OF INTEREST

①The valley below the track here has been inhabited since prehistoric times, as frequent finds of stone tools prove. It was also an important settlement in medieval days, and the field below the junction is still called 'vineyard' by local people – a verbal record of a long-forgotten use. The valley is now one of Britain's major producers of sweetcorn and garlic.

②Lower Knighton Farm, to the left, has an 18th-century weather-boarded granary supported by staddle stones. These stones, which look like toadstools, kept vermin and damp from reaching the grain.

③The railway was the Sandown-to-Newport line, which closed in 1956. The Island once had 56 miles of railway, but in the 1950s they were cut by more than half as trade was lost to the more convenient bus services. Further closures in the 1960s left only the stretch from Ryde to Shanklin open.

④Valued in *Domesday Book* at 40 pence, Alverstone Mill continued to grind corn until 1950. The building is now part of a private house.

Alverstone is famous locally for its wild flowers, which are especially lush along the river banks

ROUTE DIRECTIONS

Allow 3 hours
Start from the National Trust car park at The Duver (grid ref. SZ637892).

Leave by the interpretation board. Cross the road and, keeping to the right of the bushes, follow the track to the old Mill Dam①.

Cross the Dam and turn right up Mill Road to St Helens Green②.

Turn left along Lower Green Road, bearing right across the green to the Vine Inn. Take the concrete path by the inn, and go through a small housing development, bearing slightly right by the school playing-field to the main road.

Turn left, and at the right-hand bend continue ahead on the track signed R63. Follow this for ½ mile to a downhill right bend and leave the track to continue ahead through the gateway.

Follow the obvious track to the far side of the field and the junction with a signpost. Turn right along the track B12 to Park Farm. Go through the yard, keeping the house on your left, to the access drive. 100yds beyond the sign R62, take the track right (R61).

Follow this to the end and continue along the field edge. Pass through a small gate and cross the paddock to the far right-hand corner and two gates to the private drive. Continue to the road and turn left to the Wishing Well pub. Take the track in front of the pub (R59), which reaches the road at Flamingo Park③.

Turn right and descend to the sea-front, and right again along the toll road. As the road turns right into Salterns Road, continue ahead along the sea-wall to the road. Turn left along Seaview Esplanade, enter High Street and take the third left (Pier Road)④.

Fork right opposite the last house on the seaward side, and follow the road to its end, continuing to Seagrove Bay.

Turn right along Fernclose Road (signed R74) and the track beyond. At the far end, turn left along a track and then right over a private drive, past the Holiday Centre entrance. Go through the kissing gate on your left (R85) to the footbridge and stile at the bottom of the meadow. Turn left along the side of the field to a stile in the far left corner. Cross into Duver Road and follow this back to the car park⑤.

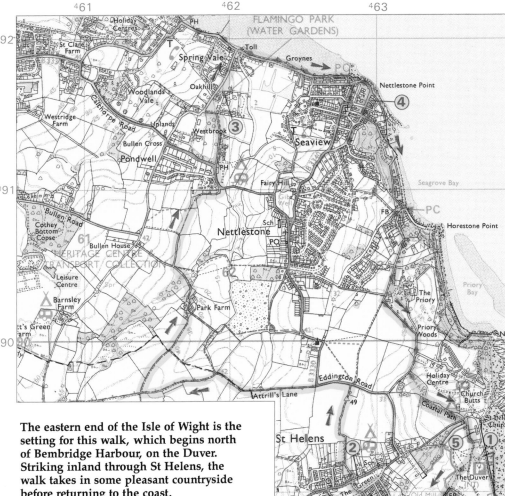

The eastern end of the Isle of Wight is the setting for this walk, which begins north of Bembridge Harbour, on the Duver. Striking inland through St Helens, the walk takes in some pleasant countryside before returning to the coast.

POINTS OF INTEREST

①More than 250 different species of plant grow on the broad expanse of grass and dunes known as The Duver. This was the site of the Royal Isle of Wight Golf Club from 1882 until 1961, when this very special strip of coast passed to the National Trust.

②Surrounded by a pleasing jumble of houses, the nine-acre Green was once the centre of village life in St Helens, grazed by flocks of geese and the site of nine wells. Today it offers cricket and football pitches, a children's playground and seats.

③Peacocks, flamingos, macaws and many varieties of geese and ducks can all be seen at close quarters at the Flamingo Park bird sanctuary.

④Seaview's pier, where steamers from the mainland once tied up, disappeared in a storm in 1951, but visitors come today for the sailing and windsurfing as well as the fine seaside walks.

⑤The remains of 12th-century St Helen's Church can be seen on a short detour to the beach. The rest of the ancient building was washed into the sea in 1703.

Flamingo Park, Seaview's bird sanctuary

ROUTE DIRECTIONS

Allow 2½ hours (longer if you are visiting the windmill which is open in summer only)
Start outside the Royal Spithead Hotel (grid ref. SZ642887).

Go up the gravel road opposite the Pilot Boat Inn, signposted Coastal Path BB33 Foreland, and at the junction with the unmade road turn left towards the sea, then right along footpath BB6, signposted to Foreland①.

Follow the wooded track past the Sailing Club start hut; then the path joins the top of the shingle bank. Follow the shingle bank, then the sea wall as far as the Lifeboat Station②.

Leaving the Lifeboat Station car park, walk along the seaward edge of the green, turn right, passing the entrance to the Chalet Hotel, and follow the footpath between fences.

Turn left along the gravel road signposted Coastal Path, turn right at Forelands Farm, passing Paddock Drive, turn left along Beachfield Road (signposted Coastal Path) and at the end turn right, past the Coastguard Lookout to the Crab and Lobster. Walk across the pub car park towards the sea and at the top of the steps turn right along the footpath following the top of the coastal slope.

Cross the gravel car park and follow the coast path for ¾ mile past open fields and through woodland until you emerge on to Bembridge School playing-fields. Continue to the far end of the playing-field and at this point, near the buildings, leave the coast path by turning right along the public footpath with the flat-roofed building on your left.

Join the school drive, then leave it by branching left by the 'Private' sign and follow the footpath through the trees to the road. Turn left down the hill and after 110yds turn right along the footpath by the camping site, passing into a wood. Cross the road and follow the footpath opposite through the wood. At the junction with the bridleway turn right up the hill to the windmill③.

Continue ahead down the High Street then turn left opposite The Courtyard public house down the path signposted to Bembridge Point. Turn right at the bottom of the hill and follow the path through the woodland④.

Join the unmade road and follow it back to the car park.

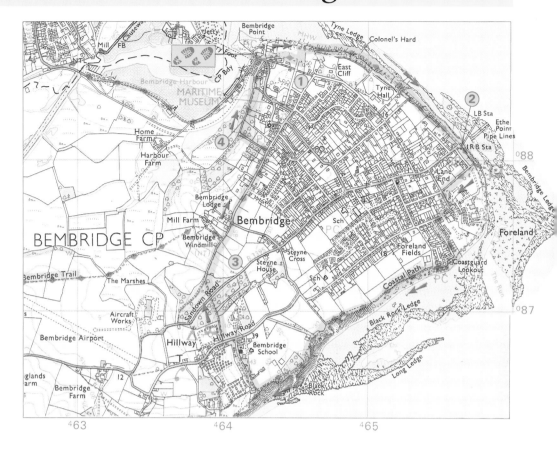

Plenty of sea air, and a visit to the Isle of Wight's only remaining windmill, are the highlights of this easy walk at the Island's eastern tip. Though the route encircles Bembridge and is never far from a built-up area, some of the walking is through woodland.

POINTS OF INTEREST

① A well near the shore here was much used by the Navy in earlier centuries because of its remarkable properties. Ships would anchor offshore to replenish their water supplies from it, for the water was said to keep fresh throughout a voyage round the world.

② Bembridge Ledge has always been treacherous to shipping, claiming hundreds of lives over the centuries. A lifeboat has been stationed here since 1867. Today the lifeboat station, on its long jetty, is sometimes open to the public.

③ At one time Bembridge Windmill, probably built around 1700, was one of seven windmills on the Island. Now it is the only one. Renovated in 1957, it has kept much of its original wooden machinery. The mill is in the care of the National Trust and is open in summer.

④ This path follows part of the old harbour wall. At one time Bembridge Harbour reached inland as far as Brading, but a large area was reclaimed as meadowland about 100 years ago. The history of the harbour is illustrated in Bembridge Maritime Museum.

Bembridge Windmill. Last used in 1913, it is now one of the Island's showpieces

Allow plenty of time to appreciate the splendid scenery on this short but enchanting walk in an unspoilt part of the Island's popular south-east coast. Energetic walkers can add to the route by making the steep descent through Luccombe Chine to the beach.

POINTS OF INTEREST

① The Devil's Chimney, a deep, narrow gap in the cliff, was probably cut at the time of the great landslip. A huge mass of land collapsed towards the sea, forming the Undercliff towards which the steps descend.

② The huge ivy-clad boulders to the left of the path plunged from the sandstone cliff during the landslip. One of them, a little further on, is marked 'Wishing Seat'. Here generations of children have sat and made a wish. To the right are some particularly ancient oak trees twisted into fantastic shapes. One of them has grown out of a cleft in a huge boulder and its roots now engulf the rock; others have ferns growing from their gnarled branches.

③ Fishermen and their families lived in five cottages at the foot of the Chine until less than a century ago, when they had to move out because of the risk of further landslides. The Chine was undoubtedly a smugglers' route, and the rocks to the north are called Johnny New, after a man who used to sink his contraband there.

④ Hydrangeas used to be grown commercially near Luccombe. The moist, mild climate and sheltered aspect proved ideal for this unusual crop, and 'escaped' hydrangeas are still to be seen growing wild in the area.

The Landslip; its windswept sea edge (below) and its famous Wishing Seat (above)

ROUTE DIRECTIONS

Allow 1¼ hours, or 1¾ hours including the Luccombe Chine detour
Start from Nansen Hill (the Landslip) car park by the picnic site (grid ref. SZ581789).

Enter the grounds of Smugglers' Haven tea gardens, pass across the lawn in front of the café, then turn left down the steps by the shelter. Turn right and follow the winding path with the stone wall on your left. Descend the Devil's Chimney steps through a cleft in the rock ①.

Continue down the steps through the trees. Half-way down ignore the side paths and continue down the steps to the shelter in the Lower Landslip. Turn left along the footpath signposted to Luccombe and Shanklin ②.

At the far end of the Landslip, by Loafer's Glory, continue straight on to Dunnose Cottage. About 110yds past the cottage turn left at the narrow road. (At this point you may turn right down Luccombe Chine to the beach, then return to the same spot.) ③

About 55yds up the road branch right over the stile by the National Trust sign, and walk up across the field towards the little red-roofed barn of Luccombe Farm ④.

Cross the stile to the left of the barn, turn left, and follow the track with the hedge on your left until you reach the narrow road by the white-painted Luccombe Farm Cottages. Go straight across and follow the steep footpath to the right of the cottages, signposted to Bonchurch, and climb the steps back to the main road. Turn left and return to the car park.

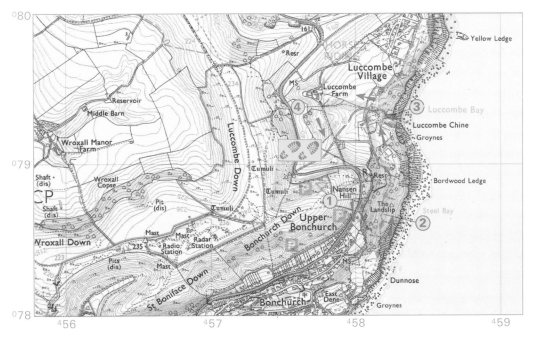

Beginning and ending in Wroxall, a village set in a lovely green fold of the Downs, this circuit follows some of the many footpaths that criss-cross the hillsides in this area. Views across the Island and out to sea are magnificent, so choose a clear day if you can.

POINTS OF INTEREST

① The old farming hamlet of Wroxall was transformed by the coming of the railway. Many of the cottages in the main street were built for workmen building the nearby 1,300yd tunnel – constructed in the 1860s at the insistence of Lord Yarborough of nearby Appuldurcombe, who did not want the railway spoiling his land. Stone from the tunnel was used to build Wroxall church, with its distinctive conical tower. The old station is now a community centre.

② An area of raised ground in the far corner of the field is all that remains of Cook's Castle, a mock ruin built as part of Capability Brown's extravagant landscaping to improve the view from Appuldurcombe House. Built in 1710, Appuldurcombe can be seen to the west, beyond Wroxall. It was once the finest private house on the Island, but is now only a shell.

③ From the path along the crest of Luccombe Down you can see both ends of the Island: Culver Cliff in the east and The Needles in the west.

④ The large area of heather, a comparative

rarity on the Isle of Wight, is growing on the acid, flinty soil that caps the chalk here. The gorse is a breeding site for the rare Dartford warbler, and this area is a designated Site of Special Scientific Interest.

⑤ Wroxall Manor Farm was an important manor at the time of the Domesday Survey in 1086 and was valued at £20. The house has changed little since 1770 and the exceptionally long barn is particularly interesting.

ROUTE DIRECTIONS

Allow 2½ hours
Start from the car park in Station Approach, Wroxall, near the church (grid ref. SZ551799) ①.

Leave the car park and walk up Station Road past the school. At the top of the hill, branch right over the stile opposite Castle Lane and follow the V30 footpath uphill. Cross two more stiles, then keep to the left-hand edge of the next field, ignoring the path that descends to the lower level ②.

Cross a stile, continue ahead for 220yds, then turn right over a stile under a larch tree. Turn left and follow the edge of the field for 45yds, then turn right to cross the field uphill to a bridlegate in the fence on the far side. Pass through and continue uphill, following the left-hand lip of the old quarry. On the top, branch left round the contour, following bridleway V45, signposted to Luccombe Down.

Pass through a bridlegate then continue straight ahead to a signpost on the skyline. On reaching it, turn right and follow bridleway V40. Keeping the hedge on your left, pass through a gateway and continue straight ahead along this bridleway, which becomes V43 ③.

At the far end of the long field pass through the gate and continue ahead along the flinty track through gorse ④.

Keep to this track (ignoring the left turn) until you reach the boundary fence of the radar station. Turn right and follow the track (becoming a road) with the radar station fence on your left.

About 220yds past the radar station, turn right down bridleway V8, signposted to Wroxall, descend steeply through Wroxall Copse, and follow the bridleway straight downhill to Wroxall Manor Farm ⑤.

Pass through the farmyard out on to the road and turn left, following the road to the Star Inn. Go straight down the High Street, up the other side towards the church, and turn right at the newsagent's to return to the car park.

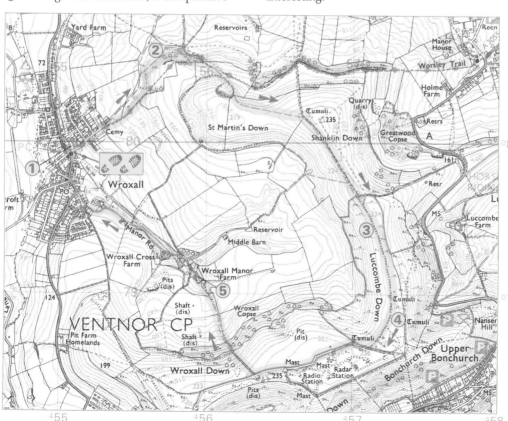

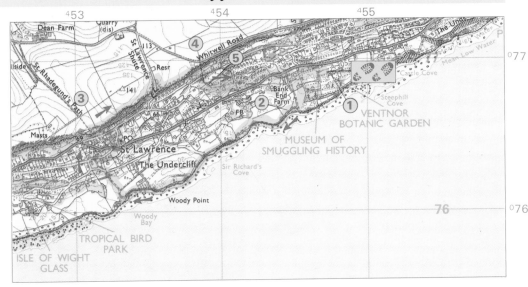

ROUTE DIRECTIONS

Allow 1¾ hours (longer if you are visiting the Botanic Gardens or the Museum)
Start from the car park at Ventnor Botanic Gardens (grid ref. SZ547769) ①.

Leave the western end of the car park, passing the Temperate House, and follow the sign pointing across the meadow to the coastal footpath ②.

Pass Orchard Bay House and, keeping the sea on your left, follow the coast path for the next ⅝ mile to the old coastguard cottages at Woody Bay. Keep to the seaward side of the cottages and about 220yds past them turn inland up footpath V97, signposted to St Lawrence.

About 55yds past the signpost turn left off the farm track, keeping the fence on your left and the sea behind you. Cross the stile and climb the steep path to Wolverton Road.

Turn left along Wolverton Road then right up to the main road. Cross over and go up Spindlers Road, turn left along Seven Sisters Road, then right up the footpath signposted to Whitwell and Niton ③.

Climb the steps to the top and turn right along the path towards Ventnor. After 600yds go over the stile down the bank to the road at St Lawrence Shute, climb up the other side, and turn right along the path towards Ventnor.

Follow the fenced-in path and near the end of the first field turn right down footpath V76, signposted to St Lawrence. Descend the rough steps built through a cleft in the rock ④.

Follow the steps down to the right and continue down the winding path to a metal kissing-gate followed closely by another ⑤.

After the second kissing-gate, descend the winding path into Pelham Wood and when you see the houses in front of you, join the estate road by the green signpost. Turn right down the road to the main Undercliff Drive. Turn left for 55yds, cross over, and go down footpath V92, signposted to Orchard Bay. When it joins the road turn left across the meadow back to the Botanic Gardens.

Ventnor's sea front and pier — originally built to land visitors direct from the mainland

The enchanting St Lawrence Undercliff is the setting for the first part of this walk, which returns along the clifftop. The walk is fairly short, but has a steady climb halfway and a steep descent towards the end. Take care with children and dogs on the cliff path.

POINTS OF INTEREST

① A worthwhile addition to the walk is a visit to Ventnor Botanic Gardens, where rare trees, shrubs and other plants thrive in an almost Mediterranean climate. A growing collection of exotic plants from around the world is on display in the recently opened Temperate House. A unique attraction in the car park of the Gardens is the Museum of Smuggling History, whose underground vaults contain displays on smuggling through the centuries.

② Stretching along the Island's south-east coast between Niton and Luccombe, the remarkable Undercliff is fascinating to walk through. Protected from cold northerly winds, the south-facing coastal strip is host to a huge variety of plant life and the jumble of soil types resulting from long collapsed cliffs enables acid-loving as well as chalk-loving species to find a place – sometimes side by side.

③ The steps on the footpath here are known as St Rhadegund's Path – part of the old route from St Lawrence to Whitwell, whose church is dedicated to Saints Mary and Rhadegund.

④ The 'shelves' in the Greensand cliff are formed by harder bands of a rock called Chert which are left protruding as wind and rain erode the soft sandstone in between.

⑤ The kissing-gates mark the site of a level crossing on the old railway from Ventnor to Newport, which closed in 1952.

ROUTE DIRECTIONS

Allow 2½ hours (longer if you visit Appuldurcombe House) Start from Godshill car park (grid ref. SZ530817).

Cross the main road, go up the narrow road opposite and turn left over the stile behind the Griffin, signposted to Beech Copse. Follow the stiles to Beech Copse and on entering the wood bear right, with the ditch on your left. Cross the ditch on the sleeper footbridge and climb the steep bank to the bridleway on top①.

Turn right along the bridleway leading out of the copse and continue ahead to Sainham Farm. Cross the stile, follow footpath GL56 through the white gate and turn left up footpath GL58, signposted to Gatcliff.

Follow the track uphill, along the level, then round to the right up the next hill, with the hedge on your left. Follow the track into the copse then turn right at the signpost and follow bridleway GL49, signposted to Stenbury Down. Keep the stone wall on your left for the next mile and climb to the top of Stenbury Down, emerging on to the roadway by a cattle-grid②.

Turn right, passing the radio station, and follow the road as it bends round to the left and descends to the foot of the down. At the T-junction opposite the cottages, turn left, leave the road at the corner and walk into the farmyard, passing Span Lodge on your left. Pass the barn and keep straight ahead along the track until you reach the rear entrance to Appuldurcombe House③.

Keeping the railings on your left, follow the footpath round the edge of the grounds and emerge on to the farm road by the main entrance to the house. With your back to the main gates, follow the farm road ahead, go past Appuldurcombe Farm on your left, then follow the edge of the field to the three arches of the Freemantle Gate④.

Pass through, continue ahead downhill past Godshill Park Farm, and go straight on to join the main road. Turn left back to the car park.

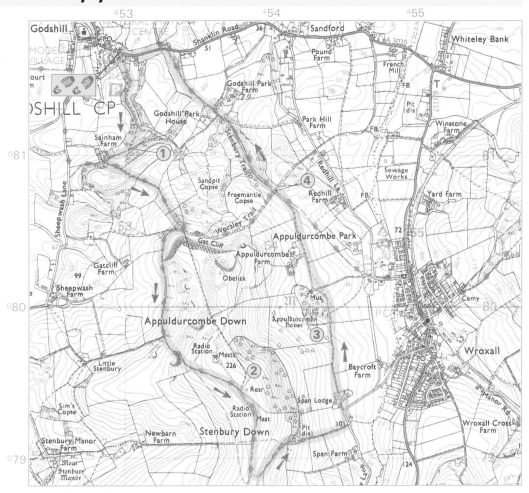

A steady climb from Godshill through woods and across farmland is rewarded by wide views from Stenbury Down. The walk returns past the ruined 18th-century mansion of Appuldurcombe House in its magnificent downland setting.

POINTS OF INTEREST

①Despite its name, the predominant tree species in Beech Copse is the sweet chestnut, planted to provide fencing stakes. Now seldom used for this purpose, the trees have been allowed to grow towards maturity and in November the nuts provide rich pickings. In May the woodland floor is covered with bluebells.

②The long stone wall, originally 6ft high, was built 250 years ago to enclose Appuldurcombe Park and prevent the deer from escaping into surrounding farmland.

③Appuldurcombe – 'the valley of the apple trees' – was for 300 years the setting of a priory. Together with a Tudor house that stood here, this was demolished to make way for the present mansion, built for the Worsley family in the 18th century. It was later owned by Lord Yarborough, founder of the Royal Yacht Squadron at Cowes. Since it was gutted by a landmine in World War II, Appuldurcombe has remained a magnificent ruin. Naturally, it is said to be haunted – by a monk carrying a handbell.

④The Freemantle Gate was the main gate to Appuldurcombe from Godshill. The Ionic triumphal arch is thought to have been designed by James Wyatt.

Appuldurcombe – now only a shell but with beautiful grounds by Capability Brown

Many generations of mariners have been guided by a lighthouse on St Catherine's Point, the most southerly headland on the Island. This walk looks down on the 19th-century lighthouse before climbing the hill on which its 14th-century predecessor, known as the Oratory or the 'Pepper Pot', still stands. Nearby is a third lighthouse, begun in 1785 but never completed.

St Catherine's 1323 Oratory

POINTS OF INTEREST

①From the seat there are views out to sea over Chale Bay and along the Island's south-west coast.

②St Catherine's Lighthouse, below, was completed in 1840 following the tragic wreck of the *Clarendon* in Chale Bay when all passengers and all but three of the crew were lost. The lighthouse greatly reduced the number of shipwrecks – prior to its building as many as 14 wrecks occurred in Chale Bay in one night.

③Bury Lane probably takes its name from the Bronze Age barrow that used to stand near the top before it was ploughed out. The old name for a barrow was a 'bury'.

④The detour to Hoy's Monument is along an area of National Trust land with fine views to either side from the ridge. The monument itself was built by Michael Hoy, a merchant of Russian origin, to commemorate the visit of Tsar Alexander to England in 1814.

⑤Dating from 1323, the old lighthouse is said to have been built by Walter de Goditon as a penance following his theft of 53 casks of Church wine from a wrecked ship. The 'Pepper Pot' was in use until 1638. Nearby, on the hilltop, stands the stump of its never-to-be-completed successor – the 'Salt Cellar' or the 'Mustard Pot'.

ROUTE DIRECTIONS

Allow 2 hours (or 3, including the Hoy's Monument extension) Start from the viewpoint car park above Blackgang (grid ref. SZ491767).

Go up the steps at the back of the car park by Hawks Ledge and follow the path to the seat on the cliff-top promontory①.

Turn left along the cliff-top path towards Niton②.

After the second stile beyond the radio station, turn immediately left over another stile and head inland, keeping the fence and sparse hedge on your right. At the far end of the field cross a stile and branch slightly left, as waymarked, to a further stile in a hollow 55yds on. After crossing this stile descend to the road, turn right, and follow it round to Niton church. Turn left at the lych gate and go up Pan Lane. At the end of the road go straight up bridleway NT53, signposted to St Catherine's Down③.

Turn left at the top and follow the track to the gate. Go through and continue along the track ahead, as indicated by the blue arrow, to the next gate and cattle-grid. Pass through the gate then turn immediately left and follow the fence-line uphill to the Oratory. Alternatively, branch half right across the field to the gate and, keeping to the left-hand fork, follow the ridge leading north to Hoy's Monument④.

Return from the monument by the same route, and then climb to the Oratory⑤.

Cross the stile leading out of the Oratory enclosure and head across the field towards the sea to a stile on the far side midway between two telegraph poles. Cross this stile and branch slightly left, as waymarked, and descend the well-trodden path across the next two fields straight towards the car park, now clearly visible.

The lantern on St Catherine's Lighthouse can be seen for 18 miles – on its first night in action cows on the nearby Downs ran riot in fear!

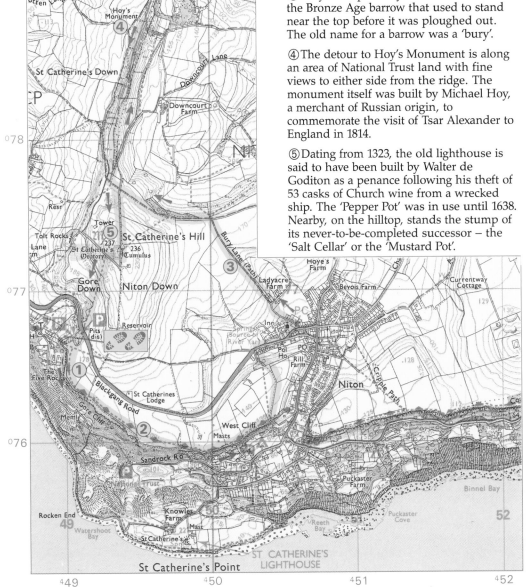

WALK 14K · *Barrows & Brighstone*   ISLE OF WIGHT

The Long Stone, beneath Mottistone Down. Red squirrels may be glimpsed near by

ROUTE DIRECTIONS
Allow 2¾ hours
Start from the National Trust car park on the Calbourne-to-Brighstone road (grid ref. SZ420846).

Take the obvious path westwards to the summit of Mottistone Down①.

Pass straight over and descend to the gate. After it, take the first forest ride left and then left again. Follow the broad grassy track along the contour of the Down, gradually descending to a T-junction on a gravel track. Turn left round the edge of the woods and continue the short distance to the Long Stone②.

Cross the stile in the fence ahead and keep straight on over a further stile and a track to the road. Turn right and, soon after, take the path to the left running up a gravel track to the woods.

Cross the stile and turn right along a broad grassy track. The track gets narrower as it descends and bends gradually right to emerge at the south-east corner of the woods. (Ignore footpaths leading right into the woods.)

Cross a stile, walk along the edge of the field to a further stile and take a narrow path that descends to the lane. Turn right and in about 130yds, after a slight bend, take an inconspicuous path left (BS64) and follow this to the road, where you turn left. After a further 130yds take a path right (BS39) to Moortown Lane.

Turn left and then take a hairpin right turn into Upper Lane. Ignore Hollis Drive to the left, continue for ½ mile or so to the first road junction and take bridleway BS81 left③.

Follow an enclosed track upwards, bearing round right to the top of the Down④.

Continue over the top of the Down on a grassy path, and turn left at the T-junction to follow the broad track along the edge of a large field, to the gate. Pass through this and maintain direction, by bearing round to the left on the obvious track up to the top of the Down and a field-gate. Turn left, follow the track to the road and cross to the car park from where the walk started.

The downland ridge above Brighstone commands spectacular views of most of south-west Wight. Along the way there are prehistoric monuments to visit, before the walk descends towards Brighstone, an interesting village conveniently placed for a half-way stop. Walking is good, but parts can be muddy after rain so stout footwear is advisable.

POINTS OF INTEREST

① At the top of Mottistone Down are four Bronze Age barrows; there are well over 200 such burial mounds on the Island's chalk downs. These ones were adjacent to the local community of Harboro, thought to have been here around 1500BC. Its name survives on the map.

② The Long Stone is, in fact, a Neolithic long barrow, now partly destroyed by quarrying. At its eastern end are two large blocks of sandstone, one upright and the other lying on its side. They were probably never part of the burial chamber itself, but their size and arrangement has made them the subject of many colourful theories.

③ At this point a short detour can be made into Brighstone village, where pub, post office and public conveniences are all within three minutes' walk. The 'Three Bishops' after whom the pub is named are commemorated by a monument in Brighstone's outstanding medieval church. The village was once notorious for smuggling, and – more respectably – boasted the Isle of Wight's first lifeboat. Its coxswain was James Buckett, a reformed smuggler. Other fascinating facts about the church and village are in the parish books, which, prior to 1588, mention preparations at the village to combat the increasing threat of the Spanish Armada.

④ On the climb from Brighstone, pause for splendid views of the coastal plain, from Blackgang Bluff in the east to the Tennyson cliffs in the west.

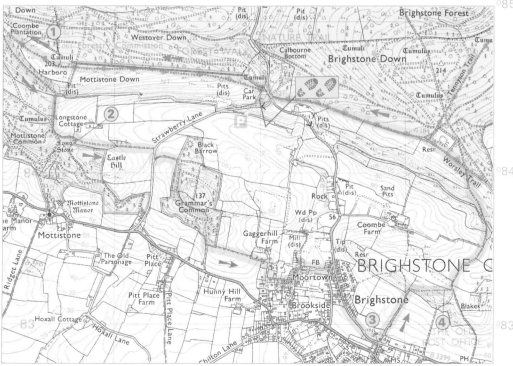

WALK 14L · Compton Bay   ISLE OF WIGHT

Compton Bay, where the wildlife includes the Island's own Glanville fritillary butterfly

Sea and downland complement each other on this bracing walk on the Isle of Wight's south-western coast. At its best on sparkling-clear summer days, when views are far-reaching and downland flowers in bloom, this is not a walk for wet, windy weather.

POINTS OF INTEREST

① Looking back from the stile towards Brookgreen, the roofless shell of the old lifeboat house can be seen – a reminder of the days when Brook was an important lifeboat station on this hazardous coast, which was once the haunt of smugglers.

② Serious coastal erosion along a ¾-mile stretch of Compton Bay has caused the loss of many acres of fields within living memory. Nevertheless the beach remains popular, not least with surfers. This area is good for wildlife: amphibians like the watery wilderness of the landslip area, while many migratory butterflies make their first landfall along this coast.

③ At Compton Chine the sandstone cliffs give way to chalk. On descending to cross the chine stream, note the route of the old sunken highway ahead on the side of the Downs and its crossing over the existing road to disappear at the cliff edge.

④ The chalk track over the Downs, now part of the Tennyson Trail, is an ancient highway. From it there are splendid views. To the north is the River Yar valley, with Yarmouth and the Solent beyond. To the north west lie the low white ramparts of Golden Hill Fort, and jutting out from the mainland shore, Hurst Castle, where Charles I was held prisoner before being taken to Westminster and the block.

⑤ On Brook Down, the track passes close to a group of excavated Bronze Age round barrows near the hilltop, which is crowned by a triangulation pillar.

⑥ As the track descends, Brook Hill House can be seen in its forest setting across the valley. Once the home of J B Priestley, the house was – understandably – marked as a fortress on German wartime maps. It survived hostilities, only to suffer the onslaught of students and weather before being sold and converted into flats.

ROUTE DIRECTIONS

Allow 3 hours
Start from the National Trust car park on the Military Road at Brook (grid ref. SZ385835).

Leave by the beach gate, taking the path along the bank on the right. Join the cliff-top path over the stile and follow this westwards, **keeping a safe distance from the eroding cliff edge**①.

After about ½ mile cross Shippards Chine car park (public conveniences at the road entrance), continuing westwards on the obvious cliff path②.

Reach the stile and paths to the beach and road. Follow the road path as it bears round right, mount the left-hand bank and continue along the cliff. After crossing over Compton Chine stream, look for the steps to the roadside as you climb the slope③.

At the top of the steps turn left, crossing the road after 220yds to the bridleway over the sunken track diverging away from the road. Follow to the point where it converges with the chalk track (at a sign board). Take the hairpin turn right and follow the obvious track over Afton Down across the golf course④.

Continue on the chalk track, passing through a gate to maintain the same direction over the grass track through the gorse scrub⑤.

Keep to the right of the knoll and the National Trust plinth, continuing around the side of the Down to descend to the double power-line post immediately ahead⑥.

Take a hairpin right turn just before the power-line post and follow the rough track keeping the power lines on the left. Shortly after the point where the power lines are overhead, diverge left through a gate to the signpost. Turn left (bridleway BS86A) to follow the good track, descending to cross the tarmac access road on to the grass track between the fence and hedge (bridleway BS52).

After 440yds turn right along the broad enclosed track and then left at the pair of stone cottages. Follow to the T-junction with the narrow lane by a white house and continue over the stile opposite the Military Road and your starting point a short distance to your left.

ROUTE DIRECTIONS

Allow 3 hours
Start from the National Trust car park on Mill Road, Shalfleet (grid ref. SZ414895).

Walk back from the car park to the main road, cross over and follow the lane to a T-junction. Turn left①.

At the end of the houses, continue round a left-hand bend to a copse and take the path on the right, signed S15 Ningwood. Keep left through the copse and after the first stile cross the field diagonally right by the electricity pole in the centre, and cross a second stile about half-way along the hedge from the copse.

Continue in the same direction over the next field to a gate in the corner, turning right along the edge of the adjoining field to reach a gate.

Keep to the left edge of the next field and then head for the right side of the house across the next field. When you get there, turn left and then right to the road. (Take care: it is a blind exit on to a fast main road.)

Cross the road and go left for 220yds to Hamstead Estate Road (signposted) on the right. Follow this road for about ¾ mile and then take the obvious right fork to Creek and Lower Hamstead Farms (S28). At Lower Hamstead Farm continue through the gate towards Newtown River, over the stile on your left②.

Follow an enclosed path to a stile on your right and continue along the edge of the tidal inlet and over the footbridge. Take a hairpin turn right over another bridge, go along the slight embankment and then cross further bridges and continue until you reach a stile into a field. Turn right and then left along the side of the field to a stile on your left.

Cross the adjoining field diagonally right to the catwalk, continuing along the side of the field to another stile. Descend to the beach and turn left③.

Follow the track, diverging away from the beach upwards to Hamstead Farm④.

Continue past the farm on the main track, which soon passes Hamstead Grange on the left. Follow the road back to the stone bridge and shortly after it take the signposted path left (S11) to the footbridge.

Keeping the hedge on your left, follow the boundaries of two fields to the main road. Turn left and walk back to the car park.

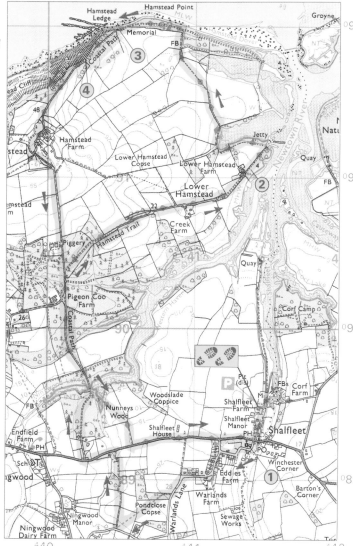

Shalfleet, situated on a finger of the Newtown Estuary

Catwalks and bridges are a charming feature of this walk

The whole of the estuary of the Newtown River – an area particularly rich in birdlife – is protected by the National Trust. Starting from the old creekside village of Shalfleet, this walk explores the woodland and farmland on the western side of the estuary. It includes an intriguing series of catwalks, bridges and embankments on tidal inlets.

POINTS OF INTEREST

① Much of this southern part of Shalfleet consists of new housing, but the church dates from the 12th century. The Norman tower has walls 5ft thick and no outer entrance, recalling its use as a refuge in bygone centuries, when French invasions of the Isle of Wight were a very real danger. In Elizabethan times, each parish was issued with its own brass cannon for defence purposes. It is said that in the 19th century the people of Shalfleet sold theirs, together with the church bells, to raise money to add a steeple to the church.

② From the old quay there is a fine view of the acres of mudflats and saltmarsh which attract huge flocks of waders and wildfowl to this estuary in winter. Wigeon, shelduck, black-tailed godwits and brent geese are among the species likely to be seen, while terns have bred here in summer.

③ Stretching away north-west is Hamstead Ledge, an outcrop of resistant Bembridge limestone. Particularly strong currents prevail offshore. Before leaving the beachside, look left and you will see a small stone memorial to three young men lost at sea locally in 1932 and 1934.

④ Shortly after the path leaves the seashore, there is a concrete ramp to the beach – a remnant of wartime when tanks landed here. Before Hamstead Farm there are fine views to the south and east of the Newtown River complex, where fingers of water feel their way through Hamstead clays.

ROUTE DIRECTIONS

Allow 3½ hours
Start from the car park on
Whitcombe Road, Carisbrooke
(grid ref. SZ489876).

Cross the road to a narrow lane on the south side of St Dominic's Priory. Shortly after the end of the perimeter wall take footpath N26 left, following the track to the cemetery wall①.

Return to the road. Turn left and almost immediately right, following the path by the gate to the castle, bearing left along the southern ramparts. Follow the path round to the right and at the car park turn sharp left and almost immediately right to descending path N88②.

Bear right on reaching a narrow lane and take the left fork (Clatterford Shute) over a ford to the main road. Cross right into Nodgham Lane and later turn left into Down Lane (Tennyson Trail)③.

Follow the enclosed track for about one mile to a metal gate④.

Continue in the same direction through a gate (bridleway N128), turning diagonally left through a further gate at the end of the field. Pass along the enclosed track and through two more gates⑤.

Continue to the next gate and a five-way signpost. Turn left along an enclosed track (N135) and when the track bends right take a field track forking left⑥.

After the next gate take the right fork and go on to another gate, then follow a chalky track to the road. Cross diagonally left (bridleway N137a), running along the field edge to the gate.

Maintain direction along the edge of the next field to a gate on your right. Pass through the gate and turn left along a broad chalky track to a T-junction. Turn left along a track towards Bowcombe Farm. Just before the farmhouse turn right along an enclosed lane, and right again at the T-junction near Plaish Farm.

Follow this lane to the stile on your left along the side of the water meadows. Keep going to a lane. Turn right, and keep right at the bend and a path junction. Follow the tarmac lane over the ford, bearing left at Froglands Farm to the main road and the car park ahead.

Views, both near and far, of the Island's best-known historic building dominate this walk. From its beginning close to the castle the walk goes along the castle ramparts before starting to climb towards the breezy uplands of Bowcombe Down. Magnificent views characterise this part of the walk, which returns through peaceful water meadows.

Stout footwear is advisable, as parts of the walk can be muddy. Please close all gates, since this is sheep and cattle country.

POINTS OF INTEREST

① A short detour to an excellent viewpoint can be made by turning right and walking to the end of the cemetery wall. A panorama over Newport and the River Medina opens up at the top of Mount Joy. On the descent, the television masts at Chillerton (left) and Rowridge (right) are clearly visible.

② The gates of Carisbrooke Castle can be seen by turning to the right after entering the car park. Perhaps most famous as the prison where Charles I was held for 10 months before his execution, Carisbrooke is the Isle of Wight's only medieval castle. Early Norman in origin, the building has been adapted to suit changing defence needs down the centuries. There are two medieval wells, one of which has a winding wheel powered by donkeys. Visitors can still see the window in the north curtain wall through which King Charles tried, unsuccessfully, to escape, and can follow in his footsteps on the walk he took daily round the battlements.

Carisbrooke Castle, where holes in the medieval drum towers were used for archery

③ The Tennyson Trail, one of the Island's long-distance footpaths, runs for some 15 miles from here to Alum Bay near the Needles.

④ An open stretch on this part of the walk offers fine views back to Carisbrooke Castle and southwards across the Bowcombe Valley to Chillerton Down.

⑤ The view northwards from the second gate extends over the Solent, with the mudflats and creeks of the Newtown Estuary to the left, and the chimneys of Fawley oil refinery on the mainland.

⑥ The chalk of Culver Cliffs, far away to the east, can be seen from here through a gap in the hills slightly to the right.

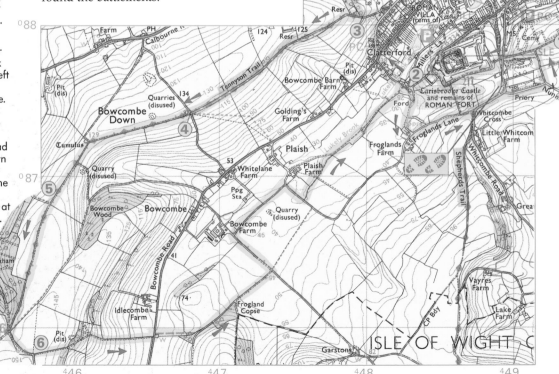

TOUR 15 · A Sussex History Tour

ROUTE DIRECTIONS

The drive starts from Chichester ①.

From the eastern side of the ring road follow signs for Bognor Regis, A259, and at the Four Chestnuts public house keep forward, no sign, into Oving Road, the B2144. In ½ mile, at the traffic-lights, go forward across the Chichester bypass, signed Oving. In another ½ mile keep forward again, unclassified, signed Tangmere. Just over a mile farther bear left ②.

At the end of Tangmere village turn right on to the main A27 Worthing road. After a further 3 miles pass the edge of Fontwell, famous for its racecourse. At the roundabouts follow the Worthing signs. In 3¾ miles, at the roundabout, take the second exit, unclassified, to enter the town of Arundel ③.

Return to the roundabout junction with the A27 to continue the main tour. Here take the exit signed London/Dorking to leave by the A284. Ascend through woodland, skirting the Arundel Castle estate on the right, and after 2½ miles, at the roundabout, take the third exit, B2139, signed Storrington. There are pleasant views as the drive descends into the Arun Valley at Houghton. The river is crossed prior to Amberley Station, beyond which is the Amberley Chalk Pits Museum (right). Shortly pass the turning to the village of Amberley on the left ④.

Continue along the foot of the Downs to reach Storrington. Here turn left on to the A283, signed Petworth and Pulborough. One mile farther pass the entrance to Parham House and Gardens ⑤.

In another mile turn left on to an unclassified road, signed Greatham, and enter Northpark Wood. Continue with the Coldwaltham road and later recross the River Arun at Greatham Bridge.

On reaching Coldwaltham turn left on to the A29 Bognor Regis road. Shortly pass through Watersfield and in ½ mile turn right on to the B2138, signed Petworth, then almost immediately turn left on to the unclassified West Burton/Bignor road. Half a mile farther turn left and continue to West Burton. Here turn right, signed Roman Villa and Bignor. After a mile pass the entrance to Bignor Roman Villa and Museum, right ⑥.

At the edge of Bignor village bear right, then at the church turn right, signed Sutton. Proceed to Sutton where the drive again turns right, signed Petworth. In 1¾ miles at the crossroads turn left.

One mile farther turn right on to the A285 and later cross the River Rother before reaching the outskirts of Petworth ⑦.

The main drive turns left on to the A272 Midhurst road (for the town centre keep forward). Continue through Tillington and later enjoy a delightful drive through Cowdray Park before Easebourne. Here bear left and shortly recross the River Rother to enter Midhurst ⑧.

Follow Chichester signs to leave by the A286. Pass through Cocking, then enter thickly wooded downland *en route* to Singleton. At the far end of the village turn left on to the unclassified Goodwood road. Almost immediately pass the Weald and Downland Open Air Museum on the right ⑨.

Alternatively, remain on the A286 for a mile to visit the gardens at West Dean ⑩.

The main tour ascends with extensive views to the left, passing beneath a hill called The Trundle (675ft). The grandstand of Goodwood Racecourse is then seen, and later the wooded grounds of Goodwood House are passed on the left ⑪.

One mile beyond the entrance to the house turn right, signed Chichester. Half a mile farther, at the roundabout junction with the bypass, take the third exit on to the A285, and return to Chichester.

There are many places of historical interest which may be visited during this drive – a Roman villa, a Norman castle, a medieval town, a stately home, an aviation museum and an open-air museum.

POINTS OF INTEREST

① The beautiful city of Chichester dates back to Roman times. The cathedral is mainly Norman and contains works by 20th-century artists. The Mechanical Music and Doll Museum is a real must.

② You will pass, on the right, the famous World War II fighter airfield of Tangmere. Now disused, it is the site of the Military Aviation Museum.

③ The imposing, much restored Norman castle at Arundel is the ancestral home of the Dukes of Norfolk. Other notable buildings are the 19th-century Roman Catholic cathedral and the 14th-century Church of St Nicholas.

④ An exceptionally pretty village, Amberley consists entirely of old stone, flint and half-timbered dwellings. The Chalk Pits Museum is an open-air museum of industrial archaeology.

⑤ Parham House is a splendid Elizabethan mansion with beautiful gardens standing in a deer park. The house contains a fine collection of paintings, furniture, carpets and rare needlework.

⑥ A Roman site was discovered on the West Burton side of Bignor in 1811 and has some of the finest mosaic pavements in the country. The museum contains models, pictures and objects from the site. Bignor itself is a pretty village; its mainly 13th-century church has a Norman chancel arch and nearby is a superb Sussex yeoman's cottage.

⑦ This medieval town of narrow winding streets crowds up to the walls of Petworth House (National Trust), a large 17th- to 19th-century mansion situated in a great park.

⑧ Midhurst has many fine buildings including a 17th-century cottage in Knockhundred Row which houses the public library and, close by, in Market Square, a timber-framed Elizabethan house with a 16th-century mural.

⑨ On a 40-acre site in the beautiful Lavant Valley, the famous Weald and Downland Museum has a unique collection of 30 historic buildings that were rescued from their original sites when threatened with destruction. The museum is also known for its demonstrations of rural crafts and industries.

⑩ West Dean Gardens cover about 30 acres and feature a wild garden, a walled garden, a pergola and various summerhouses. There is also an interesting Museum of the Garden which includes antique lawnmowers.

⑪ Goodwood has been the imposing seat of the Dukes of Richmond since 1697 and is frequently visited by royalty for the Goodwood Races.

Petworth House and its beautiful 700-acre deer park. Turner immortalised the estate in his paintings

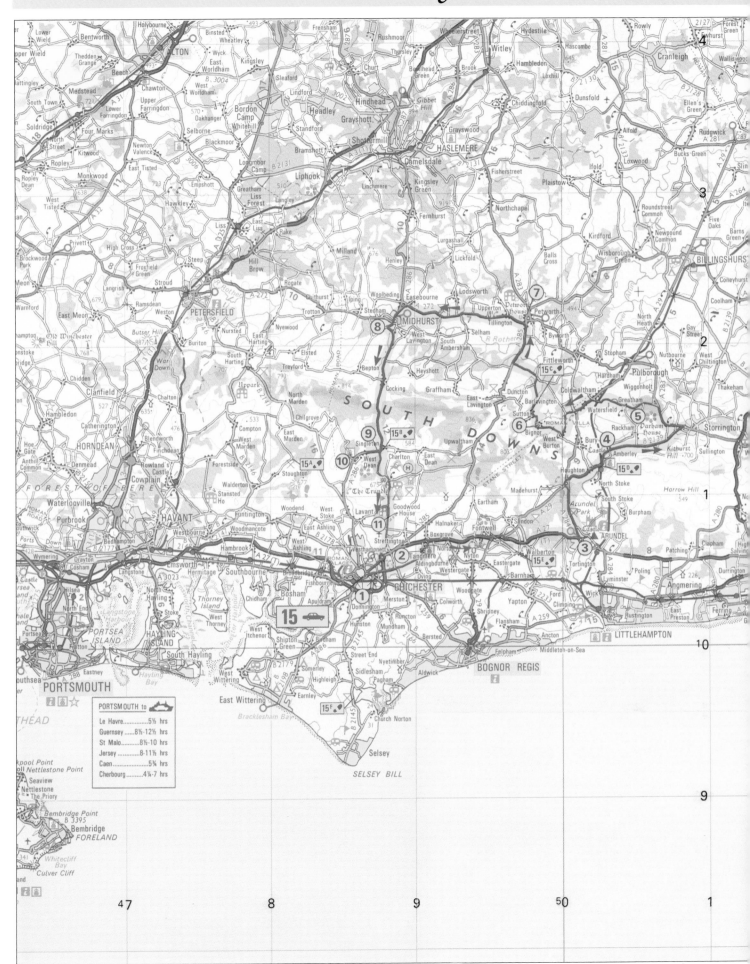

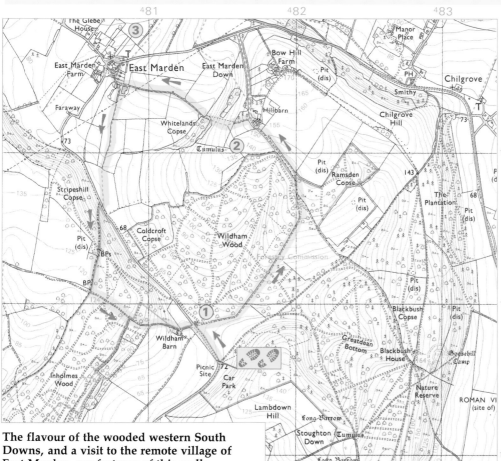

The flavour of the wooded western South Downs, and a visit to the remote village of East Marden, are features of this walk, which follows a circular route, much of it through Forestry Commission broadleaved woodland.

POINTS OF INTEREST

① Commercial forestry is an important economic activity on the South Downs, and is well demonstrated at Wildham Wood which is of planted beech ranging between 25 and 40 years old. Most of the plantation occupies an ancient woodland site that was formerly managed with oak and ash standards over an understorey of hazel. Beech woodland under the control of the Forestry Commission in the area covers some 1,000 acres.

② A rest on the short downland turf of the escarpment above Whitelands Copse offers an opportunity to enjoy the views across the valley to East Marden, with its red-roofed cottages. The Mardens – a family of villages which also includes North, West and Up Marden – belong to one of the most remote and beautiful parishes in the South Downs.

③ Snug in its south-facing hollow in the chalk, East Marden is an enchanting little village of flint cottages, farms and a simple medieval church. Completing the picture is a much-photographed well with a thatched roof. However, walkers visiting the village

may wish to be forearmed with the advice of E V Lucas, that East Marden 'has no inn and is therefore not the best friend of the traveller'.

The thatched well head at East Marden. Picturesque cottages and a tiny church complete the village scene

ROUTE DIRECTIONS

Allow 1¾ hours
Start from the Forestry Commission car park below Stoughton Down, about a mile north-east of Stoughton village (grid ref. SU815126).

Walk up the road towards East Marden and after 200–300yds turn right and follow a footpath along the southern edge of Wildham Wood, resisting an early opportunity to turn left into the interior ①.

As it climbs towards East Marden Down, largely following the edge of the wood, the path becomes steeper, affording views back over the wooded western downland. Just past Hillbarn, turn left along a footpath between a field and a copse, climb a stile and follow the path down a steep hillside ②.

Press on towards the village, following the path through a farmyard, and join a road by Postman's Cottage. Here turn left and visit the church and the village well ③.

Retrace the route to the farmyard and take the path due south between the hay-barn and the stockyard. Climb a stile into the following field, walk south to another stile on the right, cross this into the adjacent field and continue straight on (south), keeping the hedge to the left. Finally, cross an open field to reach the road by a large beech tree.

Cross the road and take the path opposite to continue straight on into the wood, climbing. At the top of the hill, after a large field opens out on the right, turn left at a junction to continue along a bridleway which follows a broad ride through the woodland.

Ignore all paths to the right and left, descending through the wood to a road by Wildham Barn, and a brick-and-flint house with pretty Victorian gables. Turn right and walk back along the road to the car park.

ROUTE DIRECTIONS

Allow 1¾ hours
Start from a parking spot near Singleton church (grid ref. GR878131)①.

Take the footpath east from the churchyard, pass through modern housing and cross open fields to the Charlton Estate②.

Reach the road in Charlton and turn left, then at the main road turn left again③.

After 100yds take a steep path right on to Levin Down. Climb a stile, then after a short while another, and ascend the eastern

Splendid downland is a major attraction of this walk, which explores famous hunting and racing country in the heart of the South Downs, while affording views across the valley of the Lavant to Goodwood and The Trundle.

POINTS OF INTEREST

① Once owned by Earl Godwin, father of King Harold, Singleton came to more recent prominence when Goodwood race-course was opened in 1801. In 1880 the railway arrived and a fine station (now a winery)

The open-air Weald and Downland Museum gives a glimpse of everyday life in past centuries

was built between Singleton and West Dean. Visited on more than one occasion by royalty, the village claims to have formed the first Women's Institute in England, in 1915. Today Singleton is best known as the home of the superb Weald and Downland Museum. This unique collection of historic buildings includes a watermill, a 15th-century Wealden farmhouse, a Victorian village school and a market hall – all rescued from threatened demolition.

② The Lavant chalk stream flows between Singleton and Charlton – though not always in summer, since it is a 'winterbourne', appearing above ground only when the water-table rises in the wetter months of the year.

③ In the 18th century Charlton was renowned as the home of the first and most famous regular foxhunt in England, with more than 150 horses stabled here at one time. Its crowning glory was a 10-hour chase in 1738.

④ Views south from Levin Down take in Goodwood race-course and the radio masts on the 600ft-high hill crowned by The Trundle. This was a large and elaborate Neolithic causewayed camp which later became an Iron Age hillfort. Archaeological finds from the site can be seen in the museum at Lewes.

face of the down, forking left after a few yards.

After some time, as the chalk track comes into sight in the valley below, bear right into a wood, following the footpath. When the path emerges from the wood, continue beside an open field. Keep the Old Charlton Hunt waypost to the left and walk straight ahead (north) following the bridleway.

At the T-junction, before the bridleway enters Singleton Forest, turn sharp left to Broadham House. Go through the field gate by the farm and turn left up the chalky track. At the waypost, go through a bridlegate and turn left, then pass through the field gate past a 'Boundary of Open Country' sign (these signs show that public access to Levin Down is by agreement between the landowner and the county council). Walk over the Down in a generally south-westerly (diagonally-right) direction. At the top, go through a field gate and make for a signpost on open downland, then head in the same direction to another signpost④.

Go left over the stile above the school, then descend to the village and car park.

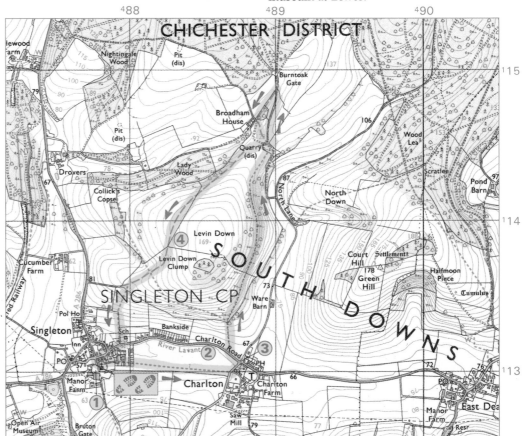

WALK 15C · Bignor Hill   WEST SUSSEX

ROUTE DIRECTIONS

Allow 2½ hours
*Start from Sutton village, where
there is parking near the White
Horse (grid ref. GR978153).*

Take the path to the right of a
thatched cottage opposite the
pub, and cross the field. Cross a
stream by two footbridges and
climb along its bank through
woods to a road①.

Turn right and just past
Malthouse Cottages take a
footpath to the right – then turn
almost immediately left. At the
next junction bear left along the
hedge line and, following the
path, ascend the hill.

Reach a stile at the fringe of
the wood, cross a track and pick
up the path again on the other
side – slightly to the right. Climb
steeply through the woods in a
diagonally-right direction and
meet the road. Turn right and
walk up the road to a waypost
by the National Trust car park, at
the top of Bignor Hill.

From the car park take a chalky
track past the National Trust 'no
cars' sign, cross Stane Street on its
embankment and continue with
radio masts to the left②.

Keep straight on where a
bridleway joins from the left and
walk down the hill. After about
½ mile turn right on to a
signposted bridleway through
woodland. After about 30yds,
where the path divides into three,
take the extreme left-hand fork
and follow it generally straight
on between two fields. Go
through the gate and follow the
track uphill among beech woods.

Cross a bridle gate at the top
and descend over an open field.
At the bottom of the field cross a
track, ignore the first path to the
right into the woods and take the
second, a few yards further on.
This descends to Barlavington.
Follow the path to the road and
walk up the no-through road to
Barlavington church③.

Pass through the churchyard
and along a farm track, then
turn right by a row of trees and
walk towards Sutton church. Turn
right over a stile into a field,
cross the stream, climb through
woodland and out into the field.
Keeping the hedge line to the
left, take the bridleway left to
Sutton at the T-junction④.

Join the village street by the
church, turn right and walk back
to the White Horse and the car.

**A strenuous climb up Bignor Hill – one of
the highest summits of the South Downs –
is rewarded by a gentler stroll along the
escarpment and an easy descent to the
downland villages of Barlavington and
Sutton. Lovely views, peaceful country
churches and some interesting relics of
Roman times make this a walk to
remember.**

POINTS OF INTEREST

①This road is the west side of a square of
lanes that make up the pretty downland
village of Bignor. Just north of the junction
here is the 13th-century church which,
though much restored, has kept its Norman
chancel arch. The village centre is to the
east of the route, and further east still is the
famous Roman villa, which is well worth a
visit. One of the excavated rooms is now
used as a museum, and items found on the
site include animal skulls and bones. A
model indicates how the villa might have
looked.

②Stretching south west for 3½ miles, this
is the longest surviving section of Stane
Street, the Roman road, built around AD70,
that ran from Billingsgate in London to the
East Gate of Noviomagus, now Chichester.
Although its name is derived from the Old
English for 'stone', the road is unlikely to
have been paved with stone. This section,
bounded by banks, was surfaced with chalk
and flint, both readily available locally.

③The steep scarp of the Downs, clothed by
the woods of Barlavington Hanger, shelters
the hamlet of Barlavington, whose name is
pronounced 'Barlton'.

④Dedicated to St John the Baptist, Sutton
church is Early English in style, with large
windows that give the simple interior a
light, airy atmosphere.

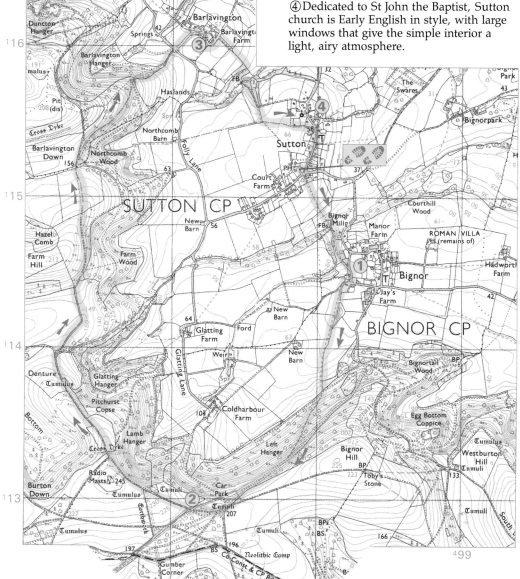

WALK 15D · Amberley Mount WEST SUSSEX

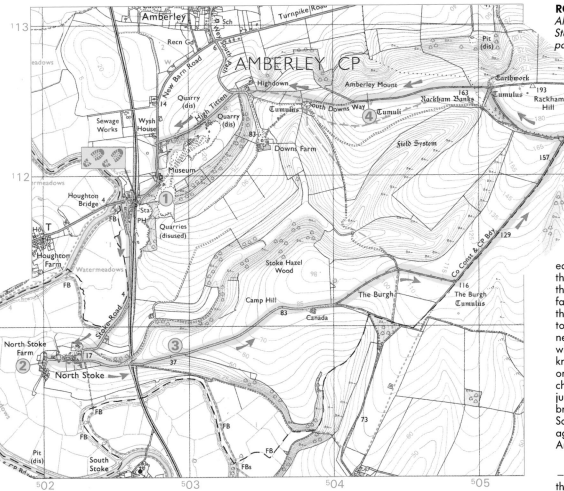

ROUTE DIRECTIONS
Allow 2½ hours
Start from Amberley station car park by the entrance to the Chalk Pits Museum (grid ref. GR026118) ①.

Walk down to the road, turn left and walk under the railway bridge. Turn left again after the bridge, pass the Bridge Inn and walk down a lane to North Stoke. At the T-junction by the telephone box, turn right to visit North Stoke church②.

Retrace the route to the telephone box and junction, then continue straight up the road in a gentle ascent③.

After a very long but quite easy climb, pass Canada Barn on the right and bear left, following the road as it degenerates into a farm track. Carry straight on at the path crossroads towards the top of the hill, turn left at the next junction and head up the hill with a stand of trees ahead known as Rackham Clump — once the home of Sussex charcoal-burners. At the next junction turn left and follow a bridleway to its junction with the South Downs Way. Here turn left again and follow the Way to Amberley Mount④.

Descend Amberley Mount and — keeping alongside the fence to the right and ignoring all left turns — continue with Downs Farm to the left. Walk on past Highdown and along the surfaced road of High Titten, peering down into the Chalk Pits Museum in the quarry to the left. Join the very busy main road at the bottom and, exercising great care, turn left and return to the station car park.

Industrial memorabilia in the Amberley Chalk Pits Museum

Amberley's award-winning open-air museum is the starting point for this route. A long but gentle climb through open farmland towards Rackham Hill affords good views across the River Arun. For the return, the walk joins the South Downs Way to cross Amberley Mount.

POINTS OF INTEREST

① Allow at least two hours for a visit to Amberley Chalk Pits Museum, a fascinating and varied trip into the industries and transport of bygone days. Opened in 1979 in a disused chalk quarry, the museum tells the story of the chalk-burning industry which flourished here for over 100 years. Traditional craftsmen demonstrate skills from wood-turning to printing, and working transport exhibits include an industrial narrow-gauge railway.

② Domesday recorded a church at North Stoke in 1087, but there is nothing in the present building earlier than the 13th century. The windows in both transepts have some of the best early tracery in southern England, and there is a crude sundial scratched fairly high up on the outside wall of the south transept.

③ As the walk climbs from North Stoke, spectacular views of the Arun Valley open out to the south, with the 'Alpine' spire of the church at South Stoke on the other side of the river. Beyond is Arundel Park, and in good weather it is possible to glimpse the distinctive outline of Arundel Castle.

④ Traces of prehistoric huts and field systems attract archaeologists to Amberley Mount, while naturalists came here for the rich downland flora, including wild thyme, milkwort and yellow rattle as well as juniper which, is not at all common.

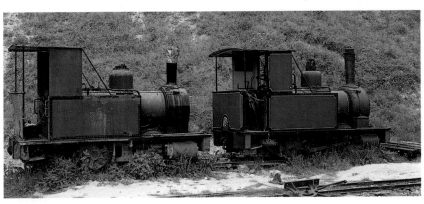

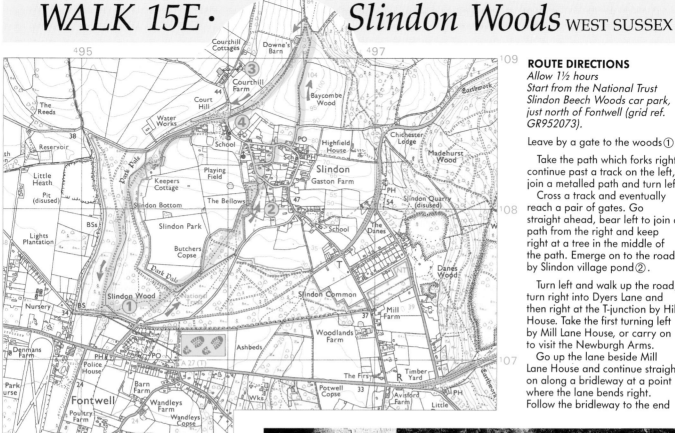

Allow 1½ hours

Start from the National Trust Slindon Beech Woods car park, just north of Fontwell (grid ref. GR952073).

Leave by a gate to the woods①.

Take the path which forks right, continue past a track on the left, join a metalled path and turn left.

Cross a track and eventually reach a pair of gates. Go straight ahead, bear left to join a path from the right and keep right at a tree in the middle of the path. Emerge on to the road by Slindon village pond②.

Turn left and walk up the road, turn right into Dyers Lane and then right at the T-junction by Hill House. Take the first turning left by Mill Lane House, or carry on to visit the Newburgh Arms.

Go up the lane beside Mill Lane House and continue straight on along a bridleway at a point where the lane bends right. Follow the bridleway to the end

Easy and level, this walk explores picturesque Slindon village, much of which is part of the National Trust's Slindon Estate. Famous for its beech woods, the 3,500-acre estate offers plenty of interest, both natural and man-made – from woodland wildlife to a substantial piece of Roman road and several of the prehistoric sites that abound along the South Downs.

POINTS OF INTEREST

①Few large estates on the South Downs were without a beech wood, for the tree thrives well even in poor, chalky soil, producing a crop of strong, hard timber. The wood had many uses, from tools and bowls to flooring and chairs. Beech trees are less attractive to wildlife than oaks, partly because of the dense shade they cast; nevertheless many species of bird including warblers and woodpeckers may be seen in Slindon Woods. Wood anemones and other spring flowers thrive before the trees come into leaf, and in autumn various kinds of fungi may be seen here, including the funnel-shaped horn of plenty.

②Brick and flint – building materials so typical of chalk country – are used in many of Slindon's cottages, most of which date from the 17th century. The village and the huge area of National Trust land that surrounds it have a much longer history, however. Slindon was an important estate of the archbishops of Canterbury in medieval times and, much earlier still,

Beech woods on the 3,500-acre National Trust Estate to the west of Slindon village

Neolithic people had settled at Barkhale, a hilltop site at the northern end of the Slindon Estate near Bignor. Near by, a 3½-mile surviving stretch of Roman road – Stane Street – recalls the Roman legions.

③Courthill Farm, in the valley to the right, was the home of Hilaire Belloc and his wife when they were first married. The author had a great affection for this part of Sussex, having spent part of his childhood in Slindon – though he was born in France.

④The college occupies Slindon House, an Elizabethan building which retains some traces of its medieval predecessor.

of the wood and then take a 'U' turn left to Downe's Barn.

Follow the bridleway south west, diverting – if too muddy – on to the parallel permissive footpath at the National Trust 'no horses' sign③.

Emerge on the road opposite the entrance to Slindon College and turn right, following the road for about 200yds④.

Turn left at the National Trust sign into Slindon Woods and follow the track round to the right. Pass Keeper's Cottage, take the right fork and after 200-300yds take the path forking down to the right. Keep straight on in a southerly direction to return to the car park.

ROUTE DIRECTIONS

Allow 2 hours
Start from the information centre at Sidlesham Ferry (grid ref. SZ856967); parking is available nearby in the nature reserve car park.

From the information centre, follow a surfaced path signed Pagham Harbour and Sidlesham Mill①.

Go through the gate at the end of the path and turn left②.

Meet a road, turn right and walk to the quay③.

Take the shoreline footpath to the right of the brick and sandstone garage, noting a warning that the path floods at high tide. Keeping the hedge and wall close to the left, follow the path round the harbour on to Pagham Wall④.

On Pagham Wall, almost due south of Honer Farm, turn left off the coastal path and take a footpath north into a field. At the top of the field, follow a footpath left before reaching the farm, climb over a stile, then cross a field and enter a wood. Cross a footbridge and continue west (straight on) along the path across an open field.

Continue with a footpath sign, climb a gate and join a grassy track past a barn on the left, with Marsh Farm away to the right. After the barn, the track becomes a concrete road. Follow this for about 150yds and turn left into a field.

Continue along a path south, negotiate New Barn and reach a road. Cross over and pick up the path almost immediately opposite. Follow the path as it bears left beside a wall, and eventually emerge on to the road by Old Mill Farm.

Turn right and walk along the road for about 200yds to the junction with the path from the information centre. Turn left on to the path and follow it back to the car park.

Footbridge over Bremere Rife, just west of Honer Farm. The river flows into Pagham Harbour

The tidal flats and saltmarshes of Pagham Harbour are one of the south coast's principal havens for birdlife, so a pair of binoculars will add greatly to the pleasure of this walk. Sections of the path flood at or near high tide, so consult tide tables – such as those in the *AA Members' Handbook* – before setting out.

POINTS OF INTEREST

①A visit to the information centre at the start of the walk is well worth while. Built on reclaimed land near Sidlesham Ferry

Pool (always a good spot for birdwatchers), the centre is run by the county council, who manage the whole of the 1,000-acre nature reserve of Pagham Harbour.

②This path follows part of the old tramway route from Chichester to Selsey.

③The quay is still accessible by boat at high tide, although landing is now controlled in the interests of nature conservation.

④The harbourside path offers excellent opportunities to observe wildfowl and wading birds at close quarters. Winter flocks will probably include shelducks, brent geese and black-tailed godwits. Pagham Harbour is also one of Britain's principal sites for wintering ruffs – though at this time of year they lack the extraordinary, colourful plumage which gives them their name. Spring and autumn bring many an unexpected migrant, while at high tide in summer little terns, which breed on the shingle, may be seen feeding in the harbour. Typical lower saltmarsh plants to be seen on the reserve include sea purslane, seablite and glasswort or marsh samphire. The ash of this edible plant was mixed with sand in early glass-making.

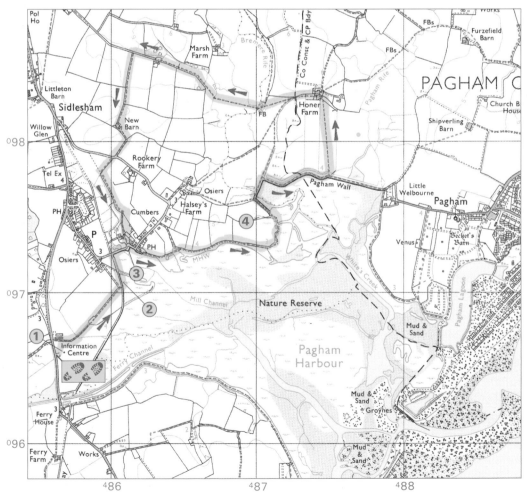

ROUTE DIRECTIONS
The drive starts from Brighton ①.

From Brighton follow the signs to Lewes to leave by the A27. After 3 miles the drive leaves the built-up districts and passes Stanmer Park, the home of the University of Sussex. Here branch left on to the B2123, signed Falmer, Rottingdean, then at the roundabout turn right to cross the main road, still signed Rottingdean. An ascent is then made, crossing pleasant downland to reach a height of 536ft before descending past the residential area of Woodingdean into the village of Rottingdean ②.

At the far end turn left at the traffic-lights on to the A259, no sign, and proceed, with views of the chalk cliffs and the sea, through Saltdean, Telscombe Cliffs and Peacehaven. After a short climb, later descend to the busy cross-Channel port of Newhaven in the Ouse Valley ③.

At the one-way system turn left then bear right, following the Seaford and Eastbourne signs. Cross the River Ouse and skirt Denton then Bishopstone before entering the residential town and resort of Seaford ④.

Follow the main A259 Eastbourne road through the town and in just over ¾ mile turn left on to an unclassified road, signed Alfriston. After a further 1½ miles there are fine views of the Cuckmere Valley from the High and Over Viewpoint, on the right. There is a steep descent of 1 in 5 followed by an ascent before reaching Alfriston ⑤.

At the market cross bear right and in 1¼ miles pass Drusilla's Zoo Park, on the right ⑥.

At the next roundabout take the first exit to join the A27, signed Lewes, and follow the northern slopes of the Downs. Four miles farther a short detour can be made by turning left on to an unclassified road to visit Firle Place ⑦.

This alternative can be extended by proceeding southwards to climb to the top of the Downs at 713ft near Firle Beacon.

For the main tour continue along the A27 and in a mile turn right, unclassified, signed Glynde and Ringmer. Shortly enter the village of Glynde and keep forward, passing Glynde Place on the right ⑧.

In ¾ mile bear left, signed Ringmer. Pass Glyndebourne ⑨.

On reaching the junction with the B2192 turn left, signed Lewes. There are fine downland views on the left and across the Ouse Valley to the right before turning left after 1½ miles on to the A26 in order to visit Lewes ⑩.

On entering the town keep forward at the mini-roundabouts,

signed Town Centre, and cross the River Ouse. Turn left then right with the one-way system and ascend the main street. At the far end branch right, signed London/East Grinstead, then, at the T-junction, turn right again to leave by the A275. Later descend beneath the slopes of Offham Hill into Offham, then in ½ mile turn left on to the B2116, signed Hassocks. The route again follows the foot of the Downs to pass through Plumpton, famous for its racecourse, 1½ miles to the north.

Continue along the B2116 to Westmeston and here go forward with Underhill Road, unclassified, signed Narrow Lane. In ¾ mile turn left, signed The Beacon, and ascend a narrow winding road (1 in 10) to the summit of Ditchling Beacon ⑪.

Descend across undulating downland and in 2¼ miles pass a picnic site on the left. At the next T-junction turn left then turn right, no sign, and continue the descent to enter the suburbs of Brighton. After 3 miles turn left at the roundabout, signed Town Centre, then at traffic-lights turn right, A27, for the return to the start of the drive.

Newhaven — built about 400 years ago to replace the harbour at Seaford which became blocked when the Ouse changed course after a storm

POINTS OF INTEREST

① In Regency times Brighton became the most fashionable resort in England, and its centrepiece today, as it was then, is the Royal Pavilion. There is something for everyone here – beach, good shops, entertainment and nightlife.

② Old buildings line the High Street in the attractive village of Rottingdean where an early Georgian house contains the Grange Museum and Art Gallery.

③ The busy port of Newhaven is the start of the crossing to Dieppe and the only Sussex Channel port of importance. Of interest in the town is a coastal artillery fort and a museum near by.

④ Good shops and a 3-mile-long promenade are Seaford's attractions. The Martello Tower, part of a chain of defences built to defend the coast against Napoleon, now houses a fascinating Museum of Local History.

⑤ Alfriston is considered to be one of the most attractive villages in Sussex with several old buildings, notably the 13th-century Star Inn and the 14th-century Clergy House (National Trust).

⑥ Drusilla's is a small zoo with rare breeds, an adventure playground, a butterfly house, crafts and a bakery.

⑦ Home of the Gage family since the 15th century, Firle Place contains notable collections of Old Masters, porcelain and furniture.

⑧ Glynde Place is an Elizabethan manor house with high yew hedges, imposing gateways and a portrait-hung long gallery.

⑨ The opera house in the partly Tudor mansion of Glyndebourne opened in May 1934 with *The Marriage of Figaro*. Today it accommodates 830 people and attracts artists from all over the world.

⑩ Among the many interesting features in Lewes are the Norman castle, with its Barbican Museum of Sussex Archaeology, and the Museum of Local History in Anne of Cleves' House. The town is famous for its Bonfire Night celebrations when there is a great procession along the High Street.

⑪ At 813ft, Ditchling Beacon (National Trust) is one of the highest points on the South Downs and on a clear day affords views to the sea and across the Weald.

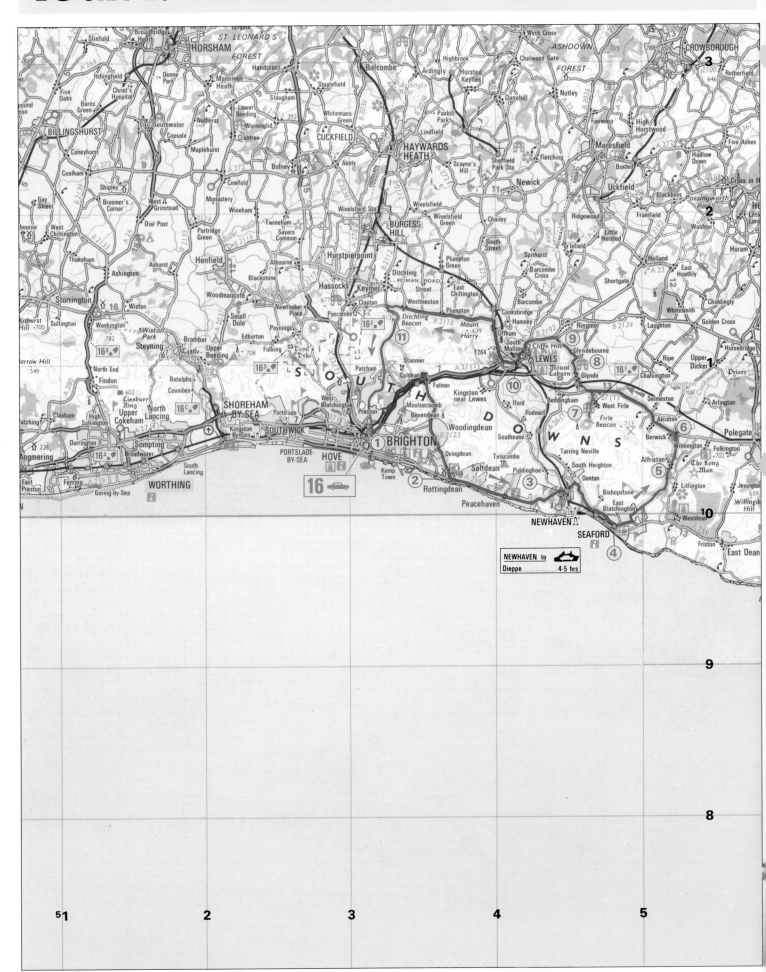

ROUTE DIRECTIONS

Allow 2½ hours
Start from the public car park at the far end of the recreation ground in Hillbarn Lane, off the Broadwater roundabout on the A27 north of Worthing (grid ref. TQ143055).

Walk back along Hillbarn Lane to the A24 and turn right at the roundabout①.

Continue beside the main road for about 300yds, then turn right up a bridleway. Walk straight up the bridleway towards the Downs for about half an hour, with the golf course mainly to the right. At the top, where a footpath joins from the left, go through the bridlegate②.

Bear centre-left across the grass to a fence stile, climb over and follow the path up steps to the top of the rampart③.

Bear left and follow the path around the monument④.

Continue over sheep-cropped turf to the north-eastern portal of the monument, at which point leave through a gate and bear right to head south-east along a grassy track to a bridlepath signpost.

Go straight ahead through a gate and follow the bridleway south along the eastern edge of the golf course. After a while pass a brick-and-flint barn, then houses and gardens on the left.

Reach a T-junction and turn right on to a metalled road, past a waterworks. The car park is at the end of the road on the left.

Cissbury Ring – 603ft high on the Downs behind Worthing

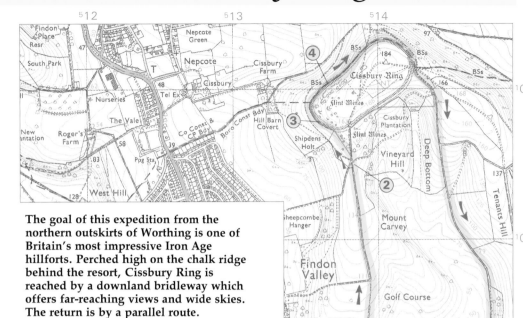

The goal of this expedition from the northern outskirts of Worthing is one of Britain's most impressive Iron Age hillforts. Perched high on the chalk ridge behind the resort, Cissbury Ring is reached by a downland bridleway which offers far-reaching views and wide skies. The return is by a parallel route.

POINTS OF INTEREST

① The Broadwater roundabout is at the edge of one of several villages that are now part of Worthing's urban sprawl. Broadwater was the original settlement, and retains something of a village atmosphere – helped by its fine late Norman church, ½ mile south-east of the roundabout. Two of the most widely read countryside writers of the late 19th and early 20th centuries – Richard Jefferies and W H Hudson – are buried in the churchyard.

② It is worth pausing at the bridlegate to take in the view. To the north loom the great ramparts of Cissbury, while to the east, beyond an old beech wood, lie Vineyard Hill and a sheltered valley known as Deep Bottom. Below, to the west, spreads the built-up area of the Findon Valley along the A24 out of Worthing.

③ Although Cissbury Ring is thought to be named after a Saxon king, Cissa, its history goes back much further. Around 3000BC Neolithic man had established flint mines here, and evidence of these can still be seen at the western end of the enclosure.

④ From the northern ramparts of Cissbury Ring there are views north to Chanctonbury and east to Truleigh Hill and Newtimber Hill. As a defensive position, Cissbury protected a very large area, far surpassing other Sussex hillforts in scale. Its ramparts are a mile long, and enclose an area of 60 acres. They are highest on the eastern side.

ROUTE DIRECTIONS

Allow 2½ hours
Start from the small car park off the access track to Washington Lime Quarry, east of the A24 at Highden Hill (grid ref. TQ121119).

Following South Downs Way signposts, climb a track to the 750ft hilltop①.

Turn left towards Chanctonbury Ring②.

Walk on to Chanctonbury Ring③.

Continue on the South Downs Way to a junction. Turn sharp left, leaving the Way, and follow the path downhill through Chalkpit Wood.

At the bottom of the hill turn left on a bridleway, past a brick-and-flint cottage. Walk on past Owlscroft Barn, through the northern fringe of the wood and eventually emerge at a footpath crossroads. Here go straight ahead across two open fields, then follow the path along a hedge line, past Tilley's Farm to the road④.

Turn left and walk back up the road to the quarry access track and car park.

Possibly a sacred meeting place in Neolithic times, Chanctonbury is said locally to have a strangely disturbing atmosphere

Views from prehistoric Chanctonbury Ring are well worth the steep climb necessary to reach it. The going is easier on the descent through beech woods to the village of Washington whose inn, according to writer Hilaire Belloc, served the very best beer in Sussex. Parts of the route can be very muddy.

POINTS OF INTEREST

①Near the summit of Chanctonbury Hill, pause to look at the dewpond on the left of the path, originally constructed in 1870 and restored by the Society of Sussex Downsmen. Dewponds, built to provide drinking water for cattle and sheep on the Downs, were lined with puddled clay to retain rainwater.

②On the ridge between Chanctonbury Hill and Chanctonbury Ring, look out for the remains of a cross-dyke at right angles to the track. Its bank is more than 200yds long, and has a ditch on its western side. The presence of a similar bank and ditch on the other side of Chanctonbury Ring suggests that these earthworks were part of the fort's defences.

③The small Iron Age hillfort of Chanctonbury Ring owes its fame as a South Downs landmark chiefly to the beech trees which crown its hilltop site. They were planted in 1760 by Charles Goring of nearby Wiston House.

④A short detour into Washington village is worth while – whether to visit the Frankland Arms for refreshment, to see St Mary's Church, or simply to enjoy the pleasant jumble of cottages, whose varied building materials – flint, brick, chalk and sandstone – are a reminder that the Downs meet the Weald not far from here.

Downland supports some of the richest flora in Britain

ROUTE DIRECTIONS

Allow 2 hours
Start from the telephone box below the church and Church Farm at Coombes, off the A27 west of Shoreham (grid ref. TQ192082).

Walk up the footpath to the church①.

Go through the churchyard and continue up through a copse to a footpath junction. Here turn right, go through a gate and turn immediately left to follow a fence across the hillside towards Coombehead Wood, with a good view of Coombes down to the right.

Cross the cattle grid and follow the bridleway along a farm track towards Steep Down. Eventually, after another cattle grid, leave the track where it bears right and head left under an electricity power line.

Climb up the field to a footpath signpost distantly visible on the skyline. At that junction turn right and follow a broad, grassy green lane for some distance. Emerge at a road, turn right and after 100yds turn right again on to the South Downs Way②.

Follow the Way for about a mile, passing Bramber Beeches③.

After climbing the hill, reach a junction and turn left along the South Downs Way, then descend past farm buildings to the entrance of Tin Pots Cottage. Here, where the track bears left, almost immediately leave the South Downs Way on a bridleway to the right, through a narrow belt of trees. Emerge from the trees and turn immediately right, passing the cottage and keeping close to the wood.

Follow the path to the right of a disused tip, climb through scrub and turn left at the top of the hill, by the pylon. At the road turn right and walk the short distance back along it to the car④.

Tucked into a fold of the Downs above the Adur Valley, the delightful hamlet of Coombes is the starting point for this walk. The ascent of Annington Hill is bracing but fairly gentle, with views to the sea and across the valley. Northward views open up on the return along the South Downs Way.

POINTS OF INTEREST

①The simple, tiny church at Coombes seems almost to have grown out of the steep hillside into which it is built. Parts of the building are Norman, with later additions made over the centuries. The fragments of wall paintings may be as much as 900 years old.

②The junction where the South Downs Way meets the road is at the top of Annington Hill, offering views in all directions. To the north is Steyning Bowl, a great combe sweeping down to the old town from which it takes its name (pronounced 'Stenning'). A prominent landmark away to the south-east is Lancing College, famous for its handsome neo-Gothic chapel.

③Bramber Beeches were planted by the county federation of Women's Institutes to mark their jubilee. Fine views continue on the descent of Annington Hill. Steyning and Bramber can be seen to the north, while Upper Beeding's cement works is

The long, straight pull up to Steep Down

clearly visible across the Adur Valley to the east. To the left and behind it is Truleigh Hill.

④Church Farm, Coombes, welcomes visits by school parties and organised groups, who are taken on a guided tour of the farm. Enquiries by post, or telephone Shoreham-by-Sea (0273) 452028.

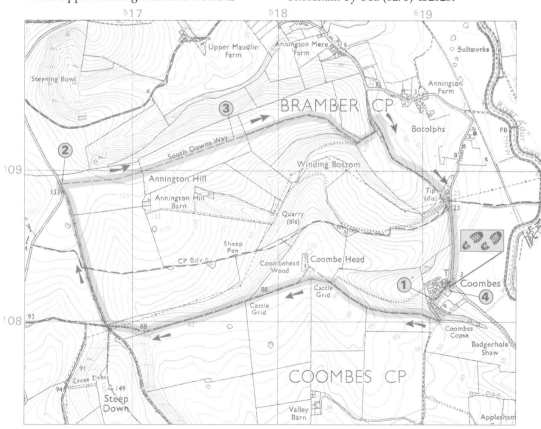

WALK 16D · Devil's Dyke   WEST SUSSEX

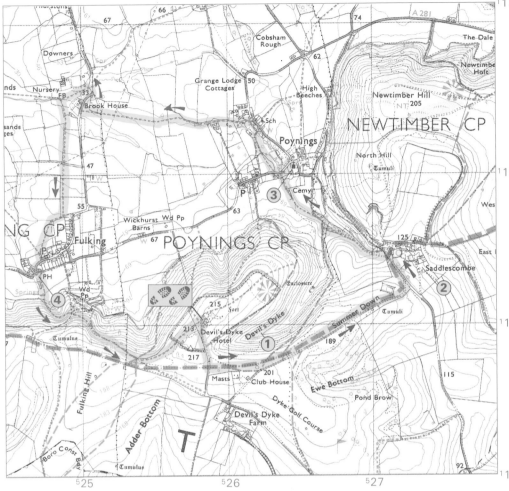

From a stunning 700ft-high viewpoint above the famous Devil's Dyke, this walk descends quite gradually to villages nestling along the springline at the foot of the Downs. A stiff climb leads back to the summit.

The Devil's Dyke has always attracted tourists, and at one time it could be crossed by cable car

POINTS OF INTEREST

①From the South Downs Way you can look down into Devil's Dyke, a ¾-mile-long dry cleft in the escarpment. The legend that goes with the name is that the valley was the start of an unsuccessful attempt by the Devil to cut a dyke through the South Downs so that the sea would flood the churches of the Weald. The hill towering above it, crowned by an Iron Age hillfort, is a popular spot for hang-gliding, or for flying model aircraft and kites.

②A charming memoir of 19th-century downland life called *A South Down Farm in the Sixties* describes Saddlescombe Farm, which still has a donkey-driven winding wheel in its well-house.

③The handsome flint church at Poynings was built with money left by Michael of Poynings, a local landowner who had fought at Crécy and Poitiers, and who died in 1369. Do not miss the interesting display about Dr Samuel Holland.

④Fulking's Shepherd and Dog inn is a reminder that the village used to earn its living from the thousands of sheep that once grazed the Downs.

ROUTE DIRECTIONS

Allow at least 2½ hours
Start from the Devil's Dyke Hotel, at the end of an unclassified road north-west of Brighton (grid ref. TQ258111).

Leave the car park, walk back along the road and turn left along the South Downs Way①.

Follow the Way to the main road, opposite Saddlescombe Farm②.

Take the path into the field on the left and walk round the wood. Follow the rather obscure signpost, keep to the right of the field, descend into a muddy hollow and cross the stile. Turn right down the path. Very soon leave the path by stile on left, keeping a stream on the right.

Climb the grassy bank, keeping close to the right of the field, and cross meadow-land to reach the road via a stile. (There may be temporary fencing.) Turn right for Poynings church③.

Return and take the path on the right, off the road, passing through a gate into the field. Keep to the right of the field, through an iron gate, and bear right following a close-boarded fence where the paths converge.

Go through a wicket gate, cross the stream footbridge and turn left at the signpost to follow a surfaced twitten (alleyway) to its junction with Mill Lane. Turn left. Follow road by stream.

Pass a sewage works and a small dam, then leave the stream at a wooden footbridge and follow the path over a field, through an iron gate, over a stile and into a big, open field. Keeping Chanctonbury ahead to the left, arrive at a road.

Turn right and walk past a house with a tennis court. Cross the stream and turn left on to the footpath by Brookside Liveries. Follow the path by the stream, cross bridge and head south.

At the corner of the field turn right over a stile, and after 100yds turn left round the edge of the field. On the far side, cross a stile over a post-and-rail fence. Join the road and turn right to the Shepherd and Dog④.

Walk across the pub car park (under the trellis) and follow the public path, then turn right and begin the climb up to the Dyke Hotel. Ascend steps and head for the prominent signpost on the skyline, then continue straight up the chalky track to the summit. Go through the gate and follow path along crest to the hotel.

ROUTE DIRECTIONS

Allow 2½ hours
*Start from the public car park
beside Jill Mill (grid ref.
GR303135).*

*To find it, leave the A273 near
Clayton, turn into Mill Lane and
drive up the hill①.*

Walk up the track, past Jack Mill,
and turn left at the junction with
the South Downs Way, where
there is a stone bridleway
marker. Walk along the Way for
nearly two miles to Ditchling
Beacon car park, ignoring all
paths to the right②.

Return from Ditchling Beacon
car park along the main track,
passing first a triangulation point
and then a scrub-filled dewpond
on the left. At the old pond turn
left on to a gated bridleway and
follow it between large fields③.

Keep straight on through
double gates, and where another
gated bridleway joins from the
left, then descend steeply to a
metal field gate and bear
diagonally right, signposted
Lower Standean. Follow the
centre of a sheltered valley,
winding right and leaving the
field through a metal gate.

Continue along the valley, or
combe, and where it swings left
go through a wooden gate with
a blue waymark and turn sharp
left to follow the fence. Ascend a
chalky path and cross a ridge to
Lower Standean Farm.

At the bridleway junction, turn
right, signed Keymer Post. Pass
brick-and-flint buildings on the
left, ignore a left turn and follow
the track through a hedgeline.

Climb up out of the valley,
following the bridleway signposts
and at the crossroads turn right
through a hedge boundary and
continue across open fields. Soon
Jack Mill can be seen ahead to
the left.

Rejoin the South Downs Way
at Keymer Post④.

Turn left to the car park.

Clayton's famous windmills – Jack and Jill – and
one of the marvellous views from Ditchling Beacon

**Beginning at a familiar Sussex landmark –
the Clayton windmills, affectionately
known as Jack and Jill – this bracing walk
follows the South Downs Way along the
escarpment to Ditchling Beacon. The
contrasting return follows bridleways along
the sheltered valleys of the south-facing
dip slope, which falls away to the sea.**

POINTS OF INTEREST

①Probably among England's most famous
windmills, Jack and Jill worked together
here until about 1907. Jill, the white post-
mill, was originally built in Brighton in 1821
and was moved here, dragged by teams of
oxen, in 1852. Today her sails turn again,
working to produce the stoneground
wholemeal flour which is sold when the
mill is open, normally on Sundays.

②At 813ft, Ditchling Beacon is the third
highest point on the South Downs. Views
from the summit stretch across the Weald to
the North Downs, with Ashdown Forest
and Crowborough Beacon visible nearer at
hand. The site of an Iron Age hillfort, it was
also one of a chain of summits on which
beacon fires were lit to warn of the Armada.

③The fields to either side of the bridleway
are a good place to see flints, the irregular
stones composed almost entirely of silica
which occur in the chalk and have been
used by man since earliest times.

④Topped by an acorn finial, the Keymer
Post marks the county boundary between
East and West Sussex. On this stretch of the
South Downs Way note the fine downland
turf and look out for dewponds,
constructed by farmers to provide drinking
water for their sheep.

WALK 16F · Firle EAST SUSSEX

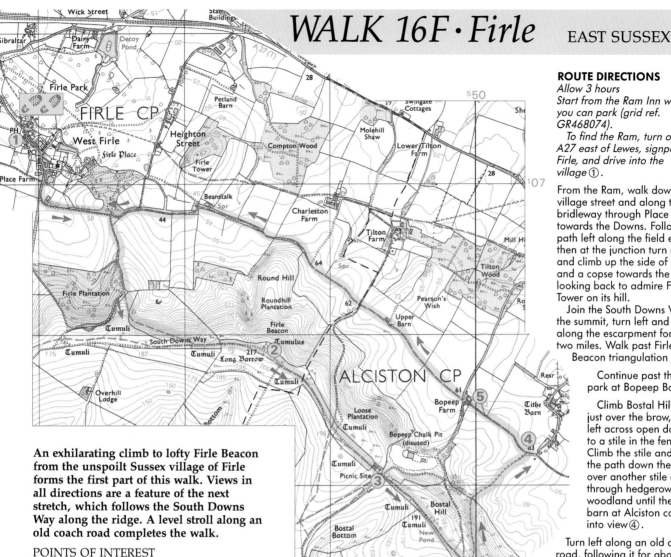

ROUTE DIRECTIONS

Allow 3 hours
Start from the Ram Inn where you can park (grid ref. GR468074).

To find the Ram, turn off the A27 east of Lewes, signposted Firle, and drive into the village ①.

From the Ram, walk down the village street and along the bridleway through Place Farm towards the Downs. Follow the path left along the field edge, then at the junction turn right and climb up the side of the field and a copse towards the top, looking back to admire Firle Tower on its hill.

Join the South Downs Way at the summit, turn left and walk along the escarpment for about two miles. Walk past Firle Beacon triangulation point ②.

Continue past the car park at Bopeep Bostal ③.

Climb Bostal Hill and, just over the brow, bear left across open downland to a stile in the fence. Climb the stile and follow the path down the hill, over another stile and through hedgerow woodland until the tithe barn at Alciston comes into view ④.

Turn left along an old coach road, following it for about two miles to Firle. (Be careful not to go straight on towards the tithe barn) ⑤.

Walk past Bopeep Farm, Upper Barn and the old Beanstalk — formerly an inn on the coach road and now a pair of cottages — below Firle Tower. Bear left and then right at the Beanstalk, and follow the track straight on to the village and back to your car.

An exhilarating climb to lofty Firle Beacon from the unspoilt Sussex village of Firle forms the first part of this walk. Views in all directions are a feature of the next stretch, which follows the South Downs Way along the ridge. A level stroll along an old coach road completes the walk.

POINTS OF INTEREST

① The Ram takes its name from the crest of the Gage family, who have lived at Firle Place since the 15th century. The house is open to the public in summer, and has a splendid collection of porcelain, paintings and furniture. Sir John Gage and his wife, Philippa, are the subjects of the beautiful alabaster effigies in St Peter's Church, which also has several very good brasses. These can be rubbed for a small fee.

② Firle Beacon, and the village of Firle far below, derive their name from an Old English word meaning oak tree. From the 718ft Beacon there are views north to the Weald and south to the sea. The chalk ridge between Firle Beacon and Bostal Hill is good for wild flowers.

③ Bostal is the Sussex term for a road or track which ascends the scarp of the Downs. From the car park there are views south to Newhaven, Cuckmere Haven and the Seven Sisters.

④ Alciston's magnificent 14th-century tithe barn is one of the longest in the country, at 170ft. This little hamlet became known as the forgotten village after its population fled before the Black Death.

⑤ The coach road under the Downs carried all traffic until 1812, and its often muddy condition gives a good idea of travel problems in days gone by.

The pub sign at Firle — Southdown rams do not have horns, but the artist added them for effect

ROUTE DIRECTIONS
The drive starts from Eastbourne ①.

From the seafront follow the B2103 towards Beachy Head. After a winding ascent turn sharp left on to an unclassified road, signed Beachy Head. This road soon reaches the summit of Beachy Head.

Continue along the unclassified road past the disused Belle Tout Lighthouse to Birling Gap. Between here and Seaford are the chalk cliffs known as the Seven Sisters (National Trust).

The drive veers inland to East Dean ②.

From East Dean, a left turn is made on to the A259 Seaford road. Ascend (1 in 6) to Friston and 2 miles farther descend (1 in 7) into the valley of the Cuckmere River. At Exceat, at the foot of the hill, is the entrance to the Seven Sisters Country Park. Opposite is the Living World Museum of natural history ③.

Take the next turning right on to an unclassified road, signed Litlington and Alfriston. In just over ¼ mile a short diversion to the right may be taken to the village of Westdean ④.

The main drive continues along the winding road. A car park and forest walk are passed at the edge of Friston Forest on the right, and across the valley to the left a figure of a white horse cut into the hillside can be seen.

Proceed through Litlington and in ½ mile turn left, signed Alfriston. A detour (¼ mile) ahead leads to Lullington Church ⑤.

In ¾ mile bear left and cross the Cuckmere River then, at the T-junction, turn right, signed Berwick Station and Dicker. Alternatively turn left for Alfriston ⑥.

The main drive heads northwards and in ¾ mile passes the Drusilla's Zoo Park, on the right ⑦.

From Beachy Head, the drive passes one of England's smallest churches, an Augustinian priory and the Royal Observatory at Herstmonceux to reach Pevensey, landing place of William the Conqueror.

At the next roundabout take the second exit and later go over the level crossing at Berwick Station. Two and a half miles farther the drive reaches Upper Dicker. Here a short detour to the right leads to Michelham Priory ⑧.

The main drive turns left, signed Golden Cross. In 1¼ miles turn left on to the A22 and nearly ½ mile farther take the next turning right, unclassified, signed Gun Hill. Continue with the Horam road and in 3¾ miles turn left on to the A267 and enter Horam. Branch right with the B2203, signed Heathfield, and proceed for 3 miles to the outskirts of Heathfield. At the junction with the A265 turn right, signed Hawkhurst, and follow a ridge of the Sussex Weald through Broad Oak, Burwash Weald and on to Burwash. Before Burwash, a turning to the right leads to Bateman's (National Trust) ⑨.

In Burwash turn right on to an unclassified road, signed Wood's Corner. After crossing the River Dudwell gradually ascend and in 1 mile turn right. Continue the ascent, passing close to a gypsum mine, on the left, and near the 646ft summit go forward over the crossroads. Shortly, at the T-junction, turn right and then descend to Wood's Corner. At the Swan Inn turn right then immediately left, signed Bodle Street. In ¾ mile continue with the Ponts Green/Ashburnham road through pleasant countryside, then follow the Ninfield signs.

Three miles farther at the junction

with the B2204 turn right, signed Boreham Street. In another mile turn right again on to the A271 to reach Boreham Street. Half a mile beyond the village turn left, unclassified, signed Royal Greenwich Observatory and Pevensey. After another mile, on the right, is the entrance to Herstmonceux Castle ⑩.

Continue to Wartling and at the Lamb Inn bear right, signed Pevensey. The low-lying Pevensey Levels are then crossed to reach the edge of Pevensey ⑪.

The main drive turns right on to the A259 (roundabout due for completion) then left at the traffic-lights, signed Pevensey Bay. Alternatively keep forward for the village and castle. At Pevensey Bay turn right for the return to Eastbourne.

POINTS OF INTEREST

① George III gave Eastbourne the royal seal of approval in 1780 and it's been a popular holiday resort ever since, with its elegant Victorian and Edwardian seafront, 200 acres of parks and gardens, splendid pier and safe sands.

② East Dean has a picture-book village green with a pub, flint cottages and a general store. The whitewashed Tiger Inn, built in 1298, was once a famous smugglers' haunt. The 11th-century church has a Saxon tower.

③ The excellent Living World Museum, with its living displays from the countryside and seashore,

is part of the Seven Sisters Country Park, which covers about 700 acres around the Cuckmere Valley.

④ Westdean is a secluded little village in the heart of Friston Forest. It is thought that Alfred the Great kept a fleet here and that his palace stood where the ruins of a medieval manor now lie.

⑤ Lullington church is only 16ft square and has no more than 20 seats making it one of England's smallest churches. Services are still held there on the first Sunday of the month.

⑥ A picture-book and one-time smuggling village, Alfriston has a street lined with medieval timber-framed houses, flint cottages with overhanging tiles, and a spreading chestnut tree in its small square.

⑦ Known to be the best small zoo park in the south, Drusilla's attractions include over 400 animals and birds, a beamed restaurant and a Japanese garden.

⑧ Founded by the Augustinian monks in 1229, Michelham Priory is a peaceful spot, with ducks on the moat and a 15th-century mill.

⑨ Seventeenth-century Bateman's was Rudyard Kipling's home for some years. The watermill, installed by Kipling, is one of the oldest working water-driven turbines in the world.

⑩ The beautiful, red-brick, moated Herstmonceux Castle has long been the home of the Royal Greenwich Observatory. The Welcome Stranger, in the village, is one of the smallest inns in Sussex.

⑪ William the Conqueror landed at Pevensey in 1066, and the moated castle stands within Roman walls. There are several interesting buildings in the village, including the old Minthouse, built in 1342 and now a museum.

First built by William the Conqueror's brother, Pevensey Castle was refortified as recently as 1940

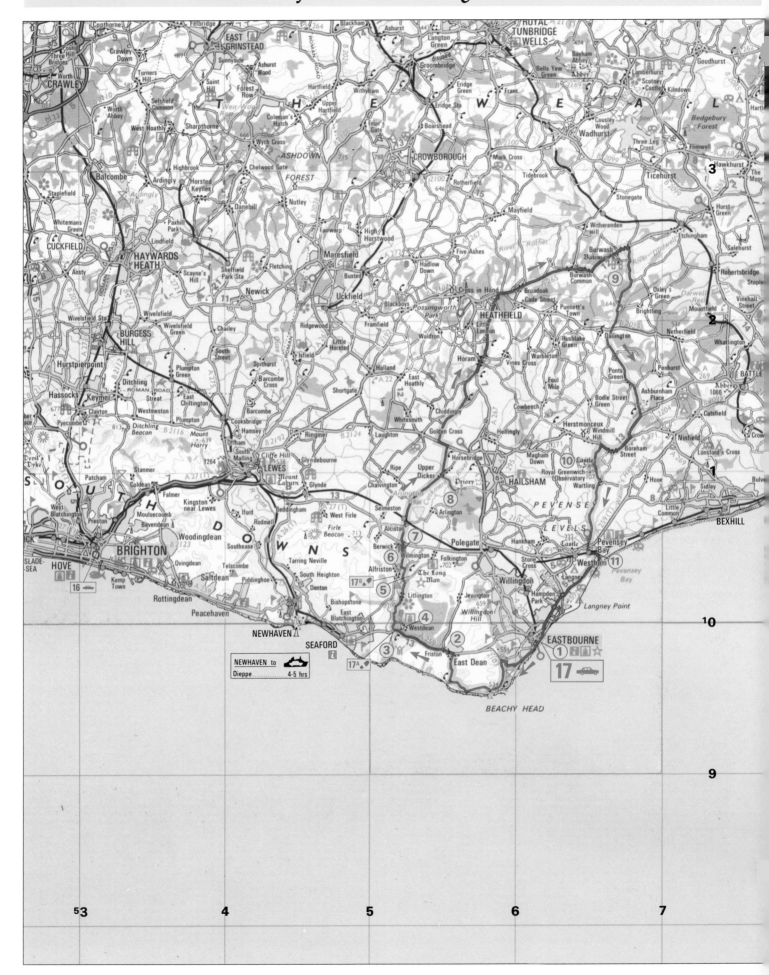

WALK 17A · Seven Chalk Cliffs   EAST SUSSEX

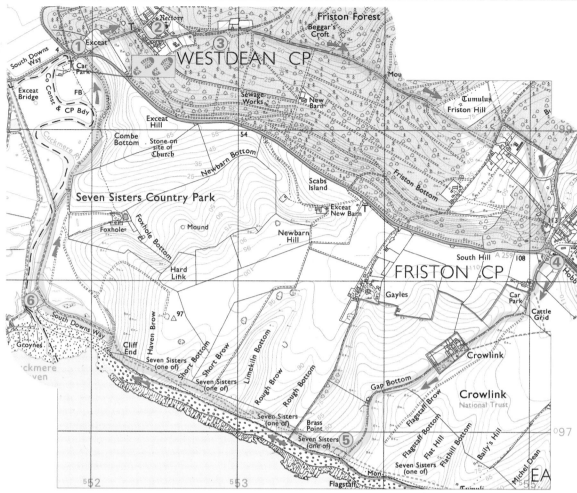

ROUTE DIRECTIONS
Allow 3 hours
Start from the public car park south of the A259, at the Seven Sisters Country Park Centre at Exceat (grid ref. GR518995) ①.

Cross the road with care and follow South Downs Way signs up the hill to the right of the centre. Climb over the flint wall at the top and go straight on, soon climbing down a stepped slope through woodland to Westdean village②.

Turn right by the pond, signed Friston and Jevington. Follow the road and – where it curves left – continue straight on into Friston Forest③.

After a pair of white cottages and a vineyard, bear right up a chalky track signed Friston. Follow the broad forest ride for about half an hour, ignoring all paths to the right and left.

Eventually, reach a road opposite a brick-and-flint barn and turn left, signed Friston. Follow this uphill to a gate and stay with it as it swings sharply downhill to the right. Half-way up the subsequent rise turn right over a stile into a field, signed Friston and East Dean.

Cross the field to a gate, cross a road and continue on the path through the next field. Climb over the stile and walk up steps through a wood. Climb the wall steps to emerge on the busy A259 opposite Friston church, cross the road and take the no-through road beside the church to Crowlink④.

Walk through the National Trust car park, bear right and follow the road through Crowlink to a grassy gated track, which leads to a dewpond. There ascend diagonally right to the cliff top and continue right over the testing summits of the Seven Sisters to Cuckmere Haven⑤.

Descend from Haven Brow by the South Downs Way to a raised causeway alongside the shingle beach, and walk along to the river⑥.

Turn right on to a gravel path, which becomes a grassy track and eventually a concrete road, all the time heading north towards the head of the valley and the car park.

Exploring perhaps the most famous section of downland in Sussex, this classic route visits Friston Forest, the Seven Sisters, Cuckmere Haven and the Cuckmere Valley.

POINTS OF INTEREST

① Some 700 acres of outstanding coast and downland make up the Seven Sisters Country Park, whose visitor centre is here in the tiny riverside village of Exceat. A beautifully converted 18th-century barn houses an exhibition about the Downs and the excellent Living World Museum.

② Church, duckpond and flint cottages make an idyllic picture at this secluded little village in Friston Forest. It is thought that Alfred the Great had a palace here.

③ Most of the trees in Friston Forest are beech, with other species such as Corsican pines planted to give them shelter from the salt-laden sea winds.

④ Standing on its own beside a pond, Friston church dates partly from 1042. Its door is dedicated to the 20th-century composer Frank Bridge.

⑤ Almost as famous as the White Cliffs of Dover, the Seven Sisters present a challenge to even the most energetic walker. Seabirds including fulmars nest on the cliffs themselves, while chalk-loving wild flowers and cropped turf carpet the Down above.

⑥ Backed by water meadows and the silver meanders of the river, Cuckmere Haven is a completely unspoilt estuary. Various habitats, including salt-marsh, a lagoon and shingle banks, attract many species of bird.

The Seven Sisters chalk cliffs, from Exceat

Partly on the high, bare downland of East Sussex and partly in one of England's areas of undisturbed chalk heath, this walk visits the curious Long Man of Wilmington chalk figure before exploring the exquisite village of Alfriston, on the Cuckmere River.

POINTS OF INTEREST

① Topped by a weatherboarded belfry, Lullington's tiny flint-and-stone church is the smallest in Sussex, measuring only about 16ft square. The reason is that it is the chancel of a once larger church. Services are held once a month, and there is a solitary grave in the churchyard.

② Below, on the north face of Windover Hill, is the Long Man of Wilmington – a figure 240ft high, outlined originally in chalk. His origins are obscure, one story being that he was cut by the monks of the Benedictine priory at Wilmington – the ruins of which can be seen adjoining the farmhouse in the valley below.

③ Lullington Heath is protected by the Nature Conservancy Council as the classic example of a rare habitat known as chalk heath. Here the chalk is mixed with sandy soil, so typical downland plants such as wild thyme grow happily side by side with acid-loving species such as ling.

④ Allow time at the end of the walk to explore the exceptionally pretty (if popular) riverside village of Alfriston, whose dignified 14th-century church is known by

The mysterious Long Man of Wilmington

the Cathedral of the South Downs. Near by stands the famous Clergy House, timber-framed and thatched, and as old as the church. It was the first building to be acquired by the National Trust, and is open daily in summer. Across the village green, known as The Tye, a street of delightful old cottages leads to the market cross. Alfriston has several teashops and inns, some of which have been giving hospitality to travellers and pilgrims for centuries. Many of today's customers are walkers on the South Downs Way.

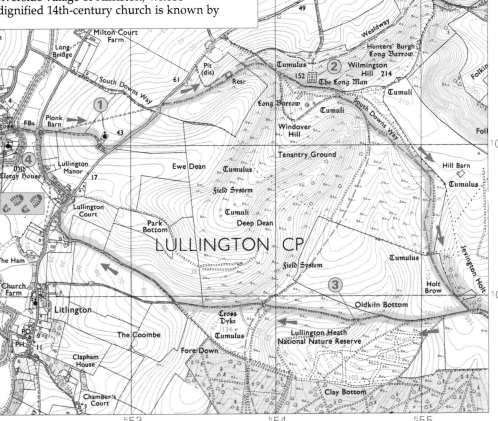

ROUTE DIRECTIONS

Allow 2½ hours
Start from the church at Alfriston (grid ref. TQ522030).

Cross the Cuckmere River by the white bridle-bridge near the church and follow a metalled path to the road. Cross the road by Plonk Barn and take the footpath signed Lullington Church. Continue to the church, ignoring a sign to the South Downs Way ①.

Return to the brick path and continue left to the road. Turn left and follow the road for about 400yds to the hill crest, then turn right and join the South Downs Way. Towards the top of the hill keep straight on, even though the South Downs Way bears right, and follow fence line ②.

Keep straight on beside the fence to a gate, then bear right alongside another fence to rejoin the South Downs Way through a bridlegate in about 20yds. Follow the Way partly round the rim of a deep combe for about 300yds, then strike off diagonally left to pick up a concrete South Downs Way marker. Continue to a second marker, then uphill over open downland to a fence. Follow the fence right, then near a roofless barn continue right past a wood to a crossroads.

Turn right, leaving the South Downs Way, and walk through the edge of Lullington Heath National Nature Reserve, following signs to Litlington. Avoid the path left into the nature reserve, signed Charleston Bottom ③.

At the next junction, as views of Alfriston and the Cuckmere Valley open up, bear right on a path signed Lullington Court. Join the road at Lullington Court, turn right and then left, signed Alfriston. Walk along the road to Plonk Barn, turn left and follow the path back to the village ④.

ROUTE DIRECTIONS
The drive starts from Ipswich ①.

Follow signs to Colchester (A12) to leave by the London Road, A1214. In 2 miles, at the traffic signals, turn right on to the A1071, signed Hadleigh. Half a mile further, go forward at the roundabout. Later, pass through Hintlesham, then in

This tour visits the beautiful Suffolk countryside which Constable captured in his paintings. Places such as Flatford Mill, Lavenham and Long Melford have hardly changed at all since the artist's time, some two hundred years ago.

⑤ At the northern end of Long Melford is a large green beside which stands the fine 15th-century church. Old buildings include the Tudor red-brick Melford Hall, and the Elizabethan Kentwell Hall. The Bull Inn dates from the 15th century.

3¾ miles turn left on to the B1070 and enter the market town of Hadleigh ②.

At the T-junction turn right, signed Lavenham. Keep left across the river bridge, then bear right. Almost ½ mile further on, turn left, then immediately right, to join the A1141. In ¾ mile turn left on to the unclassified Kersey road, then in another ¾ mile turn right and enter Kersey ③.

Descend through the watersplash, then ascend. Almost 1 mile further on, turn left to rejoin the Lavenham road, A1141. In 3½ miles, at the crossroads, keep left to Monks Eleigh, then continue past the edge of Brent Eleigh to reach Lavenham ④.

Follow signs Sudbury, to leave by the B1071. In ½ mile, at the outskirts of the town, turn right on to the unclassified Long Melford road. After 2¾ miles turn right again, and continue to the village of Long Melford ⑤.

Leave by the Sudbury road, A134. In 1¾ miles at the roundabout, take the second exit, A131, and enter the Stour Valley market town of Sudbury ⑥.

Follow signs Bures to leave by the B1508, and head down the Stour Valley to Bures ⑦.

In the village, turn left at the church on to an unclassified road, signed Nayland. Follow this by-road, narrow in places, for 4½ miles to the junction with the A134. Turn right here, and immediately left, on the B1087, to enter the old village of Nayland ⑧.

Proceed to Stoke-by-Nayland and turn right, B1068, signed Ipswich. Continue through Thorington Street and Higham, then in 2 miles turn left on to the A12. Half a mile further on, branch left, B1070, signed East Bergholt, then turn left again. In another mile, at the Carriers Arms, turn right, unclassified, and enter the village of East Bergholt ⑨.

On reaching the church, bear left, then in ½ mile pass the turning, on the right, which leads to Flatford Mill ⑩.

The drive continues on the Manningtree road, and, in almost another ½ mile, rejoins the B1070. In 1¼ miles, turn left on to the A137, signed Ipswich, and pass through Brantham. One mile further, at the Bull Inn, turn right on to the Holbrook road, B1080. Beyond Stutton the road runs through the grounds of the Royal Hospital School, to reach Holbrook. In 1¾ miles take the B1456, signed Ipswich, and later drive alongside the River Orwell to pass beneath the Orwell

Road Bridge. At the roundabout, turn right on to the A137 for the return to Ipswich.

POINTS OF INTEREST

① Little remains of medieval Ipswich, the county town of Suffolk, which today is a predominantly Victorian town. Twelve medieval churches survive, however, as does the 16th-century Ancient House, a rich merchant's house with oriel windows and magnificent coloured pargeting. Christchurch Mansion, an Elizabethan house, has a fine collection of china and glass.

② The important provincial town of Hadleigh was once a Viking stronghold and later became one of the most prosperous towns in the country. It retains a variety of Suffolk architecture.

③ Kersey is one of the prettiest of the Suffolk wool towns, with its street of timber-framed, colour-washed cottages and their pantile roofs. The street rises to a Saxon church.

④ One of the most famous historic wool towns in England, Lavenham is rich in old timbered houses, such as the Guildhall (National Trust) dating from 1529. The church is one of the finest in East Anglia.

Flatford Mill inspired many of Constable's paintings

⑥ An ancient market town on the River Stour, Sudbury was Charles Dickens' 'Eatanswill' in *The Pickwick Papers*. It is also the place where, in Gainsborough Street, Thomas Gainsborough was born in 1727. The house is now a museum and art gallery.

⑦ To the north-east of Bures is St Stephen's Chapel, a small thatched building thought to stand on the site where St Edmund was crowned in 855.

⑧ A delightful village, Nayland's Parish Church of St James contains one of Constable's only two religious works. The mainly Perpendicular church is full of monuments to wealthy clothiers.

⑨ John Constable was born in East Bergholt in 1776. Although you can no longer see the house in which he was born, his studio is still standing, as part of the Post Office.

⑩ Flatford Mill, built in 1773, is owned by the National Trust. Nearby is a study centre. From the car park here, a path winds to the Stour. Along the right bank you can see the side of the Mill, with its sluice gate and trees overhanging the river bank.

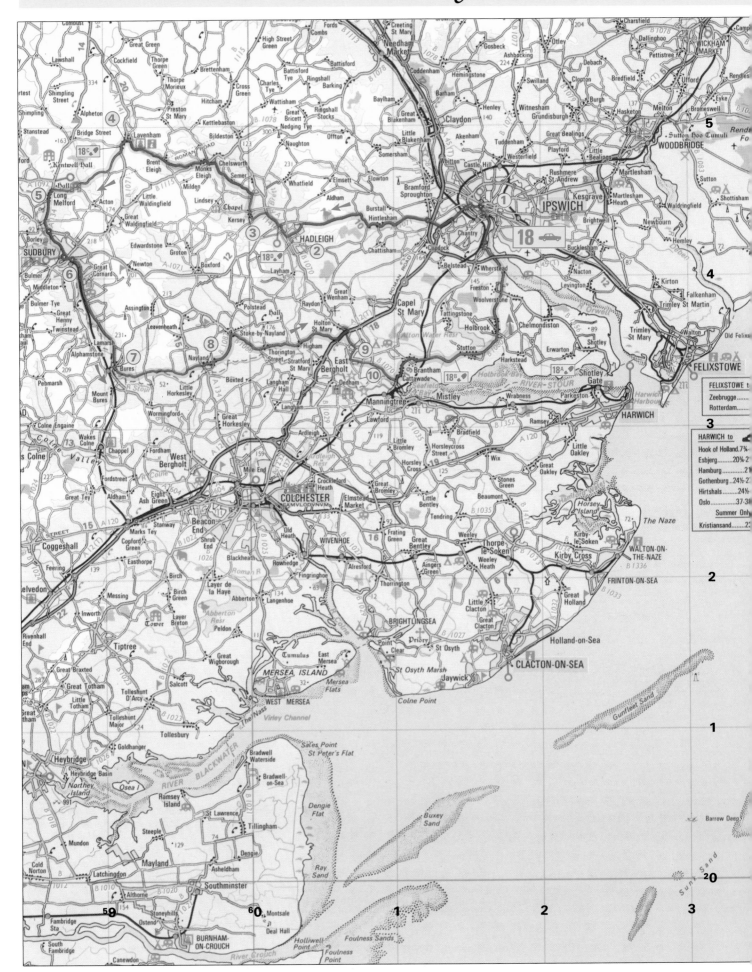

WALK 18A · The Orwell & the Stour   SUFFOLK

Commercial boats still use these waters, but the older ones have become pleasure craft

ROUTE DIRECTIONS

Allow 3 hours
Start from Shotley Post Office; parking is available in the side road at the rear (grid ref. TM233351).

Walk down the main street, with the Post Office on your right.

Turn left along a metalled footpath between houses and the village hall. Cross the road and turn right, then turn left between the bungalow numbered 26 and a row of four garages.

The footpath continues between fields. At the field boundary, turn right, then left, over a footbridge. The footpath continues diagonally across the corner of a field, rejoining the boundary hedge, and becomes a well-marked track①.

When the track meets a road turn right②.

Go past the church③.

Going downhill, turn right, and then climb over a stile into a meadow. Follow the path straight to the river estuary, go over a second stile and up on to the top of the river bank. Turn right and follow the path alongside the Orwell④.

Continue round Shotley Point towards Shotley Gate⑤.

Take the path around the marina, passing the Bristol Arms. Bear left along a footpath beside the River Stour. After 750yds turn right up some steepish steps to the road; turn left here.

At the end of the road, go across a grassy area, and then take the path through a wood, along a field edge. After passing some cottages and caravans, turn right at cross tracks, up a wide rough track, passing Shotley Cottage on your right.

Continue along this path to the road. At the main road turn left, and return to the car park.

The banks of two of East Anglia's principal rivers provide most of the walking on this route. As well as a chance to see a variety of seabirds, there are views across the estuary to the harbours of Felixstowe and Harwich, always busy with Continental shipping.

POINTS OF INTEREST

① As the track approaches the road, there are good views over gently undulating farmland with the River Orwell to the north and east.

② Shotley Hall, on the north side of the road, is a handsome timber-framed farmhouse. It has retained one of its original 16th-century gables, but much of the building was added in the 19th century.

③ From Shotley church there are good views out to sea across the marshes. The building has a Georgian chancel, and the churchyard contains the graves of a great many sailors, including the whole ship's company of HMS *Gypsy*, which was blown up by a magnetic mine in the Orwell near here.

④ The lower reaches of the Orwell are a hive of activity, with coastal shipping travelling up to Ipswich, and yachts plying to and from the marina at Levington, upstream on the opposite bank. The estuary is also good for seabirds. Cormorants can often be seen here, and many waders fly upstream to feed on the mudflats where the river widens around Pin Mill. The Orwell joins the Stour at Bloody Point.

⑤ The modern village of Shotley Gate is dominated by HMS *Ganges*, an onshore training centre for the Navy. The centre takes its name from the 19th-century ship which was moored here and used for training recruits before the shore station was founded. A ferry used to operate between Shotley Pier and Harwich, clearly visible across the Stour. Like the Orwell, the Stour (which divides Suffolk from Essex) is good for birdwatching: shelduck, wigeon, black-tailed godwits and brent geese are all numerous in winter.

VEHICLE (V) & FOOT PASSENGER (F) FERRY SHIP	
Esbjerg (V/F) (Summer only)	20 hrs
Hamburg (V/F)	19–21½ hrs
Hook of Holland (V/F)	6½–8½ hrs
Gothenburgh (V/F)	23–25 hrs

ROUTE DIRECTIONS
Allow 2½ hours
Start from the car park at the
Stutton Community Centre
(grid ref. TM143347)①.

From the car park turn right into the road, passing the Gardeners' Arms on your left. Turn left into the driveway to Stutton Hall, passing the lodge cottage at the entrance②.

At a cross tracks, turn right and at the next junction, turn left and follow the winding lane to Stutton Mill and the River Stour③.

Go through the white gates. The path continues in front of the mill house. Go up on to the bank. The path goes either along the field edge at first, then down along the river shore; or immediately along the river shore, going first through high reeds for a very short distance④.

The driveway leading to 16th-century Stutton Hall

Stutton lies close to the River Stour and the walk follows its banks, with superb views along the way. The Stour Estuary has been designated an Area of Outstanding Natural Beauty, and the region is excellent for bird-watching – many species of waders and water birds can be spotted. Over the farmland, hares chase one another.

POINTS OF INTEREST

①Stutton is a pleasant village with modern houses blending in well with the old timber-framed and pink-washed cottages, some with thatch. To the east, Stutton House, opposite the church, was built as the rectory in 1750. St Peter's is also worth a visit and there are lovely views from the top of its 15th-century tower.

②Built in the mid 16th century, Stutton Hall has a lovely walled garden and fine views across the estuary. Originally timber-framed, it was rebuilt in brick in the late 19th and early 20th centuries.

③The lane leading to Stutton Mill affords superb views over rolling countryside in all directions. The mill itself, now a private house, stands overlooking the river.

Along the banks of the Stour Estuary

④This idyllic waterside scene has many interesting features. Colourful barges can be seen moored at low water in the estuary, and, looking across to Jacques Bay, trains can be seen (and heard) travelling to Harwich Harbour. Oystercatchers, shelduck and redshank are among the many birds that can be spotted along this stretch of the river walk.

⑤At Stutton Ness, the large clock tower of the Royal Hospital School towers over the trees; the chimes of the clock can be heard ringing out over the water.

About 20yds beyond a bird-watchers' hide, on the left, climb a bank and cross a wooden bridge. Follow the path at the edge of a wood, then enter a field. Before the next stretch of woodland, bear right down to a track beside the river. Go around the point at Stutton Ness, then turn left up on to a wide path, alongside the edge of a field⑤.

The track winds and turns left, leaving the river to go inland. Walk past farm buildings and Crepping Hall. The path continues along a driveway lined with poplars and holly trees. At a road, turn left and return to the Community Centre.

After passing a thatched house on the left, keep the Tudor house on your left and go along a road signed Lavenham. Cross the main road and continue up a narrow lane, with the Cock Inn on your right. Immediately after crossing the stream, turn right along a path at the field edge. Follow the yellow footpath markers. Ignore a stile on the right leading to the lake area.

At a farm track turn right then almost immediately left, keeping the hedge on your left and a plantation of poplar trees on your right. At the end of the plantation, a footpath crosses to the left bank of the stream. Continue along the edge of the stream for 650yds, ignoring the first footpath indicated to the right and taking the second one, turning sharp right uphill, then left along a track to a farm, ignoring the path ahead. At the pond turn right, skirting around the farm house to join a lane. At the lane turn right. Pass a pink thatched cottage, and then some new houses. As the lane bears right, turn left up a narrow metalled footpath to return to the car park.

This pleasant stroll takes in the historic town of Lavenham – whose layout has hardly changed since the Middle Ages – and the surrounding farmland where apple orchards can be seen.

POINTS OF INTEREST

① Lavenham has some exceptionally beautiful timbered houses and inns dating from the days when it was a centre for the cloth-weaving industry. Two of its finest buildings are the 16th-century Guildhall – now housing a museum – in the Market Place and the Old Priory, which has a lovely herb garden and is also open to the public.

② Along this stretch of the walk there are tremendous views over the flat countryside. Clay Lane is an ancient routeway and the hedges contain a great number of plant species such as hazel, spindle, field maple, honeysuckle, dog's mercury and even some wetland species. As Spragg's Wood is approached, look out for primroses and bluebells in season.

③ The village of Brent Eleigh takes its name from *Illeleya*, derived from *leah*, the estate or land of a Saxon landowner. One of its most imposing buildings is Brent Eleigh Hall, now a herb-growing centre. St Mary's Church has interesting old box pews and fine medieval paintings on the east wall.

One of Lavenham's four guilds, the Guild of Corpus Christi, built the 16th-century half-timbered Guildhall, whose uses have ranged from prison to school. It now houses a museum featuring the cloth trade

ROUTE DIRECTIONS

Allow 2¼ hours
Start from the free car park nearly opposite the church and next to the thatched Cock Inn (grid ref. TL915490).

Turn right down Church Street passing the timber-framed houses, then right along Water Street, passing the Priory①.

Turn left along a by-road, passing a postbox on a telegraph pole and keeping the playing field on your right. Turn right into the lane leading to Clayhill Farm. Cross the river by a bridge. Continue up the bridleway, passing a farm on your left and one mile or so further along, apple orchards on your right②.

At a by-road turn right towards Brent Eleigh village. Go down the hill, passing Brent Eleigh Hall and the church on your right③.

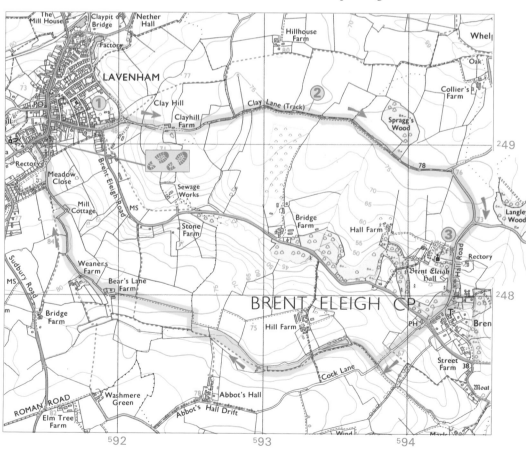

WALK 18D · Hadleigh and the Brett   SUFFOLK

ROUTE DIRECTIONS

Allow 2½ hours
Start from the free car park in Magdalen Road, Hadleigh (grid ref. TM028425).

Leave the car park by the Exit sign and turn left, passing the bowling club. At the T-junction turn left into Station Road, then right along the path signposted Railway Walk①.

Ignore all paths to right and left along the old railway track. After passing apple orchards on the left, continue along the path until you reach a footpath signed Benton End. Turn right here and follow a path between fields.

At the top of the hill, by a marker post in a field, turn right and follow the yellow markers across the field to pylons②.

Just after the pylons, go a very short distance along the top fence line to a stile. Climb this and go diagonally down an avenue in a new plantation. Keep just to the left of the pylon base. Go down through the hedge line and climb a stile to reach a track.

Turn right along this track and, just before a gate, turn left along a path between field and barns. Turn right by a large chestnut tree to reach the road. Turn right on to the road and after 100yds, at a footpath sign, climb a stile on the left and cross a wet meadow to a river bridge.

Go over the bridge and then half right to a gate. Cross stiles and meadows to reach an arable field. Cross this field, keeping the hedge on the right, to reach a minor road, and turn right.

At the sports ground entrance turn right and go across the car parking area. Turn left along a narrow path to an iron gate on the right, with tennis courts on the left. Go through the iron gate and continue along a narrow path to the river. Turn left by river to Toppesfield Bridge③.

Cross the road and continue along the riverside path to a track. Turn right along the track.

Just before the main road turn right across the green, cross a bridge and go through a car park to the road.

Turn right and go along the High Street④.

Turn right into Queen's Street then left to St Mary's Church⑤.

Leaving the church and Guildhall, go along Church Street. Cross High Street and walk along George Street back to the car park.

Tudor and Georgian houses at Hadleigh

The lovely medieval wool centre of Hadleigh is the starting point for this town and country walk. A footpath along an old railway line leads out of the town while the return, never far from the River Brett, is mainly across farmland. The final section of the walk explores some of Hadleigh's old streets.

POINTS OF INTEREST

①Formerly a branch of the main east coast line from London to Norwich, the railway ran from Hadleigh through Raydon to join the main line between Ipswich and Colchester. The route is now a delightful footpath, rich in wildlife and commanding extensive views of the surrounding countryside.

②As the route crosses fields and new plantations, there are fine views across the valley of the River Brett to the outlying farmsteads on the hills beyond.

③Triple-arched Toppesfield Bridge dates from the 14th century. The original stone bridge was widened in brick in the 16th century. Close by stood two watermills, now gone, but the riverside path is a delight, with many marsh-loving plants growing beside the river.

④Many of the handsome buildings along the High Street are decorated with pargeting. Hadleigh's affluence grew from the woollen and cloth trade and in 1834 there was a flourishing silk factory.

⑤The area around the church was the heart of medieval Hadleigh. Until 1838, when Queen Street was built, a tithe barn was part of the cluster of lovely old buildings here. The half-timbered Guildhall, with its peg-tiled roof, started life in 1438 as the Market Hall. Near by is the sharply contrasting Deanery Tower, with its fine display of 15th-century diamond-patterned brickwork, arches, battlements and polygonal turrets. St Mary's spire has dominated the town since about 1250.

Beginning in Norwich, this tour visits the seaside resorts of Great Yarmouth and Cromer and crosses the flat countryside to the east of the Broads, with its many windpumps.

ROUTE DIRECTIONS

The drive starts from Norwich ①.

Leave Norwich by the Yarmouth road, the A47, and pass through Thorpe St Andrew. Later join the Acle Bypass and, at the roundabout, turn right. From here the road enters flat marshland, and after 2¾ miles it passes Stracey Arms windpump on the left ②.

Continue along the A47 to the town of Great Yarmouth ③.

Leave Great Yarmouth by the A149, signed Caister, and in 2 miles take the second exit at a roundabout, into an unclassified road, to enter Caister-on-Sea ④.

From the town centre turn left, signed Acle and Norwich, and pass on the right the excavated ruins of Caister Roman Town. At the next roundabout take the second exit on to the A1064, then in ¾ mile you will pass, on the left, the road to Caister Castle ⑤.

Take the next turning right on to an unclassified road, signed Ormesby. A mile further on, at a T-junction, turn left on to the A149 to enter Ormesby St Margaret. At a memorial turn right, signed Scratby, on to an unclassified road alongside the green, then turn left. At the following T-junction turn right, signed Hemsby. Continue to Hemsby and at the end of the village turn left on to the B1159, signed Mundesley. A winding road then leads through Winterton-on-Sea to West Somerton. Continue with signs for Cromer and pass, on the left, Horsey Windpump, from the top of which there are fine views across Horsey Mere (National Trust), situated off to the left ⑥.

After skirting Horsey, you see high coastal dunes on the right before reaching Sea Palling, the scene of severe flooding in 1953. In 1¾ miles, turn right, and continue through Lessingham to reach Happisburgh ⑦.

In 1½ miles, at some crossroads, turn right for Walcott, from where there are fine marine views. At Bacton pass, on the left, the remains of a priory which was, in the Middle Ages, one of the holy places of Europe. In ¼ mile turn right, and in a further 1¼ miles pass through the installations of the North Sea Gas Terminal. Later, pass Stow Windmill before entering the small resort of Mundesley.

Follow signs for Cromer, crossing higher ground with occasional views before passing through Trimingham and skirting Overstrand to reach Cromer ⑧.

Leave the town on the Norwich road, the A149, and in 2¼ miles bear left, signed North Walsham. Continue through Thorpe Market to the outskirts of North Walsham.

At the traffic signals, a diversion can be made by going forward on to an unclassified road, into the town centre ⑨.

The main drive turns right at the traffic signals, and in ½ mile, at the next traffic signals, turn right again, signed Norwich, along the B1150. Continue through some wooded countryside to Coltishall on the River Bure. Cross the river to Coltishall's twin village of Horstead. The drive continues through pleasant country to Norwich.

POINTS OF INTEREST

① The ancient capital of East Anglia and county town of Norfolk, Norwich contains within its walls many impressive buildings, including 33 medieval churches, the finest of which is St Peter Mancroft. The Norman castle, with its 12th-century keep, houses a museum and art gallery. The Cathedral is one of the finest ecclesiastical buildings in England.

② The Stracey Arms windpump is one of the most impressive of those surviving in East Anglia, where they have been an important feature of the landscape since medieval times. This stretch of road is below sea level in places. The numerous windmills in this area bear witness to the need for draining the marshes.

③ Formerly a busy herring-fishing port, Great Yarmouth is now a popular seaside resort with two piers and many amenities. The restored 14th-century Tollhouse, the 114ft-high Nelson's Tower and the Maritime Museum of East Anglia are among the buildings of interest.

④ Caister-on-Sea was an important Roman station and naval base, and the foundations of a few Roman buildings are open to view. There are still fishermen's flint-faced cottages to be found.

⑤ The 15th-century moated ruins of Caister Castle contain a collection of vintage cars. The castle was built by Sir John Fastolf (Shakespeare's model for Falstaff in *Henry IV*) on his triumphant return from Agincourt in 1415.

⑥ Horsey Mere stands where the Broads come to within 2 miles of the sea and is popular with sailors and winter wildfowl. It is designated a Site of Special Scientific Interest because of its range of flora and fauna.

⑦ Pronounced 'Haisboro', Happisburgh is a small resort dominated by a tall red and white lighthouse. The 15th-century church has a fine rood screen and a magnificent carved font.

⑧ Cromer is a popular resort with a pier, good bathing from a sandy beach, and high cliffs nearby. The 15th-century church tower of St Peter and St Paul, once used as a lighthouse, rises to 160ft and is one of the highest in Norfolk.

⑨ Devastated by fire in 1600, North Walsham is now suggestive of Georgian prosperity. The parish church is the second largest in Norfolk and was built in the 13th century. The market cross dates from the 16th century, but has been restored.

First a fishing village, then a select watering place, Cromer today is a favourite traditional resort

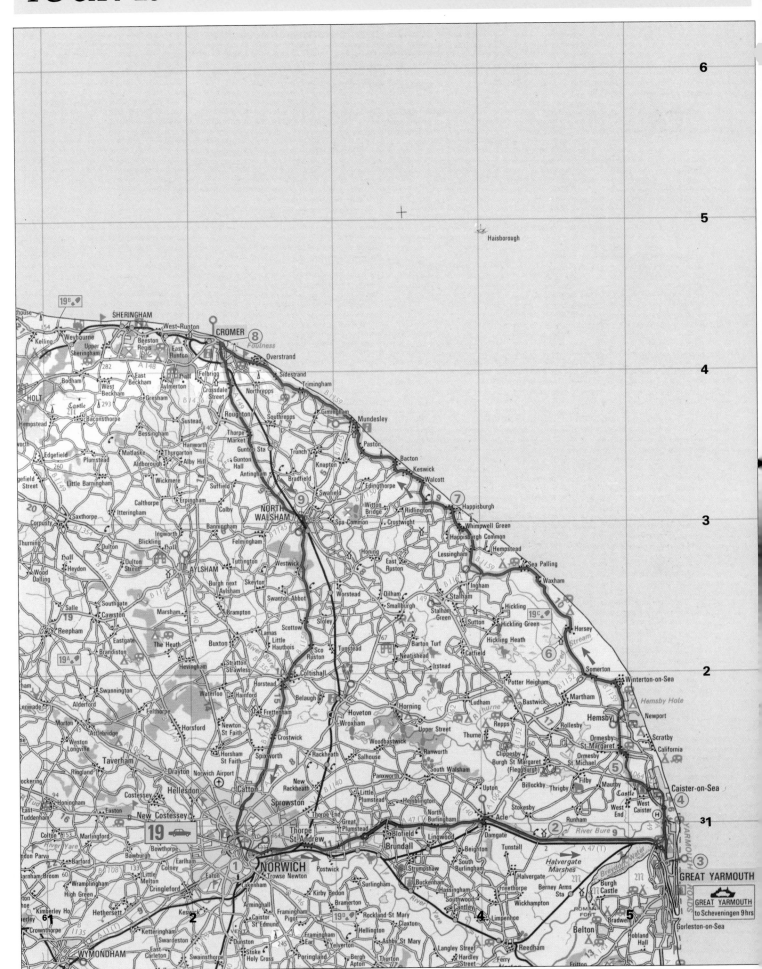

Delightful cottages line the streets of Reepham, which once consisted of three parishes — Hackford, Whitwell and Reepham

ROUTE DIRECTIONS

Allow 2 hours
Start from the free car park off Station Road (grid ref. TG099229).

Go to the far corner of the car park and turn left, away from the town, into hedged Chapel Walk, then turn right into Old Brewers Lane, strolling left into Ollands Road①.

At the main road junction, turn right over the railway bridge. Go straight ahead, signed Salle, then turn left into World's End Lane. At World's End Cottage keep right of the hedge and go over the stile into the meadow. Go straight down over the streams. At the high hedge turn left, keeping the hedge on the right, and cross the stile. At the road, turn left under the railway bridge, then bear right. After 50yds, turn right into Catchback Lane.

If it is exceptionally wet, continue up the tarmac road, turning right into Smugglers Lane and right again, past the police station, left into Park Lane, and straight past Grosvenor House. At the end of the bungalows, the path narrows. Turn right at the T-junction. At the far end of a wire fence, turn left to rejoin the main walk.

At the end of Catchback Lane, turn right into the road, then left opposite Winks Cottages into a rough track. Reaching the corner of the playing-field, turn right along the path in the meadow, keeping the tall hedge on your left. At the left-hand corner of the field, the path narrows, with woodland on the right. At the road, turn left uphill, and after 300yds turn right on to a grassy track②.

At the road turn left, signed Cawston. Turn right into a tree-lined path, emerging into Whitwell Street, with pretty cottages. Turn into Bar Lane, with Reepham church ahead. Reaching Back Street, turn left③.

Turn right up Pudding Pie Alley. At Market Square, between the butcher's shop and The Chimes, take Fisher Alley back to the car park.

This walk winds along hedge-lined lanes and tracks and through the quaint old market town of Reepham, with its delightful street names.

POINTS OF INTEREST

①At one time Reepham was made up of three parishes: Hackford, Whitwell and Reepham, one belonging to each of three sisters who had her own church. Two of these churches remain. Built back to back, their towers are visible above the rooftops.

②From a gap in the hedged track there is a view of arable land sloping to the Wensum Valley. At the bottom of the track a cluster of buildings includes Eade's watermill, on the River Eyn.

③Reepham's very old Back Street has a timber-framed building standing among whitewashed cottages, some of which take their names from the early trades practised in Reepham, like Greyhound Inn and the Old Bakery. The old market square contains buildings of many different ages, including the Brewery House, dated about 1700.

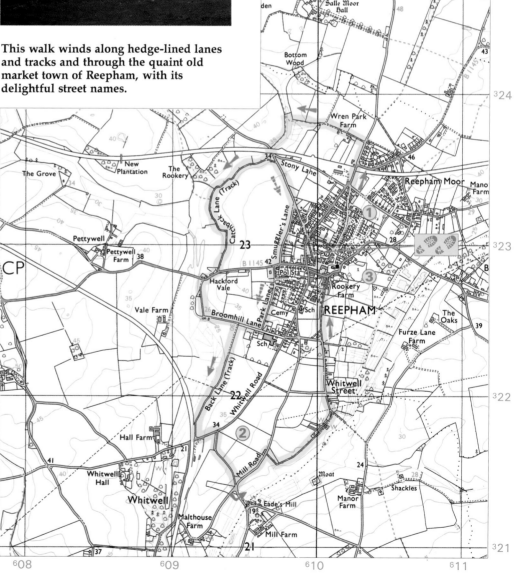

WALK 19B · Weybourne Hope   NORFOLK

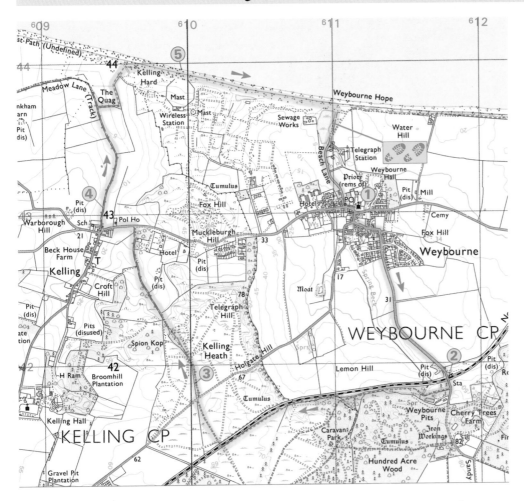

ROUTE DIRECTIONS

Allow 2½–3 hours
Start from the free car park at the beach in Weybourne (grid ref. TG110436).

Walk up Beach Lane and turn left. Take the path through the churchyard and go along the road, following the 'North Norfolk Railway' sign①.

Leaving the village behind, cross over the railway bridge, which gives good views of the track, station and countryside②.

Shortly afterwards, turn right on a wide track passing Springs Farm. The path narrows, entering woodland and leading to a picnic area. Just after the wildlife pond, turn right. The narrow path runs alongside the preserved railway line. Go between the 'Ski' notice and tyres, and immediately bear right uphill on the narrow bracken and heather path.

Continue along the wide path to the white gate of the railway crossing. Stop, look and listen before crossing. Keeping the bungalow on your left, go straight ahead (north) across Kelling Heath, on the wide track and over the by-road③.

At the cross tracks on the heathland turn left, and after 10 paces, turn right down a narrow bracken-lined gorge. At the main road (A149), turn left. After 250yds turn right, passing Meadow View House and the playground of a flint school built in 1876, along the Norfolk Heritage Path④.

At the fork turn right to the seashore, then, keeping the fence on your right, take the coast path back to the car park⑤.

Weybourne Hope, situated at the point where cliffs rise from the coastal marshland, was used as an embarkation point for troops off to France during World War I. The beach is more popular with fishermen than bathers, and wildlife abounds along the coast.

POINTS OF INTEREST

①Weybourne itself is very pretty, with flint-built cottages typical of many villages in the district of North Norfolk. The 11th-century All Saints' Church has a brick and flint chequer-work porch, added in the 15th century. All around it are the ruins of an Augustinian priory founded in 1200.

②The North Norfolk Railway is a preserved line now operating steam trains between Weybourne and Sheringham during the summer. Weybourne station was built in 1900.

③Kelling Heath covers a wide area and is very pretty, especially when the gorse and heather are in bloom. A mile down the road are Kelling Aviaries, which have a large variety of birds on show.

④The Norfolk Heritage Path has bird reserves by a shingle bank, and common seals may occasionally be seen in the sea; they breed just along the coast at Blakeney Point. Boat trips are available to the Point from Blakeney and Morston.

⑤During World War II, remote-controlled target planes called 'Queen Bees' were flown from what is now a modern radar station on the coast.

Extensive views of Kelling Heath

Horsey Mere, a Site of Special Scientific Interest because of its wide range of flora and fauna, is one of the largest areas of open water on the Broads and a favourite place for sailing boats. Horsey is thought to mean Horsa's Island; a Danish king named Horsa once settled here. Wet-weather footwear is essential in all but the driest spells.

POINTS OF INTEREST

① The 100 acres of Horsey Mere, administered by the National Trust, offer a peaceful haven to over wintering wildfowl. The reedbeds and the proximity of the sea make it an attractive place for migrating birds. A panoramic view of the area can be enjoyed from its eastern end and throughout the whole walk keep an eye out for marsh harriers and listen for the booming cry of the bitterns.

Horsey windpump, also owned by the National Trust, was built to help drain the surrounding marshes by lifting water from the dykes into the river. It is open to the public between April and October. The staithe has been the landing place for thatching reeds for over 150 years.

② There have been serious invasions of the sea along this coast. In 1953 it broke through the dunes, and in 1938, 5ft of

water was recorded at Horsey and water travelled 10 miles inland. Two hundred years ago, before the marshes were drained, the only road to Horsey from Sea Palling was the track behind the dunes.

③ East Anglia is renowned for its delightful churches and All Saints at Horsey is no exception. Dating from the 11th century, its round tower is crowned by a thatched octagonal top with battlements. A stained-glass window of 1890 commemorates an artist by the name of Miss Catherine Ursula Rising.

Horsey's windpump and dunes. There are superb views of the Broads from the windpump gallery

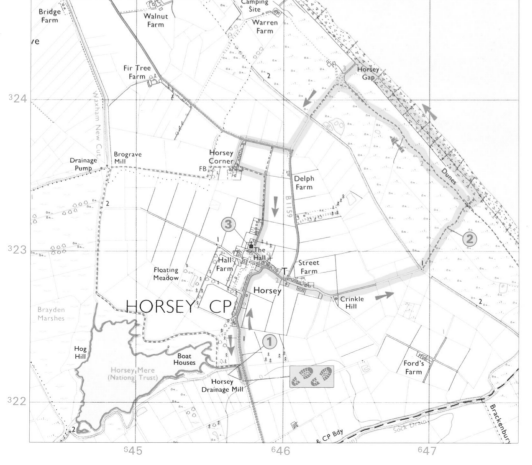

ROUTE DIRECTIONS

Allow 1½ hours
Start from the car park at Horsey windpump by Horsey Mere (grid ref. TG457222) ①.

Turn left into the road, past thatched houses. Where the road bears sharp left, go straight up the signed by-road passing an old barn dated 1742 and the Nelson's Head public house. Go left at the fork, passing the nature reserve. Take the path through the dunes on to golden sands, or walk behind the dunes if it is windy②.

Continue along the beach for ¾ mile, then turn left through the concrete-walled opening in the dunes and follow the hedged path to the road. At the road, turn right and walk westwards until you see the track into Horsey Corner. Turn left and walk southwards through the village, bearing left where the houses give way to open countryside. The path runs through farmland to Horsey③.

Once back on the main road it is a short walk back to the windpump.

WALK 19D · Green Lanes & Villages   NORFOLK

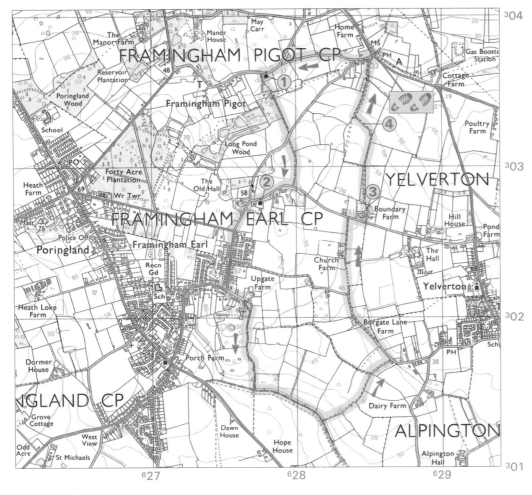

627   628   629

This walk takes you through the rural landscape of South Norfolk. Every turn brings pastoral scenes, quiet lanes and attractive houses with colourful gardens, and the tree- and hedge-lined tracks are a haven of wild flowers. Some sections may be muddy in wet weather.

The church at Framingham Pigot

POINTS OF INTEREST

① Framingham Pigot's knapped-flint Church of St Andrew with its unusual spire and clock was built a hundred years ago. The ornamental ironwork on the entrance gates is particularly fine.

② The church at Framingham Earl, also dedicated to St Andrew, has 15th-century stained-glass windows, a Saxon chancel and a Norman tower and nave. The walk takes you through the modern part of Framingham Earl, which has colourful gardens, hedges and trees.

③ Although mud may cause a problem on wet days, it is worth persevering towards the pond at Boundary Farm in order to catch a glimpse of the many beautiful birds to be found on or near the water's edge. Norfolk is particularly rich in birdlife because its location attracts many birds as they move down Britain's east coast in autumn, or fly directly across the sea from Scandinavia.

④ There is a glorious view from this point, and the white face of the Gull Inn can be seen across the valley, signifying that the walk has come full circle.

ROUTE DIRECTIONS

Allow 2½ hours
Start from the well-defined lay-by with grass between it and the busy main road, just past the Gull Inn on the A146 (Norwich to Beccles) road (grid ref. TG285037).

Walk towards the Gull Inn. Cross to the road, and take the metalled lane between white iron posts, passing houses with a stream on your left. After 200yds fork right, signed Framingham Pigot. At the junction turn left towards the church①.

Turn left along the footpath, keeping the churchyard railings on your left. Just after the wooden garage go through a gate on the left into a meadow, and cross to the edge of the wood. Go over a broken stile into the field, and just after an old ivy-covered barn in the wood turn right over the stile taking the path through woodland. Pass into the field, crossing over the stile into Gull Lane. Turn right, then after 50yds turn left into a path between trees leading into a field. At the road turn right towards Framingham Earl②.

At the road junction, turn left, signed Poringland. Go along Hall Road, leading into Upgate. As the road bends right, turn left, continuing along Upgate. Where the road turns left, turn on to the track. Follow the bridleway sign along the sunken track.

Just after Poringland Hall, turn left into a field, between posts. Follow it down the right-hand edge. Further along, rejoin the sunken path (it can be muddy in wet weather). At the T-junction, turn left. **Fox snares are used around here, so keep your dog on its lead.** Ignore the track to your left. After 700yds turn left into a field and follow the path uphill, around a small wood on the right, and down to the road. Turn left, passing Orchard Farm bungalow. When the road bends left, turn right on to the metalled farm track, and go through the farm. Turn right at the road, then left at Boundary Farm③.

Continue along the track to the brow of the hill, then swing left, keeping the field boundary hedge on your left④.

At the far hedge, turn right with the hedge on your left. This path continues between trees to the road. Turn right to go back to the starting point.

TOUR 20 · The Vale of Evesham GLOUCESTERSHIRE

ROUTE DIRECTIONS

The drive starts from Moreton-in-Marsh ①.

Follow the Oxford road, A44, for 1¾ miles. Here the road passes the Four Shires Stone where the counties of Gloucestershire, Oxfordshire and Warwickshire (and, before the last boundary changes, Worcestershire) meet. After ¾ mile turn right on to an unclassified road for Chastleton ②.

Half a mile on turn left and cross a cattle grid, then at the end turn right on to the A44. Beyond the Cross Hands public house turn left on to an unclassified road, signed Rollright. After 2 miles, on the right, lie the Rollright Stones ③.

In ¾ mile turn left on to the A34, signed Stratford, and descend to Long Compton, then continue to Shipston-on-Stour. Turn left on to the Campden road, B4035, and after 1¾ miles cross the main road. In 1½ miles keep forward on to an unclassified road to Charingworth and the pretty village of Ebrington. At the end of the main street bear right and then right again, signed The Hidcotes. After 2 miles a detour can be made by keeping forward and following signs to Hidcote Manor Gardens ④.

Opposite Hidcote, on the unclassified road, is Kiftsgate Court garden ⑤.

The main tour turns left, signed Mickleton. In 1 mile turn right and immediately right again on to the B4632 (formerly A46), signed Stratford, to enter Mickleton. At the end of the village bear left, then in ½ mile go forward on to an unclassified road, signed Long Marston. Continue through Long Marston to Welford-on-Avon. After crossing the river, turn left on to the A439 to reach the edge of Bidford-on-Avon.

At the roundabout take the first exit on to the B4085, signed Broadway, and cross the 15th-century bridge. After ½ mile turn right for Cleeve Prior and South Littleton. One mile beyond South Littleton go over a level crossing, then take the first turning left on to an unclassified road, no sign, to reach Bretforton, where the B4035 is joined, and continue to Weston Subedge.

At the Seagrave Arms turn right on to the B4632 (formerly A46), signed Cheltenham, pass through Willersley, and in 1¾ miles, at the T-junction, turn right on to the A44 into Broadway ⑥.

By the Swan Hotel turn left on to an unclassified road, signed Snowshill. Ascend and later bear right into the village of Snowshill ⑦.

Turn left at the church, then at the top go forward over the crossroads, signed Chipping Campden and

The steep escarpment of the Cotswolds contrasts with the timber and thatch of the Vale of Evesham on this tour. The route veers north for a taste of Shakespeare country and returns via Chipping Campden.

Broadway Tower (care required). After 1¼ miles turn left, signposted Broadway, to Broadway Tower ⑧.

In ½ mile cross the main road, signed Saintbury, and pass the Fish Hill Picnic Area. After another ¾ mile turn right, signed Chipping Campden. Continue for 1½ miles and at the crossroads turn right for Chipping Campden ⑨.

Leave the town by Sheep Street, B4081, signed Broad Campden, and after ¼ mile turn left on to an unclassified road for Broad Campden. In the village turn right then shortly right again and climb to Blockley ⑩.

Turn left then shortly right on to the B4479, signed Moreton-in-Marsh. After 1½ miles, at the T-junction, turn left on to the A44 to pass through Bourton-on-the-Hill ⑪.

Continue on the A44 to return to Moreton-in-Marsh.

POINTS OF INTEREST

① A small, busy town of the northern Cotswolds, Moreton-in-Marsh is on the route of the Roman Foss Way, which forms its wide main street. The bell in the 16th-century Curfew Tower was tolled daily until 1860.

② The scenic village of Chastleton contains Chastleton House, a notable Cotswold-stone building dating from 1603. It has a secret room in its walls where a fugitive from the Battle of Worcester hid from Cromwell's soldiers.

③ The Rollright Stones are two curious Bronze Age clusters of stones, on the sides of the road between Great and Little Rollright villages, that assumed their identity in medieval myth.

④ Cultivated by an American and now owned by the National Trust, Hidcote features a series of small gardens, each given over to a theme or kind of flower.

⑤ The attractive gardens at Kiftsgate Court are renowned for their collection of roses and unusual trees and flowers, and command superb views over the countryside.

⑥ William Morris is said to have discovered Broadway, a village of corn-coloured stone whose 'broad way' is lined with red chestnut trees. Other Pre-Raphaelite artists followed. Charles I and Cromwell used the 17th-century Lygon Arms.

⑦ An isolated little hill village, Snowshill's history goes back 1,000 years. Snowshill Manor House (National Trust) dates back to around 1500 and has a lovely terraced garden and a collection of toys, clocks and musical instruments. It is open two days a week.

⑧ At over 1,000ft, the views from the 18th-century Broadway Tower are magnificent. Other attractions are an adventure playground and a collection of rare animals and birds.

⑨ A former centre of the wool industry, Chipping Campden has an impressive 15th-century 'wool' church and a fine Jacobean market hall. Traditional crafts are kept alive at the pottery and the Campden Weavers.

⑩ Blockley's 19th-century silk-throwing mills harmonise well with contemporary cottages and add character to this attractive village.

⑪ With its steep cottage-lined street leading to a lovely old church, Bourton-on-the-Hill is an artist's delight. St Lawrence's holds many treasures, the Winchester Bushel and Peck being of special interest.

Kiftsgate Court garden: worth seeking out for a rich variety of roses and rare plants

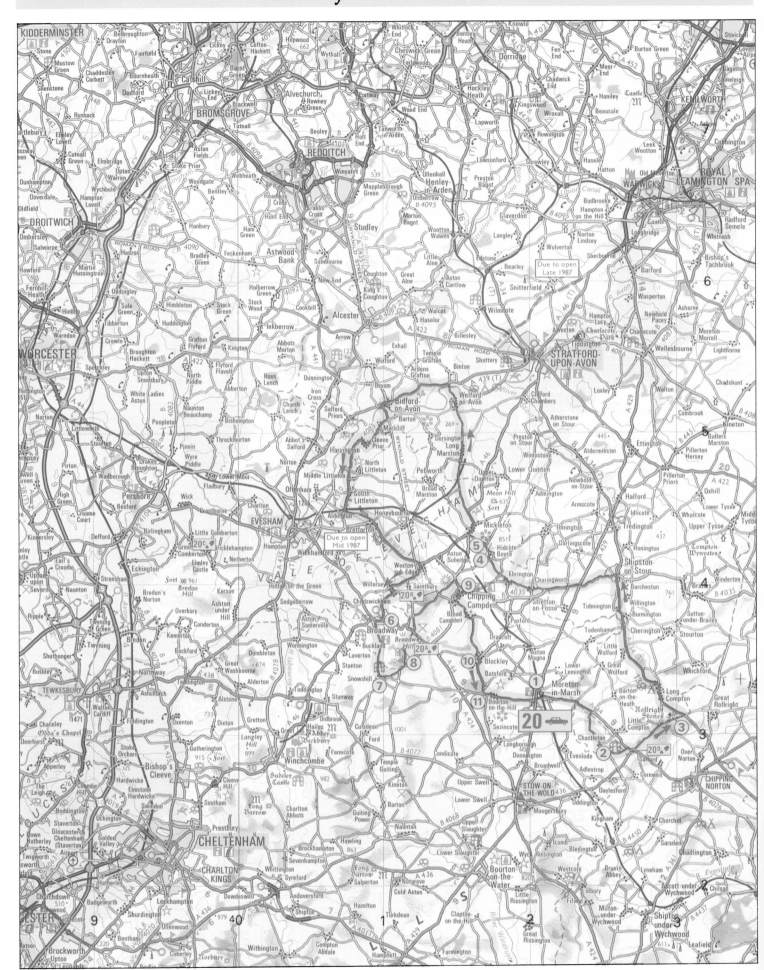

WALK 20A · Broadway Tower

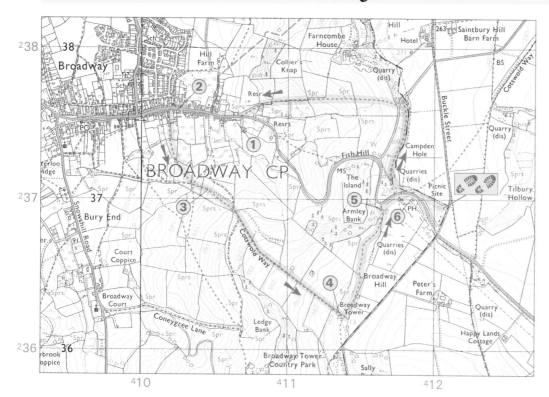

ROUTE DIRECTIONS

Allow 2½ hours
Start from the Fish Hill picnic site (grid ref. SP120369).

Follow the 'Woodland Walk' footpath sign, past the Don Russell memorial topograph, and into the quarries along a clearly waymarked path. Continue high through Campden Hole beech woods, following the signs for Broadway.

In due course the path descends to a stile and crosses the minor road by the entrance to Farncombe House.

Cross the stile, descend the pasture, slanting gently down from the fence to a stile vividly painted red and white. Occasional waymark posts plot the line of the footpath via a gateway and stile down to Pike Cottage ①.

Continue down Broadway's main street ②.

Leave the main street at Peartree House. A Cotswold Way footpath sign directs along a lane and over two stiles/gates into a small pasture. The well-trodden footpath is easy to follow as it slants left via stiles and up old ridge and furrow ③.

Steadily gain height, keeping alongside a wall through arable fields to enter the Broadway Tower Country Park through the hunting gate ④.

Leave through the hunting gate to the east of the tower, slipping through the scrubby lateral valley. Follow the route to a stile/gate to the Armley Bank woodland ⑤.

Proceed along the Cotswold Way to cross Fish Hill road by the Fish Inn ⑥.

Cross the road (with great care because it is usually very busy) to the picnic site.

A visit to one of the most popular Cotswold villages is followed here by a strenuous climb up the escarpment to the fine viewpoint of Broadway Tower, now the focal point of a country park. It is said that 12 counties can be seen from here on a clear day.

POINTS OF INTEREST

① Set on the main route between Oxford and Worcester, Broadway owes much of its early development to the stage-coach trade. Fresh horses were always in demand here for the long haul up Fish Hill on the eastbound route. Pike Cottage is so called because near here stood the turnpike gate. Today, the houses in upper Broadway are very grand, and houses such as Top Farm and Orchard Farm are far removed from the serviceable agricultural dwellings they may once have been. However, all the buildings in this part of the village suffer from clamorous traffic throttling up in preparation for the ascent of the long and steep Fish Hill.

② The spacious, tree-lined main street makes it easy to see how Broadway got its name – though the original 'broad way' may have been Snowshill Road, where the old parish church is situated. It is worth strolling through the village to take in the pleasant, harmonious mixture of Cotswold cottage and house styles. The Lygon Arms is a particularly fine building, and there are plenty of inns and teashops where walkers can re-fuel themselves.

③ Ahead, Broadway Tower makes a fine objective, dominating the scarp at 1,027ft. It was built in 1798 for the Countess of Coventry.

④ Nature trails, an adventure playground and a collection of farm animals are among the outdoor attractions of Broadway Tower Country Park, while the tower itself houses exhibitions including a permanent one on William Morris.

⑤ 'Armley' is derived from the Saxon word for 'wretched', so Armley Bank may have been a refuge for beggars and outlaws.

⑥ Originally a summer-house for Farncombe House, the quaint Fish Inn later became an ale-house catering for weary travellers at the crest of Fish Hill.

The view from Broadway Tower extends as far as Warwick Castle and Worcester Cathedral

The Cotswold Edge near Dover's Hill is the setting for this short walk, which gives memorable views northwards over the Vale of Evesham. The walk can conveniently be extended (more than doubling its length) to visit the medieval wool centre of Chipping Campden. Stout shoes or wellingtons are advisable, as the long grass on the hill may be wet and the wood muddy.

POINTS OF INTEREST

① The extensive westward views from the scarp feature Dumbleton and Bredon Hills

Hay tossing at the annual 'Olympicks' on Dover's Hill

ROUTE DIRECTIONS

Allow 1 hour
Start from the Dover's Hill National Trust car park (grid ref. SP136395).

Go through the kissing-gate and follow the escarpment edge straight ahead①.

At Bold Gap the path descends slightly towards a wooden squeeze stile. Do not cross this stile; instead, descend the pasture, passing a waymark post, to reach a stile into The Lynches Wood②.

The Ordnance Survey map shows none of the paths within this wooded spur, so follow the yellow-painted waymarks along the main path round the spur. Cross a heavily used path, and where the path forks go left, then after a short descent turn sharp left at the path junction. The route rises gradually, beneath sweet chestnuts and laurel bushes, until it turns left up recently set steps. Swing right at the top, following a fence-line and still within the wood, to a stile.

Go over the stile and take an old cart track, just discernible ahead and right, following the fence up the pasture near the woodland③.

The track mounts the rough, hummocky slope. It then slants right about the woodland, rising above a scrub-surrounded spring pool. Just before the road divert left along a waymarked hollow way to the topograph④.

A fine way of extending the walk from this location is by following the Cotswold Way waymarks to Kingcomb Lane, then down Hoo Lane to explore Chipping Campden. Stroll along the curving High Street to the church, returning by Sheep Street, Westington and Blind Lane⑤.

Return along Dyer's Lane to Dover's Hill.

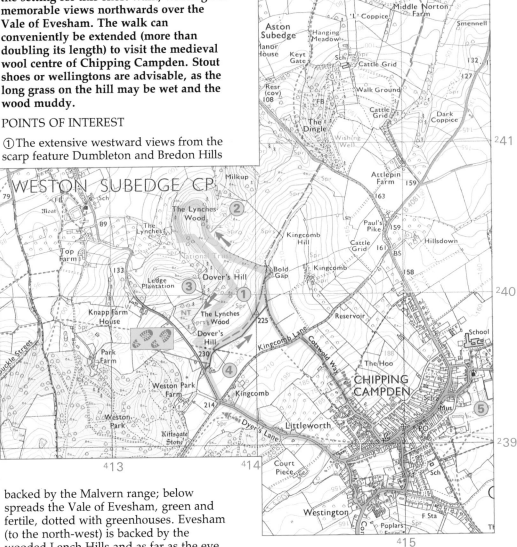

backed by the Malvern range; below spreads the Vale of Evesham, green and fertile, dotted with greenhouses. Evesham (to the north-west) is backed by the wooded Lench Hills and as far as the eye can see stretches the undulating countryside of Worcestershire and Warwickshire.

② The term 'lynches' suggests a terraced hillside – a feature sometimes found on chalk escarpments. There is no obvious sign of these ancient cultivation strips here, but it is thought that these strip lynchets were often used for vineyards during the Romano-British period. Possibly this was the original use of the fruit orchards that still exist just below the woodland.

③ Notice the old ridge and furrow on the shallow slope just above The Lynches Wood.

④ Resembling a garden sundial stand, the elegant topograph commemorates the efforts of F L Griggs to acquire this estate for the public when hotel development threatened it in the 1920s. The splendid natural amphitheatre of Dover's Hill, now

protected by the National Trust, is the venue, every summer, for the 'Cotswold Olympicks' – Robert Dover's Games. Founded in 1612 as a protest against Puritanism, the Games include rural sports such as tug-of-war, greasy pole and shin-kicking together with dancing and other entertainment.

⑤ Chipping Campden could scarcely have a more appropriate town motto than 'History in Stone'. The glow of Cotswold limestone is everywhere, from pubs and teashops to St James's Church – one of the finest Cotswold 'wool' churches. Treasures inside include a huge brass of William Grevel and his wife, whose house, a 14th-century gem, can be seen in the High Street. A short distance away is the delightful Jacobean market hall, and near it the Woolstaplers' Hall, now a museum and information centre.

Bredon Hill is the literal and metaphorical high point of this walk. The climb to it is steep initially, but well repays the effort for the panoramic views – to 'see the coloured counties and hear the larks so high', as A E Housman put it in a poem from *A Shropshire Lad*.

POINTS OF INTEREST

① Northward views open up as the path climbs, extending in clear weather as far as the Wrekin, and the Clent and Lickey Hills, south of Birmingham.

② Erected by the owner of Woollas Hall, the viewing platform at Parson's Folly sets the spectator at 1,000ft. Unfortunately the tower is now used for some serious purpose and it hums with electrical apparatus. Nevertheless, the views from Bredon are unquestionably stunning, with fields, woodland and orchards spreading out in a patchwork effect below. The hillscape includes the Cotswold edge to the south-east, the Forest of Dean and the Monnow Hills south-west across the Severn, and the Malverns to the west. The summit of Bredon is hemmed in by double ramparts on the south and east, earthworks of an Iron Age fort. The Banbury Stone, near the look-out, was probably connected with this. Archaeological evidence suggests that the fort came to a violent end shortly before the Romans arrived in Britain. A number of human skulls found during the

Looking north-east from Bredon – a good view is always a handy excuse for a rest!

excavations were probably trophies displayed by the fort's inhabitants.

③ Away to the left on the descent from Bredon Hill are the massive bracken-covered earthworks of 12th-century Beauchamp Castle.

④ Allow time after the walk to explore Elmley Castle, a quintessentially English village where children dance round the maypole on Oak Apple Day (29 May).

ROUTE DIRECTIONS

Allow 2½ hours
Start from the broad main street of Elmley Castle (grid ref. SO982412).

Take the road leading north-west from the Queen Elizabeth, passing the former post office and several delightful half-timbered cottages.

Bear left with the lane to Hill House Farm.

A bridleway leads on up a hollow way to a gate. Stay on the main track climbing between Doctor's Wood and Fox Hill Wood to a stile/gate at the edge of Even Hill. At this point, where the track peters out, turn sharp left along the top side of Doctor's Wood.

Join the green track which rises out of the wood, gaining height steadily, until, at a gate into Long Plantation, you turn right up the worn path by the short edge of woodland. Keep right, away from the wood above the scrub line, on course for the scarp edge ①.

Follow the scarp-top track via two gates to accompany the wall to Parson's Folly ②.

Retrace your steps, keeping to the wire fence and skirting the top of Long Plantation, until the Wychavon Way waymarks (yellow crown) direct you left down through the scarp woodland and rough pastures by two hunting gates ③.

Eventually reach the Kersoe road and turn left to return to the village ④.

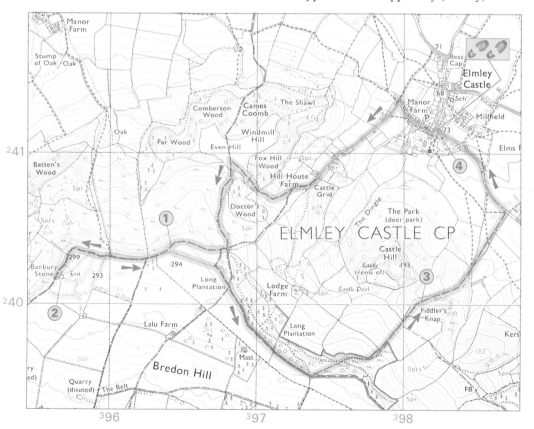

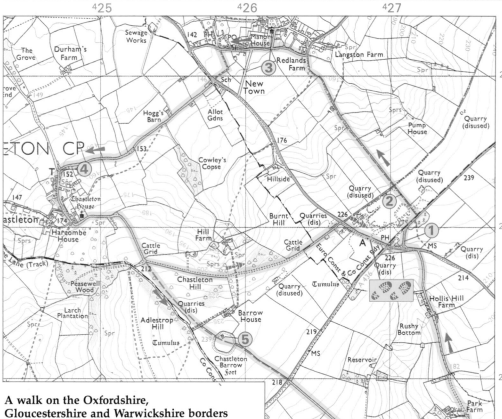

A walk on the Oxfordshire, Gloucestershire and Warwickshire borders with many fine ingredients to recommend it – superb views over three counties, remains of the Iron Age and three magnificent manor houses, all distinctly different.

POINTS OF INTEREST

① The first part of the route is along the Cotswolds' continuous spine of hill country, which has constituted a safe, dry passage for travel and trade since Neolithic times.

② Ahead a breathtaking view reveals Ilmington Downs, Dover's Hill, Batsford Hill and Bourton Downs with the vale of the Stour leading north towards Stratford-upon-Avon and Warwickshire.

Built in the 17th century, Chastleton House was stormed by Cromwell's men in the Civil War

③ Little Compton's Parish Church of St Denys with its saddleback tower, the handsome manor house and a few cottages form a very pleasing group.

④ Chastleton has several attractive thatched cottages and farmhouses, but the stately Chastleton House transcends all in its magnificence. Built soon after 1602 by the wool merchant Walter Jones, this Jacobean masterpiece has frequently been used in the filming of period dramas. It is not open to the public.

⑤ Chastleton Barrow is one of the many Iron Age hillforts to be found in this area. Their banks are now gently sloping, grass-covered mounds and their interiors seem featureless, to the extent that some have thought them to be cattle enclosures.

⑥ In 1936 Clough Williams-Ellis was given liberty to re-model the estate village of Cornwell, together with much of the manor house. He was able to bring together elaborate formal gardens and beautiful sweeping vistas to enhance the fine setting.

ROUTE DIRECTIONS

Allow 2¾ hours
Start from the lay-by west of the Cross Hands Inn, where you can leave your car (grid ref. SO269289).

Walk back past the inn taking the minor road left, signposted Rollrights. ①.

Two hundred and fifty yards on the left, a hunting gate (bridleway sign) gives access to a track leading north west past Newman's Quarry ②.

The bridleway descends for ¾ mile; on entering Little Compton through a gate, turn left along the minor road. The second turning right leads to the church ③.

Return to the street, going right, until you reach the wicket gate left, close to the telephone box. A tarmac path leads to a kissing gate, then the route crosses the A44 at the primary school with its distinctive monkey-puzzle tree. Proceed along the quiet road to Chastleton, turning left at the junction ④.

Continue up the road to a sharp corner junction, cross the cattle grid left then the stile immediately right. Alternatively, at this point the walk can be shortened by simply following the unenclosed road directly to the Cross Hands Inn. Ascend the pasture, admiring the view north featuring Brailes Hill with the spinney on top. Advancing parallel with the county boundary road, go through the gate on to the Barrow House drive, turning left then first right over a gate, following the fence to a metal gate into Chastleton Barrow ⑤.

Pass diagonally through the circular tree-fringed earthwork to a further metal gate. The bridleway follows the hedge down to the A436 (Jurassic Way). Go down the single-track road to Cornwell with views east to Chipping Norton and south to Churchill. Where the road bends, after the sawmill, follow the track left, branching right diagonally across the apple orchard, shielded by a tall hedge, to a kissing gate. Turn sharp right down the field to join the fenced path to the church where the metal fencing begins ⑥.

Descend the parkland pasture to a passage between gates over a bridge, rising to a further kissing gate into a lane. Go left to end the walk via Hollis Hill.

ROUTE DIRECTIONS

The drive starts from Burford ①.

From the Corner House Hotel halfway down the High Street follow the Swinbrook road, unclassified, and after 1 mile turn left. After another mile continue straight over the crossroads, signed Asthall. The drive then skirts Asthall.

At the T-junction turn right, signed Witney, and at the top of an ascent turn left on to the B4047. In 1¾ miles at the White Hart Inn turn left, unclassified, signed Leafield. Descend and cross the river bridge then pass the old village of Minster Lovell ②.

In 1¾ miles, at the crossroads, go forward to reach Leafield. Turn left, signed Shipton, then bear right. In 2 miles cross the main road and continue on into Shipton-under-Wychwood ③.

Here the drive turns right on to the A361 and continues to Chipping Norton ④.

Follow the Stow road, B4450, via Churchill and Bledington, and later join the A436 for Stow-on-the-Wold ⑤.

From the town square turn right on to the A429, then turn left, signed Tewkesbury, B4077, and immediately branch left, B4077, for Upper Swell. The B4077 continues through Ford, then after 1½ miles descends to the Stanway war memorial. Here turn right at the crossroads, signed Stanton, on to an unclassified road. Pass the gatehouse and grounds of Stanway House ⑥.

After 1¼ miles turn right for Stanton ⑦.

Bear left, signed Broadway, then after ¾ mile turn left on to the Cheltenham road, B4632 (formerly A46). Go straight over the Toddington roundabout and after 1 mile take the second turning on the left on to an unclassified road for Hailes Abbey (National Trust) ⑧.

Return for 200 yards and turn left, then follow a narrow by-road to climb on to the Roel Hill ridge, nearly 1,000ft, from where there are fine views. At the T-junction turn left, then take the next turning right. At the next T-junction turn left and continue to Guiting Power. After ½ mile, at the T-junction, turn right, signed Andoversford, then take the next turning on the left, signed Stow. After 1¾ miles a detour can be made by turning left at the crossroads to the Cotswold Farm Park ⑨.

The main drive keeps forward and follows a quiet country road to Lower Swell. Here turn right on to the B4068, then left on to an unclassified road, signed The Slaughters, and enter Upper Slaughter ⑩.

At the end of the village, turn left for the neighbouring village of Lower Slaughter ⑪.

Cross the bridge, then turn right and at the end right again on to the A429, signed Cirencester. Turn left after ½ mile on to an unclassified road into Bourton-on-the-Water ⑫.

At the post office turn right into the village centre, then at the crossroads turn left on to the unclassified Sherborne road. Cross the river and bear right, then ascend and, after 3½ miles, turn left for Sherborne. At the end of the village turn right and continue to the village of Windrush ⑬.

Keep left and after ¾ mile turn left at the T-junction to Great Barrington. At the war memorial bear right for Taynton. At the end of the village follow the signs for Burford, and, after 1 mile, join the A424. In ¼ mile, at the mini-roundabout, turn right on to the A361 and cross the river bridge for the return to Burford.

POINTS OF INTEREST

① Grey-gabled houses, shops, tearooms, hotels and old inns line Burford's main street, which descends steeply against a backdrop of wold and water-

From Oxfordshire to Gloucestershire this drive passes through several villages along the River Windrush, also taking in the hill towns of Chipping Norton and Stow-on-the-Wold.

Minster Lovell Hall, whose ruins are steeped in legend

meadow. The town was important in the coaching era.

② Minster Lovell is an enchanting stone and thatch village containing the ruins of what was once a magnificent manor house, built in the 15th century by William Lovell.

③ Originally set in Wychwood Forest, the large village of Shipton boasts a 600-year-old hostelry formerly used as a guesthouse for Bruern Abbey.

④ There are many historic buildings and points of interest in Chipping Norton which evolved as a typical wool town. Its most notable landmark is the tall chimney stack of the 19th-century Bliss Tweed Mill.

⑤ The highest town in the Cotswolds at nearly 800ft, Stow-on-the-Wold is a good antiques centre and hosts two annual horse fairs.

⑥ Stanway House is an exquisite Jacobean manor with a beautiful gatehouse and a magnificent 14th-century tithe barn used for music and arts festivals.

⑦ Stanton is the perfect Cotswold village, thanks to architect Sir Philip Stott, who allowed nothing to spoil its simple, classic lines whilst he owned the estate. Its long main

street is lined with beautiful houses.

⑧ Haunting ruins are all that remain of 13th-century Hailes Abbey which once drew royalty and pilgrims alike. A small museum contains exhibits excavated from the site.

⑨ The Cotswold Farm Park is an adjunct to the working Bemborough Farm, the centre and shop window of the Rare Breeds Survival Trust near Guiting Power. The Park offers the chance to see ancient breeds of farm animals and fowl in a natural farm environment.

⑩ Upper Slaughter is a completely unspoilt village. It has an Elizabethan manor house and several bridges over the Eye stream fringed with wild flowers.

⑪ Downstream, Lower Slaughter is the pretty sister where the water flows broad and shallow. There are many good houses, and the red brick-built corn mill with its tall chimney and waterwheel is an attractive corner.

⑫ There is something for everyone at Bourton-on-the-Water: Birdland Zoo Gardens, a Village Life exhibition, a scale model of the village, a motor museum and a perfumery.

⑬ The church at Windrush preserves a splendid Norman doorway and the churchyard contains some remarkable Baroque table tombs.

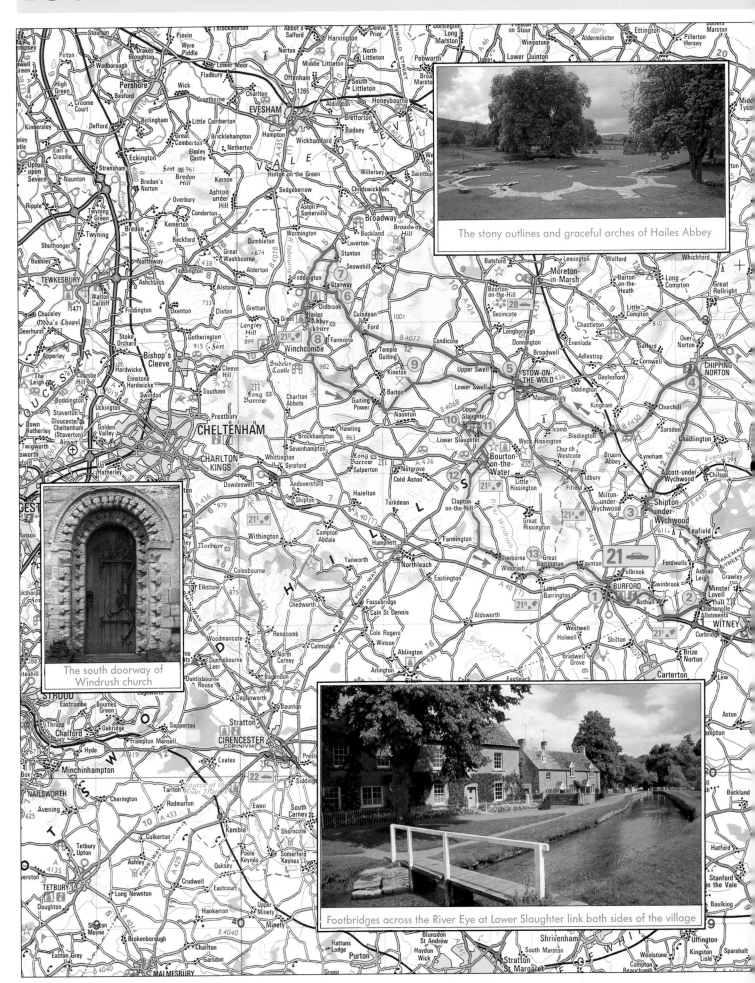

The stony outlines and graceful arches of Hailes Abbey

The south doorway of Windrush church

Footbridges across the River Eye at Lower Slaughter link both sides of the village

WALK 21A · *Herbert's Heath* OXFORDSHIRE

ROUTE DIRECTIONS

Allow 2½ hours
Start from the lay-by on the A424 just south of the Merrymouth Inn (grid ref. SP234182).

Go north towards the inn, turning right through the gateway on to a bridleway track that leads over the skyline and down to the road to Fifield. Turn left, then first right to pass the parish church①.

Swing left along the street, branching down right at the bridleway sign, and follow the lane to a gate labelled 'Fifield Parish Common'②.

Approaching Herbert's Heath the lane narrows. After passing through a gate opt either to turn left along the south fringe of the woodland to a hunting gate and thence to Idbury, or to continue along the path to explore Foxholes Nature Reserve. (If you are daunted by the many paths in the wood, choose the former, shorter route)③.

The longer route follows an open ride via Snow Hill and, after crossing a track, soon diminishes to a path that slips out of Roughborough Copse at a partially overgrown white gate. Now follow the edge of the woodland to a gate left, and re-enter the wood continuing on the bridleway for 400yds. Turn left at the path junction then fork right, shortly afterwards passing an old shepherd's hut.

On reaching a path junction turn left to pass a hunting gate, working round Wetpool Corner under the horse barrier and over a duckboard by the pool to follow the horse track from a second hunting gate, or take the firmer path under the fence to a hardcore track, then turn right.

While winding through Starveall Wood diverge from the track at a sharp left bend, to follow a confined path to the right, out of the wood. The path follows the wood south.

Upon reaching the hunting gate (where the longer and shorter routes rejoin) turn right, skirt round the headland to a gateway then cross the unploughed strip on to a track. On first glimpsing Idbury church, turn right at the gate, walk up the pasture to a double gate, then on to the road by the Old School House④.

Take the lane left from a post box. On reaching the wall stile go right, cross the tiny stream

then slant diagonally across the ridge-and-furrow pasture to a gate. Continue via another gate before descending first to a concealed footbridge, located where the ridge and furrow alters orientation.

Rise with the faint bank, pass through the old rank hedge and drop down to cross the next dingle via two hunting gates. Continue across the long pasture to reach a metal kissing-gate, and proceed along the confined path to another kissing-gate leading into Fifield.

Turn right, passing the village post office/shop, continue straight on at the village crossroads until you reach the junction by the Merrymouth Inn, cross the road, then turn left to reach your car.

Still on the oolitic limestone of the Cotswolds, but well east of the more rugged hills of the scarp slope, this is a gentle, rural ramble, passing through two charming springline villages, to explore pastures and woodland on lias clay near the River Evenlode. Some tracks in the wood are used by horses, making them muddy, so wear wellingtons after wet weather.

Near Idbury, a beautifully constructed drystone wall shows fine traditional craftsmanship

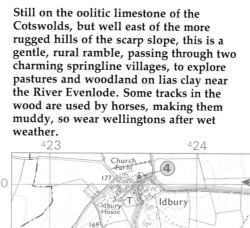

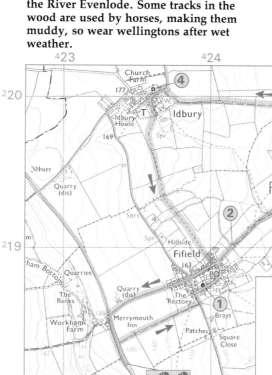

POINTS OF INTEREST

① The most striking feature of Fifield's Church of St John the Baptist is its unusual, octagonal west tower. It dates from the 14th century.

② Though the land on Fifield Common is no longer regularly grazed, it is invaluable as a wildlife habitat, notably for insects.

③ A reserve of the Berkshire, Buckinghamshire and Oxfordshire Naturalists' Trust, Foxholes is a marvellous combination of unimproved, flower-rich

meadow and deciduous woodland. Many of the trees are oaks, but there is also ash, birch and hazel, as well as some areas of planted conifers. Warblers of several kinds are attracted by the insect life and by the sometimes dense nesting cover among brambles, hawthorn and coppiced hazel. This shrubby understorey also encourages small mammals, which in turn attract predators such as weasels and stoats.

④ An Iron Age hillfort above Idbury is considered to be the origin of the place name 'Ida's Burg'. Idbury House, an imposing three-storeyed Tudor manor house, was once the home of J W Robertson Scott, the original editor of *The Countryman* magazine. St Nicholas' is an appealing little church. Look for the blocked Norman north doorway and, in the churchyard nearby, a grandiose memorial to Sir Benjamin Baker, architect of the Forth Bridge.

This not too strenuous walk takes in three enchanting Cotswold villages and their churches, two mills on the River Windrush, and an 18th-century mansion in its landscaped parkland setting. Much in evidence everywhere is some of the very finest Cotswold stone, quarried locally and used in Oxford colleges and St Paul's Cathedral.

POINTS OF INTEREST

① Take time to look at St Peter's Church, which encapsulates the essence of local style and form: Baroque table tombs, a Perpendicular 'wool' tower and an early Norman south doorway carved with two complete rows of beakheads. The cottages to the north and east of the church make a delightful composition; notice particularly the pointed arch doorway, a 14th-century survival.

② You can visit Little Barrington church by following the Upton (Middle) Road, but for many the visual charm of the upper terrace of cottages, each subtly different from its neighbour yet harmonious as a group, will be the real pleasure to savour.

③ The scene at Barrington Mill seems to have changed little since the days when horses and wagons trundling up loaded with sisal sacks of grist were a familiar sight here.

④ The route passes the sadly neglected old school and village hall – superb buildings crying out for use, neither at present

having a role to play. From here there are lovely views of the Windrush Valley.

⑤ The completely restored cottage opposite the path makes a striking contrast with the exteriors of most other houses. Architecturally, Great Barrington is assuredly homogeneous, an estate village with little desire to forsake its agricultural roots. However, in recent decades, with the swing away from a labour-intensive industry, the village has lost its purpose though not its vernacular beauty.

⑥ Take the opportunity of visiting St Mary's, a large Norman church with Bray and Talbot monuments. Barrington Park, the great mansion adjoining it, was built for Earl Talbot in 1736–38 by William Kent.

⑦ Strong's Causeway was named after Thomas Strong, master mason to Sir Christopher Wren, who lived at Little Barrington and left money in his will for the repair of this road for funeral cortèges.

The peaceful old path between Little and Great Barrington

ROUTE DIRECTIONS
Allow 2¼ hours
Start near the Windrush Eater (grid ref. SP189125).

Go right almost immediately and descend the unsignposted minor road off the A40, passing Glebe Farm, to the green in front of Windrush church①.

Go right, where the road bends, through a kissing-gate, opening up a view of Barrington Park. Cross the pasture to a gate followed by a fenced passage for cows, and continue onward via stone and wooden stiles into the lane next to Green Drive Farm house. Follow the lane around to the left, passing the post office②.

Cross the foot of the sloping green and then the road to follow the byway on to a confined footpath. Go left across the river to reach Barrington Mill via the stile and lane③.

Pass in front of the mill building and ascend the mill lane to Great Barrington. On meeting the road, turn right④.

Go left along the short path on to the main street⑤.

Go left along the main street and then left again at the monument⑥.

Descend beneath the high garden wall to cross the mill stream on to Strong's Causeway⑦.

The route passes the Fox Inn. Go right along the road.

Look out for a stone stile on the right to take you on course for Windrush Mill, reached via three stiles. Go left up the mill lane, then left over a stone stile, with 'Windrush' on the step.

Go straight across a paddock, over a stile and into a lane rising into Windrush village, going left on to the road and then right, back to the A40.

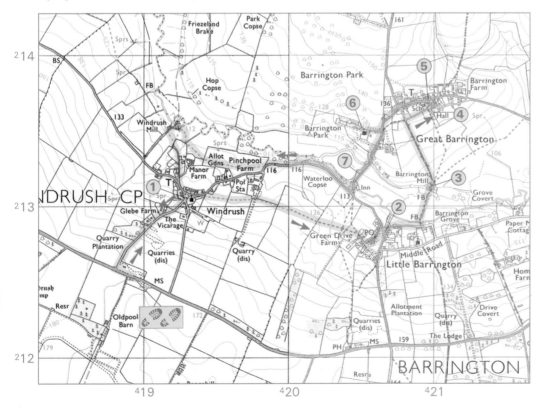

ROUTE DIRECTIONS

Allow 2½ hours
Start from the large car park (small fee April to September) in Bourton-on-the-Water (grid ref. SO171205).

Follow the path beside the river, cross the first bridge left and keep on the streamside path to the road bridge at the Motor Museum (former mill). Go right to the road junction and turn left. Turn right along the metalled path passing the parish church①.

The tarmac footpath leads past Bourton Vale School left on to Station Road. Turn right along the path beside the Fosse Way (A429). Approaching the Coach and Horses cross the main road on to a tarmac footpath, which leads to Lower Slaughter across fields and enters the village along the east bank of Slaughter Brook②.

Keep with the stream and go towards the right past the mill, Collett's bakery and the post office, then turn left between the buildings. Go through two kissing gates, past the long millpond, then slant up over ridge-and-furrow pastureland via stiles and gates before descending to a short lane on to the road, right, at Upper Slaughter. Over the road bridge follow the road left, marked 'no through road', then left over the footbridge by the ford and up the rise③.

From the triangular 'square' turn right to the road junction. The gate opposite leads on to a bridleway, which you ascend. At the top turn right through a gate and go diagonally across a field into a lane to the right of the farm. At the road junction turn left and follow Buckle Street past Brassey's Buildings.

Continue along the road until a signposted bridleway lane forks right, descending via gates towards Aston Mill. At the foot of the lane, before entering Aston, go left to a gate, briefly following the old Banbury-to-Cheltenham railway, then over the Windrush meadows (passing through several gates)④.

Follow Lansdown Road into Bourton-on-the-Water, turning right at the footpath sign opposite Hill Cottage. Pass some delightful back gardens before going through kissing gates into the village street. Turn left past the Trendy Duke and retrace your steps down the main street to the car park.

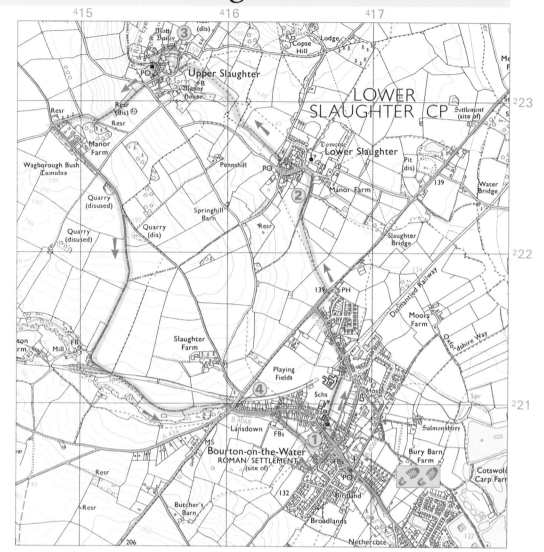

'Slaughter' may have been the name of the stream now flanked by Upper Slaughter's cottages

A fairly leisurely walk, much of it on level ground, linking three of the most popular – and picturesque – Cotswold villages: Upper and Lower Slaughter and Bourton-on-the-Water, site of a Roman settlement.

POINTS OF INTEREST

①In 1784 Bourton-on-the-Water's Norman church, built on Saxon foundations, was demolished, and a Georgian church was built on to the preserved chancel.

②In Lower Slaughter the stream flows broad and shallow between neatly mown grass banks, and many houses retain their traditional features. Notice the attractive red brick-built corn mill with its tall chimney and waterwheel. The 19th-century church now has its elegant spire capped with fibreglass and the 17th-century manor house is a hotel.

③The architectural touches of Edwin Lutyens are evident in the cottages by the church and in the strangely sunken path. Upper Slaughter was the home of a family called Slaughter in the 16th century, but the site has been inhabited since early times.

④A stone plaque on Bourton Bridge commemorates the Roman Second Legion, who built this section of the Fosse Way.

Beginning at Hailes Abbey, a place of pilgrimage for three centuries, this walk takes in part of the Cotswold Way, an ancient drove route to Chipping Campden and a former salt way to Lechlade.

POINTS OF INTEREST

①Hailes Abbey is a hauntingly beautiful ruin. Despite its remoteness, it drew royalty and pilgrims alike in its heyday, mainly because Edmund, Earl Richard of Cornwall's son, presented the abbey with a phial authenticated as containing the blood of Christ. This was later found to be false. Graceful arches and stony outlines of the ground plan are all that remain of the building today, but in the adjacent museum many exhibits indicate its former glory.

②The four-acre site of Beckbury hillfort is protected by natural scarp defences on two sides. It is thought that the smaller

enclosures such as this were probably the fortified residences of petty chieftains.

③Along Campden Lane sheep were driven and wagons drawn, relaying the fleeces to Chipping Campden. From there they went to be graded, known as 'stapling', by the local medieval merchants before despatch to London and Southampton, where they would await the export ships to France and Italy. Under Norman rule the export of wool increased considerably to meet the demands of Flemish weavers. The Cotswold, an ancient breed descended from the Roman longwool sheep, became the largest sheep in England.

④As its name suggests, Salter's Lane was once a 'salt way'; a route on which salt was carried from Droitwich to Lechlade, then to London on barges down the River Thames.

Rich and poor once flocked to Hailes Abbey, where a phial was said to hold Christ's blood

ROUTE DIRECTIONS

Allow 2¼ hours
Start from the Hailes Abbey car park (grid ref. SP051301) ①.

Follow the road east and at the Hayles Fruit Farm continue up the waymarked, roughly cobbled track. The lane leads up between Hailes Wood and fruit orchards to a stile and signpost to Beckbury Camp, left. You may prefer to shorten the walk to Lynes Barn by following the lane through the medieval grange of Great Farmcote to visit the Norman chapel of ease.

The main route ascends the pasture from the lane. Cross to a gate at the end of a fence, then via a stile head up into Cromwell's Clump, the monument at the north-west corner of Beckbury hillfort ②.

The route follows the Cotswold Way keeping to the scarp wall. Just short of the old wooded quarry go through a gate, left, keeping to the stone wall. On joining the trackway, turn right through the gate ③.

The main track branches left, but go through a gate on to the bridleway, where it can get muddy in places. Beyond a small freestone quarry you reach the Farmcote road and bear left towards Winchcombe. Continue downhill to Lynes Barn, and, a few yards beyond the road junction, go through the gate, right. Follow the waymarked track along a strip lynchet shelf (terraced hillside), past a Dutch barn to a double gate. The route proceeds by gates through a short section of woodland, following the contours to Little Farmcote Farm. Through the iron gate keep right, round the new barn, before walking up through the farmyard and right on to the concrete road. Turn right on the tarmac Salter's Lane, descending over a cattle grid ④.

Turn right just beyond the few houses on the right along a short lane, following the Cotswold Way, and from the gate cross the pasture diagonally to another gate to return to Hailes Abbey.

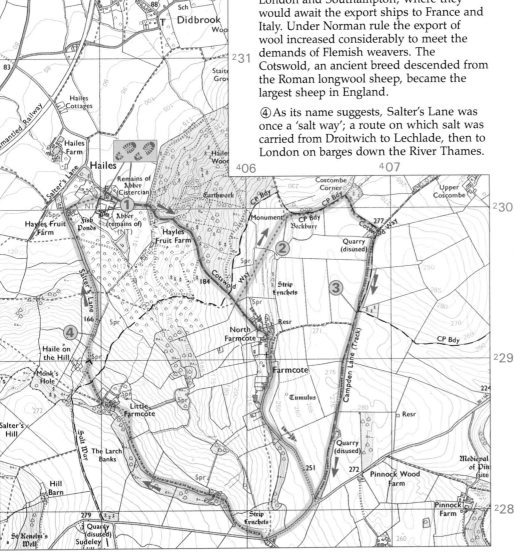

Although quite close to Cheltenham, at the foot of the Cotswold escarpment, this is a high wold walk in an area which has a surprisingly remote feel to it. Stretches of woodland around the route shelter songbirds and small mammals, and there are fine views.

POINTS OF INTEREST

① The curious name given to the group of trees on the hilltop is St Paul's Epistle – possibly something to do with the custom of beating the bounds of Dowdeswell parish, during which passages were read from the Bible. The 948ft hill is a good viewpoint: the panorama stretches across the Vale of Gloucester to the Malverns in the north-west, and in the opposite direction to the Thamesdown Hills above Swindon.

② The route accompanies the ridge wall with fine views over Foxcote and the upper valley of the River Coln, which rises just a few hundred yards east of the footpath. The richly textured woodland of Foxcote Grove is a pleasant feature on the nearer slope.

③ The name of Smoke Acre is thought to be derived from land rented for payment in money (known as 'smoke pennies') in place of tithewood.

④ The wooded hillsides above Hilcot Brook are alive with birdsong in spring and early summer: Pinchley Wood derives its name from the Old English word 'pinca', meaning finch. The steep slope to the west is known as Breakneck Bank, while Ratshill Bank, further along, speaks for itself – though you are more likely to see 'tree-rats', or squirrels, along this woodland way.

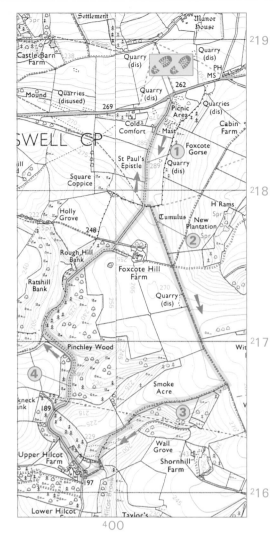

Along the breezy ridge wall as it passes Foxcote Grove

ROUTE DIRECTIONS

Allow 1¾ hours
Start from the Kilkenny Viewpoint car park (grid ref. SP004186).

Walk up the Hilcot road, passing the mast and a larch clump on a mound①.

Branch from the road just prior to entering a belt of beeches, go left to a stile, then, keeping strictly to the footpath, go through the tiny reservoir enclosure via stiles②.

Join a track leading on over Withington Hill, alongside a fence to a gate. Go immediately right through the gate and follow the track leading down beside Smoke Acre③.

The track passes through a new gate (beneath the word 'Acre' on the map), continuing under power-lines.

Leave the track at a metal gate left, shortly before the track veers right following the field boundary. The path goes right, along the top of the bank, through the scrub, which appears more impenetrable than it actually is.

Entering a narrow cultivated strip, the path slants down the steep bank left, where the bracken ceases, to reach a hunting gate at the foot of a dry valley. A lane crosses the Hilcot Brook with its pretty pond, and rises via a gate to the road. Go right, past the attractive buildings of Upper Hilcot Farm.

The walk follows the minor road for Cold Common, initially beside Hilcot Brook, sheltered by wooded banks④.

The road rises by Rough Hill Bank to regain the open road on Cold Common and return to the car park.

The larches called 'St Paul's Epistle', perhaps read here in the beating of the bounds

WALK 21F · Meadow Way OXFORDSHIRE

ROUTE DIRECTIONS

Allow 2½ hours
Start from the Windrush Valley Park, Asthall Barrow, where parking is available (grid ref. SP290102).

Go left, descending the minor road to Asthall, and fork right to enter the village①.

Go right at the Maytime Inn, formerly the Three Horse Shoes②.

Cross Asthall Bridge to a stile left into the meadow③.

Look for a stile to the left of some bushes among old gravel pit hollows and maintain course across the ensuing meadow to join a hedge-line leading to two stiles enclosing a stone slab. Proceed past a cottage on the left, reaching the road next to the Swan Inn. Go right carefully round the sharp corner, passing a superb Cotswold barn, and keep left at the junction. Ascend the steps left into Swinbrook churchyard④.

Cross the stile and advance to a waymark post; ahead, beyond the cattle grid, is Widford church⑤.

Returning to the waymark post ascend Dean Bottom via two new stiles on to a minor road. Go right to the brow of the hill, branching left down a leafy lane. From the bridgegate veer right down the valley, but keep to the left of the rushes to avoid the springs on the right. Pass between a thorn bush and a fence, and slant right at a drystone wall. Cross over a little stream by a telegraph pole and continue straight to a gate on to the valley road. The road accompanies the clear stream passing attractive 17th- and 18th-century cottages into Swinbrook. At this point you may retrace your steps to the car park through Swinbrook and Asthall or make a detour on to higher ground for a more scenic view of the Windrush Valley.

Cross the stream beside the ford and go left up the hill, continuing out of the village on to Chalk Hill, then turn right and descend to Asthall Bridge⑥.

Leaving the village via the beech avenue, retrace your steps up the road to Asthall Barrow car park.

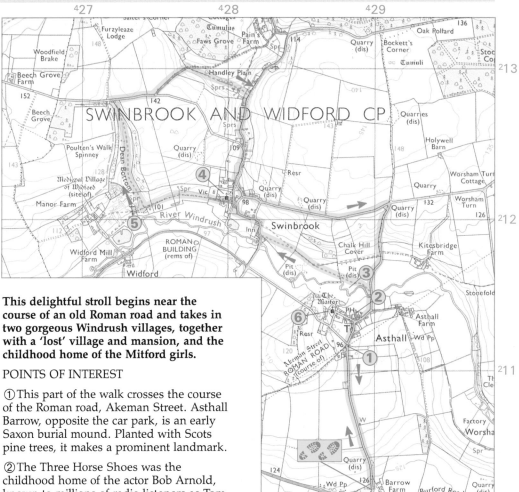

This delightful stroll begins near the course of an old Roman road and takes in two gorgeous Windrush villages, together with a 'lost' village and mansion, and the childhood home of the Mitford girls.

POINTS OF INTEREST

① This part of the walk crosses the course of the Roman road, Akeman Street. Asthall Barrow, opposite the car park, is an early Saxon burial mound. Planted with Scots pine trees, it makes a prominent landmark.

② The Three Horse Shoes was the childhood home of the actor Bob Arnold, known to millions of radio listeners as Tom Forrest of *The Archers*. His father was once the publican here.

③ The River Windrush lives up to its name at this point, as it winds through the rushes, though like most river names it has changed radically from its Celtic origins. Seen from the meadow, Asthall can readily be appreciated as a topographical name for the church and manor clearly shelter on the east side of a wooded bank.

④ There are fine table tombs in Swinbrook churchyard and the clear glass east window pours light upon the Tudor and Stuart Fettiplace monuments within the church. The Fettiplace mansion is lost along with the notable family line, but as you leave the churchyard by a narrow walled footpath on course for St Oswald's, the old terraced gardens and fishpond at the foot of the hill readily reveal its location.

⑤ Seemingly remote from all habitation, Widford church is all that is left of a medieval 'lost' village, confirmed by tell-tale hummocks in the adjacent pasture. Box pews fill the nave, while the chancel harbours fragments of floor mosaic, indicating that a Roman villa stood here.

⑥ Back in Asthall are the church and the manor house – where Nancy Mitford and her sisters spent their childhood.

The blue flash of a kingfisher in flight can often be seen along the banks of the Windrush; perched motionless, they are surprisingly difficult to spot

ROUTE DIRECTIONS

The drive starts from Cirencester ①.

From Cirencester follow the signs The South West and Chippenham to leave by the A429. In 1½ miles go forward on to the A433, signed Bristol. After another mile, in the meadows to the right, beyond the turning for Coates, is the reputed source of the River Thames. Pass under a railway bridge and turn left on to an unclassified road for Kemble. Cross the main road into the village, then go over the staggered crossroads, signed Ewen. The infant Thames is first seen before reaching Ewen.

Continue with the South Cerney signs and keep forward at all crossroads to reach South Cerney ②.

In South Cerney turn right at the war memorial into Broadway Lane, and in ¾ mile pass, on the right, the Cotswold Marina. This is part of the Cotswold Water Park ③.

Half a mile farther, at the crossroads, turn right, B4696, signed Ashton Keynes. In 1¼ miles turn left and shortly branch left, unclassified, to reach Ashton Keynes. The stripling Thames, only a few feet wide, flows through the village and is spanned by small bridges.

At the end of the village turn left on to the Cricklade road then bear right. Two miles farther, at the crossroads, turn left on to the B4040, and after another 1½ miles turn left again to enter Cricklade. At the clock tower turn right and follow signs Swindon, then in ¾ mile join the A419. One mile farther turn left on to an unclassified road for Castle Eaton. This pleasant Thames-side village is skirted by continuing with the Highworth road to pass through Hannington. In 1¼ miles turn left on to the B4019 for Highworth ④.

Turn left on to the Stow road, A361. After 4½ miles, on the left, a riverside park is passed before crossing the old Halfpenny Bridge into Lechlade ⑤.

Turn right, then right again to leave by the Faringdon road, A417, and in ¾ mile cross St John's Bridge ⑥.

Two miles farther the drive passes the grounds of Buscot House ⑦.

Keep straight ahead to Faringdon. From the Market Square branch left on to the Bampton road, A4095, and after passing the church turn left. In 2½ miles cross Radcot Bridge ⑧.

At Clanfield the drive goes forward on to the Burford road, B4020, for Alvescot. In ¼ mile turn left, unclassified, to Kencot, and in 1¼ miles at the crossroads turn right into Filkins ⑨.

In the village turn right and in 1 mile, at the T-junction, turn right on to the A361, signed Stow. In 2 miles at the crossroads turn left, unclassified, signed Wildlife Park, and pass the entrance to the Cotswold Wildlife Park ⑩.

In ½ mile go over the crossroads, signed Eastleach Martin, then at the end of a tree-lined road, ½ mile, branch left and follow a narrow by-road to the twin Eastleaches. At Eastleach Martin cross the River Leach into Eastleach Turville, then keep right through the village on the Hatherop road. In ½ mile, at the T-junction, turn left, then in ½ mile turn right, and 2 miles farther turn right again into Hatherop. Turn left for Coln St Aldwyn ⑪.

Turn left, signed Fairford, then cross the River Coln and ascend into Quenington. At the green turn left, then at the end of the village recross the Coln and continue to Fairford ⑫.

The drive returns to Cirencester by following the A417 through the pleasant villages of Poulton and Ampney Crucis.

POINTS OF INTEREST

① The Roman capital of the Cotswolds, Cirencester is a pleasant market town with a Norman abbey gateway and a 15th-century 'wool' church with a magnificent three-storeyed porch. The 3,000 acres of Cirencester Park near by are open to the public.

② By the end of the 1980s it is estimated that around 4,000 acres of lakes will have been created from gravel pits around South Cerney. The village itself retains its Cotswold heart and has three manors.

③ The Water Park – a series of 100 man-made lakes – attracts human and wildfowl visitors alike, offering water sports, angling and sailing.

④ Highworth is a hill-top town with some 17th-century houses and a 15th-century church which still bears the marks of a Civil War cannon ball.

⑤ The rivers Coln and Leach join the Thames at Lechlade, a popular boating and fishing spot. Shelley composed his *Summer Evening Meditation* in Lechlade churchyard during 1815.

⑥ An Augustinian hospital gave its name to the 13th-century St John's Bridge, the street leading to it and to St John's Lock, beyond which point motor cruisers and narrow boats cannot navigate the Thames.

⑦ Built in the Adam style in 1780, Buscot House is surrounded by landscaped gardens, including a formal Italianate water garden.

⑧ The 14th-century Radcot Bridge is the oldest recorded bridging point on the Upper Thames and was built by the monks of Beaulieu Abbey.

⑨ Huge rectangular slabs of stone edge the cottage gardens in Filkins. The Cotswold Woollen Weavers keep old skills alive in an 18th-century barn, and there is a small museum and an old village lock-up.

⑩ Set in 200 acres of lake-watered wooded parkland, the Cotswold Wildlife Park contains animals and birds from all over the world. There is also an adventure playground and a narrow-gauge railway.

⑪ Sturdy stone cottages set in pretty gardens line Coln St Aldwyn's main street. Barns, cottages and a manorial farm group with the mainly Norman church are to the west; to the east is Williamstrip Park, a classical 17th-century mansion.

⑫ The magnificent stained-glass windows of the late 15th-century church at Fairford are the only complete set of their period to survive intact in the British Isles.

From Cirencester, the route follows the Thames from its reputed source, through Ewen and Ashton Keynes to its confluence with the Coln and the Leach at Lechlade, passing some pretty villages on the way.

Pleasure craft now ply the River Thames at Lechlade, where working boats once carried Cotswold stone to London

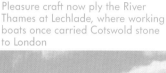

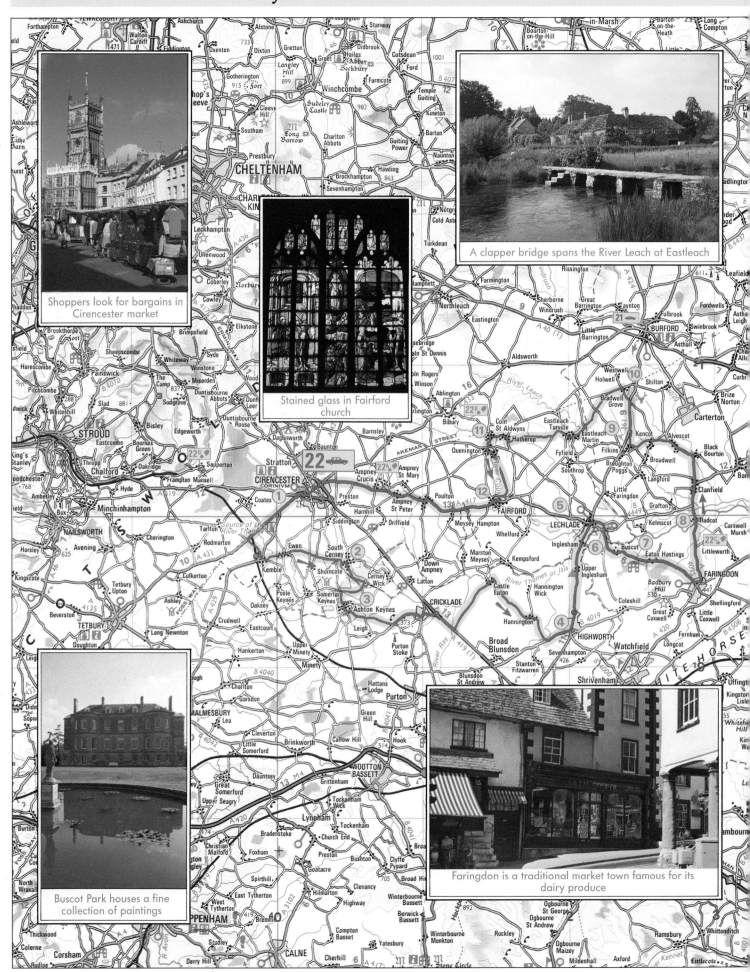

Shoppers look for bargains in Cirencester market

A clapper bridge spans the River Leach at Eastleach

Stained glass in Fairford church

Buscot Park houses a fine collection of paintings

Faringdon is a traditional market town famous for its dairy produce

Leafy lanes between Cotswold villages provide most of the walking here, and the route also passes two churches, one isolated in a field, the other in a beautiful village setting. Short sections of the walk run alongside the busy A417 Cirencester–Fairford road, so take care with young children.

POINTS OF INTEREST

① St Mary's Church was originally surrounded by the village of Ampney St Mary, but it is presumed the community suffered when the Black Death struck in about 1349 and the village found a new site ¾ mile away. The mainly Norman church, entered through a massive 14th-century elm door, contains some splendid medieval wall paintings. Outside, above the blocked north door, is a tympanum of a lion trampling upon a two-headed serpent, a motif unique in England.

② Among Ampney St Peter's delightful collection of Cotswold cottages, notice the second house on the right in the main street, which has the unusual vernacular feature of double string courses. The house at the fork in the road has a sundial on its right-hand wall.

③ St Peter's Church has a pleasant, low west tower at the end of its late Saxon nave. The 14th-century churchyard cross, with neatly restored gable head, is contemporary with that at nearby Ampney Crucis.

The Ampneys take their name from the little Ampney Brook, which once linked all three villages

④ Though now in Gloucestershire, Poulton – whose name means 'farmstead by a pool' – was formerly a detached parish of Wiltshire. Among the village's farmhouses and cottages stands a fine late 17th-century manor house, while Poulton Priory, ¾ mile to the south-west, was built in 1895 on the site of a medieval Gilbertine priory.

West of the village is the Neolithic encampment of Ranbury Ring, which is looped around by the circuit of this walk – like the village, it is a reminder that many generations have walked here before.

ROUTE DIRECTIONS

Allow 2½ hours
Start from the large lay-by on the A417 near Ampney Crucis (grid ref. SP073018).

From the west access to the lay-by, cross the main road and climb over the wooden field fence opposite (no stile or sign). Slant left across the arable field and follow the stream to a footbridge over an ancient ford. A stile and a wicket gate give access to St Mary's churchyard ①.

Cross the A417 once more and go right along the pedestrian walk to Ampney St Peter, turning left up the attractive village street ②.

Take the right fork to pass the church ③.

Continue along the lane, beyond the Rectory, turning right into the tree-shaded lane behind Eastington House. Enjoy the views of Ashbrook on the way to the Red Lion public house junction.

Go left down the minor road, and at the Ampney St Mary signpost turn right along the lane to Poulton. Turn right into the village, passing Prescott's shop and the Falcon Inn ④.

Follow the A417 on the pedestrian walk until the 'Hartley Ayrshires' farm sign. Enter the farmyard here (permissible right of way), pass the farmhouse and continue along the lane to its junction with Charlham Lane.

Go right, soon to accompany Ampney Brook past The Moor, a precious remnant of common land, to reach the A417 again. Conclude by crossing the road and returning left, along the pedestrian walk.

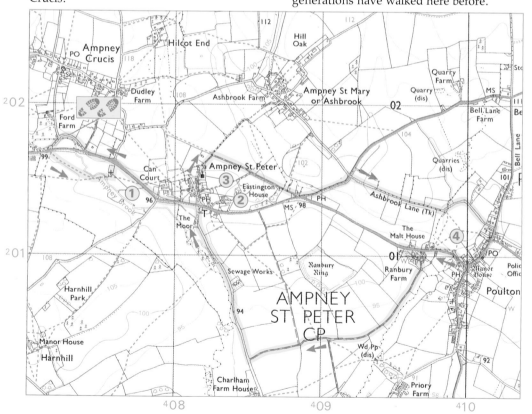

WALK 22B · Beage's Stronghold

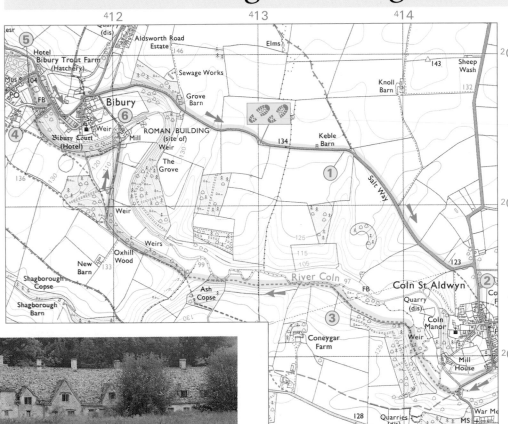

Allow 2¾ hours
Start on the minor road between Bibury and Coln St Aldwyn, which offers good car parking (grid ref. SP130064).

Leave your parking place, and walk eastwards along the road, then continue to follow it as a track enters sharply from the left①.

Turn right at the T-junction to reach the Green crossroads in the little village of Coln St Aldwyn. Facing the crossroads are two shops②.

Proceeding down the village street, pass the New Inn and the old mill. Follow the causeway road and cross the bridge over the river.

At Yew Tree Lodge turn right and pass through two gates to a footpath sign. Advance along the river meadows to a gate with a bold Williamstrip signboard into mature woodland. Emerging shortly at a further gate, the obvious track leads to the banks of the Coln③.

The footpath goes through three gates to reach Shagborough Bottom and then crosses a stone stile, ascending the steep bank beside woodland to a wicket gate which has a Bibury Court Estate notice. Keep to the clear track above Oxhill Wood.

Take the obvious right turn via double gates down the lane towards Bibury Mill. Walk on beyond the gate by the sheep pen to a footpath sign which directs left up to a gate. Pass to the right of the cricket ground, admiring the views through the trees to Bibury. Slant right to either the kissing-gate or, lower down, a stone stile, from where a path leads right, down to the rear of the row of cottages (Arlington Row)④.

Go left in front of the cottages and along the footpath beside the mill stream and Rack Island⑤.

Go right, crossing the smart footbridge by the Swan Hotel. Turn right along the pedestrian walk beside the Coln. Continue into the quieter section of the village to visit the parish church⑥.

Go back up to the main road, turn right past the entrance to Bibury Court Hotel, and follow the road right beyond the mill lane. This road will lead you back to the starting point.

Much-photographed Arlington Row, Bibury

One of the best-loved of English villages, Bibury's name derives from 'Beage's Burg' – the stronghold of Beage, who with her father, a Saxon earl named Leppa, was granted some land here by the River Coln. This walk explores the village and the lovely environs of the Coln, whose clear waters run through river meadows sheltered by woodland and backed by cornfields and sheep pastures.

POINTS OF INTEREST

①From the road there are good views across the spacious wold landscape and into the Coln Valley to the south. The track that joins the road east of Keble Barn is the Salt Way, used in medieval times by pack ponies conveying this essential commodity from Droitwich to Lechlade, and on by boat down the Thames to London. The final stretch of road before the T-junction follows the course of Akeman Street, the Roman road that ran from St Albans to Cirencester.

②Nestling behind the 16th-century manor house, the Church of St John the Baptist is well worth a visit. Formerly dedicated to St Ealdwine (the derivation of Coln St Aldwyn's name), the church has some Norman features and a fine tower topped by gargoyles.

③Approaching the river, the track crosses the line of Akeman Street again. The rushy banks of the Coln here are popular with fly fishermen, and walkers are advised to avoid the water's edge.

④Totally renovated in the late 1970s, the former weavers' cottages of Arlington Row are now owned by the National Trust.

⑤The meadow known as Rack Island takes its name from the time when it was a drying place for cloth woven at Arlington Row and fulled at the mill opposite. On reaching the main road, you are near the Arlington Mill Museum, a 17th-century mill which houses a stimulating farming and folk collection. Across the river from here is Bibury Trout Farm, also open to visitors.

⑥St Mary's was a large Saxon church, and though later additions have left little Saxon work visible outside, the interior has kept several features which may be over 1,000 years old. The fine collection of sheep corbels is a testimony to later wealth – that of the medieval wool industry.

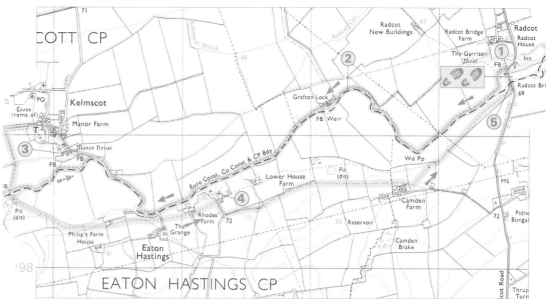

Footbridge at Kelmscot

ROUTE DIRECTIONS

Allow 3 hours
Start from the riverside meadow to the north-east of Radcot Bridge (grid ref. SU286995; small parking fee).

Cross the navigation bridge and go through the wicket gate on the north side①.

Walk alongside the river, via stiles and gates and passing several war-time pill boxes and Grafton Lock②.

After 2½ meandering miles join a track leading from the river into Kelmscot③.

Take the lane to the right of the Plough Inn (a useful stopping point halfway through this walk), and where this enters an arable field go left along the hedge-line to a footbridge on course for the wooden Thames footbridge. You may prefer at this point to return along the Thames bank. The main walk crosses the Thames to enter the scattered parish of Eaton Hastings.

Diverge from the track left to a stile, follow the dyke beside arable fields and then a pasture, crossing three stiles (one a covered barbed-wire affair), and rise across a track to a remote cottage. Cross the rails, turning immediately right to a stile.

Head east across arable land to a stile and a footbridge, rather overgrown, over a brook north of The Grange. Continue to pass in front of Rhodes Farm, reaching a gate on to the road to Eaton Hastings church④.

Go south along the road, branching left on to the Lower House Farm access road. Continue east via gates by Camden Farm, slant left to a stile beyond the wind pump. Two further stiles lead to a long pasture, and thence follow the fence to a stile by Radcot Bridge⑤.

The navigation bridge at Radcot

Radcot, scene of many battles over the centuries, is the oldest recorded bridging point on the upper Thames. From here, this walk follows the river upstream to Kelmscot, William Morris's home for 25 years, before returning through the scattered parish of Eaton Hastings. This stretch of the Thames is the scene of much pleasure-boat activity, and in summer it is possible to replace the first part of the walk by a river cruise to Buscot Lock.

POINTS OF INTEREST

① The navigation bridge and locks were constructed in 1787 by the Thames and Severn Canal Company.

② Fishermen ensconce themselves in hollows along the banks of the Thames here, sharing the river with pleasure boats and wildfowl. In high summer, nettles on the corner approaching the lock may be a problem for walkers – though not for the butterflies that feed on them.

③ Beyond an old stone barn a high wall shields one of the Cotswolds' famous houses, Kelmscot Manor. From 1871 to 1896 this was the country home of William Morris, the pre-Raphaelite socialist advocate. The 16th- and 17th-century Manor was restored by the Society of Antiquarians and is open to the public occasionally.

④ Unlike Kelmscot, Eaton Hastings seems to have suffered cruelly in the 14th century from the Black Death, which virtually destroyed the community, clustered since at least the 11th century around the church. Eaton meant 'river farmstead', and today all that remains are amalgamated farms cropping vast acreages of wheat.

⑤ The earliest known reference to Radcot Bridge dates from AD958, but the present bridge with its two pointed arches and later central arch was built in 1317 by the monks of Beaulieu Abbey.

ROUTE DIRECTIONS

Allow 1¾ hours
Start from the Broad Ride where you can park your car next to the road (grid ref. SO947028)①.

Go past the Manor Farm and the Glebe estate, then descend the footpath, right, into Sapperton village street, opposite the school and post office (there is no shop). Go right, then fork left down the 'no through road' to the Parish Church of St Kenelm②.

Continue down the passage beside the church to a stile slanting below Upper Dorvel③.

Go over the stile, bearing right toward the sheep pens but keeping above them. go through the third pen on to the steep road then left down a footpath, which is prone to run as a watercourse after heavy rain. The footpath enters Dorvel Wood and becomes muddy. Take the main, steep path upward and turn left along a main cross track, which is also muddy in places. Continue until you descend to the Dane Lane minor road just above Daneway House④.

Cross the road to a stile and, keeping to the left track, proceed across Daneway Banks, a precious unimproved calcareous grassland, protected as a National Nature Reserve. Continue to a gate then cross a minor road on to the obvious track through Siccaridge Wood – scrub woodland alive with wildlife. After a while descend to where three paths diverge. Take the sharp left down, eventually climbing a locked gate and crossing a pasture to reach Dane Lane next to the Daneway Inn⑤.

Take the footpath in the valley, left by the bridge, signposted to Sapperton. Cross the stile marked 'Canal Walk'. Climb above the tunnel entrance to a stile, slanting up to the pasture and keeping right of the old pump house, to a stile leading into Sapperton. Keep on the main road, past the village hall, Bell Inn and Glebe Farm, and continue to the road junction, where you go right. Notice the tiny railed enclosure left containing the precise Ordnance Survey datum 594.88ft. Then go right again into the Broad Ride to conclude the walk.

Sapperton and the Daneway represent an important focus of Cotswold industrial ambition, with their late-18th-century canal tunnelling and the early-20th-century Arts and Crafts revivalism, practised by Gimson and the Barnsley brothers. The walk takes a dive into the wooded Frome Valley, and there are some steep and muddy places so it is advisable to wear stout boots or wellingtons.

POINTS OF INTEREST

① Broad Ride extends from Sapperton Common east through Lord Bathurst's Cirencester Park – 10,000 acres of the finest surviving example in England of geometrical landscaping, where great rides meet and grand vistas appear unexpectedly. Only this length, west of Sapperton Park, is freely open to the public.

② St Kenelm's Church belongs principally to the 14th century, although the Atkyns family of Pinbury Park made embellishments around 1730. Sir Robert Atkyns, whose monument adorns the south transept, was the author of *The Ancient and Present State of Gloucestershire*, a famous early historical treatise. Pinbury was also the home of John Masefield, made Poet Laureate in 1930.

③ The house, Upper Dorvel, was formed and extended from two cottages by Ernest Barnsley around 1901 and has a striking topiary.

④ Daneway House dates from around 1250. It was the home of the Hancox family continuously from 1397 to 1860, then at the beginning of the present century it became the workshop and showroom of the Gimson/Barnsley woodcraft partnership.

⑤ The Daneway Inn was built for the refreshment of bargees and 'leggers' who worked the Sapperton Canal Tunnel until the Great Western Railway was built in 1911.

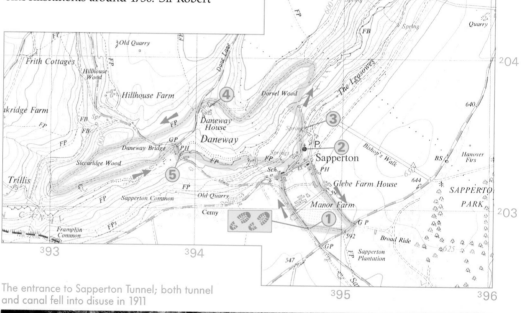

The entrance to Sapperton Tunnel; both tunnel and canal fell into disuse in 1911

TOUR 23 · In the Heart of the Forest   GWENT

ROUTE DIRECTIONS
The drive starts from Monmouth ①.

Follow Chepstow signs to leave by the A466, cross the River Wye, then bear right and follow the river to Redbrook. At the Bush Inn turn left on to the B4231, signed Lydney. Beyond the village enter England and continue through hilly countryside to Newland②.

Remain on the B4231 to Clearwell where, at the Wyndham Arms, go forward on to an unclassified road. Shortly to the right are the Clearwell Caves Ancient Iron Mines③.

In almost ½ mile cross the main road then, in ¼ mile, turn right, signed Ellwood. Take the next turning right and ½ mile farther at the crossroads turn left, signed Parkend. In almost another ½ mile join the B4431 and proceed through woodland to Parkend. To the right along the Lydney road, B4234, is the northern terminus of the Dean Forest Railway④.

Continue along the Blakeney road, B4431. Then in 1¼ miles turn left on to an unclassified road, signed Speech House. A fine run is then made through more forest scenery, passing several picnic sites, before reaching the Speech House Hotel⑤.

Turn right with the Cinderford road, B4226, passing an arboretum, and continue through the forest. Two miles farther the drive reaches the outskirts of Cinderford. From here a diversion to the right along the B4227 Blakeney road leads through Ruspidge to Lower Soudley. Nearby

is the Dean Heritage Museum and Craft Centre⑥.

The main drive continues forward and ascends to skirt the town of Cinderford. Later turn right on to the A4151, signed Gloucester, then descend to Littledean. At the T-junction turn right with the unclassified Newnham road and shortly pass Littledean Hall⑦.

There follows a long descent with views across the River Severn to the distant Cotswold Hills. At Newnham on Severn turn left on to the Gloucester road, A48. The River Severn is then followed for a short distance to Broadoak. One mile farther turn left on an unclassified road, signed Mitcheldean, and proceed along a pleasant by-road to Flaxley⑧.

In a mile bear right and continue to the outskirts of Mitcheldean. Here turn left on to the Monmouth road, A4136, and ascend. This undulating main road, passing through attractive scenery along the northern extremity of the Forest of Dean, with the occasional evidence of old mine workings and quarries in places, is followed for the next 9 miles to reach Staunton⑨.

A long descent is then made

through beautiful wooded countryside, and after 3 miles a worthwhile detour to the left can be taken along a side road to Kymin Hill (National Trust)⑩.

Continue the descent, and at the foot turn right on to the A466 for the return to Monmouth.

This drive into the Forest of Dean offers an insight into the Forest of the past – the ancient mines at Clearwell, the Verderers' Court, the Dean Heritage Museum and the historic Flaxley Abbey.

POINTS OF INTEREST

① An interesting former county town, Monmouth contains several Tudor and Georgian buildings within a network of old streets. The museum has a collection of Nelson mementoes as well as items of local history.

② The attractive village of Newland, on the edge of the Forest of Dean, is noted for its fine 13th- to 14th-century church – known as the 'Cathedral of the Forest'. It also has a number of Stuart and Georgian houses, 17th-century almshouses and the original Bell's Grammar School.

③ The Mines include exhibits of local mining and geology from the Forest of Dean area. During the summer months, visitors may enter the mines and go underground to a depth of 100ft.

④ The Dean Forest Railway runs from Lydney Junction to Parkend and was part of the Severn and Wye Railway.

⑤ Built in 1680 as a hunting lodge for Charles II, Speech House Hotel later housed the court room of the Forest Verderers. The Verderers' Court still meets in the dining room.

⑥ Surrounded by magnificent woods, the Dean Heritage Museum and Craft Centre reflects the unique heritage of Dean and its ancient laws and customs.

⑦ The remarkable Littledean Hall depicts the evolution of a manorial hall from the early Norman period, and is claimed to be the oldest known house in the country. Other points of interest in Littledean include the gaol, a motte-and-bailey castle and a fine church.

⑧ Behind the church at Flaxley is Flaxley Abbey, founded in the 12th century by Cistercian monks who both farmed in the valley and smelted and forged iron.

⑨ Staunton is a small village perched high over a deep valley. Its church has a corkscrew staircase. A short walk leads to Buck Stone, the view from which is one of the finest in the county.

⑩ Standing at 800ft, Kymin Hill affords good views over the Wye and Monnow valleys. Near the summit there is a 'naval temple' built in 1800 as a memorial.

The Monnow Bridge Gateway in Monmouth is the only remaining fortified bridge gate in Britain

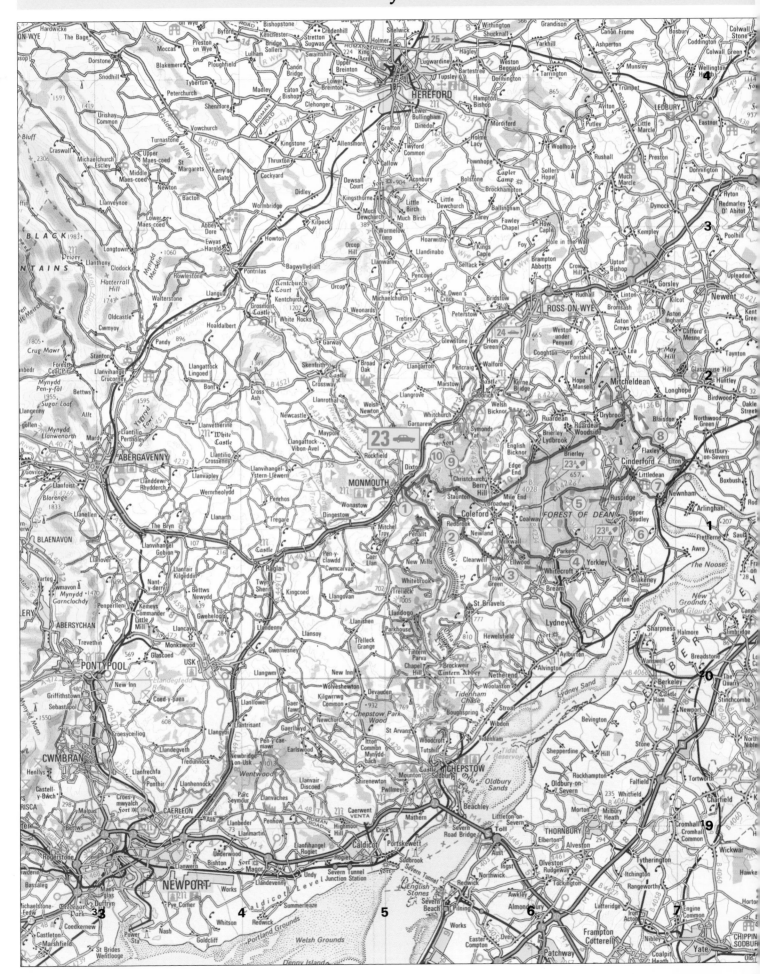

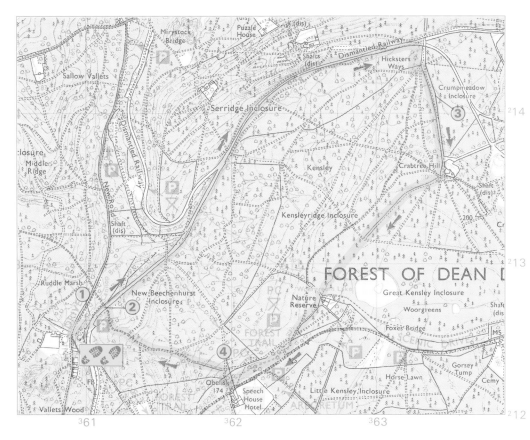

Follow the Lydbrook road for 50yds, passing a deep pool fed by the Cannop Brook. Turn right along a forest trail waymarked with yellow arrows over Cannop Brook (via stepping stones) and towards a railway bridge①.

Scramble up the embankment and follow the track to the left through woodland②.

Continue ahead along the railway track, passing under a brick and stone bridge, then through the wooded slopes of Serridge Inclosure.

The waymarked route of the forest trail goes right over a stile parallel to the railway line then bears right through woodland. At a main track turn left and left again, leaving the waymarked path. On reaching a metalled road turn right and continue to Crabtree Hill③.

At the top of the hill the path veers right alongside a patch of cleared woodland with delightful views. Well to the right of Woorgreens Lake the path joins a wide forest track, descending past Kensley Lodge and continuing over a step stile to the picnic site at Speech House④.

Keep to the right of the picnic site and follow the way as directed by yellow arrows, going sharply right opposite the hotel. After the thick yew trees, planted in 1902, the path opens up offering scenic views and a close-up of a massive oak sculpture, The Giant Chair.

After a gentle descent do not miss a left fork along a rocky track which becomes soft and muddy and descends to the railway embankment. Continue up and over this to return to the car park.

Forestry and mining have long gone hand in hand in the Forest of Dean. This walk begins by following one of the railways, now disused, that served the mining industry here. Woodland tracks then lead to the Speech House, at the centre of the Forest, from where a waymarked trail returns towards the starting point.

POINTS OF INTEREST

①Rivalry between the inhabitants of East Dean and those of West Dean has long been a Forest tradition, and it is the Cannop Brook that divides the two halves. Running north-south through the heart of the Forest, the Cannop Valley was one of the most important coal-mining areas, with seams frequently breaking the surface. The old Cannop Colliery (now a county council depot) had its own reservoir for the water used to generate the steam that powered the winding gear.

②The route briefly joins the Sculpture Trail, which includes a collection of seven works commissioned by the Arnolfini Gallery in collaboration with the Forestry Commission and Henry Moore Foundation.

③To the left of the road between the old railway and Crabtree Hill is Crumpmeadow Inclosure. These now peaceful woods were at one time a traditional haunt of the Forest gypsies – Romany people who originally lived in tents and only later, when

commonland became more scarce, in caravans. They practised woodland crafts such as charcoal-burning, making pegs and baskets from coppiced hazel and gathering berries and herbs for use in medicines.

④Now a hotel, the Speech House is an imposing building of local stone, dating from the late 17th century. Formerly known as the King's Lodge, it is reputed to have played host to Charles II and Nell Gwynne in 1680. It is the traditional meeting place of the Verderers' Court. Verderers are still elected and, in theory though not in practice, meet every 40 days. Their courtroom, now the hotel dining room, can still be viewed by visitors.

On the Sculpture Trail, which encourages artists to interpret the Forest of Dean in new works

ROUTE DIRECTIONS

Allow 2 hours
Start from the Forestry
Commission car park opposite
the entrance to Mallards Pike
Lake picnic site (grid ref.
SO638088).

Cross the road and enter the site
by following the tarmac lane up
to the picnic site and lake①.

Keep to the left of the lake,
following a path which becomes
narrow and uneven as it winds its
way under conifers along the
water's edge②.

On reaching the Blackpool
Brook, which feeds this lake, turn
left beside the wooden bridge
and follow the yellow arrows of
the forest trail③.

Our route now follows this
waymarked trail to Staple Edge.
From the bridge go left then right
along a forest track to cross the
brook. Turn immediately left
through a spruce plantation
where the path bears right and
continues through woodland
before joining a broad path.
Follow this to the right, and at
the next crossways turn right
descending to a main forest
track. Be careful to continue
ahead along a narrower path
which then bears left, becoming
broader as it gently climbs
between spruce plantations to a
clearing at Staple Edge.

At the junction of numerous
paths and tracks, turn right and
right again to follow the
waymarked route along a grass
path. Where the waymarked trail
bears right, continue ahead④.

Ignore all turnings as the path
gently descends towards
Mallards Pike. Cross over a main
track where the narrowing path
offers glimpses of the tree-
shaded lake below. Once back at
the picnic site proceed ahead,
cross a stone railway bridge and
return to the car park.

Designated picnic sites – where camp fires can be
lit – are a popular feature of the Forest of Dean

**A ramble in the scenic Forest of Dean leads
alongside a picturesque lake at Mallards
Pike, then along a waymarked forest trail
with a strenuous climb to Staple Edge.
Here far-reaching views may be enjoyed
before returning down an attractive
woodland path to the car park.**

POINTS OF INTEREST

① Mallards Pike is a purpose-built
recreational lake. It was constructed by the
Forestry Commission in 1982, and,
although swimming is not allowed, sailing
and canoeing are permitted on this

delightful pool, surrounded by shady Scots
pine trees.

② Along the first stretch of this walk, traces
of the old industrial heritage of this area are
still evident. Coal has been taken from the
Forest of Dean since Roman times, and in
the 19th century up to a million tons of coal
a year were mined and transported on a
network of tramroads and railways. The
landscape round about still bears the scars.

③ This 'yellow arrow route' through the
Forest of Dean was created by the Forest of
Dean Group of the Ramblers' Association.
Their policy is to lay out a system of paths
and trails using coloured arrows and
signposts in order to lead walkers through
scenic areas they would be unlikely to find
without help. With the Forestry
Commission, they also produce useful
leaflets guiding visitors through forest trails.
This walk follows part of a 10-mile circular
route through East Dean, which can be split
into three shorter rambles offering a variety
of glorious views and a selection of pools
and many acres of woodland to be explored
along the way.

④ Along this delightful path lined with
holly, larch, spruce, gorse and bracken,
forest sheep forage. Residents of this
ancient woodland since about 4000BC –
when the New Stone Age people, who
were the first real farmers, displaced the
Middle Stone Age settlers – sheep have
long been part of life and the landscape of
the Forest of Dean.

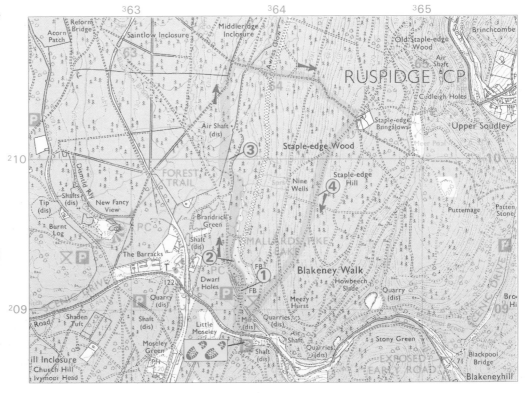

TOUR 24 · Lower Wye Valley   HEREFORD & WORCESTER

ROUTE DIRECTIONS

The drive starts from Ross-on-Wye ①.

From Ross follow signs to Monmouth (A40) to leave by the B4260. Descend and cross the River Wye, then at the roundabout turn left on to the A40. There are occasional views of the river before this scenic dual carriageway main road crosses higher ground and continues past the turning to Whitchurch. From here a short detour to the left along the Symonds Yat West road, B4164, leads to the Jubilee Maze and Museum of Mazes ②.

Remain on the A40 for 2½ miles and enter Wales, then rejoin the River Wye and proceed towards Monmouth ③.

Approaching the town go forward at the roundabout (for the town centre turn right). At the next traffic signals turn left on to the A466, signed Chepstow. Cross the river and bear right to enter the lower reaches of the picturesque Wye Valley. Pass through Redbrook, then in 3½ miles cross Telford's Bigsweir Bridge to reach Llandogo. Continue down the valley and later pass, on the left, a picnic site and interpretation centre situated in an old railway station before entering Tintern ④.

An ascent is then made through pleasant woodland, and 3 miles farther a turning to the right may be taken to visit the fine viewpoint at Wyndcliff (footpath on the final approach).

Beyond St Arvans, pass Chepstow Racecourse, then at the roundabout take the first exit, B4293, to enter the historic fortress town of Chepstow ⑤.

Turn left through the archway, then descend through the town and in the square keep left. Shortly cross the River Wye to re-enter England. Ascend, and in ½ mile turn left with the B4228, signed St Briavels. Continue through undulating countryside for 7 miles to St Briavels, then branch left on an unclassified road to enter the village ⑥.

At the end of the village turn left at the crossroads to rejoin the B4228, signed Coleford. Two miles farther turn left on to the B4231, signed Clearwell, then in ¾ mile pass Clearwell Castle on the left ⑦.

In Clearwell turn right at the Wyndham Arms on to an unclassified road and shortly pass the Clearwell Caves Ancient Iron Mines ⑧.

In ¼ mile turn left on to the B4228 and continue to the small former mining town of Coleford. At the roundabout take the second exit, signed Ross, then in ¼ mile turn right. In just over another ½ mile cross the main road for Christchurch. Here turn left on to the

---

This tour includes some of the best-known places in the area: busy Ross-on-Wye, historic Chepstow, the ancient mining centre of Clearwell and the spectacular viewpoint at Yat Rock.

Symonds Yat road, B4432. Almost 2 miles farther is the car park for Yat Rock ⑨.

Continue forward on an unclassified road, narrow in places, and descend steeply (1 in 5). Later cross the River Wye by Huntsham Bridge, then at the T-junction turn right on to the B4229 for the outskirts of Goodrich. Here bear right with the B4229. Alternatively branch left on an unclassified road to visit Goodrich Castle ⑩.

After about ½ mile the main drive crosses Kerne Bridge over the River Wye for the last time. At the next T-junction turn left with the Ross road, B4228. Proceed through Walford before returning to Ross-on-Wye.

POINTS OF INTEREST

① Ross-on-Wye is an ideal tourist centre for the Wye Valley and the Forest of Dean. The town is attractively situated above a bend of the Wye and from the Prospect, near the churchyard, there is a splendid view of the river and surrounding countryside. An 18th-century benefactor, Thomas Kyrle, is called the 'Man of Ross'.

② The Jubilee Maze is a superbly presented hedge maze laid out in 1977 in celebration of the Queen's Silver Jubilee.

③ There are scant remains of the 12th-century castle at Monmouth, but the unique 13th-century fortified Monnow Bridge is still in use today.

④ Standing serenely on the banks of the Wye, the 13th-century Cistercian Tintern Abbey is noted for its majestic arches, fine doorways and elegant windows.

⑤ Chepstow's grand Norman castle has a 13th-century chapel and looks down on Chepstow's steep, medieval streets. The 16th-century town gate still survives and there are extensive remains of the town walls. Also of interest are the fine Norman church and the local museum.

⑥ The middle of St Briavels is delightfully compact with a castle, a large Norman church and a pub. The surviving part of the castle is now a youth hostel. A unique ceremony takes place every Whit Sunday when bread and cheese are distributed to the villagers after the evening service.

⑦ Built around 1727, Clearwell Castle is the earliest example of neo-Gothic architecture in England. It is now a hotel.

⑧ This unique museum records the history of iron-mining in the Forest of Dean. Eight large caverns are open to the public. The caves were mined from Iron Age times to the 20th century.

---

⑨ The AA Viewpoint on Yat Rock offers fine Wye Valley scenery where attractive woodland forms a backdrop for this great bend in the river. This is a popular spot, with many facilities provided for the visitor. The area is also a good touring base.

⑩ The ruins of Goodrich Castle, with its massive Norman keep, rock-cut moat and shaded lawns, stands on a high bluff overlooking the Wye affording breathtaking views over the river. Goodrich was slighted in the Civil War.

Chepstow Castle was one of the first Norman strongholds to be built from the outset of stone rather than earth and wood

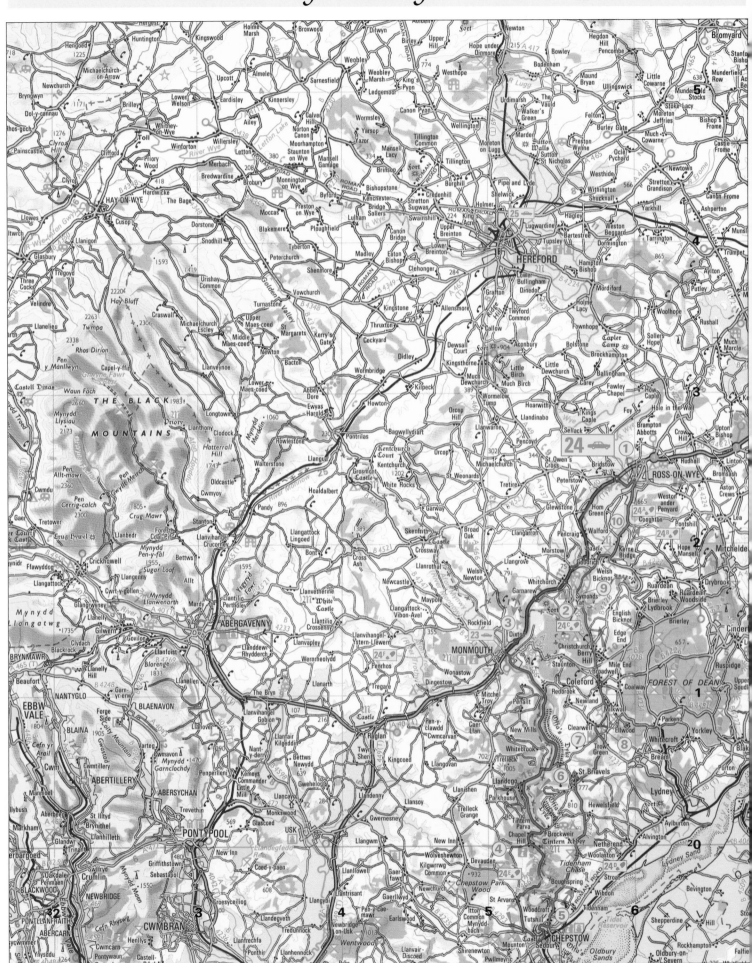

WALK 24A · Around Ross

ROUTE DIRECTIONS

Allow 3½ hours
Start from the public car park at Mill Pond Street in Ross-on-Wye (grid ref. SO601244) ①.

Turn left out of the car park and left again on to the footpath. Continue alongside a dismantled railway track and the narrow Small Brook. Cross the footbridge and turn left along a lane passing a short stretch of industrial Ross. Keep straight ahead where the right of way crosses a stile through low-lying fields until reaching steps up and over a new relief road. (This new road is not shown on the map.)

Proceed immediately over a step stile and alongside the Rudhall Brook, lined with alders and willows, and watch mallards enjoy this quiet backwater. Cross the solid bridge over the brook where the path keeps to the right of a drainage ditch, soon crossed by a bridge on the left. Walk diagonally right across the field to join a farm track leading to the road at Rudhall ②.

From Rudhall turn right along the road, which continues for 1½ miles, following road signs to Weston-under-Penyard ③.

Beside the inn at Weston-under-Penyard cross the main Ross-to-Gloucester road and follow the lane ahead towards St Lawrence's Church. The lane becomes an unmade track winding its way up Penyard Hill between thick conifer plantations before reaching Lawns Farm. Continue past the farm, through a meadow to a stile in the right-hand hedge. Before crossing, glance back to admire the superb views and catch a glimpse of Penyard Castle ④.

Follow the narrow footpath skirting the woods of Penyard Park. At a forest track turn right till a stile is reached on the left. Cross a field to a solitary oak where the route of the Wye Valley Walk is met. Follow the yellow arrows right through more woods and down across a sloping meadow to a kissing gate. Go on to the outskirts of Ross and Alton Court. The lane leads to Alton Road. Turn right to a turning on the left called Waterside which leads to Gloucester Road. Cross and continue ahead along Smallbrook Road to a mini roundabout. From here retrace the route back to the car park.

From the historic market town of Ross-on-Wye the walk follows the banks of the Rudhall Brook to Rudhall, from where country lanes lead through Kingstone and on to Weston-under-Penyard. From here a steep climb up the wooded slopes of Penyard Hill offers splendid views of Ross and the surrounding hills.

Ross-on-Wye's sandstone in the evening light

POINTS OF INTEREST

① Rising in a series of terraces from its mound of sandstone above a loop of the Wye, Ross-on-Wye has become a tourist centre for the Wye Valley. Many Georgian and earlier houses line the steep streets and the gabled Market Hall dominates the market place.

② In a hollow, partly hidden by trees and a high stone wall, lies Rudhall House – a 14th-century building with later additions; altogether a pleasing mixture of architectural styles.

③ The road to Weston-under-Penyard leads past some interesting buildings, including the mock 18th-century castle at Bollitree which is said to include medieval material from Penyard Castle and a Bristol church.

④ The scanty remains of Penyard Castle are visible from this point of the walk. It is thought that the castle was built in the 14th century as a medieval hunting lodge, but by the 1600s it was in ruins and a house was built on the site.

This short, hilly ramble explores the delightful countryside south of Ross-on-Wye. From the elevated hamlet at Howle Hill quiet lanes, footpaths and bridleways lead across wooded hills, offering sweeping views as well as sites to interest the local historian and please the photographer or artist.

POINTS OF INTEREST

① Built as a chapel of ease over 100 years ago, the small, stone-built Church of St John was paid for by a lady living in this parish of Walford. The Crown Inn dates back to 1857 when it was called Kiln Cottage, suggesting its connection with either lime-burning or brick-making. Remains of both these local industries can be clearly identified on this hill, where a network of deep sunken lanes scores the landscape, connecting lime kilns, pits and quarries in a series of scars.

② Known as 'Dib Dean' in the 18th century, Deep Dean was the spot where the turnpike road from Ross-on-Wye terminated. The original route across Chase and Penyard Hills became so difficult for wheeled traffic that it was abandoned in 1791 and replaced by an easier route through the Coughton Valley. A better road system was necessary owing to increased industrialisation.

③ As this attractive lane levels off there are far-reaching, glorious views of Deep Dean and the surrounding hills in all directions.

④ The Iron Age camp at Great Howle stands in a commanding position at over 600ft, although its ramparts enclose a relatively small area for a fort of this kind.

Great Howle: during the Early Iron Age many hilltops were fortified by encircling them with ramparts and ditches – possibly to protect land and livestock from invaders

ROUTE DIRECTIONS

Allow 2 hours
Start from the telephone box at Howle Hill, where there is limited parking (grid ref. SO606204).

From the crossroads follow the tarmac lane to Howle church, passing several dwellings, including the Crown Inn, before reaching a small stone-built church ①.

Just past the entrance to a house called Wooleys, the lane bears right. Continue ahead here to the road at Deep Dean ②.

Turn right along the road where a few scattered cottages add to the charm of this pretty wooded valley. Shortly after passing Deep Dean Cottage, opposite a small reservoir, turn sharp right to follow a signed bridleway leading steeply up a lane ③.

Before reaching the next building be careful not to miss a stile on the left. Here the footpath leads straight across fields and over stiles to the right of a wooded earthwork at Great Howle ④.

From here follow the right of way which continues ahead alongside the right-hand hedge. The road is met at a gate opposite Great Howle Farm. Here turn right to the crossroads at Howle Hill.

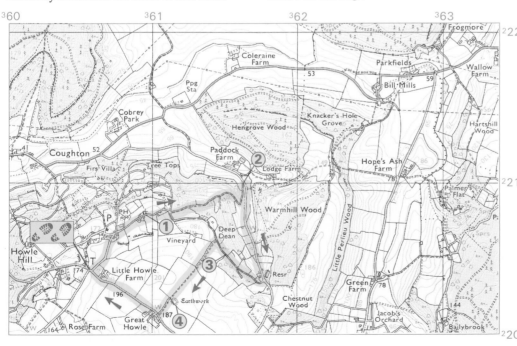

WALK 24C · To Symonds Yat GLOUCESTERSHIRE

Peaceful woodland, riverside paths and the Wye's most famous viewpoint, Symonds Yat Rock, combine to make this an energetic but worthwhile and very enjoyable walk. The route is easily followed on waymarked forest trails and a section of the Wye Valley Walk, but there are a number of steep climbs and descents.

POINTS OF INTEREST

① Highmeadow Woods, owned by the Forestry Commission, covers 3,500 acres between Symonds Yat, Monmouth and Coleford. At least 20 different types of tree can be identified, and this encourages a variety of wildlife. Fallow deer are common and can be seen at dawn or dusk.

② The path meets the Wye on one of several huge loops in this part of the river. The suspension bridge just downstream links a network of footpaths and forest trails on both sides of the Wye. On the opposite bank are the twin hills of Great Doward, known for its rare wild flowers, and Little Doward, topped by an Iron Age hillfort. Below them, the river is overlooked by the limestone outcrop of the Seven Sisters and by King Arthur's Cave, where bones of prehistoric animals such as mammoth and woolly rhinoceros have been found.

③ This is among the most beautiful stretches of the whole Wye, much loved by Victorian tourists in their pleasure boats, and equally popular at one time with coracle fishermen. The river is forced through a steep-sided gorge between wooded hills. Above the path are the steep cliffs called The Slaughter, and, further along, the river rushes through the impressive rapids of New Weir.

④ Soaring to 504ft above a great loop in the Wye, Yat Rock is a truly magnificent viewpoint. It is seldom a peaceful spot, however. Tourists have flocked here for well over a century, and their numbers have been swelled in recent years by birdwatchers who come to see the peregrine falcons that nest here. A toposcope, erected by The Automobile Association, helps interpret the view.

Take binoculars to make the most of Yat Rock's stunning views

ROUTE DIRECTIONS

Allow 3 hours
Start from the small picnic site at Ready Penny, near the village of Christchurch (grid ref. SO568132).

Follow the track on the right leading to a 'no through road'. Observe the first of the yellow arrows indicating a route through Highmeadow Woods. A narrow path shortly leads down to a wider track where the path follows a stone sign to Buckstone along an avenue of trees①.

Before reaching the road at Bracelands turn sharp right and follow a white-arrowed path which gradually descends between conifer and oak plantations. It becomes steeper and rockier before reaching a swift-flowing brook, the banks of which are now followed down to the River Wye at The Biblins②.

At the riverside turn right and follow the shorter yellow arrows of the Wye Valley Walk for about a mile, to the Royal Hotel at Symonds Yat③.

Leave the Wye Valley Walk and follow the longer yellow arrows of the forest trail, which bears right beside the left-hand wall of the hotel. A steep zigzag path climbs to Yat Rock. Wooden seats and steps ease the ascent.

At Symonds Yat picnic site bear left to walk across the road bridge to enjoy the view④.

Retrace the path back across the bridge to rejoin the waymarked path which leaves the car park to the right of its exit. A pleasant 1¾-mile walk can now be followed through mixed woods called Mailscot.

At a cottage called Mailscot Lodge the waymarked trail bears left then continues ahead, leading back to the stone sign at Ready Penny. Here turn left and walk back to Ready Penny.

ROUTE DIRECTIONS

Allow 2½ hours
Start from the Forestry
Commission car park at
Tidenham, a few miles north of
Chepstow on the Gloucestershire
side of the River Wye (grid ref.
ST559993).

From the car park a footpath sign to the Devil's Pulpit directs the way along a spongy waymarked path through thick conifer plantations known as The Park. On reaching a narrow lane turn right and after about 300yds turn left over an unusual stone and wood stile①.

From here a clearly marked footpath leads across pleasant level pastures to the steep wooded slopes of the Wye②.

Walk north for about 1½ miles along the waymarked Offa's Dyke Path③.

At a wooden barrier leave the Dyke Path by turning right over a stile beside a huge boulder. The right of way is followed along the left-hand side of the field to a gate.

Here, by a fence, turn sharp right up the slope to Beeches Farm where yellow arrows direct the way around the farmyard to join a lane ahead. This wide, grassy byway, known as Miss Grace's Lane, narrows and continues along a pleasant stretch before returning to the conifer plantations of The Park.

Follow the first wide track on the left which leads past the triangulation point where the way is easily retraced back to the car park④.

This is an invigorating ramble over mixed terrain. Peaty forest tracks and level pastures lead to a magnificent view of the Wye Valley and Tintern Abbey from the Devil's Pulpit. After a magical woodland stroll along a short stretch of Offa's Dyke Path, pleasant footpaths lead back across farmland and along old lanes.

POINTS OF INTEREST

① The woodlands on this part of the walk belong to Tidenham Chase, a large

Tintern Abbey is surprisingly intact and elegant

afforested area, in the parish of Tidenham, now managed by the Forestry Commission. Walkers using the trails here today are unlikely to encounter a danger that drove away a vicar of Tidenham in 1445 – wolves!

② A detour of about 100yds to the left leads to a rocky outcrop known as the Devil's Pulpit, from which there is a memorable view of the Wye Valley and Tintern Abbey below. Legend relates that from this eminence the Devil preached to the monks working in the abbey grounds, hoping to take their minds off their work. Immortalised in the title of one of Wordsworth's most famous poems, Tintern Abbey was founded in 1131. However, the great crumbling church that stands beside the Wye today dates from the early 14th century, a most evocative ruin.

③ Offa's Dyke was constructed in the 8th century by a King of Mercia to form the boundary between his kingdom and Wales. The great bank has all but disappeared in some places, but the stretch north of the Devil's Pulpit is still substantial. The path alongside it winds northwards, beneath yew, holly and beech trees – probably ancient woodland.

④ From a viewpoint opposite the Tidenham car park, visitors can admire the panorama to the south-east over the Severn estuary. Near by is Poor's Allotment, a nature reserve with a small pond. The unusual combination of sandy heath with limestone grassland has given rise to a fascinating flora here.

There are spectacular views of the lower Wye Valley from the steep limestone crags of the Wynd Cliff, which rises to over 700ft. From here the walk continues along the cliff top through attractive beech woods. Ancient cart tracks and quiet lanes lead back amid a serene landscape of gently undulating fields dotted with mature hardwoods.

POINTS OF INTEREST

① The Wye Valley Walk follows the footsteps of 18th- and 19th-century poets, writers and artists who toured this area during the Romantic period when it was fashionable to discover places of 'untamed beauty'. The 365 steps leading down the Wynd Cliff were constructed in 1828 as a tourist attraction and renovated in 1971 by the Beachley Army College Apprentices. The look out known as the Eagle's Nest is set 700ft above the River Wye where there is a famous and magnificent view of the Wye Valley. The stone seat commemorates a Wye Valley warden who was involved in the planning and construction of the Wye Valley Walk.

② Glorious scenic views across the Wye Valley can be glimpsed through the mixed woodland of holly, yew, beech, oak and ash trees. The sheer limestone cliffs of the valley provide ideal nesting sites for corvids and raptors, and jackdaws and kestrels commonly breed here.

③ The remains of wood and earthwork hillforts are a familiar feature of the landscape where Wales and England meet. They were mainly the work of the Celts who moved across into Wales prior to the Roman invasion.

④ This track, once described as a packhorse road, was widened to accommodate iron-shod traffic carrying lime and iron ore down to the barges at the riverside and to the iron furnaces at nearby Tintern. Consisting of one long main street, the village was an important industrial centre in the 17th century, with wire works, furnaces and forges which gradually ceased production during the latter part of the 19th century. Today Tintern is best known for its ruined but still superb Cistercian abbey.

An impressive view of the River Wye from the Eagle's Nest look out on Wynd Cliff

ROUTE DIRECTIONS
Allow 2½ hours
Start from the Upper Wynd Cliff car park, which is on a minor road three miles north of Chepstow (grid ref. ST524973).

Follow the yellow arrows of the Wye Valley Walk, winding along the top of the Wynd Cliff towards the fascinating 365 steps and the Eagle's Nest viewpoint①.

Continue along the waymarked path through a variety of woodland. **Young children should be carefully supervised along this stretch, where the cliffs fall dramatically and steeply to the river**②.

After Blackcliff Wood the uneven path rises over an enchanting outcrop of mossy boulders, the site of an ancient settlement③.

After a steep and rocky descent the Wye Valley Walk turns right then left before leaving these attractive cliff-top woods.

Yellow arrows direct the way over a solid stile and across a sloping field to another stile leading into the dark Limekiln Woods, where a steep and narrow path joins an old cobbled track. Leave the Wye Valley Walk by turning left up this old forgotten by-way④.

Rough and uneven, the track rises and continues between hedges which enclose undulating fields offering a more comforting landscape. On meeting a tarmac lane turn left where a steeper climb passes one or two isolated cottages. At a T-junction keep to the left, and left again at Wyndcliffe Court where the lane returns to the car park.

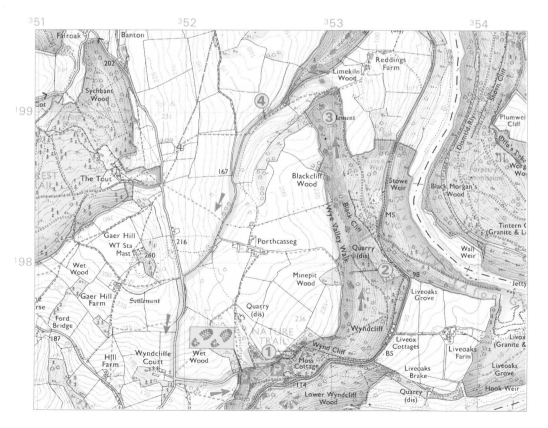

ROUTE DIRECTIONS

Allow 1½ hours
Start near Abbey Bridge, about 5 miles west of Monmouth, where there is limited verge-side parking beside an Offa's Dyke Path finger-post (grid ref. SO447134).

Opposite Abbey Cottage the waymarked Dyke Path leads across fields to the left of a corrugated barn and proceeds through a meadow to a footbridge over a small tributary of the Trothy. Here turn right over a stile, then bear left to walk alongside the River Trothy①.

The path continues through riverside meadows which provide ideal sheltered pastures for sheep. After passing the whitewashed farm called Sunnybank, the waymarked route follows the track to a tarmac lane, which proceeds straight ahead.

Soon another Offa's Dyke Path finger-post directs the way right around the isolated church at Llanvihangel-Ystern-Llewern. Here leave the path by bearing left through the churchyard②.

Leave the graveyard by the other gate, and turn right to follow a quiet lane steeply climbing a hairpin bend③.

A pleasant oak- and beech-covered ridge leads to a crossways. Turn left here towards Hendre, following a switchback lane for ¾ mile. At a T-junction keep left where a downhill slope leads back to Abbey Bridge④.

Ynyr, King of Gwent, is reputed to have founded the church at Llanvihangel-Ystern-Llewern

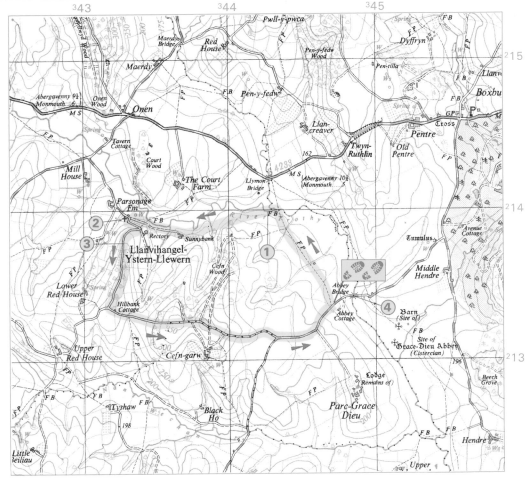

This attractive short walk follows Offa's Dyke Path along the banks of the River Trothy to the pretty, remote parish church at Llanvihangel-Ystern-Llewern. The return route is via hilly lanes amid the rolling country of the Welsh Borders.

POINTS OF INTEREST

①The Trothy drains the lovely countryside between Monmouth and Abergavenny and enters the Wye a mile below the bridge at Monmouth. The banks of this stretch of the river are lined with alders – among the most handsome of Britain's native tree species, especially in spring when the long, golden male catkins contrast strikingly with the rich purplish-brown of the small female cones.

②The medieval stone-built church of Llanvihangel-Ystern-Llewern, with its tiny turret and timbered porch, stands on rising ground amid rows of lichen-covered tombstones.

③As the road climbs a spur between two north-facing valleys, views open up over undulating Welsh countryside dotted with isolated farmsteads and surrounded by tree-topped hills.

④Abbey Bridge itself is some 200yds east of the walk's starting point. The neat stone structure is believed to be about 200 years old, as are several other bridges spanning the Trothy. This bridge takes its name from Grace Dieu Abbey, a 12th-century Cistercian foundation which lay a few hundred yards to the south-east. Today nothing remains of either the Abbey or its barn, though the sites of both are marked on some Ordnance Survey maps.

ROUTE DIRECTIONS
The drive starts from Hereford ①.

From Hereford follow signs to Brecon to leave by the A438. During the first 10 miles there are occasional views of the Wye before reaching Letton. In 1¾ miles turn left into Willersley, then continue through Winforton and Whitney-on-Wye. In ½ mile turn left on to the B4350, signed Hay, and cross Toll Bridge, to reach Clifford where there are the remains of an 11th-century castle. In 2 miles enter Wales and Hay-on-Wye ②.

On reaching the Blue Boar Inn, turn left on to the Peterchurch road, B4348. Re-enter England, then in 2½ miles turn right, signed Ross. The drive then enters the attractive Golden Valley to Dorstone and bears left at the church. In just over ¼ mile turn right and continue to Peterchurch ③.

Two miles farther turn right on to the B4347, signed Pontrilas, to reach Abbey Dore ④.

Continue to Ewyas Harold ⑤.

Bear left over the river bridge. In ¾ mile cross the main road and then the River Dore, then turn right signed Monmouth. In 1½ miles bear right, cross the River Monnow into Wales and ascend to Grosmont ⑥.

Continue through pleasant hilly countryside and in 4¼ miles, at a T-junction, turn left on to the B4521, signed Ross, to reach Skenfrith. Cross the River Monnow then ascend, and in 1¾ miles, at the crossroads, turn right on to an unclassified road signed Welsh Newton. After 1½ miles, to the left, lies Pembridge Castle ⑦.

On reaching the main road turn right on to the A466 into Welsh Newton. Here turn left on to an unclassified road signed Llangarren to reach the village of Llangarren. At the church bear right, signed Ross, and in 1½ miles cross the main road for Glewstone. In 1 mile turn left, joining the A40 to reach the Wilton roundabout, where the drive takes the third exit, B4260, to enter Ross ⑧.

Leave by following signs to Gloucester (A40). In just over ½ mile, at the roundabout, turn left on to the A40, signed Monmouth. Almost a mile farther, at another roundabout, turn right, A449, signed Worcester. At the next roundabout take the first exit, then in 1¾ miles branch left to join the B4224 signed Hereford. A quarter of a mile farther turn left, following a pleasant road with distant views to the left, to reach Fownhope ⑨.

The Wye is touched again before Mordiford where it is joined by the River Lugg ⑩.

This drive goes west from Hereford through the Wye Valley to Hay-on-Wye, then south-east through the Golden Valley to Skenfrith. After Ross-on-Wye, it passes pretty villages before returning to Hereford.

Hereford Cathedral and The Wye. Nell Gwynne, David Garrick and Edward Elgar are among the famous names linked with the town

At the Moon Inn bear left and cross the Lugg to Hampton Bishop. Continue back to Hereford.

POINTS OF INTEREST

① Hereford is full of rural charm and beautiful buildings. The Church of All Saints has a memorable twisted spire and among the Cathedral's many treasures are the Norman font, the Mappa Mundi and the largest chained library in the world. There are a number of museums, including a fascinating Cider Museum.

② A busy market town set beneath the Black Mountains, Hay-on-Wye is best known today as a centre for second-hand books, and even over a hundred years ago Francis Kilvert walked here from Clyro to attend the annual Book Club sale at the Rose and Crown.

③ Peterchurch is the main village in the valley, and has a large, well-preserved Norman church and a 14th-century hall-house, Wellbrook Manor.

④ One of the finest Cistercian abbeys, Abbey Dore was founded in the 12th century. The church, renovated in the 17th century, is one of the most outstanding in England with its Early English architecture and magnificent wooden roof of Herefordshire oak.

⑤ The remains of Ewyas Harold Castle, built in the 11th century and one of the most important castles along the Welsh border, can be seen to the west of the much restored Early English church.

⑥ Picturesquely situated high above the River Monnow, Grosmont village contains the ruins of the Norman castle, one of the trilateral castles originally built to guard against Welsh raids from the west.

⑦ Still a family home, Pembridge Castle is a good example of a small castle farmhouse dating from the 13th century.

⑧ The best-known view of Ross is of the town rising in a series of terraces from its mound of sandstone above a loop in the Wye. The spire of St Mary's is one of the most famous in England.

⑨ Fownhope was once a centre for commercial trade and for the pleasure boats of the Wye Tours. The village stocks and whipping post are preserved in the churchyard wall of the Norman church, and inside is a 12th-century tympanum which is widely held to be one of the most splendid in England.

⑩ A pretty village with a 14th- and 16th-century bridge, Mordiford's village church had, until 1811, a large green dragon painted on its west end which was said to represent a dragon that once inhabited the woods near the village.

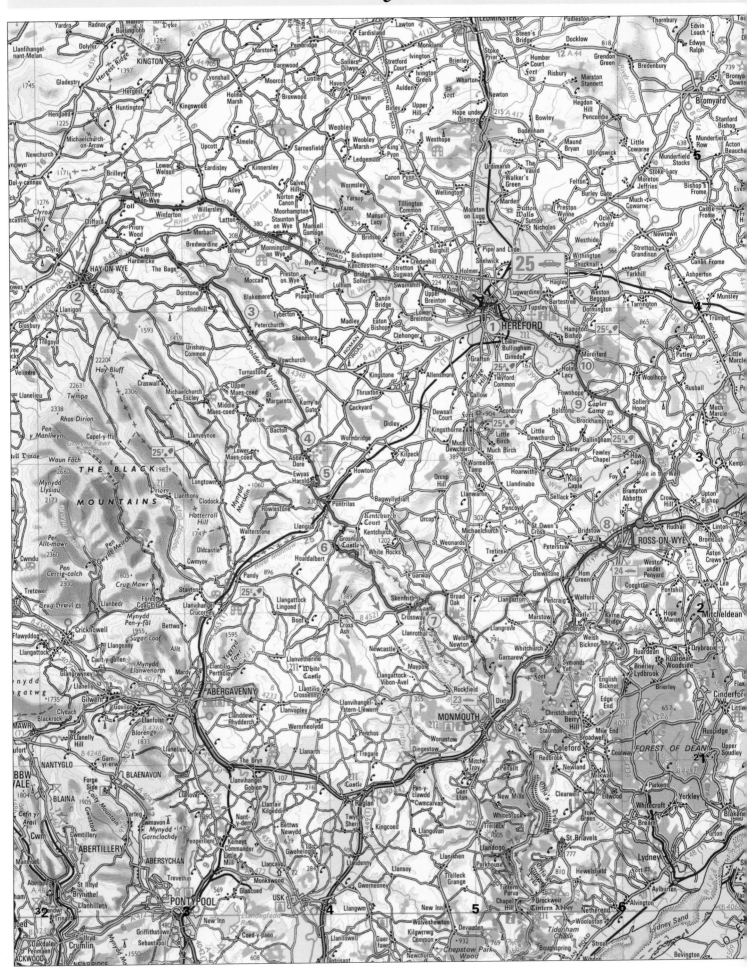

WALK 25A · *Dinedor Hill* HEREFORD & WORCESTER

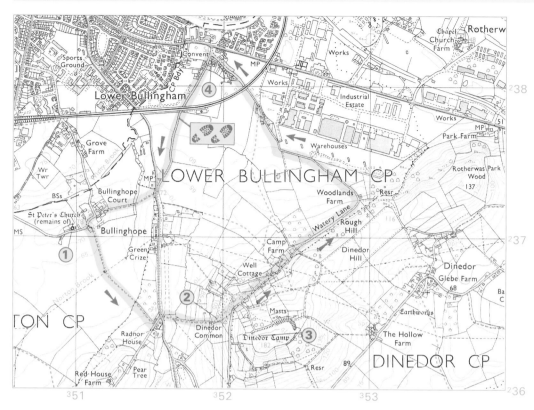

Church ruins in a Bullinghope garden

From the outskirts of Hereford city this attractive walk follows lanes and field paths to the Victorian church at Bullinghope. The highest point is the wooded hillfort of Dinedor, approached by a sharp climb. The return is by a gentle downhill path which joins a tarmac road leading back to the car.

POINTS OF INTEREST

①The ancient parish of Bullinghope is a pretty place. St Peter's, designed by F R Kempson, was built in the Early English style in 1880 at a cost of £2,000, replacing a ruined Norman church. The remains of this earlier building can be seen in a nearby garden belonging to The Cedars.

②As the path climbs more steeply up the western side of Dinedor Hill, views open up northwards over Hereford and the River Wye. To the west are the Black Mountains, straddling the Welsh border and rising to 2,660ft.

③Formerly known as Oyster Hill, Dinedor rises to nearly 600ft, making it a good vantage point for this part of the Wye. Fine mature beech trees on the summit cover the ramparts of an Iron Age hillfort, believed to have been occupied between 300BC and AD100. An area of 12 acres is enclosed by a bank and ditch which are most clearly visible on the north-eastern side. Views from the top take in the Black Mountains, Aconbury Hill to the south (also topped by an Iron Age fort) and the

Malverns. Nearer at hand the city of Hereford spreads out below.

④Two crosses shown on the map near the junction with Lower Bullingham Lane mark the chapels of two convents, both built of brick in Victorian Gothic style.

Hereford and its cathedral from Dinedor Hill

ROUTE DIRECTIONS

Allow 2½ hours
Start from the lay-by on the south side of the railway bridge spanning Lower Bullingham Lane (grid ref. SO517378).

Walk south along the narrow lane which shortly joins the Hoarwithy road at Green Crize. Cross this road and follow the signed footpath ahead which crosses fields and Norton Brook before reaching the farmyard at Bullinghope Court.

Continue through the farmyard on to a lane at Bullinghope which is followed to the left①.

About 100yds east of the church, turn left over a solid stile to the left of a black and white cottage. A well-used and clearly defined footpath leads through fields, and re-crosses the Norton Brook to join a tarmac lane beside some houses. Turn left along the lane to a road which is then crossed.

A signed right of way is followed over a stile, through a small paddock and across the Red Brook. In the next field the path steeply ascends the slopes of Dinedor Hill. From the next stile the walk offers scenic views②.

Cross an unmade track where a worn but unsigned narrow right of way bears slightly left uphill through woodland. At a tarmac lane turn left, then right within 50yds to reach the summit of the hill③.

Retrace the way back from the hill camp and continue along the lane which soon becomes an unmade track passing several isolated cottages. After the sign 'Unsuitable for Motorists' it descends through woods.

At a modern house follow a tarmac lane to the left leaving the slopes of Dinedor Hill. After ½ mile or so the walk comes to the railway bridge, then Lower Bullingham Lane④.

Turn left back to the lay-by.

Utter calm within a few miles of Hereford: the peaceful parish of Little Birch. St Mary's is a Victorian church on an old site

Six miles south of Hereford lies the scattered parish of Little Birch, where a maze of lanes and paths lead from the slopes of Aconbury Hill to the thick plantations of Athelstan's Wood. This pleasant ramble from the quiet village of

ROUTE DIRECTIONS

Allow 3 hours
Start from the post office at King's Thorn (grid ref. SO498319).

North of the post office and general stores turn right along Aconbury Close where a signed footpath leads down steps to join a rough track to the right. This leads on to a tarmac lane and a right turn is made at a T-junction. The lane is followed for a further 500yds from Wriggle Brook Cottage.

Beyond the next stone-built cottage turn left, go through a gate and follow the signed path across a meadow to a wooden bridge over the Wriggle Brook. Continue ahead where the right of way climbs steeply to the top of the field.

Turn right through the gate and continue ahead to another gate leading on to an enclosed track. This turns left at the crossways to meet a tarmac lane, which is followed to the right past Little Birch church①.

After passing the church and the Old Rectory, the lane becomes a rough track which proceeds between woods and open farmland for about a mile. Beyond the woods turn left at a T-junction on to a partly metalled lane which winds past Rowlston's Barn before descending to another brook.

Do not cross the bridge, but bear left, passing an isolated cottage called the Crickets, and follow the path along the left bank of the stream through Athelstan's Wood②.

Within a mile, at the outskirts of the woods, the route turns sharp left climbing gently to a larch plantation. Turn right along a narrower path and out of the woods. Cross an iron hurdle and follow a green lane which passes Green Farm before continuing through Little Birch to join the road at the Methodist Chapel③.

Cross the road and alongside the chapel follow a well-defined path on the left below Aconbury Hill④.

Take the next track left past Warren Farm and descend to the road. Turn left along the road and return to the post office.

King's Thorn, now bypassed by the main road, includes varied, undulating countryside and shady streams.

POINTS OF INTEREST

① Dedicated to St Mary, the church at Little Birch was rebuilt in 1869 at a cost of £3,500, paid by a long-serving rector of the parish. Built in the Geometric style, with a bellcote and polygonal apse, it contains a tall, wrought-iron screen of about 1870.

② A mixture of conifer plantations and native deciduous trees, Athelstan's Wood is managed by a private forestry group, but is accessible by public footpaths.

③ Founded in 1834, the Primitive Methodist Chapel of Little Birch was rebuilt in 1858 but still has the arched windows typical of the earlier 19th century.

④ The wooded slopes of Aconbury Hill rise to 904ft, making it a fine strategic site, especially in ancient times when most of lowland Herefordshire was densely forested. The single bank and ditch of an Iron Age hillfort enclose an area of 17½ acres on the summit, and pottery found on the site suggests that it was also occupied in Roman times. Archaeological finds from Aconbury are on display in Hereford Museum.

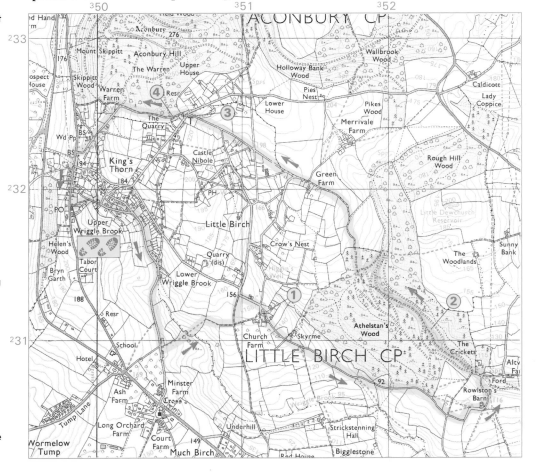

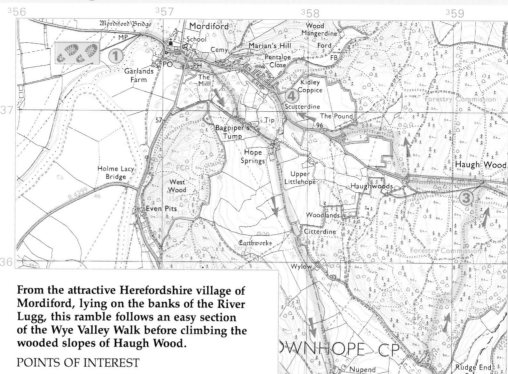

ROUTE DIRECTIONS

Allow 3 hours
Start from the western end of Mordiford Bridge, where parking is available (grid ref. SO569375).

Follow the yellow arrows of the Wye Valley Walk across the ancient bridge leading to Mordiford①.

Turn immediately right along a track which bears left to cross the road, then leads through the yard of an old mill and continues through pleasant orchards to Bagpiper's Tump. From here a lane is followed before bearing right and passing the farm at Hope Springs. The Wye Valley Walk continues along a well-defined bridleway through fields to join the road near Nupend Farm. Turn left along the quiet road, leaving the route of the Wye Valley Walk. At Rudge End investigate the Tom Spring Memorial, indicated by a sign on the right②.

Return to the road and beyond Hill View Cottage turn left to follow a track steeply ascending to Haugh Wood. Take the left fork, then bear right to enter the woods by a barrier where the stony track climbs to a junction beside thick spruce plantations. Here turn right following a wide winding track which reaches a road opposite the Haugh Wood car park and picnic site③.

Cross the road to the picnic site, but turn immediately left along a narrow woodland path running parallel to the road. At a forest track turn left to join the road which is followed to the right. At the next entrance into Haugh Wood on the right follow a path leading diagonally left through the deep conifer forest. At the outskirts of the wood keep left where the path follows the banks of a brook to a gate leading on to the road④.

In the village turn right then left to return to the bridge via the churchyard.

From the attractive Herefordshire village of Mordiford, lying on the banks of the River Lugg, this ramble follows an easy section of the Wye Valley Walk before climbing the wooded slopes of Haugh Wood.

POINTS OF INTEREST

①Mordiford's powerful, well-proportioned stone bridge was built in the 14th century to carry the Hereford-to-Gloucester road over the swiftly flowing River Lugg.

②A memorial to colourful local character Tom Spring, landlord at a nearby Fownhope inn and celebrated bare-fist prize fighter (he became Champion of England in 1823), is at Rudge End. After his death in 1851 his fellow 'countrymen of the land of cider' erected this memorial at his place of birth.

③Managed by the Forestry Commission, the mixed woodland of Haugh Wood (pronounced 'Hoff', from a Saxon name) is host to a small herd of fallow deer. Squirrels, voles, mice and a wide variety of bird and plant life are also to be found. Fallow deer are thought to have been introduced into Britain by the Romans.

④There is delightful scenery as one drops into Mordiford with its inn, school and 13th-century church. An interesting stone font stands in the porch of the church alongside a 'Record of Occurrence' telling how a storm in 1811 drowned four people in the village and swept away a barn, cider mill and adjoining cottage. The slopes of Haugh Wood rise steeply behind Mordiford.

Fallow deer make their home in Haugh Wood

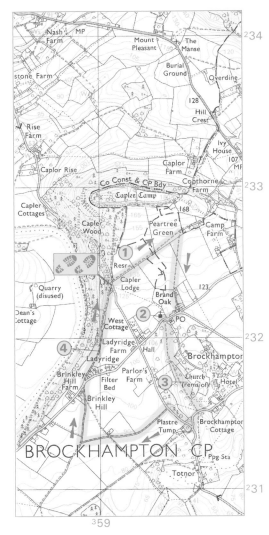

Capler Camp, a strategically placed hillfort on a ridge above the River Wye

This is a lovely walk through beautiful, unspoilt countryside between Ross-on-Wye and Hereford. Starting at a magnificent viewpoint high above the meandering Wye, the route climbs the slopes of Capler Hill before passing one of the prettiest churches in Herefordshire, at Brockhampton. After crossing a delightful

Brockhampton's enchanting little church

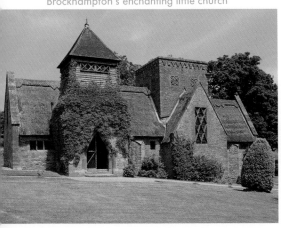

valley, the walk follows the familiar arrows of the Wye Valley Walk back along well-defined tracks above the river.

POINTS OF INTEREST

①Capler Camp, which can be seen on the left, is an Iron Age hillfort standing at just under 600ft. At this oval site of 10¼ acres enclosed by double ramparts, Roman coins and traces of medieval buildings were discovered during the 1920s. From its slopes there are panoramic views.

②All Saints is the delightful and unusual parish church of Brockhampton-by-Ross (as it is sometimes known, to avoid confusion with another Brockhampton, near Bromyard, to the north). Although the building has all the atmosphere of a medieval country church – even a thatched roof and a lych gate – it was built in 1902, and embodies many of the ideas of the Arts and Crafts Movement of that time. Local wild flowers, an appropriate motif, are everywhere inside the church: carved on the choir stalls and embroidered on the altar cloth and the hymn-book covers.

③The remains of Holy Trinity, Brockhampton's medieval church, can be seen in a clump of evergreens in the grounds of Brockhampton Court, a 19th-century Tudor-style house. Services are still held once a year in the roofless ruin.

④This stretch of the Wye Valley Walk is almost 200ft above a great sweeping curve of the river, so there are superb views whenever there is a gap in the trees. Below, peaceful pastures line the meandering Wye, while more distant views take in the Black Mountains to the west.

ROUTE DIRECTIONS

Allow 2 hours
Start from the small scenic parking site opposite Capler Lodge on a minor road at Brockhampton, a mile south of Fownhope (grid ref. SO591324).

Cross the road and follow an unsigned footpath starting from the field gate to the right of Capler Lodge①.

Keep straight ahead close to the right-hand hedge. Cross a dividing fence, then a makeshift stile, and turn almost immediately sharp right to cross a rickety stile beside a gate.
From here the right of way continues diagonally right over a stile in the hedge and across the next field to a hurdle beside a house and barn at Brand Oak. Follow the track to the road and turn right to visit the church at Brockhampton②.

Opposite All Saints follow another unsigned path through a wooden gate and straight across a delightful valley of sloping pastures③.

At a tarmac lane turn right, then right again at the junction. A short road section of the Wye Valley Walk has now been joined; follow it for 200yds before turning left along a pleasant track which eventually bears right through a field and along another track leading to houses at Brinkley Hill.
Cross the road and follow the well-defined track, passing the old school and several cottages④.

A short climb leads back to the parking site.

ROUTE DIRECTIONS

Allow 3 hours
Start from the northern end of Llanfihangel Crucorney, where you can park in the side road beside the letter box (grid ref. SO327207).

Cross the busy A465 and climb over the stile ahead, where the right of way goes diagonally left across the orchard towards a whitewashed cottage. Left of the cottage cross two footbridges before reaching a tarmac lane. Turn right here and ascend past Llanteens Cottage and farm buildings at Whitehouse.

After 600yds turn left to follow the clearly waymarked Offa's Dyke Path①.

Descend sloping pastures, with remarkable views of Skirrid Fawr and Hatterrall Hill②.

Continue following the Dyke Path across the A465, over the River Honddu and the railway track. Beyond Tre-fedw Farm bear right across a hilly field to rejoin a lane beside a stone barn. Here proceed right, past the entrance to Little Llwygy. At the next crossroads turn left.

Pass barns and buildings on the right, and within 200yds follow an unsigned footpath on the left through a gate. Keep to the right side of the fields, crossing old stone and timber stiles. On reaching a gate in the right corner turn sharp left, heading for the bridge at Pont-Rhys-Powell③.

Do not cross the stile on to the lane, but turn left along the banks of the Honddu to a stile and footbridge over a brook. Keep ahead across the next field to a coppice, where another footbridge followed by a stile leads back to the riverside.

Follow the banks of the river until you reach a footbridge. Here bear left to the cottage and join a woodland path. On reaching fields, the footpath keeps to the right hedge until it reaches a gate. Here bear slightly left across a field towards the farm at Llwygy. Turn right through the yard towards the house.

Before reaching the farmhouse turn right through a gate on the right. The undefined path descends through fields and over stiles to the railway track. Turn right over a stile then across the railway lines on the left. The path continues along the right-hand side of the next meadow to the road. Turn right, cross a stone bridge, then turn left, and left again to return to the car④.

From the Welsh borderland village of Llanfihangel Crucorney, this invigorating walk leads up to Offa's Dyke Path, from where there are commanding views of the Black Mountains. Narrow lanes and hilly paths then lead beside the pretty Honddu River, where there is a splendid variety of flowers in spring.

POINTS OF INTEREST

①For much of its length, Offa's Dyke Path follows the line of the 8th-century earthwork that was built to divide Celtic Cymru from Saxon Mercia. However, several alternative routes here in the Black Mountains area offer walkers a choice of scenery, meeting the Dyke again south of Monmouth.

②Rising to 1,595ft, The Skirrid or Ysgyryd Fawr is easily recognised by its unusual outline. The story that the ridge owes its shape to a massive landslide at the time of the Crucifixion has given The Skirrid the alternative name of Holy Mountain. A ruined medieval church stands on the summit.

③During the early months of the year, primroses, bluebells, stitchwort, violets, vetches and forget-me-nots line the wayside banks. Beside the water courses, eye-catching marsh marigolds glow above abundant beds of watercress.

④The tiny but busy village of Llanfihangel Crucorney advertises its long history in its pub sign: The Skirrid claims to be the oldest inn in Wales, dating back to the 12th

The Skirrid pub, named after the nearby mountain

century. Executions took place here during the visit of the notorious Judge Jeffreys, following Monmouth's rebellion in 1685.

A worthwhile short detour from Llanfihangel Crucorney is to the Tudor house called Llanfihangel Court, just southeast of the village. Sometimes open to the public, the house stands in fine gardens and has a superb staircase, oak panelling and Jacobean plaster ceilings.

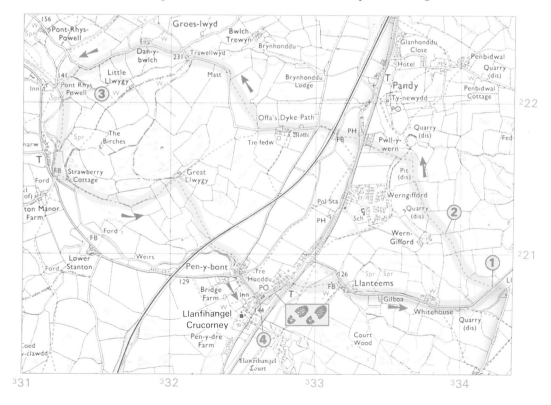

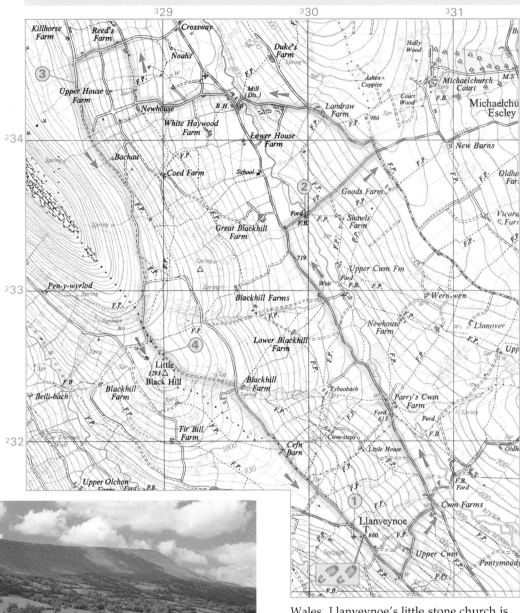

ROUTE DIRECTIONS

Allow 3½ hours
Start from the telephone box opposite the church at Llanveynoe (grid ref. SO304314); roadside parking is available ①.

Walk southwards and, at a recently restored cottage, turn left. This lane winds steeply down to join the Craswall road. Follow this to the left for about a mile alongside the little River Monnow. About 500yds after passing the sign to Blackhill Farm, leave the road and follow a green lane on the right leading to a footbridge crossing the River Monnow ②.

After crossing the footbridge, continue ahead to a T-junction. Here turn left towards Craswall. Cross the stone bridge and at the junction turn right. Within 100yds, beyond Rose Cottage, turn left following an unsigned but well-defined bridleway, which becomes rocky underfoot as it climbs uphill.

By a derelict barn at New House turn right through a gate, keeping left of stone farm buildings. The right of way continues ahead through open fields, crossing two tricky stone slab stiles, keeping right of the hill farm before meeting a metalled lane which is followed to the left.

A short climb leads to a T-junction where a well-used bridleway is followed to the left. After passing through a gate the open mountainside is reached, and the route continues for at least a mile along this scenic stretch of remote, bird-haunted hillsides ③.

From a small picnic site a rocky route follows the ridge to join Offa's Dyke Path at Hay Bluff. At the picnic site follow the tarmac lane, but before it bears right turn left to follow the right of way straight across unfenced rough pastures ④.

Cross the right-hand gate and walk diagonally right across a patch of waste land covered with fallen trees. Reaching an open field, follow the fence on the right to a gap where an irregular track leads downhill through rough wooded pastures. It crosses a brook to reach a gate leading on to a rocky path. Turn right and immediately go through another gate leading on to an unclassified road which descends to the church at Llanveynoe, and your starting point.

Hay Bluff: the view from the route

The valleys that drain the eastern slopes of the Black Mountains make up a little-known and totally unspoilt corner of England. This delightful but demanding walk, suitable for more experienced ramblers, begins at the tiny, hidden hamlet of Llanveynoe. From here quiet lanes and tracks lead to the slopes of Black Hill, offering stunning views.

POINTS OF INTEREST

① Looking across the remote Olchon Valley to the wild ridge that divides England from Wales, Llanveynoe's little stone church is memorable chiefly for its setting. The building itself is mostly 19th- and 20th-century, but inside is a carved panel which may date from Norman times.

② The Monnow is one of several parallel rivers fed by the streams of the eastern Black Mountains. Here little more than a brook, it is joined further downstream by all the others, and its lower reaches mark the English-Welsh border.

③ The track follows the side of Black Hill, which rises to over 2,000ft and is known locally as 'The Cat's Back'. It is the setting for Bruce Chatwin's novel *On the Black Hill*. On this stretch of the walk, listen for the 'mew' of buzzards and the unmistakable deep 'cronk' of ravens.

④ Just above is the 1,293ft summit of Little Black Hill, commanding good views over the tranquil Monnow Valley.

ROUTE DIRECTIONS
The drive starts from Brecon ①.

Leave by the B4601, signed Cardiff (A470), and in 1 mile, at the roundabout, take the second exit on to the A470. Proceed to Libanus and ¼ mile beyond the church turn right, unclassified, signed Mountain Centre. After 1½ miles turn right to visit the Brecon Beacons Mountain Centre②.

From the entrance return to the road junction and turn right (no sign), then follow a narrow by-road for ½ mile to a T-junction. Here turn left and continue along another narrow road, with views of the Brecon Beacons to the left. After 1¾ miles turn left on to the A4215 (still no sign). In just over ½ mile turn left again. The drive then gradually descends into the Tarell Valley, with more views ahead of the Beacons.

On reaching the A470 turn right, signed Merthyr Tydfil, and follow the long ascent (with Fan Fawr, 2,409ft high, ahead) to the summit at 1,440ft. There follows a descent along the Taf Valley, passing three reservoirs.

A turning on the right before the last reservoir leads to the Garwnant Forest Centre beside Llwyn-on Reservoir③.

Continue to Cefn-coed-y-cymmer, on the outskirts of Merthyr Tydfil. Here turn left on to an unclassified road, signed Talybont. Alternatively, keep forward with the A470 for a short diversion to visit Cyfarthfa Castle and Museum at Merthyr Tydfil④.

The main tour continues through a quarrying area, later keeping left before proceeding to Pontsticill. Remain on the Talybont road and beyond the village bear left. The turning on the right leads across the Pontsticill Reservoir⑤.

Continue down to the Brecon Mountain Railway Centre⑥.

The drive now heads northwards through the wooded Taf Fechan Valley to follow a narrower road alongside the shore of Pontsticill Reservoir.

After 1¾ miles turn left, then in another mile turn right and descend. Pass the Taf Fechan Picnic Site and ascend on to higher ground, then descend through attractive woodland to follow the valley of the Caerfanell River. Continue alongside the Talybont Reservoir and at the far end pass the dam.

In 1¼ miles bear right and almost ½ mile further cross the Monmouthshire and Brecon Canal by a lift-bridge, then turn right on to the B4558 (not shown) to enter Talybont-on-Usk. At the far end keep forward with the Crickhowell road along the Usk Valley. After 3 miles bear right and cross the canal bridge into Llangynidr. In 1 mile turn right on to the B4560, signed Beaufort. The drive now ascends, with hairpin bends, to a summit at 1,460ft. From here there are magnificent views across the Usk Valley to the Black Mountains⑦.

Beyond the quarry turn left on to an unclassified road, signed Llangattock. A gradual descent is then made to re-enter the Usk Valley at Llangattock. Cross the hump-back bridge and turn left into the village. Later turn left again on to the A4077 (not shown) then, at the traffic signals, turn right and cross the River Usk. On the far side bear left, signed Brecon A40, for the edge of Crickhowell⑧.

Leave by the Brecon road, A40, to follow the north side of the Usk Valley. After 1½ miles the A479, to the right, may be taken to visit Tretower⑨.

The main tour continues with the A40 and eventually ascends to Bwlch, a good Usk Valley viewpoint. Beyond the village turn right on to the B4560, signed Llangorse. Later, to the left of this road, is Llangorse Lake. Pass through Llangorse village and near the end turn left, unclassified, signed Brecon. Shortly, to the left, is the turning which leads to the lakeside⑩.

In ¾ mile keep left and continue to Llanfihangel Tal-y-llyn. Keep left into the village and at the end bear right. In 2¼ miles, at the T-junction, turn left, pass under the bridge and turn right to join the A40. After another ¾ mile, at the roundabout, take the second exit on to the B4601 for the return to Brecon.

Several different features of the Welsh landscape are taken in during this drive – including sweeping mountain roads, the head of the South Wales valleys, and natural and man-made lakes.

POINTS OF INTEREST

①Brecon is the main centre for touring the Brecon Beacons National Park. Its history stretches back to the 12th century. The impressive Priory of St John the Evangelist was designated Brecon Cathedral in 1923.

②Opened in 1966, the Mountain Centre covers almost every aspect of the 519 square miles of the National Park; exhibits include geological specimens, a relief model of the Park and illustrations.

③Llwyn-on Reservoir, bordered by a mature conifer forest, offers 150 acres of high-quality brown and rainbow trout fishing.

④Cyfarthfa Castle was built in the 19th century as the home of the Crawshays who took over the Cyfarthfa Ironworks. They were started in 1766 and employed 1,500 men by the turn of the century.

⑤Pontsticill Reservoir is now part of the Taf Fechan Reservoir, completed in 1927, the last in a chain of four reservoirs built to supply water to the industrial valley around Merthyr Tydfil.

⑥The narrow-gauge Brecon Mountain Railway follows a 2-mile route from Pant into the foothills of the Brecon Beacons. The train is pulled by a vintage steam locomotive.

⑦The Black Mountains area is in the most easterly part of the Brecon Beacons National Park, with Hay-on-Wye at its northern tip and Abergavenny at the south. On the western side is Maen Llwyd which, at 1,880ft, is the highest standing stone in Wales.

⑧The small country town of Crickhowell contains some Georgian houses, a restored 14th-century church and some remains of a ruined 13th-century castle.

⑨Ruins of a 13th-century castle can be seen at Tretower as well as Tretower Court, a well-restored 14th-century fortified manor house. The castle's huge, single tower can be seen looming over the fields.

⑩Llangorse Lake is the second largest natural lake in Wales and its attractions include sailing, canoeing, rowing, water skiing and windsurfing. Legend has it that a once-thriving town lies beneath the lake; its tolling bell can be heard when the water is rough.

A mystery to puzzle over: the bridge at Crickhowell has 12 arches on one side, but 13 on the other

ROUTE DIRECTIONS

Allow 3½ hours
Start at the Mynydd Du Forestry Commission car park at Pont Cadwgan in the Grwyne Fawr Valley (grid ref. SO267252).

From the car park go straight across the road and follow a forest drive to ascend gently through the woods. On reaching a cleared area, and the junction of tracks, bear left①.

Continue past plantations of fir trees, through a gate and on past Ffordd-las-fawr farmhouse. The track leads on to the edge of the forest at Cwm Ffrwd. Go through a hunting gate, ford the stream and continue beside a stone wall with views of the prominent cairn of Garn Wen and the sharp ridge of Chwarel-y-Fan.

At a gate the track descends to join a road. Turn right here, descend into the Nant Mair Valley, and go over a stile on the left above the church of Partrishow②.

Leave the church through a gate at the eastern end of the churchyard and cross a field to join a track leading down past Ty'n-y-llwyn farmhouse③.

Immediately after the farmhouse turn left through a gate and cross a field. Then go over a stile and bear right down to another gate in the corner of a field. From there, go diagonally left to pass between two ruined buildings and down to a stile. Cross a road and, shortly, go over a bridge to pass the Tabernacle Baptist Chapel (1837). Follow the lane past Tŷ Mawr to Upper House and continue between the house and a barn to follow the track up to another gate. The track ascends beside a fence and passes through two gates. Follow a rutted path up to the crest of the ridge④.

Now bear left and follow a track heading towards a stone wall (on the right). Follow a path along the western slopes of the ridge, enjoying views into the valley. After reaching a track junction go left to traverse the hillside and descend into Cwm Nant Brân. Cross a stream and go through a hunting gate, then go on past Cadwgan farm. Keep left at the next junction and descend through the wood to reach the car park.

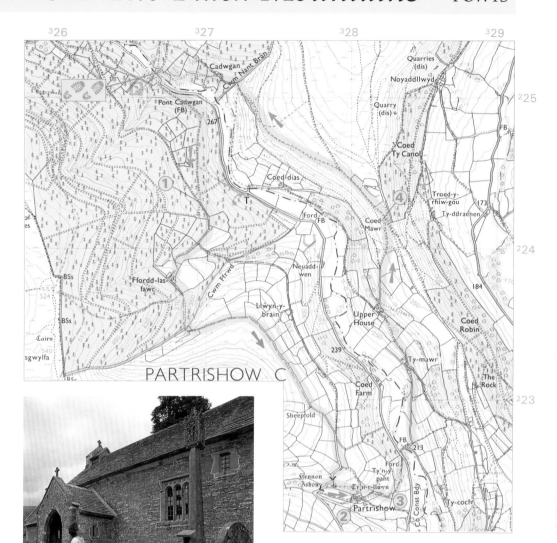

Secluded and intriguing, Partrishow church houses a wealth of historical curiosities

The Grwyne Fawr Valley passes through the heart of the Black Mountains and contains the forest of Mynydd Du. This walk takes in both sides of the valley and includes a visit to the secluded little church of Partrishow.

POINTS OF INTEREST

① From a clearing in the woods above Grwyne Fawr Valley an open view takes in the valley itself and the Iron Age fort of Gaer Hill.

② Partrishow's isolated little church is set 1,000ft above sea level. The church is thought to have been founded in the 11th century, and the enormous font's Latin inscription claims that 'Menhir made me in the name of Genillin' – the latter being Prince of Powys before the Norman Conquest. Dedicated to St Issui, Partrishow contains a beautiful 15th-century carved oak screen and two stone altars. On the west wall of the nave is a 'Doom Figure', discovered during restoration work in 1909. It shows a skeleton with scythe and hourglass which is reputed to have been painted in human blood. At the west end is an old double bell-cot with two bells, one dated 1708.

③ Ty'n-y-llwyn farmhouse, whose name means 'the house in the grove', is an attractive 15th-century building.

④ From the ridge of the hill above Upper House, a small stone pillar can be seen. Standing about 3ft high, this is the Dial Garreg (stone of revenge). It is said to mark the scene of an ambush in 1135 when the Norman marcher lord, Richard de Clare, and his party were massacred by a band of Welshmen.

ROUTE DIRECTIONS

Allow 2¼ hours
Start from the roadside, where there is parking, just beyond the cattle grid on the road that connects Llangattock village with the B4560 (grid ref. SO183168).

Walk up the road a few yards and turn left along a cart track. Go through two gates, then turn right through a gateway and follow a stone wall downhill. Turn left through yet another gateway and pass a ruined barn. Head across a field to a stile, then go across the next field to a gate. From here, cross two more fields and make for the floor of the valley where a track follows the stream. Pass through a gate and follow the track through the valley ①.

Cross a stile in a wall on the right, then cross a stream on stepping stones. Follow an ascending track to the left, ignoring the lower track by the stream. In due course, a 'platform' between two industrial inclines is reached ②.

Turn right and ascend the upper incline. Now follow the tramroad to the right ③.

Look out for a narrow path on the right which leaves the quarry track and diagonally descends the hillside below ④.

The path keeps parallel with the escarpment, passes through a wooded area and crosses a boulder-strewn slope, to lead across to the left-hand side of the mire called Waun Ddu (Black Bog). By the remains of a stone building, follow the track up to a fence. Continue beside the fence and bear left to return to the start.

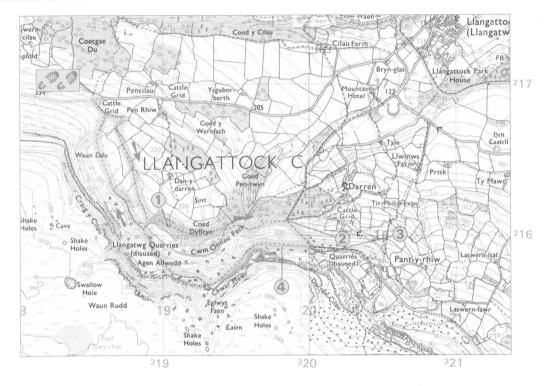

Craig y Cilau, with its amphitheatre of limestone cliffs, screes and trees, is an impressive sight, and Cwm Onneu below often echoes with the sound of the rushing waters of the Onnau Fach.

POINTS OF INTEREST

① In 1959 the 400ft-high limestone escarpment of Craig y Cilau and part of the valley below were declared a National Nature Reserve. It contains several caves, rich flora and a number of uncommon trees, including several species of whitebeam. These grow here, in the beechwoods of Cwm Clydach and in the Taf Fawr Valley – all nature reserves – and nowhere else in the world. The finest limestone vegetation – the richest in the Brecon Beacons National Park – is preserved on the Craig y Cilau precipices. It makes a marked contrast with the duller shades of peat vegetation such as matgrass and heather.

② Between two industrial inclines on the hills above Cwm Onneu, a brake wheel once controlled the descent of trams loaded with limestone down into the valley below. The tramroad then runs on to meet the canal at Llangattock wharf.

③ From the tramroad to Llangattock, an extensive view takes in, from right to left: Skirrid Fawr, Sugar Loaf, Gaer Hill, Hatterall Ridge, Table Mountain, Pen Cerrig Calch, Castell Dinas, Mynydd Troed, Mynydd Llangorse and Allt-yr-Esgair. The steepness of the terrain here protects the rich limestone vegetation even from cropping by Welsh sheep.

④ Mynydd Llangattock is a cavers' paradise, with several large systems still being developed and explored. These include Ogof Agen Allwedd and Ogof Darren Cilau, as well as Eglwys Faen – which translates as Stone Church – just behind a bay in the cliff. The presence of limestone in the hills produces the swallow- or sink-holes which are particularly common all over the Brecon Beacons National Park. These little pits are formed by rainwater or streams, and by the collapse of the Basal Grit into the limestone below.

Rich vegetation covers the limestone escarpment of Craig y Cilau, which was made a National Nature Reserve 30 years ago

ROUTE DIRECTIONS

Allow 3 hours
Start from Talybont-on-Usk
village (grid ref. SO115226).

Walk past the side of the White Hart Inn to cross a stone bridge over the canal. From here a lane leads on to join the Bryn Oer Tramroad, passing above the Afon Caerfanell. On crossing another bridge look down to see the track of the old Merthyr to Brecon Railway passing below①.

Continue to the right along the tramroad②.

The tramroad gently ascends the side of the valley and provides views into the eastern cwms of the Brecon Beacons and, below, of the Talybont Reservoir dam③.

Teal, the smallest of the duck family, are among the residents of Talybont Reservoir

Almost level with the dam, a track leads up on the left to a stile. Go over the stile and follow the path up through the trees to reach a field. Continue across the field to a gate, then turn right on to a road by a cattle grid. Cross the road to follow a track to a gate. Cross a sloping field towards a wood. Go through a gate and walk through the next field to join a rutted track. Pass through a gate and then carry on past a gate marked 'Private'. Keep beside the hedge to reach another gate. Cross a stream and go on to a gate at the corner of a wood directly ahead. Shortly afterwards, cross another stream and bear right to go over a stile. Then turn left to join a track leading down to the canal. Cross a girder bridge (which obscures an older stone construction) and a stile on the right, giving access to the canal towpath, which is then followed back to Talybont④.

Follow the towpath, to return to the starting point at Talybont-on-Usk.

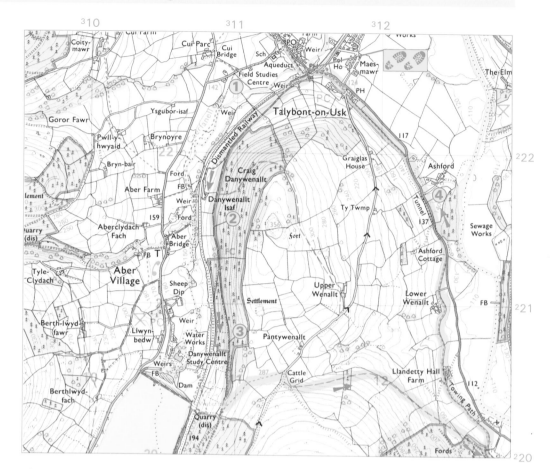

This route provides an opportunity to walk a short section of the Bryn Oer Tramroad, once an important industrial link between Tredegar and Talybont-on-Usk. There are views of the eastern end of the Brecon Beacons as the walk crosses the ridge above Talybont Reservoir and then returns along the towpath of the Monmouthshire and Brecon Canal.

POINTS OF INTEREST

①The Merthyr to Brecon Railway opened in 1865 and closed in 1963. From Talybont it climbed steeply for seven miles up to Torpantau, and passed through the highest railway tunnel in Britain.

②The Bryn Oer Tramroad, opened in 1815, carried coal and lime from Brynoer, near Tafarnaubach, to the canal at Talybont. Stones set in the ground along the tramroad once held the saddles, or supports, which kept the rails in place.

③Talybont Reservoir, fed by the Afon Caerfanell, was constructed in the 1930s to supply water to Newport. Its 318 acres provide excellent fishing: brown and rainbow trout swim here; and the reservoir is also a major haunt of winter wildfowl, with a small passage of waders.

④As the Monmouthshire and Brecon Canal towpath makes its way to Talybont, the 375yd-long Ashford Tunnel is passed. Horses pulling the canal narrowboats had to be led over the tunnel, as the boats were 'legged' through by men lying on their backs, or 'shafted' with poles pushed against the walls.

Talybont Reservoir in the Caerfanell Valley

A striking view of Pen y Fan from Corn Du, one of the main Brecon Beacons summits

ROUTE DIRECTIONS

Allow 3 hours
Start from the Pont ar Daf lay-by on the A470 (grid ref. SN988199).

From the lay-by, go up the track on the left to reach a gate. Ford the river (quite shallow) and head up the obvious track leading towards the table-like summit of Corn Du①.

On reaching the col of Bwlch Duwynt follow a track to the left around the side of Corn Du. Directly below in the Taf Fechan Valley are the Upper and Lower Neuadd Reservoirs. These are the highest of all the Beacons reservoirs. Stay on the main path at the next junction and head straight up to the col. **Keep well away from the north side for it is precipitous.** In the event of weather deterioration or poor visibility on reaching the summit of Pen y Fan, walkers with limited navigation experience are advised to retrace their outward route back to Pont ar Daf and to leave the section over Corn Du and Y Gyrn for another day②.

Return to the col and ascend the rocky crest of Corn Du③.

Descend with special care the ridge of Craig Cwm Llwch on the north-west end of Corn Du and head for a stone pillar which can be seen in the distance on the ridge above Llyn Cwm Llwch④.

Follow a path down into the head of the Taf Fawr Valley below, and continue over Y Gyrn and down to the Storey Arms⑤.

Follow the grass verge back to the start at Pont ar Daf lay-by.

An ascent of the two highest mountains in South Wales is easily made from the A470, which is one of the highest trunk roads in Britain. This is an area where the weather can change suddenly, and even in good weather walkers need suitable footwear, waterproofs, a map and a compass.

POINTS OF INTEREST

① The National Trust and National Park Service have worked hard to combat erosion on the track to the Corn Du summit. Drainage channels have been cut, and the surface improved with natural materials and stones, laid into the ground in jigsaw fashion. A plaque on the edge of the track notes the Eagle Star Insurance Company's gift of the Brecon Beacons to the National Trust in 1965.

② Pen y Fan is the highest Old Red Sandstone mountain in Britain, formed from the sand and mud of a great marine estuary which covered the Brecon Beacons area in Devonian times – about 300,000,000 years ago. During the Ice Age a huge ice cap covered the mountains and a glacier, making its way down to the coast, slowly scoured out the landscape, leaving distinctive U-shaped valleys.

③ On the summit of Corn Du is a recently excavated burial cairn. It was found to contain a stone cist, which archaeologists have dated to about 200BC.

④ The stone pillar on the ridge above Llyn Cwm Llwch is the Tommy Jones Obelisk. It was erected in memory of a five-year-old boy who died after losing his way between Cwmllwch farm and the Login in 1900. No one could ever explain how the little boy had managed to reach the spot where his body was found: 2,250ft above sea level – a climb of 1,300ft from the Login.

⑤ The Storey Arms, which is at the highest point of the A470, is an activity centre, taking its name from the old coaching inn which stood a few hundred yards away.

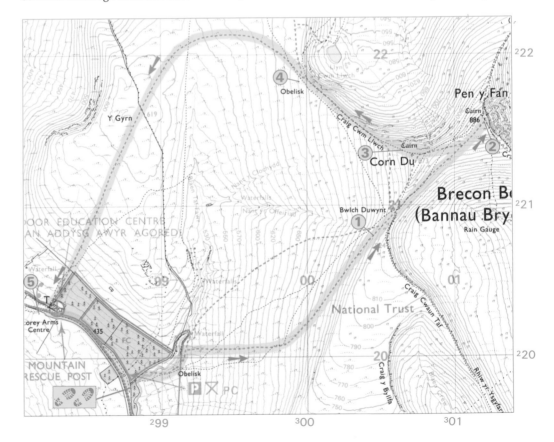

ROUTE DIRECTIONS

Allow 2¾ hours
Start from Porth yr Ogof car park (grid ref. SN928124).

Cross the road and follow a signposted footpath which follows the old river bed①.

From here the path joins the river bank. Follow this to a footbridge spanning the river. Don't cross it, but take the path to the left, following a waymarked route to reach a point above the Upper Clun-gwyn fall②.

Continue along the path, crossing a couple of streams, and then bear left at the next junction, keeping to the waymarked path which avoids the more dangerous places. Turn left up a side valley and at a fence follow it to the right③.

A junction is reached, where a diagonal path leads down the slope to river level. Turn to the right and go back up the river to reach the Middle Clun-gwyn fall. Then retrace your steps and continue along the river bank following a broad path to reach the third of the Mellte falls, called Sgwd y Pannwr④.

From here the track crosses an area of rocks. Keeping the river on the right, follow a path up over the rocks opposite the falls to reach a plateau where good views may be obtained across the Mellte Valley and south to the Vale of Neath.

Continue along the waymarked path and bear left to reach the high-level path once more. Turn right and soon the thunder of Sgwd yr Eira fall on the Afon Hepste will be heard⑤.

A stile is reached on the left. (Just beyond this point a path leads down steeply on the right to the waterfall. If you descend you must return to this point.)

Go over the stile and into the wood to follow a track winding dimly through the trees, providing a strange contrast to the previous scenery. Leave the plantation to enter a clearing and turn right up a short slope, then go left along a broad track⑥.

On reaching a gate across the track continue past a farm; go over a stile and on beside a fence in front of the farmhouse. A lane is then joined which is followed back to the start⑦.

One of the waterfalls carved in the limestone by the Afon Mellte

The Afon Mellte tumbles down from the upland expanse of Fforest Fawr – 'the great forest' – in a spectacular series of waterfalls which make this a walk to remember. A visit to another of the natural wonders of the Brecon Beacons – Porth yr Ogof Cave – can be added on to the end of the walk.

POINTS OF INTEREST

①At one point the path drops down into a hollow where the underground river can be glimpsed on either side. Shortly afterwards the river reappears.

②A short diversion from the path leads down to a viewing position above the single-leap upper waterfall of Clun-gwyn, one of a series of three falls on this part of the Mellte.

③This high-level path provides tantalising glimpses into the valley of the Mellte, the best known of the headstreams of the River Neath. Lovely limestone woodlands cover the gorges and ¾ mile north-east of Ystradfellte is the ruin of Castell Coch (Red Castle), built of red river boulders.

④Look out for dippers, which are sometimes seen on the stretch of the river around the falls. These enchanting little birds, dark brown with a large white bib, can walk underwater in search of food.

⑤On reaching a gap in the trees a good view may be obtained of Sgwd yr Eira, in the valley far below. Cattle, sheep and ponies were once driven across the ledge behind the fall's curtain of water.

⑥From the track here there are good views across the valley towards Fforest Fawr, originally a royal hunting forest.

⑦Porth yr Ogof Cave may be visited by

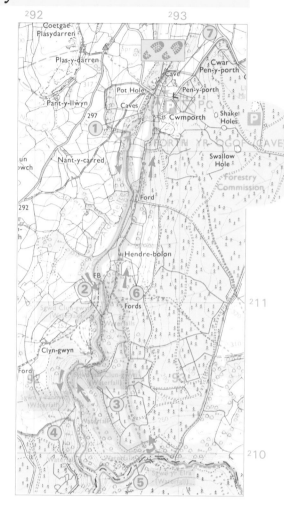

following a path down from the car park. It has the largest cave entrance in Wales and the initial chamber can be explored, but deep pools soon bar further progress. The side passages should only be entered by experienced and properly equipped cavers.

Sarn Helen, part of a rich Roman legacy

This walk explores the limestone country to the north of Ystradfellte, on the southern edge of Fforest Fawr. The outward route is along moorland tracks, passing a small Iron Age hillfort, while the return follows a section of the Roman road called Sarn Helen.

POINTS OF INTEREST

① Below a limestone cliff on the left near the top of the climb, look out for a well-preserved lime kiln. Used to burn limestone in order to produce building lime, such kilns are known to have been used in Roman times, and most medieval building contracts included the construction of one or more kilns. They were in common use as recently as the early 19th century.

② Also known as shake-holes or swallets, swallow-holes are a familiar feature of limestone scenery. They are found where surface water has gradually dissolved the limestone. Surface streams suddenly disappear through the resulting holes to run underground.

③ Iron Age hillforts were fortifications built on hills of middling height to act as refuges and cattlepounds for tribes, clans or family groups, who cultivated the land below or grazed their cattle around them. Some forts were permanently occupied by family groups living in circular houses constructed of wood or stone.

④ The ancient route known as Sarn Helen ran from Neath via Coelbren to the Roman fort of Y Gaer, near Brecon. 'Sarn' means causeway and, according to Welsh tradition, the road is named after a Welsh princess. Alternatively, Sarn Helen could be a corruption of Sarn y Lleon, meaning 'the way of the Legions'; and yet another theory suggests that the name derives from the Welsh *sarn heolen*, 'paved causeway'.

⑤ Just before the straight section of Sarn Helen changes direction slightly, a slender standing stone can be seen on the right. Marked on the map as Maen Madoc, this 9ft stone bears an inscription *Dervacus filius Justi ic jacit*; a Latin memorial to 'Dervacus, son of Justus. He lies here'.

ROUTE DIRECTIONS

Allow 2½ hours
Start from Blaen Llia car park off the Heol Senni to Ystradfellte road (grid ref. SN927166).

Walk up to the road and follow it to the left for about ½ mile. On reaching a sharp bend, go straight on to follow a stony track between two stone walls. It becomes a smooth grass path and ascends gently to the ridge above.
　Go through a gate and keep straight on, ignoring the path on the right ①.
　Pass between two limestone outcrops and continue to a gate set in a wall. The path then crosses the open moorland and forks left to another gate, set in the corner of a stone wall. Do not go through it, but make an elbow turn to the right and head across to a circular fence enclosing a deep swallow-hole ②.
　Continue across the moorland to cross a track and reach a stile in a stone wall on the western skyline. Climb past the edge of an Iron Age fort on the crest of the ridge ③.
　Carry on beside a stone wall to pass through a gap in another wall, directly ahead. Descend, keeping right, to an opening in a field boundary.
　Further on, cross two stiles and join a road. Turn right and follow the road to Blaen-nedd Isaf farm. Enter the farmyard and, at a footpath signpost, turn left and go through a metal gate to the left of a stable.
　Cross a footbridge, continue up, then turn right to follow the old Roman road known as Sarn Helen ④.
　Descend once more into the valley to cross a ford and then follow the Roman road up the hillside. After heavy rain this ford may be difficult to cross, in which case it may be necessary to return via the outward route ⑤.
　After passing the standing stone the Roman road runs through a Forestry Commission plantation and over the site of a Roman camp to join the Ystradfellte road. Turn right here and return to the car park at Blaen Llia.

ROUTE DIRECTIONS

The drive starts from Brecon ①.

Follow High Street Superior, B4520 (not shown), signed Brecon Cathedral. In ¼ mile turn left, signed Upper Chapel, and shortly pass Brecon Cathedral on the right ②.

Continue through pleasant hill scenery following the Honddu Valley, later passing through Pwllgloyw and Lower Chapel to reach Upper Chapel. In ½ mile turn left on to the B4519, signed Llangammarch Wells. This road may be closed occasionally, as it passes through an army firing range. An alternative route is to remain on the B4520 to Builth Wells and then to follow signs to Llandovery (A483) to Llanwrtyd Wells. The main drive crosses the upland moorland area of Mynydd Eppynt, and from the 1,500ft summit there are fine views to the north across the Irfon Valley.

At the foot of the descent turn left at the crossroads on to an unclassified road to reach Llangammarch Wells ③.

Bear right to cross the River Irfon, then pass beneath the railway and turn left, signed Llanwrtyd Wells. In ¾ mile turn left and continue along this by-road for a further 3½ miles before turning left again, on to the A483, to enter Llanwrtyd Wells ④.

This drive uses narrow and winding roads in places – with unprotected drops. Although these provide spectacular views they may be unsuitable for nervous drivers or passengers.

Here turn right, unclassified, signed Abergwesyn and follow the wooded Irfon Valley (narrow road in places). In 1¼ miles cross the river, then turn right. A number of picnic sites are passed before reaching the hamlet of Abergwesyn ⑤.

The drive turns left here, signed Tregaron, and continues up the valley along a narrow road, passing through open and dramatic scenery. The Irfon is crossed three more times before the ascent of the Devil's Staircase (1 in 4, with hairpin bends). After the 1,550ft summit there is a 1-in-4 descent before turning left, signed Llandovery. The drive now continues through the extensive Tywi (Towy) Forest and in 2 miles it starts to run high above the Llyn Brianne Reservoir. This well engineered road follows a winding forest route for some 4 miles, with occasional glimpses of Llyn Brianne ⑥.

Later, open moorland is crossed before making a long descent in order to pass a turning, on the right, to the 300ft-high Llyn Brianne Dam and viewing point ⑦.

The main drive continues descending into the attractive Tywi Valley. A mile beyond Llyn Brianne is Ystradffin ⑧.

Continue for 4 miles to reach Rhandirmwyn ⑨.

Later, approaching Llandovery, turn right and immediately left across the main road, signed Brecon, to enter the town centre, then turn left on to the A40 (not shown). Shortly join the deep, wooded valley of the Afon Gwydderig for a long, gradual ascent. After 2½ miles pass the 'Coachman's Cautionary' ⑩.

Beyond Trecastle the Upper Usk Valley is joined for Sennybridge ⑪.

Remain on the Brecon road (A40), and in 6 miles pass a picnic site beside the Usk (on the left). Shortly, skirt Llanspyddid and in 1¼ miles at the roundabout take the first exit, B4601, for the return to Brecon.

POINTS OF INTEREST

① Brecon is full of interesting reminders of its 700-year-old history and St Mary's Church makes a good starting point to explore. The Old County Hall now houses the Brecknock Museum and contains a wealth of local history.

② The impressive Priory of St John the Evangelist, built in the 13th and 14th centuries, became Brecon Cathedral in 1923 and reflects a good deal of the town's history.

③ Situated at the confluence of the Rivers Irfon and Cammarch, Llangammarch Wells has springs containing barium chloride, said to be especially effective in heart disease.

④ The sulphur well which brought fame to Llanwrtyd Wells, the smallest town in Britain, is still much in evidence by sight and smell alongside the River Irfon. The old village is further up the valley from the modern settlement.

⑤ Standing at the edge of one of the wildest parts of Mid Wales, Abergwesyn forms a gateway to the impressive mountain road to Tregaron.

⑥ The spectacular 520-acre Llyn Brianne Reservoir occupies a once remote part of the country rich in wildlife. Before the existence of the reservoir local inhabitants would travel on horseback to the adjacent Camddwr Valley, where the chapel of Soar y Mynydd is situated halfway between Rhandirmwyn and Tregaron.

⑦ Said to be the largest rock-filled dam in Europe, the 300ft-high Llyn Brianne Dam is capable of holding 13,400 million gallons of water.

⑧ Ystradffin is associated with the Welsh Robin Hood, Twm Siôn Catti, whose hide-out can be seen by following a nature trail alongside the Tywi.

⑨ Rhandirmwyn, a village set around the bend of the river and once an important lead-mining centre, is a good starting-point for exploring the valley. There are still surface workings and ruins to be seen nearby.

⑩ The 'Coachman's Cautionary' is an obelisk marking the point where a stagecoach plunged over the side of the road in 1835, the driver apparently being intoxicated.

⑪ Sennybridge was mainly developed in the 19th century, when it took hold of the sheep and cattle market once held in Defynnog, before the turnpike road was opened.

The making of Llyn Brianne Reservoir brought good roads to a very remote part of Wales

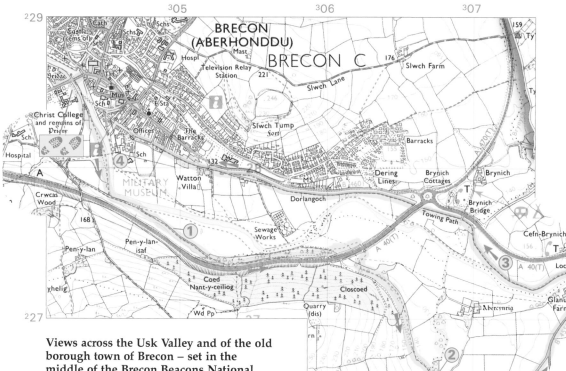

Views across the Usk Valley and of the old borough town of Brecon – set in the middle of the Brecon Beacons National Park at the confluence of the rivers Usk and Honddu – can be enjoyed on this walk. Brecon is the terminus of the Monmouthshire and Brecon Canal system.

POINTS OF INTEREST

①Below the beautiful wooded slopes of Coed Nant-y-ceiliog there are pleasant views across the valley floor to Brecon and its two Iron Age hillforts of Pen-y-crug and Slwch Tump. The former is a splendid fortress, defended by five ramparts and ditches. Constructed by the Celts in about 100BC, it is oval in shape and about ⅓acre in area.

②The remains of a stone bridge can be seen near the old Abercynrig Mill. This bridge came to grief some years ago when it was demolished by the Afon (River) Cynrig in flood.

③The Mon and Brec Canal, as it is locally known, was once two waterways – the Monmouthshire Canal and the Abergavenny Canal, both opened in the late 18th century, and joined in 1812. The Canal carried iron ore from the south and brought back limestone and coal. But by the late 19th century competition from railway companies was taking its toll, and by the beginning of World War II commercial traffic had ceased. Now over 30 miles of navigable water have been restored, from Brecon to Pontypool.

④The historic town of Brecon, known in Welsh as Aberhonddu ('the mouth of the Honddu') has a 13th-century cathedral which houses a great rood, the Crog (cross)

Aberhonddu, celebrated by 15th-century Welsh bards. The main castle ruins, in the grounds of the Castle Hotel, date from a reconstruction during the reign of Edward I. Opposite the hotel are the motte and part of the bailey of the original 11th-century castle, built by Bernard Newmarch, half-brother of William the Conqueror.

Against the backdrop of Pen y Fan, the market town of Brecon nestles in the Usk Valley

ROUTE DIRECTIONS
Allow 3 hours
Start from the car park on the west side of the river in Brecon (grid ref. SO043285).

From the car park, follow the lane to reach a metal kissing gate, just to the left of a lodge house. Continue beside the river to reach a stile, then go over a small footbridge spanning a stream. Follow a path up to a lane and turn left①.

Soon the lane rises beside the A40, and then descends. Go through a gate and across a field to make for an underpass beneath the A40. Then go over a ladder stile and turn sharp right, keeping a fence on the right. Continue over another ladder stile and follow a broad track. Where the path divides, keep along the lower route, just above the fence line, and cross a stile into a field. Continue over two more stiles to pass between two hedges and then cross an attractive wooden bridge②.

Traditionally carved love spoons can be seen in the Brecknock Museum, Brecon

Follow the lane to the left to reach a junction, and keep straight on. On reaching a road junction keep straight on to reach a T-junction and turn left. At the next junction continue along the B4558 to reach Lock Bridge. Having crossed the bridge, turn left just past Lock Cottage. Go through a gate and follow the canal towpath③.

Follow the towpath all the way to the end of the canal at Brecon basin. Complete the walk by continuing through Brecon④.

Go down to the river and cross the bridge, and turn left to reach the starting point.

ROUTE DIRECTIONS

Allow 2¾ hours
Start from the public car park near Carreg Cennen Castle (grid ref. SN666194).

From the car park, follow the lane towards the castle, passing through a farmyard and two kissing gates. Continue along a tarmac path for a short distance directly beneath the castle. At a bend descend to the left, following a broad track across a wooded slope leading down into the Cennen Valley. On reaching the floor of the valley, turn right to follow the Afon Cennen①.

Cross a stile on the left, go down some steps and then on beside the river to cross another stile; go through a gate, and then turn left over a stile to follow a farm lane leading to Hengrofft Farm. Walk through the farmyard and pass between the house and a barn to follow a cart track up the hillside. Where the track divides, keep right and, at a junction on a corner, carry straight on. From here there are excellent views of the castle②.

Go through a gate and across a field, keeping the fence on the right③.

Continue straight on to a gate, where the track becomes more defined, then go through another gate to follow a stone wall. Cross a limestone-scattered landscape to meet a mountain road. Turn right here and, after a short distance, go over a stile on the right. Bear left, passing two large mounds, and make for another stile near two swallow-holes (sometimes referred to as sink-holes or shake-holes).

Bear to the left to join a wall. The track now broadens and descends to pass above the source of the River Loughor④.

The broad track continues beside the river for a short way and then leaves it to pass through two gates. At the second gate turn right and follow the track down over a stream towards Cwm Cennen. On reaching Llwyn-bedw farm, turn left and descend through a field to reach a stile. Further on, cross a footbridge over the river. The path then ascends the bank on the other side via three stiles to join the road above. Turn left and follow the road uphill to a junction. Go right and return to the car park.

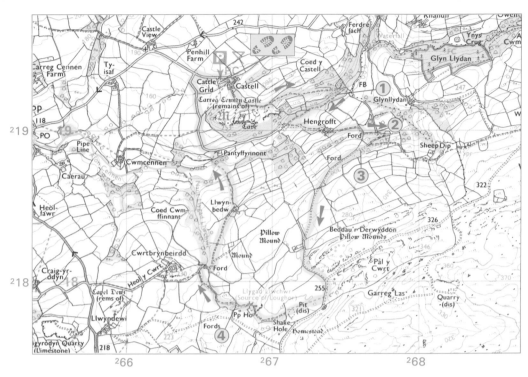

Impressive views of Carreg Cennen Castle, standing in solitary splendour on an outlier of Carboniferous limestone above the lovely Cennen Valley, are features of this walk near the western boundary of the Brecon Beacons National Park.

POINTS OF INTEREST

① According to legend, the Welsh hero Owain Lawgoch (Owain of the Red Hand) sleeps in a cavern on the banks of the Cennen with his band of 51 men, waiting to be summoned to his nation's aid.

② Carreg Cennen Castle, perched on the summit of a 300ft precipice, is perhaps the most romantic in Wales. It is said to be built on the site of another fortification, erected by Sir Urien, one of King Arthur's knights. The spectacular crag was certainly fortified long before the 13th century, when the present castle was built. The Edwardian layout consists of a single ward, curtain walls and towers; and the most remarkable feature of the ruins is a long, dark passage cut through the solid rock and lighted by loopholes.

③ On the Black Mountain, above the Cennen Valley, can be seen two groups of prehistoric sites: Tair Carn Isaf and Tair Carn Uchaf (Three Lower Cairns and Three Upper Cairns). These rough stones heaped into large piles could be burial sites or some form of memorial.

④ The River Loughor (Llwchwr) issues from a limestone cave known as Llygad Llwchwr (Eye of the Loughor), about ½mile to the south east of Carreg Cennen Castle.

Just above the cave – whose entrance should only be negotiated by experienced and equipped cavers – are the remains of an old limestone kiln.

By tradition the dramatic Carreg Cennen Castle is believed to date back to King Arthur's day

TOUR 28 · Journey to the Marcherlands POWYS

ROUTE DIRECTIONS

The drive starts from Builth Wells ①.

Follow signs for Brecon to leave by the A470. This road follows the tree-lined River Wye between 1,400ft hills and later passes through Erwood to Llyswen ②.

At Llyswen keep forward with the A479, signed Abergavenny, and in just over ½ mile bear right and ascend. There are good views ahead towards the Black Mountains before reaching the junction with the A438.

At this junction turn right and enter Bronllys, then turn left following the A479, still signed Abergavenny. Half a mile further, on the left, are the remains of Bronllys Castle ③.

In ¾ mile, at the outskirts of Talgarth, turn left on to the A4078, signed Hereford (A438) ④.

After another 2¼ miles turn right at the T-junction to join the A438 and pass through Three Cocks (Aberllyfni). One mile beyond the village go forward with the B4350 along the Wye Valley to visit Hay-on-Wye ⑤.

In the town turn left on to the B4351, signed Clyro, and cross the River Wye. In 1¼ miles bear right across the main road on to an unclassified road and enter Clyro ⑥.

At the church turn left, signed Painscastle, then in ½ mile turn left again and start a long ascent. Half a mile further bear right and continue the climb across the Clyro Hills before proceeding to Painscastle ⑦.

In the village turn right on to the B4594, signed Newchurch. Pass through the secluded communities of Rhos-goch and Newchurch, then continue with the secondary road amid hilly Welsh Marches scenery to Gladestry. In 2¼ miles bear right and 1 mile further, with views ahead of the Stanner Rocks, turn left on to the A44, signed Rhayader. Beyond Walton the route by-passes New Radnor and gradually climbs on to the upland area known as Radnor Forest ⑧.

Continue to Penybont and on to Crossgates. Here, turn left at the roundabout with the A483, signed Llandrindod. The valley of the River Ithon is then followed for the short distance to Llandrindod Wells ⑨.

Remain on the A483, signed Builth Wells. After 7 miles, at the roundabout, take the first exit and shortly cross the River Wye for the return journey to Builth Wells.

This drive passes through the beautiful pastoral scenery of the Welsh borderlands, includes Hay-on-Wye, the ideal town for booklovers, and takes in spectacular mountain views.

POINTS OF INTEREST

① Builth Wells is a pleasant mountain town on the River Wye and a former inland resort with saline and sulphur wells. The Royal Welsh Agricultural Show is held here annually.

② The name Erwood is a corruption of 'Y Rhyd' – Welsh for 'the ford' which cattle drovers once crossed on their journey over the Wye to England.

③ Bronllys Castle dates from about 1200 and stands, with its single round tower, on a mound surrounded by trees – evidence of the need for strong defence at the northern end of the gap between the Usk and Wye valleys.

④ Talgarth church contains a 14th-century sepulchral slab where Hywel Harris, father of the Welsh Methodist movement, is buried.

⑤ With its old buildings and pretty streets, Hay-on-Wye is an attractive market town on the English border. It is remarkable for the number of its second-hand bookshops.

⑥ The Romans used Clyro as a stopping point *en route* to the west, though its main claim to fame is its connection with the well-known diarist, Reverend Francis Kilvert, curate of Clyro from 1865 to 1872.

⑦ The early Norman motte-and-bailey castle at Painscastle, now in ruins, is ascribed to Payn de Quercis (1130). The castle has a keep and deep earth banks.

⑧ Radnor Forest has never been a wood in the modern sense; in medieval times 'forest' meant unenclosed land used for hunting. The highest summits – The Black Mixen and Great Rhos – rise to over 2,000ft. The north is now heavily planted with conifers. The Water-Break-Its-Neck waterfall has a 90ft plunge.

⑨ The county town of Powys, Llandrindod Wells is a pleasant Victorian and Edwardian spa town. Its springs were found to have healing powers in the 18th century, but the town came into its own with the railway age.

Hay-on-Wye, reputed to have the world's largest concentration of used books in its shops

Radnor Forest is, in fact, a heart-shaped mass of hills. Roughly eight miles wide and six miles deep, they are formed of Silurian limestone. The names of the summits are a strange mixture of Welsh and English.

POINTS OF INTEREST

①New Radnor actually dates back several centuries, and was once surrounded by town walls and dominated by a Norman castle, around which its streets were arranged in a chessboard pattern. The castle, whose few ruins now stand in their commanding position above the town, was built in the 11th century. Demolished by King John, it was restored by his son Henry III. Owain Glyndŵr, the leader of the 15th-century Welsh uprising, came here in 1401 and destroyed the fortress so entirely that it was never rebuilt.

②The hills of Radnor Forest were not originally, as the name might imply, an area of woodland. This was a forest in the medieval sense of the word: that is, a hunting ground. Over the past few decades the Forestry Commission has planted conifers in the area. From the Mynyddyreithin plateau it is possible to see the prominent dome known as Whimble.

③The crest of the Bache Hill ridge is the highest point of the walk and offers extensive views of the Black Mountains and the Shropshire summits. Radnor Forest at its highest – Great Rhos is the highest point of all – reaches 2,166ft.

④The Radnor Forest pondlife is varied and interesting. It is particularly worth keeping a lookout for dragonflies, which feed on various insects up to the size of butterflies. Dragonflies are among the fastest-flying and oldest insects in the world: estimates of their speed vary from 35mph to 60mph, and fossilised remains have shown them to have been in existence for 300,000,000 years. Their speed of flight enables these colourful insects to catch their food on the wing, seizing the prey with their legs.

ROUTE DIRECTIONS

Allow 3 hours
Start in the main street of New Radnor (grid ref. SO213608).

Go up the street towards the castle①.

Turn right and then left to follow a lane named Mutton Dingle. At a fork, bear left and follow a cart track beside a fence, on the edge of a forestry plantation. On reaching a gate the gradient eases and the views start to expand. Unfortunately the gradient increases again until the plateau of Mynyddyreithin is reached②.

Follow the track past the base of Whimble and into the next valley where a broad path can be seen continuing past Whinyard Rocks to the top of a pass directly ahead. At the top of the pass go through a gate and follow a fence. On reaching the edge of a wood turn right through a gate and follow a broad path through the bracken to cross the western part of Bache Hill③.

Carry on down the broad, heather-lined track. On reaching a gate, go right along a gravel track to another gate, near a large agricultural building beneath the eastern side of Whimble. Now follow a forest road for about 150yds and then take a grass track on the left which descends through a break in the plantations. Further on, cross two forest roads and continue beside a plantation and past a pond④.

Turn right at the end of the plantation and follow a fence to reach a gate. On the other side, a green lane is joined which descends to the road in Mutton Dingle, leading back to New Radnor.

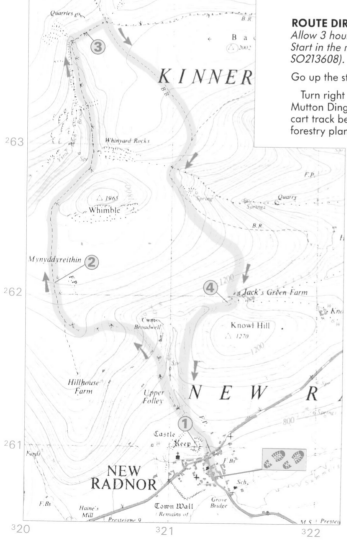

Visitors expecting tree-covered ground at Radnor Forest will be surprised to find bare hills, over 2,000ft high, offering superb views

ROUTE DIRECTIONS

Allow 4 hours
Start from the square by the Swan Hotel in Kington (grid ref. SO299567).

Go up Church Street, past the church①.

Follow the A44 for a short way. Turn left up a narrow road signposted Hergest Croft and Offa's Dyke Path②.

Follow the road up the crest of the ridge to reach a gate across the road. From here continue along the ridge to enjoy fine views on either side③.

The wide green path follows the centre of the ridge, giving views on the left of the mass of the Black Mountains of Powys and Gwent④.

Continue past a pool to reach a crossing of tracks. Turn right and descend towards Hanter Hill – a bracken-covered mound on the right. On reaching a col follow the track round the right-hand flank of the hill, obtaining green and pleasant views down the valley. Descend to join a track beside a fence and turn left. Continue past a cottage and on to reach Lower Hanter Farm. Go through a gate and follow a track around the left side of Worsell Wood to reach a footbridge, which crosses the Gilwern Brook beside a ford⑤.

Follow the lane to a gate and turn right by an old railway station and walk with care along the grass verge of the A44⑥.

Go through a gate on the right opposite the turning to Dunfield House, and cross a field and a footbridge; go through another gate and over the old railway track to reach Bestrey Farm. Turn left and continue through the farmyard to follow a lane back to Kington.

Hergest Ridge, commanding panoramic views of England and Wales, lies on the waymarked Offa's Dyke Path which follows the Welsh border

Hergest Ridge is a fine viewpoint on the border of Wales. From its heights on a clear day the Clee Hills in Shropshire can be seen, as well as the Malverns in Hereford and Worcester and the Black Mountains and Radnor Hills of Powys.

POINTS OF INTEREST

①Kington is a small market town on the Welsh/English border, with attractive Georgian houses. Mrs Siddons made her debut in a barn there in the 1770s, and the church contains a 15th-century alabaster tomb of one of the Vaughan family of Hergest. Margaret Vaughan was the wife of Elizabethan adventurer Sir John Hawkins, and founded a grammar school here in 1632.

②Hergest Croft is well known for its beautiful gardens of rhododendrons and azaleas. The Vaughans of Hergest had their family seat at Hergest Court, a moated manor house built around 1430 near the road to Hay.

③The fine views from Hergest Ridge include Bradnor Hill, which lays claim to the highest golf course in England (Nantyglo in Wales is higher).

④The old Kington racecourse forms a track encircling the top of Hergest Ridge, and to the right a slight detour leads to the Whetstone. This is a rectangular stone, composed not of the native Ludlow shale, but of a hard igneous rock which must have been deposited here during the glacial period.

⑤Directly ahead of the Gilwern Brook are Stanner Rocks, where it was said the Devil had his garden on the summit.

⑥An old boundary stone on the verge of the A44 marks the county boundary, as well as the point where England and Wales meet.

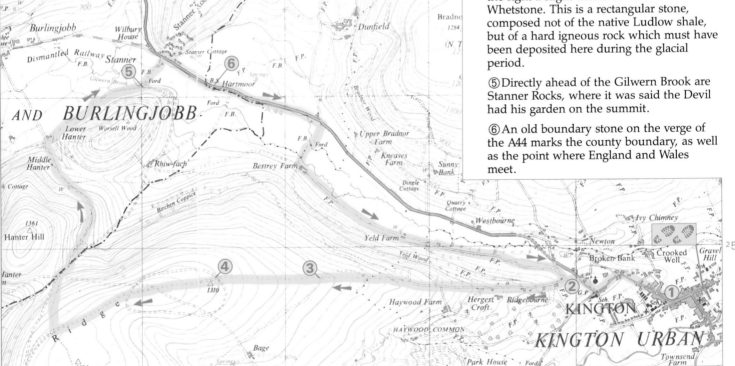

The narrow and most easterly ridge of the Black Mountains is called Crib y Garth, but is more popularly known by its English name – the Cat's Back.

POINTS OF INTEREST

①Hatterall Ridge, which can be seen to the west of the Cat's Back, marks the route of the Offa's Dyke Long Distance Path. Built as a line of demarcation, this long dyke is named after the Mercian King Offa and was constructed in about 784. It runs from the coast near Prestatyn southwards across Wales to Chepstow, and still marks the Welsh/English border. The place names to the east are generally English and those to the west largely Welsh. Many sections of the dyke are still visible and the waymarked path follows its length of 167 miles.

②Birds likely to be spotted on Black Hill include the buzzard, distinguished by its broad, rounded wings, short tail and soaring flight; the little brown meadow pipit, and the skylark, with its warbling song. The ring ouzel may be seen in spring and summer, and very often large flocks of lapwings, or peewits, can be seen during late summer and autumn.

③To the left of Hay Bluff – otherwise known as Pen-y-Beacon – is Y Twmpa, often referred to as Lord Hereford's Knob. Below, to the right, is the Monnow Valley and the tiny hamlet of Craswall, which has a quaint old pub called the Bull's Head and a church.

There's a grand view to be had from the summit of Black Hill and buzzards (inset) may often be seen circling high above

ROUTE DIRECTIONS

Allow 2 hours
Start from the small car park and picnic site just to the north of Little Black Hill, at the foot of the Cat's Back (grid ref. SO288328).

Go over a stile and head up the hillside following a well-defined path, which is quite steep at first. When the ridge is gained, the walking becomes easier①.

The ridge becomes stepped and rocky. It then narrows for a short distance before broadening into Black Hill, where the summit is marked by a trig. point②.

Follow a well-trodden path in a north-westerly direction towards Hay Bluff, until the head of the Olchon Valley is reached③.

Turn left and follow a track descending into the valley. On reaching a road, turn left and follow it back to a junction where a turning leads up to Black Hill car park.

A circuit of Mynydd Llangorse provides panoramic views to the largest natural lake and the loftiest mountains in South Wales. At the highest point of the walk the view takes in the Rhiangoll Valley and the westerly ridges of the Black Mountains.

POINTS OF INTEREST

①Mynydd Llangorse and Allt-yr-Esgair are the hills which guard Llangorse Lake on the east and south; the other side is open. Llangorse Lake is the second largest natural lake in Wales and its waters are dammed behind a barrier of glacial gravel. Great crested grebe and other fish-eating birds breed there, white and yellow water lilies can be seen on the water, and pikes and eels have been caught in the lake.

②Llangorse Lake is a lake of legend. One tells of a once-thriving township which, destroyed by an earthquake, now lies beneath the lake. The tolling of church bells is said to be heard on occasion. According to another legend, the Old Woman of Llangorse reaches out from the submerged church tower to take disobedient children back with her under the water. An artificial island in the lake is marked on the map as Bwlch. Such islands, known as crannogs, are believed to have been used as ancient Celtic dwellings. In 1925 a dug-out canoe, hewn from a single oak log, was found in the lake, and is now housed in the Brecon Museum.

③Three stones set in the ground at the Cwm Sorgwm pass are inscribed with names and dates; but these are not gravestones. They are boundary stones, marking the junction of three estates.

Windsurfing, boating, sailing, canoeing and water ski-ing can all be enjoyed on Llangorse Lake

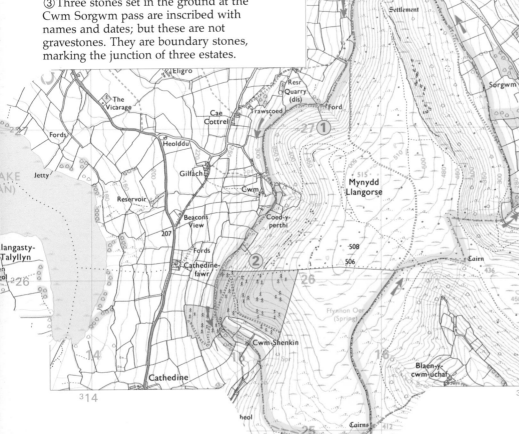

ROUTE DIRECTIONS

Allow 3 hours
Start from the small parking area at the summit of the pass in Cwm Sorgwm (grid ref. SO161283).

Follow the path in a southerly direction and head for the fence on the right to pick up a path which leads round the western slopes of Mynydd Llangorse①.

The mountain slopes provide level walking at an altitude of over 1,000ft, with good views of Llangorse Lake②.

After two miles or so of steady walking, reach a hunting gate, where the path enters the edge of a wood. It then ascends and crosses a diagonal track. Soon another hunting gate is reached, and from there the path follows a stone wall for a short way. On emerging from the wood, cross a field and go past an isolated cottage named Cwm-Shenkin. Then cross another field to pass through a gate and from there follow a diagonal path leading up the hillside.

Curving around to meet a fence, the track then joins the crest of the ridge and a cairn. Turn left here and follow the ridge track for a short distance then fork right along a narrower path. The path skirts around the head of two side valleys and reaches another cairn. From here descend on a zigzag path into Cwm Sorgwm to join a track heading in a northerly direction back up the valley. It joins the road just below the summit of the pass, which completes the circuit③.

ROUTE DIRECTIONS

The drive starts from Machynlleth ①.

From the town, follow the signs Dolgellau, A487, and after crossing the River Dovey (Dyfi) turn left on to the A493, signed Aberdyfi. Continue through well-wooded country and in 3 miles, beyond Pennal, the drive reaches the estuary, with fine views across to Borth. Enter Aberdyfi②.

Continue, away from the shore, to Tywyn (Towyn)③.

Turn right into the town centre, passing St Cadfan's Church④.

Continue with the A493 to Bryncrug, then turn right on to the B4405, signed Abergynolwyn. In 3 miles, on the right, is a track up to the famous Dolgoch Falls. The Tal-y-Llyn Railway now runs parallel to the road to reach Abergynolwyn. A detour can be made here by remaining on the B4405 for 3 miles to reach the picturesque Tal-y-Llyn Lake, set below Cadair Idris, 2,927ft⑤.

The main drive turns left on to a narrow unclassified road, signed Castell y Bere, and passes through a deep valley. In 1½ miles another detour can be made by turning right to reach Castell y Bere⑥.

The main drive turns left, signed Llanegryn, and soon the massive Bird Rock towers up ahead. At the foot of the rock turn right, crossing the Dysynni Valley to reach Llanegryn. In ¼ mile, at a T-junction, turn right, rejoining the A493, signed Dolgellau. Beyond Rhoslefain the drive reaches the coast then follows it north through Llwyngwril to the edge of Fairbourne⑦.

Continue with the A493. There are views towards Barmouth and Barmouth Bridge on the left before passing through well-wooded country. One and a half miles beyond Penmaenpool turn right on to an unclassified road to enter Dolgellau⑧.

From the town centre follow through-traffic signs and leave by crossing the seven-arch Wnion Bridge, dating from 1638. At the first T-junction turn right, signed Machynlleth, and in ¾ mile, at the next T-junction, turn right on to the A494. Another T-junction is reached in ¼ mile and here the drive turns left on to the A470, up a long ascent. In 2 miles the B4416 is passed on the left. This leads to a footpath known as the Torrent Walk and follows the Afon Clywedog down to the Wnion Valley.

Continue to the Cross Foxes Hotel and turn right on to the A487, signed Machynlleth, and continue the ascent. The eastern end of Cadair Idris is now dominant on the right.

Later descend, with views ahead

After visiting the resort of Aberdyfi (Aberdovey) the drive enters the Tal-y-Llyn Valley. The coast is rejoined before the route follows the Mawddach Estuary and finally re-enters the Dovey Valley.

of the Tal-y-Llyn Lake, before ascending a low pass to reach Corris Uchaf where there are extensive remains of former slate quarries. After a further 1¼ miles, an unclassified road on the left leads into Corris⑨.

Continue down the winding and thickly wooded valley and after 2¾ miles an unclassified road on the left leads to the Centre for Alternative Technology, set in a slate quarry. The drive soon enters the Dovey Valley and recrosses the river, back into Machynlleth.

POINTS OF INTEREST

① A pleasant market town and touring centre, Machynlleth is dominated by a massive clock tower. The Owain Glyndwr Institute stands on the site of the meeting place of the last independent Welsh Parliament in 1404. The town is also an angling centre.

② Aberdyfi is a popular and attractive resort with extensive sands and a sheltered estuary that is ideal for yachting. Regattas are held here in the summer. The Boys' Outward Bound Sea School is situated here.

③ Tywyn has fine bathing sands and is the starting point of the narrow-gauge Tal-y-Llyn Railway to Nant Gwernol. Opened in 1865 to carry slate from quarries near Abergynolwyn, it was the first ever to be preserved by enthusiasts in 1951 and it has the oldest passenger coaches still in service in the world.

④ St Cadfan's Church is partly Norman and contains the ancient St Cadfan's Stone which bears the earliest-known Welsh inscription.

⑤ There are many beautiful little lakes in North Wales, and the Tal-y-Llyn is considered to be one of the most beautiful. It is also well known for its sizeable trout.

⑥ The ruins of Castell y Bere are perched high on its lonely hill. Built by Llywelyn the Great in 1221, the castle was captured some 60 years later by Edward I, who partly rebuilt it. It is now in the care of *Cadw*: Welsh Historic Monuments.

⑦ Fairbourne is a holiday village with fine beaches whose main summer attraction is its narrow-gauge steam railway, the tiniest of the 'Great Little Trains of Wales'. It also has a Butterfly Safari.

⑧ The town is a market centre of grey stone buildings. Experts disagree as to what Dolgellau means in English, the most romantic translation being 'cottages in a meadow'. Gold was discovered in the district in 1844 and the mines worked until 1966. Queen Elizabeth

II's and the Princess of Wales' wedding rings are made from the gold they yielded.

⑨ Corris consists of two parts, Corris 'upper' and Corris 'proper', both lying at the southern limits of Snowdonia National Park. Slate-quarrying was the traditional industry, as the heaps of quarry waste testify. A craft centre has opened recently and there is a railway museum.

Tal-y-Llyn and Cadair Idris – it is said that anyone who sleeps a night at a certain spot on the mountain will wake up either mad or a poet

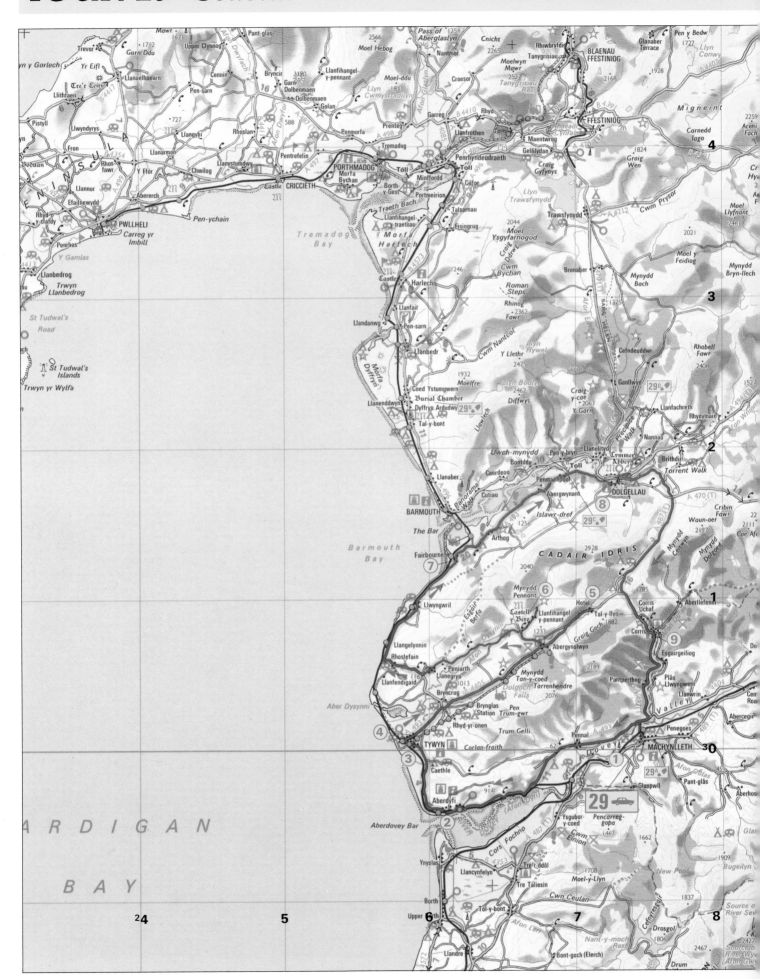

A 19th-century clock tower stands at the meeting-point of the principal streets of Machynlleth, a market town on the River Dyfi

Among the lovely green hills to the south of the pleasing little market town of Machynlleth, the effects of some of the pressures being put on the countryside are revealed. Despite these aspects, this walk still takes in some beautiful woodland, rich in a variety of plant- and birdlife.

POINTS OF INTEREST

① Machynlleth is a popular centre with several interesting features. The Owain Glyndŵr Institute in Maengwyn Street is a 16th-century building, said to occupy the site of Glyndŵr's first parliament in 1404. The Dyfi Bridge, north west of the town, was first built in 1533, and reconstructed in about 1800.

② Cadair Idris (Chair of Idris) is named, according to tradition, after a warrior, poet and astronomer. The path above Machynlleth has suffered from heavy erosion, due to its illegal use by motorcyclists.

③ A lot of felling has recently taken place on the hills above Machynlleth, leaving extensive scars. It will certainly take many years to regenerate growth.

④ Roads such as the unmarked route to Llyn Glanmerin proliferate throughout Mid Wales, made possible by EEC subsidies and the lack of applicable planning regulations.

⑤ The hillside leading to Llyn Glanmerin – a popular venue for anglers – is on one of the most frequented routes for low-flying military aircraft.

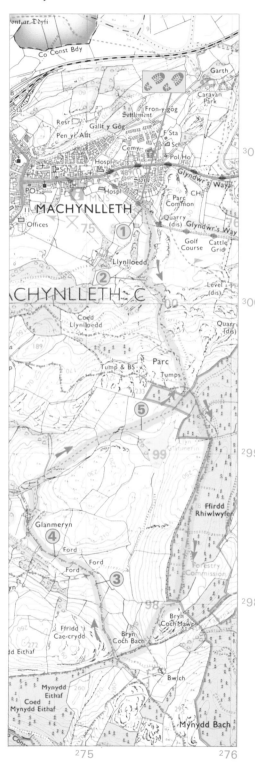

ROUTE DIRECTIONS

Allow 3 hours
Start from the lay-by in front of the council houses opposite the British Telecom depot in Machynlleth (grid ref. SH753007) ①.

A footpath sign on the south side of the road points the way, over a stile and along the line of a fence to the perimeter of the golf course. The path goes right, then zigzags up steeply to the left, with views to the north over the town to the Tarrens and Cadair Idris ②.

At the brow of the hill another path joins in from the valley to the left, and other paths veer off right towards the top corner of the forest. Ignore them, and keep straight on to a gate in the left side of an angle of the forest verge. (There are a stile and directional arrows a little further down to the right, but this is the path along which the return route emerges.) Go through the gate into the wood and continue for 400yds. The path arrives at a stone wall by the edge of the wood. Go through it, into the trees again.

Continue on for ¾ mile through a muddy, sterile tunnel in the trees. Make sure you take the right fork after a particularly boggy section. The path comes to a gate, beyond which there is recently cultivated land. Bear off right, then go down and round a steep spur to the left, which leads to a green track. Turn right and continue to a gate where a track comes in from the left ③.

Just beyond the gate is another gate on the right, bearing the legend 'Footpath only – no vehicles'. The path it gives on to leads down to a junction with a new road at SN748983. Take care, because this road, which leads up to Llyn Glanmerin, is not marked on the map ④.

Turn left to Glanmerin, where a path beyond the first building rises on the right to reach the bottom of a copse, climbs left to the top of more forest, then breaks right across some rather boggy sections to reach Llyn Glanmerin ⑤.

The path arrives at a rhododendron thicket, and then heads left into the forest, shortly emerging again at the stile mentioned previously. From here, a one-mile downhill walk leads back to the lay-by.

ROUTE DIRECTIONS

Allow 4 hours
Start on the road, where there is parking, just east of Cors y Gedol Hall (grid ref. SH603232).

Follow a broad track that runs east from the road, beyond a gate with a 'no vehicles' sign. After 150yds, over the wall on the right, just before a waterworks, the remains of a hut group can be seen①.

After two miles, just before the end of a larch plantation on the side of Moelfre (to the left), a marshy track leads off right, with a stumpy stone standing 100yds along on its right. Follow it down to Pont-Scethin②.

Coetan Arthur — an ancient burial chamber

The old road continues in a great zigzag up the side of the hill to the south. The rampart of the hillfort of Craig y Dinas is clearly visible across to the right in the final stages of the ascent to the ridge top. Once there, head south along the nearside of the wall that is reached. This ridge is a broad, grassy whaleback which should be followed over Llawlech, with its summit cairn, before descending 1½ miles to Bwlch y Rhiwgyr. From here, a path leads down the narrow, stony gully to the right, through one gate and on to another marked by a white post. Keep to the obvious route, and after 1½ miles reach the Pont Fadog③.

From Pont Fadog, above its rocky stream, climb the track to Llety Lloegr④.

About ¼ mile beyond Llety Lloegr (on the left) is the cromlech. This is known variously as Arthur's Quoit, Cader Arthur, Coetan Arthur or Carreg Arthur⑤.

A few minutes' walk from Coetan Arthur leads back to the start.

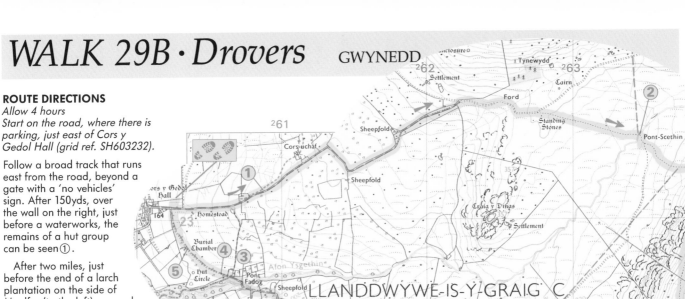

This walk in the southern Rhinogydd offers gentle slopes and firm ground, and on a fine, clear day it is as memorable as any in Wales.

POINTS OF INTEREST

① The track running east from Cors y Gedol is a remnant of the days when cattle were driven regularly on long, hard journeys to the English markets. The ruined huts on its verge were once drovers' inns, or *lletiau*.

Pont-Scethin, once part of a major highway

② The hump-backed bridge at Pont-Scethin once carried the main London to Harlech stagecoach traffic.

③ At Pont Fadog is a memorial stone inscribed 'WV 1762 HE SAER'. *Saer* is the Welsh word for architect, and WV is William Vaughan of Cors y Gedol, the Elizabethan and Jacobean house where this walk starts.

④ Once an inn for English drovers (its name means England Inn), Llety Lloegr is now a teashop.

⑤ Coetan Arthur is a huge slab propped up by a single upright, and dating back to 2000–1500BC. From it can be seen Pen y Dinas hillfort and the long cairns of Carneddau Hengwm to the south and Craig y Dinas to the east.

WALK 29C · *Birds and Sandflats*   GWYNEDD

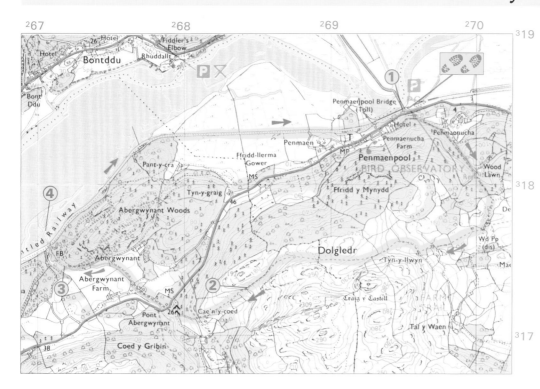

According to John Ruskin, there was only one finer walk in the world than that from Barmouth to Dolgellau, and that was the walk from Dolgellau to Barmouth. The following circuit gives you the best of both, with Cadair Idris towering high above on the outward journey, and an astonishing variety of birdlife in the Mawddach Estuary on the return to Penmaenpool.

POINTS OF INTEREST

①The old railway at Penmaenpool ran from 1865 to 1965, starting as the Aberystwyth and Welsh Coast Railway. A signal box has now been made into a bird observatory by the Royal Society for the Protection of Birds and the North Wales Naturalists' Trust.

②Mine entrances can still be seen in the rock outcrops to the left of the new farm road beyond Tyn-y-llwyn. These were trial shafts sunk during the mid-19th-century gold rush which centred around Dolgellau. From this road there are spectacular views of Cadair Idris.

③A curious structure between the path and stream in Abergwynant Woods was probably an ice-store for Abergwynant Hall.

④The Penmaenpool to Morfa Mawddach Walk, a dedicated right of way, runs along the Mawddach Estuary. It offers excellent opportunities to study birdlife. Many species of duck and wading birds frequent the estuary, and the old railway above the wetlands and saltings is an ideal viewpoint.

ROUTE DIRECTIONS

Allow 2½ hours
Start from the car park by the bird observatory on the old railway near the toll bridge at Penmaenpool (grid ref. SH695185).

Return to the road from the bird observatory①.

Walk to the right for 100yds to a footpath sign on the left, half-hidden in a rhododendron bush. After 150yds this path goes through a gate to a road. Follow it left for 200yds to a track which branches off right. After 500yds there is a pond on the left. Go straight over the junction ahead, and in a further 300yds emerge from the wood at a gate.

A track leads round behind a tall-chimneyed cottage and passes a barn to arrive at a gate and stile. Follow it further, alongside a fence, to a farm – Tyn-y-llwyn – and on entering the farmyard turn right past a barn and up left, towards a further barn across the field. Just before the second barn, a marked track leads off right through a gate and up to a ridge where a path joins in from the left. From here, bear up right, with occasional posts marking the way, to a second ridge and descend from this (to the left) to a stile of protruding rocks near the corner of the wall ahead. The right of way now joins a new farm road, which offers an easy descent down the valley ahead②.

The new road joins the tarmac road running up from the A493 at an ornate old schoolhouse, now offering accommodation for walkers. Follow the minor road down from here, and at the main road go left, then right, to gain the track down to Abergwynant Farm. The track runs under magnificent trees planted at the time of the building of Abergwynant Hall. Pass the farm, keeping the stream on your left, and go through a gate (with an owl carved on one post) into a wood③.

Beyond the ice-store pass a deep green pool before crossing an area of waste ground and a footbridge to reach the old railway track④.

Two miles of level walking along the old track, leads back to the car park at Penmaenpool.

A toll bridge runs across the Mawddach Estuary to Penmaenpool, a shipbuilding base before the silting up of the estuary

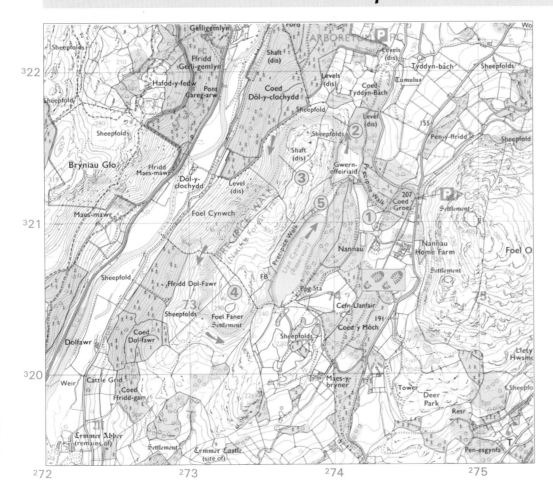

ROUTE DIRECTIONS
Allow 2 hours
Start from the car park at Coed Groe (grid ref. SH746212).

Turn left and walk along the road for 50yds to the first track leading off on the left①.

The track runs through a wood for 200yds, and then turns right along its south-western margin to reach the small cottage of Gwern-offeiriaid, in front of which it ascends left, to a stile. Beyond the stile, a path curves to the right around the hillside and emerges on to open land at the northern end of Llyn Cynwch. A wall runs up to the right and the path follows it, turning right and keeping to its top edge. The route now gently curves around the broad northern spur of Foel Cynwch②.

The path turns south and continues across an area of scree③.

The steepest section of hillside traversed by the path is barely 300yds long, and at its end, just before a wall, there is a belvedere (turret) on a level spur over to the right④.

Beyond the wall, the route slips round the southern spur of Foel Faner. There is a small valley running down towards Dolgellau on the right, but the path leaves this behind and arrives back at the southern end of Llyn Cynwch, which is skirted by an often puddly track on the left, through native oakwood⑤.

Just beyond the end of the lake, the path rejoins the route up from the car park, only a few minutes' walk away.

The unmistakable grandeur of Cadair Idris, viewed across Llyn Cynwch

Despite its fearsome name, this delightful circuit around Foel Cynwch should hold no fears for those who are reasonably steady on their feet. The outlook is continually magnificent.

POINTS OF INTEREST

① The courtesy path through the Nannau Estate started life as a sheep track. Nannau Park is the ancient seat of the Vaughan family. A sign issuing dire warnings about the unsuitability of the path for some people errs heavily on the side of caution.

② On a clear day the views to the north from Foel Cynwch are wonderful. Snowdon is the dominant peak to the left of the ugly reactors of Trawsfynydd Nuclear Power Station, clearly visible in the middle distance. The complex landscape of river valleys closer at hand is given over almost entirely to conifers, but the planting is more varied and pleasing to the eye than many such forests.

③ The precipice which gives the walk its name is a fairly steep slope of heather dropping into the flat bed of the Mawddach Valley below. The path across it is entirely level and quite wide, and the extraordinary panorama of Cadair Idris, with the Mawddach Estuary in the foreground, should distract even those of the most nervous disposition.

④ Both Foel Faner, on these slopes, and Foel Offrwm, on the other side of Llyn Cynwch, were populated in Neolithic times, and there are traces of settlements on the summits.

⑤ From the northern end of Llyn Cynwch, the view of Cadair Idris across the tree-fringed waters of the lake is one of the finest in Snowdonia.

ROUTE DIRECTIONS
The drive starts from Caernarfon ①.

From Caernarfon follow the signs to Bangor, to leave by the A487. There are views across the Menai Strait before reaching the former slate port of Port Dinorwic②.

In 1½ miles, at the roundabout, turn left, signed Holyhead, and in ¾

From Caernarfon this drive crosses the Menai Strait and reaches the superbly scenic Pass of Llanberis. There are splendid views of the Snowdon Peaks before the road skirts Beddgelert Forest.

Caernarfon Castle, where Edward I presented his first-born son to the Welsh and set a precedent for the present Prince of Wales

mile, at the next roundabout, take the first exit to join the A5. One mile further, cross the Britannia Bridge for the Isle of Anglesey③.

On the far side branch left, then turn right on to the A4080 and continue to the outskirts of Menai Bridge Town. Follow signs to Bangor and cross Telford's famous Menai Suspension Bridge, then at the roundabout join the A5122 for Bangor④.

Follow signs to Betws-y-coed (A5), to leave by the A5122. In 2½ miles pass the entrance, on the left, to Penrhyn Castle Estate⑤.

In ¾ mile, at a roundabout, take the second exit on to the A5 and almost immediately turn right on to the B4366, signed Caernarfon. In 3½ miles, at a roundabout, turn left on to the B4547, signed Llanberis. Three and a half miles further, at the T-junction, turn left on to the A4086. A detour can be taken by turning right on to the A4086 to visit Bryn Bras Castle and its grounds which lie to the south of Llanrug. The main drive continues with the A4086, skirting the shore of Llyn Padarn and Llanberis⑥.

Continue on the A4086 and pass, on the left, the 13th-century

Dolbadarn Castle⑦.

At Nant Peris the drive begins the ascent of the Pass of Llanberis, where at the summit, 1,169ft, the Pen-y-Pass car park is the start of the Miners' Track nature trail and path to Snowdon. There are fine views on the descent from the pass and after a mile, at the T-junction by the Pen-y-Gwryd Hotel, turn right on to the A498, signed Beddgelert.

Continue the descent, passing an excellent viewpoint of the Snowdon Peaks, before Llyn Gwynant. Beyond the scattered hamlet of Nantgwynant the road follows a narrow valley skirting Llyn Dinas. After the lake the drive passes the turning, on the left, to the Sygun Copper Mine before reaching Beddgelert⑧.

Keep forward on the Caernarfon road, A4085, and gradually ascend, skirting Beddgelert Forest⑨.

Pass by the shores of Llyn Cwellyn, then continue through Betws Garmon and Waunfawr. Two miles further, at the roundabout, go forward for the return to Caernarfon.

POINTS OF INTEREST

①The county town of Gwynedd, Caernarfon is famous for its magnificent 13th-century castle,

scene of the investiture of the present Prince of Wales. On the south-eastern outskirts of the town lie the remains of the Roman fort of Segontium, with a museum of excavated relics. Also of interest is the maritime museum at Victoria Dock.

②Known officially as Y Felinheli, Port Dinorwic has provided seafarers with a sheltered anchorage on the Menai Strait for 1,200 years and has a large marina.

③Britannia Bridge, Stephenson's tubular railway bridge spanning the Menai Strait, was opened in 1850, but it suffered a disastrous fire in 1970 and was rebuilt with the addition of a road deck.

④A cathedral city, university town and cultural centre, Bangor is a good base for touring north-west Wales. Its pier is acknowledged to be one of the finest in Britain and the Museum of Welsh Antiquities is well worth visiting.

⑤Penrhyn Castle is one of the most magnificent stately homes in North Wales. Built in the 19th century in neo-Norman style, the interior is equally grand and contains a collection of industrial locomotives and a doll museum.

⑥Right on the edge of the National Park, Llanberis is one of the most well-known places in Snowdonia. At the far end of the village is the terminus of the Snowdon Mountain Railway and the easiest walking route to Snowdon follows the railway. To the left lie the Welsh environment interpretation centre, *Oriel Eryri*, and the Dinorwic Quarries, now the site of the Welsh Slate Museum. Adjacent are the narrow-gauge Llanberis Lake Railway and the Llyn Padarn Country Park.

⑦Built by Llywelyn the Great in the late 12th to early 13th century, Dolbadarn Castle's 40ft-high circular keep still guards the approach to the winding, narrow Pass of Llanberis.

⑧Beddgelert is a beautiful wooded village at the junction of the Afon (River) Colwyn and Afon Glaslyn. In a field nearby is the reputed grave of Llywelyn the Great's dog, Gelert, with stones erected during the 18th century.

⑨Beddgelert Forest is the site of several Forestry Commission picnic areas and forest walks. From Rhyd-Ddu, a footpath to the right leads to the summit of Snowdon.

WALK 30A · *Llanddwyn Island*   GWYNEDD

Despite its popularity and carefully defined rights of way, Llanddwyn Island, with its rich texture of ecclesiastical, maritime and natural historical interest, is well worth a visit. It is a perfect place for an evening walk.

POINTS OF INTEREST

① The woodland of Newborough Forest, leading down to Llanddwyn Beach, is chiefly of Corsican pine, planted on the former sand dunes of Newborough Warren. Villages existed here in the Middle Ages but were later buried by the windblown sand.

② Nowadays Llanddwyn Island is cut off only at the highest tides. A detour along Malltraeth Sands to look for oystercatchers, dunlins and redshanks is well worthwhile. It is also possible to see a wreck protruding from the sand in Malltraeth Bay.

③ From the bay behind Trwyn Ffynnon-y-Sais, a path takes walkers past enclosures which often contain the native Soay sheep in summer. This wild breed was interbred with the Roman-imported white-faced sheep, to produce the smallest of British breeds – the Welsh Mountain sheep.

④ The 16th-century church on Llanddwyn Island is built on the site of an earlier church, dedicated to St Dwynwen, the 5th-century Welsh patron saint of lovers. Beyond are the cottages of pilots who guided boats into harbour over Caernarfon Bar, and, beyond them, the 1845 lighthouse.

Newborough Warren, stretching to the south west of Newborough, where thousands of acres have been used for afforestation

ROUTE DIRECTIONS

Allow 2 hours
Start at the car park in Newborough Forest (grid ref. SH405634).

Take the forest track signposted Rhodfa Coedwig/Forest Walk that heads off right. After nearly ¾ mile, join another track, bear left, and after a further 200yds, arrive at a smaller car park. From here follow a sandy track that leads down to the beach ①.

Head right along the beach and in a little more than 200yds arrive at the remnants of the causeway, built to give high-tide access to the former inhabitants of Llanddwyn ②.

If a detour has been made along the sand, the main right of way along the spine of rock which is Llanddwyn Island can be rejoined from the small bay behind the fretted curtain of rock called Trwyn Ffynnon-y-Sais. A path then leads alongside two enclosures ③.

The main path passes by the chancel ruins of a church ④.

Return to the car park along the main island track to Newborough Beach.

ROUTE DIRECTIONS

Allow 3½ hours
Start at the Forest Walk car park and picnic site in Nantmor, Gwynedd (grid ref. SH621468).

Walk 100yds north up the road to a footpath sign on the left. Cross the footbridge and the field beyond, to a stile left of the barn. After this the path climbs up through an oak wood and mossy boulders. Do not go right, but follow the top edge of the wood, and where a path joins in from the left, climb over a stile and go though a gate to join a track which is followed to the right ①.

The track bears left to a gate, and leads beyond this to the farm of Carneddi ②.

From the farm a tarmac road leads down towards the village of Nantmor. Opposite the first house on the left, go diagonally down the field on the right, over a stream, through a gate and across another field, to a track which leads down to Nantmor village. Turn right on the road, and at the end of the village, turn right again on to the old railway track. At the mouth of the tunnel, turn right, signposted Cwm Bychan. Follow the path as it forks right beyond the pylons for the old copper mine cableway ③.

At the top of the col (pass) keep right again, and take a further right fork in the valley ahead, which leads to a steep descent to Llyn Dinas. Follow the lake-shore path to the right, and after a gate in a wall, climb up right to a small col and ruin beyond. Keep this on the right, and follow the path until a branch leads off right, into the wood. Above the wood the path emerges on to open slopes and continues, clearly marked, to a stile beyond a small stream. Further on, there is a tunnel through rhododendrons, which leads to the garden of a small cottage ④.

From Hafod Owen, keep straight ahead to a stile. Here, bear right, and cross a track. About 200yds beyond, cross a stile on the right, to a path leading uphill to the left, and then go down right to the Nantmor road at a white house. Turn right here and follow the road down past an old quarry to a bridge. A footpath sign points up the track to the right here.

Follow this to just before a house, where the path branches left into the wood. Continue downstream past the old farmhouse of Buarthau, and through the gorge. The path comes out of the wood on the first stage of the walk. Turn left, and cross the bridge to return to the car park.

Majestic scenery can be enjoyed on this walk in the region east of Beddgelert. Some sections can be muddy, so boots are advisable.

POINTS OF INTEREST

① The oak woodland in the area above Nantmor is the typical native vegetation of Snowdonia, and once grew up to the 2,500ft contour. Much timber on Snowdonia's slopes was lost in heavy fellings during World War I, and some natural erosion has also led to deterioration on higher ground, with rain washing the soil down to the lower slopes.

② At Carneddi Farm the rather incongruous sight of grazing llamas can greet visitors. They have been kept at Carneddi for many years. The farm's own story has been described in *Place of Stones* and *Hill Farm Story*, written by the present occupant, Ruth Janette Ruck.

③ The copper mines in Cwm Bychan enjoyed their heyday during the last two decades of the 18th century, when copper prices were very high.

④ Hafod Owen cottage is closely associated with the great climbing pioneer and writer Menlove Edwards, who lived here during the war years. After his suicide, his ashes were scattered from the tree-covered knoll above.

Approaching Nantmor from Carneddi

ROUTE DIRECTIONS

Allow 3½ hours
Start from the Beddgelert Forest car park by Hafod Ruffydd Isaf (grid ref. SH574502).

A path by the public conveniences leads on to a forestry track. Go left on this, pass a track on the right and bear right on a second track, to pass the house of Hafod Ruffydd Ganol on the left. Just beyond a further track on the right, cross a stile and take the indistinct path to the right of Hafod Ruffydd Uchaf into the forest①.

The path soon mounts a rocky bluff, crosses a forestry track, and plunges into the trees beyond. Take the right fork where it divides, to meet a further track on a bend, and leave this again by a path on the left after 25yds. This climbs to a further track after 150yds, and 20yds left along this track a blue post on the right marks the continuing path. It leaves the wood at a stile and crosses open moorland before re-entering forestry.

When the path joins a track, turn left and after 50yds look for a boggy path on the right which leads out of the forest, crosses a broken wall to the left, and threads its way into the wild and lovely Cwm Trwsgl. Follow this path round to the quarry incline and descend to the bottom. From the flat area behind the ruined slate mill, a stile allows access to the old tramway which runs to the copper mine workings at Cwm Dwyfor②.

Look out for the Bronze Age house platform and enclosures (SH543477). Half a mile beyond these, a path comes up through a gap in the low wall from the farm of Cwrt Isaf, and climbs to the left past a hawthorn to a stile. Keeping the stream on the right, it is now an arduous climb of a mile or so up to Bwlch Meillionen. Stay with the natural line up the valley, passing on the right, near the top, the workings of the old Moel Hebog copper mine③.

At Bwlch Meillionen, cross the stile and the wall on the left, and follow the top edge of the wall round to a point below a dripping, black cliff④.

The path into the forest from here lies 100yds to the east of where the right of way is marked on the map. (The right of way is now obliterated, so follow the old footpath marked on the map instead.) The path follows a stream for most of its length. At the fifth forestry track, turn left, and take the second track right after ½ mile. This leads down past Hafod Ruffydd Uchaf to a further track. Turn left along this track, and retrace the first ½ mile of the walk back to the car park.

Owain Glyndŵr's cave near Beddgelert

The most graceful hills in North Wales are those immediately west of Snowdon, the setting for this walk. Good boots are needed.

POINTS OF INTEREST

①Beddgelert Forest is named, as is Beddgelert village, after the legend of Prince Llywelyn's hound Gelert, killed when his master wrongly suspected him of killing his baby son. The faithful Gelert had, in fact, saved the child's life.

②The 2ft-gauge railway at Cwm Dwyfor once carried passengers and goods round to Cwm Ystradllyn and down to Porthmadog. The line closed in 1882.

③In the mid 19th century there were reports of gold finds at the copper mine on Moel Hebog – which means 'Bare Hill of Hawks'. The reports appear to have been fraudulent.

④The chest-high cave at Moel yr Ogof – 'Bare Hill of the Cave' – is reputed to have been a hiding place for the Welsh leader Owain Glyndŵr.

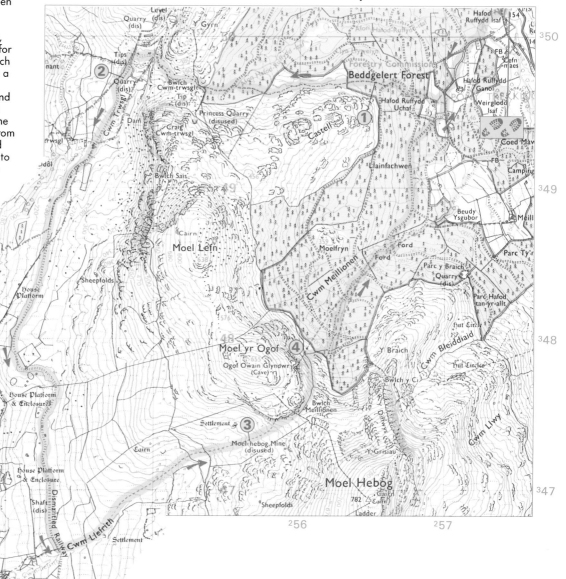

WALK 30D · Iron Age City   GWYNEDD

ROUTE DIRECTIONS

Allow 2 hours
Start at the kissing gate where a footpath leaves the B4417 less than a mile south west of Llanaelhaearn (grid ref. SH378442). There is ample roadside parking just to the east of the gate.

Go along the footpath, which climbs by a wall and through a further gate to veer round to the left in front of a rocky outcrop. Where it forks on the shoulder of the hill, keep right①.

The path from Llithfaen soon joins in from the left. Zigzag up through the defensive walls encircling Tre'r Ceiri②.

From the summit cairn follow the north-western rampart round in an anti-clockwise direction (it is at its highest here, reaching 15ft in places) for 150yds, to a staggered gateway through both inner and outer walls. A narrow path cuts through the heathery basin between the east and central summits to lead left across the hillside ahead③.

Follow the path as it climbs steadily, always well defined, to the brow of the hill. From here, a short ridge leads to the summit cairn-shelter④.

From the summit, return to the car by taking the path leading off south in the direction of the pimple-topped hill, Mynydd Carnguwch. The path crosses a fence and leads down by a wall to a stile on the left. Cross the stile, and follow any of the paths on the right to return to the starting point.

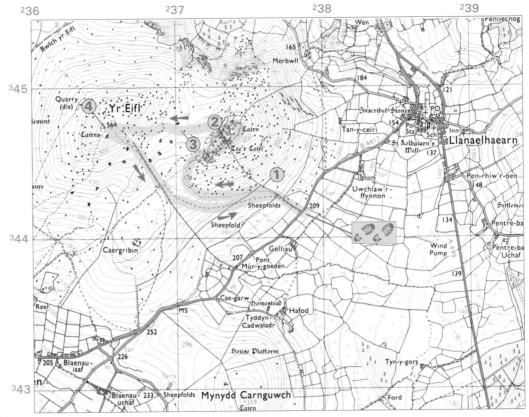

This walk takes in one of the most spectacular viewpoints in Wales, and visits the ramparts and hut circles of an extraordinarily impressive Iron Age village. The walking is not unduly rough, but visitors should note that it does involve an ascent of over 1,000ft.

Tre'r Ceiri, the hillfort on the lower peak of Yr Eifl, whose name is usually translated either as 'the town of giants' or 'the town of stones'

POINTS OF INTEREST

①Yr Eifl is a hill named for its three peaks; the Welsh name means 'The Forks', though it has frequently been anglicised into 'The Rivals'. Rising to 1,850ft above sea level on the north coast of the Lleyn Peninsula, Yr Eifl is an outlier of the main mountain groups of Snowdonia.

②The magnificent fortification of Tre'r Ceiri covers an area of five acres. There are about 150 circular and rectangular huts within its walls, dating from 400-150BC. From the summit cairn the street plan of a deserted town spreads out to the south and west.

③Below the central peak of Yr Eifl and to the south west is Nant Gwrtheyrn, also known as Vortigern's Valley. This 5th-century leader was said to have been destroyed by heavenly fire. The valley's old quarrying village, deserted in 1954, is now being restored as a Welsh language study centre.

④On a clear day, the view from the summit cairn-shelter on Yr Eifl is breathtaking. To the south across Cardigan Bay is Mynydd Preseli, from where the uprights and slabs of bluestone were taken to build Stonehenge. To the west, across the Irish Sea, are the Wicklow Hills. The peaks of Snowdonia are ranged along the eastern horizon; and the west coast of Anglesey stretches round to the north.

ROUTE DIRECTIONS

The drive starts from Betws-y-coed ①.

Leave by the Llangollen road, A5. Cross Waterloo Bridge and turn right, then immediately right again on to the A470, signed Dolgellau. Pass by the entrance to the Fairy Glen on the left and then cross the River Conwy to follow the thickly wooded Lledr Valley to Dolwyddelan ②.

The landscape becomes wilder as the road climbs Crimea Pass to its 1,263ft summit. On the descent into Blaenau Ffestiniog, the drive passes the Gloddfa Ganol Slate Mine, on the right, and the Llechwedd Slate Caverns, on the left ③.

Enter Blaenau Ffestiniog ④.

At the edge of the town turn right, signed Porthmadog, on to the A496. Cross the railway bridge and bear right, then keep left. After almost 1 mile, pass, on the right, the entrance to Ffestiniog Power Station at Tanygrisiau ⑤.

Continue with the Maentwrog–Porthmadog road down the valley of the Afon Goedol. Two and a half miles further turn sharp left on to the A4391 and climb to Ffestiniog ⑥.

The drive rejoins the A470, signed Bala, then passes under a railway bridge and turns left on to the A4391, still signed Bala. The road climbs on to high open moorland and in 2 miles passes, on the right, a viewpoint near the Rhaeadr-y-cwm waterfall. Continue to cross open moorland and in 5¾ miles turn left on to the A4212. Pass by the Llyn Celyn reservoir and descend to the hamlet of Frongoch. Here turn left on to the B4501, signed Cerrigydrudion. Cross more high ground and after 6¼ miles turn left on to the A5, signed Betws-y-coed. Half a mile further, branch right on to the B4501 (no sign) and enter Cerrigydrudion ⑦.

Go forward through the village, signed Denbigh and Llyn Brenig, then in 3 miles pass a road on the left to the Alwen Reservoir visitor centre, picnic site and forest walk. One mile further on, a road on the right leads to the Llyn Brenig visitor centre and park. Continue through well-wooded country and after 3¾ miles, at the T-junction, turn left on to the A543, signed Pentrefoelas ⑧.

The road crosses the moors for nearly 8 miles before it turns right on to the A5, signed Betws-y-coed, to reach Pentrefoelas. Continue along a winding road through the Conwy Valley, later passing the Conwy Falls and the Fairy Glen before turning left to recross the Waterloo Bridge and re-entering Betws-y-coed.

Blaenau Ffestiniog, with its famous railway, is just one of the fascinating places of interest on this drive, which crosses moorland, cuts through woodland and passes the highest public house in Wales.

POINTS OF INTEREST

① Attractively situated in the wooded hills of the Gwydyr Forest, with four rivers converging nearby, Betws-y-coed is an excellent touring centre for Snowdonia. Just outside is one of its main attractions, the spectacular Swallow Falls.

② Dolwyddelan has a 16th-century church, and beyond the village to the right is the 12th-century castle where Llywelyn the Great, Prince of Wales, is reputed to have been born. Northwards towards Dolgarrog in the Conwy Valley stretches Gwydyr Forest.

③ The Gloddfa Ganol Slate Mine is the world's largest slate mine with huge underground caverns, a floodlit trail, narrow-gauge railway centre, and quarrymen's furnished cottages. A miners' underground tramway takes you through a re-creation of Victorian conditions at the Llechwedd Slate Caverns.

④ Blaenau Ffestiniog is world-famous for its slate-quarrying industry and for the narrow-gauge Ffestiniog Railway which recently re-entered the town. The railway is one of the earliest of its kind and is 13½ miles long. Main stations are Blaenau and Porthmadog, where there is a small museum. The drop of 700ft between stations was overcome with a maximum gradient of 1 in 68.

⑤ Guided tours are available of the Ffestiniog Hydro-Electric Generating Station, and from the Stwlan Dam, above, there are excellent views to the south. Nearby is Tanygrisiau Station on the Ffestiniog Railway.

⑥ The large village of Ffestiniog is set amidst superb mountain scenery. Beyond the village to the east lies Migneint Moors crossed by a winding but spectacular road that can be treacherous in winter. To the south, in the deep valley of the Afon (River) Cynfal, is the spectacular 300ft waterfall, Rhaeadr Cynfal.

⑦ Cerrigydrudion is a moorland village with an attractive group of 18th-century almshouses. The height of the area, and the comparative absence of nearby hills, give it an outlook of wide horizons. It is an excellent centre for walking on the moors and around the Brenig Reservoir.

⑧ The drive passes the Sportsman's Arms, which is the highest public house in Wales, and then goes over the lonely Mynydd Hiraethog (Denbigh Moors).

Betws-y-coed is celebrated for its bridges. This one, Pont-y-Pair, was designed by a local mason

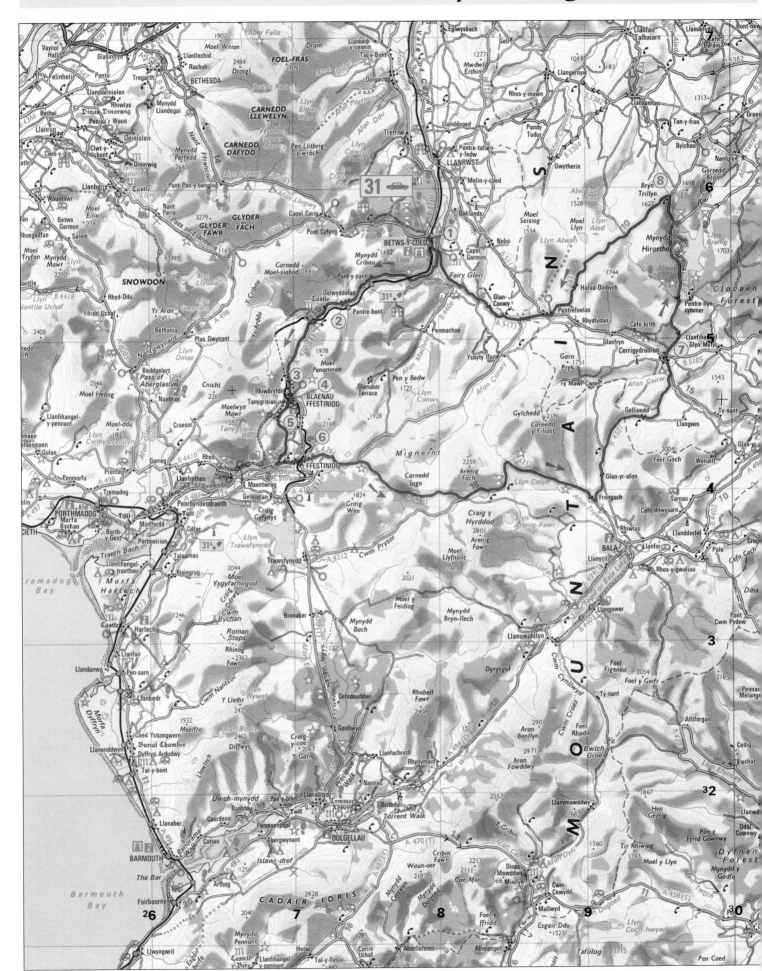

Traces of prehistoric life — the remains of a Bronze Age hut circle in the Rhinog Hills

At the northern end of the Rhinog range of hills the country is wild and boggy. This is high, lonely terrain, where good boots and clear visibility are necessary.

POINTS OF INTEREST

① From Caerwych Farm the views open out to the west across short-cropped upland turf, and along The Lleyn, the 25-mile-long peninsula jutting into the Irish Sea.

② The Bronze Age burial cairn of Bryn Cader Faner has a distinctive circle of 15 upright stones leaning outwards within the body of the mound. This cairn was one of the best-preserved monuments of its period in Snowdonia, before it was vandalised by soldiers on an exercise some years ago.

③ The green pathway at Bryn Cader Faner was a major line of communication in pre-Roman times between the port at Mochras and the Dee Valley.

④ Portmeirion is an Italianate private village with a small harbour, created by the Welsh architect Sir Clough Williams-Ellis. It was built in two phases — one before the war and another after 1954. The well-known Portmeirion pottery is on sale throughout the north west of Wales.

ROUTE DIRECTIONS
Allow 2½ hours
Start from the road junction just beyond Llyn Tecwyn Isaf (grid ref. SH633370). Limited roadside parking is available.

Take the narrow road leading south east for 200yds to a gate giving on to a track on the left. This zigzags steeply uphill through birchwood by a stream, to the farm of Caerwych. Keep to the right of the farm and 50yds beyond it turn right, just past a barn, along a field track ①.

After ½ mile, beyond a third gate and a rocky outcrop, the path curves round left, up to a fourth gate with a stream coming down from the valley ahead on the right. Follow the path and, where it levels, cross a slab-bridge on the right, turning left almost immediately to keep close to the stream. A better path re-appears after an area of bog. It leads past a particularly fine Bronze Age ring cairn on a level shelf on the other bank of the stream, before becoming indistinct again at a boggy area. Cross this and keep along its far side to a valley leading out on the left. The path now crosses a stream and climbs, sunken and well defined, round to the right up a broad ridge, passing a very clear Bronze Age circle on the left. As the path runs down into an area of red bog, Bryn Cader Faner stands out on the skyline ahead. Make your way towards it ②.

Return to join the green pathway ③.

After a mile the path meets a wall, and a track joins in from the left. Follow it through a gate, but bear right on an indistinct path immediately before a second gate. Portmeirion is now in sight ahead ④.

After a narrow opening in a wall, cross the stream on the right and head for Moel-y-geifr, the house with a fir plantation above it. Go round to its right and cross a stile in front of the house. Turn right along the wall to a gate, beyond which the path curves to the right to meet a wall, and follow it down to Caen-y-bwlch Uchaf. Continue down the path, but where it turns up right look for a stone stile in the angle of the wall. Cross the stile, go diagonally down a rough field, and pick up a better-defined path running down between rectangular enclosures on the right and a low line of rock on the left. This path soon joins a muddy farm track running down to Coetty-mawr. Go down the steep track and then down the road for about 10 minutes to return to the starting point.

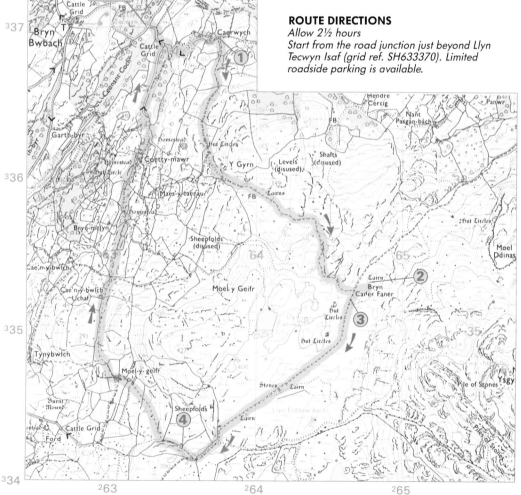

WALK 31B · *Along the Lledr* GWYNEDD

The beautiful Lledr Valley offers a variety of landscapes, ranging from picturesque greenery to open moorland and wilder, rocky countryside

ROUTE DIRECTIONS

Allow 3 hours
Start at Pont-y-pant station (grid ref. SH753536).

Take the minor road that heads south west, soon becoming a track which leads under the railway and arrives at the farm of Hendre. Just beyond, go under the railway again and cross a small stream in front of a barn, to reach the foot of a disused quarry incline. Climb up this to a forestry track, turn left and cross two tiny streams to just before a third in a slatey bed. (The track bends left beyond it.) Follow an indistinct path beside it into the trees. After 100yds cross the stream below a miniature torrent and keep straight ahead, up an overgrown firebreak. This soon emerges from the forest by a ruined building①.

Cross the clearing to the corner of a wood beyond and follow its northern edge, past sheep pens, for 300yds to the top. Diagonally right across the moor is a lone cypress. Head for this, and after 150yds pick up a path leading left through the heather. The peaks of Snowdonia, with Moel Siabod nearest at hand and Snowdon itself peering over its shoulder, rise magnificently behind you②.

Beyond a rocky outcrop the path dips into a wood. Bear left by a ruined sheep pen, and pass an abandoned house on the right. The path crosses a forestry track and continues down to Pwll-y-gâth③.

From Wybrnant take the road leading downhill towards the Lledr Valley. At the white-painted chapel house, a track branches left into the trees. After 800yds it crosses a forestry track and goes under the railway to Tan-aeldroch Farm. A series of stiles in front of the house leads to the riverbank path. Follow it upstream④.

The path climbs into trees beyond a ladder stile. The main path rejoins the river in a few hundred yards, soon curving away in front of an ornate black-and-white house to join a track and then a road, which leads back to Pont-y-pant station.

An ancient trackway across high moorland, with panoramic views of the Snowdonia peaks, is the way to the secluded valley of Wybrnant. The return route passes through the sylvan gorge of the Afon Lledr. Encroachment of forestry on to rights of way in the early stages of this walk makes precise navigation necessary.

POINTS OF INTEREST

① This farm may have been a *hafod*, or summer dwelling, where shepherds lived when their flocks were grazing. The same practice of alternating between uplands and lowlands according to the season still takes place in Switzerland.

② The track followed over the moor on this walk is typical of what would have been the normal lines of communication between valleys before motorised transport.

③ A short diversion to the right from Pwll-y-gâth leads to the birthplace of William Morgan, Ty-Mawr, now restored as a museum. Morgan, who became Bishop of St Asaph, translated the Bible into Welsh in 1588 – 23 years before the English Authorised Version, which was the work of 54 translators.

④ There are otters still living on the Lledr, and dippers may be seen foraging among the boulders.

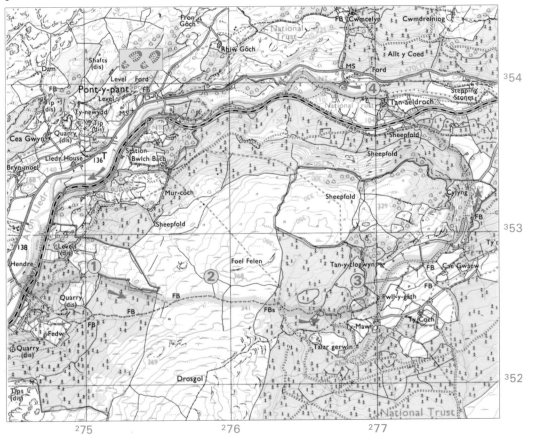

TOUR 32 · *Peak Miniatures* DERBYSHIRE

Winding through the south-eastern corner of the Peak District National Park, this tour visits a great diversity of places: stone-built cottages and rocky valleys, relics of early industry, grand houses and great churches.

The Heights of Abraham — landscaped woodlands above Matlock Bath — can be reached by a cable car ride over the steep-sided Derwent Valley

ROUTE DIRECTIONS
The drive starts from Matlock ①.

From Matlock, follow the signs Derby to leave the town by the A6, winding through a limestone gorge to the neighbouring spa village of Matlock Bath ②.

Continue along the A6 to Cromford ③.

In the village turn right on to the A5012, signed Newhaven, then turn right again for a long, winding climb through woodland on the Via Gellia valley road. After 4 miles reach crossroads and turn right on to the B5056, signed Bakewell. Continue across open countryside for 1¾ miles, then turn right on to an unclassified road signed Winster. Descend steeply into Winster ④.

Leave Winster by the Bakewell Road, then ½ mile farther turn right and rejoin the B5056. Follow an undulating course for 2¾ miles, then cross a river bridge and turn right. Almost a mile farther on turn left on to the A6, signed Buxton, and shortly pass the car park for Haddon Hall ⑤.

Continue along the A6 to Bakewell ⑥.

Leave Bakewell by King Street, signed Monyash B5055. In almost ¾ mile turn left on to an unclassified road signed Youlgreave. At the next T-junction turn right and continue over higher ground for 1¾ miles before descending a 1-in-5 slope to cross the River Lathkill. Beyond the bridge take the next turning left to reach Youlgreave ⑦.

At the church turn right (no sign), and in ¾ mile bear right signed Newhaven. After another ½ mile keep left, and in 2¾ miles pass on the left a turning into a picnic site. At the next T-junction turn right on to the A5012, then shortly turn left to join the A515, signed Ashbourne.

Pass the Newhaven Hotel and after 6 miles, at crossroads, turn left on to an unclassified road signed Tissington. Drive through parkland to Tissington ⑧.

Return through the parkland, then turn left on to the A515 Ashbourne road and continue to Fenny Bentley. Continue past the village for ½ mile, then turn left on to the B5056, signed Bakewell. After 2¾ miles turn right on to an unclassified road signed Bradbourne. At the post office in Bradbourne village turn right signed Carsington, and follow a pleasant byroad, narrow in places, for about 1¾ miles, then turn left on to the B5035 Wirksworth road. After another 1¾ miles drive alongside the northern extremity of the new Carsington Reservoir. Stay on the B5035 for a further 1¼ miles, then turn right signed Wirksworth (unclassified; light traffic only). Descend into Wirksworth ⑨.

In the town centre turn left, then immediately right, with the B5035, signed Crich. Ascend on to higher ground, then follow a long descent into the Derwent Valley with views across to Crich Stand, 940ft. At the foot of the descent turn right on to the A6, then cross the River Derwent and immediately go forward with the B3035, still signed Crich. At Crich turn left at the village cross (unclassified) and follow signs to the Crich Tramway Museum ⑩.

Continue with the unclassified road to Holloway and turn right into Church Street, signed Riber. In ¾ mile go over crossroads into Riber Road. Follow that byroad for 1½ miles, meet a T-junction and turn left, then ¼ mile later keep left and pass on the right the turning to Riber Castle Wildlife Park ⑪.

Descend steeply through hairpin bends, and at the foot of the slope turn right. Later turn left on to the A615 for Matlock.

POINTS OF INTEREST

① Matlock is in fact a collective name for a loose gathering of individual settlements that were welded together into a single spa resort in the 18th century.

② There's lots happening in Matlock Bath in and around the Pavilion by the Derwent, including the Peak District Mining Museum. The impressive Heights of Abraham can be ascended by cable car.

③ Cromford was where Richard Arkwright built the first successful water-powered cotton mill in 1771. Two of his houses are also here.

④ Winster has a charming 16th-century market hall and a number of 18th-century buildings. Lots of little alleyways, or 'ginnels', run off Main Street and up the cliffs.

⑤ Magnificent Haddon Hall is noted in particular for its chapel, its long gallery and its great chamber. The terraced rose gardens are also delightful.

⑥ Bakewell is famous for the dessert sweet known as Bakewell Pudding, which can still be bought in the town. Bakewell is full of good old buildings, many dating from around 1700.

⑦ A charming, extended linear village, Youlgreave's church has a splendid Perpendicular tower and there are some rather grand Georgian houses nearby.

⑧ Tissington is considered to be the most beautiful village in the National Park and has everything except an inn. The Norman church faces a splendid Jacobean manor house.

⑨ Once a great lead town, Wirksworth has been reborn as an important tourist centre. Its splendid church is in a charming circular mini-close and has the Peak's earliest Christian monument, a coffin lid dating from the late 7th century.

⑩ The Museum is sited in an old limestone quarry and visitors are carried in trams past Edwardian street advertisements and out along a ridge which affords superb views.

⑪ The Park is a Rare Breeds Survival Trust Centre where colonies of European lynx live and other endangered species breed in natural surroundings.

The crag of High Tor rises nearly 400ft above the River Derwent and there are magnificent views from its summit. Across the gorge are the Heights of Abraham

Arkwright's Masson Mill stands beside the A6

Snowy owl — one of the inmates at Riber Castle

ROUTE DIRECTIONS

Allow up to 3 hours
Start from the National Park Blore Pastures car park and picnic site (grid ref. SK136497).

Walk north from the car park and descend via stiles through pasture to an unenclosed but metalled road. Here turn right to continue downhill to a cattle grid. Cross this, then walk over Ilam Bridge into Ilam①.

From the bridge go straight ahead into the village, meeting a drive to Ilam Hall. Follow this, then very shortly and before the gates fork left on to the Dove House drive. At the gates to Dove House turn left to follow a field-edge track to the church②.

The route can continue by descending steps to join the Paradise Walk near St Bertram's Bridge – or by crossing the terraced gardens, passing the tea rooms and slanting down towards the river on a wooded path which skirts a stone grotto. Either way, the Paradise Walk is joined and followed upstream through the Manifold meadows and past the Battle Cross (read the plaque) to a footbridge③.

Either cross the footbridge and make the energetic climb direct from here to Musden Grange, or continue along the river to River Lodge to cross a private garden to the road.

Once on the road, continue alongside the river to Rushley Bridge. Cross this and ascend the track through Rushley Farm, bearing left to Musden Grange.

Keep right of the grange buildings then, where the track switches right, slant left by an ascending wall. Go through a hedge gap above a small, tree-filled enclosure and ascend diagonally to a fork.

Keep left here and continue to climb diagonally and reach a gate with scrub on the left. Cross a stile here and walk uphill to a stile into the yard of Upper Musden farmstead④.

Cross the stile left of the barn, then immediately cross another adjacent to it. Descend pasture along an old and sparse hedge-line to a gate and horse jump, then climb via gates along an obvious bridleway above Hinkley Wood⑤.

On reaching a minor road turn left and proceed for about 150yds to a gate and stile. Cross the stile and descend ridge-and-furrow pasture for the return to the car park.

The beautiful scenery of the Manifold Valley is the backdrop to this walk. First descending to the river and the well-known Victorian village of Ilam, the route then crosses the parkland of Ilam Hall and follows the river for some distance before climbing to return over the hillside.

POINTS OF INTEREST

① One of only two villages in the narrow Manifold Valley, Ilam was 'moved' in the 19th century as part of the grand design of shipping magnate Jesse Watts-Russell when he had Ilam Hall rebuilt. The re-sited village has a school, a hall and a collection of tile-hung, bargeboarded cottages.

② An ancient building with a distinctive saddleback tower, Ilam church was heavily restored in the mid-19th century. It has kept two fine chapels, as well as two Saxon churchyard crosses. Nearby Ilam Hall, rebuilt in Tudor Gothic style in the 1820s, was rescued from demolition in 1934 and given to the National Trust. The hall itself is leased by the Youth Hostels Association and is not open to the public, but its 84 acres of lovely parkland are managed as a country park and is open all year.

③ During dry weather, the River Manifold sinks into its limestone bed several miles upstream at Wettonmill, to reappear just across the meadow from Paradise Walk at

The River Manifold to the south of Ilam

the Boil Hole (no public access). Its tributary, the Hamps, whose name means 'summer-dry', does the same trick, disappearing underground at Waterfall.

④ Now derelict, Upper Musden has suffered the fate of many farms that cannot be reached by road. However, note the solid construction of the buildings, the tree-shelter belt and the circular mere – all vital elements for such an exposed farmstead.

⑤ Hinkley Wood is a Site of Special Scientific Interest. Its tree species include the small-leaved lime, often found on limestone cliffs but not very common elsewhere in the wild.

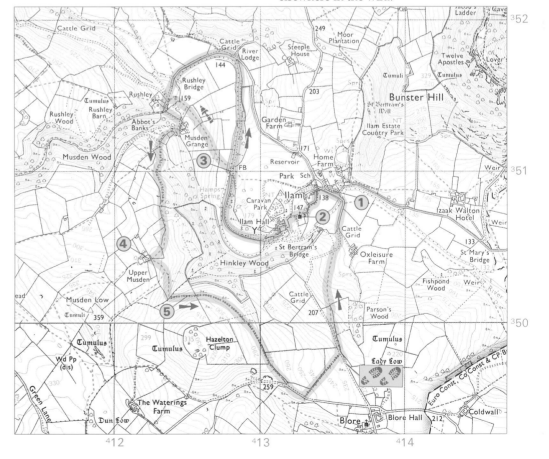

ROUTE DIRECTIONS

*Allow at least 3½ hours
Start from the National Park car park in Alstonefield (grid ref. SK131556).*

Turn right out of the car park, then after a very short distance right again into a road signposted 'Wetton' ①.

Continue forward to a T-junction and turn left – then almost immediately left again past cottages into a green lane. Follow this to a sharp right-hand bend, where the route continues straight on downhill beside a wall to the right. Bear right with the wall and descend very steeply to cross a minor road in Hopedale, then continue up the other side along a green lane to Stanshope.

On reaching the road in Stanshope turn left past the farm and immediately left again – also past the farm – on a rough track. A little way along find on the right a signpost indicating Dovedale. Follow the path into Hall Dale via a series of easily seen stiles, then follow Hall Dale itself to the River Dove. At the river turn right through a wall 'squeeze' stile and follow the bank to a footbridge below Pickering Tor and Ilam Rock ②.

Cross the Dove footbridge and turn left to Dove Holes ③.

A choice of route can be made here – along an even path directly to Milldale, or by a more arduous route to the same destination up Nabs Dale. This dry valley is entered by branching right at Dove Holes and making a stiff climb through rocky woodland to a stile at the edge of a field. Cross this and walk straight ahead to a double finger-post waymark. Facing the post, turn left and cross a stile opposite the farmhouse. Skirt Hanson Grange Dairy Farm to join the farm-access track, and turn right to follow the track to a four-way fingerpost. From here leave the track by following the Milldale sign to the left and descend via stiles to the viewpoint of Hanson Toot. From here the path zigzags down to cross the bridge, then leaves the valley along Millway Lane – which is signposted on the shop as the way 'to the Chapel in the valley'. Actually, it goes all the way to Alstonefield church ④.

From here the green, the George Inn and the car park are easily found.

With a bit of effort a far more balanced view of Dovedale and its attendant valleys can be enjoyed by approaching it from Alstonefield rather than by the usual routes from Thorpe or Ilam.

POINTS OF INTEREST

① Standing at 900ft between the Dove and the Manifold, Alstonefield is a charmingly unspoiled village. Several of its mullioned-windowed houses form a delightful group with The George around the village green, between which and the church is the Hall – formerly the Rectory – of 1587. Behind this is a tithe barn, featuring an internal wall of wattle and daub and a spiral stone staircase.

② Hall Dale narrows into a deep, wild gorge with limestone terraces and buttresses towering either side of a steep path – often scattered with scree – that plunges through woodland to join Dovedale. The main dale is guarded by the huge pinnacle of Pickering Tor and the spire of Ilam Rock.

③ Dove Holes, the last vestiges of an enormous cave system eroded by glacial melt waters, attracts visitors in thousands. The caves mark the junction of Dovedale and Milldale.

④ There has been a church at Alstonefield since at least 892, but the present building dates from around 1100, with a mixture of Norman, Decorated and Perpendicular styles and a profusion of 17th-century woodwork. The elaborate grey-green pew belonged to the Cottons of Beresford Hall – birthplace of Izaak Walton's friend Charles Cotton, who wrote the second part of *The Compleat Angler.*

The River Dove from Dove Holes, a cave system inhabited by man at the end of the glacial age

ROUTE DIRECTIONS

Allow at least 3½ hours
Start from the National Park car park in Wetton (grid ref. SK109552).

Head a short way south to the nearby road junction, turn right, then meet a second junction and turn left along a green lane signposted 'concessionary path to Thor's Cave'. Follow this to a stile and gate, cross the stile, then follow a sign right to another stile. Keep close to the upper wall, descending briefly before ascending to a fence stile, from which an often slippery path runs to the cave①.

Descend from the cave, initially with promising-looking steps but subsequently down a steep scramble to the valley floor. At the bottom go straight ahead to the footbridge over the Manifold.

From the footbridge cross the Manifold Track and climb the slope opposite through Ladyside Wood, with views of the Thor's Cave outcrop behind②.

Reach a field edge, cross to the wood edge on the left and re-enter the wood by a ladder stile. Continue for a fair distance along a level though rocky path to another stile by a stone trough. Cross this, slant left up pasture to a hedge stile and cross a tiny rivulet before crossing a gate and stile into a short lane. Turn right here and continue to Grindon③.

Cross the green in front of the church and meet a road opposite a skimpy modern mere and a new picnic site. Turn right down the road, then before Ossom's Hill Farm branch left over a stile by a gate and descend through fields into the Hoo Valley via stiles and gates.

Cross a footbridge and follow the stream down the valley (beware of bulls), by means of further stiles and gates, to Wettonmill Camping Site. Meet the road by a ford, go left and cross Wettonmill Bridge, then turn right to Wettonmill yard④.

A gate beyond and behind the millhouse gives access to a ridge that must be crossed to reach a bridlegate half obscured by vegetation. Follow the path from this gate into a broad valley and ascend gently to a gate and stile by Ecton Manor House.

Go right opposite the house, cross the stream and then ascend alongside a wall before following a line of stiles over the shoulder of Wetton Hill and on to a lane leading into Wetton village⑤.

This is a long and in places energetic walk, with areas that can be slippery and potentially tricky in wet weather. However, given these cautions, it is one that will be remembered for the great gap of Thor's Cave, yawning out over the thickly wooded Manifold Valley. Particular care must be taken on the path to the cave, and the ensuing descent to the valley bottom.

POINTS OF INTEREST

①Set in a lofty limestone cliff high above the Manifold, Thor's Cave offers marvellous views over the woodlands of the valley below. Some walkers climb to the top of the crag above the cave for even better views, *but the ascent is tricky and could prove very dangerous in wet weather.*

②Running for 8 miles from Hulme End to Waterhouses, the Manifold Track was, from 1904 to 1934, part of the Manifold Valley Light Railway. The track bed was

Thor's Cave in the great crag above the Manifold

later surfaced by the county council to make a pleasant path beside the river.

③Topped by a prominent spire, Grindon church stands beside the wide village green. A memorial inside commemorates six RAF men who died, with two press photographers, in a plane crash near here in the severe winter of 1947. They had been parachuting food supplies to the people of Grindon and neighbouring villages which were cut off by the blizzards.

④Wettonmill is known as the place where the Manifold disappears underground in dry summer weather. The Wettonmill swallow-holes, known locally as 'swallets' or 'shack-holes', are unfortunately on private land, though others can be seen from the Wetton road about ¼ mile downstream. Experiments have shown that the water in the underground stream takes up to a day to re-emerge in the grounds of Ilam Hall, only about 4 miles away (see Walk 32A).

⑤Like Grindon, Wetton sits high above the Manifold Valley, too narrow to accommodate settlements of any size. The graves in Wetton churchyard include that of Samuel Carrington, a village teacher who discovered and excavated several local archaeological sites.

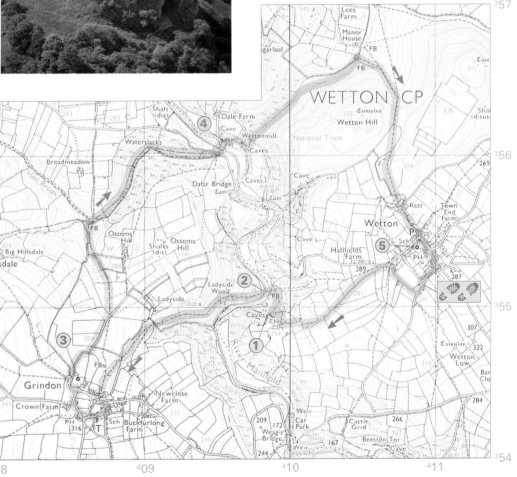

WALK 32D · The High Peak Trail DERBYSHIRE

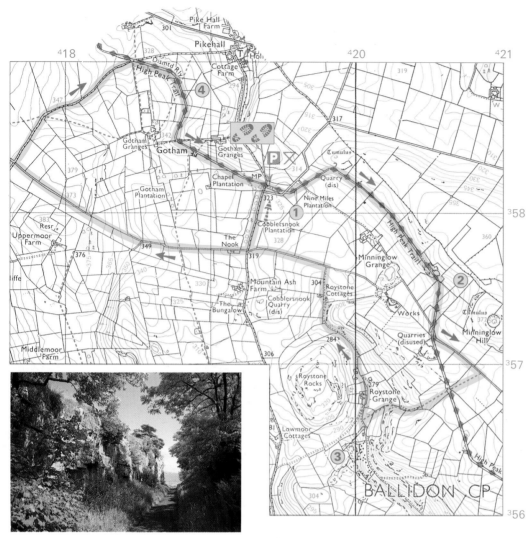

A cutting on the Trail near Minninglow Hill

After the closure in 1967 of two railways that crossed the heart of the White Peak, the Peak Park Board realised the recreational potential of the disused track beds and turned them into long-distance trails for walkers, horse-riders and cyclists. About half of this walk follows a section of one of them, the High Peak Trail. The remaining half is along farm tracks and paths, following part of the Roystone Grange Archaeological Trail.

POINTS OF INTEREST

① Opened in 1830–31, the Cromford and High Peak Railway was the first to link east with west across the Pennines – from Cromford to Whaley Bridge. Although it enabled coal, stone and other minerals to be transported much more easily in a remote area, the line was not a great financial success. Now the old track bed has found a new use, and the 17-mile High Peak Trail is immensely popular.

② Relics of past industry survive along the course of the old railway. There are numerous quarries as well as workings to extract silica sand, and brickworks where this was used. Just past Minninglow Hill is the stone beehive shape of an old lime kiln. Much earlier settlers knew Minninglow Hill: this prominent landmark is crowned by a large neolithic burial mound, dating from about 2,000BC.

③ A left turn along the track offers a short detour to see the remains of a medieval farmstead – the predecessor of 18th-century Roystone Grange, just to the north. The ruined buildings were owned by a Cistercian abbey in Leicestershire, and include a dairy that has been excavated. Evidence of even earlier farming can be seen on the hillside nearby, where a Roman field system has been discovered.

④ In its day the Gotham Curve, which turns through 80 degrees, was the tightest bend on any railway in Britain. Only short-wheelbase locomotives and rolling stock could use it.

ROUTE DIRECTIONS

Allow 2½ hours
Start from Minninglow car park near Pikehall, by a railway bridge over which the Cromford and High Peak line once ran (grid ref. SK195582).

Begin by walking to the farthest end of the car park from the entrance and follow 'Roystone Grange Trail' signposts①.

Follow the track bed round towards a large stone railway embankment below Minninglow Hill, passing quarry workings on the left and Minninglow Grange to the right②.

After the lime kiln meet a gate bearing a yellow waymark superimposed by a black 'R', blocking the track bed next to a National Park signpost. Cross this and note on the left another gate, also with a yellow mark bearing a black 'R'. This is the way the walk continues (the inviting gate and track diagonally opposite on the right should be ignored).

Turn left to cross the waymarked gate and a wall stile into Gallowlow Lane. Ascend past two fields on the right, and at the third follow waymarks to the Trail Bridge.

On emerging from the Trail Bridge continue downhill through pasture to an end wall near the field's bottom left corner. Cross this by a stile and follow the wall on the left through fields and over stiles to a farm track③.

The main route is continued by turning right where the cross-country path meets the farm track, and runs through the farmyard of the present Roystone Grange.

Continue through gates, past Roystone Cottages, then meet Minninglow Lane and turn left.

Continue to Cobblersnook crossways, where a choice of routes may be made. By turning right alongside Cobblersnook Plantation the metalled lane may be followed back to the car park.

A longer alternative is straight ahead at the crossways to follow Cobblersnook Lane past The Nook cottage and up on to Upper Moor. In just under ½ mile keep right at a fork in the lane and later continue straight on to the lane at the intersection of two ancient packhorse ways.

Turn right and follow Green Lane to rejoin the High Peak Trail after less than a mile.

The walk is concluded by following the track bed to the right round the Gotham Curve and back to the start④.

WALK 32E · Valley of the Upper Dove DERBYSHIRE

ROUTE DIRECTIONS

Allow up to 3 hours
Start from the picturesque market
square in Hartington (grid ref.
SK128604) ①.

Head north along Dig Street,
which becomes a gated road
that is followed all the way to a
group of farm buildings on the
right – the hamlet of Pilsbury ②.

Just beyond Pilsbury farmstead
a track leading on from where
the real road hairpins back on
itself leads past an open-sided
barn on the left to the earthworks
of Pilsbury Castle ③.

Return along the track to the
road, and just beyond the
Pilsbury farmhouse turn right and
descend along a pasture edge to
a footbridge over the Dove.
Cross this and turn immediately
right to climb a track for a short
distance ④.

On the left of the track, just a
little way up from the river and
opposite a fixed gate, is a stile.
Cross this and ascend diagonally
to another stile that can be seen
in the distance. Cross this,
continue uphill to a wall and
follow this along the side of the
hill and cross another stile.

Keep left to the first gateway,
cross a stile near a barn in trees
and cross another stile on to the
Sheen road. Turn left along the
road, and at a corner enter
Harris Close farmyard, on the
left.

The footpath is marked by a
sign on the right-hand corner of
the farm building farthest to the
right. Between this and a stone
wall is an unlikely-looking gap
that is the path entrance.

Continue along the downhill
side of a curiously banked wall,
crossing two gates and two stiles
before descending through
pasture to another stile.

After a while follow the edge
path through the uphill fringes of
a conifer plantation – watching
out for slippery roots in wet
weather – and on leaving the
plantation slant gradually down
the scarp bank through
hawthorn scrub to the Sheen
bridleway. Cross this track to a
stile and gate.

Cross the stile, the subsequent
meadow and a footbridge over
the Dove. Continue over more
stiles to the car park of J M
Nuttall's milk-processing
factory ⑤.

Turn left along the access road
to reach the market square in
Hartington.

While south of Hartington the banks of
the River Dove are being trodden into
mud by visitors flocking into Beresford
Dale, the wider valley to the north is
comparatively unfrequented, even though
the walking is good.

POINTS OF INTEREST

① Though today Hartington is usually
referred to as a village, the little market
place is one of several clues to its former
status: it received its charter as a market
town in 1204. The battlemented medieval
church was once the centre of a very large
parish, and the manor house, Hartington
Hall – now a Youth Hostel – was built in
1611.

② About half-way to Pilsbury, on the right
at the third gate, is a cave-like entrance.
This is an adit, tunnelled to drain lead-
mine shafts near by.

③ The hill on which Pilsbury Castle stands
is a fine strategic position commanding the
Upper Dove, but it is not known for certain
who built the fortifications here. Evidence
suggests that a Norman motte-and-bailey
castle was built on a Saxon site.

④ Crossing the footbridge takes the walker
from Derbyshire into Staffordshire, and
from carboniferous limestone to the coarser
gritstone evident on Sheen Hill.

⑤ Hartington's cheese factory is the only
one left in Derbyshire. It is known for its
Stilton, which can be bought from a dairy
shop near the village mere.

The road to Pilsbury, near Hartington

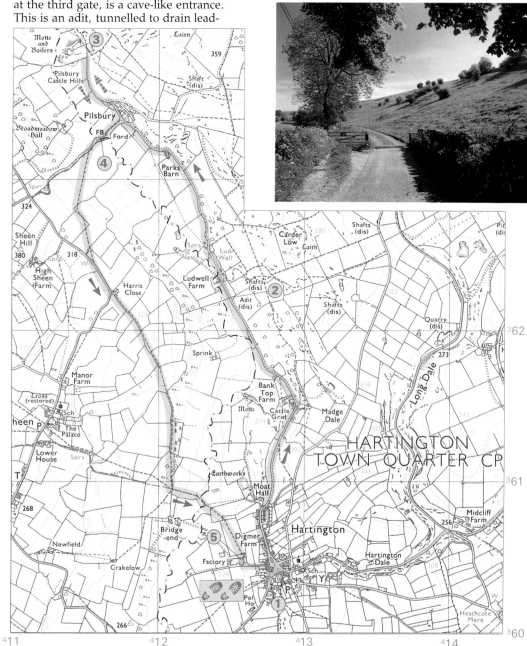

WALK 32F · Stanton Moor   DERBYSHIRE

Stanton Moor's Nine Ladies – a stone circle

Moorland walks always exert a particular fascination, but when the moor is remote and rich in the relics of prehistoric peoples its air of mystery becomes intensified. That is certainly the case on Stanton Moor, an isolated gritstone 'island' known for its quality building stone and revered in the Bronze Age as a magical place.

POINTS OF INTEREST

①Just to the right of the track junction beyond the Cork Stone is a burial mound whose size and form are still evident, despite the ravages of time and clumsy excavation. In its central cist, cremation remains of a dozen interments, with food and personal tokens, were found.

②Along this stretch of the walk are several Bronze Age features, including a sizeable ringwork to the left, just before a birch wood. In an enchanted setting within the wood is the Nine Ladies stone circle.

③Erected by the Thornhills of Stanton Hall in tribute to Earl Grey, who carried the Reform Bill through Parliament in 1832, the Reform Tower has no public access.

④Behind the pub lie Rowtor Rocks, which are well worth a visit. These curious formations include a 'rocking stone', which has a nearby farm named after it.

ROUTE DIRECTIONS

Allow 2 hours
Start opposite the west entrance to Ann Twyford's Birchover Quarry, on the Stanton in Peak-to-Birchover road, where suitable car parking can be found (grid ref. SK241624).

Facing the quarry entrance, turn left and walk along the road for about 400yds towards Stanton in Peak, then cross the road to the old New Park Quarry access track, between the posts of which is a large boulder. Follow the track to a stile and gate, cross, and ascend to the Cork Stone. Continue to the next track junction and turn left①.

Continue north (left) along the track, flanked each side by heather moor②.

Prehistoric cairns can be found scattered over Stanton Moor

After about 50yds turn right and follow a track to a stile. Cross this on to a path passing beneath the Reform Tower③.

Further on, the edge path meets the Cat Stone, which crudely resembles a feline profile. After the Cat Stone continue on the edge path to leave this spur and forge south, with views to the left over Darley Dale and the ugly fluorspar works around the former Millclose Mine. Follow close to a fence – passing deep (and dangerous) heather-covered quarry workings – to reach a minor road. At the road turn right, and at the next road junction either turn right again to the starting point or turn left and descend Birchover village street to The Druid pub④.

The return from there is by a path which dips down and then climbs east between Dungeon Plantation up on the left and old quarries down to the right.

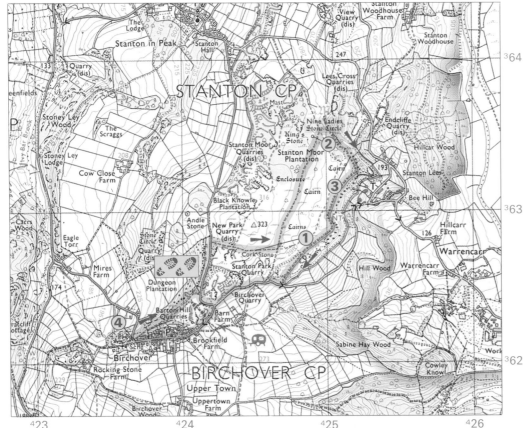

ROUTE DIRECTIONS
The drive starts from Bakewell①.

Leave Bakewell on the A6, signed Matlock, and in nearly 2 miles reach the entrance to the mansion of Haddon Hall②.

Continue to Rowsley③.

The valley of the River Wye is thickly wooded and a haven for wildlife. The combination of trees, clear water and weathered stone attracted the Dukes of Rutland and Devonshire to build great houses here.

complete an example of the neo-classical style as Haddon is of the medieval.

⑥A good 18th-century bridge spans the River Derwent at Calver which is overlooked by an austerely handsome Georgian cotton mill which was Colditz Castle in the TV series *Colditz*.

Pass The Peacock Inn and turn left on to the B6012, signed Baslow. Pass the edge of Beeley④.

Cross the River Derwent and enter the park of Chatsworth House⑤.

Leave Chatsworth Park and continue to Baslow. Leave by the A623, signed Stockport and Manchester. Follow the Derwent Valley to Calver⑥.

Meet traffic lights and turn left on to the B6001, signed Bakewell. Continue to Hassop, about 2 miles, and there branch right on to an unclassified road signed Great Longstone. On reaching that village meet a T-junction and turn right, then continue through Little Longstone to reach the Monsal Head Hotel. Here turn right on to the B6465 Wardlow road, passing on the left a point which affords magnificent views of the great, horseshoe curve of Monsal Dale. Continue to Wardlow, and beyond that village turn left on to the A623, signed Stockport. In 1½ miles turn left again on to the B6049 and pass through the village of Tideswell⑦.

Stay on the Buxton road and in 1 mile pass on the left the Tideswell

picnic area, then descend into Miller's Dale. Pass beneath a railway viaduct and turn right on to an unclassified road signed Wormhill, then climb steeply with good views of Chee Dale to the left. Beyond the hamlet of Wormhill bear left, signed Peak Dale, and after a mile note, on the left, the extensive limestone workings of Great Rocks Dale. Continue with the Buxton road and descend, then climb and after a mile keep left. After another mile turn left on to the A6 for Buxton⑧.

Leave Buxton by the A6 Matlock road, following a winding course through the attractively wooded gorge of the River Wye. Later, climb out of the valley to reach the outskirts of Taddington, at 1,139ft above sea level, one of the highest villages in England. After a short stretch of dual carriageway descend through wooded Taddington Dale, then 3 miles farther turn left on to an unclassified road signed Ashford village⑨.

Turn right through the village, and at the end turn right again, following Matlock signs. Re-cross the River Wye and turn left on to the A6 for the return to Bakewell.

POINTS OF INTEREST

①Bakewell is a market town well known for the dessert sweet known as Bakewell Pudding, said to have been accidentally developed by a cook in The Rutland Arms during the 19th century.

②Built by the Dukes of Rutland from the 12th to 17th centuries, Haddon Hall is everything a medieval manor house should be having escaped the classical facelifts given to many old buildings.

③Most of Rowsley's graceful houses are owned by the Duke of Rutland. The Peacock, built in 1652, as a private house, became an inn around 1828 and was described shortly after as 'the beau ideal of an English country hostelry'.

④Beeley is an estate village at the south end of Chatsworth Park, laid out by Paxton for the 6th Duke of Devonshire. Beside the inn a minor road climbs to heather-clad Beeley Moor, 1,200ft, where there are more than 30 prehistoric barrows and cairns.

⑤Known unofficially as The Palace of The Peak, Chatsworth is as

A lovely riverside path follows the Wye as it meanders through Miller's Dale and Monsal Dale — seen here from the viewpoint at Monsal Head

⑦The splendid cruciform church in Tideswell, often referred to as The Cathedral of the Peak, was built relatively quickly between 1300 and 1370, so, apart from the soaring Perpendicular tower, it is almost entirely in the Decorated style. The village itself is known for its well-dressing ceremonies.

⑧The attractive and park-filled spa resort of Buxton wears its lineage on its sleeve, for though it was known to the Romans and early royalty, its fine range of 18th- and 19th-century buildings leaves no doubt as to when it achieved its greatest popularity.

⑨Sheepwash Bridge in Ashford on the Water is the oldest, narrowest and most picturesque of several that span the River Wye. Among the many mills here, is one where the decorative limestone known as Ashford Black Marble used to be cut and polished. The village dresses six wells in an annual ceremony.

The cascades in the gardens of Chatsworth

Several public footpaths can be followed through Stand Wood which rises up behind Chatsworth House

Bakewell Pudding – a cook's mistake at The Rutland Arms

Sheepwash Bridge – the old packhorse crossing at Ashford in the Water

**This walk follows the topmost part of
Lathkill Dale, returning via Cales Dale
and then along farm tracks and lanes back
to Monyash.**

ROUTE DIRECTIONS

Allow at least 3 hours
*Start from a National Park car-
parking area in Monyash (grid
ref. SK150667).*

Head north along Chapel Street.
When the road descends to a
fork go right, then turn right
again to enter Bagshaw Dale
through a gate.

Continue along the valley floor
via stiles and gates to reach the
B5055 Bakewell road. Cross this
to a gate signposted 'Lathkill
Dale' and enter the shallow
upper dale. At a second stile the
dale narrows, marking the
beginning of the nature reserve.
Continue through the twisting
defile①.

Follow the dale down between
limestone cliffs to Lathkill Head
Cave②.

Continue to the junction with
Cales Dale, where the route
takes a footbridge to the right.
(Walkers who have arranged to
be met by transport are
encouraged to remain with the
Lathkill and follow its beautiful
course to Over Haddon or
Alport.)

The main route follows the
path up Cales Dale, climbing
through a breach in the
rockband via stiles to reach One
Ash Grange③.

Follow the farm access track
and pass Cales Farm to reach a
cattle grid at the Long Rake
road.

From here a detour can be
made to Arbor Low Stone Circle:
turn right and follow the road for
½ mile, then turn left up Upper
Oldhams Farm track④.

From the cattle grid go
diagonally left and across
pasture to a gate in the corner of
the field. Continue along a track,
dipping into an upper branch of
Cales Dale, then continuing left
beside a wall and through a
gateway to another gate into an
old way known as Derby Lane –
as confirmed by a stoop (stone
marker) to the right of the track
after the new gate.

Farther along, the lane has a
tarmac surface, then it meets
Milking Lane by the Manor
House at Rake End. Continue
along the street and go through
the churchyard⑤.

Turn left past The Hobbit to
return to the car park in
Monyash.

POINTS OF INTEREST

①The Derbyshire Dales National Nature
Reserve protects five of the White Peak's
best limestone dales, including Lathkill
Dale. The lower dale is noted mainly for its
woodlands, while the chief interest in these
upper reaches is the plant life.

②Lathkill Head Cave is so called because
in winter the River Lathkill rises here. In
summer, however, this huge cavity is
generally dry, with the river trickling from
a mine adit farther down.

③Originally a penitentiary for the monks
of Roche Abbey in Yorkshire, the attractive
buildings of One Ash Grange now include
a loft converted into a camping barn to
provide cheap, acceptable accommodation.

④The Peak District's largest henge
monument, Arbor Low consists of the
usual bank and ditch – but all 50 of its
stones are lying rather than standing.
Nonetheless, its spectacular setting makes
this fine monument well worth a visit.

⑤The spacious church at Monyash, like
that at Hartington, testifies to the village's
former days as an important market town.
There were several thriving industries here,
and Monyash had five natural meres for its
drinking water. The remote yet lovely
village still has a market twice a year, and
well-dressing takes place every May.

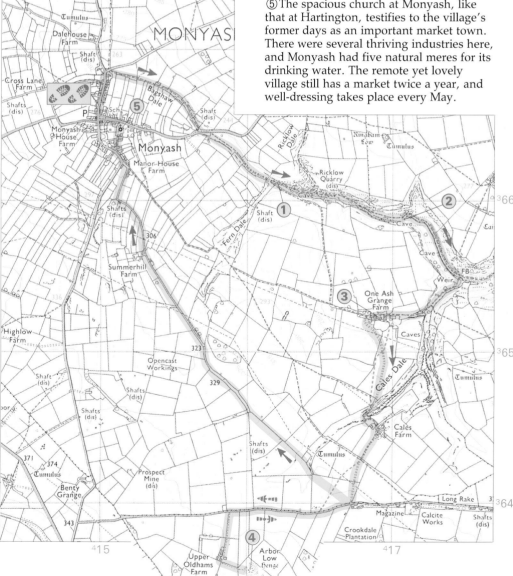

The Tissington Trail — a former railway route between Ashbourne and Parsley Hay

Delightfully named Parsley Hay is the meeting point of the two former railway lines that are now much-used trails through the White Peak. Here is a gentle circuit through the green landscapes of the plateau, setting out along the Tissington Trail then following a green lane to pick up the High Peak Trail for the return. The walking is easy and pleasant.

POINTS OF INTEREST

①In the second cutting along the Tissington Trail, fossil enthusiasts may wish to pause to search the limestone face and fallen debris for brachiopods, crinoids and corals.

②The embankment section of the track bed offers wide, open views across Long Dale westwards to the hill of Carder Low, rising to more than 1,100ft. The site of Hartington's former station, a mile north-east of the village, is now a picnic site and car park with public conveniences. The old signal box has been converted into an information centre. It still has its lever frames, and there are photographs of the railway as it used to look.

③Stone, beehive-type lime kilns, often built into the hillside, like this one, were used to burn limestone for use either in building or in farming, when it was applied to acid pasture to sweeten it.

④The green lane is an excellent example of what must once have been an important road that changing times have made redundant.

⑤At each portal of the Newhaven Tunnel are original Cromford and High Peak Railway Company plaques, dated 1825 – the year in which the building of the line was approved by Parliament. The northern of the two is the most elaborate, bearing the Latin motto *Divina Palladis Arte* and the names of principal engineer Josiah Jessop and company clerk William Brittlebank.

Fossil brachiopod shells — about one inch across — come in various shapes and patterns

ROUTE DIRECTIONS

Allow at least 1½ hours
Start from the Parsley Hay car park, picnic site and bicycle-hire centre (grid ref. SK147637).

Walk south for a short distance along the High Peak Trail, then fork right along another track bed to join the Tissington Trail and enter the impressive Parsley Hay railway cutting. Continue to the second cutting①.

Continue along a fine embankment section and, after Hartington Moor Farm, enter a third cutting before crossing the Hand Dale viaduct and entering the former Hartington Station yard②.

From the station yard go left along the approach road to join the B5054, and at that junction turn right to pass an abandoned lime kiln③.

Continue for a short way, cross the road and turn left on to a broad green lane heading away and uphill from the surfaced highway④.

Cross the busy A515 just 200yds short of the Jug and Glass pub and continue along the rough track to its intersection with the High Peak Trail.

Turn left along the track bed, pass through the thin band of Blakemoor Plantation and enter a cutting with a sharp bend — typical of this trail. Pass beneath the A515 through Newhaven Tunnel and return to the start⑤.

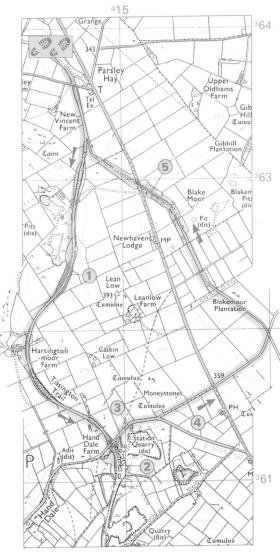

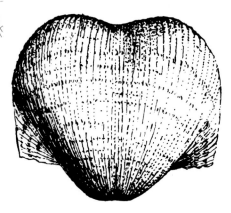

ROUTE DIRECTIONS

Allow 2 hours
Start from the telephone box in Hollinsclough (grid ref. SK066665). Parking is tricky, but space may be found along the road.

Walk north-west past a chapel building on the right and a wall post box on the left. After about 200yds, on an ascent, reach a bridlegate on the right. Cross this and descend diagonally, at first beside a wall, to a packhorse bridge over the rushing infant Dove beside a Severn-Trent Water Authority flow gauge①.

Cross the river and the gate at the end of the bridge, then slant diagonally up rough pasture on the downhill side of a wall to meet a recognisable track. Follow this left②.

Still climbing on the track, pass on the left a small collection of farm buildings known as Fough hamlet (pronounced Fuff), and continue to a cattle grid and sweeping right-hand curve that takes the route away from Booth Farm, down on the left.

Reach another cattle grid and branch right towards Stoop Farm, then just before the farm's tree-shelter belt climb diagonally left across pasture and above the farm buildings to reach another cattle grid and a track leading down to a gated road③.

Walk down the track to the unenclosed public road and turn right, passing through a gate and heading towards the access drive for Greensides Farm④.

Pass through a second gate and, staying with the road, pass on the left near a corner a sad and tree-shrouded dump that used to be Owl Hole. Descend via gates through the lovely riverless Dowel Dale⑤.

Continue through the amphitheatre, leaving by the pass, then, after crossing a cattle grid and a conduit containing the Dowel stream, branch acutely back along a track that leaves the road from the right and drops through stone gateposts topped by spheres.

Continue to a footbridge and ford on the River Dove, cross the bridge and continue alongside the river on a path that is grassy and indistinct at first, but which after a stile and gate becomes a metalled farm track. At the end of the track meet a minor road and turn right to pass the Frank Weldon Centre, thus completing the walk.

Starting from Hollinsclough, a pretty village only a couple of miles from the source of the Dove, this is a walk among grassy hills and below isolated, soaring limestone summits. The highlight is a splendid natural amphitheatre.

POINTS OF INTEREST

① The River Dove marks the county boundary for its entire length, so at the packhorse bridge the walk crosses from Staffordshire into Derbyshire.

② All along the rough road that climbs from the valley of the infant Dove there are superb views of the upper Dove Hills, dominated by Axe Edge. Rising to more than 1,800ft in the north west, this long gritstone escarpment is often snow-covered well into spring. The Dove and Manifold are among several rivers that rise on the Edge, whose open moorland contrasts sharply with the verdant, tree-filled valley below.

③ A prominent landmark to the south is the bristly, craggy crest of Chrome Hill. This is one of a succession of reef knolls – isolated peaks of a harder limestone than that of the surrounding country, so that they have weathered more slowly.

④ Opposite the track to Greensides, the roadside is pitted with curious hollows. These are the familiar 'swallets' or swallow-holes of limestone country. Surface water vanishes through these to enter an uncharted region of subterranean fissures, later to emerge as the Dowel stream.

⑤ Just above Dowall Hall is the Dowel Cave, where excavations have revealed Neolithic burials. Past the hall and a cattle grid, the Dowel – or Dove Well – gushes from a source to the right of the path and flows alongside the road through a natural amphitheatre of mini mountain peaks. At the far end is a dramatic pass between 1,417ft Chrome Hill on the right and the 1,221ft bulk of Parkhouse Hill on the left. This secret place would be worth any amount of walking to find.

Parkhouse Hill, visible to the left of the route in Dowel Dale

Plum Buttress, a steep limestone precipice, plunges into the greenery of the gorge below

Beautiful as it is, this memorable walk among woodlands, rock and tumbling water cannot be recommended to everybody. One section in particular includes stepping-stone ways through the river and rock-step clambers that can be very greasy in wet weather. However, the first part is easy, safe walking, and young or infirm walkers can complete this stretch before turning back.

POINTS OF INTEREST

①The Monsal Trail is one of the Peaks' well-known footpaths that have been made out of former railway tracks. This one runs between Buxton and Rowsley.

②This section, as far as the Chee Tor Tunnel, is flat, safe walking. After the first portal-like cutting is the dramatic peak of Plum Buttress on the right, with its wavy bedding planes of limestone.

At the river-crossing the Wye flows in a deep wooded gorge rich in plants and animals. Chee Tor is renowned for its 300ft cliff face, providing the Peaks' most challenging rock climbs.

③The path tunnels deep into the greenery of the gorge itself, with cliffs and crags looming on both sides of a cut not much wider than the river bed. Wormhill Springs is a strange area where water gushes with some force from a dozen places in the ground, and flows cold and clear across the ground into the river.

④The pasture between the river and the first wall features small stone enclosures, typical of the Peak District. They mainly date from the Enclosure Movement of the late 18th and early 19th centuries.

ROUTE DIRECTIONS
Allow up to 3 hours
Start from Wye Dale car park on the A6 opposite Topley Pike Quarry (grid ref. SK103724).

Follow a riverside track running downstream through woods. Just before the third viaduct, climb steps in the bank to the track bed of the Monsal Trail①.

At the top of the steps turn right. Pass through a cutting and alongside high crags, then cross the Wye. Continue through two short tunnels to the sealed Chee Tor Tunnel, under Chee Tor②.

It is suggested that young or infirm visitors turn back at the second short tunnel.

Before reaching the sealed entrance to Chee Tor Tunnel, leave the track bed along a permissive path to the right and cross a footbridge just before passing beneath a railway bridge. Descend to the water's edge, and continue over stones below the cliffs. After negotiating rough rock 'steps' above the river cross two small footbridges to skirt Wormhill Springs③.

After another rock step continue across a footbridge. Climb directly up the slope opposite until about halfway, then veer slightly right to a stone wall④.

Cross this and the following one at stiles, then continue alongside a wall to the right. As it turns right join a gated lane leading through Blackwell Hall farmyard.

Past the farmyard to reach a junction and bear round right, eventually passing a farm shop and camping site on the right. Just after the site reach the gated entrance of a green lane on a left bend. Follow the green lane to its end, then continue to a stile by a ruined barn. Cross this and head for a wall stile in the bottom-left corner of the pasture. Continue along the foot of the next field to another stile leading to rough ground a few paces from Plum Buttress.

Instead of crossing the stile above the precipice, slant left on a path which descends steeply to join the main path. Descend right to the main valley floor and cross a stile next to the old railway bridge to rejoin the trail. From here retrace steps upstream to the Wye Dale car park.

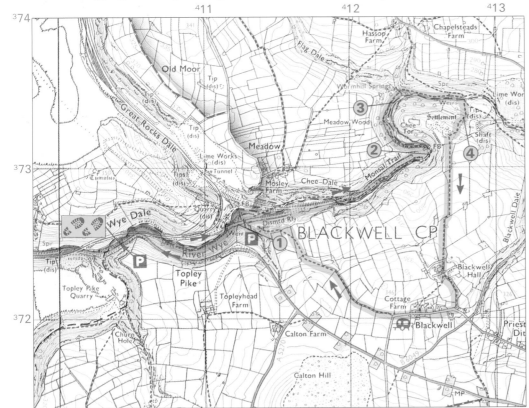

ROUTE DIRECTIONS

The drive starts from the huge industrial city of Sheffield ①.

Leave Sheffield along the A625 with Chapel-en-le-Frith signs, and climb through the western suburbs before reaching open countryside after 4 miles. After 2 miles farther keep forward, signed Castleton, to remain on the A625. Enter the Peak District National Park, shortly crossing into Derbyshire, and after another mile reach the Surprise View ②.

Descend into the Hope Valley and Hathersage ③.

Stay on the A625 to Hope ④.

Continue along the attractive valley to Castleton ⑤.

Follow the main road through the village and in almost ½ mile turn left on to an unclassified road signed Speedwell Cavern After a short distance pass the entrance to the Cavern ⑥.

Climb through the gorge of Winnats Pass and at the top turn right. In ¼ mile turn left to rejoin the A625 Chapel-en-le-Frith road.

Continue west on the A625, beneath Mam Tor ⑦.

Winnats Pass, a former coach road, is designated a Site of Special Scientific Interest

The Peak District's great scenic contrasts are appreciated on this drive: urban sprawl to a wild, open landscape, dark and mysterious caverns beneath lofty hilltops soaring above village and valley.

Pass a picnic site and an Edale turning on the right ⑧.

Continue towards Chapel-en-le-Frith.

After 3¾ miles turn left, signed Buxton, and join the A6. In nearly 1½ miles turn left again on to the A623, signed Chesterfield. Continue to Sparrowpit and at The Wanted Inn, turn right, and later pass through the straggling village of Peak Forest. After 5 miles pass on the right the B6465 turn to Wardlow, then in ¾ mile turn left on to an unclassified road signed Foolow. Shortly turn left again to reach Foolow ⑨.

Turn right in the village and continue to Eyam ⑩.

At Eyam turn right on to the B6521, signed Bakewell, and enter wooded Middleton Dale. Reach a junction with the A623 and turn left, signed Chesterfield, and continue to Stoney Middleton ⑪.

Continue to Calver. At the traffic lights turn left on to the B6001. Then turn right with the B6054, signed Sheffield via Frogatt Edge. Later cross the River Derwent, pass through attractive woodland and climb towards Totley Moor. The ascent affords spectacular views left along the Hope Valley, with the Frogatt and Curbar Edges to the right.

Near the summit pass on the left the entrance to Longshaw Country Park (National Trust) ⑫.

Branch right, signed Dronfield. Continue across open moor to a junction with the A621, and at the gyratory system take the Sheffield road. Enter the southern fringe of the city, passing through the suburb of Abbeydale before reaching the city centre.

POINTS OF INTEREST

① Sheffield has been famous as Britain's capital steel city for centuries. The City Museum has the best collection of silver and

plate but there are several other museums and art galleries here which repay a visit.

② At this point along the A625 the whole of the Hope Valley suddenly opens up, with the 2,000ft ridge of the Dark Peak's Kinder Scout in the distance.

③ Hathersage is a large village whose main tourist attraction is the so-called grave of Little John – Robin Hood's friend – which is in the churchyard.

④ Hope is the educational centre for the valley with its fine Hope Valley College. Of the original church, mentioned in the *Domesday* survey, only the Norman font remains. A century ago it was one of the largest parishes in the country.

⑤ Castleton is well-known both on the ground and below, for here are the famous caverns where the mineral Blue John was worked. The best known is the Blue John Mine, but the Speedwell and Treak Cliff are also worth a visit. Peak Cavern is one of the area's most spectacular limestone caves.

⑥ One of the great attractions of the Speedwell Cavern is a half-mile underground canal along which visitors can travel by boat to investigate an old working face.

⑦ To the north is Mam Tor – known as the Shivering Mountain because the limestone scree on its slopes is continually moving.

⑧ Civilisation ceases at Edale, for the road stops at the top of the village and the skyline is jagged with the highest, wildest hills of the mysterious Dark Peak. The Pennine Way starts at the Nag's Head.

⑨ Now a commuter village, Foolow was once a lead-mining centre and is unusual in being built compactly round a village green – something of an oddity in the Peak.

⑩ Eyam is a very typical mining and quarrying settlement with a fascinating history. There is an excellent exhibition in the church about the plague which struck Eyam in the 17th century.

⑪ Stoney Middleton is a pleasant village, especially around the Nook, a charming square where two wells are dressed in July and August. Close by is a rare octagonal church.

⑫ The Park comprises over 1,500 acres of open moorland and woodland, at the heart of which is the former shooting lodge of the Dukes of Rutland.

Peveril Castle, onetime hunting lodge

Only a small part of Peak Cavern is open to the public

Mam Tor, above Castleton, is now in the care of the National Trust. With the Winnats, it forms part of their 30,000-acre holding known as the High Peak Estate

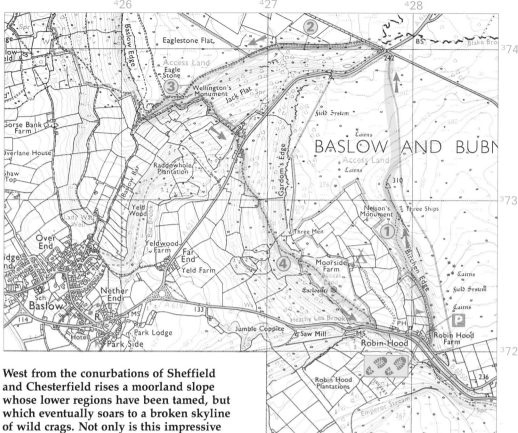

The skylark — whose glorious song is one of the delights of moorland walking — often flies too high in the sky to be seen

ROUTE DIRECTIONS

Allow 2½ hours
Start from the Birchen Edge car park just above the Robin Hood Inn (grid ref. SK281722).

Follow the B6050 left to a stile on the left, signposted Birchen Edge. Follow a clear path from the stile, through birchwood and boulders, to an outcrop beneath Nelson's Monument. Climb to the crest of Birchen Edge①.

Follow the Edge north, joining an evident path beyond the 1,017ft OS trig. pillar. Descend along the path, sometimes over wet moorland, to a ladder stile. Cross this on to a minor road and go left. Cross the A621 at crossroads and climb past the infant Bar Brook to a gate on the left, from which continue along a track known as the Chesterfield Road②.

Continue towards the Wellington Monument③.

As the track descends it becomes rougher near an old quarry at the end of Baslow Edge. Here veer sharp left and follow the wall round and down to a narrow passage, via stiles, and to an old packhorse footbridge over Bar Brook. Cross and climb to the A621. Cross the road, and round Cupola Cottage via two stiles, thereafter ascending a clear path beneath Gardom's Edge. At the third gap in the wall a diversion can be made to the left, climbing to the Three Men of Gardom viewpoint④.

The main route continues over the shoulder of the hill, crossing a Bronze Age ring enclosure. The walk now picks up the A619 Chesterfield road at a stile. Turn left here for the return to the car park.

West from the conurbations of Sheffield and Chesterfield rises a moorland slope whose lower regions have been tamed, but which eventually soars to a broken skyline of wild crags. Not only is this impressive feature very beautiful, but — particularly in this century — it provides abundant recreational opportunities to visitors from town and country alike.

POINTS OF INTEREST

①By Nelson's Monument, erected in 1810 by John Brightman of Baslow, stand three isolated boulders on which have been incised the names *Royal Soverin* (sic), *Reliance* and *Victory*. Known collectively as the Three Ships, they commemorate Nelson's successes at the Battles of the Nile and Trafalgar. There are several easy lines of ascent to the edge, but also huge slabs of rock popular with climbers.

②An interesting relic of bygone days along this old way is a stone marker, or stoop, which dates from when the track was the main horse road between Chesterfield and Baslow.

③The 10ft-high obelisk was raised in 1816 to the memory of the Duke of Wellington. Some 200yds north-west is the Eagle Stone — the name is a corruption of 'eccles' and may signify that it was a place of early Christian gatherings.

④Gardom's 'Three Men' are ancient cairns. The function of relics such as these is still an enigma, but they probably date from around 2000BC and had a ceremonial significance.

Rugged gritstone gives way to a softer, rolling limestone landscape at Baslow Edge

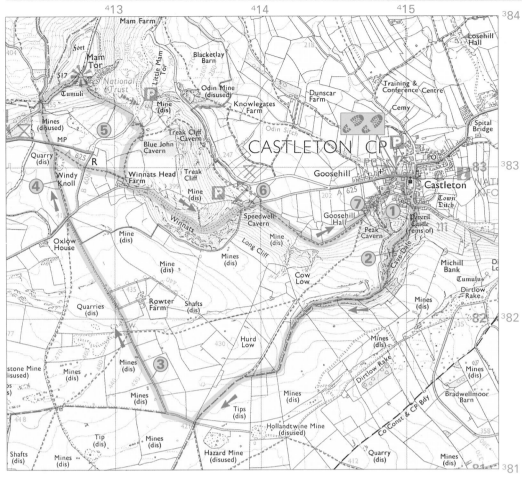

ROUTE DIRECTIONS

Allow 2½ hours
Start from Castleton's main car park (grid ref. SK149830).

From the car park's entrance go left into the village and turn right into Castle Street – where there is an information centre. Ahead is ruined Peveril Castle①.

Go left across the Market Square to the unobtrusive entrance of Cave Dale, which is to the right, off Bargate②.

The walk route continues along the dale and progresses through several metal gates. Cross a large pasture – passing a mere – and enter a small passage lane (note the sheep pens) to join Dirtlow Rake Lane. Turn right here, continue to where the lane widens and take the right-hand track along Rowter Lane③.

Continue beyond the Rowter Farm access on to a metalled surface, reach a cattle grid and cross the B6061 to climb Windy Knoll before descending to the right④.

A short, stiff climb from Windy Knoll leads to the summit of Mam Tor, **but care is required.** A stepped path which descends alongside the slippery scree to the Blue John Mine and Treak Cliff Cavern makes an interesting addition to the walk⑤.

Castleton is a Peakland resort of the best kind – offering plenty of scenic variety, both above and below ground. Many fascinating geophysical secrets are revealed by close study of limestone bluffs that are effectively great fossil reefs.

POINTS OF INTEREST

①Peveril Castle, begun in 1176 by Henry II, possibly on an Iron Age site, stands proudly on its still impressive natural bastion. It was named for William de Peveril, who acted for Henry as forest bailiff.

Landslips on Mam Tor have left the rock exposed

②Cave Dale's tiny entrance leads into a beautiful, secluded valley. Streams come and go along the dale – disappearing into the swallow holes typical of limestone country.

③From Bradwell to Eldon Hill the upland is streaked with lead veins which have been exploited since at least Roman times. More recently many of the spoil heaps have been re-worked for fluorspar.

④The limestone outcrop of Windy Knoll includes the Bone Cave, where excavations by Victorians uncovered the bones of bison, brown bear, reindeer and wolf.

⑤Known as the 'Shivering Mountain' because its layers of soft shale are constantly crumbling, Mam Tor is crowned by an Iron Age fort. The Blue John and Treak Cliff caverns feature spectacular stalagmites and stalactites.

⑥Speedwell Cavern is reached by a 104-step descent and a boat trip along an underground canal.

⑦Peak Cavern, below Peveril Castle, is so huge that it once sheltered cottages. Peakshole Water, a tributary of the Derwent, emerges from its mouth. Tours are available.

Blue John, a beautiful mineral once mined locally

This and the main walk meet at Winnats Head Farm. A minor road descends Winnats Pass from here to the Speedwell Mine⑥.

At Winnats go through a gate and keep right, following a track to reach Goosehill Bridge. Peak Cavern can be reached from the bridge along a narrow path running to the right⑦.

Cross the bridge and follow the path downstream alongside Peakshole Water.

WALK 34C · *Ladybower Reservoir*   DERBYSHIRE

Woodlands and water predominate on this walk in the Upper Derwent Valley, sometimes known as the Lake District of the Peak on account of its three big reservoirs: Howden, Derwent and Ladybower. Ridge-top vantage points offer splendid views of the reservoirs and the forestry plantations on their shores.

POINTS OF INTEREST

①Fairholmes is a good base for exploring the popular Upper Derwent Valley, being on a small promontory between the Derwent and Ladybower Reservoirs. The car park has an information centre and facilities for cycle hire.

②A detour to the right at the cross-tracks leads to the shores of the Derwent Reservoir at the foot of Ouzelden Clough. The Derwent was constructed between 1902 and 1916 – some 30 years before Ladybower Reservoir.

③From the ridge path along Open Hagg there are views west into the Woodlands Valley. Through it flows the River Ashop, a tributary of the Derwent that feeds Ladybower Reservoir. Upstream is the notorious Snake Pass, offering an exhilarating drive in fine weather but frequently closed by snow in winter. The valley is overlooked by the shadowy northern edges of Kinder Scout.

④The signpost is a relic from the days before the village of Derwent was drowned, after Ladybower Dam was built. The isolated community was one of two villages that were sacrificed in the project to provide drinking water for Derby,

The triple chain of Howden, Derwent and Ladybower Reservoirs, known as 'the Dams', have also been dubbed the Peak's Lake District

Nottingham, Leicester and Sheffield. Also lost were 17th-century Derwent Hall and Derwent's Parish Church of St John and St James.

⑤Bridge End is so called because it was here, before the reservoir was created, that the old road crossed the River Derwent. Ahead, on the skyline of Derwent Edge, are the Wheel Stones – sometimes known as the Coach and Horses, because in profile they are said to resemble a coach in mad flight across the moor.

⑥The woodlands beside the reservoir here are carpeted with bluebells in late spring. The ugly pipeline farther along relays water from the Derwent Dam to the Ladybower treatment works.

ROUTE DIRECTIONS

Allow 1½ hours
Start from the car park along a tarmac road above the reservoir picnic area (grid ref. SK173893) ①*.*

Cross the main approach road, adjacent to Locker Brook, and follow a signpost direction up into the Forest Walk on a concessionary footpath.
   Reach a 'leat' – which captures water from Upper Locker Brook for the Derwent Reservoir – and cross this by means of a stile and footbridge. Continue ahead along a zig-zag path, with larch-stake steps at the steeper parts, keeping right at the junction with an exclusive path for the Lockerbrook Centre.
   Continue through a broken wall and turn left to leave the plantation by a stile. Follow waymarks to a junction②.

The main route turns left at the cross-tracks. Go through a gate and climb to another cross-track junction at the ridge top. Go left here and walk along the edge of the Open Hagg Plantation③.

Continue along the high grass path to a stile and gate, where there is a signpost to Glossop and Derwent④.

Descend the bridleway into a plantation and emerge from the trees at a gate. Continue down the 'Old Road' track and descend to the reservoir road beside Bridge End car park⑤.

Go left and branch right along a concessionary path leading through the woodland between the reservoir and the road⑥.

When you pass the pipeline, angle gradually up to the Derwent Overlook car park, then continue on a path alongside the road, slanting right and returning to the Fairholmes car park.

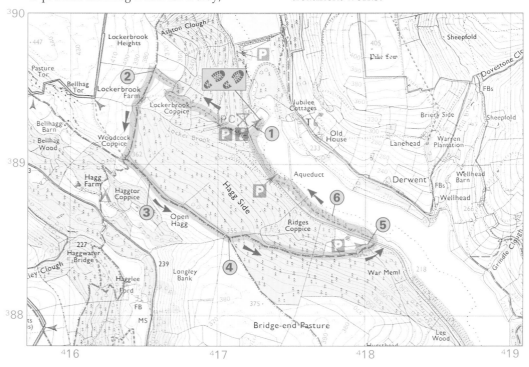

The gritstone of Over Owler Tor, weathered into strange shapes

ROUTE DIRECTIONS

Allow 1½ hours
Start from the Surprise View car park (grid ref. SK253802).

Cross a fence stile and climb a clear path through light birch woodland and gritstone boulders on to the Owler Tor edge. Continue through heather among gritstone blocks①.

Continue, noting the 'Smiling Tortoise' rock formation on the way to Mother Cap②.

Holding on to the ridge top through heather the walk eventually arrives at the gap of Winyards Nick, where the ridge is breached by an old hollow way that was used as a packhorse route③.

Identify a narrow but visible path to the right and descend it through heather, joining a more pronounced path just before a stream. Continue over close-cropped turf, dropping down to the A625 by the Toad's Mouth Rock. Go left, taking care while negotiating the sharp bend, and cross the road to a kissing gate signposted 'Padley via Padley Gorge'. Cross small cascades to a footbridge and follow the Burbage Brook downstream④.

The next right turn is marked by a simple plank footbridge, after which the walk climbs a deeply grooved packhorse route – known as the Hollow Gate – and returns to the start.

Travellers approaching Hathersage on the A625 from Fox House Inn for the first time never fail to be surprised by the sudden Derwent Dale panorama that greets them when they burst through a breach in the high Millstone Edge. The scenic thrill is enhanced for the walker who climbs to Over Owler Tor across country that is unlikely to be boggy, but has heather and boulders that demand the protection of stout shoes.

POINTS OF INTEREST

① The name 'Owler' Tor is derived from 'alder tree' and is nothing to do with owls.

Among the strange and varied gritstone shapes all around are millstones that were cut on site and then abandoned. The Millstone Grit from which they were fashioned is a coarse sandstone that forms the great edge which is crossed on the approach to Surprise View from Hathersage. In ancient times the stone was used for making corn-grinding querns, and more recently both this edge and nearby Lawrence Field were major sources of millstones. Many hundreds lie cut and forlorn in the woods below Surprise View.

② The path to Mother Cap is lined with many natural stone formations, and Mother Cap itself is a giant stack which – like the summit rocks of Over Owler Tor – survived the gruelling attentions of the Ice Age. Its name has obvious parallels with Mam Tor, since both mean 'Mother Hill' and both are associated with the sites of ancient settlements. When visibility is good Over Owler Tor is a superb viewpoint from which to appreciate the deep cut of Derwent Dale.

③ Long-distance transport relied heavily on packhorses, and their journeys across hill country well into the 19th century have left a legacy of trackways such as those on this walk.

④ This section of the route, by a babbling brook, is popular with picnickers and paddling children.

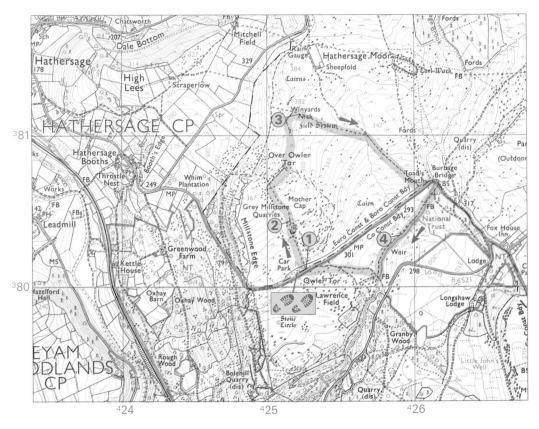

ROUTE DIRECTIONS

The drive starts from Scarborough ①.

Follow the signs North Bay then Whitby (A171) to leave on the A165. In 1 mile, at the roundabout, keep left and continue to Burniston. Here turn right on to the A171, signposted Whitby. At Cloughton bear left then pass through an afforested area before emerging on the desolate Fylingdales Moor. After 9½ miles turn right on to an unclassified road, signposted Fylingthorpe and Robin Hood's Bay. Descend a steep (1 in 4) hill with hairpin bends and fine views of the sea to reach the village of Fylingthorpe. Keep straight on to Robin Hood's Bay. The main thoroughfare is narrow and descends very steeply to the shore. From May to September there is restricted access for motor vehicles ②.

From the village follow the signs Whitby along the B1447 to reach Hawsker. Bear right, and at the end of the village turn right on to the A171. Just over ¼ mile farther turn right again on to an unclassified road, signed Whitby Abbey. There are good coastal views before reaching the cliff-top ruins of Whitby Abbey ③.

Return for ¼ mile and turn right (no sign). At the foot of the descent turn right and later cross the swing bridge into the town centre of Whitby ④.

Leave by the Teesside road, A171, and in 2 miles turn left on to the A169, signposted Pickering. Continue to Sleights. Beyond the village the road climbs on to Sleights Moor. Continue for 3 miles. Here a detour can be taken by turning right on to an unclassified road to Goathland ⑤.

Continue with the main drive, following an undulating road over bleak moorland ⑥.

Pass by the lonely Saltergate Inn then ascend. Pass, on the right, the natural amphitheatre known as the Hole of Horcum ⑦.

In 4 miles, at the Fox and Rabbit Inn, turn left on to an unclassified road, signposted Thornton Dale. Two miles father turn left, signed Low Dalby Forest Drive. Shortly join a Forestry Commission toll road. During periods of extremely dry weather the Forest Drive may be closed owing to the high fire risk. If you wish to avoid the toll road continue to the picturesque village of Thornton Dale ⑧.

Turn left on to the A170, signed Scarborough. The drive can be rejoined at Snainton. The main tour soon passes Low Dalby ⑨.

Turn left at the visitor centre and continue on the Forest Drive. This

The variety of the North York Moors National Park can be seen on this tour: the large resort of Scarborough and the small fishing village and port of Whitby; bleak moors, cool forests and picturesque villages.

A headland crowned with a ruined castle separates Scarborough's two popular sandy bays. South Bay is shown here

passes through beautiful woodland scenery in the Dalby Forest. After 5 miles, at a fire tower, turn left then in 2 miles leave the forest drive. In ¾ mile, at a T-junction, turn right, signposted Scarborough. Pass the Moorcock Inn at the hamlet of Langdale End, then in 1 mile turn sharp right signposted Troutsdale and Snainton. Proceed along an undulating and winding road through Troutsdale.

After 4 miles leave the valley, keeping left on the ascent. At Snainton turn left on to the A170, signposted Scarborough, and pass through Brompton ⑩.

Continue to West Ayton, then cross the River Derwent and turn left on to an unclassified road, signed Forge Valley. The road follows the river through the Forge Valley with thick wooded slopes on either side.

In 1¾ miles turn right, signed Lady Edith's Drive. A short detour can be made by keeping forward at this junction for a nearby picnic site and viewpoint. Continue with the main drive along a pleasant byroad through the Raincliffe Woods. Two miles farther pass a pond on the right, then in another mile, at a T-junction, turn right (A171), to re-enter Scarborough.

POINTS OF INTEREST

① Described by the Victorians as the 'Queen of Watering Places', Scarborough is England's oldest holiday resort and has something for everyone. It has the Victorians to thank for the magnificent Spa complex, the railway, the promenade, many of the shops, hotels and theatres, and the landscaped gardens.

② There is no hard evidence to link Robin Hood with this quaint seaside village, although the Bay does have a rich heritage of legends. It has fine beaches with rocky outcrops and at high tide the sea runs up the village street.

③ First founded almost 13 centuries ago, most of the present ruins of St Hilda's Abbey are in the Early English style and date from the 13th century. Beside the abbey is the unusual parish church of St Mary. From here 199 steps lead down to the town.

④ Red roofed houses separated by narrow streets cover the steep valley sides on both banks of the River Esk at Whitby. The harbour still shelters a variety of boats, a reminder of the town's long seafaring past.

⑤ Goathland is one of the most picturesque villages in the North York Moors, with superb stone houses, excellent hotels and interesting shops. It also has a station for the North York Moors Railway.

⑥ To the left there are views of the huge 'golf balls' of the Fylingdales Ballistic Missile Early Warning Station.

⑦ Also known as Devil's Punchbowl, the Hole of Horcum is a huge natural hollow in Levisham Moor. The remote and lonely Saltersgate Inn has a peat fire which is supposed to have kept alight since it was lit in 1801.

⑧ Among the most beautiful villages in Yorkshire, Thornton Dale has one of the most photographed homes in Britain, a charming thatched cottage. Other features include a 600-year-old market cross and 12 almshouses.

⑨ Low Dalby is the thriving centre for the tourist boom which has developed locally because of the recreational value of the forests.

⑩ Brompton has a special place in aviation history for it was here, in 1853, that Sir George Cayley devised a glider which flew 50yds.

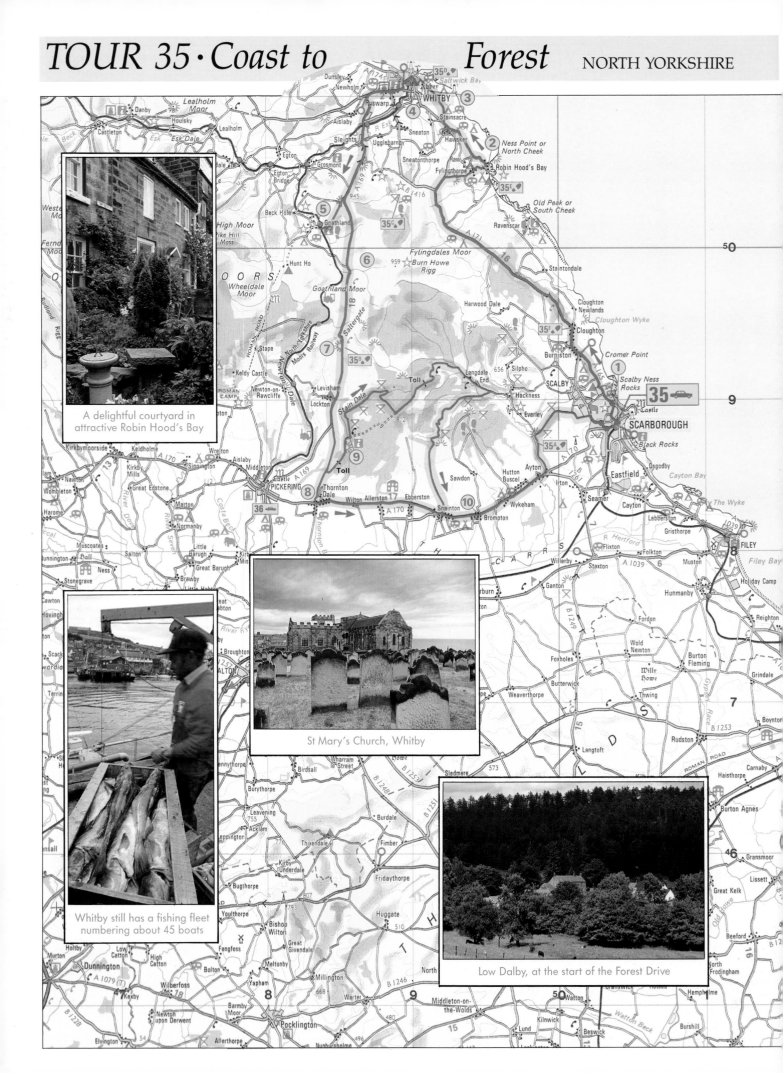

A delightful courtyard in attractive Robin Hood's Bay

St Mary's Church, Whitby

Whitby still has a fishing fleet numbering about 45 boats

Low Dalby, at the start of the Forest Drive

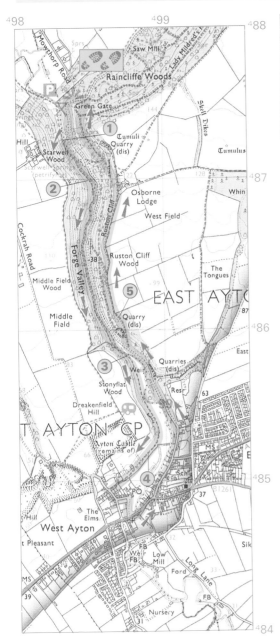

Forge Valley lies on the route of the Derwent Way — one of the local long-distance walks

This is an easy walk along river-bank and woodland paths through the steep-sided Forge Valley, much of which is now designated a National Nature Reserve. Start this walk at daybreak on a fine June morning and an unforgettable dawn chorus will be ample recompense for a very early rise.

POINTS OF INTEREST

① Close to the bridges is the site of the old forge from which the valley takes its name. A forge was as important to early travellers as a petrol station is to us today, and, with abundant limestone, wood for charcoal and ample water supply, this was an ideal site.

② The woodlands here are among the best remaining examples of mixed woodland in north-east England. A wide variety of trees, including oak, lime, wych elm and birch, is complemented by a rich ground flora of wood anemone, primrose, bluebell, woodruff, ramsons, orchids and many other species. Look for the yellow globes of marsh marigold and yellow flag (iris) growing in the river.

③ The small weir was built by the water authority to measure flow rates in the Derwent. A little downstream, although out of sight, are sink holes in the bed of the river through which some of the water percolates. After travelling underground for some miles the water is trapped in the limestone and is then tapped to supply Scarborough with its water.

④ Dating from about 1400, Ayton Castle is a ruined pele-tower – a type of fortified building that is much more common nearer the Scottish border, for most of them were built as a defence against the marauding Scots. This one stands on the site of an earlier castle: Ayton is mentioned in *Domesday Book* and its name is derived from the Old English for 'settlement by the river'.

⑤ The deciduous trees and shrubs along Forge Valley attract a tremendous variety of small birds including nuthatches, woodpeckers, several kinds of warbler and many common woodland species. For those who have experienced the full flood of the dawn chorus echoing along this ancient wooded gorge, the memory will last a lifetime.

ROUTE DIRECTIONS

Allow 2 to 2½ hours
Start from one of the two small car parks on the road out of West Ayton towards the north end of Forge Valley (grid ref. SE983874).

Walk a short distance downstream to cross one of two footbridges over the River Derwent ①.

Follow the river-bank path downstream ②.

Where the path enters a field continue straight ahead, keeping the fence on your right ③.

The path merges into a rough track which bends gradually right uphill to pass close to the ruins of Ayton Castle ④.

Continue ahead to join the road, turning left downhill then quickly left and right to the road bridge on the A170. Cross the bridge and turn left on the road to Hackness.
Follow the road as it drops back into Forge Valley and about 300yds beyond the weir (having passed one bridleway) cross the road to follow the signposted bridleway which cuts steeply uphill, bearing right of the road. Near the top of the wood where the path divides, take the left fork to follow the path along the top edge of the woods ⑤.

Pass the back of Osborne Lodge Farm and within a short distance start dropping downhill. Continue on this path, which gradually swings round to join the road near Green Gate. Turn left to return to your car.

WALK 35B · *The Hole of Horcum* NORTH YORKSHIRE

The Hole of Horcum – left by the devil when he formed the hill of Blakey Topping to the east?

ROUTE DIRECTIONS

Allow 3½ to 4 hours
Start from the car park at Saltergate (grid ref. SE853937).

Follow the road to the hairpin bend on Saltergate Bank①.

Turn left over the step stile down into the Hole of Horcum②.

Continue down the valley, passing to the right of the old farm buildings. Carry on through the middle of the fields, avoiding any routes uphill.

Where the valley narrows keep the fence and wall on the left and continue down on to the confluence of two streams. Cross both streams and turn sharp right up Dundale Griff, signposted footpath③.

On coming on to open moorland, bear right across the moors. Shortly pass Dundale Pond on your right④.

Continue up the dry valley, gradually bearing up to the left. At the corner of the walled field strike off on the path straight across the moor to reach the edge of the escarpment overlooking Newton Dale, then cut down to the right towards the ruins of Skelton Tower.

Continue along the path, bearing to the right and following the edge of the dale northwards to Yewtree Scar⑤.

Leave the broad track where it swings away from the edge of the valley and follow the path along the cliff top. **Take care if with children.**

At the north end of Yewtree Scar continue with the path as it bends right, away from Newton Dale. Go along the field side to the edge of a tributary valley and then almost immediately bear right again to cross the moor and climb towards the hairpin bend of Saltergate Bank.

Climb up to the road, keeping the fence line on the left, then turn right to the car park.

This long, exhilarating ramble on Levisham Moor sets out through the middle of the remarkable Hole of Horcum, returning along the edge of the steep gorge of Newton Dale. *Take care along the edge of Huggitt's Scar and Yewtree Scar.*

POINTS OF INTEREST

①From Saltergate Bank there is a good view northwards to an unmistakable landmark – Fylingdales Ballistic Missile Early Warning Station. Its three white radomes, resembling giant golf balls, are more than 150ft high. In the foreground is the ancient Saltergate Inn, beside the old road from Robin Hood's Bay. Fish were brought here for salting before onward transit to inland towns.

②One of the geological curiosities of the North York Moors, the Hole of Horcum is a great steep-sided bowl in the moorland. Large enough to contain two complete farms, the hollow has been sculpted over the millennia by the action of springs. Needless to say, folklore has given it more colourful explanations: it was scooped out by the giant, Wade, to throw at his wife.

③The word 'griff' is used in this area to denote a very steep-sided little valley, often with cliffs along its flanks. Another common local word is 'rigg' as in Dundale Rigg, just north of the path. This is used to describe a long, narrow hill or ridge.

④Dundale Pond was probably constructed in medieval times as a watering place for livestock.

⑤Through the remote valley of Newton Dale, below the path, runs the popular North York Moors Railway, also known as 'Moorsrail'. The 18-mile privately owned line between Pickering and Grosmont is operated by both diesel and steam locomotives. Trips along the railway show visitors some of the loveliest scenery in the National Park.

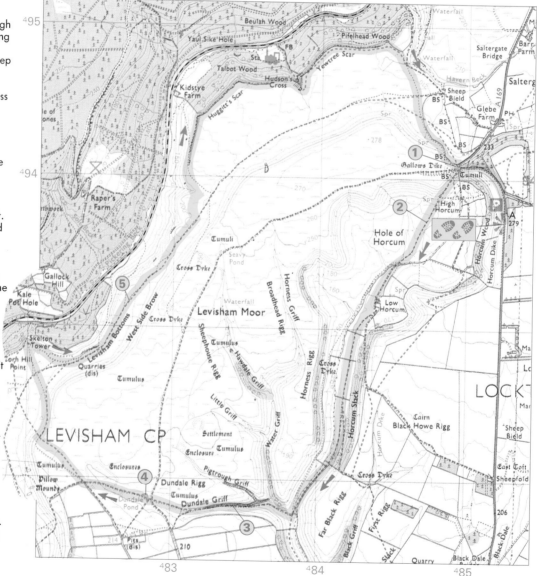

ROUTE DIRECTIONS

Allow 2½ to 3 hours
Start from a car park reached by turning off the B1416 at Redgates Corner and following the road signposted Falling Foss and Newton House (grid ref. NZ889035).

Walk down the track towards Falling Foss①.

At Midge Hall double back on the path leading alongside the gorge above the stream②.

Follow the path downstream to the Hermitage③.

Go down steeply towards the stream and pass an old alum quarry. Continue to join the road at Littlebeck④.

Turn right up the road, pass the village hall and follow the left fork for a short distance, then turn left off the road along a footpath (signposted).

Bear right and cross the top edge of three fields with the hedge on the right. Cross the two stiles and drop down the side of Low Farm.

Go through the gate, pass below the farm and continue diagonally down to the right to the track and ford. Follow the track parallel to the stream. Avoiding the footbridge (unless the stream is in spate), cross the weir and then the stepping stones.

Follow the path through the wood to a second set of stepping stones and continue downstream to a metal footbridge. Cross this and turn sharp right uphill, signposted Dean Hall⑤.

Turn right where the path joins a track which cuts up to the right between the buildings of Dean Hall and joins the road. Turn right on the road and very shortly veer forward left along the second (unsigned) bridleway towards the old quarry. Keep right at the fork and go up the side of the quarry on to the open moor, then keep right to go through the pine trees with the wall and fields on the right.

Emerging from the trees, continue ahead across the moor, still keeping the fields on the right. Gradually swing left to pass to the left of the new barn and keep forward on the track to the road.

Cross the road and follow the footpath (signposted) towards Thorn Hill, but shortly veer to the left of the buildings to follow a track over the moor to Newton House Lodge. Turn right down the road.

As enchanting as its name, the Littlebeck Valley is a haven of waterfalls and woodland tucked between the open tracts of Sleights Moor and Fylingdales Moor. This is an easy walk, setting out down the valley and returning over moorland.

POINTS OF INTEREST

①The track towards Falling Foss is part of an old coach road from Whitby over the moors towards Hackness and Pickering. The Foss itself is a very attractive waterfall, plunging 40ft among woodlands that were once part of a large private estate. The damp rocks around the fall are thick with ferns and mosses.

Secluded Littlebeck in its wooded valley

②Midge Hall was the keeper's cottage. At one time it had a double-seater outdoor privy which was virtually suspended over the waterfall.

③Carved out of solid sandstone, the Hermitage was built about 200 years ago and will accommodate about 20 people. On its top are two stone armchairs, and in front is a small balcony from which the steep valley sides can be fully appreciated.

④The enchanting hamlet of Littlebeck grew up around a quiet pool in the stream from which the settlement takes its name. Its charming houses enjoy a seclusion rarely found nowadays, for it is reached only by tiny, steep, tortuous lanes.

⑤The path leading up out of the valley is a paved 'trod' or pannierway. There are many of these early routeways, slabs of sandstone laid in lines, in the Whitby area. Often running for many miles, they are probably of medieval date.

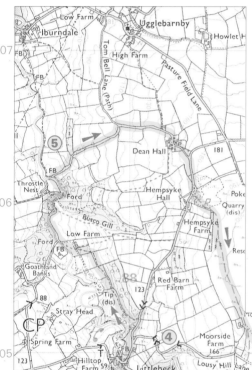

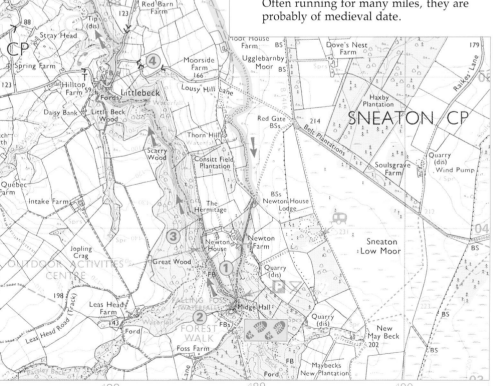

ROUTE DIRECTIONS

Allow 2 to 2½ hours (a good half day for the longer walk) Start from the swing bridge in the centre of Whitby (grid ref. NZ899111).

Go up Bridge Street and turn left to walk along Church Street and up to Whitby Abbey①.

From the abbey, cut through the car park and turn right to take the cliff path in front of the coastguard lookout②.

The path (signed the Cleveland Way) continues along the cliff and through a caravan site③.

Continue on the site road and cross a stile on to the Cleveland Way again to go along the cliff edge. Follow the path to the hilltop just beyond the Fog Horn Station and lighthouse, from where there is a good view down the coast. (Those walking to Robin Hood's Bay should continue on the coast path.) Most of the remainder of the circular route is on tarmac and some may prefer simply to retrace their steps to Whitby.

If completing the circular route, follow the tarmac lane from the lighthouse via Brook House to the road and turn right. Continue, with views ahead of Whitby Abbey. Just past the track to Knowles Farm (on the right) look for a narrow path on the left which goes towards New Gardens. Go through a gate and continue straight ahead, joining a narrow road. Where this bends right, continue straight ahead along a narrow path to join the road. Turn left downhill and right along the harbourside④.

From the harbour return to the town centre.

This two-in-one walk gives the option of a cliff-top walk from Whitby to Robin Hood's Bay, returning by bus, or a short easy walk never far from Whitby. In either case allow extra time to explore Whitby Abbey, the nearby parish church and some of the hidden alleys and courtyards of the old town. If intending to take the longer route, check the bus times in Whitby before setting off.

Surrounded by moors on three sides and by the North Sea on the fourth, Whitby has a rich maritime past — and excellent kippers

POINTS OF INTEREST

①This walk often takes longer than expected, such is the wealth of interest on the way, including the Tuscan-style old 'town hall', which dates from the late 18th century, and the interesting shops along Church Street selling Whitby jet or 'black amber' jewellery. Incidentally, tradition demands that you count the church steps; if you do not count 199, start again!

Dating from about 1110, the unique Parish Church of St Mary has a magnificent tiered pulpit with ear trumpets, box pews and a fine Norman chancel arch. Near by are the imposing ruins of Whitby Abbey, refounded in 1078 to replace the famous earlier foundation of St Hilda, dating from 657. It was St Hilda who gave her name to a local ammonite or 'snakestone'. These flat, coiled fossils are found in rocks below the abbey.

②From the cliff top the remains of a wreck can be seen, a reminder of the many maritime disasters which have occurred along this coastline.

③The 93-mile Cleveland Way, the second long-distance footpath to be established by the Countryside Commission, was opened in 1969.

④Whitby Harbour was the birthplace of the three ships, *Endeavour, Resolution* and *Adventure,* that carried Captain Cook around the world on his three great voyages of exploration.

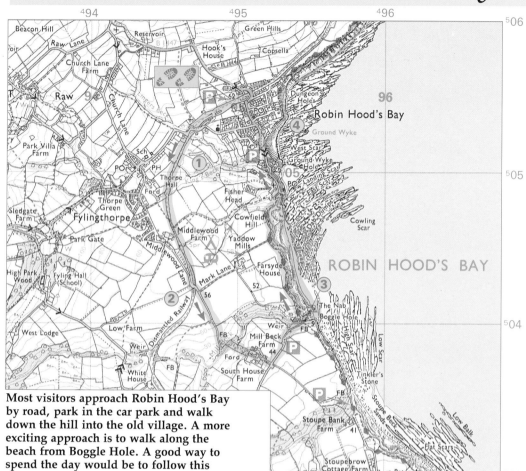

Robin Hood's Bay from Stoupe Brow (above) and the quaint town (left) of the same name

Most visitors approach Robin Hood's Bay by road, park in the car park and walk down the hill into the old village. A more exciting approach is to walk along the beach from Boggle Hole. A good way to spend the day would be to follow this walk in the morning and spend the afternoon exploring the delights of the seashore and the old village.

POINTS OF INTEREST

①The Scarborough-to-Whitby railway line was opened in 1885. In the short distance between Ravenscar and Robin Hood's Bay the line drops some 400ft and sweeps inland to avoid some of the steep-sided valleys draining into the bay. The track bed is now a walkway.

②The old railway continues southwards past Fyling Park. On local maps the word 'park' appears several times, a sure indication that there was a medieval deer park here. Earth embankments are the only evidence of it today.

③Boggle Hole was once a mill, one of several in the area, and is now a popular Youth Hostel. The word 'boggle' is a local name for a hob or goblin once said to frequent this area. If the tide is out the bay's reefs are clearly visible. Formed from the oldest rocks in the area, they are a paradise for fossil hunters, and contain hundreds of fascinating rock pools. The bird life of the shore can be equally interesting, with several species of gull and wader. Until quite recently the southerly approach to Robin Hood's Bay was by a

steep track from Ravenscar. This descended to the shore at Stoupe Beck and from there followed the beach to the village.

④Wedged between cliffs and sea, the delightful fishing village of Robin Hood's Bay is a warren of steep streets and passageways, whose houses often seem to be built almost on top of one another. There is no real evidence to link the place with the famous Sherwood Forest outlaw whose name it bears, but centuries of fishermen's and smugglers' tales have ensured that Robin Hood's Bay has a folklore all of its own. Aspects of its history are illustrated in the small local museum, open in summer.

ROUTE DIRECTIONS

Allow 2 to 2½ hours
Start from the old station car park (pay and display), on the western edge of Robin Hood's Bay village (grid ref. NZ949055).

Leave the car park by the lane at the opposite end to the main entrance. Join the road and turn right to Fylingthorpe and almost immediately opposite follow the track bed of the old Scarborough-to-Whitby railway line①.

The bridge over Middlewood Lane has been removed. Drop down here to the road and continue ahead along the lane signed 'Unsuitable for Motor Vehicles'②.

The lane drops steeply to a ford and footbridge and then climbs up between the buildings of South House Farm to join the road. Turn left down the road to Boggle Hole③.

If the tide is out you can walk along the shore back to Robin Hood's Bay. If the tide is in, cross the footbridge by the Youth Hostel and follow the cliff-top path to the village④.

Looking back towards the cliffs and Salt Pans at Cloughton Wyke from the coastal path

Footbridge on the Cleveland Way at Hayburn Wyke

One of the attractions of this easy walk is the shore at Cloughton Wyke and Hayburn Wyke. With children it would be wise to allow extra time to explore the boulder-strewn beaches. The route follows the Cleveland Way coastal footpath and returns along the track bed of the old Scarborough-to-Whitby railway.

POINTS OF INTEREST

① The sheltered inlet at Salt Pans is called Cloughton Wyke. The word 'wyke' is of Scandinavian origin and is used at several locations along the Yorkshire coast to denote a narrow inlet.

② The steep climb from Salt Pans gives extensive views south towards Scarborough, Filey and, on a clear day, the distant headland of Flamborough. A broad ledge well below the cliff edge but above sea level is a veritable jungle and a haven for wildlife. This tree-covered, boulder-strewn platform is known as the undercliff.

③ Hayburn Wyke is a delightful and secluded bay with woodland coming right down to the shore and a twin waterfall. Much of the woodland here is a nature reserve managed by the National Trust and the Yorkshire Wildlife Trust.

④ The track bed of the old Scarborough-to-Whitby railway makes an ideal walking route and was acquired for this purpose by Scarborough Borough Council in 1975. Walkers can now follow the route from the outskirts of Scarborough to the viaduct at Whitby, a distance of some 20 miles.

ROUTE DIRECTIONS

Allow 2 to 2½ hours
Start from the lane that runs down by the side of Cober Hill, off the A171 (grid ref. TA012947). Parking is available at the bottom.

Go through the gate by the farm and follow the lane down to the cliff top at Salt Pans①.

Turn left to follow the Cleveland Way cliff path to Hayburn Wyke②.

At Hayburn Wyke the path drops down through the woodland, bearing right to reach the shore③.

Return from the shore by the same route but only a short distance, where the Cleveland Way turns left, continue straight ahead. At the edge of the wood cross the stile and continue uphill through the field, gradually bearing left to pass between the farm buildings and out in front of the Hayburn Wyke Hotel.

Continue a short distance up the road and turn left along the track bed of the old railway to return to Cloughton④.

Leave the railway at the bridge over the track bed and turn right to the car park.

ROUTE DIRECTIONS
The drive starts from Pickering ①.

Follow the Whitby road, A169, gradually climbing towards the moors. After 4¾ miles pass a turning on the left to Lockton. A detour can be made to visit the hilltop villages of Lockton and Levisham on the edge of the Tabular Hills ②.

Descend to the steep valley of Newton Dale. Continue the main tour, climbing to 920ft on Lockton Low Moor and passing on the left the Hole of Horcum ③.

Descend to the Saltergate Inn. Continue on the A169 for 2¾ miles before turning left on to an unclassified road, signed Goathland ④.

Cross Goathland Moor before descending to Goathland. Bear right and pass the Mallyan Hotel to enter the village ⑤.

Follow signs for Whitby and cross the railway. Climb steeply on to the moors and after 2 miles turn left on to the A169. In another ¼ mile turn left again on to an unclassified road, signed Grosmont and Egton. The road crosses Sleights Moor. Later there are fine views to the right along Esk Dale. Descend steeply into Grosmont ⑥.

Proceed over the level crossing and River Esk then ascend steeply (1 in 4) to Egton ⑦.

In the village bear right and, at the Wheatsheaf Inn, turn left, signed Glaisdale. Continue with the Castleton road and in 1 mile bear right. In another ¾ mile, at the T-junction, turn right for Lealholm. Recross the River Esk then turn left, signed Danby. Continue through Esk Dale for 3½ miles to reach the Moors Centre ⑧.

Keep left to reach the village of Danby ⑨.

Go over the staggered crossroads and continue to Castleton. Follow the Rosedale signs and in ½ mile bear left to climb along the 1,000ft-high Castleton Rigg. After 4 miles turn left, still signposted Rosedale ⑩.

Cross the plateau of Rosedale Moor for 4 miles and then descend into Rosedale before turning left for Rosedale Abbey ⑪.

At the end of the village turn right and ascend Rosedale Chimney Bank (1 in 3) ⑫.

Cross Spaunton Moor. On the descent there are fine views ahead. After 3 miles, at the T-junction, turn right for Hutton-le-Hole and the Ryedale Folk Museum ⑬.

Turn left on to the Kirkbymoorside road. In 2¾ miles, at a T-junction, turn left on to the A170, signed

On this drive exhilarating high moorland with superb views contrasts with green dales and pretty villages. The many places well worth stopping to visit include the Moors Centre at Danby and the Ryedale Folk Museum.

Scarborough. Return through the agricultural countryside of the Vale of Pickering, passing through the villages of Wrelton, Aislaby and Middleton to Pickering.

POINTS OF INTEREST

① Pickering's now ruined castle was used as a hunting lodge by English kings between 1100 and 1400. Also of interest are the Beck Isle Museum of Rural Life and the southern terminus of the North York Moors Railway.

② Lockton and Levisham are a pair of tiny villages separated by a deep and spectacular valley. Lockton's church has a squat, 15th-century tower, a medieval nave and chancel and a 14th-century arch.

③ The Hole of Horcum is a spectacular natural hollow that is popular with hang-gliders. See also Tour 35.

④ The three huge white 'golf balls' which can be seen to the right of the A169 are the fibreglass radomes

(protective coverings for radar equipment) of the Fylingdales Ballistic Missile Early Warning Radar Station. See also Tour 35.

⑤ Goathland has a station for the North York Moors Railway and there are several attractive waterfalls nearby. Mallyan Spout, 70ft, can be reached by a footpath which starts near the Mallyan Hotel. See also Tour 35.

⑥ The village of Grosmont developed in the 19th century to house miners for the local iron mining industry. The northern terminus of the North York Moors Railway is here.

⑦ Egton, from Egetune, meaning town of oaks, stands on the hill above Egton Bridge – one of Yorkshire's prettiest villages. The Egton Bridge Old Gooseberry Society holds a show of giant gooseberries every August.

⑧ The Centre is an information and interpretation centre for the North York Moors National Park.

⑨ Of interest in Danby are the remains of 14th-century Danby Castle and the high-arched Duck Bridge over the River Esk, built in 1386.

⑩ On the left pass a small medieval white cross known as Fat Betty with a separate round headstone sitting on top of the main 'body'. Coins used to be left under the top stone for poor travellers.

⑪ Rosedale became a busy mining centre after the discovery of ironstone in 1856. Next to the church are the scant remains of the 12th-century Cistercian nunnery after which the village of Rosedale Abbey was named.

⑫ Named after a previous landmark, a remnant of the iron industry, the view from the summit of Rosedale Chimney Bank, 1,022ft, is superb.

⑬ One of the showpieces of the Moors, Hutton-le-Hole's houses, inn and shops surround a spacious and undulating village green. A major attraction is the Ryedale Folk Museum, showing life as it was on the moors in times gone by.

The impressive ruins of Pickering Castle, dating back 800 years, are in the care of English Heritage and can be visited all year round

Remains of Rosedale's 12th-century Cistercian nunnery

Viking crosses in Middleton church

Superb views from Rosedale Chimney Bank's 1,022ft summit

ROUTE DIRECTIONS

Allow 2 to 2½ hours
Start from the river bridge at
Sinnington (grid ref.
SE745858) ①.

Follow the road from the bridge to the right past the school, on the east side of the river ②.

Bear left down the no-through-road. Where the road ends, continue down the bridleway to the river bank. The bridleway is signposted left but continue straight ahead along the footpath into the woods, gradually climbing and then dropping to a field gate and through a meadow. About three-quarters of the way across the meadow cut up right to the corner of the wood and cross a stile to follow a path through the wood high above the river ③.

Descend to the river bank but then follow the right-hand edge of a field, climbing steeply uphill after about 150yds. At a crossroads of paths turn right and continue to climb steadily to the top edge of the wood. Ignore the path to your left and follow the path to the right as it gradually descends. Leaving the wood, continue over an open area and bear left along a field-side to a track. Turn right and after about 100yds turn sharp left towards Hall Farm. Join the road where it bends and continue between the buildings, past the church and downhill to return to Sinnington ④.

From the centre of Sinnington this walk goes through pleasant woodland often close to the River Seven. Above Appleton Mill the route climbs steadily to the top edge of the woods and then gradually descends towards the Hall and Sinnington church.

POINTS OF INTEREST

① Many villages along the southern edge of the moors have names ending with -ton, a sure indication that they were established by invading Angles in the 6th and 7th centuries. Sinnington has been by-passed by the A170 and is now a quiet, pleasant village on the River Seven.

In the centre is a maypole, one of only a few remaining in this area. In 1708 the Quakers made several attempts to stop the fun and games around the maypole, but not, it seems, with much success.

Close by is a low hump-back bridge spanning a dry ditch which may have once been a flood channel or possibly an old water-course that conveyed water to a mill wheel. This bridge is medieval in origin but the bridge across the River Seven dates from 1767.

② Fed by moorland streams, the River Seven flows through the lengthy, pleasant valley of Rosedale which extends from the centre of the North York Moors National Park to its southern boundary.

Sinnington, whose name carries echoes of the Angles' invasion 13 centuries ago, sits astride the River Seven on the southern edge of the North York Moors

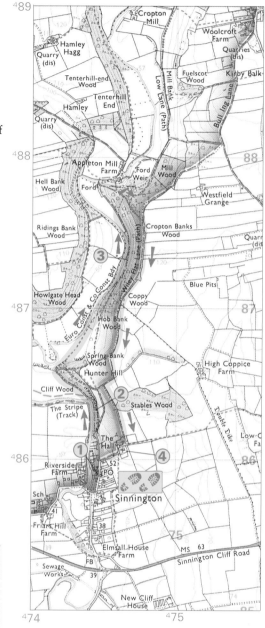

③ These woodlands are a pleasure to visit at any time of year, but particularly so in the spring. Before the leaves are fully open on the trees the ground is a carpet of early spring flowers including primroses, violets, wood sorrel and wood anemones. Later in the season bluebells, woodruff and wild garlic are found. The woods are also home to much wildlife, including badgers and a variety of birds.

④ The Church of All Saints has many original features dating from Saxon and Norman times, although it was restored in 1904. The old Hall near by has high Perpendicular windows. It dates from the 12th century, when it was built by the de Clere family.

Railway remains in Rosedale

ROUTE DIRECTIONS

Allow 2½ to 3 hours
Start at the village green in
Rosedale Abbey (grid ref.
SE724959).

Take the path between the school and church①.

Cross the road and take the footpath straight ahead into the caravan site and turn right along the track through the site. Approaching the end of the site pass through a metal gate (footpath signed) to continue the walk over fields.

About 15 minutes from the start of the walk the path descends to a footbridge over the River Seven②.

Go across the field to steps over a stone wall and turn right along Daleside Road.

Just before Thorgill turn right down a track and follow the signs through Low Thorgill Farm. Following the direction of a yellow arrow on a post, cross a field and continue over a footbridge across a stream. Proceed towards Hill Cottages③.

Cross another footbridge and continue across two fields, then along a track which bears left. Pass through a gate and continue up to the cottages.

Cross the road and follow the track up towards the white house. Turn sharp right before you get to the house, over a stile next to a small red-tiled outhouse and right again immediately, over a fence and on to a rough track.

Continue through a wooden gate and bear left (crossing a fence just before the house). Cross a fence again just after the house (this part of the path is overgrown). Bear left (crossing another fence) into a young conifer plantation. Continue up to the old railway track bed④.

Follow the track bed round the head of a steep-sided valley and round the contour towards Knottside, bearing right, with young conifers on the left. Reach

mature conifers and climb over a rough fence, continuing through the wood. Turn left up a track, to cross a fence and reach the road.

Cross the road and follow the bridleway (signed) down to the left and then turn right on to a footpath, with the derelict farmhouse and pond on the left. The path goes gradually downhill.

Bear right by a hawthorn tree and continue downhill to a road and a stream. Pass through a gate and go right up the road for about 50yds, then bear left on the path parallel to and above the stream, crossing the bottom of two fields. Just after leaving the second field, keep the stone wall on the left and continue down to a wooden gate, crossing the footbridge.

Continue through a larger gate, crossing the corner of the field diagonally to a bridlegate.

Go across the next field to reach a gate. In the next field drop down to reach a ladder over the stone wall in the corner of the field.

Continue, following a well-marked path parallel to the stream, through several more fields, to return to the village.

Less than a century ago, the peaceful landscape of rural Rosedale was the backdrop to a thriving ironstone industry. The slopes of this lovely valley are still peppered with old workings, ruined kilns and other reminders of a past way of life.

POINTS OF INTEREST

①Rosedale Abbey's Victorian church stands on the site of the 12th-century Cistercian nunnery from which the village takes its name. A few fragments of this earlier building, including part of a staircase, can still be seen near the church. A famous landmark connected with the iron industry stood for many years at the top of Chimney Bank, a 1-in-3 hill south of the village. Visible for miles, the 100ft-high chimney was demolished in 1972.

②Here little more than a stream, the River Seven is one of several parallel rivers that drain the southern half of the North York Moors. All join the Derwent to flow out to the sea along the Humber Estuary.

③The route climbs the hill on an old paved way. Sections of such tracks, known here as 'trods', can be found in many upland regions of Britain and are often difficult to date accurately. In Rosedale, a paved way like this would probably have been constructed to serve the early mining industry.

④The railway track bed is a later legacy of the ironstone extraction industry. Ironstone from Rosedale was found to be very rich in ore, and the area was conveniently close to the Tees-side blast-furnaces.

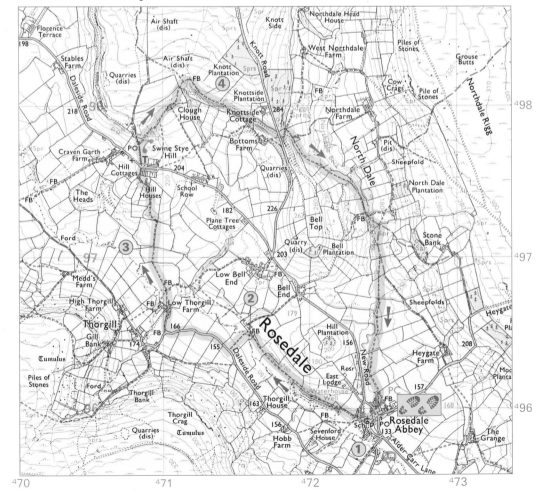

WALK 36C · *Ainthorpe Rigg* NORTH YORKSHIRE

A breezy moorland walk followed by easy going along a country road. Broad views along the Esk Valley and Little Fryup Dale, a high-arched medieval packhorse bridge and a detour to the Moors Centre at Danby are some of the attractions of this moderately easy walk in the heart of the North York Moors National Park.

POINTS OF INTEREST

① Opposite the Fox and Hounds in Fryup is the village quoits pitch. The ancient game of quoits is becoming increasingly popular in villages throughout the length of the Esk Valley. A pitch 11yds long has a square bed of clay at each end in which is set an iron post or hob. Basically the game involves throwing a bevelled metal ring or quoit from post to post.

② At this point there are extensive views from the path, which further on is clearly marked with a line of stone cairns. The North York Moors are rich in prehistoric remains, particularly from the Bronze Age, and hundreds of burial mounds can be found on the high moorland.

③ William le Latimer built Danby Castle – a 14th-century palace-fortress. Tradition suggests that Henry VIII stayed here, but in fact there is no evidence that he ever travelled further north than York. The building is not open to the public.

④ Duck Bridge is a fine example of a medieval packhorse bridge and one of three remaining in the Esk Valley. The bridge was built in about 1386 and has low walls leaning out over the water.

⑤ The Moors Centre was previously a shooting lodge on the estate of Lord Downe, but since 1976 it has been used as a visitor centre by the National Park Authority. A detour to view the exhibition, visit the grounds or enjoy the refreshments is well worthwhile. Admission is free and the centre is open daily from Easter to October.

ROUTE DIRECTIONS
Allow 2½ to 3 hours
Start from the railway station in Danby (grid ref. NZ708084).

From the station, turn right to follow the road which crosses the railway and the River Esk. Follow the road into Ainthorpe and turn left up the road to Fryup①.

Just past the tennis court the road bends left. Take the bridleway (signed) to go straight forward up Ainthorpe Rigg and on to the moor. Pass through a gateway②.

Reach the edge of the hill, with views over Little Fryup Dale through a gap, into Great Fryup Dale. Where the path forks, take the left path down to the road junction and turn left along the road. Further on, pass Danby Castle③.

Just beyond the castle, turn sharp right down the road to Duck Bridge④.

Do not cross Duck Bridge, but continue to follow the road as it bears left.

On the opposite side of the river stands Danby Lodge, now known as the Moors Centre. Cross a stile on the right to follow a public footpath to the centre, but take care crossing the railway and do not allow children to run on ahead⑤.

Retrace your steps to Easton Lane and turn right. Keep bearing right, over the railway, to return to the car park.

The Moors Centre (left) in Danby (below) contains a wealth of information about the North York Moors National Park

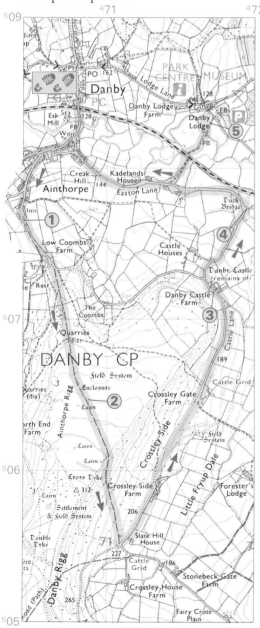

ROUTE DIRECTIONS

Allow 2½ to 3 hours
Start in Goathland, opposite the
church (grid ref. NZ828007) ①.

Follow the footpath down the
right-hand side of the Mallyan
Hotel, signposted Mallyan Spout
Waterfall. At the stream turn left,
signposted Mallyan Spout.

On reaching the waterfall
there is a scramble over boulders
which can be very slippery ②.

The path passes in front of the
fall and continues to meander by
the side of the stream. There are
more boulders along the way
and in places the path is very
muddy, even on a hot day ③.

Reach the road and go straight
ahead (left). At the second bend,
just before the cattle grid, turn
right past the house and follow
the path over the moor towards
Hunt House.

From the lay-by near Hunt
House turn right down the track,
cross the first footbridge and turn
right along the stream bank. Go
left uphill, signposted Roman
Road.

Turn right over the stile at the
top and bear left along the wall
side to join the Roman road.
Follow the road as it climbs
gradually to the moor ④.

Follow in the Romans'
footsteps, cross the step stile and
continue ahead for about 200yds
before doubling back on a path
(left) and dropping to the
stepping stones over Wheeldale
Beck. The route of the Lyke Wake
Walk continues straight up the
moor but take the more gentle
route to the left ⑤.

Follow the track past
Wheeldale Lodge to Hunt House.
A few yards along the tarmac
road cut forward (right) up the
moor. The track climbs gradually,
in a straight line, to the rocky
outcrop and then follows the
edge of the hill towards
Goathland ⑥.

Bear gradually right and pass
to the right of a small tarn before
going downhill to Goathland.

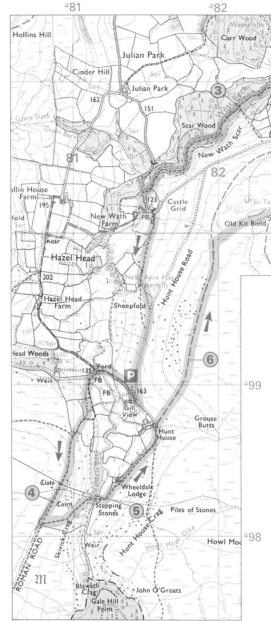

Here is a walk that could easily make an
all-day family excursion. The steep-sided,
wooded valley of West Beck is ideal for
games or a picnic, and good for
birdwatching too. The route later follows a
Roman road before returning over open
moorland. The walk is of moderate
difficulty, and includes a scramble across
boulders below Mallyan Spout. In poor
weather it is advisable to return from Hunt
House along the road.

POINTS OF INTEREST

① Goathland's late Victorian church is
dedicated to St Mary, as was the 12th-
century hermitage recorded at 'Godeland'

Mallyan Spout on West Beck — one of the Moors'
few waterfalls, and the highest

that was one of its predecessors. The
village itself is among the prettiest in the
North York Moors, with fine stone houses,
broad grass verges grazed by sheep, and a
station for the North York Moors Railway.
Near the church is the old village livestock
pound, in use until 1924.

② With the lowest rainfall of Britain's
National Parks, the North York Moors is
not noted for its waterfalls. However,
several falls can be reached from
Goathland. Mallyan Spout, at 70ft, is the
highest.

③ The West Beck is a delightful stream
tumbling amongst huge boulders beneath
tree-covered hillsides. Woodpeckers are
common, and you may see the white-
fronted dipper flitting low above the water,
or perched on a rock in mid-stream.

④ Often called Wade's Causeway after the
legendary giant who supposedly built it,
this is one of the best-preserved sections of
Roman road in the country. Built as a
military project about AD80, it probably fell
into disuse some 40 years later. The road
has been traced from near Malton, a
Roman town, to the lower slopes of the
moors above Pickering.

⑤ The Lyke Wake Walk takes its name
from an old Cleveland folk song which
describes a journey over the moors
supposedly made by departed souls. The
strenuous, 40-mile walk from Osmotherley
to Ravenscar was established in 1955, and
the traditional challenge is to complete it
within 24 hours.

⑥ The rocky outcrops are inhabited by
adders, but they usually disappear before
you have a chance to see them. Britain's
only poisonous snake, the adder has a
characteristic zig-zag line down its back and
a V-shaped mark on the back of its head.

ROUTE DIRECTIONS

The drive starts from Helmsley ①.

Follow the signs Stokesley to leave by the B1257. Ascend and, in 1½ miles, turn left on to an unclassified road, signposted Scawton. Descend steeply through thick woodland before turning right by the near side of the river bridge, signed Rievaulx Abbey. Follow the River Rye to Rievaulx ②.

Continue with the unclassified road and ascend through the woods to the junction with the B1257. To the right is the entrance to Rievaulx Terrace ③.

To continue with the main drive turn left, signed Stokesley, and rejoin the B1257 which climbs to over 800ft, with fine views from the Newgate Bank Picnic Area. Descend into Bilsdale. Here the moors rise to over 1,100ft on both sides of the dale.

Pass through the hamlet of Chop Gate (pronounced 'Chop Yat') to reach the 842ft road summit of Clay Bank. The Forestry Commission car park has panoramic views towards Middlesbrough and Roseberry Topping, a distinctive conical hill. To the east is Botton Head, 1,489ft, the highest point on the moors.

Descend through a forested area to Great Boughton. Two miles farther, at a roundabout, take the second exit to enter Stokesley. Leave by following signs to Thirsk (A172) and in ¾ mile turn right on to the A172. Follow the foot of the Cleveland Hills for 8 miles before branching left to join the A19. In ½ mile a road to the left can be taken to visit Mount Grace Priory ④.

Remain on the A19 for ½ mile then branch left on to the A684, signposted Northallerton, and continue to Northallerton ⑤.

Follow the signs Thirsk to leave by the A168 and continue through agricultural countryside. In 7 miles turn right on to the B1448 to enter Thirsk ⑥.

Follow the signs Scarborough to leave by the A170 and approach the escarpment of the Hambleton Hills. Beyond Sutton-under-Whitestonecliffe pass a turning, on the right, to Osgodby Hall ⑦.

Begin the steep ascent of Sutton Bank with gradients of 1 in 4 and hairpin bends ⑧.

In just over ¼ mile turn right on to an unclassified road, signed White Horse Bank. One mile farther begin the descent of White Horse Bank (1 in 4). The huge figure of a horse was cut into the hillside in 1857. At the foot of the descent keep forward for the village of Kilburn ⑨.

Continue with the Coxwold road and in 1½ miles bear right, then at the T-junction turn left. Pass Shandy

This drive through hilly country includes fine viewpoints and has a particular appeal for those interested in the rich Christian architectural heritage of the Moors area.

Pronounced Reevo, Rievaulx Abbey was founded in 1132 — the first Cistercian house in Yorkshire

Hall before entering Coxwold ⑩.

At the crossroads turn left, signed Byland. Alternatively keep forward with the Oulston road to visit Newburgh Priory ⑪.

Continue with the main drive to Byland Abbey ⑫.

At the village of Wass turn right for Ampleforth ⑬.

At the end of the village bear right signposted Oswaldkirk and pass Roman Catholic Ampleforth College. Reach Oswaldkirk and keep forward, joining the B1363 signposted Helmsley. In ¼ mile turn left on to the B1257. At Sproxton turn right on to the A170, signposted Scarborough, for the return to Helmsley.

POINTS OF INTEREST

① One of Yorkshire's prettiest country towns, Helmsley's handsome houses and inns are built of local yellow stone with red pantile roofs. Ruined Helmsley Castle stands in the grounds of Duncombe Park (now a school).

② Many of the houses in the small village of Rievaulx were built with materials from the 12th-century Cistercian abbey, but despite this there are impressive remains of Rievaulx Abbey in a splendid setting.

③ Rievaulx Terrace is a 1½-mile-long grass terrace completed in 1758, with classical temples and superb views.

④ The spacious and beautiful ruin of Mount Grace Priory is the largest and best preserved of all English Carthusian houses and the only one in Yorkshire.

⑤ An important road and rail junction, the market town of Northallerton is situated on rising ground east of the River Wiske, outside the National Park.

⑥ Thirsk is an old market town astride the God Beck with a fine 14th-century church, some interesting historic houses and inns, and a well-known racecourse to the west.

⑦ A small, elegantly proportioned Jacobean manor house, Osgodby Hall retains several interesting features, including a walled forecourt and a 17th-century staircase.

⑧ The peak of the escarpment known as Sutton Bank affords the finest views in Yorkshire, if not England, stretching from the Pennines in the west into Cleveland in the north and across to York in the south.

⑨ The village of Kilburn was the home of woodcarver Robert Thompson, 'The Mouseman of Kilburn'. Oak furniture is still hand-made by Robert Thompson's Craftsmen Ltd.

⑩ Rich with places of interest, Coxwold is small, compact and highly attractive. At one end of the village stands the literary shrine of Shandy Hall, the home of vicar and writer Laurence Sterne.

⑪ Standing in grounds containing wild water gardens, Newburgh Priory is a large 17th- and 18th-century house with some fine rooms. Opening times are limited.

⑫ The considerable remains of the Cistercian church and monastic buildings of Byland Abbey date mainly from the late 12th and early 13th century. The glazed tiles are of particular interest.

⑬ Known for its modern Benedictine Abbey and College, Ampleforth's main street stretches for almost a mile. St Hilda's Church has a 17th-century register, a Norman font and a 12th-century doorway.

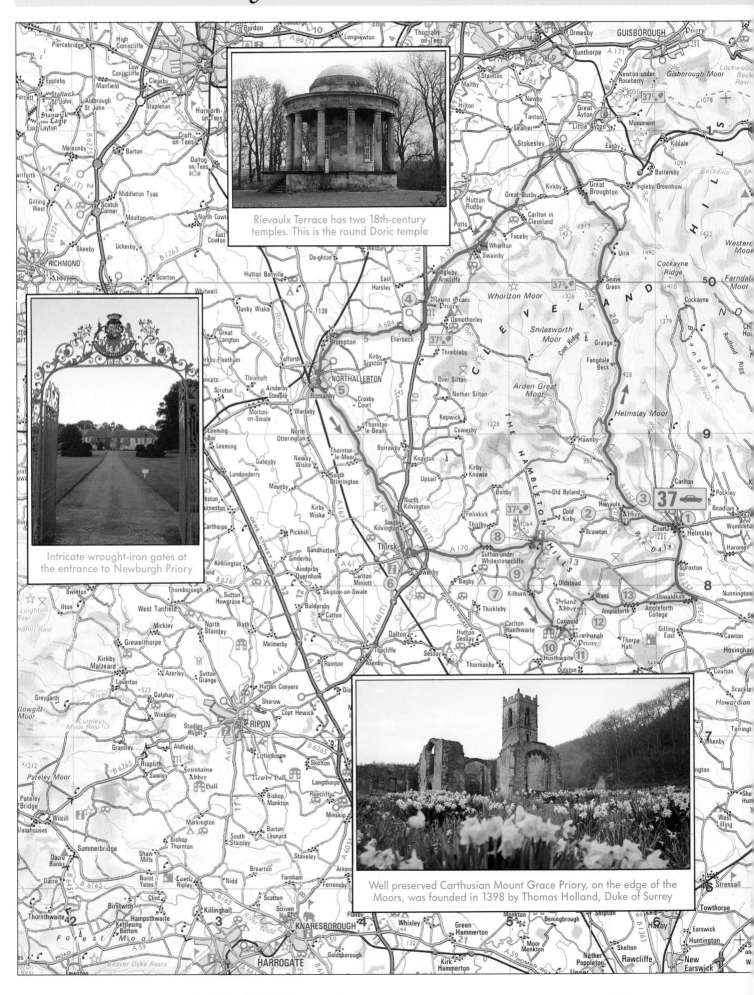

Rievaulx Terrace has two 18th-century temples. This is the round Doric temple

Intricate wrought-iron gates at the entrance to Newburgh Priory

Well preserved Carthusian Mount Grace Priory, on the edge of the Moors, was founded in 1398 by Thomas Holland, Duke of Surrey

WALK 37A · Sutton Bank   N YORKS

Gormire Lake below Sutton Bank

On a clear day, the view from Sutton Bank, where this walk begins, is perhaps the finest in Yorkshire. The route down towards Gormire Lake is steep but not difficult and the path back along the top of the escarpment gives ever-changing views.

POINTS OF INTEREST

① As well as being justly famous for its views, Sutton Bank is notorious for its gradient. The A170 climbs the escarpment in a mile-long ascent with gradients up to 1 in 4. At the top, the viewpoint car park has a picnic site and a telescope with an explanation of the panorama.

② From the path there is a view down to Gormire Lake. In the distance the Pennines can be seen, while to the south the cliffs of Roulston Scar provide a good take-off platform for gliders from the Yorkshire Gliding Club.

③ The path descends the escarpment through pleasant woodland which provides cover for a wide range of birds, animals and insects, including deer, foxes and badgers. Garbutt Wood is a reserve of the Yorkshire Wildlife Trust.

④ Formed by glacial action, Gormire Lake is rich in wildlife and is remarkable because no streams flow into or out of it. Local legends about the lake include the story that the devil leapt from Whitestone Cliff on a white horse and disappeared into a hole in the ground. This filled with water to form the supposedly bottomless lake.

⑤ The 93-mile-long Cleveland Way, opened in 1969, runs from Helmsley right round the western, northern and eastern margins of the National Park to end at Filey. Part of the Way here in the Hambleton Hills follows the route of the old Hambleton Drove Road, which was used between the 17th and 19th centuries by Scottish drovers bringing their livestock to sell at southern markets and fairs.

ROUTE DIRECTIONS

Allow 3 to 3½ hours
Start from the Information Centre at Sutton Bank (grid ref. SE515831) ①.

Walk to the edge of the escarpment and turn right along the Cleveland Way ②.

Follow the path of the Sutton Bank Nature Trail to where a narrow path (marked number 3) branches off to the left ③.

Continue down to the edge of Gormire Lake, passing on the way a standing stone ④.

Turn right along the lake side, and just beyond the end of the boardwalk turn left to Southwoods Lodge and then right, through a gate and along a broad bridleway.

Approaching Southwoods Hall walk straight over the crossroads and continue up the tarmac road to where it bears right towards the Hall. Continue through trees and a field gate, gradually turning left downhill, then go through a gateway and up a grassy track. At the top of the rise turn sharp right. Go through a field gate and then turn forward left to Tang Hall. Keep the farm on the left then turn sharp right over the cattle grid up to Greendale.

Approaching Greendale Farm pass through a field gate on the left of the farm entrance and go up the field to a bridlegate on the edge of the wood. Turn left uphill and then right at the first junction of paths.

Pass through a young forestry plantation and then go over a stile into scrubland. Bear forward right to re-enter the forest and continue uphill.

Cross the broad forest track and, a little way uphill, bear right alongside an old wall. Follow this until you emerge on to the Cleveland Way ⑤.

Continue along the edge of the escarpment back to Sutton Bank.

WALK 37B · The Drovers' Walk   NORTH YORKSHIRE

A gradual climb from Osmotherley reaches a high point with panoramas of the distant Pennines, then the path descends to Sheepwash, a favourite picnic place. The route of an ancient cattle-droving road is then followed before the path curls back to Osmotherley.

POINTS OF INTEREST

① Osmotherley is an attractive village with much to interest the visitor. One of the first Methodist chapels in the Moors was built in a cobbled alley; John Wesley preached from the stone table in the market place.

② The Cleveland Way is a long-distance walk (93 miles) crossing both the Cleveland and the Hambleton Hills. It starts at Helmsley, reaches the coast at Saltburn, then heads south to Filey.

③ Down on the left of the path are the ruins of Mount Grace Priory. Founded in 1398, this is one of only nine Carthusian priories left in England.

④ After leaving Arncliffe Wood there are distant views towards Live Moor and Carlton Moor, the onward route of the Cleveland Way.

Mount Grace Priory's fine, spacious ruins

⑤ Hambleton Drove Road was used to drive cattle and sheep from Scotland and the northern counties to markets in London and the south. Drove roads were used for many centuries before the development of a railway network in the early 19th century.

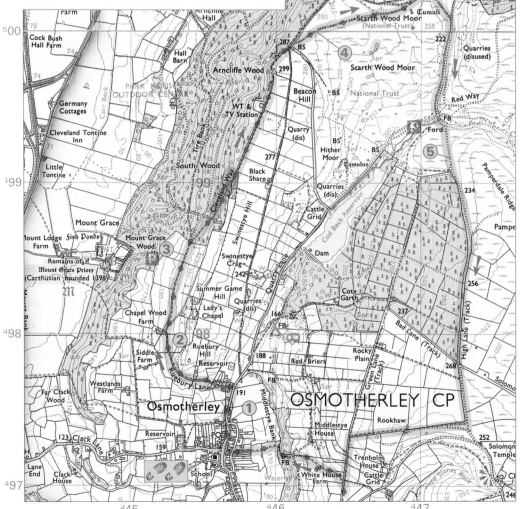

ROUTE DIRECTIONS

Allow 3 to 3½ hours
Start from Osmotherley (grid ref. SE457973) ①.

Leave the centre of Osmotherley and follow the Swainby road uphill, turning left into Ruebury Lane at the edge of the village. The route is now following the Cleveland Way ②.

Follow the track, gradually bearing right. Pass to the right of Chapel Wood Farm and continue across the fields ③.

Enter the conifer plantation and take the path forward right, gradually climbing to the top of the hill. Go through scrub woodland and past the TV station. Passing through two bridlegates on to the open moor, take the right-hand of the two paths, gradually veering away from the trees ④.

Approaching Scarth Nick, leave the Cleveland Way and take the obvious path sharp right down to the road and follow this to Sheepwash. Cross the footbridge and follow the broad track uphill. This is the line of the old Hambleton Drove Road ⑤.

Continue along the track, which becomes a tarmac road. Just before a junction turn right on to a path with a field on the right and moorland on the left. Go through the right-hand of two facing field gates and continue through the field with the wall on the left. Turn left along the track, going downhill to rejoin the Cleveland Way at a good farm road. Turn sharp right, pass on the right of White House Farm and go downhill to cross the footbridge and follow the path uphill through the woods. Cross the field towards the church and return to Osmotherley.

WALK 37C · *Roseberry Topping* NORTH YORKSHIRE

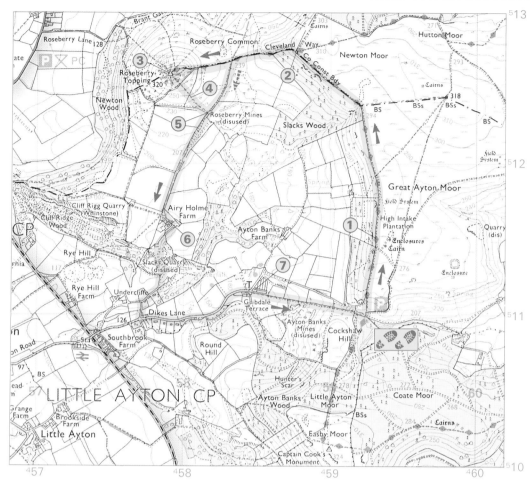

Roseberry Topping. Local people watch the summit for signs of bad weather

Beginning at Gribdale Gate car park, this moderate walk follows the escarpment to a 'miniature Matterhorn' – perhaps the most prominent landmark in the North York Moors. The short but stiff climb to the summit of Roseberry Topping is optional, but those who do reach the top will be rewarded by fine views.

POINTS OF INTEREST

①On Great Ayton Moor, to the right, is an important archaeological site excavated during the 1950s and now known to be a complex burial site dating from the New Stone Age and Bronze Age. Prehistoric remains of this period are abundant on the North York Moors, and though there are few large or spectacular monuments, the number of barrows and cairns in the area runs to several thousand.

②This part of the walk follows the county boundary between North Yorkshire and Cleveland.

③Though only 1,057ft high, Roseberry Topping's craggy south-west face gives this charmingly named cone of rock something of the grandeur of a much higher mountain. Views from the top take in the sea, clearly visible to the east beyond

Guisborough, and the industrial complex around Middlesbrough to the north-west. Closer at hand is the village of Newton under Roseberry. Not surprisingly, Roseberry Topping has been used as a beacon station and, many centuries before the Spanish Armada, was occupied by prehistoric herdsmen and hunters. The hill is now protected by the National Trust.

④Erected in 1827 to commemorate Great Ayton's most famous son, Captain James Cook, the 50ft stone obelisk on Easby Moor is a landmark for many miles around.

⑤The lower slopes of Roseberry Topping have for centuries been worked for the alum and ironstone they contained. In fact it was early mining activity which led to the collapse of the hillside, giving the hill the dramatic rock face we admire today.

⑥As a boy in the 1730s Captain Cook lived with his family here at Airy Holme Farm, where his father worked. The young James went to school in Great Ayton. He later moved to Staithes and then Whitby before joining the Navy.

⑦The houses of Gribdale Terrace were built to accommodate the ironstone miners who worked the rich ores in the vicinity.

ROUTE DIRECTIONS
Allow 2½ to 3 hours
Start at Gribdale Gate, which can be reached on a narrow road from Great Ayton by following signs for the station. Approaching from Great Ayton, park in the first car park at the top of the hill (grid ref. NZ593110).

Cross the cattle grid and turn left up the hill, following the Cleveland Way. The path levels out at the top of the hill to follow the edge of the escarpment①.

Keep the stone wall (conifer plantation boundary) on the left and go through the bridlegate in the wall which crosses the path just above Little Roseberry②.

Drop downhill before climbing Roseberry Topping③.

(If you decide not to climb Roseberry Topping turn left through a field gate on the level ground before the hill and follow the track towards Airy Holme Farm.)
From the summit drop down the steep south-east slope, towards the Cook Monument high on distant Easby Moor④.

Pass through a bridlegate and down towards the old mines⑤.

Turn right along the track towards Airy Holme Farm, turning left to pass in front of the farm and join the tarmac road⑥.

Continue down to the crossroads at Dikes Lane and turn left up the road to reach Gribdale Terrace⑦.

The road bends sharp left here, but follow the track straight ahead with the Terrace on the left and continue straight up the fields to return to Gribdale Gate.

CLEVELAND WAY

ROUTE DIRECTIONS

Allow 4 to 5 hours
Start from the car park at Chop Gate (grid ref. SE559994).

Walk up the road into the village. Turn left on the road to Carlton and almost immediately right up a track by the Wesleyan Chapel①.

Follow the path through the gate up to the moor and, leaving the stone wall on your left, climb up the ridge. At the first cairn the path bends slightly to the right to follow the edge of the hill overlooking Bilsdale②.

The path now joins a broad track. Follow this straight over Cold Moor to join the Cleveland Way at the escarpment overlooking Great Broughton③.

Turn right along the Cleveland Way, dropping down steeply then climbing up between the Wainstones on Hasty Bank④.

Follow the track on the edge of the hill before dropping steeply down to the left towards the road. Towards the bottom of the hill climb the step stile and turn immediately right down the wall side, avoiding the more obvious forest track.

Cross the B1257 and continue along the Cleveland Way, which climbs the hill opposite. Keep the wall on the left and, when you reach the second bridlegate across your path, pass through and then bear right along the edge of the hill, leaving the Cleveland Way on the left⑤.

The path now becomes indistinct but follows the prominent earthwork (ridge and ditch) around the contour of the hill to Medd Crag⑥.

At the old quarry near Medd Crag turn right downhill with the old barn on your right. Continue on an obvious track which bends downhill to Bilsdale Hall, where you turn left down a tarmac lane to Seave Green and the B1257. Turn left along the main road to return to Chop Gate.

The Cleveland Way – a well signposted long-distance footpath

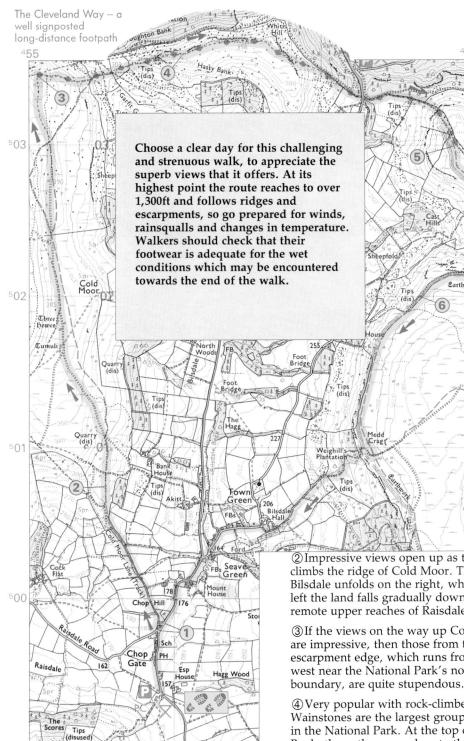

Choose a clear day for this challenging and strenuous walk, to appreciate the superb views that it offers. At its highest point the route reaches to over 1,300ft and follows ridges and escarpments, so go prepared for winds, rainsqualls and changes in temperature. Walkers should check that their footwear is adequate for the wet conditions which may be encountered towards the end of the walk.

POINTS OF INTEREST

①Chop Gate is one of only two tiny villages in Bilsdale, a peaceful, green valley whose farmlands were once cultivated by the Cistercian monks of Rievaulx Abbey. Pronounced locally as 'Chop Yat', the name of the village is thought to be derived from Chapman's Gate – 'chapman' being an old name for a pedlar.

②Impressive views open up as the walk climbs the ridge of Cold Moor. The head of Bilsdale unfolds on the right, while to the left the land falls gradually down into the remote upper reaches of Raisdale.

③If the views on the way up Cold Moor are impressive, then those from the escarpment edge, which runs from east to west near the National Park's northern boundary, are quite stupendous.

④Very popular with rock-climbers, the Wainstones are the largest group of rocks in the National Park. At the top of Hasty Bank, the path passes close to the edge of quarries, *so take care – especially with children.*

⑤The Cleveland Way continues south-eastwards, soon reaching the highest point in the National Park, 1,490ft, on Urra Moor.

⑥The long bank-and-ditch earthwork on the side of Urra Moor is one of hundreds to be found throughout the North York Moors. They may have been defensive works, boundaries or cattle enclosures.

ROUTE DIRECTIONS
The drive starts from Skipton ①.

From the roundabout near the castle follow the signs Harrogate (A59). In ½ mile turn left with the unclassified Embsay road. The former British Rail Station at Embsay is now the headquarters of the Yorkshire Dales

The serene priory ruins of Bolton Abbey in its romantic riverside setting and the harsh lines on the horizon left by the lead mining industry are contrasting features of this spectacular drive.

Arncliffe's porched barn seen across the village green. It is a good example of the local style and bears a datestone of 1677

Railway. Near the end of the village turn left, signed Eastby and Barden. Pass through Eastby and ascend on to high ground from where there are good views. The drive then gradually descends into Wharfedale to reach the junction with the B6160. Here turn right, signed Bolton Abbey②.

Continue to the Devonshire Arms at Bolton Bridge and turn left on to the A59, signed Harrogate. A climb is then made on to Blubberhouses Moor. The drive enters a rocky valley before the descent into the Washburn Valley to Blubberhouses Church, at the head of the Fewston Reservoir. Here, cross the river bridge and turn left on to an unclassified road, signed Pateley Bridge. This road crosses more high ground for some 7 miles before reaching the junction with the B6265 where the tour turns left, signed Grassington.③.

Remain on the B6265 and later pass through Hebden before entering Grassington④.

At Grassington go over the crossroads on to an unclassified road, signed Conistone. This pleasant by-road passes through attractive woodland and runs alongside the River Wharfe to the hamlet of Conistone⑤.

Here keep left, signed Kilnsey and Kettlewell, and cross the river bridge. On reaching the T-junction turn right on to the B6160 and shortly pass beneath the impressive Kilnsey Crag. After another ¾ mile turn left on to an unclassified road, signed Arncliffe. The drive now follows the valley of the River Skirfare to reach the grey stone village of Arncliffe⑥.

Turn right, signed Litton and Halton Gill, and continue up the valley into Littondale. Pass through the hamlet of Litton and on to Halton Gill, an isolated farming settlement near the head of Littondale. Here turn left, signed Stainforth and Settle, and climb on to open moorland. This narrow, and occasionally gated, by-road reaches a height of over 1,400ft.

After 6 miles turn left, signed Malham. Cross more high ground and in 2¾ miles bear right. Half a mile farther go over the crossroads with the Grassington road and in 1 mile pass the car parking area for Malham Tarn (National Trust)⑦.

Later bear right, signed Malham, then descend and at the foot of the hill turn right for Malham⑧.

At the Buck Inn turn left and continue to Kirkby Malham. Here

turn left with the Gargrave/Skipton road and follow the valley of the River Aire to Airton. In ¾ mile bear left and cross the river bridge, then pass through attractive countryside. After 2½ miles turn right and continue to Gargrave. Turn left on to the A65, still signed Skipton. In 2¾ miles, at the roundabout, take the second exit for the return to Skipton.

POINTS OF INTEREST

① A busy market town beside the River Aire and the Leeds-Liverpool Canal, Skipton's most notable feature is the castle dating in part from the 12th century. Other places of interest include the Craven Museum in the Town Hall which covers local history.

② The Strid Wood Country Park lies to the left of the road before reaching Bolton Abbey. Here the attractive 12th-century priory ruins stand in a superb setting beside the River Wharfe.

③ Disused lead workings can be seen on the left before passing the entrance to Stump Cross Caverns, once populated by wolverine, bison, fox and reindeer. Some of Britain's finest stalactite and stalagmite formations are shown to wonderful effect by electric coloured lighting here.

④ The upper Wharfedale village of Grassington contains a Yorkshire Dales National Park Centre. It is the main tourist spot in the area, with good shops and amenities.

⑤ Conistone's farmhouses, barns and houses are built of local limestone, with rendered walls and dressings of sandstone. The farmhouses and barns are mainly late 17th century.

⑥ Arncliffe is splendidly situated on a well-drained gravel delta above the flood plain of the River Skirfare. The houses, cottages, farms and barns face inwards towards a spacious green.

⑦ The actual tarn – or lake – lies to the left of the road and is a lonely sheet of water set among the moors at an altitude of 1,229ft. It can only be approached on foot.

⑧ The pleasant village of Malham, on the Pennine Way footpath, offers fine walks to two spectacular beauty spots – Malham Cove and Gordale Scar. The Cove (to the north of the village) is a limestone amphitheatre with cliffs nearly 300ft high. Gordale Scar (to the north east) is a wild defile containing waterfalls. In the village there is a Yorkshire Dales National Park Centre.

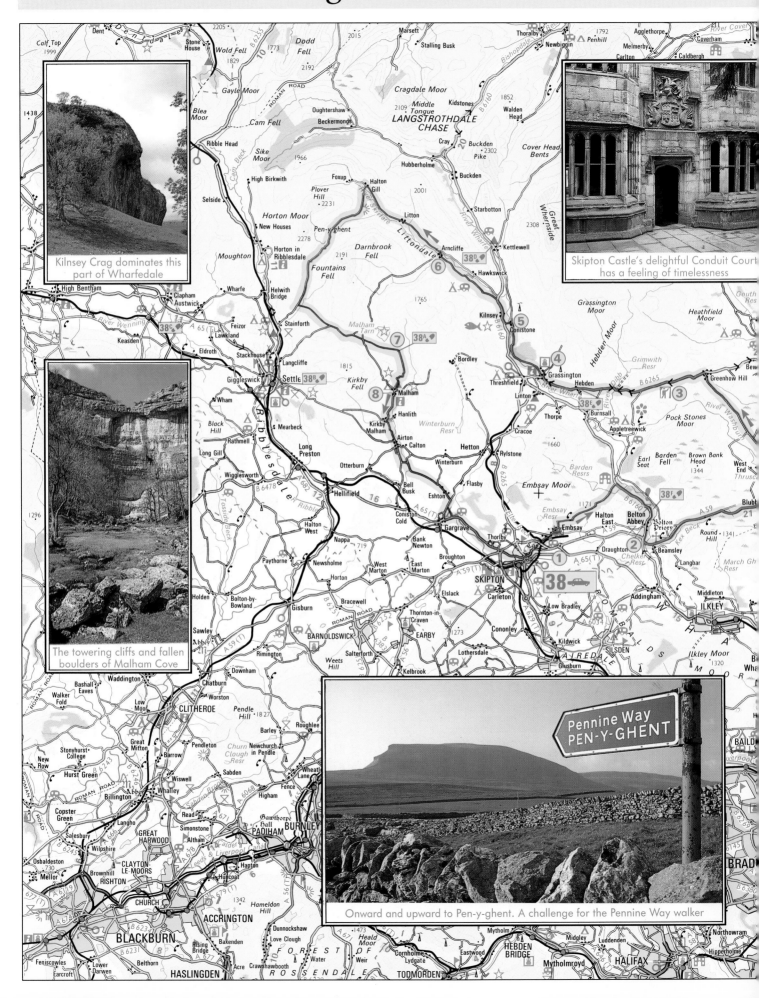

Kilnsey Crag dominates this part of Wharfedale

Skipton Castle's delightful Conduit Court has a feeling of timelessness

The towering cliffs and fallen boulders of Malham Cove

Onward and upward to Pen-y-ghent. A challenge for the Pennine Way walker

WALK 38A · *Malham Tarn* NORTH YORKS

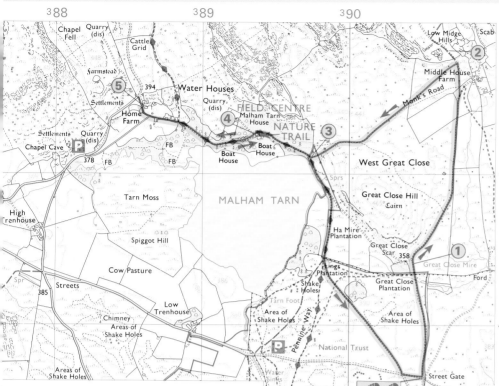

Shovelers breed on Malham Tarn

ROUTE DIRECTIONS

Allow 2 to 3 hours
Start from Street Gate, where parking is available (grid ref. SD903656).

Walk up the metalled road beside the wall towards Great Close Scar (left) and Great Close Mire (right)①.

The road continues past Middle House Farm to Middle House②.

Just beyond Middle House Farm, a stile on the left leads across West Great Close to the edge of Malham Tarn③.

The nature trail follows the track on the north shore of the tarn past Tarn House. (Public conveniences are provided for walkers at the side of the track behind the house)④.

The nature trail continues past Tarn Moss to the estate cottages and farmhouse of Water Houses⑤.

The trail ends here. It is possible to continue the walk by metalled roads past Higher Tren House and Water Sinks Gate back to Street Gate. But a more congenial route, strongly to be recommended, is to retrace one's steps through the nature trail to its official start at the corner of Ha Mire Plantation, then follow the Tarn House road back to Street Gate.

Malham Tarn

Some of Britain's finest limestone country is to be found near Malham. Part of this route follows the Malham Tarn Nature Trail, for which leaflets are available at Ha Mire and Water Houses.

POINTS OF INTEREST

① Great Close Mire is a former glacial tarn whose shores were frequented by hunters and fishermen of the Middle Stone Age. It retains a swampy character and is a haven for many rare and interesting plants.

② Middle House is the site of an old building which, at one time, housed the shepherds who tended the flocks of Fountains Abbey, a former owner of Malham Tarn and the surrounding land.

③ One of Yorkshire's few natural lakes, Malham Tarn is about ½ mile square and nowhere more than 15ft deep. It sits on a bed of slate amid the porous limestone, and its water is held back by glacial debris or moraine. The lake is the focal point of a 4,000-acre National Trust estate, part of which is a nature reserve.

④ Set in the woodlands between the lake shore and the limestone crag of Highfolds Scar, Malham Tarn House is let by the National Trust to the Field Studies Council. Residential courses are held here in term time, and there are also holiday courses.

⑤ According to its date-stone, the imposing old farmhouse of Water Houses was built in 1635. It is extremely well preserved and a good example of the vernacular architecture of its day.

Setting out from the unassuming old market town that is the southern terminus of the famous Settle and Carlisle railway, this is a gentle, easy walk in mid Ribblesdale. Sheltered lanes and flower-studded pastures command views over the dale and into the county of Lancashire.

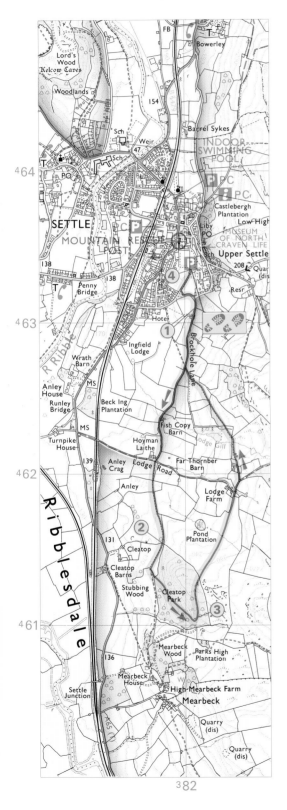

POINTS OF INTEREST

①Beyond the allotments on the left as the path leaves Settle are terraced fields – a relic of medieval strip farming. Each strip, called a lynchet, was of a size able to be tilled by a man and his ox-drawn wooden plough in one day. It was believed to be sufficient to sustain a good husbandman and his family throughout the year.

②Pause for a while on the approach to Cleatop Park to take in the view. The south-western horizon is dominated by the dark, heathery Bowland Hills of Lancashire, while to the north the white limestone of Giggleswick Scar and Settle's Castlebergh cliff frame the rugged splendour of Pen-y-ghent.

③Cleatop Park is an old wood now owned by the Yorkshire Dales National Park. Its trees are of many different species and ages, and there is a great variety of woodland plants and birds. In places, clusters of upright, pole-like growth from gnarled stumps reveal the traditional woodland craft of coppicing.

④Allow time at the end of the walk to explore Settle. This pleasant country town has a long tradition of hospitality towards visitors to the Yorkshire Dales. It owes its Georgian buildings to the prosperity it gained when the Keighley-Kendal Turnpike first brought coaching traffic here, and today the town copes with a lot of motor traffic on the A65. Nevertheless, Settle has kept its friendly atmosphere and its independent shops – often selling the work of local craftsmen.

Settle's bustling Tuesday market originates from a charter of 1249

ROUTE DIRECTIONS

Allow 2 to 2½ hours
Start from Settle's Greenfoot car park, best approached from the A65 at the southern end of Settle, turning into Butch Lane immediately north of the prominent Falcon Hotel. It is 400yds along this lane on the left-hand side (grid ref. SD821632).

From the car park entrance walk 100yds left along Butch Lane, then take the walled path on the right, signed Mearbeck①.

At the end of the walled lane, beside Hoyman Laithe (laithe=barn), cross Lodge Road and follow field paths (in single file) indicated by stiles, to the corner of Cleatop Park②.

Continue below this mixed wood to enter by the gate half-way along. Follow the diagonal path up through the wood to meet another path joining from a small footbridge on the right③.

The route takes a dog-leg to the left, up through the pine trees to leave the north-eastern side of the wood by a small gate. Head across the rough pasture to the field gate just to the right of Lodge Farmhouse. Turn right along the lane for 100yds, then take the walled lane on the left. A clearly defined path now angles down across fields to Brockhole Lane. Turn right and retrace the outward track back to the Greenfoot car park④.

WALK 38C · *Clapham & Clapdale* NORTH YORKSHIRE

The nearby geological wonders of Ingleborough Cave and Gaping Gill, together with the National Park Centre, attract thousands of visitors every year to Clapham, the starting point of this walk. This route follows old bridleways up Clapdale and down Crummack Dale.

POINTS OF INTEREST

① The upper part of Clapham village was transformed in the 19th century by local landowners, the Farrer family. They built estate cottages, rebuilt Ingleborough Hall, and dammed Clapham Beck to create a lake, planting thousands of trees on its shores. The Reginald Farrer Nature Trail was established in 1970 in memory of the family's most famous member, a respected botanist of the early 20th century.

② From the beginning of Long Lane the North Craven Fault can be seen stretching away to the east below Norber. Massive earth movements long ago created this line of limestone cliffs, which runs right across the National Park. Further up the lane are Thwaite Scars. Glacial erosion and more recent weathering have formed the cliffs and screes here.

③ In Clapham Bottoms, to the left, low rudimentary walls outline ancient field systems, while sink holes indicate the presence of eroded limestone.

④ On the descent towards Austwick, the squat, wooded hill of Oxenber stands out to the south east. Its slopes have the characteristic 'frilled' appearance of hillsides that have been terraced.

⑤ On Nappa Scars, note the breccias or crushed fragments of rock between the base of the Great Scar limestone and the much older Ordovician rocks.

⑥ Perched on the limestone shelves of Norber Brow, just above the path, are the huge stones known as the Norber erratics. These dark gritstone boulders were lifted by Ice Age glaciers on their way down Crummack Dale and deposited here.

A Norber erratic, perched on its limestone pedestal

ROUTE DIRECTIONS

Allow 3 to 3½ hours
Start from Clapham National Park Centre car park (grid ref. SD745693).

Turn right out of the car park, up the village①.

At the church, take the lane to the right signed Austwick. At the corner of Thwaite Plantation turn left into Long Lane, signed Selside②.

At the end of the walled lane a clear broad green track heads just below a large cairn on the skyline ahead③.

At a point where the 'lion couchant' shape of Pen-y-ghent just appears ahead, another bridleway joins from the right. Turn along this springy turf track, passing below a band of limestone pavement (not shown on the map), then continue past Crummack Farm for the road to Austwick④.

As the road sweeps sharply right beyond Sowerthwaite Farm entrance, a stile on the right, signed Norber, leads to Nappa Scars⑤.

Continue westwards through a stile on to the open fell⑥.

From the wall below Norber Brow follow the footpath past the foot of Robin Proctor's Scar, then diagonally across the field, skirting an old mere to the right, to Thwaite Lane, thence back to Clapham.

Despite tourism, Kettlewell is still essentially a farming community

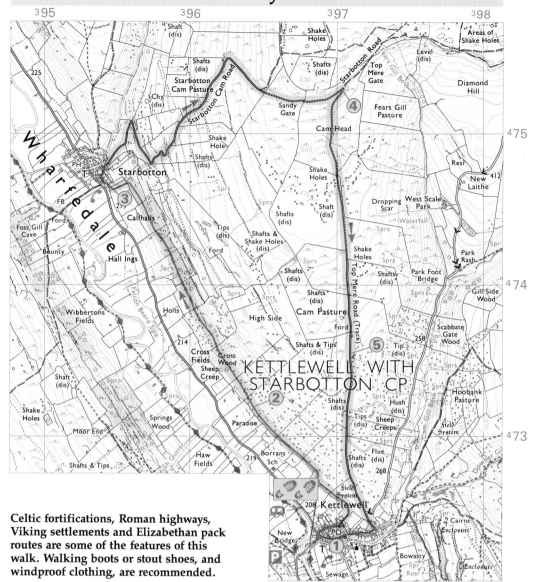

ROUTE DIRECTIONS

Allow 3 to 4 hours for the longer route, 1½ to 2 hours for the shorter
Start from Townfoot Bridge car park in Kettlewell (grid ref. SD967723)①.

Cross the small bridge into the village, and follow the road to the left side of the Bluebell Hotel. Where the road turns right, go straight ahead, over a stile, then turn left alongside the wall. The path continues roughly at this level all the way to Starbotton②.

At the third barn (Calfhalls) after the wood, bear left down to Starbotton village③.

At Starbotton, those choosing the shorter walk must cross the road (B6160) and follow the very attractive and well signposted Dales Way back to Kettlewell. Sturdier souls will bear right through the village, past the mullioned cottage dated 1656, to a walled track on the right winding steeply up the hillside – Starbotton Road. At an airy 1,600ft where the walled lane (and the climb) ends, a stile leads to a springy turf path with Great Whernside looming ahead, and mid Wharfedale laid out like some gigantic three-dimensional map. Almost unexpectedly, as a track goes off to the right, the peak of Little Whernside appears left ahead, and much nearer, the semi-amphitheatre of Ta Dyke, commanding the head of the tributary valley to the north east of Kettlewell④.

Extra time should be allowed for a diversionary close examination of Ta Dyke, but the descent to Kettlewell should be taken from this point, where a green track runs straight down the ridge to the right⑤.

The track, Top Mere Road, joins the metalled Park Rash Road just above Kettlewell, and a choice of downhill lanes leads back to the car park.

Celtic fortifications, Roman highways, Viking settlements and Elizabethan pack routes are some of the features of this walk. Walking boots or stout shoes, and windproof clothing, are recommended.

POINTS OF INTEREST

① Kettlewell is an Anglian name meaning a bubbling spring. A market was established here in the 12th century but most of the buildings date from the last two centuries.

② The route between Kettlewell and Starbotton follows the line of a Roman road from Ilkley, up Wharfedale, over Stake Pass to Bainbridge and on to Catterick.

③ Picturesque Starbotton has cottages dating back to the 17th century – survivors of a dreadful flood in 1686 during which many buildings were destroyed.

④ Ta Dyke, a ditch and earth bank, was built by the Brigantes in about AD70 to prevent the Romans invading Wensleydale.

⑤ On the way down to Kettlewell there are superb views of Wharfedale. At the gate to the walled lane, note the lead-mining bell pits to the left and, further on, the top of an old flue from a lead-smelting mill.

Kettlewell's beautiful setting draws many visitors wanting to explore Wharfedale

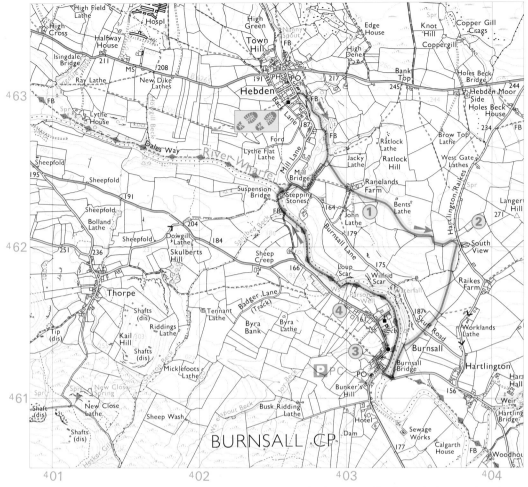

ROUTE DIRECTIONS

Allow 2 hours.
Start from Hebden village, where parking space is available in the broad street near the old school (grid ref. SE027629).

Take the descending footpath just beyond the old school. After the footbridge follow the finger-post signed Hartlington Raikes across a rough track to a stile to the left of the field gate.

Cross the next field diagonally to the right-hand corner of Ranelands Farm. Through the farmyard's three gates the path continues in roughly the same direction①.

A field gate in the top right-hand corner of the field extends the path, rising gently, towards a finger-post at the wall side above the gate. Follow this wall to the left to the A-stile at its top right-hand corner②.

Follow the path, crossing two more A-stiles, to the A-stile opposite South View Farm on Hartlington Raikes (road). Do not cross the stile, but follow the path at right-angles indicated by the finger-post signed Burnsall. It descends through hay meadows, the route indicated by stiles marked with yellow discs, to Skuff Road.

The stile immediately opposite leads down to the riverside and Burnsall Bridge. Here you can either follow the riverside path northwards from immediately across the bridge, or walk up the road into Burnsall village③.

A path just above the church leads down to join the riverside path which continues past Wilfrid Scar to Loup Scar④.

The path continues to the Hebden Suspension Bridge. After negotiating it, the path goes straight ahead to Mill Lane. Across Mill Bridge to the right, the footpath on the left leads back between two modern bungalows and ultimately over Hebden Beck, back to the village.

This is a pleasant country ramble between two peaceful, unpretentious villages in lower Wharfedale. The fairly easy ascent from Hebden, at the start of the walk, is rewarded by splendid views over the River Wharfe and beyond. Then, after an optional visit to Burnsall and its church, the return route runs right beside the river back to Hebden.

POINTS OF INTEREST

① As the path climbs up the side of Wharfedale, you may be glad of the excuse to stop and admire the view behind. Hebden village nestles comfortably above its beck, with Grassington Hospital beyond. The River Wharfe trickles gently down from Linton, and on its opposite bank the limestone reef knolls of Elbolton and Kail Hill assert themselves at the foot of the more substantial Thorpe Fell. As the map demonstrates, this part of Wharfedale is liberally scattered with the typical isolated stone barns of the Dales country, most of them still known by their Old English name of 'lathe'.

② At just under 800ft, the first A-stile is the highest point of the walk, so make the most of the views, which now begin to include Burnsall village, below and to the right.

③ The road into Burnsall winds past stone cottages and the handsome Old Grammar School, endowed as a boarding school in 1602 by Sir William Craven of nearby Appletreewick. Ten years later he was Lord Mayor of London: inevitably, he has been nicknamed 'the Dick Whittington of the Dales'. Just above the school is St Wilfrid's Church. The oldest parts of the building are 12th century, but even these probably replaced an earlier church, which would account for the very old font, the fragments of Anglo-Saxon crosses and the Viking tombstones.

④ Below Wilfrid Scar and Loup Scar the river has cut a deep channel through the limestone to leave contorted cliffs to the sides and a narrow course of turbulent water swirling erratically over deeply rounded potholes in its bed. A very little distance beyond, it resumes its more customary local demeanour – a calm, unhurried flow.

Burnsall, from the walk's junction with Skuff Road

WALK 38F · Bolton Priory WEST YORKSHIRE

ROUTE DIRECTIONS

Allow 1½ hours (with 20 minutes in the priory)
Start from the riverside car park (Cavendish Pavilion) just north of Bolton Abbey (grid ref. SE078552) ①.

Cross the narrow bridge opposite the café. Take the path to your right to the ford. Up the road, 50yds beyond the ford, take the obvious footpath to the right. There are other paths, but this one offers the best views of the river and priory ②.

The path descends to a sturdy footbridge across the River Wharfe. Adventurous spirits will take up the challenge of the alternative stepping stones ③.

From the west door of the priory, take the drive north, up the road, then the footpath to the Cavendish Memorial at the top of the road to the car park ④.

The path slopes gently down to the picnic area and car park at the riverside ⑤.

The River Wharfe surges through the Strid Gorge (below) and flows past the remains of Bolton Priory (below right)

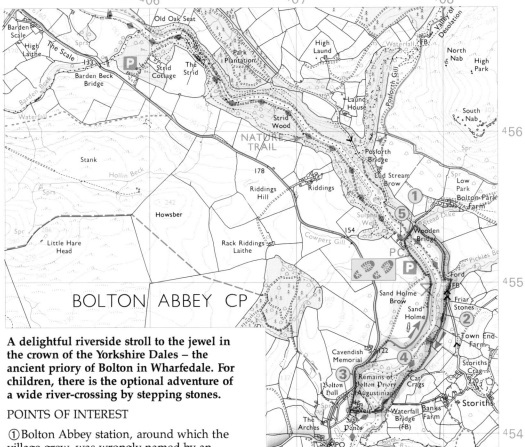

A delightful riverside stroll to the jewel in the crown of the Yorkshire Dales – the ancient priory of Bolton in Wharfedale. For children, there is the optional adventure of a wide river-crossing by stepping stones.

POINTS OF INTEREST

① Bolton Abbey station, around which the village grew, was wrongly named by an official of the railway company – there is a priory here, not an abbey, but the name has stuck.

② From this path there is a spectacular view of Bolton Priory in all its dignified dilapidation. Beyond it, Bolton Hall – shooting lodge of the Dukes of Devonshire – is built round the 14th-century priory gatehouse. To its left can be seen the high wall that surrounds the priory. The outlines of the former fishponds can just be made out astride the path to Bolton Abbey village.

③ Bolton Priory was built from 1155 onwards by the religious order of Augustinian Canons. Despite their black monastic dress, the canons were not monks. They were ordained priests whose mission was to go out daily into the surrounding area preaching the gospel and ministering to the needs of the people. The dissolution by Henry VIII of all religious foundations between 1536 and 1539 was not allowed to interrupt this function, and the priory nave has continued to this day as the parish church. Construction of a tower at the west entrance began in 1520 but the dissolution interrupted its completion. After 463 years as a ruin the tower was eventually roofed over.

④ The memorial is a drinking fountain in memory of Lord Frederick Cavendish, brutally murdered in 1882.

⑤ If time allows, follow the nature trail from here to the Strid – a deep, narrow gorge studded with potholes and whirlpools. Although stony, this path is passable for wheelchairs and pushchairs.

ROUTE DIRECTIONS

The drive starts from Hawes ①.

Leave by the Sedbergh road, A684, and near the end of the main street turn left on to an unclassified road, signed Gayle and Kettlewell. Shortly cross the Duerley Beck, at Gayle, and follow a steep ascent through Sleddale. Fells rise to over 2,000ft on either side before reaching the summit where there is a good viewpoint at 1,934ft, this being the highest road in North Yorkshire.

A long descent is then made into the valley of Oughtershaw Beck. Beyond the hamlet of Oughtershaw follow the Kettlewell road alongside the river and enter Langstrothdale to reach the George Inn at Hubberholme. Here keep forward and continue to the Upper Wharfedale village of Buckden. Turn left on to the B6160, signed Aysgarth, and climb out of the valley to over 1,300ft along the Kidstones Pass. A descent is then made into Bishopsdale to reach the edge of West Burton ②.

Turn left here, then branch on to an unclassified road, still signed Aysgarth. In ¾ mile turn left on to the A684, and ¼ mile further turn right on to an unclassified road, signed Aysgarth Force. On the steep descent the drive passes the Yorkshire Museum of Carriages and Horse-Drawn Vehicles ③.

Cross the River Ure. After a short distance there is a Yorkshire Dales National Park Centre, on the left ④.

Continue with the unclassified road and in ¾ mile turn right, signed Castle Bolton, and enter Carperby ⑤.

Two miles farther turn left for Castle Bolton ⑥.

From this picturesque village follow the Reeth/Redmire road for ¾ mile, then at the T-junction turn left, signed Grinton and Reeth. A long climb is then made on to the lonely Redmire and Grinton Moors. After the summit at over 1,500ft there are fine views on the descent into Swaledale.

Near the foot of the hill turn left to reach Grinton ⑦.

Turn left at Grinton on to the B6270 and cross the River Swale to Reeth ⑧.

At the Buck Hotel turn right on to the unclassified Langthwaite road and climb above the valley slopes of Arkengarthdale. Half a mile beyond Langthwaite keep forward, signed Tan Hill. The drive then crosses the desolate Arkengarthdale Moor for 7½ miles to reach the Tan Hill Inn ⑨.

At the Inn turn left (no sign) and follow a moorland road to enter West Stones Dale. Later there is a steep descent, with hairpin bends,

The market town of Hawes is the starting point for a tour which passes through Langstrothdale, and much of Wensleydale. It visits several waterfalls as well as the historic village of Castle Bolton.

before crossing the River Swale and turning left on to the B6270 to reach the edge of Keld ⑩.

To visit the waterfall of Kisdon Force enter the village and follow the signs. Continue along the B6270 to Thwaite ⑪.

Beyond this hamlet turn right on to an unclassified road, signed Hawes, and ascend the Butter Tubs Pass. After the summit at 1,726ft the drive descends into Wensleydale again. Proceed through the hamlet of Simonstone and in ½ mile reach a T-junction. From here a short detour to the right may be made to visit the 100ft-high waterfall of Hardraw Force. Access is via the Green Dragon Inn at Hardraw. The main drive turns left, then takes the next turning right for the return to Hawes.

POINTS OF INTEREST

① Hawes is the friendly market town for upper Wensleydale and the Yorkshire Dales National Park Centre is housed in the former station yard. Shops and amenities in the town are good.

② West Burton encapsulates all the essential attributes of a village in the Dales and the whole area merits Conservation Area status. It has the bonus of a charming waterfall at the end of the village.

③ An old stone mill at Aysgarth Falls now houses over 60 horse-drawn vehicles including some splendid carriages and relics of the era of horse-drawn transport.

④ The Centre provides a convenient car park in order to explore the nearby Aysgarth Force waterfall. Facilities for the disabled make it possible for visitors in wheelchairs to view the Lower Falls with ease.

⑤ Carperby was an important Wensleydale centre of Quakerism in the 17th century and the biggest building today is the Classically-styled Friends' Meeting House of 1864.

⑥ The impressive 14th-century stronghold at Castle Bolton was once the prison of Mary, Queen of Scots who spent several months here in the troubled 16th century.

⑦ Grinton's Church of St Andrew was the mother-church for the whole of upper Swaledale until Tudor times. Fragments of the original Normal church survive but the long, low, broad building is largely 15th century.

⑧ The small Swaledale village of Reeth, formerly a lead-mining centre, stands at the confluence of Arkle Beck and the River Swale. Its superb setting makes it a popular stopping place.

⑨ At 1,732ft, the isolated Tan Hill Inn on the route of the Pennine Way footpath is reputed to be the highest inn in England.

⑩ The riverside scenery at the tiny grey stone village of Keld is superb. Cottages cluster around a tiny square and two chapels, the school and the Youth Hostel at Keld Green are the biggest buildings in this remote place.

⑪ Thwaite is a rugged, charming, remote Dales village; a couple of farms, former lead-miners' homes and the well-known Kearton Guest House make up the friendly community. The Kearton brothers were born here and a modern lintel over a cottage doorway commemorates their birthplace.

The Middle Falls on the Ure at Aysgarth. They can be reached by following signposted paths through Freeholders' Wood

TOUR 39 · Falls, Fells and Fortress

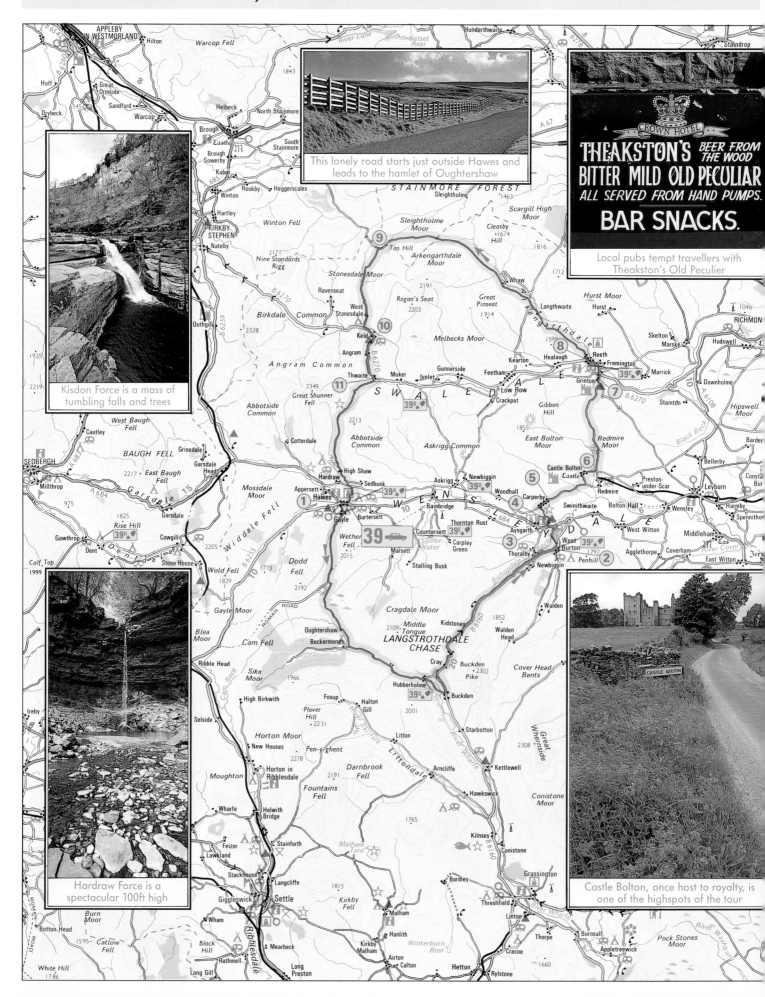

This lonely road starts just outside Hawes and leads to the hamlet of Oughtershaw

THEAKSTON'S BITTER MILD OLD PECULIAR BEER FROM THE WOOD ALL SERVED FROM HAND PUMPS. BAR SNACKS.

Local pubs tempt travellers with Theakston's Old Peculier

Kisdon Force is a mass of tumbling falls and trees

Hardraw Force is a spectacular 100ft high

Castle Bolton, once host to royalty, is one of the highspots of the tour

Hawes, near the head of Wensleydale, has high fells to the north and east

ROUTE DIRECTIONS

Allow 3 to 4 hours
Start from Hawes National Park Centre car park (grid ref. SD876899).

Walk through the town and take the steps and path up in front of Liverpool House between the church and the old schoolroom①.

Join the paved Pennine Way briefly to Gayle Lane, then follow the road left to Gayle Bridge②.

Go up Hargill, a cobbled lane in front of some cottages, along Gaits and straight ahead through the village to the T-junction. Turn left, then right along Bands Lane to the Old Cam Road. Go left up the track③.

A stone at the junction with a distinct path joined acutely declares the identity of the Pennine Way and points the return route to Hawes along a well-defined track④.

Making Wensleydale cheese. The Creamery at Hawes is one of three in the area

It is well worth allowing extra time on this walk to explore the little Wensleydale market town of Hawes and its older neighbour, Gayle, an enchanting village of alleyways and cottages. From here it is a long haul (but worth it for the views) up the Old Cam Road to the spur of Dodd Fell called Ten End. The return is a fine downhill coast along the Pennine Way.

POINTS OF INTEREST

①A large and busy livestock market, and a commanding position where several routes meet, have firmly established Hawes as the centre for upper Wensleydale. It received its market charter as late as 1700, and was given a further boost when the railway (now closed) arrived in the 1870s. The old railway buildings have been put to good use: the station houses the National Park Centre, while the engine shed is now the Upper Dales Folk Museum.

②Gayle Beck tumbles through the village over its limestone bed in a series of steps and falls. Downstream is the mill-race of a former cotton mill, built in the late 18th century. The tall houses upstream on the Beckstones were formerly combing-houses for the mill.

③The stony track known as Cam Road affords splendid views back to Hawes and Hardraw. Beyond, to the north, the Butter Tubs Pass divides the vast upland area of Abbotside Common into Stags Fell (east) and Great Shunner Fell (west). Due west, Widdale Fell rises towards its summit at Great Knoutberry.

④The most striking feature of the descent is the view of the clearly stepped terraces of Wether Fell, with their chequerwork of rectangular walled hay meadows. Approaching Hawes, two of the town's main industries are in evidence. The further one is Hawes Auction Mart, while closer at hand is the Wensleydale Creamery – home of the famous white cheese.

Approaching Muker. The village is the largest of a trio – the others are Thwaite and Keld – clustered near the head of Swaledale

This easy walk runs along the elevated flank of Ivelet Moor, commanding exquisite views, before returning through tranquil riverside meadows.

POINTS OF INTEREST

① Muker's grey stone buildings huddle beside Straw Beck, which joins the Swale near by. The village is backed by traditional hay meadows – especially lovely when they are filled with flowers in midsummer. Muker church was first built in 1580 but most of the present building is Victorian, as is the curious Literary Institute near by.

② Staring blindly down the valley from the north is the derelict farm of Crackpot Hall. It is surrounded by lead-mining disturbance, the legacy of an industry that flourished around here from about 1750 to 1850. The landscapes of upper Swaledale are peppered with the traces of old workings.

③ The field gate below Ivelet Wood leads Muker's Annual Fell Race competitors on to the fell side, whence they go directly up to Ivelet Boards before a heady downhill fling back to the village showfield.

The unfenced metalled road affords spectacular views of Satron, Oxnop and Muker Sides across the dale.

④ Continuing eastwards, the valley widens into rich meadows divided by white stone walls and dotted with numerous field barns. Tucked to one side is Gunnerside village, protected by Brownsey Moor behind.

⑤ With its graceful arch, Ivelet Bridge is probably the most attractive limestone bridge in the area, despite the headless dog reputed to haunt it. The flat stone at its north-eastern corner is where mourners used to rest coffins on the long 'Corpse Way' to Grinton, which until Tudor times had the only church in upper Swaledale.

ROUTE DIRECTIONS

Allow 2 to 2½ hours
Start from Muker village, where you may be able to park, with care, near the old school (grid ref. SD910978) ①.

Take the road up past the Literary Institute and the Public Hall, keeping the latter to your right and the Post Office to your left, to the start of the field path signed Gunnerside and Keld. The stiled path is unmistakable ②.

A footbridge takes the path across the juvenile Swale towards Ramps Holme. Turning to the right, the path forks after 200yds. Follow the left-hand track, signed Gunnerside via Road, to reach the tractor track from Ivelet Wood ③.

Above Calvert Houses the main route can be shortened by following the path that runs steeply down to the riverside, but the extra ½ mile to Gunnerside Lodge pays rich dividends and needs little additional effort ④.

The road falls sharply to Gunnerside Lodge. Take the right fork steeply down past Ivelet, then go along the riverside to Ivelet Bridge ⑤.

From here a distinct and delightful path on the north bank of the river leads gently back to Ramps Holme Bridge, then by the outward route back to Muker.

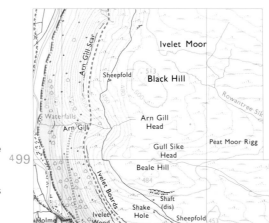

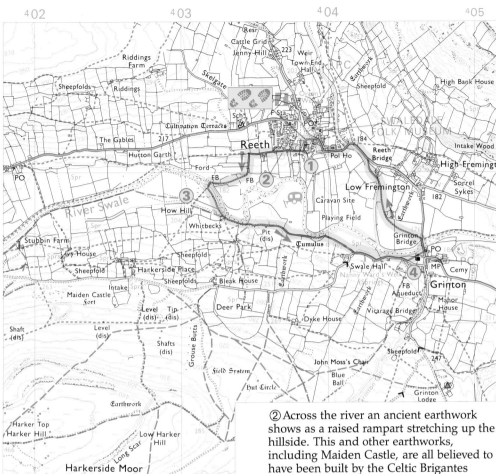

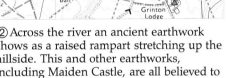

From the former lead-mining capital of Swaledale, this riverside stroll follows easy paths between Celtic earthworks to the 'Cathedral of the Dales' at Grinton.

POINTS OF INTEREST

① Once an important farming and industrial centre, Reeth is now popular for its superb setting. The Swaledale Folk Museum, housed in the Methodist Schoolroom, recalls the local history of the neighbourhood.

② Across the river an ancient earthwork shows as a raised rampart stretching up the hillside. This and other earthworks, including Maiden Castle, are all believed to have been built by the Celtic Brigantes about AD70 as defences against the Romans.

③ From this point, the view back across the river reveals medieval cultivation terraces and also Reeth Friends' School. Now a primary school, it was founded by the Quaker Raw family in 1785. The old spoil heaps from lead-mining on Fremington Edge are also just visible.

④ The Parish Church of St Andrew at Grinton was founded in the early 12th century. Scratches around the porch show how retainers sharpened their arrows while their lords were at service.

ROUTE DIRECTIONS

Allow 1¾ hours
Start from Reeth Green, where you can park on the cobblestones (grid ref. SE038993) ①.

At the south side of the green take the narrow road between the Congregational church and the Literary Institute to Back Lane. Turn right along this lane, bearing left at the fork ②.

At a fingerpost signed Harkerside and Grinton, follow the lane downhill to the left, then the well-trodden path directly to the Reeth Suspension Bridge. Cross the bridge and follow the river's edge to the left ③.

The Reeth Suspension Bridge – a footbridge over the River Swale

After the second stile, the track goes straight ahead while the river executes an extravagant bow to the left, to be rejoined a little further on before meeting the minor road and turning left to Swale Hall. About 400yds along the road enter the churchyard by the gate on the left ④.

Leave the churchyard by the path at its east end and turn left, noting the 17th-century Blackburn Hall opposite the Bridge Hotel. Over Grinton Bridge, a footpath on the left leads across the meadows. The path continues past Fremington Mill, still retaining its mill race, a discarded millstone and, out of sight, the crumbling remains of its waterwheel. Turn left at the road, and cross Reeth Bridge over Arkle Beck to return to the green.

Reeth enjoys a scenic setting on the lower slopes of Calva

Legend claims that flat-topped Addlebrough, visible on leaving Askrigg, was the home of a giant

An easy, leisurely stroll past an imposing fortified farmhouse, through sleepy hamlets and peaceful meadows.

POINTS OF INTEREST

① Elegant three-storey houses line Askrigg's main street, presenting an almost urban appearance. An iron ring set into the cobbles near the market cross was where dog-baited bulls were tethered.

② 'Skeldale House' was the home of Siegfried Farnon and James Herriot – familiar to television viewers of *All Creatures Great and Small*. It is now a community home belonging to the Askrigg Foundation.

③ Standing virtually unaltered from its original conception, Nappa Hall (not open) is a fine example of a 14th- and 15th-century defensive stone house.

④ On the side of the valley beyond Nappa Scar the long, shallow scar woods typify Wensleydale scenery, while beyond Bainbridge Fort the Roman road strikes an unerringly straight line over the southern shoulder of Wether Fell.

⑤ The last house on the right before the fell road in Askrigg is the subject of *Yorkshire Cottage* by Ella Pontefract and Marie Hartley – two local ladies who chronicled the life and times of the Dales in the last century.

ROUTE DIRECTIONS

Allow 1½ hours
Start from Askrigg market place, where parking is available near the church (grid ref. SD948910) ①.

Opposite the market cross, take the lane alongside the three-storey Cringley House, a residential home sometimes masquerading under a more famous name, 'Skeldale House' ②.

The lane leads to a narrow walled lane with Penhill looming ahead like some bulky ziggurat and Addlebrough sitting squatly to the far right. At the end of the lane, a stile on the right gives access to a field path continuing on the same line to the Worton road. Across this road, take the left fork to the bridge and the ford at the entrance to Nappa House. At this point the path and stile to the left of the barn lead towards a gate diagonally across the field. At the next field gate, turn left up the track to Nappa Hall ③.

Date-panels above doorheads – such as this one in Askrigg – are a decorative feature of Dales houses rebuilt between about 1630 and 1730

At the road above the hall go left for 130yds, then turn up the metalled road on the right. Immediately beyond the last house and barn of the hamlet of Nappa Scar, take the stile to the left. After an initial diagonal uphill slant, the path continues along the high sides of the fields past the front of two barns ④.

A succession of stiles gives way to field gates approaching the tiny village green of Newbiggin. Across the green and over the bridge into the lane, a stile on the left takes the path diagonally across the corner of the first field over a number of stiles down into Upper Askrigg ⑤.

From here the road runs past interesting old buildings and alleys back to the starting point in the market place.

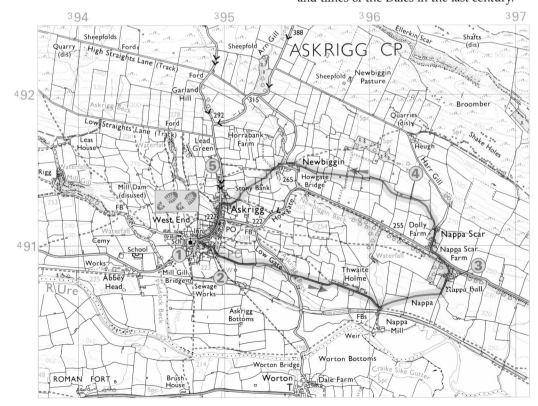

WALK 39E · *Around Semer Water* NORTH YORKSHIRE

The wide, steep-sided valley of Raydale, off Wensleydale, is a fine setting for the shallow glacial lake of Semer Water. Though sometimes marshy in places, this is an easy walk, offering views across the lake as well as visits to the old village of Countersett and to a ruined church.

POINTS OF INTEREST

①The Carlow Stone and the two smaller Mermaid Stones near by are huge pieces of granite left by melting glaciers at the end of the Ice Age. Local folklore attributes them to a stone-throwing fight between the Devil and a giant who lived on the hill of Addlebrough, to the east.

②One of Raydale's three villages, Countersett is a very old settlement with strong Quaker associations. Past the former inn and 17th-century Countersett Hall, a path on the left leads to the Friends' Meeting House.

③The '-sett' ending of Marsett and Countersett is derived from an Old Norse word meaning 'hill pasture'. It is also found in the names of two nearby Wensleydale hamlets: Appersett and Burtersett.

④Stalling Busk's little church stood here from 1603 and was rebuilt in 1722. Not

Semer Water from a point near Thwaite End House

until 1909 was this church replaced by one in the village itself, after which the older building fell into ruin.

⑤The favourite legend about Semer Water runs as follows. An old man, visiting a town that once stood here, asked the inhabitants for food and shelter. All refused, except an aged couple in a poor cottage on the hillside, who took him in for the night. Next morning the beggar pronounced a curse on the town:

> 'Semerwater rise, Semerwater sink
> And swallow all save this li'le house
> That gave me meat and drink.'

It rained and rained, flooding the valley and leaving only the cottage where he had stayed. The cries of the drowned, and the town bells, can supposedly still be heard on quiet, dark nights! A tall story, perhaps, but considerable traces of prehistoric settlement were found when the level of the lake was lowered in 1937, leaving scope for conjecture. Today Semer Water attracts windsurfers, swimmers and anglers – and, in winter, large numbers of wildfowl.

The Friends' Meeting House at Countersett

ROUTE DIRECTIONS

Allow 2½ hours
Start from the north-eastern shore of Semer Water, where parking is available off the road, near the large boulders known as the Carlow and Mermaid Stones (grid ref. SD922876) ①.

Cross the bridge over the River Bain (England's shortest river) and climb up the steep hill, turning right at the top into Countersett②.

  Return to the crossroads and continue along the metalled Marsett Lane③.

  Cross Marsett Bridge and turn left along the track that follows the beck's natural fish nursery. Stalling Busk can be seen at the head of the lane.

  Stay on the lane over a footbridge then a ford to a stile by a barn on the left. (A footbridge slightly downstream offers a dry crossing and a short cut!) The path follows a fairly level course through a chain of stiles to a ruined church④.

  The path continues to the lake⑤.

  The road beside Low Blean marks the end of the path, from which an easy few minutes' walk will take you back to the car.

Near Nancy Nick, on High Lane

ROUTE DIRECTIONS

Allow 2½ to 3 hours
Start from West Burton, where
you can park beside (not on) the
village green (grid ref.
SE017867) ①.

At the bottom of the green, take
the track to the right past the old
mill to a packhorse bridge and a
spectacular waterfall. Cross the
bridge and follow a well-trodden
footpath up to a stile, marked
with a yellow disc, at the corner
of Barrack Wood.

Turning right over the stile, the
path heads straight up to the
right of Knarlton Knot, then as it
becomes less steep, south-
eastwards towards a finger-post
in the wall at the entrance to the
disused Hudson Quarry. Follow
the quarry road left to join
Morpeth Gate above Morpeth
Scar ②.

The lane, now known as High
Lane, winds round the broad
terrace below Dove Scar. A
walled lane on the left leads
down towards Swinithwaite
below, with views of Bolton
Castle across the valley ③.

Where the track, now
concreted, swings sharp right, go
left across the field between two
plantations. In the bottom right-
hand corner, a field gate gives
access to, and sight of, the
ruined chapel across the next
field ④.

From the chapel cross the lane
and follow a level grassy path
above Spring Bank Wood ⑤.

Beyond a gate in line with the
path, it descends to a slightly
lower level before emerging on
to Morpeth Gate. Follow the lane
down to the foot of Barrack
Wood. Go through the wood
over the stile on the left, then
back by the outward route.

Magnificent views of mid Wensleydale
will be a lasting memory after this walk
from the tucked-away village of West
Burton, at the foot of Bishopdale. An airy
upland track follows a natural hillside
terrace on the flanks of Penhill before
descending to the mysterious ruins of the
'Crusaders' Chapel'.

POINTS OF INTEREST

① Stone cottages – many of them the
former homes of miners and quarry-
workers – surround the spacious green at
the unspoilt village of West Burton.
Peacefully situated off the road through
Bishopdale, the village was in existence
before the Norman Conquest. The obelisk
on the green is of more recent date – 1820 –
but it may have replaced an earlier cross.

② The gentle descent down the quarry
road affords extensive views up
Waldendale, Bishopdale and Wensleydale.
The long riggs (ridges) sloping evenly
down between the tributary valleys to
Wensleydale below illustrate clearly the
effects of glacial sculpturing.

③ The huge ruin of Bolton Castle
dominates much of mid Wensleydale from
its commanding position above the valley
at its junction with Bishopdale. The castle

was built in 1379 as a fortified manor
house, and survived more or less intact
until after the Civil War. From July 1568 to
January 1569, Mary, Queen of Scots, was
imprisoned in the castle, which is now
open to the public.

④ Described on the map as a preceptory,
the name given to a subordinate
community of Knights Templars, the ruins
here at the foot of Penhill are of a building
dating from the early 13th century – some
50 years after the Order of the Knights
Templars was established.

This chapel was used by the order for a
little over a century, until its transfer on
dissolution to the Knights Hospitallers. In
ruins for over 300 years, it was uncovered
in 1840.

⑤ Go quietly along the path beside Spring
Bank Wood, and you may be rewarded by
a glimpse of one of its resident roe deer.

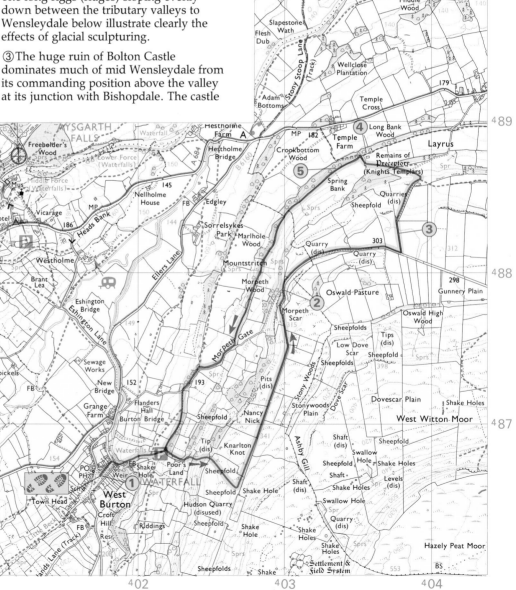

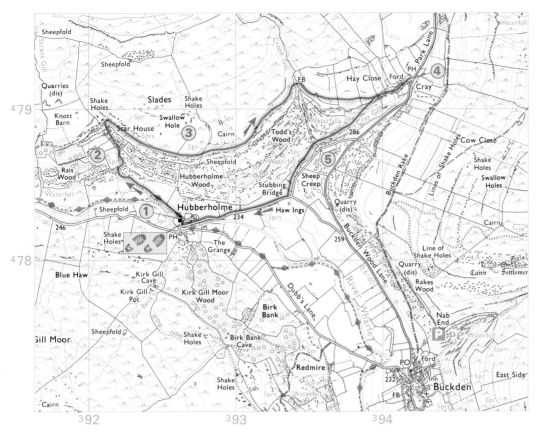

ROUTE DIRECTIONS

Allow 2 hours
Start from Hubberholme church; parking may be available in the quiet road over the nearby bridge (grid ref. SD926783) ①.

From the field gate next to the church, walk up the drive to Scar House ②.

The path weaves between the house and a barn, then turns sharply right up a few limestone rocks on to the soft, springy turf. It stays at this level right along the top of Hubberholme Wood ③.

Crook Gill is crossed by a footbridge, after which the path rises slightly, past the front of a barn, to culminate beyond a farmyard in Cray ④.

The return journey retraces the outward through the farmyard, bearing left in front of the last cottage to descend to Cray Gill. Following the gill with its numerous cataracts, the path crosses the tributary Crook Gill by an old packhorse bridge ⑤.

The gillside path joins the quiet road at Haw Ings. It is only a short distance along to the right to Hubberholme.

Starting and ending at Hubberholme's fascinating church, this is a gem of a walk in idyllic surroundings. Its easily gained altitude affords panoramic views of Langstrothdale Chase, a former hunting forest, and of upper Wharfedale's stepped hillsides and small lush meadows. The gentle descent is by the banks of Cray Gill.

POINTS OF INTEREST

① Rebuilt in 1734, Hubberholme Bridge used to be on an old and important route between Lancaster and Newcastle. St Michael's Church stands beside it, in a wonderful riverside setting backed by a wooded hillside and distant fells. The church will unfold its own wonders to the curious visitor, but features to look out for include its rare rood loft dated 1558, its unusual font – and mice running up and down the ends of the pews! These wooden carvings are the 'signature' of Robert Thompson, who made almost all the 20th-century oak woodwork in the church.

② The view up Langstrothdale gradually unfolds to reveal bright pastures studded with limestone boulders and rugged outcrops, with hanging woods clinging to the hillsides along the rich limey escarpments. Scar House, with its two date stones, 1698 and 1876, has seen many

alterations, but its sturdy construction from local stone, its mullioned windows and its stone slab roof set it clearly in the Dales tradition.

③ Hubberholme Wood consists primarily of indigenous trees – ash and wych elm interspersed with hazel, holly and blackthorn, with a sprinkling of oaks and sycamores. Gradually Buckden Pike appears ahead, and the long glacially widened valley of the Wharfe emerges from the screen of trees, revealing the villages of Buckden and Starbotton melting into their surroundings. After a while a limestone pavement is passed. The grikes (channels) are havens for a variety of flowers – safe from the ever-nibbling sheep.

④ Cray is an old British river name aptly meaning 'clean and fresh'. The village inn here offers morning coffee, lunchtime snacks and evening meals.

⑤ The bed of Crook Gill, often cut deep into the limestone, is studded with potholes and displays many fossils.

Many people visit Hubberholme church especially to see the distinctive woodwork inside by Robert Thompson – the famous Mouse Man of Kilburn

ROUTE DIRECTIONS

Allow 2 to 2½ hours
Start from Dent car park (grid ref. SD704871).

Follow the cobbled street to the Adam Sedgwick stone ①.

Turn right into another cobbled lane past the Post Office and Village Reading Room, then take the farm track over the cattle grid on the right. The metalled track goes past a modern bungalow and a second cattle grid to Throstle Hall ②.

An A-stile across the field to the left (south east) indicates the initial direction to be taken. Thereafter yellow disc markings draw the walker on in the same direction ③.

From West Banks the path passes above East Banks, then approaching Near Helks descends to a concrete road through the farmyard in front of the house.

The track then goes slightly right up to a stile on the left just before a barn, and diagonally across the pasture to the edge of the gill wood below. The path descends to a footbridge, then proceeds to meet the road at Coventree.

Follow the road up to a stile on the left opposite the cottage entrance, then the wall-side footpath to a second road below. Go along this road to the right for 300yds, then take the footpath on the left, signed Church Bridge ④.

Follow the riverside footpath (Dales Way) alongside Deepdale Beck and the River Dee, then turn left on to the road leading into Dent. Go through Dent churchyard to the church and car park ⑤.

Adam Sedgwick, the famous geologist, is commemorated in Dent by this stone

Here is an easy walk from the delightful village of Dent. A metalled road leads up the valley side, giving access to field paths that join old farmsteads strung along the fellside. There are impressive views over Dentdale before the descent to join the Dales Way, which follows the banks of Deepdale Beck and the River Dee.

POINTS OF INTEREST

① Roughly hewn out of pink Shap granite, the Adam Sedgwick memorial commemorates Dent's most famous son, the revered early geologist, who was born at the Parsonage in 1785 while his father was vicar here. A committed Dalesman and a friend of Queen Victoria, Sedgwick was Professor of Geology at Trinity College, Cambridge, for 55 years and had a profound influence on his specialised science. Among his writings is a pamphlet illustrating 19th-century life in Dentdale.

② As the track climbs, there are bird's-eye views of Dent – the only village in this remote western dale – and the rolling Howgill Fells beyond.

③ The path leads in front of derelict West Banks, a splendid example of traditional Dales architecture, using local stone and timber, and adapting contemporary national designs to regional climatic considerations. From here upwards the valley follows the Norse settlement pattern of isolated farmsteads.

④ The riverside path back to Dent is part of the Dales Way, a long-distance footpath which runs from Ilkley to Windermere, in Cumbria.

⑤ St Andrew's Church was founded in Norman times and probably maintained by the monks of Coverham Abbey. The building has seen many structural restorations. Worthy of note is the chancel floor of 'Dent Marble' – a hard limestone capable of being worked to a fine polish that reveals the intricate fossil crinoids (sea-lilies) of its Carboniferous origins. In the churchyard is the old grammar school where Adam Sedgwick's father, Richard, was schoolmaster as well as parish priest.

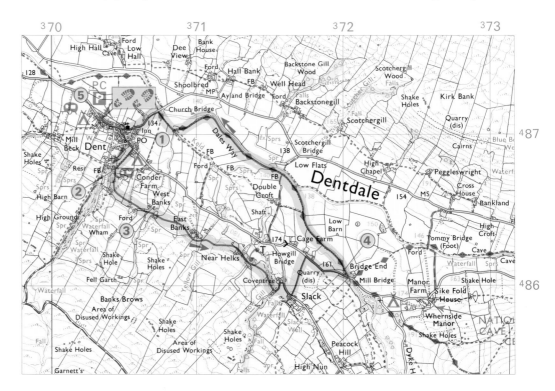

This tour visits Wast Water and the beautiful Dunnerdale; climbs the heights of Hardknott Pass by way of numerous hairpin bends; and visits Muncaster Castle and the Ravenglass and Eskdale Railway.

ROUTE DIRECTIONS

The drive starts from Broughton-in-Furness ①.

Leave by the Workington road, A595. After the ascent turn right, then descend to Duddon Bridge②.

By the nearside of the river bridge turn right on to an unclassified road, signed Ulpha and Seathwaite. The drive now heads northwards along a hilly road through Dunnerdale.

After 3 miles cross a river bridge and turn right for Ulpha. Here keep forward signed Seathwaite. Continue up Dunnerdale through woodland and fell scenery to Hall Dunnerdale.

Bear right then left across the River Duddon and later pass through Seathwaite③.

Proceeding northwards, the road skirts Dunnerdale Forest with Harter Fell, 2,129ft, prominent to the left.

One and three quarter miles beyond the Dunnerdale Forest Picnic Area turn left across the river bridge, signed Hardknott Pass. An ascent is then made of the notorious Hardknott Pass. This narrow road has several hairpin bends and a gradient of 1 in 3. Although the scenery is magnificent it is possibly the most difficult pass in the Lake District. After the summit at 1,291ft there are good views on the descent down into Eskdale. The drive continues through picturesque Eskdale, passing the edge of Boot village④.

The drive passes Dalegarth Station⑤.

In 1¾ miles, at the George IV public house, turn right, signed Whitehaven, to reach Eskdale Green⑥.

More high ground is then crossed, with the forested slopes of Irton Fell on the right, to reach Stanton Bridge.

On the nearside of the river bridge turn right, signed Wasdale. Almost 2 miles farther cross the River Irt and turn right, signed Wasdale Head, then turn right again. Shortly this road runs along the shore of Wast Water⑦.

One mile after joining the lakeside turn left, signed Gosforth. (Alternatively keep forward to visit Wasdale Head.) The final part of the drive heads westwards and passes under the high crags of Buckbarrow before entering gentler countryside. Enter Gosforth⑧.

At Gosforth turn right, signed Seascale. In ¼ mile turn left then shortly cross the main road and join the B5344 to reach Seascale⑨.

Follow the B5344 southwards and pass through Drigg⑩.

Continue on the B5344 to reach Holmrook⑪.

Turn right here on to the A595. This part of the drive is mainly through agricultural countryside just inland from the west Cumbrian coast.

Ascend on to higher ground and pass the turning, on the right, to Ravenglass. ⑫.

The main drive keeps left with the Barrow road and in ½ mile passes the entrance to Muncaster Castle ⑬.

Shortly descend, then in 1¾ miles branch left on to an unclassified road, signed Broughton-in-Furness, Scenic Route. An ascent is then made along a moorland road to cross Corney Fell where there are good views at over 1,300ft.

Later bear left down the long descent and in 2¼ miles turn left on to the A595, signed Barrow. Cross Duddon Bridge and ascend for the return to Broughton-in-Furness.

POINTS OF INTEREST

① Broughton-in-Furness retains its character as a compact 18th-century market town. The 11th-century church features some Saxon walls and a Norman archway. The splendid Broughton Tower and dungeon are all that remain of the old castle.

② Although there are only a few houses around Duddon Bridge, it is of great strategic importance. Wordsworth wrote a series of 34 poems on the theme of the Duddon.

③ In the Holy Trinity Church at Seathwaite is a memorial plaque to Reverend Robert Walker (1709 – 1802), known as 'Wonderful Walker' because of his good works.

④ One of the features of Boot village is the Eskdale corn mill, restored in 1975. A corn mill has been operating in the area since the 13th century. It is now open to the public and there is an exhibition explaining the method of milling.

⑤ Dalegarth Station is the terminus of the Ravenglass and Eskdale Railway, with its steam engines and delightful old-fashioned rolling stock.

⑥ Eskdale Green is a good centre for exploring the valley and fells, on which there are many prehistoric cairns. The Ravenglass and Eskdale Railway stops here.

⑦ Wast Water is perhaps the wildest of all the lakes. There is a magnificent view across the lake, with The Screes sloping steeply down towards the water, backed by Sca Fell.

⑧ Gosforth is notable for the 10th-century cross in the churchyard. Of national importance, this 14ft-high cross has pagan and Norse devices on one side and Christian symbols on the other.

⑨ Seascale retains its character as a seaside village despite its proximity to Calder Hall Power Station and the associated works of British Nuclear Fuels Ltd.

⑩ Drigg's main attraction is sand dunes which contain the Ravenglass Gullery and Nature Reserve. It has a large black-headed gull colony and is a stronghold of the rare natterjack toad.

⑪ Holmrook is on the western boundary of the National Park. To the east is Irton Cross, an outstanding example of a pre-Norman sculpted stone cross.

⑫ Ravenglass is an attractive village within the National Park. The terminus of the Ravenglass and Eskdale Railway is here, the departure point for an old-fashioned trip to Dalegarth.

⑬ Muncaster Castle has been the home of the Pennington family since the 13th century. It is full of fine furniture, paintings and tapestries.

The Ravenglass terminus of the Ravenglass and Eskdale Railway; the line served the Nab Gill mines at Boot

Wast Water, with the slopes of Yewbarrow coming down to the lake edge and Great Gable beyond

England's highest mountain – Scafell Pike – and deepest lake – Wast Water – lie within a couple of miles of each other here in south-western Lakeland. This walk takes in two classic views of Wast Water and the fells around it – one from the lake foot and the other across the lake to the Wasdale Screes, 1,700ft high.

POINTS OF INTEREST

① Formerly known as Strands, and marked as such on some older maps, Nether Wasdale is the gateway to the remote, awe-inspiring valley that shelters Wast Water. It is the only hamlet in Wasdale apart from the tiny settlement of Wasdale Head, six miles away at the other end of the lake.

② Most of Wasdale is protected by the National Trust – even the bed of the lake. Beyond the expanse of inky water, and mirrored in it on calm days, are the slopes of Yewbarrow (2,058ft), Kirk Fell (2,630ft) and Great Gable (2,949ft). Lingmell, a spur of Scafell Pike, is just to the right. This is a place to linger and take photographs.

③ Built in 1826, Wasdale Hall is now a Youth Hostel. The child of one of its early occupants was accidentally drowned in the lake, and the area is said to be haunted by the mother and child, sometimes seen in broad daylight.

④ The remarkable Wast Water Screes are immediately opposite the lakeside road just here. The fell was undercut by the slowly moving glacier that scooped out the 258ft-deep lake at the end of the Ice Age. Sometimes a mass of rock fragments thunders down the unbelievably steep slope, but local people can point out huge boulders which have been seemingly poised precariously for many years.

Although not rich in animal and plant life like some shallower lakes, Wast Water supports trout and char (above) and can be fished by permit from the National Trust.

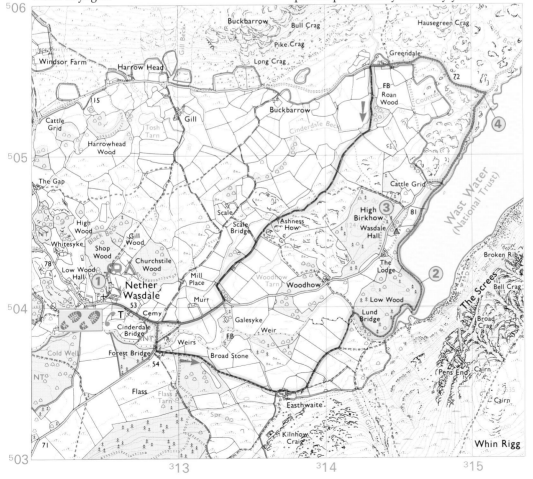

ROUTE DIRECTIONS

Allow 2¼ hours
Start from Nether Wasdale (grid ref. SD126040) ①.

Walk eastwards for ¼ mile to the road junction, go right and over the bridge, then immediately left along the track to Easthwaite Farm.

Go left at the farm buildings. In ¼ mile, at a junction in the path, bear left to cross the bridge then turn right to follow the path to the lake shore ②.

Go along the shore and in front of Wasdale Hall ③.

Emerge on to the road and walk right for about ½ mile to the first junction ④.

Turn left and follow the roadside. In ½ mile cross the bridge at Greendale, then turn left on to a signposted footpath. Follow the path straight through until it goes between walls and emerges after 1¼ miles on to a minor road. Turn right to return to the starting point.

Stone footbridge over the River Duddon near High Wallowbarrow

ROUTE DIRECTIONS

Allow 3 hours
Start near the valley head from a car park made by the Forestry Commission by Hinning House Close (grid ref. SD235995).

Walk along the road southwards for a short distance to Birks Bridge on the right①.

Cross the bridge and follow the path ahead, then in 200yds fork left for Birks. Follow a forest track, bearing left for Grassguards. Go through the yard and follow the path between two typical Cumbrian stone walls.

Leaving the forest, head for Stonythwaite Farm, but in ¾ mile fork left just before to descend to High Wallowbarrow. Turn left here and follow the path along a grass terrace. Go over an arch bridge②.

Follow the path over more small bridges to emerge at Seathwaite③.

Go left up the road for ¼ mile then turn right between walls; keep left. In ¼ mile join a road and turn left then immediately right for Long House.

Cross a bridge then go left between walls. Go on to Tongue House farmyard. From Tongue House go left along the lane for a short distance then turn right across a footbridge, past the front of the house, cross the stile and climb through the woodland.

Walk on in the direction of the head of Dunnerdale and in ½ mile join the road. Turn right on to the road to return to the starting point.

There is a lot to see and enjoy on this walk in upper Dunnerdale, the valley of the River Duddon. Ten miles long from fell to sea, this is perhaps the prettiest of the five unspoilt valleys of the lesser-known western Lake District. The tumbling rivers, scattered woodlands and soaring crags that characterise the walk make it easy to see why the Duddon held a special appeal for Wordsworth.

POINTS OF INTEREST

①Birks Bridge is famous for the deep clear rock pools below it, hollowed and smoothed by abrasive pebbles swept through the narrows when the river is in flood. Sometimes the floods can rise swiftly to sweep above the bridge itself. Downstream is an unusual rock which has been shaped by the river in such a way as to earn it the nickname of the Giant's Leg.

②Just upstream from this bridge is the romantic Wallowbarrow Gorge, where the River Duddon is squeezed between two craggy hills. The stepping stones a short way downstream are described by Wordsworth in one of his sequence of 34 sonnets on the River Duddon, published in 1820.

③Not to be confused with Seathwaite in Borrowdale, this village was the home of the remarkable Reverend Robert Walker (1709–1802), known as 'Wonderful Walker' because, as Wordsworth put it, his 'good works formed an endless retinue'. During his long life Walker was curate, farm labourer, teacher and doctor here. He is commemorated by a plaque in Seathwaite's Church of the Holy Trinity, built in 1874 to replace the earlier church. A chair made by Walker can be seen in the church, while an inscription on a stone outside the porch records that he clipped sheep there. He and his wife died in the same year, both aged 92, and are buried in Seathwaite churchyard.

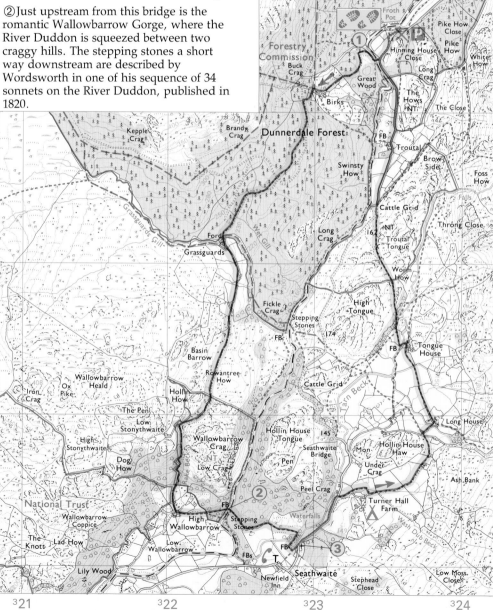

ROUTE DIRECTIONS
The tour starts from Coniston ①.

From Coniston follow the signs Broughton to leave by the A593. To the right of the road is the massive bulk of the Old Man of Coniston.

In 2½ miles enter Torver ②.

Turn left on to the Lancaster road, A5084. After another 1½ miles the road runs alongside Coniston Water and then passes a car park with a lakeside picnic area. Continuing southwards the drive leaves Coniston Water and enters the pleasant valley of the River Crake. The wooded Furness Fells rise to the left.

At the edge of Lowick Green turn left on to the A5092, then in just over ¼ mile turn left on to an unclassified road, signed Spark Bridge. At Spark Bridge cross the river and turn right, signed Newby Bridge. In ½ mile go over the crossroads and in another ½ mile bear right. At the next T-junction turn left on to the A590, signed Lancaster. To the right of this level main road there are occasional glimpses of the head of Morecambe Bay.

In 1¾ miles pass the southern terminus of the Lakeside and Haverthwaite Railway ③.

The drive then follows the valley of the River Lune to reach Newby Bridge. Here turn left on to an unclassified road, signed Lakeside, Hawkshead, and cross the bridge. On the far side turn left, then bear right. (The turning on the left leads to Rusland Hall ④.)

Coniston Water and Lake Windermere are visited by this tour, which skirts the huge Grizedale Forest. A highlight is the detour to The Tarns. The houses of Beatrix Potter and John Ruskin are also visited.

Continue to Lakeside and in ¾ mile bear right, passing a restored bobbin mill. This winding road heads northwards through more thickly wooded countryside alongside the western shore of Lake Windermere ⑤.

In 2¼ miles pass Graythwaite Hall Gardens (on left) ⑥.

Branch right, signed Far Sawrey. Later descend (1 in 6), then in 1¾ miles turn left and continue to Far Sawrey. Here bear left, then turn left on to the B5285, signed Hawkshead, to reach Near Sawrey ⑦.

The drive then follows the northern shoreline of Esthwaite Water with fine mountain views ahead, including the peak of the Old Man of Coniston (2,631ft). The drive continues to Hawkshead ⑧.

At the edge of Hawkshead turn right, signed Coniston. Skirt the village and in ½ mile turn left. After ¾ mile, at the top of the ascent, branch right on to an unclassified road, signed Tarn Hows. Another ascent is made to Tarn Hows ⑨.

Beyond the car park join the one-way system and in 1 mile turn right on to the B5285, signed Coniston. Almost ½ mile farther an unclassified road on the left leads along the eastern side of Coniston Water to the car park for lake steamers. The main drive returns to Coniston.

POINTS OF INTEREST

① Coniston stands at the northern end of 5½-mile-long Coniston Water. Its most famous resident was the Victorian writer John Ruskin, whose home – Brantwood – is open to the public. There is also a Ruskin Museum with samples of Ruskin Lace on display.

② Torver's present church was built in 1833 on a site where there has been Christian worship since the 12th century. Just south of Torver, at Brocklebank, is the Fell Workshop where pottery and wood products are made.

③ The steam engines and carriages of the Lakeside and Haverthwaite Railway are kept in sheds and sidings at Haverthwaite and there are always engines to be seen, often from the road, and with steam up.

④ Rusland Hall, no longer open to the public, was built in about 1720 and extended in the 1840s. On either side of the approach road to Rusland are the Rusland Woods – some 400 acres of broadleaved deciduous woodlands.

⑤ Windermere is a lovely stretch of water which is excellent for sailing. The famous round house on Belle Isle in the middle of the lake was built in 1774 and is now open to the public.

⑥ The seven-acre landscaped gardens at Graythwaite Hall contain shrubs, azaleas and rhododendrons.

⑦ Near Sawrey, a village on the edge of Esthwaite Water, has been immortalised by the fame achieved by Beatrix Potter, who lived at 'Hill Top', a 17th-century farmhouse which is now a museum containing her original drawings.

⑧ Hawkshead is a picturesque village in the Vale of Esthwaite with whitewashed buildings, archways, stone steps and squares. Buildings of interest include St Michael's Church and the Old Grammar School, founded in 1585 and open to the public. William Wordsworth was educated here.

⑨ Situated in woodland overlooking The Tarns, Tarn Hows is a tree-lined lake considered to be one of the prettiest beauty spots in the Lake District.

View of Coniston Water from Brantwood, former home of Ruskin

The first public steamer on Lake Windermere was launched in 1845. Today a regular service operates daily

WALK 41A · *Coniston Water Woodlands* CUMBRIA

Starting near the head of Coniston Water, this is a mainly woodland walk in the northern part of Grizedale Forest, a huge wooded area between Coniston and Windermere. Some steady climbing is repaid with fine views over the lake.

POINTS OF INTEREST

① From the edge of Black Dyke Moss there are views over Coniston Water to the Coniston Old Man range. At 2,631ft, the Old Man itself is the highest of the group.

② Between the path and the lake is Monk Coniston Moor. The name is derived from this area's association with Furness Abbey, which owned land here for four centuries, prospering from its fishing, mining and woodland industries. The moor in the abbey's days was probably open woodland.

③ Built on high ground and commanding views in all directions, the fire tower is manned by foresters during periods when there is a high risk of forest fires.

④ From the edge of the wood near Lawson Park there is a good view over Coniston Water. Craft on the 5½-mile-long lake in summer may include the National Trust's Victorian steam yacht *Gondola*, which has been completely renovated and operates a timetabled service for up to 86 passengers.

⑤ From 1871 to 1900 Brantwood was the home of John Ruskin, the influential Victorian art critic and man of letters. Now administered by an educational trust, the lakeside house is open to the public. Memorabilia include Ruskin's own paintings and manuscripts as well as works by his protégé, Turner. There is a Ruskin museum in nearby Coniston village.

Coniston Water, known for its associations with Donald Campbell who was killed on the lake in 1967

ROUTE DIRECTIONS

Allow 2¾ hours
Start from Monk Coniston car park at the north-eastern end of Coniston Water (grid ref. SD316978).

Walk eastwards for about 30yds then go left on a footpath between fences. At the end of the path go through a gate into a field. Cross the field, climbing to a step gate.

Walk straight ahead, skirting a farmhouse, and on to a minor road. Go left at the minor road to the junction with a 'B' road and turn right. In ¼ mile, at High Cross, turn right on to a forest road. Follow this to the first junction, then bear right. Continue past an open area ①.

At the next junction go left (be careful not to miss this; it appears on the left-hand side shortly before the trees again close in) and climb to a T-junction and go right. In 200yds there is a crossroads. Go straight ahead ②.

When a forest road is reached go across it to follow a path along a fire-break between the trees and past the fire tower ③.

In 1 mile the path finishes at a junction with a forest road. Turn left. Two junctions follow; bear right at each. The road rises, and just as it falls, look for a path going down to the right. Follow this to Lawson Park ④.

Walk past the buildings on your left and bear right on to the path which leads through pasture above Brantwood towards Coniston ⑤.

The way goes through a wood and joins a road. Turn right along it and in about ½ mile, at the next junction, turn left back to the starting point.

Bowness-on-Windermere is a pleasant little lakeside town. In summer its quaint narrow streets are busy with anglers, sailors, walkers and tourists who come here just for the beauty of the surroundings. This is a varied walk including a ferry trip, lakeshore lanes and hill and woodland paths.

POINTS OF INTEREST

①The first mention of a ferry at Bowness was in 1454; the present diesel boat takes 10 cars and (weather permitting) operates a frequent daily service. Motor launches operate from Bowness Pier to Belle Isle, an enchanting 38-acre island in the middle of Lake Windermere. The house (open to the public) on this unusual estate was the first completely round building of its type erected in England and contains interesting collections of furniture, portraits and miscellanea.

②The broadleaved woodland coming down to the lakes is one of the Lake District's delights, and it is one of the few remaining English habitats of the red squirrel. Although they are very shy, there is a good chance of seeing one of these delightful creatures beside Windermere.

③The rough track to the left of Belle Grange used to be an old cart road. It leads up to Long Height, following the line of the Belle Grange Beck.

④Crier of Claife is a hidden quarry, so called because it was here, in the 18th century, that a ghost which terrorised the area with its chilling screams was finally put to rest by an exorcising priest.

Bowness, on the south-eastern shore of Lake Windermere

ROUTE DIRECTIONS

Allow 4½ hours
Start from Bowness Pier (grid ref. SD401968).

From Bowness Pier walk south-west past the Information Centre and the shoreside business premises. At the far end an iron gate leads on to a footpath which goes round the lakeshore and joins the road to the ferry. Cross the lake by the ferry①.

Disembark and walk by the buildings of Ferry House to pick up a footpath going right, by the lakeshore side of some fish tanks. Turn right on to a lakeside road which becomes a track through woodland②.

Continue until the wall of Belle Grange is reached③.

Take the rough track going upwards on the left. In less than ¼ mile, near the top of the hill, a path is seen joining from the left across a stream. Take this route. This climbs for a while then levels out on to a terrace walk. Shortly the path passes Crier of Claife④.

The path comes to some rocky knolls and to a T-junction. Turn left and descend to follow a woodland boundary. The track is joined by another from the right. Continue for a further ¼ mile to a T-junction, and go left. Continue without deviation. The path dives down through a wood. After ⅓ mile watch for and take a path turning sharp right down to the shore road. Descend and after ¼ mile join the shore road, cross by the ferry, turn left by the car park and continue past the cemetery to the pier and the starting point.

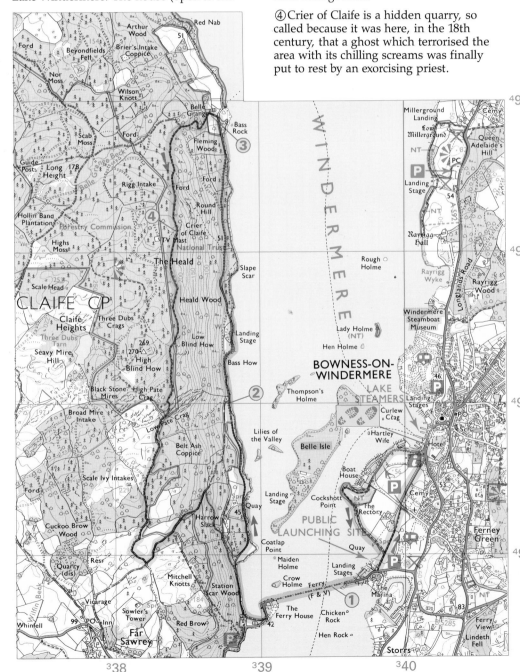

ROUTE DIRECTIONS

The drive starts from Ambleside ①.

Leave Ambleside on the Kendal road, A591. The early part of the drive winds along the shoreline of Lake Windermere and after 2½ miles passes the entrance to the Lake District National Park Centre at Brockhole②.

One mile beyond the centre turn left on to an unclassified road, signed Troutbeck. A winding valley route following the Trout Beck is taken to reach the hillside village of Troutbeck③.

Keep forward through Troutbeck and in 1 mile turn left on to the A592, signed Kirkstone. An ascent is then made of the Kirkstone Pass over wild and exposed mountain scenery.
Continue through Patterdale④.

Shortly reach Glenridding⑤.

The drive now follows the wooded shore of Ullswater with the huge mass of Martindale Common towering above the lake to the right, and the rugged peaks of Matterdale Common to the left.
Two and a quarter miles beyond Glenridding turn left on to the A5091, signed Dockray, Keswick, and then ascend. Continue through Dockray and Matterdale End⑥.

Great Mell Fell (1,760ft) can then be seen on the right and on the descent there is an excellent view ahead of Saddleback (2,847ft).
On reaching the junction with the A66 turn left, signed Keswick. There are more panoramic views ahead of the central Lake District mountains with, on the left, the conical shape of White Pike (2,382ft) easily distinguished. At the edge of Threlkeld the road passes beneath Saddleback⑦.

After passing the turning to Threlkeld turn left on to the B5322, signed Windermere A591). The drive now proceeds along St John's Vale and as the valley narrows the road follows close to the banks of St John's Beck which is flanked by rocky crags and thick woodland.

After 4 miles turn right on to the A591 (no sign), then turn left on to an unclassified road, signed Public Road Round Lake. In ¾ mile keep left⑧.

At the far end of Thirlmere turn right on to the A591 (no sign). An ascent is then made over Dunmail Raise, with fine mountain scenery all around, before the gradual descent into the valley of the River Rothay.
Pass the turning to Grasmere village⑨.

Continue along the A591 through Rydal⑩.

The final part of the drive passes by the two smaller lakes of Grasmere and Rydal Water before returning to Ambleside.

A drive through the heart of Lakeland from the shores of Windermere, over the Kirkstone Pass to Ullswater and with superb views of the central mountains. Wordsworth's favourite haunts are also visited.

The Saddleback Massif, passed at the northern end of the tour

POINTS OF INTEREST

①Ambleside is a good base for a touring, walking or climbing holiday. Many buildings date from the 17th century, including the tiny Bridge House over the Stock Ghyll. St Mary's Church has a 180ft spire, unusual in the Lake District.

②The Visitor Centre is in a 19th-century house in 32 acres of gardens and woodland and comprises audio-visual displays, films, a 'Living Lakeland' exhibition and a bookshop.

③The village of Troutbeck is a Conservation Area and contains one of the finest examples of a yeoman farmer's house in the Lake District. The Queen's Head Inn is the venue for an annual mayor-making ceremony which goes back to 1780.

④Patterdale is named after St Patrick who is said to have walked here after being shipwrecked on the Duddon Sands in 540AD. St Patrick's Church is notable for tapestries by Ann Macbeth.

⑤Once a mining village, Glenridding is now almost wholly geared to the tourists who come here for the fells and the lakes. Seven-mile-long Ullswater is the second largest lake in the Lake District.

⑥Matterdale End is known primarily for its old and beautifully located church from which there are splendid views across the lake to Place Fell and High Street.

⑦Threlkeld's church has a font made from Threlkeld granite. The village is well known for the August Sheep Dog Trials, and the kennels of the Blencathra fell pack – Lakeland's premier fox-hunting pack – are also in the village.

⑧This winding road follows the western bank of the Thirlmere Reservoir. Thick woodland stands above the road to the right, and to the left, beyond the far shore, is the massive bulk of Helvellyn, 3,116ft.

⑨Grasmere's most famous resident, William Wordsworth, lived here from 1799 to 1813. He lived at Dove Cottage until 1808 and wrote his best-known poetry there. He then moved to Allan Bank, now owned by the National Trust. He described the Church of St Oswald as a 'building of rude and antique majesty'.

⑩Rydal was the home of William Wordsworth from 1813 until his death in 1850. His house, Rydal Mount, contains fine portraits, furniture, and first editions. Just beyond is the Church of St Mary where Wordsworth worshipped; the Wordsworth pew is in front of the pulpit.

The Kirkstone Pass, with the small lake known as Brothers' Water in the distance. At its summit the Pass reaches 1,476ft

Grasmere Island, where the Wordsworths spent many happy hours picnicking

Dove Cottage at Grasmere

A walk around Grasmere is essential for anyone wishing to capture the true atmosphere of Wordsworth's Lake District. It could be combined with a visit to the poet's home, Dove Cottage, and the museum nearby.

POINTS OF INTEREST

①Rowing boats can be hired at various points around Lake Grasmere, and canoeing and sailing are permitted – for a small charge – between Easter and October.

②From the viewpoint on White Moss Common, Rydal Water can be seen. This beautiful little lake is now owned by the National Trust.

③The wood on the right beyond White Moss Common was John Wordsworth's favourite spot when he visited his brother, William. John was a ship's captain who was tragically drowned at sea and the wood became known as 'John's Wood'.

④Dove Cottage, by the foot of the hill, is open to the public. Here William and his sister Dorothy settled in 1799. Later William married and brought his wife Mary here, but the house became too small for a growing family so they left in 1808. However, during his time at Dove Cottage, Wordsworth wrote some of his greatest works, including *Intimations of Immortality, The Prelude* and many shorter works. Next to Dove Cottage is an excellent museum and gallery with an extensive library of documents and manuscripts.

⑤Wordsworth chose a modest resting place in St Oswald's churchyard (the grave can be found towards the back). His wife is buried with him and Dora, their daughter, lies in the next grave.

ROUTE DIRECTIONS
Allow 2 hours
Start in Grasmere village (grid ref. NY336075).

From Grasmere village take the minor road south west for Langdale. After climbing for a mile, pass the Hunting Stile junction, then watch for and go left down a path to the lake shore①.

The walk rounds the end of the lake past a weir. Cross the footbridge into the wood opposite and bear right up a stepped footpath. After 300yds this emerges on to a field; walk on beside the river to White Moss Common. Walk up to the left and cross the main road with care. Take the minor road a little way to the left up the hill opposite. After ¼ mile, at the top of the hill, leave the road and go right on a footpath through the bracken to the viewpoint ahead②.

Go back to the road and continue③.

At the first junction turn left④.

Cross the road with care and walk back into Grasmere village. Go into St Oswald's churchyard and turn right⑤.

Top: heading north east away from Keswick on the Cumbria Way near Whinny Brow
Above: Keswick town centre

ROUTE DIRECTIONS

Allow at least 3½ hours
Start in Station Street, Keswick (grid ref. NY268235).

Walk up Station Street by Fitz Park, round the front of the Keswick Hotel, and then round behind to go by a housing estate.

Watch for a lane on the right which runs in a straight line between hedges and fences to cross the A66 by a bridge. Follow this. Go on beyond a cottage and pick up the path round the west side of Latrigg①.

After a further ¾ mile the path begins to level and the Latrigg route leaves sharply to the right and zig-zags②.

Continue to the summit③.

Follow the path on towards Blencathra. After 300yds cross a stile and go left by a fence, then follow the path right towards the fringe of a wood. Here a track is reached. Follow this for about ½ mile to a metalled road and turn right, soon passing through Brundholme Wood. An alternative route to the metalled road through the wood is by a footpath below. It rejoins the road 1¼ miles later④.

Cross the bridge over the A66. Continue for ½ mile to a T-junction. Turn left for the return to the starting point.

Latrigg is the nearest fell to Keswick. It rises steeply to 1,203ft and looks formidable. A zig-zag track leads to the summit and is easily accomplished by the reasonably healthy of all ages. The views are superb; but the weather must be clear.

POINTS OF INTEREST

①As the path climbs, there is a view to the left, down the Derwent Valley, to Bassenthwaite, the fourth largest lake in the National Park. Views towards Skiddaw, some 2 miles north, open up after the route emerges from the trees.

②Approaching the summit of Latrigg, it is worth stopping for an occasional rest to admire the views over Keswick on the shore of Derwent Water – now far below.

③From the summit, what seems to be the whole of the Lake District is revealed in a breathtaking all-round panorama. All of Derwent Water is there, and beyond it the tree-clad crags of Borrowdale.

Newlands Valley is to the right of it. The high fells are in full view including Great Gable and, left past Scafell Pike, Bow Fell, part of the Coniston Old Man range, and mighty Helvellyn. To the right of centre are the Buttermere and Grasmoor ranges. To the north west is Bassenthwaite Lake, backed by Thornthwaite Forest. Skiddaw blocks the northern view. Its neighbour, Blencathra (Saddleback) is to its right, in the north east.

④Although Brundholme Wood is entirely planted, with no ancient woodland remaining, the tree species are those that one might expect to find here if natural regeneration were allowed: oak and birch with a shrub layer of hazel. Broadleaved woods such as this allow many wild flowers to thrive, including bluebells, wood anemones, wood sorrel and St John's wort. Below is the River Greta. The single-track railway that once followed the river is no more.

WALK 42C · *The Derwent Water Ferry*   CUMBRIA

Queen of the Lakes, and most beautiful, Derwent Water is three miles long, just over one mile wide and is very shallow at each end. It has the advantage of a boat service from Keswick that works to a timetable and circles the lake in both directions. This gives easy access to the west shore and lake head.

POINTS OF INTEREST

① Tradition has it that St Herbert's Island, opposite Hawes End, was where the 7th-century hermitage of the saint was located. St Herbert was a friend and disciple of St Cuthbert of Lindisfarne and both are said to have died on the same day. Friar's Crag, about a mile from Keswick, was probably where friars embarked when visiting the hermitage.

② Derwent Water is shallow, mainly because vast amounts of silt have been washed into it over many centuries by seasonal floods. This means that it is the first of the large lakes to freeze over in winter.

③ At Brandlehow the waste heaps of an old mine remain. Although now covered by vegetation and trees, the unnatural contours of the mounds show that they are man-made. Just above here was a once-profitable lead and silver mine.

④ The attractive land around Manesty Park was one of the National Trust's earliest acquisitions.

⑤ From the walkways at this point, some of Borrowdale's crags can be seen, including Shepherd's – one of the most popular rock-climbing crags in the country.

The whole of Derwent Water is visible from the rocky promontory of Friar's Crag

ROUTE DIRECTIONS
Allow 2 hours
Start from Keswick boat landings (grid ref. NY264227).

Take the anti-clockwise boat service to disembark at Hawes End. Go south along the lake shore①.

The path leaves the lake shore to go round a swamp and then rejoins it②.

Keep to the lakeshore path③.

The path leaves the shore at Brandlehow Bay (the point is in private ownership) and meets the shore again at Manesty Park④.

Follow the path as it takes a sweep round a wet area then returns. Later it goes along walkways and bridges⑤.

Join the road and after 200yds go left to a landing stage after the Lodore Swiss Hotel where you catch the boat back.

Another view of Derwent Water – Queen of the Lakes

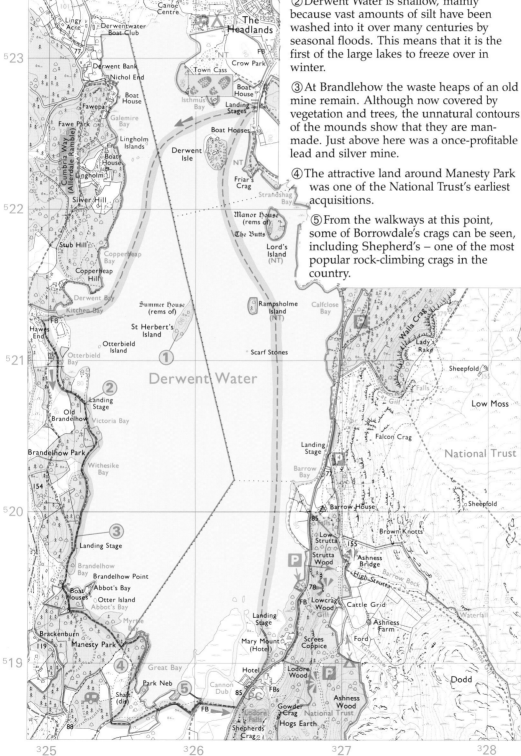

WALK 42D · *Round Hayeswater* CUMBRIA

ROUTE DIRECTIONS

Allow 2 to 2½ hours
Start from the small car park just beyond the village of Hartsop (grid ref. NY410130). This is reached by a minor road from the bend in the A592 north-east of Brothers Water.

Walk straight ahead from the car park up the track①.

Cross Hayeswater Gill by the bridge②.

Continue up 1¼ miles with the walls to the tarn. Go right, to the lakeside, and follow the lake shore anti-clockwise③.

The descent should be by the same route but can be varied by crossing the bridge over the gill by the waterworks and joining the track on the north side, rejoining the outward track for the last few hundred yards to the car park④.

Hayeswater Gill

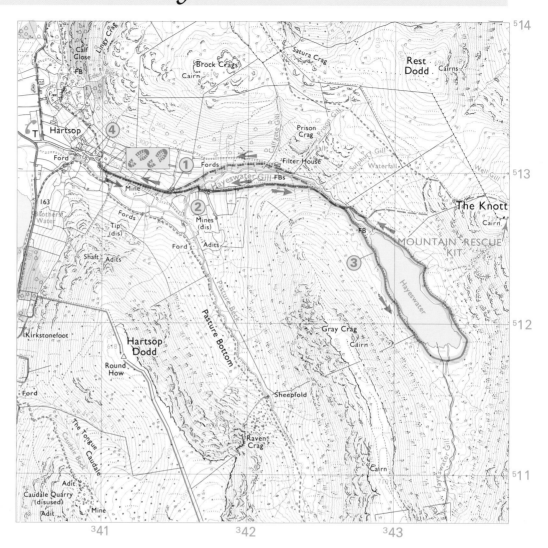

The steepish climb up to Hayeswater

Hidden away among the 2,500ft-high fells north-east of the Kirkstone Pass is the glacial lake of Hayeswater, a product of the Lake District's 'mini ice age' about 12,000 years ago. The full walk, encircling the lake, entails crossing some very wet areas, but the route can be shortened by turning back at the foot of the lake.

POINTS OF INTEREST

① To the right of the track east of Hartsop, the Pasture Beck descends from Threshthwaite Cove to meet Hayeswater Gill. This area is dotted with the waste heaps of old lead mines – a reminder that fell farming was always a precarious livelihood, and any industry that brought a little wealth into the valleys was welcome.

② Hayeswater Gill rises on the far side of Hayeswater itself, high on the slopes of beacon-topped Thornthwaite Crag. The fell country around here is crossed by High Street, an ancient British trackway which later became a Roman road. Much of this

section, which ran between Penrith and the shores of Windermere, is above 2,000ft, including a stretch across the summit of High Street itself, a ridge reaching 2,719ft just south-east of Hayeswater.

③ Hayeswater was formed several thousand years after the end of the main ice ages, when small glaciers reappeared in some of the north- and east-facing hollows of the Lake District, where the sun and thawing westerly winds could not reach. Debris scraped by the ice from the High Street crags remained trapped in the glaciers until the thaw came, when it was deposited to form a natural dam for Hayeswater. Typical vegetation around the edge of such mountain lakes or tarns is the bottle sedge, so called because of the shape of its fruits.

④ Allow time after the walk to wander down into Hartsop, an attractive fellside village of Lakeland stone. There are 17th- and 18th-century farm buildings here, and some of the cottages have spinning galleries.

TOUR 43 · Northern Lakeland CUMBRIA

From Keswick this tour quickly passes into enchanting countryside. Visiting Derwent Water and Borrowdale, it ascends Honister Pass before dropping to Buttermere. Quiet, open moorland roads lead back to Keswick.

ROUTE DIRECTIONS

The drive starts from Keswick ①.

Leave Keswick by the Borrowdale road, B5289. The drive soon follows the eastern shores of Derwent Water, with steep wooded slopes to the left. Farther on, the cliffs of Falcon Crag tower above the road and there are more excellent views over the lake.

The road then enters the attractive valley of Borrowdale, keeping to the east bank of the River Derwent. Later the conical, tree-covered summit of Castle Crag is prominent to the right, and, as Borrowdale widens out, there are panoramic views of the numerous peaks ahead.

Continue through Rosthwaite ②.

Shortly reach Seatoller ③.

Begin the ascent of Honister Pass (1 in 4). The pass, which rises to 1,176ft, offers superb mountain scenery and on the descent there is a spectacular view down into Buttermere, with steep scree-covered slopes sweeping down to the road on either side.

After the descent, follow the waters of Buttermere and remain on the B5289 through the hamlet of Buttermere ④.

The drive then follows the shore of Crummock Water, with more high peaks on either side of the road.

Almost 2 miles beyond Crummock Water, turn right, signed Lorton, Cockermouth, then in another 2 miles turn right on to an unclassified road and shortly go over the crossroads for High Lorton. At the end of the village turn right, signed Keswick, then at the T-junction turn right again on to the B5292.

An ascent is then made over the Whinlatter Pass (1,043ft) and on the wooded descent there are views to the left overlooking Bassenthwaite Lake.

Continue the descent into Braithwaite village ⑤.

Here turn left, signed Cockermouth A66, then turn left again to join the A66. Later the drive runs alongside Bassenthwaite Lake with views of Skiddaw (3,054ft) across the water.

After 3½ miles, at the far end of Bassenthwaite Lake, turn right on to the B5291, signed Castle Inn, then turn right again. In ¾ mile turn right and cross the river bridge. Later, at the Castle Inn turn right then left over the main road to join the unclassified Uldale road.

In 2¼ miles bear right. The rugged peaks of the Lakeland Fells now give way to gentler, undulating moorland scenery in the vicinity of Uldale. Continue to Uldale ⑥.

At Uldale go over the crossroads with the Caldbeck road and ascend, then in 2¼ miles join the B5299. After another 1½ miles bear left and continue to Caldbeck ⑦.

Here branch right on to an unclassified road, signed Hesket Newmarket ⑧.

At Hesket Newmarket bear left, then ½ mile farther bear right, signed Mungrisdale. In 2½ miles pass the Horse and Farrier public house, then cross the river bridge and turn right. The drive now follows a moorland road to skirt the eastern flank of the 'Skiddaw massif', passing below the sheer rock face of Carrock Fell (2,174ft).

Continue to the hamlet of Mungrisdale ⑨.

Beyond Mungrisdale there are fine views ahead of Matterdale Common, with Souther Fell to the right.

Later, at the junction with the A66, turn right, signed Keswick. The peak of Blencathra (or Saddleback) (2,874ft) is now prominent to the right, and at the edge of Threlkeld the road passes directly below it.

Nearly 3 miles after the turning to Threlkeld branch left on to the A591 for the return to Keswick.

POINTS OF INTEREST

① Capital of the northern Lake District and once a market and mining centre, Keswick is today almost solely geared to tourism. Greta Hall, a boys' school closely connected with the poets Samuel Taylor Coleridge and Robert Southey, contains exhibitions relating to them which can be visited by request. The Fitz Park Museum contains manuscripts of the poets and a good mineral collection.

② Rosthwaite lies in the middle of the Borrowdale Valley and has a number of old farms and buildings, some of which are owned by the National Trust. The Lake District Special Planning Board has a car park on the north side of the village.

③ Seatoller is home to the Lake District National Park Dalehead Base which has a blend of interesting displays and study facilities relating to the geography, geology and history of the area.

④ Buttermere, which made the national news in 1802 with the 'Beauty of Buttermere' saga, is today a centre for exploring some of the wildest and grandest scenery in the Lake District.

⑤ Braithwaite is a secluded village at the foot of the Whinlatter Pass. Its church was built in 1900 on the site of a former mission room and is dedicated to St Herbert, the local saint.

⑥ Situated on the northern fringe of the National Park, most of Uldale's buildings are 18th- or 19th-century. One mile south of Uldale is Over Water, a starting point for one of the Lake District's marathon fell runs that takes in all 27 lakes, meres and waters in the area.

⑦ Caldbeck was made famous by John Peel, the renowned huntsman who was born here in 1776 and buried in the churchyard in 1884. There is a plaque outside the house where John Woodcock Graves composed the song *D'ye Ken John Peel* in 1939.

⑧ Before the 18th century, Hesket (as it was then called) numbered only a few buildings, the most notable being Hesket Hall. It was granted its market charter in the 18th century and by 1751 had become Hesket Newmarket.

⑨ Mungrisdale consists of the old village hall, the Mill Inn and the Church of St Kentigern, otherwise called St Mungo, who gave his name to the village. The present church, rebuilt in 1756, is a low, whitewashed building which contains a fine three-decker pulpit made in 1679.

Keswick's moot hall, built in 1813, stands in the centre of the main street

Ashness Bridge with Derwent Water in the background – one of the Lake District's most famous views

WALK 43A · Ashness Bridge & Walla Crag CUMBRIA

Some will say that you have not seen the Lake District until you have seen both the view over Ashness Bridge, and that over Derwent Water and Bassenthwaite Lake from Walla Crag. This walk combines the two. It involves a fairly steep ascent, but should be within the capabilities of any able-bodied person – though the less agile may take a little longer to complete it.

POINTS OF INTEREST

① This whole area on Derwent Water's eastern shore is National Trust land. The Trust has very large holdings of land in the Lake District, more than a quarter of the National Park being in its care. Here, near the deepest part of Derwent Water, the land rises steeply to Falcon Crag, commanding splendid views over the lake.

② The viewpoint above Ashness Bridge is famous for one of the classic Lake District views: the old bridge in the foreground, with Derwent Water and the high fells rising behind. With its lush wooded shores and islands, it is easy to see why Derwent Water has been called Queen of the Lakes.

At one time it and Bassenthwaite were one huge lake, but silt gradually washed down from the fells formed an area of low-lying land between the two.

③ The view from the summit of Walla Crag is certainly worth lingering over. Derwent Water is now far below. To the south-west (left) can be seen Bow Fell, then Scafell Pike, Scafell, and Great Gable. Opposite is Catbells and behind are Eel Crag and Grisedale Pike. Northwards are Skiddaw and Blencathra, and to the south-east is the Helvellyn range. Down the crags to the left is the oddly named Lady's Rake. The story is that the Earl of Derwentwater supported the Jacobite rising of 1715 and, in spite of influence in high places, was beheaded. His young wife avoided capture when she fled Lord's Island by climbing the crag by this 'rake' (a gully).

④ Especially lovely in springtime, Great Wood is rich in wildlife and is crossed by the National Trust's popular nature walk from Friar's Crag near Keswick. Red and roe deer inhabit the wood, and there is a chance of seeing a red squirrel.

Footbridge below Walla Crag. The climb to the Crag's 1,234ft summit is well rewarded with panoramic views

ROUTE DIRECTIONS

Allow 3½ hours
Start from Great Wood car park, on the east of the Borrowdale road (B5289) just over a mile from Keswick (grid ref. NY271212).

At the back of the car park at its farther end a footpath starts left by a gate for Ashness. Follow this path up and then right along the hillside ①.

The footpath finishes after about a mile at a minor road (Watendlath road). Go left a little way and walk above Ashness Bridge to admire the view ②.

Now go back to the path and after crossing the stile this time bear right and go up the hillside. (Do not hurry this bit!) Follow the path upwards steadily until the summit cairn is reached ③.

The path continues on by a fence. Take care in steep places; otherwise there is no difficulty, and eventually a track is joined and a metalled road at Rakefoot Farm.
In 200yds cross the footbridge soon seen on the left and bear right. Soon the path goes sharp left into Great Wood ④.

Follow the path straight down to the car park.

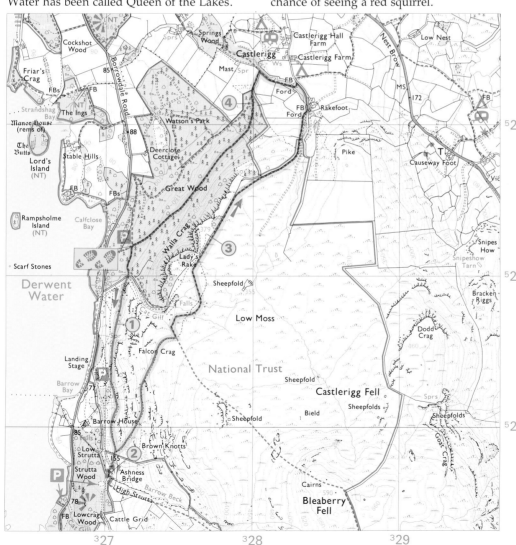

ROUTE DIRECTIONS

Allow 2¼ hours, or 3 hours with a detour to Brund Fell. Start from Rosthwaite in Borrowdale. There is a car park by the Institute on the Keswick side of the village (grid ref. NY258147).

Leave the lane from the Institute, go left and cross the road, then almost immediately go right over the bridge to pick up the clear bridletrack to the left of Hazel Bank. Follow it all the way①.

The track descends to the tarn and Watendlath②.

Retrace your steps for the return journey.

The wall on the right side of the track soon leaves and climbs the fell. The diversion to Brund Fell follows it on the left-hand side. The path is at first sketchy as it crosses wet ground. (If this is found to be too unpleasant, return to the bridletrack and continue the return journey along it; wet ground here is a sure sign of more to follow later.) The wall is followed all the way. There are a number of paths as walkers have tried to avoid wetness, but all follow that wall.

The wall meets a corner after ½ mile. Do not cross the stiles here but go left to follow the wall on and round an elbow. Cross the stile here and follow the path on up to the high points of Brund Fell ahead③.

Retrace your steps back to the last stile. Having crossed it, go right and follow the wall down for about ½ mile all the way to the bridletrack, going right for Rosthwaite④.

Right: view across Borrowdale
Below: looking down to Watendlath Tarn

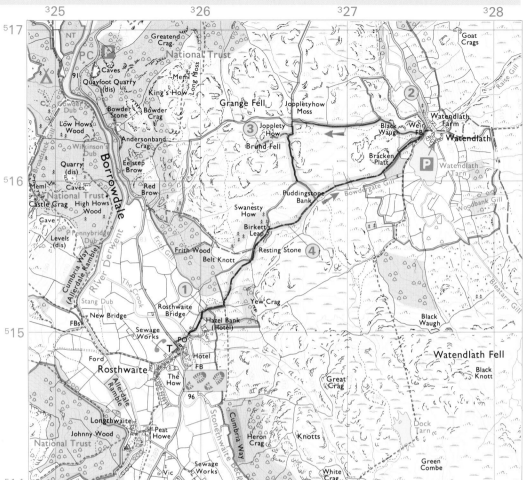

The pretty hamlet of Watendlath sits by its own tarn in a secret little valley. It is reached, on this walk, by a rough bridleway from Borrowdale which gives excellent views, especially on the return descent. The walk involves a climb of 1,000ft but is by no means formidable. It can be lengthened to take in Brund Fell, but be prepared for some wet ground if you choose this longer route.

POINTS OF INTEREST

①The bridletrack from Rosthwaite was a packhorse route from Borrowdale by Watendlath to Wythburn at Thirlmere. Times have changed: Wythburn was drowned under an enlarged Thirlmere in 1894 to supply water to Manchester. The need to maintain the track diminished, and the means – cheap and abundant labour – was lost during the Industrial Revolution.

②Only comparatively recently has mains electricity reached isolated Watendlath, a delightful group of farm buildings now owned by the National Trust.

Readers of the lastingly popular Hugh Walpole novels will seek out the house by the tarn where Judith Paris – heroine of the book of the same name – lived. Walpole (1884 – 1941) lived in Borrowdale, and set the whole of his historical *Rogue Herries* novel sequence in this area.

③Walkers are drawn to Brund Fell by the novel and rather fascinating appearance of this series of craggy peaks above Borrowdale. No rock climb is required for the highest point (1,363ft), which offers exhilarating views northwards across Derwent Water, and southwards to the highest land in England.

④On the way down the bridletrack towards Rosthwaite, take time to admire the views southwards up to the head of Borrowdale. The nearest fell is Rosthwaite Fell and behind is Great End (2,984ft), the northern extremity of the Scafell range.

WALK 43C · *Buttermere's Shore*

The lakes of Crummock Water and Buttermere – both owned by the National Trust – share a valley amid some of the Lake District's wildest and grandest scenery. Buttermere village is the starting point for this delightful walk, which follows the lake shore for most of the way.

POINTS OF INTEREST

① The long strands of falling water ahead are Sour Milk Gill, a stream which spills down the steep hillside from Bleaberry Tarn. This little mountain lake is hidden away in a combe high above, between the peaks of Red Pike and High Stile.

② Less than 1½ miles long and 90ft deep, Buttermere probably derives its name from 'Buthar's Mere', Buthar being a Norse settler. The Vikings who settled in the Lake District in the 9th and 10th centuries were not warlike invaders from Scandinavia, but farmers of Scandinavian origin who came here from Ireland and the Isle of Man. The area bristles with Norse names. The mountains are 'fells' from Norse 'fjall', streams are 'becks' (bekr), small lakes 'tarns' (tjorn), and waterfalls 'forces' (foss).

③ The path goes by Shingle Point under pine trees. Left and above the head of the lake is Fleetwith Pike. To the right of that is Haystacks and the sweep of fell side called Warnscale (Norse 'skali', summer pasture) and the peaks of High Crag, High Stile, and Red Pike. The two great hollows, or 'combes', were scooped out by retreating ice in the Ice Age.

④ The tunnel is cut through a wall of solid rock. Story has it that the one-time landowner hated to see his gardeners idle on wet days, and so he put them to the task of tunnelling to keep them occupied. The path emerges to meander through lakeside trees.

Buttermere, over 90ft deep, contains trout and char

ROUTE DIRECTIONS
Allow 2 hours
Start from Buttermere village (grid ref. NY175170).

Follow the track starting to the left of the Fish Hotel, and keep left, ignoring a right branch for Scale Force ①.

In ¼ mile go over bridges and keep left following the lake-shore path ②.

At the head of the lake turn left over the bridge and follow the path to Gatesgarth Farm and a metalled road. Turn left on to the road, follow it for ½ mile and then turn left again between gateposts on to the lake-shore path ③.

Continue on the path along a lakeside terrace before passing through a tunnel ④.

Follow the path beyond the end of the lake. Go through a farmyard back to the start.

Rowing boats for hire on Buttermere's northern shore

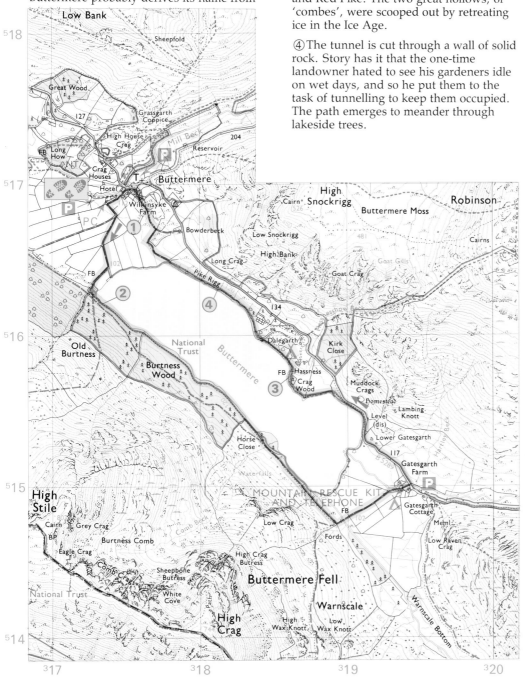

WALK 43D · *In the High Forest*   CUMBRIA

ROUTE DIRECTIONS

Allow 2½ hours, or 3½ with a detour to the summit
Start from Mire House car park, which is four miles from Keswick on the Carlisle (A591) road, and on the right just inside the forest (grid ref. NY235282).

Care is needed on the approach to Mire House car park①.

Cross the footbridge by the sawmill, climb some steps and follow the path until it joins a forest road. Turn right along this road②.

Keep on climbing, keeping to the road, which will eventually become a track. There is an optional detour along this stretch to the summit of Dodd via a signposted path which leads off to the right of the main path. There could be some wet rock and mud to cope with③.

Return to the main path by the same route. Continue on the forest road, descending. When it is joined by a road from the left, continue right④.

A road joins the track from the right, but continue descending. When the track bends very sharply to the left, look for and take an old track on the right, which ascends a little, levels and becomes a footpath. As the ravine of Skill Beck is approached, go left to descend a footpath by its side. There is then a choice of a direct steep descent to the car park, or a longer but easier route down to the left.

This walk involves a steep climb – mainly on good paths and tracks – through forest with occasional 'surprise' viewpoints over Bassenthwaite Lake to Derwent Water. An optional detour takes in Dodd summit (1,660ft).

Bassenthwaite Lake seen from Dodd Wood

POINTS OF INTEREST

①The Mire House estate, which belongs to the Spedding family, has strong literary connections. In the 19th century, literary lions such as Wordsworth, Southey, Francis Bacon, Thomas Carlyle, Tennyson and Fitzgerald – all personal friends of the Speddings – were frequent visitors to the house. The old estate sawmill, now used as a refreshment room, is by the car park.

②Thornthwaite Forest is a mixture of planted conifers and native broadleaved trees, some of which have grown naturally from self-sown seeds. The rock here is Skiddaw Slate, as Dodd is a spur from Skiddaw.

③The view from the summit of Dodd is exceptional, with views over the central fells from south to west. The whole of Bassenthwaite Lake can be seen, and to the north, on a clear day, Scottish hills are visible beyond the Solway.

④At this point in the walk there are views down to Keswick through fire-breaks, and later, views over Bassenthwaite Lake. After the Ice Age, Derwent Water and Bassenthwaite merged, but were subsequently separated by silt washed down the hills during the catastrophic storms which came later – before vegetation and trees could stabilise the soil on the mountain slopes.

ROUTE DIRECTIONS

The drive starts from Barnard Castle ①.

From Barnard Castle follow the Darlington signs along the A67. In ¾ mile turn left on to the A688, signed Bishop Auckland. In 5 miles reach Staindrop, and in ¼ mile keep left at the church. In just under a mile is the entrance to Raby Castle on the left ②.

In just over ½ mile from Raby Castle, turn left on to an unclassified road, signed Woodland, Cockfield, and after ½ mile keep forward, signed Butterknowle, Woodland. A mile further on enter Burnthouses, then after another 1¼ miles turn left on to the B6282, signed Copley, Woodland.

Pass through Copley and after a further mile reach Woodland. Turn left here, keeping on the B6282, and in about ¼ mile turn right on to an unclassified road (unsigned). In 5½ miles reach Hamsterley and turn left, signed Wolsingham. Later pass Hamsterley Forest Drive ③.

Continue for 4 miles to Wolsingham, turn left on to the A689, signed Alston, and in ½ mile pass the Windy Nook Picnic Area on the left. Continue through Frosterley and after a further 2½ miles enter Stanhope ④.

Continue along Weardale, passing through Eastgate, Westgate and Daddry Shield, to St John's Chapel. Here turn left on to an unclassified road, signed Langdon Beck. The road ascends and descends over moorland to meet a T-junction after 4¾ miles. Turn left on to the B6277, signed High Force, Middleton ⑤.

Half a mile further on, by the Langdon Beck Hotel, pass a road on the right to Cow Green Reservoir, and in 2¾ miles pass the High Force Hotel on the left ⑥.

In 1¼ miles reach Bowlees, and after ¼ mile pass the Bowlees Picnic Area on the left. Another ½ mile leads into Newbiggin. After 2¾ miles pass through Middleton-in-Teesdale ⑦.

Turn right on to the B6277, signed Barnard Castle, and in ¼ mile cross the River Tees. In ½ mile keep left, and in ¾ mile reach Mickleton ⑧.

In 2 miles reach Romaldkirk ⑨.

Two miles further on reach Cotherstone ⑩.

In 1¼ miles enter Lartington and in 2¼ miles at traffic signals turn left to enter Barnard Castle.

POINTS OF INTEREST

① The ruin of the 12th-century

Passing through undulating country to Staindrop and Raby Castle, this route skirts Hamsterley Forest before reaching Weardale, then returns to Barnard Castle via Langdon Beck and Teesdale.

castle that gives Barnard Castle its name still dominates the town. It is the administrative centre of Teesdale and has many buildings of interest; the Tudor Blagraves House was once an inn reputed to have been patronised by Oliver Cromwell, and the town's famous Bowes Museum houses important art collections.

② Raby Castle, dating back to the 12th century, is one of the finest fortresses in England. It has a great medieval kitchen, collections of furniture, paintings and other works of art; also carriages and other horse-drawn vehicles.

③ A toll here gives access to Hamsterley Forest, a Forestry Commission recreation area with several picnic sites, nature trails and walks.

④ Stanhope is the capital of the dale and the gateway to Upper Weardale. It has a 15th-century market cross, and an 18th-century castle.

⑤ This area is Teesdale; farmland and moorland on the Pennines. These beautiful remote hills have changed little since prehistoric times.

⑥ There is a car park here for people wishing to visit the famous 70ft High Force waterfall, part of the huge Raby estate which occupies a large tract of land on the north side of the River Tees.

⑦ Middleton is the capital of Upper Teesdale, and during the last century was the centre of Northumbria's lead-mining industry. The Quaker Company built virtually every 19th-century feature of Middleton; the Superintendent's House (Middleton House) is the most impressive example of its work.

⑧ Remains of prehistoric man have been discovered in the single street of the hamlet of Mickleton.

⑨ Romaldkirk's impressive church is known locally as the 'cathedral of the dale' because of its spaciousness and flamboyant style. The village consists of groups of stone cottages placed haphazardly around a series of village greens.

⑩ Of all the pretty villages beside the beautiful River Tees, Cotherstone is many people's favourite. It produces its own soft, crumbly cheese. The house styles are varied, belonging to every age and fashion, and there are many attractive walks here.

Raby Castle and its owners have lorded over the village and its residents since the 14th century

TOUR 44 · *Weardale and Teesdale*   CO DURHAM

View of Hamsterley Forest, with trails and a drive

Spectacular High Force between Durham and Yorkshire

Stepping stones across the Wear at Stanhope, set in open moorland

ROUTE DIRECTIONS

Allow 3 hours
Start from Barnard Castle, where parking is available in Galgate, Horsemarket or the main car park (grid ref. NZ049166) ①.

Go down the side road between the whitewashed Post Office and the large Methodist church at the bottom of Galgate; leave the castle on your left and follow the sign 'To the Woods'. Follow the track along the riverside when it reaches the footbridge②.

The path passes below another castle-like tower. At the end of the woodland track go on through the field gate, then turn right almost immediately through a smaller handgate and climb up the steep bank, over the stile, and turn sharp left to walk alongside the fence③.

Continue past West Holme House via gates and stiles, then where the fence curves look for the large waymarking arrow and follow the narrow path down to a slabstone footbridge. The path leads on by more gates and stiles and a sometimes slippery descent to the meeting of the waters of the rivers Balder and Tees, then by two substantial footbridges and a metalled lane steeply up to the delightful village of Cotherstone④.

Continue down the village street, turn left down a narrow lane opposite the school, and follow its winding way past houses, gardens and allotments. Then turn left to follow Mill Hill Farm track back towards the Tees, and take the footpath off to the left before reaching the farmhouse.

The path now dips down twice to the riverside, by way of Cooper House Farm and a Klondike-like log cabin, then crosses Grise Beck and rises steeply up through Towlerhill Plantation (this section can be slippery). The right of way goes to the left round the margin between crop and fence to Towler Hill, but it may be better to take the path straight across the field towards the old railway bridge, then go by farm track left to Towler Hill — use whichever route seems most walked. Go on by way of stiles and steps to descend from the old viaduct, joining the farm road leading back to Barnard Castle.

One of the elegant footbridges crossing the Tees and the Balder where they meet just to the north of Cotherstone

③ This is prime dairy land, the permanent meadows and pastures of the Raby Estate, whose farmhouses and cottages are traditionally whitewashed every year by the tenants.

④ At Cotherstone, a Norman castle once crowned the steep bank overlooking the meeting point of the rivers Balder and Tees, but all the stones are long gone into villagers' houses and barns. Cotherstone cheese is a local delicacy, still made by just a few farmers' wives.

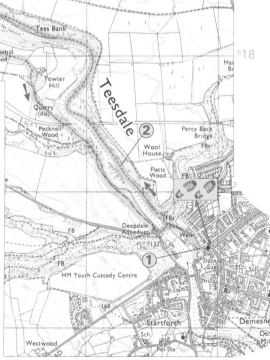

A pastoral stroll along both banks of the Tees, a meandering mature river with the turbulent ways of a mountain torrent. Walking is largely on the level and mainly on grassland which is often damp enough for stout footwear. At both ends of the walk are castles and footbridges.

POINTS OF INTEREST

① Barney, as Barnard Castle is familiarly known by all dalesfolk, is a perfect gem of a small North Pennines market town: handsome, friendly and full of character.

② The beautiful woodland beside the Tees Banks footpaths is commercially managed, and although the felling of trees and extraction of timber leave ugly scars, replanting is part of the cycle.

Spectacular, rocky river scenery and open, windswept moorland capture the spirit of Upper Teesdale on this blood-stirring walk. The circuit involves some bog and boulder-hopping and should not be undertaken lightly – you will need boots, windproof and waterproof clothing, map, compass, and a small rucksack. *Great care is needed on certain sections if children are present.*

POINTS OF INTEREST

① Open daily from Easter to late autumn, Bowlees Visitor Centre should not be missed. It gives a fascinating account of Upper Teesdale through the ages, covering the interaction of man, natural history and the elements. Some of the special plants native to the area are attractively displayed on the nature trail.

② Built in 1830 to replace England's first ever suspension bridge, Wynch Bridge, spanning the Tees, is as much a romantic landscape adornment as a river crossing. The handsome trees, dark rock and peat-brown water of Low Force complete the picture. The falls are known locally as Salmon Leap: older folk hereabouts tell tales of pools so crammed with the noble fish that they could be forked out by the barrow-load.

③ Thundering over a 70ft whinstone cliff into a long, deep gorge, the River Tees is nowhere more spectacular than at High Force – especially after heavy rain. The falls are a popular visitor attraction, but at quieter times it is worth looking out for spotted and pied flycatchers here. Both birds are summer visitors to Britain.

④ Approaching the footbridge, pause and take account of modern-day upland economics. All the ingredients can be seen: sheep, red grouse, nature conservation and recreation, and the extractive industries of water and minerals.

⑤ The Green Trod is the ancient drovers' road linking Teesdale with the Eden Valley, a centuries-old route for livestock and humans, clearly defined by the passage of countless feet. It is still used by shepherds at dipping, clipping and gathering times, and you may be lucky enough to share the trod with a flock of hill sheep on the move, attended by border collies and men on dales' ponies.

⑥ Now used only by shepherds, gamekeepers and ramblers, the Silver Bank track was made by lead-miners.

⑦ The imposing mansion is Holwick Lodge, the Earl of Strathmore's shooting house.

High Force – Durham's famous and most spectacular waterfall

ROUTE DIRECTIONS

Allow 4 hours
Start from Bowlees Picnic Area (grid ref. NY907283).

Follow the path across the beck and up the steps to the Visitor Centre ①.

Go on past the Visitor Centre, down the narrow metalled lane and cross the road by the police box to the kissing-gate diagonally opposite. Follow the path across two meadow fields to the pinch stile at the woodland edge, and continue to reach the river at Wynch Bridge near Low Force ②.

Cross the bridge, and turn right up the Pennine Way, following the clearly defined riverside path to the Upper Teesdale National Nature Reserve. Walk on duckboards through the juniper forest to High Force. The cliffs are sheer, slippery and unfenced, so take great care ③.

Continue to the footbridge, with the delicate Bleabeck Force high up on your left ④.

Walk on up Bracken Rigg, turn sharp left off the Pennine Way by the waymark post, and go through the watergate to join the Green Trod near the NNR board ⑤.

Turn left along the trod, crossing three becks by fording or boulder-hopping, then join the Silver Bank track ⑥.

Follow the track as it threads down between whinstone crags to the metalled road at the west end of Holwick, then turn sharp left along the road ⑦.

When the road bears left follow the footpath straight ahead through meadows and pastures to Low Force and so back to Bowlees.

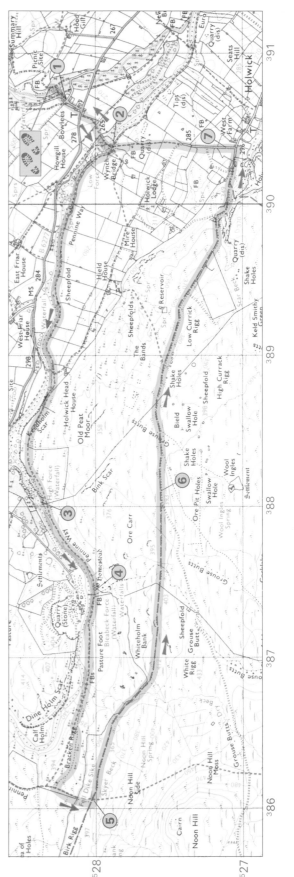

ROUTE DIRECTIONS

The drive starts from Hexham ①.

From Hexham town centre follow the Carlisle signs to leave by the A6079; cross the River Tyne and in ¾ mile, at a roundabout, take the first exit, A69. In another ¾ mile turn right on to the A6079, signed Rothbury. In just under ½ mile pass the edge of Acomb, on the right, and in 2 miles pass through Wall village and reach a crossroads at Brunton House ②.

Turn left on to the B6318, signed Chollerford, and in ¼ mile cross the River North Tyne into Chollerford ③.

At the roundabout in Chollerford take the first exit, signed Carlisle, and in ½ mile pass the entrance to Chesters Park on the left ④.

After a long ascent pass Brocolita Roman fort on the left and drive for a further 4¾ miles to reach the car park for Housesteads Roman fort on the right ⑤.

Continue along the B6318 for 2¾ miles to the Twice Brewed Inn, passing a National Park Information Centre on the left. In a further 2½ miles turn left at a crossroads on to an unclassified road, signed Haltwhistle. In ½ mile descend, and after a further ½ mile, turn right at a T-junction, signed Town Centre, and enter Haltwhistle ⑥.

In ¼ mile, at a T-junction, turn right on to the A69, signed Carlisle, and ½ mile further on turn left on to an unclassified road, signed Plenmeller, and cross the River Tyne; shortly, at a T-junction, turn left, signed Plenmeller, Whitfield. In 1 mile enter Plenmeller ⑦.

From Plenmeller there is a long ascent over Plenmeller Common. After 3½ miles turn left and in a further 2¼ miles turn right and descend to Whitfield ⑧.

From Whitfield travel forward for ¾ mile, and, at a T-junction, turn right on to the A686, signed Alston. In ¼ mile turn left across the River West Allen, on an unclassified road, signed Allendale. Almost immediately there is a hairpin bend in the road. In 3¾ miles join the B6295 and after ¾ mile enter Allendale ⑨.

Follow the B6295 as it turns right at the Hotspur Hotel, signed Allenheads, Cowshill, and in 7¾ miles reach Allenheads. A long ascent and descent is then made and after 3¼ miles at a T-junction turn left on to the A689 (unsigned). In ¼ mile enter Cowshill. In ½ mile reach Wearhead, and follow the signs for St John's Chapel, passing through Ireshopeburn after another ¾ mile.

In ¾ mile, enter St John's Chapel, and in just over ½ mile pass through Daddry Shield. A mile further on is the village of Westgate, and in

another 3 miles is its twin, Eastgate ⑩.

Some 2½ miles further on, enter Stanhope and at the Grey Bull public house turn left on to the B6278, signed Edmundbyers, and climb to Stanhope Common. In 3 miles bear right, and in practically a mile descend a 1-in-7 then 1-in-10 incline before continuing to Edmundbyers.

Turn left on to the B6306, signed Blanchland, and skirt the southern edge of the Derwent Reservoir, passing Pow Hill Country Park after a mile, on the right. In another ¼ mile pass a picnic area on the right, and 2 miles further on pass a road to Carricks Picnic Area. Cross the River Derwent in another 1¾ miles, and enter Blanchland ⑪.

Turn right, signed Hexham, and in 2¾ miles keep left. In another 2½ miles reach the edge of Slaley, and in just over 3 miles cross Linnels Bridge and continue for 2 miles into Hexham.

POINTS OF INTEREST

① Hexham, the administrative centre for Tynedale, is an historic market town built on a terrace overlooking the Tyne. Hexham Abbey was once said to be the finest church north of the Alps; much of it dates from the 12th century, but there is a superb Saxon crypt – perhaps the finest in England.

② There is a stretch of Hadrian's Wall at Brunton House, in the care of English Heritage.

③ The single-track, five-arch bridge was built after the river flooded in 1771 and washed away the previous structure. There are Roman bridge abutments about ½ mile south of the present bridge.

④ Here the Wall can be seen again, with the Roman fort of Cilurnum, excavated by a Victorian amateur archaeologist, John Clayton, who lived in the 18th-century Chesters House in the Park.

⑤ Housesteads is the most dramatically sited of the many forts along Hadrian's Wall and probably the finest. Now in the joint care of the National Trust and English Heritage, it has the only example of a Roman hospital in Britain.

⑥ Haltwhistle is associated with the Ridleys, one of the most powerful Border families. The exceptional Early English Church of the Holy

Cross is one of the best in Northumberland.

⑦ A left-hand turn at Plenmeller leads to Unthank Hall, partly 15th-century, and built on the site of an earlier house claimed to be the birthplace of Nicholas Ridley, who died at the stake with Latimer in 1555.

⑧ The village of Whitfield, scattered about the rivers of West and East Allen, is sited in one of the most beautiful parts of Northumberland.

⑨ Allendale is the capital of a district called 'the English Alps' by the Victorians, and claims to be the geographical centre of Great Britain. The Allendale Baal Fire – a festival with origins going back to the Dark Ages – is held here every New Year's Eve.

⑩ Westgate was the site of the Bishop of Durham's castle, the foundations of which can be seen at High Westgate. Eastgate and Westgate border Weardale Park, a deer park before the 16th century.

⑪ Blanchland is one of Northumberland's prettiest villages and was designated a perfect village by *Town and Country Planning*. It is thought the village is named after the white habits worn by the monks of the 12th-century abbey.

Looking east along Hadrian's Wall towards Housesteads fort

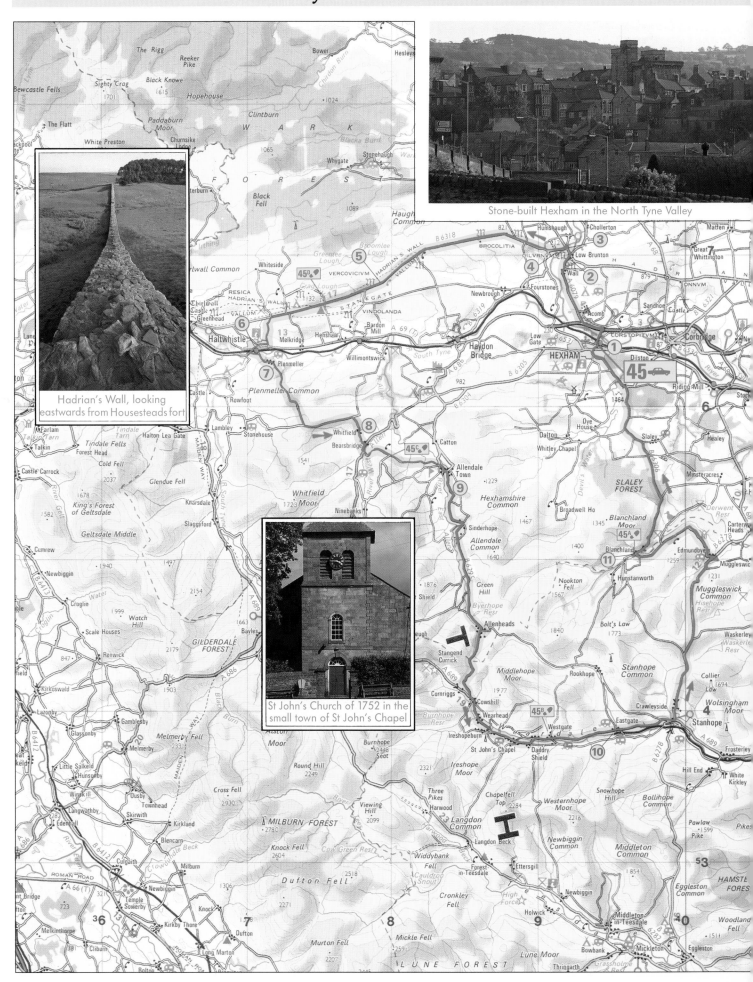

Stone-built Hexham in the North Tyne Valley

Hadrian's Wall, looking eastwards from Housesteads fort

St John's Church of 1752 in the small town of St John's Chapel

From the historic village of Blanchland, this walk leads up to open moorland which offers spectacular views, on a clear day, of the northern Pennines, before returning to the Derwent Valley. The walk is perhaps at its best in early summer, when the valley is rich in wild flowers and the moors resound with the distinctive calls of curlews and lapwings.

POINTS OF INTEREST

①In the spring and early summer the hedgebanks lining the road up the valley are thick with cow parsley, germander speedwell, greater stitchwort and meadow cranesbill. As the road passes the plantation on the right, listen for the songs of wrens, chaffinches and blackbirds and the thin 'zis' of the goldcrest.

②Shildon is surrounded by relics of lead-mining days. Spoil heaps behind the cottages remain bare of vegetation, and on the left of the track is an old smelt-mill chimney. Do not attempt to explore the workings as there are dangerous hidden shafts. Lead mining is probably Northumberland's oldest industry; it began in Roman times, and continued up to the 1920s.

③On the way past the plantation, look out, in summer, for northern marsh orchids in the ditch on your right, growing among fairy flax, birdsfoot trefoil and lady's mantle. On the approach to the moorland, listen for the bubbling call of the curlew.

④These moors also provide nesting places for lapwings, which can be seen in spring performing their spectacular aerobatic

Terraces of 18th-century cottages in Blanchland

display flights. As the track begins to lose height, the views across the northern Pennines are superb. Bolts Law on the right is the highest point on the skyline and Edmundbyers Common rises on the left.

⑤The buildings of 12th-century Blanchland Abbey suffered two centuries of neglect after the Dissolution of the Monasteries, but in the mid-18th century the site was given a new lease of life by Lord Crewe. Following the ground plan of the Abbey, and re-using some of its old stone, he built this austere but attractive village, originally consisting of lead-miners' cottages. The abbey's 15th-century gatehouse survives, and other fragments of the monastic buildings are incorporated into the Lord Crewe Arms and the church.

ROUTE DIRECTIONS

Allow 2 hours
Start from the public car park in Blanchland (grid ref. NY964505).

Turn left out of the car park on to a minor road which follows a stream①.

The road climbs up a small, steep hill to the little settlement of Shildon②.

Keep left at the road fork and continue as the track climbs steadily past a sitka spruce and Scots pine plantation on the left and a barn on the right③.

The track is gated just before Pennypie House; go through the first gate, ignore the track up to the house and go through another gate straight ahead. Turn left and cross a small plank bridge. Now follow this moorland track which is a public road④.

Go through the gate at the end of the moor and follow the track down the steep hill. Be careful going down as the loose gravel on this steep track can be slippery. Baybridge nestles at the foot of the hill.

At the road junction turn right, pass Baybridge picnic site on the right, and take the waymarked footpath for Blanchland on the left, just before the river bridge. Cross the boardwalk, turn right and follow the River Derwent back to Blanchland⑤.

Go up through the village past the old school to return to the car park.

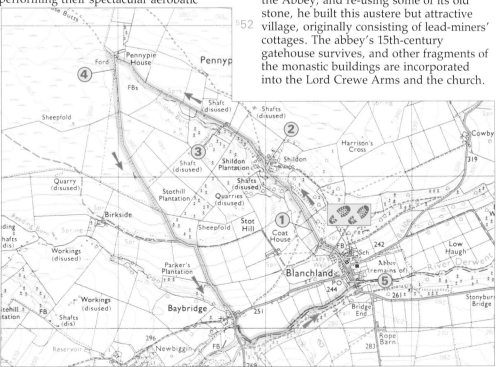

ROUTE DIRECTIONS

Allow 1½ hours
Start from Westgate; there is limited parking near the church on the A639 (grid ref. NY908381).

Walk west along the main road, taking the first right-hand turning into High Town. From the square veer left along a gravel road to the entrance to the garden of High Mill. Please respect the fact that you are now on private property①.

Walk on through the kissing-gate beside the pretty little waterfalls, and follow the path over two wooden footbridges as it criss-crosses the burn②.

Pass through the hand gate to Slit Mine③.

Follow the path beside the burn, by way of stiles over low walls, to Middlehope Shield Mine④.

Walk on up the path to the last gated mine opening on your right.

Retrace your steps from this point to Slit Mine as there is no right of way beyond. From Slit Mine take the steep path to the left until you reach a narrow gateway. To the right a dam can be seen⑤.

Go through the gateway and cross the meadow to another field gate. At the metalled road turn left and walk straight ahead through another field gate to follow the track past High and Low Crooked Well⑥.

Follow the track down through the last farm gate into Weeds farmyard, then turn sharp left over the footbridge back into High Town. Then turn right back on to the road leading to the car.

Abundant remains of old lead workings on this walk are a poignant reminder of the hidden wealth of the North Pennines and the once thriving industry that depended on it. This is an area also rich in natural beauty and wildlife. The going may be slippery and muddy in places, so stout footwear is needed.

POINTS OF INTEREST

①Two large pipes cross the burn just inside the gateway to High Mill – one carrying untreated water to Tunstall Reservoir at Wolsingham, the other, painted black, carrying treated water which serves the Wear Valley and Wearside. High Mill, one of two mills in Westgate, is visible behind the mill house as you pass through the kissing gate at the rear of the house. Corn was ground at the mill until 1918.

②The banks of Middlehope Burn rise steeply from its rocky bed, and are covered with a typical north country scrub woodland mixture of hazel, blackthorn, alder and rowan – so hazelnuts and sloes may be found here in autumn. Dippers are busy up and down the burn all year; look for them bobbing and curtseying on any rock near the stream.

③Extensive industrial remains on both sides of the path recall the days when the valley hummed with the waterwheels and hydraulic engines of Slit Mine. Its shaft was one of the deepest in the North Pennines lead industry – 585ft, which the miners negotiated by ladders. The shaft is safely capped, **but all lead sites are dangerous, so explore with caution**.

④The buildings of Middlehope Shield Mine have almost entirely disappeared, but retaining walls, dams, level mouths and bridge abutments all remain, a monument to the supreme skills of the masons. Some of the unfenced drops are hazardous; be careful where you stand.

⑤Water supplying this dam travelled 12 miles from the head of Weardale at Burhope and Kilhope. It marks one end of the Great Weardale Water Race.

⑥There are plans to renovate the stoutly-built old houses of High and Low Crooked Wells which have fallen into ruin – although in fact High Crooked Well is still occupied. Mountain pansy flourishes along here in season.

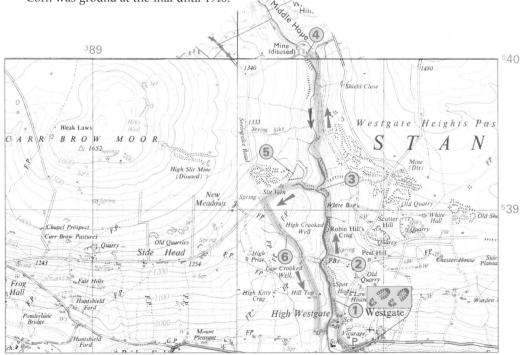

Cupola Bridge over the fast-flowing River East Allen which meets the West Allen near by

An exhilarating walk high on the valley side, overlooking the meeting point of two lovely rivers – the East and West Allen.

POINTS OF INTEREST

① The house that lies at the end of the track is Hindley Wrae and derives its name from 'the hill where the hinds graze', indicating that red deer may once have featured in the landscape here.

② From this cobbled path, the views over the West Allen Valley are excellent with the wooded valley sides falling away steeply to the fast-flowing river below. The variety of trees makes a splendid show of colour in the autumn.

③ The name of the house, Harlowbank, relates to a gathering of people. Harlow Bower, less than ½ mile away, means the cottage where people assembled.

④ On reaching the road there is a good view; the cluster of houses in the valley to the south is Whitfield. Lead-mining was a principal industry in the Allen valleys in the last century and ore was brought from Alston to be smelted at Whitfield. Two miles downstream was one of the principal mills, and Cupola Bridge, carrying the A686, takes its name from a type of furnace used in the smelting process.

ROUTE DIRECTIONS

Allow 1½ to 2 hours
Start from the crossroads near Keenleywell House (grid ref. NY798569).

Take the minor road signposted Oakpool, then turn down the first road on the left. Enjoy good views of the River East Allen which has carved a valley on the right. Keep on this road as it passes a house on the left and a coniferous plantation a little further on. At the bottom end of the plantation turn left through a gate ①.

Follow the line of the drystone wall on the right and at the end of the wall follow the track to the small hawthorn tree in the corner of the field, over to the right, and go through the gate beside it. Look through the trees on the right for a view of the meeting point of the Allen rivers. Now follow the line of the track on to a cobbled path which is an old drovers' road ②.

As the path leaves the wall, pass beneath an avenue of trees and then go through the gate ahead (beware of the wet patch). The path now crosses a small burn and turns slightly right to head up through the field, in front of a small cottage. Turn left through the gate and then bear right in about 15yds along the fence line to continue parallel with the river valley. Cross an old field boundary and head for the large ash tree ahead; just to the right of the tree, the roof of a house called Harlowbank comes into view. Keeping the row of trees and hawthorns on the right, walk along to the end of the field, through a gate and turn right in front of Harlowbank ③.

Bear left up the track (by kind permission of the owner), being sure to fasten the gate on to the road ④.

Turn left up the road and in about 30 paces cross a stone stile built into the drystone wall on the right. Now walk straight up this field (it is quite steep) keeping in a line parallel with the conifer plantation to the far right. At the end of the field is a gate beside a wych elm; go through this and keep the wall on the right.

At the top of this field cross the ladder stile. The farm on the right is Harlow Bower. Turn left along the track. In about ½ mile, where it joins the road, turn right for a short distance to return to the crossroads.

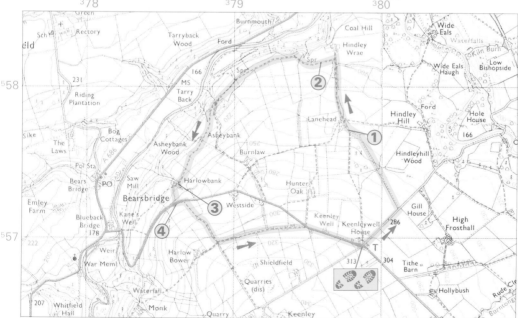

WALK 45D · Along the Wall NORTHUMBERLAND

A milecastle on the Wall

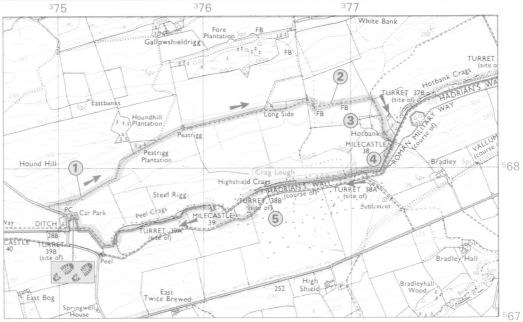

ROUTE DIRECTIONS

Allow 2 to 2½ hours
Start from the National Park car park at Steel Rigg (grid ref. NY751677).

Turn right out of the car park's main entrance on to a minor road. At the bottom of the hill turn right and go over the ladder stile, waymarked 'Hotbank'. Follow the track①.

The track passes a plantation and a barn on the left and continues straight ahead. Cross two ladder stiles, then bear right and follow the path over a small stream and up through a meadow, taking care to keep to the footpath②.

Cross a step stile, then make for the gate and stile almost straight ahead. Cross the stile, turn right through a gate and head towards Hotbank farm③.

Keep straight ahead through a gate, with the farm on the right; ignore the gate on the right to the farmyard and cross a stone step stile built into the wall. Now turn right and walk along the line of Hadrian's Wall④.

Continue along the Wall to a ladder stile, cross this, turn right over another ladder stile, turn left and climb up the path as it rises above Crag Lough⑤.

Once over the ladder stile, follow the footpath diversion down to a further stile in the wall (not the gate). Cross this and keep to the path. Bear right back on to the Wall.

The path now undulates but the climbs and descents are short. At the next step stile, beware: the path descends via slippery steps.

After the descent, the path may be diverted once again to allow fresh archaeological work to be carried out. Follow the small valley on the right back towards Steel Rigg car park. After about 50yds, step down through the wicket gate and take the path back into the car park.

The impressive crags of the Great Whin Sill, topped by the best remaining Roman monument in Europe, make this an exciting and dramatic route, with fine views from both sides of Hadrian's Wall. The track is prone to flooding and unless the ground is very dry, good boots or wellingtons are advisable.

POINTS OF INTEREST

①In the evening, when there are long shadows, the columnar structure of the Great Whin Sill is revealed. The sill is a wedge of volcanic rock which was forced in molten form through existing layers of sedimentary rock. It is at its most impressive here, forming continuous crags for several miles. The sill stretches in an arc from Teesdale through the south of Northumberland right to the Farne Islands.

②The low nutrient value of the soil means that grass growth is meagre here and farmers have to buy in winter feed for their animals. Therefore the hay crop is very important and should not be trodden on.

③On the approach to Hotbank farm look to the right for a good view of Crag Lough. This shallow lake, owned by the National Trust, is a good habitat for summer flowers and winter birds. The flat, marshy land to the right indicates the lake's former area. It is gradually silting up and will eventually disappear as the reeds are succeeded by mosses, birch and alder trees.

④A short distance along Hadrian's Wall is the site of Milecastle 38, now an overgrown ruin. It was built in AD122–26 to shelter the troops who patrolled the Wall. There was a milecastle every Roman mile (1,620yds) along the Wall and two turrets on each stretch between milecastles.

⑤At the top of the rise, the path levels out and the views are exhilarating with sheer crags falling away to the Lough below. The structure of Hadrian's Wall can be appreciated in a newly excavated section which is clearly visible from the top of the next ladder stile. There are properly faced outer sandstone blocks with awkwardly shaped chunks of whinstone used as the infill.

Hadrian's Wall at Highshield Crags

This route takes in part of the beautiful coastline, before turning west from Bamburgh Castle to sample the foothills of the Cheviots and the delights of Coquetdale. The drive returns to Alnwick via Warkworth.

ROUTE DIRECTIONS

The drive starts from Alnwick ①.

From Alnwick town centre follow the signs for Morpeth, and then Bamburgh to leave the town by the B1340. Cross the River Aln by Denwick Bridge for Denwick. At Denwick Church keep left, then branch right on to an unclassified road signed Longhoughton. In 2½ miles turn left on to the B1339 and enter Longhoughton. After 1 mile turn right. In another ¼ mile keep forward on to an unclassified road and a mile farther pass the entrance to Howick Hall on the left ②.

Turn sharp right, signed Craster, and after ½ mile turn left at a T-junction. In 1½ miles turn right at a crossroads, and in ¼ mile turn right at a T-junction for Craster village ③.

From Craster return for ¼ mile, then keep forward, signed Embleton, and in just over ¼ mile turn right; keep on for ¾ mile and turn right again at a T-junction. About 1½ miles on, at Embleton Church, turn right on to the B1339, signed Beadnell. Minor roads lead from Embleton to its golf course, and to Dunstan Steads on Embleton Bay, and the coastal footpath.

In 1¼ miles keep forward on the B1340, and in nearly 3 miles, at a crossroads, turn right. In 1½ miles pass the edge of Beadnell and continue for nearly 2 miles to Seahouses ④.

At a mini-roundabout in Seahouses turn right, then left at the War Memorial, signed Bamburgh. In 3 miles pass Bamburgh Castle ⑤.

In ¼ mile reach Bamburgh town and branch right on to the B1342, signed Belford. In 2½ miles, at Budle Bay, turn left. In 1¾ miles the road traverses a level crossing; ½ mile onwards turn right, then left to join the B6349 for Belford ⑥.

Leave by the Wooler road, B6349, then in ¾ mile turn left on to an unclassified road, and after 3 miles, turn right at a T-junction on to the B6348, signed Chatton. In 2 miles the Percy Arms public house at Chatton is reached.

At the end of Chatton turn left on to an unclassified road, signed Chillingham. In 1½ miles, at Chillingham, pass a road to the ruined Chillingham Castle – a short detour to the left ⑦.

From Chillingham village continue for just over 4 miles to join the B6346, then proceed ahead for nearly 2 miles to the edge of Eglingham. Turn right on to an unclassified road, signed Powburn ⑧.

In just over a mile, branch left, signed Glanton, and in 2½ miles cross the main A697. More than ½ mile further on enter Glanton. From this village, 500ft up in the Cheviot foothills, there are good views over the valleys of the Rivers Breamish and Aln.

Turn right in Glanton, and then left, signed Whittingham. After 1½ miles enter Whittingham; cross the river bridge and take a right turn, signed Rothbury, and pass the entrance to Callaly Castle 2 miles further on, on the right ⑨.

In ¼ mile bear left, and 1¾ miles later, turn left at a T-junction. In just over ½ mile take a left turn, signed Thropton, Rothbury, and just over 3 miles further on, reach the edge of Thropton ⑩.

Turn left at a T-junction on to the B6341, signed Rothbury, and in 1¾ miles enter Rothbury ⑪.

From Rothbury drive for nearly ½ mile and bear right on the B6344, signed Morpeth. In another mile pass the National Trust's Cragside estate on the left ⑫.

In 1¾ miles pass Brinkburn Priory, on the right, and in 1¼ miles turn left, signed Coldstream, and join the A697. Less than 1¼ miles further on turn right on to the B6345, signed Felton; in 2½ miles bear right, and in just under 2 miles enter Felton.

Turn right, signed Morpeth, Newcastle, and in ¼ mile the B6345 turns very sharply left, signed Amble, Warkworth. In 2 miles keep left, still on the B6345, signed Acklington, and later enter Acklington. Continue through the village, and in 3 miles turn left on to the A1068 and enter Amble. Turn left and, in ¼ mile, pass Amble Braid Picnic Site on the right. In a further mile at a T-junction turn right into Warkworth ⑬.

In 3½ miles, at the Hipsburn Roundabout (Alnmouth is to the right), take the second exit, and in nearly ½ mile on the edge of Lesbury keep left and in 3¾ miles re-enter Alnwick.

POINTS OF INTEREST

① A delightful grey stone market town on the River Aln, Alnwick is dominated by the medieval Alnwick Castle, home of the Percy family, and is often described as the 'Windsor of the North'. The annual medieval costumed fair is held in the cobbled market place.

② Howick Hall was built in 1782 and has long associations with the Northumberland Grey family. Its garden is noted for its beauty.

③ Craster is a fishing community famous for its oak-smoked kippers. The coast from here to Dunstanburgh is wild and beautiful.

④ Seahouses is the embarking point for the Farne Islands, and is a yachting and holiday centre. Much of the beautiful coastline between Beadnell and Seahouses is owned by the National Trust.

⑤ The massive Bamburgh Castle is visible for miles across the countryside. The present castle dates from the end of the Norman period, and is still the home of the Armstrong family.

⑥ Belford was once a famous coaching stop on the Great North Road. Just outside the town is the 18th-century Belford Hall.

⑦ The 600-acre medieval park of Chillingham Castle is home to a very rare herd of wild white cattle.

⑧ At this turning is a glimpse of Eglingham Hall, mostly early 18th century, with some parts dating back to the 16th century.

⑨ Callaly Castle stands on the site of a 13th-century pele tower which became a Border fortress in the 15th century and is incorporated into a fine 17th-century mansion.

⑩ The village of Thropton is divided in two by the Wreigh Burn, and has a footbridge over the River Coquet. It also has an early 15th-century fortified house, Thropton Tower.

⑪ Rothbury, the capital of Coquetdale and a market town since 1205, is a perfect centre for exploring the Cheviots and the Northumberland National Park.

⑫ Cragside House and grounds were built by the 1st Lord Armstrong, the Victorian industrialist. The house was the first in the world to be lit by electricity.

⑬ Another Percy stronghold, Warkworth Castle, is here. Three scenes from Shakespeare's *Henry IV* are set here. Now in ruins, there is some fine medieval masonry and the keep has been restored.

Warkworth Castle – one of the chief baronial castles of Northumberland

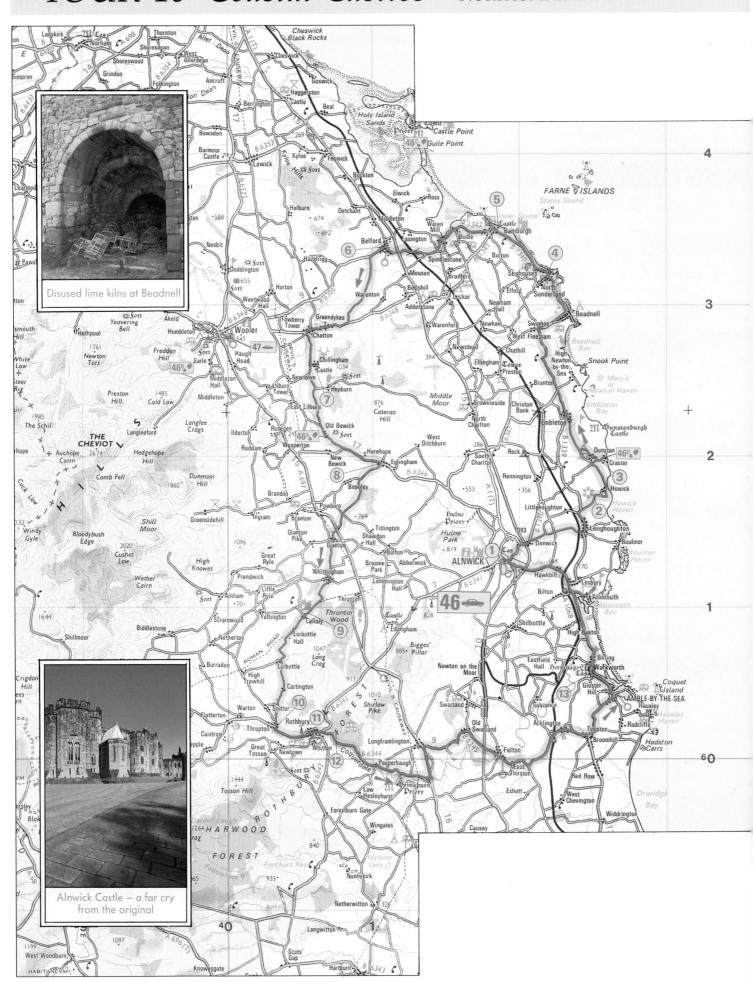

Disused lime kilns at Beadnell

Alnwick Castle – a far cry
from the original

WALK 46A · Around Bewick Hill NORTHUMBERLAND

ROUTE DIRECTIONS

Allow 2½ hours
Start from the hamlet of Old Bewick (grid ref. NU067215). Please take care not to block farm entrances.

Go up the track which runs beside a small row of cottages and through a gate①.

Go through two gates, keeping to the roughly cobbled track with a drystone wall on the left②.

The land changes at the third gate from rough pasture and bracken to rush and heather moorland. Fork right where the track divides and head for the sycamore trees which can just be seen above the rise③.

Continue up to the ruins of Blawearie④.

Retrace your steps for 40yds back down the track and follow the direction of a yellow waymarker in the bracken on the left, just before a small stream. Follow this path through the bracken (and make plenty of noise in warm weather to warn any snoozing adders of your approach).

Cross a boggy area and follow the direction of the yellow waymarker opposite which leads to a good path, marked through the heather with cairns. At the white-topped marker post, head directly away from Blawearie between two small valleys⑤.

Eventually, the path leads into a mossy area which is the meeting point of two streams. Head straight across this, towards a gate. Just before this, turn right, keeping the wire fence on the left, and go up the side of the small valley ahead.

As the path gets steeper, various small paths lead off into the bracken. Keep roughly to the valley on the left and eventually come to a fence. Follow it to a gate.

From the gate there is a choice of return routes to Old Bewick. The first option is to turn left through the gate, down the track which eventually leads to the minor road, and turn right to walk the mile back to Old Bewick.

The second is to turn right at the gate along a deeply rutted bridleway. Keep in sight of the fence on the left and, as it bends left, follow it to a wicket gate in a drystone wall. Bear left down a steep hill and right beneath an area of rhododendrons. Keep to the contour and eventually cross a stile in the fence ahead. Turn left back to Old Bewick.

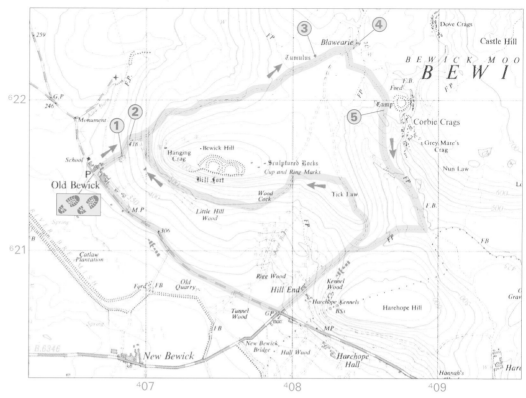

There is a feeling of great space and isolation on this moorland walk. The route takes in several prehistoric sites, in an area liberally scattered with burial mounds and hillforts. The views – across to the Cheviots and along the valley of the meandering River Till – are among the finest in Northumberland.

POINTS OF INTEREST

① The track climbs the flank of Bewick Hill, passing an old reservoir surrounded by sycamore, larch and Scots pine trees. Ahead and to the right is the flat summit, the site of a prehistoric hillfort. It is well preserved and has four ridges on the north side. This hill is part of an escarpment which extends away to the north, cloaked mainly in sitka spruce trees. This is Hepburn Wood and behind it on a hilltop is Ross Castle, another Iron Age fort.

② As the track gains height, look back at the panoramic view of the Cheviots. Hedgehope is the dome-shaped hill, and to its right is The Cheviot itself, crowning the massif at 2,674ft.

③ The pile of stones to the left of the path just beyond the fork is a Bronze Age burial mound, dating back to 1600BC. It contains three cists, or stone graves, where various treasures have been found, including a jet necklace, shell beads and a broken flint knife. As well as these remains, there are also strange rock carvings which decorate some of the moors above Rothbury. These

'cup-and-ring' carvings, as they are known, have fascinated and puzzled archaeologists for decades.

④ The lonely settlement of Blawearie has been derelict for more than 40 years. The outcrop of sandstone behind the house was once incorporated into a garden, with stone steps linking the levels.

⑤ Just before the path passes the rocky gully known as Corbie Crags (whose name is derived from the local word for crow), another prehistoric camp can be seen in the bracken on the left. Further down the valley of Stock Brook, on the right, is a reminder of more recent defensive measures – a World War II pillbox.

The ruins of Blawearie on the edge of Bewick Moor

Coldgate Water near Carey Burn Bridge

From its source high on the slopes of The Cheviot, the Harthope Burn rushes down towards Happy Valley, at the edge of the National Park. This walk follows the valley downstream, never far from the river, before returning along the opposite side on higher ground with magnificent views.

POINTS OF INTEREST

①Close to the start of the walk, the Harthope Burn joins forces with the Carey Burn to form Coldgate Water. Both tributaries have large water catchment areas and the channel ahead indicates Coldgate Water's capacity to flood. In June the bank of gorse on the left is aflame with yellow flowers whose rich scent is strongly reminiscent of coconut.

②Herons can often be seen fishing along the river beside the flat pasture known as Grimping Haugh. As you come over the rise in the path you may disturb one of these huge, graceful birds and watch it take off, flying with outstretched legs and slow wing-beats.

③Pause on the footbridge to look for dippers and wagtails. The dipper is a characteristic bird of clear, rocky streams; it looks like a chubby blackbird with a white breast.

④At the first gate on the track to Old Middleton, it is worth pausing to look back at the fine view of Bewick Moor's sandstone edge, rising steeply from the valley of the River Till.

⑤From the hilltop the red pantiled roofs of Middleton Old Town can be seen, with the tip of The Cheviot behind. The deserted houses of this remote hamlet are not of any great age, but the hummocks in the field further on are the remnants of an older settlement. The site is a scheduled Ancient Monument. A splendid drystone wall on the left at the next gate has been beautifully restored in an effort to preserve the character of the old village. A public footpath runs through Middleton Old Town if you wish to explore.

⑥Look back from Carey Burn Bridge for a fine view up the Harthope Valley, with Housey Crags high up on the left and the great dome of Hedgehope Hill beyond.

ROUTE DIRECTIONS

Allow 3 hours
Start in the Harthope Valley, where you can park on the gravel verge at the bottom of the steep hill which leads into the valley, just before Carey Burn Bridge (grid ref. NT976249).

Turn left along the road and in about 20yds, cross a stile on the right beside a gate①.

Keep to the track through the gorse to an alder grove and fork left along a path which leaves the main track and starts climbing②.

Keep straight on, more or less following the river and eventually bear left beside a plantation and go through a gate. Continue on the haugh, avoiding the sheep paths which lead up the bank on the left. Eventually the path reaches a stile. Cross this into a wood. The path is right beside Coldgate Water.

Near the end of this track, turn right through a kissing-gate and cross the footbridge③.

Bear right up the road for about ¼ mile, past North Middleton Farm, and turn right along the track waymarked 'Old Middleton, Harthope Valley and Langlee'. Follow the drystone wall uphill④.

Continue to the brow of the hill⑤.

Bear right after a gate. Go down a bank and cross a bridge at the head of a gorge.

Now go up the bank, cross the stile and keep to the fence on the right which encloses a pine plantation. Cross two more stiles and follow the side of the hill as the path begins to climb.

At the next gate, turn left to follow the yellow waymarker straight up along the edge of a field to another waymarker. This points the way across a field.

Keep straight on as the track leads through an isolated gateway and, to avoid a small marsh, keep right. Another waymarker signals the way.

Just beyond the next gate, turn left on a path through the bracken. At the bottom of this section of path, bear left over a broken wall and go over a stile.

Now keep to this path as it hugs the valley side and passes beneath a group of oaks.

Finally, the path leads down steps, across the footbridge, almost straight across a field and then over a stile on the left to come out on the road. Turn right over Carey Burn Bridge⑥.

WALK 46C · *Holy Island* NORTHUMBERLAND

ROUTE DIRECTIONS

Allow 1½ hours
Start from Holy Island car park
(grid ref. NU127422).

Turn right out of the car park
and left at the next junction.
Then turn right and sharp left to
visit the church and priory①.

If bypassing the priory, go
through the gate, keep to the
path which loops around the
church and exit via a small gate
on the west side of the church.
Turn left down the track. At the
bottom of the hill, bear left up
the steep path on to the top of
the rocky outcrop which is a
dolerite dike.
Bear left at the dip in the hill
and then right along a gravel
path to the harbour②.

At the end of the track, turn
right towards the castle and
follow the road to a kissing gate.
Go through the gate and walk
around the base of the castle③.

Turn along the old wagonway
through a kissing gate and keep
to this track which leads away
from the sea via a freshwater
pool on the left. Cross one stile
and a second kissing gate
leading into the National Nature
Reserve which extends across the
north of Holy Island④.

Turn left at the next track
crossing the path (before the
dunes) and follow this path along
the foot of the dunes. The path
will eventually lead on to a well-
defined track which turns left and
then leads directly back to the
car park.

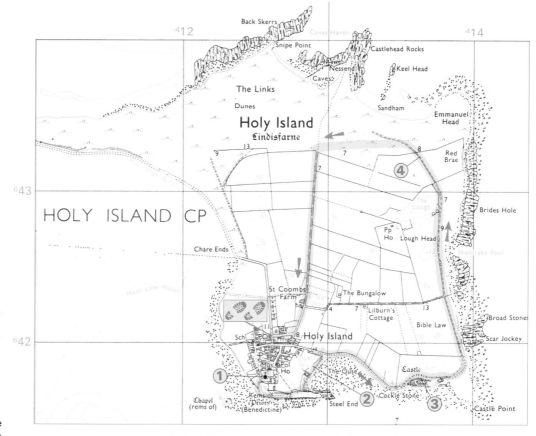

**Experience the charm of Holy Island on
this walk which takes in Lindisfarne
Priory, harbour and castle on a short but
fascinating excursion. Note: the causeway
floods at high tide, so to avoid a delay of
up to two hours, check the tide times
in advance.**

Architect Sir Edwin Lutyens turned Lindisfarne
Castle into a comfortable home in 1903

POINTS OF INTEREST

① In 634 Oswald invited the monks from
Iona to Lindisfarne and Aidan founded a
wooden monastery here. This was wasted
by Vikings in 875 and the brothers fled for
their lives. However, the monastery was
added to over the years and although now a
roofless ruin, the 11th-century remains are
still impressive.

② Lobster and crab pots are in evidence at
the harbour, even though the main catch is
now salmon. Go round the harbour,
noticing the boathouses which are listed
buildings.

③ Lindisfarne Castle was built in 1539, a
year after Henry VIII dissolved the
monasteries and the island became a
military rather than a spiritual base. It was
bought as a private house at the turn of the
century by Edward Hudson, founder of
Country Life magazine, and is now in the
care of the National Trust. The old lime
kilns a little further on were fed by
limestone from the north of the island and
the quicklime was shipped to Dundee in
return for coal.

④ Most of Holy Island is a National Nature
Reserve because of the vast stretches of
intertidal mudflats between the island and
the mainland – providing a winter home for
thousands of wildfowl – and the great
botanical interest of the island.

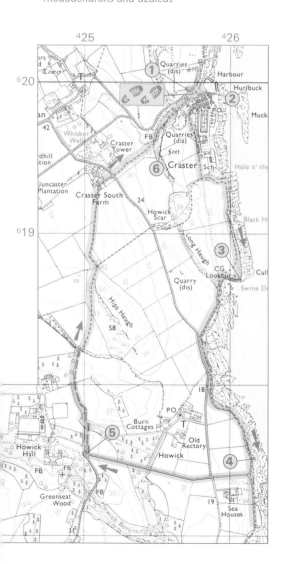

Howick Hall Gardens — renowned for banks of rhododendrons and azaleas

Lobster and crab pots — familiar in Craster

Northumberland's wonderfully unspoilt coast is the backdrop to the first stretch of this varied walk, which begins in the tiny fishing village of Craster, home of the famous kippers. There is an opportunity to visit the gardens of Howick Hall before crossing a small woodland nature reserve on the return.

ROUTE DIRECTIONS

Allow 2 hours.
Start from Craster car park (grid ref. NU257198) ①.

Leave the car park and turn right down to the harbour ②.

Turn right alongside the harbour, bear slightly right at the end of the road and go along Heugh Road before turning left on to the coast path. Follow the path past Cullernose Point ③.

Continue along the coast path from Cullernose Point, eventually passing a beautifully chimneyed house ④.

Turn right along the track waymarked Howick Burn Mouth and keep straight on at the road to reach the entrance to Howick Hall in about ½ mile ⑤.

Turn right through the car park (just before the Hall entrance) and go through a gate to follow a farm track along the edge of a wood on the left. At the end of this wood, go through a gate (ignore the stile on the left) and cross the field ahead, which has a very narrow footpath leading straight through it towards a 'heugh' or rocky outcrop of the Great Whin Sill.

Cross a stile at the end of the field and now keep to the stone wall on the left. In the corner of the field is a ladder stile on the left. Cross this, and now follow the right-hand field boundary round to Craster South Farm.

Here, turn right and go down to the road. Cross to the gate opposite and follow the footpath to a wooded heugh ⑥.

Follow this path back to Craster car park.

POINTS OF INTEREST

① Craster car park is in the village's old quarry, worked until the 1930s for its whinstone. This hard, dark stone is difficult to shape for use in building, but was good for surfacing roads. Near the coach-parking area the sheer quarried faces have found a new use — as a nesting site for fulmars.

② Craster's fishing industry is today a smaller concern than it was 70 or 80 years ago, but traditional Craster kippers are still cured in the smoke-blackened harbourside sheds of Robson and Sons, and can be purchased here during the smoking season in late summer.

③ Looking north from Cullernose Point, the coastline is dominated by ruined Dunstanburgh Castle. House martins and fulmars nest on the cliffs near Cullernose, and all along this coast you are likely to see cormorants, kittiwakes and eider ducks.

④ The clifftop cottage was built as a bathing house for the Grey family of nearby Howick Hall. On the seaward side of the promontory ahead is Rumbling Kern, a deep cleft in the cliff which earns its name from the sound effects created by an incoming tide.

⑤ Built in 1782, Howick Hall stands in beautiful gardens which are well worth a visit in spring and early summer, when the displays of daffodils are followed by rhododendrons and azaleas.

⑥ One of a series of whinstone outcrops or 'heughs', this woodland just outside Craster is a reserve of the Northumberland Wildlife Trust. It is especially lovely in spring. Several species of warbler are found here, and the reserve is often visited by rare birds on migration.

ROUTE DIRECTIONS

The drive starts from Wooler ①.

Take the A697 from Wooler, signed Coldstream. After 2¾ miles, branch left on the B6351, signed Yetholm, and follow the road for 1¾ miles to a plaque on the right ②.

Follow the B6351 for a further mile to Kirknewton ③.

This tour starts at the edge of the Northumberland National Park, skirts the Bowmont Water Valley, takes in Carter Bar and Otterburn, before passing Catcleugh Reservoir and Redesdale Forest on the return to Wooler.

⑤ The viewpoint at Carter Bar (1,371ft) is on the Border, and from the lay-by on a clear day the view reaches 50 miles away to Edinburgh and the Firth of Forth.

⑥ There is a memorial in the tiny 18th-century church at Byrness to the construction workers who died while building the reservoir.

Leave Kirknewton and after 2¾ miles, on the edge of Kilham, go forward on an unclassified road, signed Kirk Yetholm, Town Yetholm, and drive for 3 miles, to a small stream which marks the Scottish Border; 1½ miles further on is Kirk Yetholm, and the road leads on to the main village under ½ mile away at Yetholm, or Town Yetholm as it is locally known ④.

Take the B6401 from Town Yetholm, signed Morebattle, Jedburgh. In 3⅓ miles, cross a bridge over the Kale Water, and continue towards Morebattle. After ¼ mile keep left and in another ½ mile the road reaches Morebattle.

One and a half miles from Morebattle turn left along an unclassified road, signed Cessford; 1½ miles further on keep left into Cessford.

In the village bear right and after 3½ miles turn left at a crossroads, signed Oxnam. Just over a mile further on cross a narrow bridge, and in another ½ mile, at a T-junction, turn left and follow the road for ¾ mile into Oxnam. In just over 4 miles turn left on to the A68, signed Newcastle, and ascend from here 5¼ miles to Carter Bar ⑤.

The long 5½-mile descent leads past the Catcleugh Reservoir on the right to Byrness ⑥.

In a further 1¾ miles, on the right, is the Redesdale Forest Park. Follow the A68 for 3¾ miles to Rochester, the 'camp on the high rock', and, a little more than 2½ miles beyond Rochester, go forward on the A696, signed Otterburn, which is reached in 2¼ miles ⑦.

In just under a mile from Otterburn, branch left on to the B6341, signed Rothbury, and in 2½ miles enter Elsdon ⑧.

From Elsdon continue northwards on the B6341 for nearly 5 miles to reach the Harehaugh Picnic Site, on the left. After ¼ mile turn left on to an unclassified road, signed Holystone, Harbottle. Follow this road for 2¾ miles into Holystone ⑨.

Bear right out of Holystone and ¾ mile north, at a T-junction, turn left, signed Harbottle, Alwinton, to Harbottle ⑩.

A mile out of Harbottle, cross the River Coquet, and turn right after ¼ mile, signed Netherton. Follow the road for 4¾ miles to Netherton and turn left at the post office, signed Whittingham ⑪.

Leaving Whittingham, in ¼ mile turn left at a T-junction, signed Glanton, Wooler, and follow this road for almost 2 miles to Glanton. Here are lovely views over the Breamish and Aln valleys.

Turn left at the crossroads, and then bear to the right, signed Powburn, Wooler. In 1¼ miles the road reaches Powburn and joins the A697. In a further 3½ miles pass the Cat's Paw Picnic Area and the last lap into Wooler is 5 miles.

POINTS OF INTEREST

① The centre of a large farming community, Wooler is a good place from which to explore the Cheviots. It has a distinguished place in the history of wood engraving, for it was the birthplace of the Brothers Dalziel, who were responsible for a large number of the illustrations in Victorian books.

② The plaque indicates the Saxon village of Ad Gefrin, first discovered in 1955, its timber hall structures and stockades long since decayed.

③ One of the most beautifully situated villages in Northumberland, Kirknewton was once a vulnerable Border town. Its remarkable Early English church has a chancel and south transept both with pointed tunnel vaults and little, or no, vertical walls.

④ Kirk Yetholm marks the end of the Pennine Way, and is a walking and climbing centre with camp sites and fishing and riding facilities.

The stark beauty of the Upper Coquet Valley from a viewpoint above Alwinton

Byrness has a small village built for Forestry Commission employees, a picnic site and fishing facilities.

⑦ Otterburn is where James, Earl of Douglas, died at the hand of Harry Hotspur in the famous Battle of Otterburn (1388). The early 19th-century mill used to produce world famous tweeds and woollens using the fleece of local black-faced sheep.

⑧ One of the finest pele towers in the county, and the remains of a Norman motte-and-bailey, illustrate Elsdon's one-time strategic importance.

⑨ Holystone is one of the loveliest villages in Coquetdale and is famous for the holy well – known as Lady's Well – now in the care of the National Trust.

⑩ The lovely Coquetdale village of Harbottle nestles beside the river at the foot of the ruined 12th-century castle.

⑪ Whittingham's stone houses make it one of the most picturesque of Northumberland's villages. The annual fair became celebrated in folklore by the song *Whittingham Fair*, also sung as *Scarborough Fair*.

Wooler – a market town

Elsdon's spacious village green, with its church

Catcleugh Reservoir, completed in 1906

Elsdon pele tower

A view towards the moorland summits lying to the east of Clennell Street

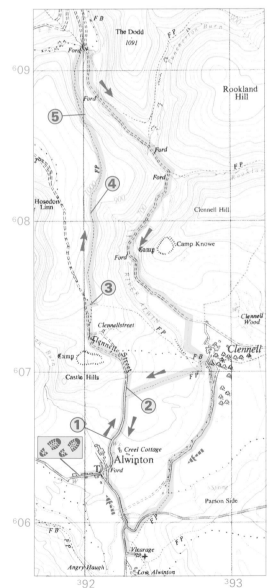

ROUTE DIRECTIONS

Allow 2 hours
Start from Alwinton car park
(grid ref. NT919063).

Turn left out of the car park and go straight across the village green over a small footbridge and turn left along the track①.

Begin the slow steady climb up the track and at the first gate across Clennell Street cross the ladder stile and take a breather②.

Continue as the track sweeps round the tiny settlement of Clennell Street. Cross the step stile over a wire fence just beyond the settlement, and follow the waymarker to another stile③.

Keep on this contour along the small, well-defined footpath above a circular stone pen, known as a stell④.

The native Cheviot, short-legged and hardy

Eventually the path goes past a stone cairn, complete with waymarker, and this points to another cairn and to the track to Kidlandlee Dean⑤.

Go through the gate at the bottom of the track and turn right to follow the river to Clennell. Keep to the main track as it skirts the hamlet and cross the cattle grid. Either keep straight on for about ¾ mile and turn right along the minor road past Alwinton church (this is of Norman origin and has the unusual feature of being separated from its chancel by about 10 steps) or take the footbridge across the river. The footpath sign points the way up a bank, over a stile and along a raised bank across a field, eventually meeting Clennell Street again. Turn left and retrace the beginning of the outward route back to the car park.

The small village of Alwinton nestles in the beautiful valley of the Upper Coquet which runs its course here between the ancient laval flows of the Cheviot Hills and the sediments of the fell sandstones. The landscape is wild, dramatic and empty but for sheep and the odd isolated farm.

POINTS OF INTEREST

① This is Clennell Street, one of many ancient roads that cross Northumberland and remain because of the isolated nature of much of the country. The Roman marching camps garrisoned here were of great strategic importance.

② The small knoll seen on the left was once the site of a well-fortified or palisaded settlement. It is about 2,700 years old and was defended by wooden barricades. The large hill on the right is Silverton Hill, and in the valley bottom on the right is Clennell Hall, which once belonged to the ancient family of that name. The name means 'hill that was clean' or 'free from undergrowth'.

③ The view back from this point is excellent, with Simonside Hills to the south east and Long Crag due east.

④ A stell such as this is a traditional gathering point for hill shepherds to herd their sheep into, for counting and checking.

⑤ Kidlandlee Forest stretches away almost to the Scottish border. This is a good point from which to view the steep valley sides of the River Alwin. The scree slopes are a relic of the last Ice Age.

Lady's Well and the statue of St Paulinus

Delightful cottage gardens and solidly built stone houses make Holystone one of the prettiest villages in Northumberland. It is the starting point for this short walk in the heart of Coquetdale, a lovely valley descending through the Cheviots from the Scottish border ten miles away. The route passes the famous Lady's Well.

POINTS OF INTEREST

①St Ninian's or Lady's Well has been a watering place since Roman times, but found fame in later centuries when Northumbria was the cradle of Christianity in Northern England. St Paulinus is said to have baptised 3,000 people here on Easter Day in AD627. Now cared for by the National Trust, the still, clear pool is surrounded by 18th-century masonry and sheltered by trees and rhododendrons. Little remains of the 12th-century Augustinian priory at Holystone, which doubtless had associations with Lady's Well.

②The hillside above the Coquet gives views across the river, to the right, towards the village of Sharperton in the north-east. The Scots pine plantation on the right is the home of red squirrels, who feed mainly on conifer seeds. The expansion of Northumberland's forests has been to their distinct advantage – but has adversely affected other forms of wildlife.

③Enjoy the view from the bridge over the Coquet, with the river sweeping in wide bends along the wide, flat bottom of the valley. It is fed by many tributaries, most of which rise in the Cheviots close to the Scottish border. Oystercatchers, grey wagtails, pied wagtails and common sandpipers may be seen below the bridge.

④On this stretch, notice the marsh between the path and the river, which is rich in wild flowers including lady's smock, lady's mantle, great willowherb, crosswort and horsetails. On the way up towards the woods, there is a fine view of the River Coquet as it meanders seawards, leaving great banks of boulders and pebbles in its wake. Downstream are workings belonging to the Ryton Sand and Gravel Company. The company has converted most of the old workings into a nature reserve. Visitors are welcome, and should contact the site manager.

ROUTE DIRECTIONS

Allow 1 to 1½ hours
Start from the village of Holystone, where roadside parking is available (grid ref. NT954027).

Take the waymarked path for Lady's Well in front of the Salmon Inn. After about 30yds, fork right over a stile and keep to this track to Lady's Well①.

Continue along the track to cross another stile. Now follow the edge of the field and, at the top of the rise, turn round for a superb view of the Simonside Hills.

Go on to a gate where it can be extremely muddy if it has rained recently, but is easily passable if it has been dry. Head straight to a squeeze stile and cross another stile immediately ahead. Now follow the line of the fence②.

Go through the gate in the corner of the field and walk along the edge of this field, keeping the hawthorn trees on your right. At the end of the hawthorns, go through the metal gate which leads to the road. Turn right and go down the hill.

Ignore the road to Holystone at the bottom of the hill and cross the river bridge③.

Continue up the road, beyond the left-hand turn to Sharperton village and, where the road bends left, go through a small gate on your right.

Go down the path but beware the strip of dock leaves; these mark the course of a tiny but deep stream. The water is obscured by the vegetation. Take a big step across to the bank opposite and climb up through the trees, keeping the fence on your left④.

Go through the gate at the top of the wood and turn right along the edge of the field down to the footbridge. Cross the bridge and take the track straight ahead across the haugh to the minor road.

The last section of the walk into the village passes a lovely water meadow on the left after a little bridge. Just beyond it, turn right into Holystone village.

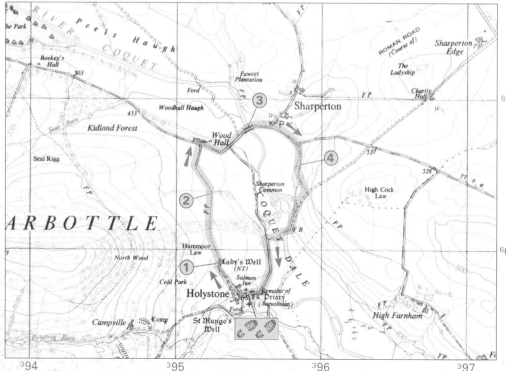

ROUTE DIRECTIONS

The drive starts from Oban ①.

Follow signs for Crianlarich to leave by the A85. After 3 miles the road to the left leads to ruined 13th-century Dunstaffnage Castle (Ancient Monument) ②.

Later, on the approach to Connel, the Falls of Lora can be seen below Connel Bridge. Continue beside the loch to Taynuilt. A 1½-mile detour may be taken from here to the 18th-century Bonawe Iron Furnace (Ancient Monument); at the crossroads turn left on to the B845, signed Village, and in ½ mile turn right, unclassified ③.

The main tour continues with the Crianlarich road, A85. Beyond Taynuilt, twin-peaked Ben Cruachan (3,695ft) rises to the left of the road. The drive then enters the wild Pass of Brander and later, on the left, are the Falls of Cruachan below the Cruachan Reservoir ④.

The road continues alongside Loch Awe and after 2¾ miles is the church of St Conan. Later, beyond Loch Awe Post Office, there are views of the ruins of Kilchurn Castle (Ancient Monument) ⑤.

Pass Dalmally, then 2 miles farther, turn left on to the B8074, signed Glen Orchy. The single-track road passes through partly forested valley scenery featuring several waterfalls. (An easier, alternative route to Bridge of Orchy is via the A85 to Tyndrum, then left on to the A82; it is 5 miles longer.)

After 10¼ miles on the B8074 turn left on to the A82, signed Fort William, and continue to Bridge of Orchy. Beyond the village the road passes Loch Tulla then climbs on to the bleak bog and lochan waste of Rannoch Moor. The Kings House Hotel, on the right, faces Stob Dearg (3,345ft), one of Scotland's most famous rock peaks, which lies in a well-known winter sports district. From here the road descends into rugged Glen Coe, overshadowed by the peaks of Bidean nam Bian, at 3,766ft the highest mountain in Argyll, and its outliers, the Three Sisters. One mile beyond Loch Achtriochtan on the right is the Glen Coe Visitor Centre (National Trust, Scotland) ⑥.

Continue down the glen to Glencoe village ⑦.

From Glencoe follow signs Oban and Fort William alongside Loch Leven. Pass the edge of Ballachulish and in 1¾ miles, at the roundabout, take the second exit, A828, signed Oban. Shortly the road runs beneath the impressive Ballachulish Bridge then past the Ballachulish Hotel. Nearby is a monument to James of the Glen ⑧.

The drive then follows the Appin shore of Loch Linnhe, through Kentallen and Duror, with views of the Ardgour Hills across the loch. Before the drive meets the edge of Loch Creran, Castle Stalker can be seen near Portnacroish ⑨.

The drive continues round the loch to the Sea Life Centre and Marine Aquarium at Barcaldine, with several picnic sites and forest walks along the way ⑩.

Later there are views of Barcaldine Castle to the right ⑪.

Continue through Benderloch, skirting Ardmucknish Bay; from here the Moss of Achnacree can be seen over to the left.

After 2¼ miles cross the cantilevered Connel Bridge. At the T-junction turn left on to the A85 for the return to Oban.

POINTS OF INTEREST

①Oban is a popular resort and the port serving the islands of Mull, Coll, Tiree, Lismore, Colonsay, Barra and South Uist. Of interest around the town are McCaig's Folly, the Caithness Glassworks, Macdonald's Mill and, a mile to the north-west, the ruins of 13th-century Dunollie Castle.

②Dunstaffnage Castle, guarding the entrance to Loch Etive, dates from the 13th century and has a 17th-century tower-house. The Campbells of Dunstaffnage are buried in the adjacent ruined chapel.

③Once the main iron-smelting centre of Scotland, Taynuilt provided the cannon and shot for the navy, and a monument near the church commemorates Nelson's victory at Trafalgar. The restored remains of an 18th- to 19th-century furnace can be seen.

④The Reservoir stands at 1,315ft and the power station and visitor centre are built deep into the mountain. The latter has displays and literature explaining the scheme.

⑤Kilchurn Castle was built in 1440 by Sir Colin Campbell of Glenorchy. It was extended in 1693 by Ian, Earl of Breadalbane.

⑥The Centre, standing in outstanding walking and climbing country, stands about half a mile from Signal Rock, from which the signal was given for the hideous massacre of the Macdonalds of Glencoe by the Campbells of Glen Lyon in 1692.

⑦Two heather-thatched cottages in the main street house the Glencoe and North Lorn Folk Museum, with Macdonald and Jacobite relics. The village is dominated by the conical peak of the 2,430ft Pap of Glencoe.

⑧James of the Glen was wrongly hanged in 1752 after a notorious trial known as the Appin murder case. The story plays a great part in R L Stevenson's novel *Kidnapped*.

⑨Castle Stalker was built at the beginning of the 16th century and has been well restored. It was the ancient home of the Stewarts of Appin.

⑩The Sea Life Centre and Marine Aquarium on Loch Creran contains the largest collection of native marine life in Britain. There are seal displays, and a tidepool 'touch tank'.

⑪Barcaldine Castle was built between 1579 and 1601 by 'Black Duncan' Campbell of Glenorchy. It has been much restored.

Oban Bay is always full of various craft serving this busy port and holiday resort

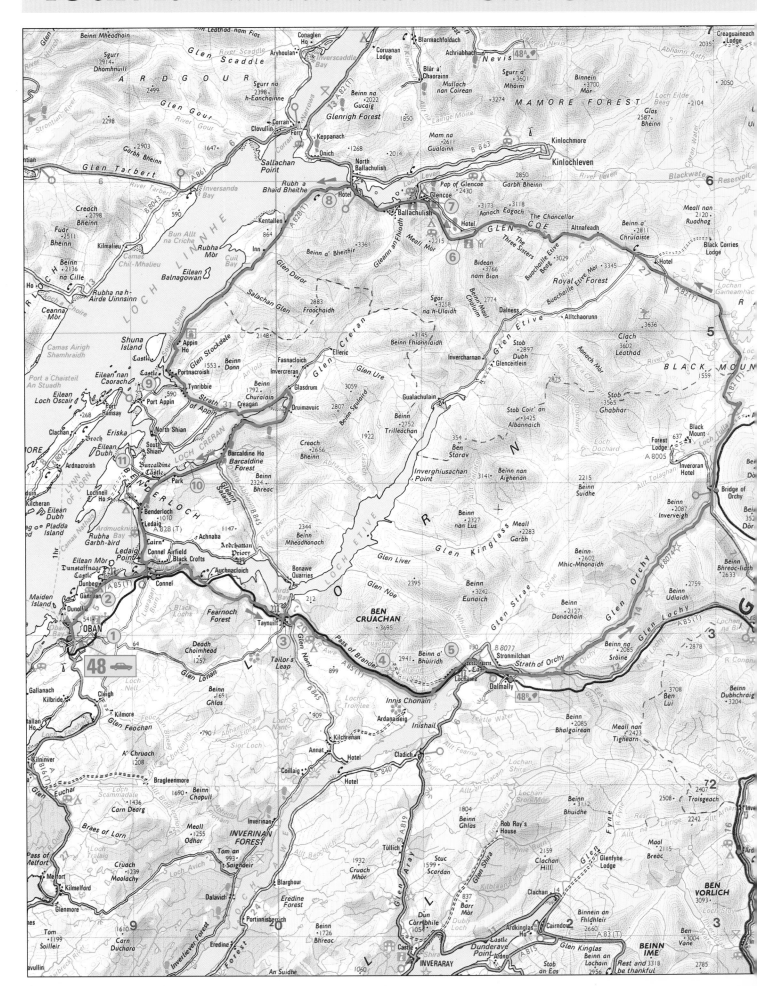

WALK 48A · *Below Ben Nevis*   HIGHLAND

This classic walk is on clear but stony, footpaths which pass through a gorge of Himalayan proportions to visit one of the country's best waterfalls. Stout footwear is advisable and the drops along the path demand caution.

POINTS OF INTEREST

① The road up Glen Nevis from Fort William (where there is an interesting museum) is twisty and narrow with some fine scenery. The road crosses the river at Polldubh and it is worth stopping to see some more falls here. Polldubh Crags above the road here are popular with rock-climbers.

② There is a slightly awkward stream to cross, and later the remains of a 23-year-old rockfall lie on the path. Where the gorge narrows, note the carved whorls and curves of water action on the rocks, even 100ft overhead. When the water is in spate this can be an awesome place. In drier conditions you will notice that the rocks in the river bed have been carved into fantastic shapes by the river.

There is a sudden change of atmosphere as you leave the gorge to stroll across a green and placid meadow, beyond which are seen the great Steall Falls, which tumble down from the Mamore Hills in a sweeping veil. A wet day ensures the most spectacular scene, so do not be put off if it is raining.

③ Although it can be rather muddy here at times, the Steall ruins, beside a river of many small falls, are a point of interest at this charming spot.

Climbers are attracted to Ben Nevis all year round to tackle the 2,000ft rock faces, gullies and buttresses of Britain's highest mountain

ROUTE DIRECTIONS
Allow 2 hours
Start from the car park at the head of Glen Nevis (grid ref. NN168691).

Beside the car park is the famous 'waterslide' which descends 1,500ft off Ben Nevis, the highest mountain in Britain①.

From the car park follow the path along into the gorge②.

The more adventurous can cross a three-wire suspension bridge to pass the White Cottage (a locked climbing hut) and reach the foot of the falls; everyone can wander along the right of way for ¼ mile③.

The path eastwards does not meet a metalled road again before two or three *days* of walking, so it is best to return from Steall!

At the mouth of the gorge, going back, there is a more challenging alternative path for fit walkers. Turn up the slope by the zigzags and follow it along and down again. From the highest point the fine view is at its most extensive. This path merges with the outward one to lead back to the car park.

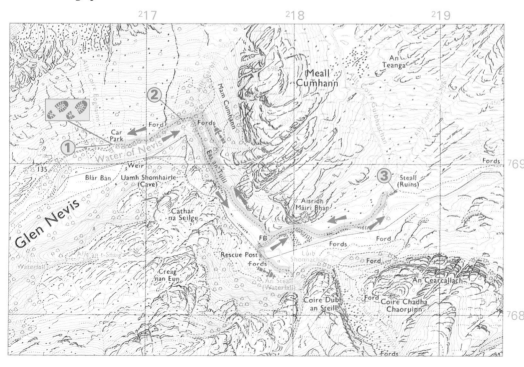

WALK 48B · *View of Glen Orchy*   STRATHCLYDE

ROUTE DIRECTIONS

Allow 2 hours
*Start from Dalmally village off
the A85 (grid ref. NN160272).
There is ample parking space at
the railway station or at the hotel
by the A85 just to the east of the
hamlet ①.*

Cross the bridge over the railway
in Dalmally village and follow
this single-track hill road, with its
steady gradient, for just over a
mile to the obvious monument,
access to which could be rather
boggy in some places ②.

Return to Dalmally along the
same route.

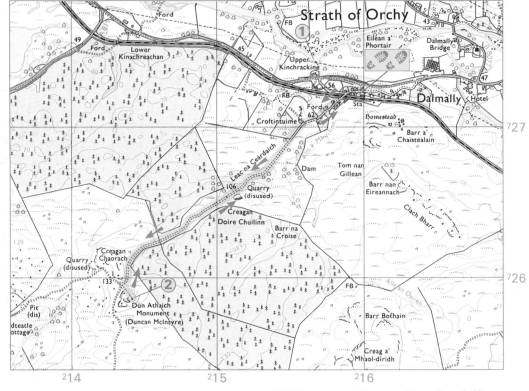

The romantic ruin of Kilchurn
Castle on the shores of Loch Awe

This is a generally easy (though uphill)
walk to a fine 'belvedere', as they used to
call such viewpoints. The scene is grand
rather than awesome, taking in a sweep of
Loch Awe, Cruachan Ben, and many other
mountains. The less fit may find the
gradient tiring.

POINTS OF INTEREST

① The River Orchy flows through Dalmally
in Strath of Orchy on its way to Loch Awe,
which lies to the west of the village.

② At the monument there is a superb
viewpoint as befits the commemoration of
one of the most famous Gaelic poets,
Duncan Ban McIntyre, 'the Burns of the
Highlands'.
   A number of interesting places, which
can be followed up once back at the car, can
be seen from the monument.
   In the corner of Loch Awe stands the
imposing ruin of Kilchurn Castle. The
massive hill range beyond the loch is
Cruachan, and the deep cleft westwards
below it is the Pass of Brander, where
Robert the Bruce had one of his many
narrow escapes in a 14th-century ambush.
Set in a hollow in the hills is the Cruachan
Reservoir. The fascinating underground
power station here is well worth a visit.
   About halfway between castle and power
station, on the left, stands St Conan's Kirk,
which must not be missed. There is no
other church quite like it!
   The walk back down to Dalmally gives
views over Glen Orchy.

ROUTE DIRECTIONS
The drive starts from Inverness ①.

Leave Inverness by the A862, signed Beauly, and follow the southern shoreline of the Beauly Firth. After 8 miles an unclassified road, on the left, leads to Moniack Castle ②.

Three miles farther cross the River Beauly and branch left on to the A831, signed Cannich. The drive then follows the thickly wooded valley of the River Beauly through Kilmorack.

After another 7½ miles cross the river by Struy Bridge and continue along Strath Glass to the village of Cannich ③.

Unclassified roads can be taken from Cannich into Glens Cannick and Affric for 10 miles, but they are not throughways for motor traffic. The highest mountain peaks north-west of the Great Glen are to be found in this area: they include Sgurr na Lapaich (3,775ft), north of Loch Mullardoch, and Carn Eige (3,880ft) and Mam Sodhail (3,862ft) to the south.

The main drive continues with the Drumnadrochit road which climbs out of the glen on to high ground. Four and a half miles from Cannich, an unclassified road on the right leads to the Corrimony Chambered Cairn (Ancient Monument) ④.

The drive then follows the River Enrick into Glen Urquhart and passes Loch Meiklie. Proceed along the pine-clad slopes of the glen and pass by Milton to reach Drumnadrochit. To the left at the junction with the A82 is the Official Loch Ness Monster Exhibition ⑤.

Turn right on to the A82, signed Fort William, to enter the main part of Drumnadrochit ⑥.

After the village of Lewiston, join the western shoreline of Loch Ness in the Great Glen passing a lay-by, on the left, which offers views over the ruins of Urquhart Castle (Ancient Monument) ⑦.

Nearly 1½ miles farther, also on the left, is a memorial to the racing driver John Cobb ⑧.

Continue down the Great Glen to Invermoriston. Here turn left with the A82 to reach Fort Augustus ⑨.

At the far end of the village turn left on to the B862, signed Whitebridge and Dores. After 3 miles the road becomes single-track before passing Loch Tarff and climbing to the Suidhe Chumein viewpoint. Continue through woodland scenery to reach Whitebridge. One mile farther turn left on to the B852, signed Foyers, and after another mile pass a picnic site beside the River Foyers ⑩.

Continue beside Loch Ness through the hamlet of Inverfarigaig ⑪.

Starting at Inverness, this drive takes you round the mysterious waters of Loch Ness and visits the Official Loch Ness Monster Exhibition. Moniack Castle, now a winery, and Urquhart Castle are also *en route*.

Remain on the B852 to Dores. Here rejoin the B862 and follow a two-lane road for the return to Inverness.

POINTS OF INTEREST

① The capital of the Highlands, Inverness is spread along the banks of the River Ness. Near the Victorian Town House is an excellent local museum and art gallery and high above the museum, on a hilltop, stands the imposing Inverness Castle.

② Once a fortress of the Lovat chiefs and their kin, Moniack Castle is today the centre of an enterprise unique in Scotland, that of commercial wine-making. The winery produces a wide range of wines including 'country wines' such as elderflower and silver birch, and two liqueurs, mead and sloe gin.

③ Cannich is the gateway to Glens Cannich and Affric. Loch Mullardoch in Glen Cannich and Loch Beinn a'Mheadhoin in Glen Affric have both been dammed for

hydro-electricity and there is a power station at Fasnakyle in Glen Affric, which has one of the most beautiful landscapes in Scotland.

④ The Corrimony Chambered Cairn is a Stone-Bronze Age burial cairn with its entrance passage still roofed. A stone circle surrounds the cairn, in which a single, crouched burial was found.

⑤ The Exhibition tells the story from 565AD to the present day and includes a scale model of the loch, equipment used in the hunt, a sonar display and models of various underwater investigations. It also encompasses the International House of Heraldry and, in summer, a glass-blowing exhibition.

⑥ Drumnadrochit, standing on the River Enrick, is a popular angling, pony trekking and hill walking centre. The vast Balmacaan Forest extends to the south of the village.

⑦ The mainly 14th-century Urquhart Castle overlooks Loch Ness and was destroyed before the 1715 Rising. It was once one of the largest castles in Scotland and is

notable for its striking position above the loch.

⑧ John Cobb lost his life while attempting the world water-speed record on the loch in his jet-powered boat *Crusader* in 1952. The memorial bears in Gaelic the words 'Honour to the brave and to the humble'.

Loch Ness under glowering skies. More than 20 miles long and just over a mile wide, its deep waters — dark with peat — have never been completely explored

⑨ Fort Augustus takes its name from the fort which was built during the 1700s by General Wade. The fort itself was named after Augustus, Duke of Cumberland, and the remains are now part of a Benedictine abbey.

⑩ The village of Foyers is noted for the first aluminium-smelting works to be built in Britain, erected in 1894. The aluminium factory closed in 1967, but in 1975 the North of Scotland Hydro-Electric Board's new pumped-storage system, situated just north of the old aluminium works, started feeding current to the Highland Grid.

⑪ The Forestry Commission has an interpretation centre at Inverfarigaig which illustrates the development of the forest environment in the Great Glen.

Inverness – the cathedral seen from the castle

ROUTE DIRECTIONS

Allow 2 hours
Start from the Inverfarigaig
Forest Centre (grid ref.
NH522237).

Turn right on leaving the car park and follow the single-track public road for ¼ mile. Do not follow the forestry signs at this stage①.

Fork right into Glen Liath, and right again after ½ mile (keep a watchful eye) and on to a rising grassy track to meet a forest road②.

Follow the forest road uphill to Lochan Torr an Tuill (look out for a yellow arrow) and 90yds beyond the lochan turn left on to a narrow path which climbs steeply to a ridge crest. Handrails assist in the climb③.

Steeply descend the north side of the ridge to reach a forest road④.

At the second crossroads turn right and left after 45yds to descend to the starting point.

Inverfarigaig, seen from one of the routes leading through the surrounding forests

The site of this walk on the east side of Loch Ness is depicted in a popular 19th-century print as a place of ambush, where claymore-wielding clansmen crouch behind massive boulders ready to surprise a drover and his shaggy herd. The gorge is an ancient glacial meltwater channel and is still susceptible to seismic disturbances associated with the Great Glen fault which is now partly filled by Loch Ness. This is not a walk for the unfit and a good pair of walking shoes is recommended.

POINTS OF INTEREST

① At the roadside beyond the Forest Centre a lichened stone commemorates the geologist James Bryce, who fell to his death opposite this spot. Further upstream the cleaner boulders of a recent rockfall have, fortunately, been intercepted by the stream-bed before they could reach the road.

② Glen Liath, the 'Grey Glen', is characterised by the massive boulders which litter the bottom. Between these boulders, road and stream pick their routes.

③ Looking back from beyond the lochan, the Monadhliath Mountains ring the horizon and beyond their tops some 20 miles of empty plateau and peat moss play host to deer and eagle before one reaches Aviemore and human habitation again.

④ By the gravelled forest road stands a stockaded log cabin, built to a *Treasure Island* design.

Fascinating scenery and a lively river form part of this walk, which is about 45 minutes' drive away from Inverness. Some parts of the walk will not suit the inexperienced, elderly or unfit. Stout shoes or boots should be worn.

POINTS OF INTEREST

①Glen Affric, one of Scotland's loveliest glens, extends into the lonely mountain country on the former borders of Ross and Cromarty. It is noted for its richly wooded scenery – old pine woods, long pre-dating the extensive areas of imported conifers that now cover much of the Highlands.

②Coire Loch is a tiny loch set in a secret bowl-shaped hollow, trapped between high ridges and gnarled sentinel pines. These display massive stabbed bark (the fissures are home for a hundred different insects) and delicate lichen structures. They are the direct descendants of the first plants to colonise this area when the last pocket of ice left its sheltering hollow some 10,000 years ago. It is not necessary to be a biologist or an earth scientist to appreciate the slightly spooky silence of the still waters of the loch. A bench high above it offers the chance to enjoy the surroundings.

Dog Fall, on the River Affric, is one of the glen's best-known beauty spots

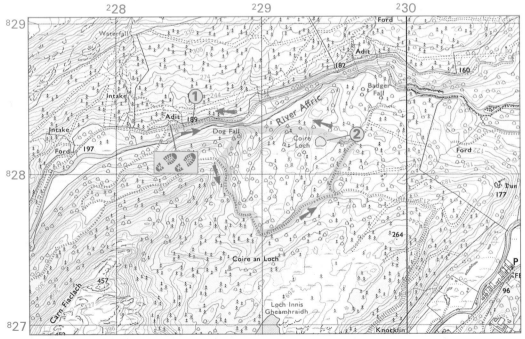

ROUTE DIRECTIONS
Allow 1½ hours
Start from the Dog Fall car park on the north bank of the River Affric (grid ref. NH284283)①.

Follow the riverside path downstream for about 330yds, then cross the road and continue on a higher level until the path returns to the river gorge and a graceful footbridge across it.
  Cross the river and climb a high stile over the deer fence, then fork right on a narrow path under birch trees. These give way to pines as the path climbs very steeply to meet a forest road.
  Turn left along the forest road and left again at the path signposted for Coire Loch②.

  From the loch, continue following the path as it descends steeply to the river bank again. Return to the car park by the roadside, stopping to enjoy views of the gorge from the various viewpoints.

ROUTE DIRECTIONS
The drive starts from Lairg ①.

Leave by the Tongue road, A836, following the shore of Loch Shin. After 2½ miles the road becomes single-track. The drive then leaves the loch and continues northwards to follow Strath Tirry. Six miles farther enter the North Dalchork Forest and beyond it pass the lonely Crask Inn. Later follow Strath Vagastie to the hamlet of Altnaharra ②.

Continue with the Tongue road through more barren country and, after 7 miles, join the shore of Loch Loyal. To the left are the peaks of Ben Loyal (2,504ft). Beyond the loch there is a short climb on to higher ground before the descent, with fine views, towards the Kyle of Tongue. At the junction with the A838 turn left and descend to Tongue ③.

Turn right, signed Durness, and in 1½ miles cross the Kyle of Tongue by a causeway built in 1971. On the far side an unclassified road to the right, signed Talmine, leads along the west side of Tongue Bay where there are magnificent sandy beaches. The main drive continues with the Durness road through desolate country and later descends to the head of Loch Hope, whose southern end is dominated by Ben Hope (3,042ft). The road becomes single-track again as it veers southwards to make the long detour around Loch Eriboll.

At Smoo, on the approach to Durness, a footpath (on the right) leads to Smoo Cave ④.

Enter Durness ⑤.

Stark mountains, sparkling lochs and rivers, acres of timberland and a rugged coast all feature in this drive, which also visits the beautiful beach of Balnakeil Bay.

To the west is Balnakeil Craft Village ⑥.

Close by is the settlement of Balnakeil at the edge of a very attractive bay ⑦.

The main drive turns southwards to leave by the Scourie road. In 1¾ miles pass an unclassified road, on the right, which leads to the Kyle of Durness Ferry (foot passengers only). A minibus service operates from here during the summer months to Cape Wrath — Scotland's most north-westerly point. Continue through mountainous scenery to Rhiconich ⑧.

Remain on the A838 and pass several small lochs before reaching the Laxford Bridge road junction. From here a 6-mile detour to the west can be made to the coastal village of Tarbet. Tarbet can be reached by turning right with the A894 then after 3½ miles right again on to a single-track unclassified road. This is the departure point for the ferry to Handa Island ⑨.

From Laxford Bridge the main drive turns left, signed Lairg, and follows the River Laxford. Later pass beneath Ben Stack (2,634ft) which overlooks Loch Stack. A further

succession of inland waters — Loch More, Loch Merkland and the small Loch a'Ghriama — leads to the long run beside Loch Shin. Near the southern end of the loch turn right on to the A836 for the return to Lairg.

POINTS OF INTEREST

① Lairg is a small town situated at the southern end of Loch Shin and popular with anglers. The Shin Valley hydro-electric scheme is one of the largest in the country. Lairg is a major road junction for the north-west Highlands and is noted for its important lamb auctions.

② Altnaharra, situated at the western end of Loch Naver, is an angling resort dominated by the 3,154ft peak of Ben Klibreck. Several prehistoric remains can be found in the area.

③ Tongue is dominated by the remains of Castle Varrich which was said to have been a Norse stronghold. The 17th- to 18th-century Tongue House, near the eastern end of the causeway, was the seat of the lords Reay (Mackay).

④ Smoo Cave is a vast cavern cut into the limestone cliff and is one of the most famous features of the landscape. Visitors can approach by

boat, but detailed exploration is for experienced potholers only.

⑤ Durness is one of the most northerly settlements on the Scottish mainland and a popular stop along the coastal road. Standing back from a rugged coast, where cliff-faces dip down to sandy coves and sea-bird colonies far outnumber human settlements, it is surrounded by crofting fields.

⑥ The RAF camp at Balnakeil was organised as a craft village in 1964 and has many individual workshops (some summer only).

⑦ The strandline of Balnakeil Bay contains an interesting range of natural and man-made objects. Ringed plovers, oystercatchers and gulls are usually present on the tidal sands, while red-breasted mergansers, shags, eiders and black guillemots may be seen just offshore. Roofless Durness Old Church, build in 1619 but on the site of a much older church, stands beside the bay.

⑧ Rhiconich is situated at the head of Loch Inchard. To the left are the high ridges of Foinaven (2,980ft) and Arkle (2,580ft).

⑨ Handa Island is a noted nature reserve and the circular walk of the island has some dramatic and unforgettable scenery. The north-west side has irregular cliffs 400ft high and the contrast between the red sandstone and the emerald water in the caves is striking.

The scattered settlement of Rhiconich beside Loch Inchard

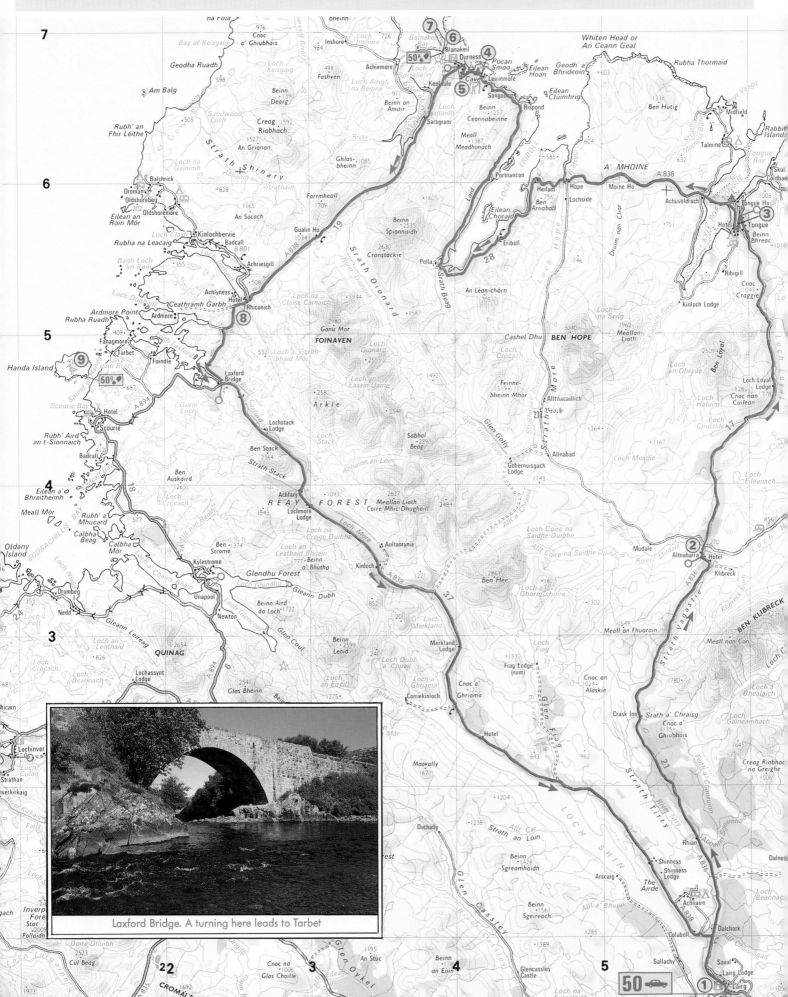

Laxford Bridge. A turning here leads to Tarbet

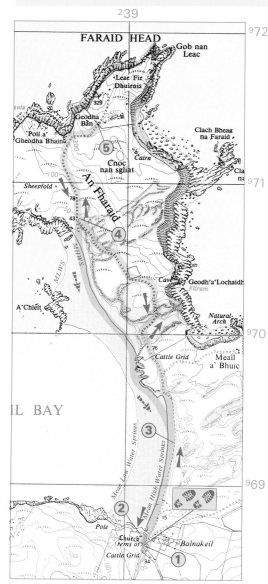

Razorbills — the largest colonies are found in northern England, Scotland and Ireland

Fulmars — perhaps Britain's longest-lived birds

A visit to an old churchyard is followed by a walk along one of the most beautiful beaches on the Scottish mainland, on to a headland where the desert-like dunes are so mobile that the road has to be bulldozed regularly. Fine views of coastal scenery and birds may be obtained at many points on the walk, culminating in superb vistas from Faraid Head. This is not an easy walk for children, however.

POINTS OF INTEREST

① Balnakeil House, to the right of the car park, was built by Lord Reay – chief of the Clay Mackay – in 1774, on the site of an older building which at one time belonged to the Bishop of Caithness. The house is now a private dwelling.

② A conspicuous granite obelisk with inscriptions in Gaelic, English, Latin and Greek marks the grave of the famous Gaelic bard Robb Donn (Robert Calder Mackay). The church itself, which gives the settlement of Balnakeil its name – Baile-ne-Cille, the Township of the Church – has within its wall the grave of a less illustrious native of the area – Donald McMurcho (or Macleod). He killed at least 18 men for his clan chief, allegedly by throwing them down the Falls of Smoo, some two miles to the east, and is said to have demanded to be buried in this position so that a witch who had predicted that she would dance on his grave would be unable to do so.

③ The shoreline along Balnakeil Bay usually has good pickings for beachcombers, although the southernmost part of the beach seems to collect flotsam and often has a heap of smelly, decaying seaweed up to 3ft high.

④ The combined effects of rabbits and wind have created a sandy 'desert' here, where even marram, the grass which usually stabilises mobile sand, has been unable to get a grip. If the wind is strong this part of the walk will involve getting stung by blown sand. Even where the road is completely covered with sand it is easy to follow its route, however.

⑤ There are fine views from the left of the road at the end of the peninsula to the west and east, and cliff-nesting seabirds which can be seen here include razorbill, rock pipit and the ubiquitous fulmar.

ROUTE DIRECTIONS

Allow 3½ hours
Start from the car park at Balnakeil (grid ref. NC391686) ①.

Enter the churchyard on the west side of the car park ②.

From the churchyard, walk northwards along Balnakeil Bay ③.

When you reach the northern end of the beach, continue northwards along the road (a continuation of a track along the beach). This takes you up over An Fharaid ④.

Once through the main 'desert' area, continue along the track, passing to the left of the enclosure. This takes you through an area of relatively stable dunes and out on to Faraid Head. Continue on until you reach the Ministry of Defence installation; this is the limit of the walk ⑤.

Return by retracing your steps until you reach the beginning of the northern beach. If the tide is very far out, and still going out, it should be possible to take a short-cut over the beach around the headland. ***Under no circumstances should this be attempted if you are in any doubt as to whether or not it is safe.*** If you decide not to go around the seaward side of the headland, do not go along the beach, but use the track as before: the climb back up to the dunes at the south end would add to the already serious erosion there.

When you get over (or round) the ridge of An Fharaid, the car park will be in full view, and the route back is straightforward. Do not be tempted to go over the dunes which back Balnakeil Bay: there are serious erosion problems on the dune front, and the areas behind the dunes are used by Balnakeil Farm for grazing its stock.

WALK 50B · *Handa Island*   HIGHLAND

POINTS OF INTEREST

① The waymarked path around the island takes in the best of the scenery and provides pleasant, easy walking – often on duckboards where the going is soft.

② Handa is now uninhabited, but in 1845 12 families lived here, ruled by a 'queen' and a 'parliament'. Potatoes, fish and seafowl were the staple foods and when the potato famine struck the islanders were forced to leave.

③ The Great Stack of Handa is a monolithic red tower of rock, pierced through by the sea at the base, which rises for some hundreds of feet with every ledge occupied by razorbills, guillemots, kittiwakes, fulmars and puffins. The Stack was first climbed by man in 1876, an escapade repeated only once in modern times.

④ At 403ft Sithean Mor is the Island's summit, with extensive views down the coast to the Old Man of Stoer and the mountains of Quinag, Suilven and Assynt. To the east the fang of Ben Stack can be seen.

⑤ Shag frequent this side of the island and seals or even whales may be spotted offshore.

ROUTE DIRECTIONS

Allow 2 to 3 hours (depending on the boatman)
Start from the car park by the jetty (grid ref. NC164488). The boat which takes visitors across the Sound to land on a sandy bay will sail only if the weather is suitable.

The RSPB warden may meet the boat, failing which, walk to the landing spot where there is a hut with information, displays and trail leaflets. Take the path anticlockwise and keep to the marked circular track to prevent disturbing the bird life①.

As you walk across the island, pass the ruins of the village②.

The island — and the path — rise steadily and as the north side is reached its big cliffs are suddenly revealed in dramatic fashion. The path follows westwards along the cliffs and in the mouth of one geo (inlet or bay) stands The Great Stack of Handa③.

The path then climbs to Sithean Mor (The Fairies' Big Hill)④.

As you walk on, the path loses height and continues around the south-west corner of the island⑤.

Continue on back to the start of the walk.

The whole of Handa Island, off the west coast, near Scourie, is an RSPB reserve, with spectacular scenery and huge colonies of seabirds. A ferry service run by fishermen operates from Tarbet between April and September, but trips do not run on Sundays.

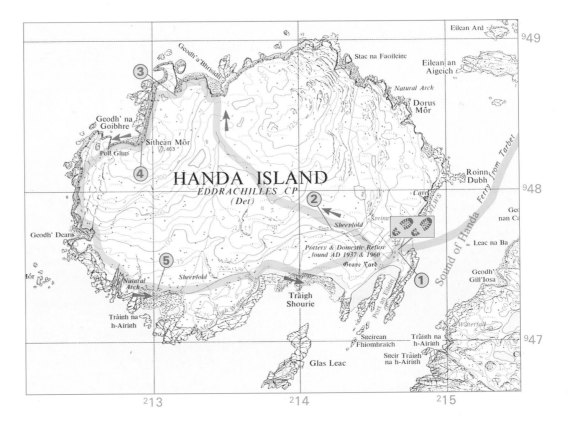

MAP SYMBOLS

THE GRID SYSTEM

The map references used in this book are based on the Ordnance Survey National Grid, correct to within 1000 Metres. They comprise two letters and four figures

Thus the reference for Brighton appears   TQ 3105

TQ identifies the major (100km) grid square concerned (see diag)

3105 locates the lower left-hand corner of the kilometre grid square in which Brighton appears

Take the first figure of the reference 3, this refers to the numbered grid running along the bottom of the page. Having found this line, the second figure 1, tells you the distance to move in tenths to the right of this line. A vertical line through this point is the first half of the reference.

The third figure 0, refers to the numbered grid lines on the right hand side of the page, finally the fourth figure 5, indicates the distance to move in tenths above this line. A horizontal line drawn through this point to intersect with the first line gives the precise location of the places in question.

TOURS

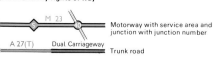

2 🚗	Start point of tour
➡	Direction of tour
▬▬▬	Featured tour
⑥	Point of Interest

TOURIST INFORMATION

⚑	Camp Site		Nature reserve
	Caravan Site	☆	Other tourist feature
	Information Centre		Preserved railway
P	Parking facilities		Racecourse
	Viewpoint		Wildlife park
✕	Picnic site		Museum
	Golf course or links		Nature or forest trail
	Castle	⅏	Ancient monument
	Cave		Places of interest
	Country park	ℭℭ	Telephones: public or motoring organisations
	Garden	PC	Public Convenience
	Historic house	▲	Youth Hostel

◆ ■ ▬ Waymarked Path / Long Distance Path / Recreational Path

⊕ Mountain Rescue Post with telephone and supervisor

Mountain Rescue Kit Equipment only

Tours 1:250,000 or 1″ to 4 miles
ROADS AND PATHS

not necessarily rights of way

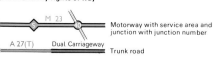

M 23	Motorway with service area and junction with junction number
A 27(T) Dual Carriageway	Trunk road

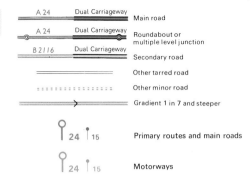

A 24 Dual Carriageway	Main road
A 24 Dual Carriageway	Roundabout or multiple level junction
B 2116 Dual Carriageway	Secondary road
	Other tarred road
	Other minor road
▬▬➤	Gradient 1 in 7 and steeper
24 15	Primary routes and main roads
24 15	Motorways

Mileages are shown on the map between large markers and between small markers in large and small type

1 mile = 1·61 kilometres

RAILWAYS

	Road crossing under or over standard gauge track
	Level crossing
	Station
	Narrow gauge track

WATER FEATURES

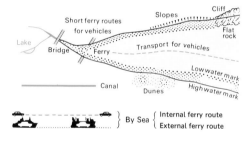

🚗 🚗 By Sea	Internal ferry route / External ferry route

ANTIQUITIES

	Native fortress
-------	Roman road (course of)
Castle •	Other antiquities
CANOVIVM •	Roman antiquity

RELIEF

Feet	Metres	
		.274 Heights in feet above mean sea level
3000	914	
2000	610	
1400	427	
1000	305	Contours at 200 ft intervals
600	183	
200	61	
0	0	To convert feet to metres multiply by 0.3048

GENERAL FEATURES

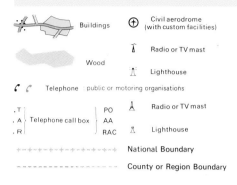

	Buildings	⊕	Civil aerodrome (with custom facilities)
	Wood		Radio or TV mast
			Lighthouse
ℭ ℭ	Telephone : public or motoring organisations		
.T .A .R	Telephone call box	PO AA RAC	Radio or TV mast
			Lighthouse
┼─┼─┼─┼─┼			National Boundary
─ ─ ─ ─ ─			County or Region Boundary

Tours 1:50,000 or 1¼″ to 1 mile
CHANNEL ISLANDS

Compiled from Ministry of Defence, United Kingdom mapping at 1/10 000, 1/10 560 and 1/25 000 scale, dated 1965-1975

ROADS, RAILWAYS, PATHS

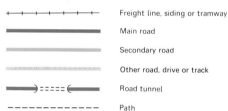

┼─┼─┼─┼─┼	Freight line, siding or tramway
▬▬▬▬	Main road
▬▬▬▬	Secondary road
▬▬▬▬	Other road, drive or track
═)══────	Road tunnel
─ ─ ─ ─ ─	Path

The representation on this map of any other road, track or path is no evidence of the existence of a right of way

GENERAL FEATURES

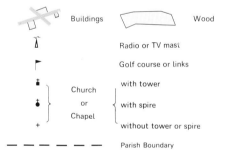

	Buildings		Wood
			Radio or TV mast
⚑			Golf course or links
ⓘ	Church or Chapel		with tower
			with spire
✛			without tower or spire
─ ─ ─ ─			Parish Boundary

ANTIQUITIES

VILLA	Roman
Castle	Non-Roman
✛	Position of antiquity which cannot be drawn to scale
⚔ 1066	Site of battle (with date)
✳	Tumulus

WATER FEATURES

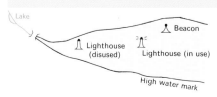

Lake	
Lighthouse (disused)	Beacon
	Lighthouse (in use)
	High water mark

MAP SYMBOLS

WALKS

 Start point of walk

→ Direction of walk

▬ Line of walk

▶▶▷ Alternative route

③ Point of Interest

1:25,000 or 2½" to 1 mile
ROADS AND PATHS

M 4	M 4	Motorway	.... Path
A 40(T)	A 40(T)	Trunk road	
A 4067	A 4067	Main road	Narrow roads with passing places are annotated
B 4520	B 4520	Secondary road	
A 40(T)	A 40(T)	Dual carriageway	
		Road generally over 4m wide	
		Road generally under 4m wide	
		Other road, drive or track	

Gradient: 20% (1 in 5) and steeper
14% (1 in 7) to 20% (1 in 5)

- - - - - Permitted path and bridleway

Paths and bridleways along which landowners have permitted public use but which are not public rights of way. The agreement may be withdrawn.

Access Land
↙ Access Point Land open to the public by permission of the owner

RAILWAYS

▬ Multiple track		▬ Level crossing	
▬ Single track		▬ Cutting	
▬ Narrow Gauge		▬ Embankment	
▬ Road over & under			
▬ Siding		▬ Tunnel	

GENERAL FEATURES

♦ Church
♦ or
+ Chapel

{ with tower
{ with spire
{ without tower or spire

Electricity transmission line
pylon pole

Gravel pit   ⇌ Railway station
Sand pit   Bus/coach station
Chalk pit, clay pit or quarry   ⊹ Site of antiquity
Refuse or slag heap   ∘ W, Spr Well, Spring

HEIGHTS AND ROCK FEATURES

Contours are at various metres / feet vertical intervals

50·} Determined { ground survey
285·} by { air survey

Surface heights are to the nearest metre / foot above mean sea level. Heights shown close to a triangulation pillar refer to the station height at ground level and not necessarily to the summit ·.

Vertical Face

Loose rock   Boulders   Outcrop   Scree

NATIONAL TRUST AND FORESTS

NT	National Trust always open	NT	National Trust always open
NT	National Trust opening restricted	NT	National Trust opening restricted
FC	Forestry Commission pedestrians only (observe local signs)	FC	Forestry Commission pedestrians only (observe local signs)

▨ National Park

PUBLIC RIGHTS OF WAY

Public rights of way shown in this guide may not be evident on the ground.

- - - - - - } Public Paths { Footpath
- - - - - - }   { Bridleway

+ + + + + By-way open to all traffic
-+-+-+- Road used as a public path

Public rights of way indicated by these symbols have been derived from Definitive Maps as amended by later enactments or instruments held by Ordnance Survey between 1st Feb 1968 and 1st May 1988 and are shown subject to the limitations imposed by the scale of mapping (Note: some walk maps do not show rights of way symbols)

Later information may be obtained from the appropriate County Council

The representation on these maps of any other road, track or path is no evidence of the existence of a right of way.

RIGHTS OF ACCESS – SCOTLAND

There is no law of trespass in Scotland. However landowners can and do impose restrictions on access such as during the grouse shooting season. They also have a legal remedy against any person causing damage on or to their land and may use reasonable force to remove such a person.

The following simple guidelines should therefore .be followed :
Obey restricted access notices and if asked to leave please do so.
Always take care to avoid damage to property and the natural environment.
Common sense, care and courtesy are the watchwords.

The representation on this map of any other road, track or path is no evidence of the existence of a right of access.

1:25,000 or 2½" to 1 mile
JERSEY AND GUERNSEY

TOURIST INFORMATION

🚌 Bus Terminus

Ⅹ Camp Site (Caravans and Motor Caravans are not permitted)

🅿 Car Park (public)

🅿 Car Park (private)

ℹ Information Centre

⊠ Picnic Site

◆ Public Convenience

📞 Public Telephone

- - - Recommended Walk

Pottery Selected places of interest

⚹ Viewpoint

ROADS AND PATHS

JERSEY   GUERNSEY

Main road
Secondary road
Other road, drive or track
Loose surface
Path

ABBREVIATIONS

CH	Club House
F Sta	Fire Station
FB	Foot Bridge
F	Fontaine
G	Garage
Liby	Library
MS	Mile Stone
Mus	Museum
PBS	Parish Boundary Stone
PC	Public Convenience
PH } Rural Areas	Public House
PO	Post Office
Pp	Pump
Sch	School
T	Telephone (public)
T(A)	Telephone (AA)
Twr	Tower
TH	Town Hall

VEGETATION

JERSEY   GUERNSEY

Coniferous trees
Non-coniferous trees
Orchard
Scrub
Rough grassland

GENERAL FEATURES

DANGER AREA — Ranges in the area
♦ Church
♦ or
+ chapel
{ with tower
{ with spire
{ without tower or spire

☒ ⚲ Lighthouse; beacon

△ Triangulation station

▭ Water

▦ Sand, sand & shingle

⬭ Quarry

⬭ Refuse tip

▧ Sloping masonry

⚘ Site of antiquity

⚐ Bus or coach station

▨ ▨ Glasshouse

— — Parish Boundary

.... Vingtaine Boundary

HEIGHTS

JERSEY
Contours are at 20 feet vertical interval

GUERNSEY
Contours are at 10 metre vertical interval

Index of Places

Index of Places

Index of Places

ACKNOWLEDGEMENTS

The Automobile Association would like to thank the following photographers and Associations for assisting us with the pictorial content of this publication:

E A Bowness
Heart of England Tourist Board
A J Hopkins
Jersey Museum
C Molyneux
D Mullins
National Park (Peak District)
Nature Photographers Ltd with contributions from: S C Bisserot, F V Blackburn, B Burbidge, C Carver, H Clark, A Cleave, P J Newman, W S Paton, P R Sterry and R Tidman
J Perrin

Also included are many photographs from The Automobile Association's photographic library with contributions from:

S Abraham, M Adelman, A Besley, J Beazley, M Birkitt, E A Bowness, R Czaja, R Eames, R Fletcher, B Johnson, S King, A Lawson, S Lund, S & O Mathews, C Molyneux, R Newton, C Nicholls, R Rainford, J Rathband, G Rowatt, T Souter, R Surman, M Trelawny, P Trenchard, W Voysey, R Weir, H Williams, T Woodcock, J Wyand